D1384718

THE
GNOSTIC
BIBLE

THE
GNOSTIC
BIBLE

EDITED BY

Willis Barnstone
and Marvin Meyer

SHAMBHALA
Boston & London
2003

Shambhala Publications, Inc.
Horticultural Hall
300 Massachusetts Avenue
Boston, Massachusetts 02115
www.shambhala.com

9 8 7 6 5 4 3 2

Printed in the United States of America

∞ This edition is printed on acid-free paper that meets the American
National Standards Institute z39.48 Standard.
Distributed in the United States by Random House, Inc.,
and in Canada by Random House of Canada Ltd

Interior design and composition: Greta D. Sibley & Associates

Library of Congress Cataloging-in-Publication Data
The gnostic Bible/edited by Willis Barnstone and Marvin Meyer.—1st ed.
p. cm.
Includes bibliographical references.
ISBN: 1-57062-242-6 (alk. paper)
1. Gnostic literature. I. Barnstone, Willis, 1927– II. Meyer, Marvin W.
BT1390.G4937 2003
299'.932—DC21
2003007148

CONTENTS

ACKNOWLEDGMENTS

We would like to acknowledge several people and organizations that have helped in the production of this volume. For a number of years Chapman University has given generous encouragement to the scholarly research of Marvin Meyer on gnostic texts by providing sabbatical leaves and financial assistance, and the work on this volume has been undertaken with the support of the Griset Chair in Bible and Christian Studies at Chapman University. Nathaniel Deutsch and Paul Mirecki have contributed insightful introductions to Mandaean and Manichaean literature in this volume, and Heather TerJung has produced an English translation of the German version of the Mother of Books. Linden Youngquist has provided essential computer expertise for formatting the texts and preparing the bibliography. The editorial staff of Shambhala Publications has taken on this large publishing project with creativity and resourcefulness. Joel Segel has brought his editorial vision to the creation of the book and has been a model of patience, persistence, and professionalism. Kendra Crossen Burroughs and Dave O'Neal have seen the manuscript successfully through press. Lastly, we recognize our colleagues, friends, and family members who have long endured our preoccupations and have offered us, in many ways, insights into wisdom and gnosis.

Willis Barnstone
Marvin Meyer

THE
GNOSTIC
BIBLE

GNOSTICISM, GNOSTICS, AND *THE GNOSTIC BIBLE*

MARVIN MEYER

*Know what is in front of your face
and what is hidden from you
will be disclosed.*

—Gospel of Thomas 5

The gnostics were religious mystics who proclaimed gnosis, knowledge, as the way of salvation. To know oneself truly allowed gnostic men and women to know god[1] directly, without any need for the mediation of rabbis, priests, bishops, imams, or other religious officials.

---

1. Throughout the present volume we have tried to avoid unnecessary capitalization of the word *god* and the names of personified spiritual powers and aeons. We are aware that the word *god* may be used as a name for the divine, but it frequently functions as a general term for the divine, so that even when "god" appears to be a name, it retains its primary nature as a term signifying the concept of divinity. For the same reason, other names of divine expressions, such as divine forethought, afterthought, and wisdom, are likewise left uncapitalized. Conversely, for the sake of clarity, when the Greek word "Sophia" is used for wisdom, that is capitalized, as are other names that are transliterated directly from other languages. We also want to avoid the common practice of singling out a particular deity, for example, the Judeo-Christian-Islamic deity, for the exclusive honor of the capitalized name "God," while other deities are relegated to the status of mere "gods" and "goddesses." We do not wish to limit the divine by restricting deity through name or selectivity. Traditionally the name and face of the divine are essentially unknowable, and so it is in this volume.

Religious officials, who were not pleased with such freedom and independence, condemned the gnostics as heretical and a threat to the well-being and good order of organized religion. Heresiologists—heresy hunters of a bygone age who busied themselves exposing people judged dangerous to the Christian masses—fulminated against what they maintained was the falsehood of the gnostics. Nonetheless, from the challenge of this perceived threat came much of the theological reflection that has characterized the intellectual history of the Christian church.

The historical roots of the gnostics reach back into the time of the Greeks, Romans, and Second Temple Jews. Some gnostics were Jewish, others Greco-Roman, and many were Christian. There were Mandaean gnostics from Iraq and Iran; Manichaeans from Europe, the Middle East, North Africa, and all the way to China; Islamic gnostics in the Muslim world; and Cathars in western Europe. The heyday of their influence extends from the second century CE through the next several centuries. Their influence and their presence, some say, continue to the present day.

Gnostics sought knowledge and wisdom from many different sources, and they accepted insight wherever it could be found. Like those who came before them, they embraced a personified wisdom, Sophia, understood variously and taken as the manifestation of divine insight. To gain knowledge of the deep things of god, gnostics read and studied diverse religious and philosophical texts. In addition to Jewish sacred literature, Christian documents, and Greco-Roman religious and philosophical texts, gnostics studied religious works from the Egyptians, Mesopotamians, Zoroastrians, Muslims, and Buddhists. All such sacred texts disclosed truths, and all were to be celebrated for their wisdom.

Gnostics loved to explore who they were and from where they had come, and hence they read creation stories such as the opening chapters of Genesis with vigor and enthusiasm. Like others, they recognized that creation stories not only claim to describe what was, once upon a time, but also suggest what *is*, now, in our own world. The gnostics carried to their reading a conviction that the story of creation was not a happy one. There is, they reasoned, something fundamentally wrong with the world, there is too much evil and pain and death in the world, and so there must have been something wrong with creation.

Consequently, gnostics provided innovative and oftentimes disturbing interpretations of the creation stories they read. They concluded that a distinction, often a dualistic distinction, must be made between the transcendent, spiritual deity, who is surrounded by aeons and is all wisdom and light, and the creator of the world, who is at best incompetent and at worst malevolent. Yet through everything, they maintained, a spark of transcendent knowledge, wisdom, and light persists within people who are in the know. The transcendent deity is the source of that enlightened life and light. The meaning of the creation drama, when properly understood, is that human beings—gnostics in particular—derive their knowledge and light from the transcendent god, but through the mean-spirited actions of the demiurge, the creator of the world, they have been confined within this world. (The platonic aspects of this imagery are apparent.) Humans in this world are imprisoned, asleep, drunken, fallen, ignorant. They need to find themselves—to be freed, awakened, made sober, raised, and enlightened. In other words, they need to return to gnosis.

This distinction between a transcendent god and the creator of the world is all the more remarkable when it is recalled that many of the earliest gnostic thinkers who made such a distinction seem to have been Jews. What might have led them to such a conclusion that seems to fly in the face of Jewish monotheistic affirmations? Could it have been the experience of the political and social trauma of the time, culminating in the destruction of the Second Temple in 70 CE, which prompted serious reflection upon the problem of evil and stimulated the production of Jewish apocalyptic compositions? Could it have been the reflection of hellenistic Jewish thinkers who were schooled in Judaica and Greek philosophy and recognized the deep philosophical and theological issues surrounding the transcendence of the high god and the need for cosmic intermediaries to be involved with this world? Could it have been that among the creative Jewish minds, representative of the rich diversity of Judaism during the first centuries before and of the Common Era, who boldly addressed the real challenges of Jewish mysticism before Kabbalah, of the wisdom and Hokhmah of god, of world-wrenching apocalyptic, of theodicy and evil in the world, there were those who finally drew gnostic conclusions? We know the names of some of these creative Jewish people: John the baptizer, who initiated Jesus of Nazareth and preached apocalyptic ideas in the vicinity of Qumran, where Covenanters and Essenes practiced their separatist, ethical dualism; Simon Magus and Dositheos, who lived about the same time as Jesus and advocated their ideas in Samaria and beyond; Philo of Alexandria, a hellenistic Jewish thinker who provided Greek philosophical perspectives on the Hebrew Bible; Rabbi Elisha ben Abuya, nicknamed Aher, "Other," who dabbled in dualism; and there were more. We shall encounter some of these Jewish thinkers in this volume. John the baptizer becomes the gnostic hero of the Mandaeans, Jesus of the Christian gnostics. Simon Magus may lurk in the background of several gnostic texts, and Dositheos is said to be the compiler of the Three Steles of Seth. Others, mostly unnamed, may have made similar contributions to the discussion of the profound question of the transcendent god and the demiurge.

The role of the gnostic savior or revealer is to awaken people who are under the spell of the demiurge—not, as in the case of the Christ of the emerging orthodox church, to die for the salvation of people, to be a sacrifice for sins, or to rise from the dead on Easter. The gnostic revealer discloses knowledge that frees and awakens people, and that helps them recall who they are. When enlightened, gnostics can live a life appropriate for those who know themselves and god. They can return back to the beginning, when they were one with god. Such a life transcends what is mundane and mortal in this world and experiences the bliss of oneness with the divine. As the divine forethought, or Christ, in the Secret Book of John says to a person—every person—in the pit of the underworld, "I am the forethought of pure light, I am the thought of the virgin spirit, who raises you to a place of honor. Arise, remember that you have heard, and trace your root, which is I, the compassionate."

Gnostic literature includes a typical cast of spiritual or mythological figures and realms, but they are referred to by different names.

Above and beyond all is the transcendent deity. In the Book of Baruch this deity is called the Good and is identified with the fertility god Priapos. In the Secret Book of John and elsewhere this deity is called the One, or monad, as well as the invisible spirit, virgin spirit, and father. It is said that the One should not be confused with a god, since it is greater than a god. Elsewhere the transcendent is called the boundless, depth, majesty, light. Poimandres reveals itself as the light, mind, first god. Mandaeans call this deity the great life and lord of greatness, Manichaeans the father of greatness, Muslim mystics the exalted king, Cathars the invisible father, true god, good god.

The glory of the transcendent is made manifest in a heavenly world of light. In the classic literature of gnostic wisdom this exalted world is often called the pleroma or fullness of god, and the inhabitants of this world are called aeons or eternal realms. The first of the aeons is usually the divine mother. For Simon Magus she is Helena, or *ennoia*, the thought of god. In the Secret Book of John she is Barbelo, or *pronoia*, the first thought or forethought of god. Thunder, in the text by that name, has certain similarities as well. Sometimes the transcendent father and the divine mother produce a child in spiritual love. Often the aeons are identified as spiritual attributes of the divine, are given names, and are joined together as couples, spiritual lovers in the fullness of the divine. In the Mandaean divine world the great life is surrounded by other lives and a host of Jordans, or heavenly waters; in the Manichaean kingdom of light the father of greatness is surrounded by 12 aeons and 144 aeons of aeons; and in the Mother of Books the exalted king is surrounded by seas, angels, lights, and colors.

Among the aeons and manifestations of the divine is often a figure who represents the divine in this world, fallen from the light above yet present as the light of god with us and in us. In many gnostic texts this is the figure called Sophia or wisdom, as mentioned above. In Valentinian traditions two forms of wisdom are evident, a higher wisdom called Sophia and a lower wisdom called Achamoth. Wisdom is closely linked to Eve in the creation stories, and Eve is portrayed as the mother of the living and a revealer of knowledge. Wisdom may also be linked to the gnostic revealer, and wisdom may take part in the process of salvation. In the Gospel of John and other texts the divine logos, or word, plays a similar role. Such is also the case with Ruha, the spirit, in Mandaean texts, and perhaps Salman, including great Salman and lesser Salman, in the Islamic Mother of Books.

As noted, the demiurge or creator of this world is commonly distinguished from the transcendent deity in gnostic texts. The demiurge is ignorant, tragic, megalomaniacal. In the Secret Book of John he is depicted as the ugly child of Sophia, snakelike in appearance, with the face of a lion and eyes flashing like bolts of lightning. He is named Yaldabaoth, Sakla, Samael, and he is the chief archon and an arrogant, jealous god. In the Gospel of Truth error behaves like the demiurge, for it becomes strong and works in the world, but erroneously. Similar, too, are the actions of nature in the Paraphrase of Shem, Ptahil in Mandaean literature, the five evil archons in Manichaean literature, Azazi'il in the Mother of Books, and Lucifer or Satan among the Cathars.

The gnostic revealer awakens people who are under the spell of the demiurge. Within a Jewish context the gnostic revealer is Seth, the child of Adam and Eve, or Derdekeas, probably Aramaic for "male child," or the first thought or the afterthought or the wisdom of the divine. Within a Christian context the revealer is Jesus the anointed, within a Manichaean context Jesus of light, as well as others. More abstractly, the call to revelation and knowledge—the wake-up call—is a winged divine messenger in the Song of the Pearl, instruction of mind in Hermetic literature, and enlightened Manda dHayye, knowledge of life, in Mandaean literature. In other words, the call to knowledge is the dawning of awareness, from within and without, of "what is, what was, and what is to come." It is insight. It is gnosis.

In gnostic literature those who come to knowledge are described in different ways. Occasionally they are specifically called gnostics; the Mandaeans are also called by the word that means "gnostics" in Mandaic. More often they are named the unshakable race, or the seed or offspring of Seth, or the generation without a king, or the elect or chosen, or, in the Mother of Books, the ones who know. With a mystical flourish the Gospel of Philip recommends that rather than be called a Christian, a person with knowledge might be understood to be at one with the gnostic revealer and be called Christ. This recalls the Gospel of Thomas, saying 108, where Jesus says, "Whoever drinks from my mouth will become like me. I myself shall become that person, and the hidden things will be revealed to that one." Such people of knowledge know how to live profoundly and well in the truth and light of god. The Gospel of Truth concludes, "It is they who manifest themselves truly, since they are in that true and eternal life and speak of the perfect light filled with the seed of the father, which is in his heart and in the fullness, while his spirit rejoices in it and glorifies him in whom it was, because the father is good. And his children are perfect and worthy of his name, because he is the father. Children of this kind are those whom he loves."

The sacred texts presented in this volume all help to clarify what gnosticism is and who the gnostics were. The similarities and differences among these texts are equally instructive, as are the connections among them, whether historical or phenomenological. The early "wisdom gospels" of Thomas and John, both perhaps dating from the first century CE, portray Jesus as a speaker of wise words or even as the divine word itself, which is itself "wisdom." These early wisdom gospels represent incipient gnostic perspectives, and they were used extensively by later gnostics, so that their impact upon the history of gnosticism was huge. The classic literature of gnostic wisdom dates from the second century CE, and some materials in the literature are probably even older. Justin's Book of Baruch illustrates a Jewish form of gnosticism with Greco-Roman allusions. So does Sethian gnostic literature, with its provocative Jewish interpretation of the opening chapters of Genesis and its emphasis on the special roles of Eve, the mother of the living, and Seth, whom the Sethian gnostics claimed as ancestor. Valentinian gnostic literature is named after the great second-century teacher Valentinos, who, along with his students, seems to have made use of Sethian insights in order to fashion an elegant gnostic system for reflecting upon the origin and destiny of true life and light. In Syria, the sacred literature relating to Thomas is closely related to the wisdom gospel of Thomas; Thomas is understood to be the twin of Jesus and the guarantor of his wisdom and knowledge.

The Hermetic literature dates from the first century CE and after. It is named after the Greek god Hermes, the divine messenger, nicknamed Trismegistos, "thrice-greatest," and depicted in a syncretistic way, once again with Jewish and Greco-Roman themes, along with Egyptian motifs. The Mandaeans consist of Middle Eastern gnostic communities that exist to the present day, now in locales around the world. The Mandaeans interpret the opening chapters of Genesis in a typically gnostic manner, but they reserve a special place for John the baptizer, whose style of Jewish baptismal piety they considered to reflect the origin of their communities. Manichaean literature dates from the time of the prophet Mani, the third-century prophet who, with his followers, created a world religion intended to be universal. Manichaeism draws from Zoroastrian, Buddhist, and Christian sources, likely including the Gospel of Thomas and other gnostic texts, in order to announce how the divine light of the cosmos may be saved from the machinations of the forces of darkness and gathered into the kingdom of light. Some of the songs in the Coptic Manichaean Songbook appear to be related to Mandaean literature, and Manichaeism and Mandaeism show connections with each other.

Such Islamic mystical texts as the Mother of Books, as well as Cathar sacred literature, are sometimes described by scholars as late gnostic or neo-manichaean, because of similarities with the traditions of Mani and his followers. The Mother of Books comes from the eighth century CE and represents a form of Islamic *ghuluw,* which literally means "exaggeration." The Cathar texts come from medieval Europe and offer a dualistic message of the triumph of light over darkness. The Cathars, too, like so many gnostics, venerated the Gospel of John. The Gospel of the Secret Supper features John and cites a portion of the Gospel of John as it announces the glory that will finally come to the children of the good god of light: "The just will glow like a sun in the kingdom of the invisible father. And the son of god will take them before the throne of the invisible father and say to them, 'Here I am with my children whom you have given me. Just father, the world has not known you, but I have truly known you, because it is you who have sent me on my mission.'"

In assembling a "Gnostic Bible," what definitions have we used? Where have we drawn the line? Let us examine our definitions more carefully.

The term *gnostic* is derived from the ancient Greek word *gnosis*, "knowledge." *Gnosis* is a common word in Greek, and it can designate different types of knowledge. Sometimes, as in the sacred texts included in this volume, gnosis means personal or mystical knowledge. Understood in this way, gnosis may mean acquaintance, that is, knowledge as personal awareness of oneself or another person or even god, or it may mean insight, that is, knowledge as immediate awareness of deep truths. These ways of understanding gnosis are not mutually exclusive, for knowledge may entail the immediate awareness of oneself or of another, in a personal union or communion that provides profound insight into the true nature of everything. As we have already noted, the Gospel of Thomas has Jesus articulate just such a mystical personal knowledge.

The gnosis sought by the authors of these texts is hardly ordinary knowledge. A text from the Nag Hammadi library, the Exegesis on the Soul (included in this volume), declares that the restoration of the soul to a state of wholeness "is not due to rote phrases or to professional skills or to book learning." Indeed, mystics commonly have emphasized, in many books, that mystical knowledge cannot be attained simply by reading books. Other texts describe this sort of gnosis by listing questions that need to be addressed if one is to be enlightened by knowledge. In the Secret Book of John the savior or revealer announces that she or he will teach "what is, what was, and what is to come," and in the Book of Thomas the revealer commands, "Examine yourself and understand who you are, how you exist, and how you will come to be." To attain this knowledge—to become a gnostic—is to know oneself, god, and everything. Or, in the words of the maxim from the ancient oracular center dedicated to Apollo at Delphi, Greece, a maxim cited frequently in the texts in this volume: *gnothi sauton*, "know yourself." According to many of these sacred texts, to know oneself truly is to attain this mystical knowledge, and to attain this mystical knowledge is to know oneself truly. Gnostic knowledge, then, relies on lived mystical experience, on knowledge of the whole timeline of the world, past, present, and future, and on knowledge of the self—where we have come from, who we are, where we are going—and of the soul's journey.

Thus, the Greek word *gnosis* was used extensively by people in the world of Mediterranean antiquity, including the people who wrote the texts in this volume, but among the heresiologists the word was employed in a particularly polemical fashion. The heresiologists were heresy hunters who, as the guardians of truth and watchmen on the walls of Zion, were trying to expose people judged to be dangerous to the masses, especially the Christian masses.

The more famous of the heresiologists include Irenaeus of Lyon, whose major work was *Adversus haereses,* "Against Heresies"; Hippolytus of Rome, who wrote *Refutatio omnium haeresium,* "Refutation of All Heresies"; Pseudo-Tertullian (an author writing under the name of Tertullian), who wrote *Adversus omnes haereses,* "Against All Heresies"; and Epiphanius of Salamis, who authored a particularly nasty piece entitled *Panarion,* "Medicine Chest," with an orthodox remedy for every heretical malady. The neoplatonist philosopher Plotinos of Lykopolis also wrote a heresiological treatise, *Against the Gnostics,* according to his student Porphyry. All these heresiologists focused, to one extent or another, upon the supposed gnosis of the heretics, and they suggested that at least some—even if only a few—of the heretics could be called *gnostikoi,* gnostics, or referred to themselves as *gnostikoi.* While these heretics used the word *gnosis,* they did not necessarily call themselves gnostics. Irenaeus wrote five volumes against heresies, and he claimed to have composed an "exposé and refutation of falsely so-called knowledge." Irenaeus and his fellow heresiologists, motivated by a religious zeal to expose and refute people with whom they disagreed, were rather sloppy and imprecise in their use of terms and their enumeration of heresies. Yet their presentations of gnosis, "falsely so-called gnosis," have played a role, albeit a polemical one, in defining the terms *gnosis, gnostic,* and *gnosticism* in modern discussions.

The widespread use of the word *gnosis* (and similar words in other languages, for example, in Coptic and Latin), and the polemical application of this word and related words among the heresiologists, have created a challenge for scholars and students who wish to understand gnosticism. What is gnosticism, the religion of gnosis? *Gnosis* is a word widely attested in the ancient world, but the word *gnosticism* itself is a term not attested at all in antiquity or late antiquity. Rather, it first was used in the eighteenth century to designate the heretical religious groups discussed by the heresiologists. Are gnosticism and gnosis valid categories for analysis? Who actually were the gnostics? These questions have become even more interesting when scholars have reflected upon gnosticism and gnosis in relation to hermetic, Mandaean, Manichaean, Shiʿite, and Cathar religions. Further, the discovery and publication in recent times of primary texts (as opposed to the secondary texts of the heresiologists) generally considered to be gnostic has raised the issues of definition and taxonomy in new and exciting ways. Among these primary texts are those from the Askew Codex (Pistis Sophia, or Faith Wisdom), the Bruce Codex, the Berlin Gnostic Codex 8502, and the Nag Hammadi library. The Nag Hammadi library is a treasure trove of Coptic texts, most previously unknown and many considered gnostic by scholars. The texts in the Nag Hammadi library were discovered around December 1945 near Nag Hammadi in upper Egypt, and they are now becoming available in editions and translations. A substantial number of texts in the present volume are from the Nag Hammadi library.

Scholars of ancient and late antique religions have attempted to sort through the issues of definition and taxonomy in order to reach some clarity regarding gnosis and gnosticism. In 1966 many of the leading scholars of gnosis gathered at an international conference in Messina, Italy, and produced a set of statements that are meant to define gnosis and gnosticism. Gnosis, they maintain, is "knowledge of the divine mysteries reserved for an élite," and this is a term of very broad application. On the other hand, gnosticism is "a coherent series of characteristics that can be summarized in the idea of a divine spark in man, deriving from the divine realm, fallen into this world of fate, birth and death, and needing to be awakened by the divine counterpart of the self in order to be finally reintegrated."[2] Gnosticism is thus a religious movement represented by religious groups that emerged in the second century CE and after, especially within the context of Christianity, groups such as the followers of Basilides and Valentinos, two particularly significant early Christian teachers of gnostic religion.

This distinction between gnosis and gnosticism resembles that of Hans Jonas in his books *The Gnostic Religion* and *Gnosis und spätantiker Geist*, in which he distinguishes between the gnostic principle—"the spirit of late antiquity"—and the gnostic movement or movements. The gnostic religion, Jonas suggests, is a religion of knowledge, with "a certain conception of the world, of man's alienness within it, and of the transmundane nature of the godhead."[3] This knowledge is communicated creatively in myths, which contain themes borrowed freely from other religious traditions and which employ an elaborate series of symbols. The end result, according to Jonas, is the expression of religious dualism, dislocation, alienation—"the existing rift between God and world, world and man, spirit and flesh."[4] Whereas Valentinian gnostics (and others) seek to derive dualism from a primordial oneness, Manichaean gnostics begin with a dualism of two opposing principles. But both options remain dualistic.[5] For Jonas, these expressions of gnostic dualism can be articulated

2. Bianchi, ed., *Le origini dello gnosticismo*, p. xxvi. On the history of the discussion of gnosticism, see King, *What Is Gnosticism?*
3. Jonas, *Gnostic Religion*, p. 101.
4. Ibid., p. 237.
5. Today scholars are arguing about whether or not the Manichaeans were truly gnostics, as Jonas affirmed.

in terms of modern philosophical existentialism. The gnostic drama highlights the self-experience of a person as *Geworfenheit,* "thrownness," abandonment of self in the world. As the Secret Book of John and other texts describe it, one is thrown into this world, into a body, into the darkness. Yet, Jonas states, "There is no overlooking one cardinal difference between the gnostic and the existentialist dualism: Gnostic man is thrown into an antagonistic, anti-divine and therefore anti-human nature, modern man into an indifferent one. Only the latter case represents the absolute vacuum, the really bottomless pit."[6] Ancient gnostics and modern existentialists may both be nihilistic, but we modern folks, in our post-Christian world, face the more profound abyss: the uncaring abyss. For gnostics, there is light in the darkness and hope in the abyss.

More recently scholars have questioned these ways of describing and defining gnosis and gnosticism. Here we shall consider three significant attempts to shed new light on the gnostic debate, those by Elaine Pagels, Bentley Layton, and Michael Williams.

1. In *The Gnostic Gospels,* Elaine Pagels admits that Jonas's book *The Gnostic Religion* remains "the classic introduction," but in her own book Pagels depicts gnostics in a different way.[7] She reads the gnostic gospels and draws conclusions about social and political concerns that motivated the gnostics. Thus, for Pagels, the gnostics formulated teachings on the spiritual resurrection of Christ that subverted the emerging orthodox church's hierarchy of priests and bishops, whose authority was—and still is—linked to the messengers or apostles who were witnesses of the bodily resurrection of Christ. The gnostic teaching on spiritual resurrection and spiritual authority, Pagels observes, "claimed to offer to every initiate direct access to God of which the priests and bishops themselves might be ignorant."[8] Again, Pagels notes that the gnostics formulated teachings on the multiple manifestations of god, the mother and the father, that subverted the emerging orthodox church's commitment—which still can be found—to the authority of one bishop, and a male bishop at that. In these and other ways, as Adolf von Harnack once said and Pagels also recalls, the gnostics may have been the "first Christian theologians," whose ideas and actions stimulated theological thinking in the Christian church. In Pagels's view, the gnostics lived as freethinking advocates of a

---

6. Ibid., p. 338.
7. Pagels, *Gnostic Gospels,* p. xxxi.
8. Ibid., p. 27.

mystical spirituality, and they talked a different talk and walked a different walk than the emerging orthodox church. To many readers of Pagels's book the gnostics seemed to advocate a more attractive sort of spirituality than that of the orthodox priests, bishops, and heresiologists, and they seemed to be on the right side of many issues that remain important issues to the present day. Pagels was accused by some reviewers of portraying the gnostics in too attractive a fashion. Nonetheless, *The Gnostic Gospels* offers a compelling portrayal of the gnostics as freethinking mystics who recommended a direct experience of god, unmediated by church hierarchy.

2. In *The Gnostic Scriptures,* Bentley Layton assembles an anthology of gnostic texts in English translations as authoritative gnostic scriptures. The title of Layton's book is close to the title of our volume, and the conception is similar, though more limited in scope. Like the scholars assembled at Messina, and like Hans Jonas, Layton distinguishes between two meanings of the word *gnostic:* "One is a broad meaning, denoting all the religious movements represented in this book, and many more besides. The elusive category ('gnosticism') that corresponds to this broad meaning has always been hard to define. The other meaning of 'gnostic' is narrow and more strictly historical: it is the self-given name of an ancient Christian sect, the *gnostikoi,* or 'gnostics.'"[9] Layton points out, as we have noted, that the words *gnostikos,* "gnostic," and *gnostikoi,* "gnostics," were uncommon in the world of antiquity and late antiquity, and that the Christian sect that called itself the gnostics has been nicknamed the Sethians, or else the Barbeloites, Barbelognostics, Ophians, or Ophites, by ancient heresiologists and modern scholars. These gnostics form the foundation for Layton's anthology, and Part One of his book, "Classic Gnostic Scriptures," is devoted to gnostic works in this limited sense of the word. The subsequent parts of his book have additional texts—texts written by Valentinians, by the followers of Judas Thomas, and by proponents of the systems of Basilides and Hermetic religion.

Michael Williams, in his book *Rethinking "Gnosticism"* (discussed next), applauds Layton's efforts to be as exact as possible in his use of terms, but he points out that the Coptic primary texts classified by Layton as classic gnostic scripture do not refer to themselves as gnostic and are not indisputably gnostic. The term *gnostic* is not used in so simple a way as Layton maintains, Williams continues; for example, Irenaeus says that the followers of a woman named Marcellina

---

9. Layton, *Gnostic Scriptures,* p. 5.

called themselves gnostics, but Layton does not include them anywhere in his anthology. Yet, in spite of Williams's protestations—and with his grudging acknowledgment—it must be admitted that Layton has convincingly demonstrated the connections among a variety of texts that are gnostic. In the present volume we too shall feature these classic or Sethian gnostic texts prominently in Part Two of our book, "Literature of Gnostic Wisdom."

3. In *Rethinking "Gnosticism,"* Michael Williams is more negative is his assessment of the word *gnosticism*. He argues for "dismantling a dubious category," the dubious category being gnosticism itself. Williams begins by giving his own definition of gnosticism: "What is today usually called ancient 'gnosticism' includes a variegated assortment of religious movements that are attested in the Roman Empire at least as early as the second century CE."[10] While he casts his net widely in his discussion of this set of religious movements, Williams does not include Hermetic, Mandaean, Manichaean, and later religions in his discussion. He does survey the use of the terms *gnosis* and *gnostic* in both the heresiological sources and the primary gnostic texts, and he finds that rarely do gnostics seem to have described themselves as such, and the occasional use of the term *gnostic* among the heresiologists is uneven, ambiguous, and contradictory. Further, the effort on the part of scholars to employ gnosticism as a typological category has also failed. Scholars have proposed, variously, that gnosticism was an anticosmic protest movement, or an innovative religion of adoption and adaptation of other religious traditions, or a religion of spiritualists who hated the body, or of ethical radicals who opted for either an ascetic or a bohemian lifestyle, and so on. Williams judges that these descriptions of gnosticism are caricatures of a diverse set of religious movements—misguided efforts to define a single, overarching category called gnosticism. Instead, Williams proposes that we jettison the category gnosticism altogether and focus our attention on specific religious movements, for instance, the Valentinians.

In addition, Williams suggests a new category to replace gnosticism:

> I would suggest the category "biblical demiurgical traditions" as one useful alternative. By "demiurgical" traditions I mean all those that ascribe the creation and management of the cosmos to some lower entity or entities, distinct from the highest God. This

---

10. Williams, *Rethinking "Gnosticism,"* p. 3.

would include most of ancient Platonism, of course. But if we add the adjective "biblical," to denote "demiurgical" traditions that also incorporate or adapt traditions from Jewish or Christian Scripture, the category is narrowed significantly. In fact, the category "biblical demiurgical" would include a large percentage of the sources that today are usually called "gnostic," since the distinction between the creator(s) of the cosmos and the true God is normally identified as a common feature of gnosticism."[11]

Rethinking "Gnosticism" is one of the more thought-provoking books to have appeared in the past several years on the topic of the definition of gnosis and gnosticism. In spite of Williams's argument, however, in this volume we shall continue to use the term *gnostic*. We do so for three reasons.

First, Williams concedes, as we have seen above, that Bentley Layton has brought some clarity to the discussion of what is gnostic, and he acknowledges with Layton that there are in fact connections among gnostic texts. The savvy of scholars from the time of the Messina colloquium and Hans Jonas to the present day is vindicated in the continual use of the terms *gnosis, gnosticism,* and *gnostic,* though now with important qualifications. We too shall continue to make use of these terms.

Second, Williams stresses the widespread diversity within the category gnosticism, and of course he is correct in doing so. Yet his recognition of gnostic diversity merely parallels the similar recognition by scholars of diversity in Judaism and Christianity. This recognition of diversity has led Jacob Neusner to suggest "Judaisms" and Jonathan Z. Smith "Christianities" as appropriate terms for these diverse religious movements. Perhaps we might also opt for "gnosticisms" or "gnostic religions" as a similar way of acknowledging the differences among religions of gnosis.

Third, we continue to use the terms *gnosis, gnosticism,* and *gnostic* with a particular understanding of comparison and classification. In *Drudgery Divine,* Jonathan Z. Smith reminds us that comparisons do not necessarily tell us how things actually are as much as they tell us about the people doing the comparisons and their assumptions and perspectives. Smith notes that statements of comparison are triadic, with an implicit "more than" and an additional "with respect to." Thus, A resembles B more than C with respect to N.

---

11. Ibid., pp. 51–52.

Seen in this light, statements of comparison are always relative and contextual. This understanding of comparison and classification may be helpful to us in our current discussion of what is gnostic.

Contrary to those who doubt whether there is any set of traits (N) that allow us to compare and classify religions of gnosis as gnostic, in this volume we wish to suggest a set of gnostic traits that in fact may be helpful in comparing and classifying texts and traditions.

To do this, we begin by building on the observation that, according to Irenaeus of Lyon, the people we here refer to as Sethians defined and described themselves as gnostics. Here is the historical basis for the use of *gnostic* as a valid term of self-definition.

Next we continue to explore who the gnostics were by identifying traits that were characteristic of these Sethians who called themselves gnostics. Irenaeus helps us by citing sacred materials that were used by Sethian gnostics, and it turns out that these materials are remarkably similar to the classic Sethian text entitled the Secret Book of John, presented prominently below. Through a careful examination of the Secret Book of John we identify five traits that we suggest are central to this gnostic text and that guide us in understanding Sethian gnostics. The Secret Book of John proclaims the importance of (1) gnosis, or mystical knowledge, (2) understood through themes of wisdom and (3) presented in creations stories, particularly in Genesis, and (4) interpreted through a variety of religious and philosophical traditions, including platonism, (5) in order to announce a radically enlightened way and life of knowledge. These five traits, we propose, may help us describe the leading features of Sethian gnostics.

Finally, we extend the use of the terms *gnostic* and *gnosticism* to other movements that appear to be linked to Sethian gnostics historically or that resemble Sethian gnostics phenomenologically. Sometimes there seem to be historical connections between Sethian gnostic texts and texts that are representative of some other sort of gnosis, and at other times there seem to be clear similarities in content and theme. This wider application of the terms *gnostic* and *gnosticism* allows us to classify comparable texts and traditions as representative of gnosticism.

In this volume, then, we understand the following to be the traits of gnostic religions:

1. While the spirit of late antiquity exhibits certain gnostic features, as Hans Jonas has shown, religious movements that are to be classified as gnostic

religions in a specific sense are those that give a primary place to gnosis, unmediated mystical knowledge, as the way to salvation and life.

2. Gnostic religions typically employ wisdom traditions that are related to the Jewish family of religions but are usually influenced by Greek thought, and wisdom (or another manifestation of the divine) is often personified as a character in a cosmic drama.

3. Gnostic religions typically present stories and myths of creation, especially from the book of Genesis, interpreted in an innovative manner, with the transcendent divine spirit commonly distinguished from the creator of the world, often to the point of dualism, in order to explain the origin, estrangement, and ultimate salvation of what is divine in the world and humanity.

4. In their explanations and interpretations, gnostic religions typically make use of a wide variety of religious and philosophical traditions and find truths in a diversity of sources, such as Jewish, Greek, and other sources, including platonism.

5. Gnostic religions typically proclaim the vision of a radically enlightened life that transcends the mundane world and attains to the divine.

These traits of gnostic religions come to expression, to varying degrees, in the sacred texts that are included in this volume: wisdom gospels, classic texts of gnostic religions—Sethian, Valentinian, Syrian, and other gnostic religions—and Hermetic, Mandaean, Manichaean, Islamic, and Cathar texts. These traits, though derived from an analysis of a Sethian text of fundamental significance from a tradition that understood itself to be gnostic, do not necessarily come to expression in a uniform way in the texts included here—recall what Jonathan Z. Smith said about the relative nature of comparisons. Yet all of the texts included in this volume address the interests of gnosis and gnosticism.

The term *bible* is derived ultimately from the ancient Greek word *biblos* (or *byblos*), meaning "papyrus," the reed used to make a primitive sort of paper in order to construct scrolls and codices, or books, in the world of ancient bookbinding. The Greek word was also written in a diminutive form, *biblion*; the plural is *biblia*, "books." Within the context of Judaism and Christianity certain books came to be associated with the sacred scriptures, which in turn were eventually referred to in the singular, the Bible. Thus, within the history of the use of the term, the Bible, or the book, designates a collection or anthology of sacred texts.

We can explain how this set of meanings came to be associated with the word *Bible* by examining the process of establishing a canon or canons within Judaism and Christianity. Organized religions usually teach that adherents to a given religion should observe the tenets of the tradition in a way that is right, proper, and correct according to a given canon. (Originally a canon was a cane or reed, a measuring stick, but the term came to be applied to any standard by which one might determine whether a person's thoughts or actions measure up to the standard of correctness in the tradition.) Judaism, Christianity, and Islam are religions of the book, and so their canons are written canons, authoritative books and anthologies. For Judaism and Christianity, their authoritative books are the Hebrew Bible (or, more exactly, the Tanakh, that is, the Torah ["law"], Neviim ["prophets"], and Kethuvim ["writings"]) and the New Testament (or the New Covenant), respectively. The Hebrew Bible was used in antiquity in Hebrew and in Greek translation. The Greek version called the Septuagint was completed in Alexandria, Egypt, by bilingual Jewish translators during the first centuries BCE. A legend emerged that the Septuagint was written in a miraculously identical fashion by seventy-two translators who labored in pairs over a period of seventy-two days. The Septuagint was the Bible of the early Christian church, which originated, after all, as a Jewish religious movement. This Greek translation of the scriptures of Judaism contains several texts not included in the Hebrew Bible—for example, Baruch, 1 Esdras, Judith, 1–4 Maccabees, Sirach, Tobit, and the Wisdom of Solomon. To this day the inclusion or exclusion of these texts contained in the Septuagint remains a canonical issue among Protestant, Roman Catholic, and Orthodox Christians.

The formation of the New Testament as the Christian Bible was a gradual process that took centuries to complete. Finally, at the Council of Trent in 1545, the Roman Catholic Church acted to recognize its list of biblical, canonical books as final, that is, closed to any additions or subtractions. (Minor changes from the work of textual critics are quietly incorporated into new printings of Bible translations.) Many Protestant denominations have never acted officially to recognize a biblical canon. While there is widespread agreement among Christians concerning what books should be included in the New Testament, the traditions of the Syrian and Ethiopic churches have claimed that different sets of texts should be included in the Christian canon. Today some are proposing the Gospel of Thomas as an authoritative Christian text, and the Jesus Seminar in Santa Rosa, California, is discussing the possibility of a new New Testament, a new Christian Bible.

Arguably the most influential person in the process of the formation of a New Testament was a second-century Christian teacher, a dyed-in-the-wool dualist named Marcion of Sinope. Marcion is sometimes included in discussions of the gnostics because of his radical dualism, but his Christian religion was a religion of faith rather than gnosis. In this volume we consider Marcion to be an unrepentant Paulinist, with a literalistic way of reading the Bible, rather than a gnostic. As one prominent scholar quipped, the only person in the second century who understood Paul was Marcion, and he misunderstood him.

Marcion was a rich shipowner turned evangelist who went to Rome in the middle of the second century in order to contribute his money and his teachings to the Roman church. Both were returned to him. Marcion preached that the good and loving god, revealed in Christ, must be distinguished from the just and righteous god, who was the god of the Jewish people. Marcion's theological dualism, with all its anti-Semitic implications, necessitated for him the creation of a new Bible, a new authoritative book for the god newly revealed in Christ. Marcion wrote a book, a rather simple-minded piece called the Antitheses, with quotations from Jewish and Christian texts that seemed to Marcion to show the striking contrasts between the Jewish god and the Christian god. Marcion also formulated a Christian canon—as far as we can tell, he was the first Christian to come up with the idea of a separate Christian Bible. He knew of a series of letters of Paul, and he knew of the Gospel of Luke, which he considered Paul's gospel, and he combined these into his New Testament. And when he read in Paul's letter to the Galatians that some troublesome people want to "pervert the gospel of Christ" (1:7), he took the words seriously and literally. He assumed that lackeys of the Jewish god were perverting the written texts by penning in words favorable to the Jewish god and the scriptures of the Jewish god. Marcion responded as a highly opinionated textual critic by removing the sections of Paul's letters and Luke's gospel that he thought needed to be erased in order to restore the texts to their original form. For Marcion's misguided efforts his foe Tertullian chided him, "Shame on Marcion's eraser!"

Marcion proved to be popular and influential as a leader of his church, but only for a time. Eventually he was rejected by many Christians, including the heresiologists, and declared a heretic. The Christians opposed to Marcion disliked his insistence on two gods and his rejection of Judaism and the god of the Hebrew Bible. Instead, such Christians looked for continuity in the history of salvation from Judaism to Jesus and beyond. Yet the Christian canonical idea of Marcion carried the day, as did Marcion's basic outline of the Christian canon, with a gospel section and an epistolary (Pauline) section. From the perspective of the Christian Bible, Marcion lost the battle but won the war.

When we refer to the texts in the present volume as *The Gnostic Bible,* we are in this world of discourse. We are presenting these texts as sacred books and sacred scriptures of the gnostics, and collectively as sacred literature of the gnostics. But in this Bible of the gnostics there is no sense of a single, authoritative collection. The sacred literature in this Bible illustrates a diversity that we have suggested is characteristic of gnostic religions. Further, the sacred literature in this Bible constitutes no closed canon. We present here what we judge to be the most significant gnostic texts, but there are other gnostic texts that have not been included. All these gnostic texts may be equally authoritative, truths may be discovered in a variety of texts and traditions, and the way to wisdom and knowledge cannot be closed. Such a sense of wisdom and knowledge has made this sacred literature attractive to free spirits in the past and equally fascinating to many in the present day.

LETTING IN THE LIGHT

Translating Holy Texts

WILLIS BARNSTONE

*Spiritual and mystical scriptures survive on the
fire of art. Without the fire the new word is dead.*

—Pierre Grange, "On Translating the Holy"

R uminating about literary translation is an ancient habit. A primary idea has been that the aesthetic of the original should shine in translation. If that old news were remembered, we might stop here. But for more than a century most versions of religious scripture have retained a formulaic, archaizing lexicon. Sadly, when the source is both religious and supremely literary, as are the canons of major religions, the aesthetic disappears in the transfer, whether out of religious faith or academic purpose. The voice, the song, the whisper go unheard. They are not treated as the holy scripture of Homer or Dante.

To maltreat Homer and Dante as the Bible has been hurt would be heresy.

To be sure, religious translation has enjoyed supreme moments. There was the plain and immeasurable beauty of the Tyndale New Testament (1536) and the holy strength of the King James Version (1611). The James, or Authorized, Version was accomplished by some forty-seven scholars, who had been instructed to revise earlier versions. With Tyndale as their main source and genius as their guide, the Authorized's scholars remade the English language and letters forever. Then, in the shadow and authority of the magnificent King James, came imitations and corrections and a plunge to the pedestrian.

Anonymous teams in the Bible industry invented a compromise English, without written or spoken precedent, but the greater readership either held to the Authorized Version or ceased reading the Bible altogether. Early in the twentieth century, the reigning poet and critic T. S. Eliot denounced Gilbert Murray's wooden versions of the Greek classics, but there was no similar regal figure to demand new, vibrant versions of sacred scripture.

Finally, late in the twentieth century came a change in climate and publishing ventures. There appeared the lovely translations of Richmond Lattimore's New Testament and Robert Alter's Genesis and 1 and 2 Samuel. Their example—of great erudition, of fresh fidelity to the complexity, range, and beauty of the word—has proved that Bible translation need not be a weak mirror of a vital past. There is every reason to expect a turn to the larger task of doing the whole Bible in a version, or versions, worthy of the past and our time. "Seamus Heaney's 'Beowolf' rises from the dead," wrote Richard Eder in his review of Heaney's new translation the Old English epic. Eder concluded (perhaps prophetically), "Translation is not mainly the work of preserving the hearth—a necessary task performed by scholarship—but of letting a fire burn in it."[1] Much scholarly translation of religious scripture sees the English version fundamentally as a crib or gloss for reading the source text. These tools are laudable for reading and understanding a foreign page. Facing-page editions are attractive, and the interlinear pony serves as a dictionary for a quick return to the source tongue. Word-for-word versions are a good initial step to converting a foreign page, but verbal misery enters when the student or scholar thinks that the English pony captures the poetry of Horace. An extreme example of literalism is that of Aquila, a second-century proselyte Jew from Pontos, who spent his life retranslating the Hebrew Bible into Greek to replace the Septuagint. He reproduced every word and idiom from the Hebrew and followed Hebrew syntax whenever possible. Of course it was authoritative, sacred, and unreadable. When today the "you" in sacred texts is translated as "you (sing.)" and "you (plur.)," Aquila from Pontos has returned, and he is not singing.

In rendering ancient languages into English, each age has its own speech and demand for a natural reading experience. Most important, if the original is worth transferring to English, it must be rich in sound and sense and sovereign in art. If scripture or myth, it has survived because of its breath and its style.

---

1. *New York Times*, February 22, 2000, p. B8.

Those prophets who spoke magical words were not literary clods. Not if they were to be heard. To make a work heard again, the translator must re-create that cunning of art. Then a text can move pleasantly from foreign obscurity into the light of our own familiar tongue.

Religious scholars have the ancient tongues to bring meaning to obscure alphabets. That is their enormous virtue and power. Sometimes they are scientists seeking information transfer, a dream of absolute denotation, which is clearly incompatible with the connotative richness of scripture. Sometimes they are scholar artists in the act of translating, which is ideal, as in the instances of Lattimore and Alter.

In contrast to the mainly dim renderings of religious texts, the last century saw classical literatures converted into vital contemporary speech. Robert Fitzgerald, Richmond Lattimore, and Robert Fagles, all meticulous scholars, have in distinctive ways given us splendid versions of Homer; and Fitzgerald has carried Virgil's *Aeneid* from Latin—the marble language, as Borges called it—into a resonant English poem. They have made Greek and Latin classics thrilling to read. Like the Bible translators, they translate largely the sacred— but the pagan sacred, not the Judeo-Christian. They renew Homer's bible and Hesiod's theogony, Aeschylus's sacramental drama and Sappho's prayer poems to Aphrodite. Those ancient religions of the Greeks are other, their creators infidel, but that was long ago, and those works that have survived the fires of iconoclasm are no longer a threat or rival heresy. So the translator is free. In contrast to later Bible translations, still profoundly affected by a history of verbal piety, classical literature introduces no authority of faith for its translator poets to contend with and resolve. The Bible did find a way into nineteenth- and twentieth-century literature, decisively and influentially, but not through any new versions. It was the venerable King James Version that held sway and passed into the hearts of Blake and Whitman, and Hopkins, Eliot, and Thomas.

There is no single secret of literary translation. In fact there are many ways, and none of them includes the notion of perfection, since perfection presumes a perfect transfer from one tongue to another, of $a = b$. Language is much too rich, on too many cognitive and aesthetic levels, to be reduced to the perfection of a formula of equality. Only in purely denotive, physically measurable matters—ten acres of land, ten tons of pure iron ore—is exact translation possible and required. Even the slippery notion of "exact equivalence," fashionable in contemporary translation circles, is deception. The ways of translation have diverse linguistic and aesthetic variables, and for literary purposes these registers, from literal to license, from close to imitation, are the subject of books and essays. As for method, closeness need not be a literary travesty, and great creative freedom may arise from the deepest understanding of the source text. In this the scholar may seem to have an advantage. But the next step is to re-create from the source, and there the writer enters. If the scholar and writer artist are one person, it is ideal. However, even the most erudite non-artist scholar, apart from creating a gloss, can only do harm to the aesthetic of the original. Likewise, if the writer artist disdains knowledge of the source text, the result may be lovely but will not go beyond imitation. A frequent solution is to put scholars and writers together, which is exactly what occurred when the forty-seven men assembled to prepare the King James Version. Some contributed Hebrew, others Greek, others the sonorous word, and the result was that grand collaboration. Sometimes one person is both artist and scholar, as Robert Fitzgerald for Homer and Virgil, and Richard Wilbur for Molière's verse plays. More commonly an informant and a writer collaborate intelligently as one voice.

Pragmatically, there must be a meeting between the original creator and the writer who re-creates. When Robert Fitzgerald went to Saint Elizabeth's Hospital, where Ezra Pound was imprisoned, and asked the older poet how to render Homer into English, Pound said simply, "Let Homer speak." It takes great courage to let the original author speak through oneself, the translator. There is always the temptation to listen obliquely or selfishly, and to convert the ancestor's voice completely into one's own. Some follow this temptation and produce masterpieces. Chaucer nobly practiced this art when he turned a Boccaccio tale into *Troilus and Criseyde* and Pound transformed the Chinese poet Li Bai into *Cathay*. More recently, David Ferry's translation of *Gilgamesh*, based on the work of earlier scholars, is a thoroughly felicitous achievement. The other Fitzgerald, Edward of *The Rubáiyát of Omar Khayyám*, in 1859 published his free adaptation from the twelfth-century Persian mystical poet. Selecting certain verses of the sequence, he arranged them in a new order. His work is praised as a classic of English literature, standing on its own, escaping the scarlet-T label of "mere" translation. It achieved the dignity of an original. So too the King James Version has for centuries been popularly received as "original scripture" containing the exact chapter and verse of "gospel truth."

Bringing words understood only by clergy into the light of common understanding has historically required not only art but great courage as well. The history of these efforts is appalling.

John Wyclif (1320–84), a master at Balliol College in Oxford, was the first to transfer the gospels into the modern vernacular. With impoverished preachers, who were called the Lollards, he took the gospels in English to the people. In 1401 Archbishop Arundel denounced Wyclif as heretical, fuming, "The pearl of the Gospel is scattered abroad and trodden underfoot by swine." Arundel further wrote in his report to papal claimant John XXIII in 1421, "This pestilent and wretched John Wyclif, of cursed memory, that son of the old serpent . . . endeavoured by every means to attack the faith and sacred doctrine of Holy Church, devising—to fill up the measure of his malice—the expedient of a new translation into the mother tongue."[2] The scholar's death saved him. Some associates were burned alive for their unauthorized vernacular renderings. Wyclif lay safely in the earth until 1424, when his bones were dug up, burned, and thrown into the River Swift.

Étienne Dolet (1509–46) translated the Bible into French, but it was for translating Plato in such a way as to subvert the notion of immortality that he was tried for heresy and taken to the stake. However, in his *Manière de bien traduire d'une langue en aultre* (1540), he did leave us five important rules of translating, of which the final one applies to all good writing: "The translator must achieve harmonious cadences, he must compose in a sweet and even style so as to ravish the reader's ear and intellect."[3]

William Tyndale dared to translate the New Testament into English. It is fair to say that he established the English language for the Bible: the King James Version of the New Testament is in large part Tyndale's phraseology. Tyndale's prose is clear, modern, minimally Latinized, and with unmatched narrative powers. Everything is fresh, including the use of very common words, unelevated for religious respectability.

For "his cunning counterfeit," which Bishop Wolsey called "persiferous and most pernicious poison," he was arrested. It is good to remember that the word once had so much power to disturb. Sir Thomas More ranted alliteratively against this "devilish drunken soul," who challenged the hierarchy with his English phrases, which the lowest figure of society would receive without mediation of Latin or clergy. In what amounted to a poem of rage, More pronounced that "this drowsy drudge hath drunken so deep in the devil's dregs that if he wake and repent himself the sooner he may hap to fall into draff that

---

2. Quoted in Barnstone, *The Poetics of Translation*, p. 201.
3. Quoted in Steiner, *After Babel*, p. 263.

the hogs of hell shall feed upon."[4] More specifically, More wrote, "Tyndale has wilfully mistranslated the scripture, and deceived blind unlearned people by teaching what he knows to be false. His life is of likelihood as evil as his teaching, worse it cannot be. He is a beast who teaches vice, a forewalker of antichrist, a devil's limb."[5]

Yet none of these attacks could erase Tyndale's genius of plain word and humble ideal, nor hush his plea for a candle and a Hebrew dictionary to continue his heretical translations as he lingered for nearly two years in his lightless cell. Tyndale's hope for a new audience coincided with that expressed by his admired Erasmus, whose work *Exhortations to the Diligent Study of Scripture* Tyndale translated in 1529:

> I wold desire that all women should reade the gospell and Paules episteles and I wold to God they were translated in to the tonges of all men so that they might not only be read and knowne of the scotes and yrishmen But also of the Turkes and the Sarracenes. . . . I wold to God the plowman wold singe a texte of the scripture at his plow-beme. And that the wever at his lowme with this wold drive away the tediousness of tyme. I wold the wayfaringe-man with this pastyme wold expelle the weriness of his iorney.[6]

Tyndale's translation of scripture into the everyday English was to expose the faithful to a forbidden text, a deed as heretical as revealing a proscribed gnostic scripture or of affirming the prime authority of Hebrew Scripture, which was routinely called "the corrupt original." For his crime, on October 6, 1536, William Tyndale was taken to the stake, strangled by the hangman, and burned.

An epilogue to Tyndale's death and his unfinished labor of Bible translation came with the King James Bible, which accomplished under royal command what William Tyndale courageously desired to do on his own. The preface to the James concludes with a line redeeming not only the vernacular version but the notion of the word as light, the *logos* as *phos*, which is also the spiritual essence of gnosticism: "Translation it is that openeth the window, to let in the light."

---

4. Quoted in MacGregor, *Literary History of the Bible from the Middle Ages to the Present Day,* p. 115.
5. Quoted in Mozley, *William Tyndale,* p. 217.
6. Quoted in Barnstone, *The Poetics of Translation,* p. 204.

These little books constituting *The Gnostic Bible* are a privilege to transfer into English. Though heterogeneous, they have a common flame of belief, a mythical memory of creation and gods, and a poetry that goes through all forms. The purpose of cosmic tale, exegesis, and sermon is to convert you, the ancient and now modern reader; to bring you along to a secret knowledge available within you. These scriptures have a generosity of spirit, and while they are not immune to issuing religious warnings, light overcomes darkness, and spirit rises internally above the confines of its earthly body. These are texts written by passionate philosophers and allegorizing exegetes. In these disparate groups, from China to Provence, who held that we are sparks of light caught in a perishable body, there is a constant excitement of the new and a freedom to invent and to contend with all dark error. The Cathars, the last major gnostic speculation, recalled and reinvented scripture, and their troubadours composed and sang with satiric fun and shocking candor—all while the swords of the Albigensian Crusade (1209) prepared to extinguish them.

Now these ancient heresies, preserved in a variety of versions, survive as profound, powerful utterances. From the first-century Gospels of Thomas and John and the Book of Baruch to the twelfth-century Gospel of the Secret Supper, these copied and recopied and translated scriptures have haphazardly come down to us. Buried by a cliff in Egypt or discovered in an Inquisition archive on the Cathars, they are as fresh as outrage. We have a world literature of cosmogonies and diatribes, delicious songs of Solomon from the Syriac, essential metaphysical speculation, and the cunning whisper of the spirit. They are not ordinary. They are for your eyes to hear.

PART ONE

Early Wisdom Gospels

INTRODUCTION

MARVIN MEYER

In the beginning was wisdom, Hokhmah, Sophia.

One of the earliest forms of exalted expression in the world of Mediterranean and Middle Eastern antiquity was wisdom. Wisdom can be both the product of experience and the gift of the gods. Wisdom is what the father teaches the son, the parent the child, the sage the student. Through wisdom and knowledge, people learn how to speak and act among family and friends and foes, in social encounters, in the political arena, on the street. Through wisdom and knowledge, people learn about the world and the ways of the world, and how to cope with it. Through wisdom and knowledge, people address the ultimate questions: Why do the wicked prosper? Why do the good suffer? What is the end of human life? Is this all there is?

ANCIENT SAGES AND WISDOM LITERATURE

From the times of the ancient Egyptians and Mesopotamians, wisdom and knowledge have been seen as keys to a good and successful life. So in Egypt an old sage, under the name of Ptahhotep, offers advice to his "son" with everyday observations and clever turns of speech: "Do not let your heart be puffed up because of your knowledge. Do not be confident because you are wise. Take counsel with the ignorant as well as the wise. The full limits of skill cannot be attained, and there is no skilled person equipped to full advantage. Good speech is hidden more than the emerald, but it may be found with young women at the grindstones." Again: "If you are a leader commanding the affairs of the multitude, seek out for yourself every beneficial deed, until it may be that your own affairs are without wrong. Justice is great, and its appropriateness is lasting; it has not been disturbed since the time of the one who made it, whereas there is punishment for one who passes over its laws. . . . The strength of justice is that it lasts."[1]

In ancient Mesopotamia, wisdom is also praised, often as a gift of the gods. In one text an unnamed sage praises wisdom and the divine lord of wisdom, here understood to be Marduk, god of Babylon, whose way is both terrible and gentle: "I will praise . . . Marduk, the lord of wisdom, the deliberate god, who lays hold of the night but frees the day, whose fury surrounds him like a storm wind, but whose breeze is as pleasant as a morning zephyr, whose anger is irresistible, whose rage is a devastating flood, but whose heart is merciful, whose mind forgiving . . . whose hands the heavens cannot hold back, but whose gentle hand sustains the dying."[2]

In the ancient Greco-Roman world, wisdom was the domain of the philosopher, the lover of wisdom and knowledge, who dispenses wisdom and knowledge. Those philosophers with Cynic proclivities, so named for their rough, doglike lifestyles, employ witty sayings with a Cynic bite in order to teach the good and noble life. Thus: "Marcus Porcius Cato, when asked why he was studying Greek literature after his eightieth year, said, 'Not that I may die learned but that I may not die unlearned.'" And: "The Pythagorean philosopher Theano, when asked by someone how long it takes after having sex with a man for a woman to be pure to go to the Thesmophoria, said, 'If it is with her own husband, at once, but if with someone else's, never.'" And again: "When Diogenes the Cynic philosopher saw a country boy scooping up water in his hand in order to drink, he threw away the cup that he was carrying in his bag and said, 'Now I can be this much lighter.'"[3]

In the world of early Judaism, sages are revered for their insight into the human condition before god, and sometimes the wisdom they proclaim is personified as Hokhmah (in Hebrew) or Sophia (in Greek), terms of feminine gender used to indicate wisdom as the female expression of the divine. The figure of wisdom in Judaism echoes the earlier goddesses of wisdom in other traditions—Maat in Egypt, Ishtar in Mesopotamia—and wisdom's career continues through the gnostic texts published in the present volume. In Proverbs wisdom herself is said to raise her voice:

1. Pritchard, ed., *Ancient Near Eastern Texts*, p. 412.
2. Ibid., p. 596.
3. On sayings of the Cynic philosophers, see Hock and O'Neil, *The Chreia in Ancient Rhetoric*.

O people, to you I call out
and raise my voice to all the living.
You the simple, learn prudence;
acquire intelligence, you the foolish.

Listen, for I have noble things to say,
and from my lips will come what is right.

Choose my instruction instead of silver,
knowledge rather than choice gold.
Wisdom is more precious than jewels,
and nothing you desire compares with her.

I wisdom live with prudence
and possess knowledge and discretion.

The lord brought me forth
as the first of his works,
the first of his acts of old.

Ages ago I was set up,
at the beginning before the world began.

I was at his side like a master worker
and was filled with delight,
rejoicing before him always,
rejoicing in his whole world
and delighting in his people.
(Proverbs 8:4–6, 10–12, 22–23, 30–31)

This ancient wisdom, which provided ideas of how people might live with insight, virtue, and happiness, proved to be compelling, and wisdom sayings were communicated both by word of mouth and in written form. In the ancient world, Egyptian, Mesopotamian, Greco-Roman, and Jewish books of wisdom were compiled and circulated widely. The wisdom literature of ancient Egypt and Mesopotamia dates back to the second and third millennia BCE with collections of wisdom sayings by sages such as Amenemhat, Amenemope, Ptahhotep, Shuruppak, and Ahikar. The Cynic sayings from Greco-Roman times were collected in textbooks called *Progymnasmata*. These sayings were called *chreiai*, "useful sayings," and they were judged useful for rhetorical instruction and for the conduct of life. The *Progymnasmata* were used within educational systems into the Byzantine period and far beyond, even into the modern world, in educational systems in Europe and the American colonies. Jewish wisdom literature is included within the Hebrew Bible and elsewhere. Some of the prominent books of Jewish wisdom are Proverbs, Ecclesiastes, Song of Songs, the Wisdom of Solomon, and Sirach, as well as the tractate *Pirke aboth* (Sayings of the Fathers), which is included in the Talmud.

JESUS THE JEWISH SAGE

Within this dynamic world of ancient wisdom, Hokhmah, Sophia, Jesus of Nazareth (or Yeshua, using his Semitic name) was born to humble beginnings in Galilee, in Israel. In later christology Jesus would attain the stature of divinity, but his actual life may have been closer to that of a wisdom teacher— that is, a rabbi. The Christian gospels and other theological statements describe Jesus as the Christ, the messiah, the anointed, the son of god and son of man (or earthly son, human son, human child—several translations are used in this collection). According to the Gospel of John, Jesus is the word of god, god in human flesh. The Apostles' Creed proclaims that he was born of the virgin Mary, raised from the dead on the third day, and taken up into heaven, and the Nicene Creed acclaims him as "true god of true god, begotten not made, of one substance (*homoousios*) with the father."[4] Thus Jesus was promoted to be a full member of the godhead, the second person of the divine trinity, composed of god the father, Christ the son, and the holy spirit. Several texts comment on the possibility of the holy spirit as the mother—the true mother—of Jesus, including the Gospel of Thomas, the Gospel of Philip, and the Secret Book of James in this collection.

But the dogmatic Christ of the Nicene Creed and the other Christian creeds is hardly the same person as Jesus of Nazareth. Precisely who Jesus was as a historical person continues to be debated among scholars, and there is no consensus. During much of the twentieth century it was assumed, following Albert Schweitzer, that Jesus was an apocalyptic visionary who foresaw—mistakenly—the end of the world and the dawning of the kingdom of god.

---

4. The Greek word *homoousios* was hotly debated at the Christian church councils, at Nicaea and elsewhere, and some people preferred the word *homoiousios*, "of a similar substance," to the word destined to be voted in as the orthodox term. What a difference a single letter in a Greek word, the modest Greek iota (*i*), can make! No wonder that some parties in the christological debate protested the use of any such Greek word in confessions about Christ. Use only biblical terms, they pleaded, but they were destined to lose the battle.

Schweitzer's paragraph in his *Quest of the Historical Jesus* presents a powerful image of the apocalyptic Jesus:

> There is silence all around. The baptizer appears, and cries, "Repent, for the kingdom of heaven is at hand." Soon after that comes Jesus, and in the knowledge that he is the coming son of man lays hold of the wheel of the world to set it moving on that last revolution which is to bring all ordinary history to a close. It refuses to turn, and he throws himself upon it. Then it does turn, and crushes him. Instead of bringing in the eschatological conditions, he has destroyed them. The wheel rolls onward, and the mangled body of the one immeasurably great man, who was strong enough to think of himself as the spiritual ruler of humankind and to bend history to his purpose, is hanging upon it still. That is his victory and his reign.[5]

That is his victory, that is his reign, that is the kingdom. Jesus was convinced that the kingdom of god would come soon, but he was wrong, Schweitzer claimed—heroically wrong, yet dead wrong.

Today many scholars are questioning whether Schweitzer and others were right in proposing that Jesus was first and foremost an apocalyptic figure. Schweitzer himself seems to have had second thoughts about Jesus as an apocalypticist. During much of his life Schweitzer focused his attention upon the sayings of Jesus—sayings of the Jewish sage—and in a later version of the preface to *The Quest of the Historical Jesus* Schweitzer suggests that Jesus' ethical teachings may be more central to his message than the apocalyptic vision. As scholars increasingly are reasoning, if the apocalyptic vision actually comes from believers in the early church, then the supposed apocalyptic preoccupations of Jesus may have been placed upon him by his biographers. Jesus may not have been a preacher of the apocalypse after all; he may have been a Jewish teacher of wisdom, a teller of stories, a sage.

There is considerable evidence to support the interpretation of Jesus as a Jewish sage. The New Testament Gospels of Matthew, Mark, Luke, and John all contain a substantial amount of material reflecting Jesus' teachings and sayings. Among the first three gospels (usually termed the synoptic gospels), Matthew and Luke have more sayings and stories than Mark, and most scholars think

---

5. Schweitzer, *The Quest of the Historical Jesus*, pp. 370–71.

this is due to an additional written source, besides Mark, that Matthew and Luke both used. In order to make the strong, relatively silent Jesus of Mark's gospel more loquacious, most scholars deduce, Matthew and Luke must have added a collection of Jesus' sayings, now called Q (from *Quelle*, German for "source"), to the story of Jesus.[6] If this is so, then Q must antedate the Gospels of Matthew and Luke as a gospel of the wisdom of Jesus, and thus it may have originated in the middle of the first century, only a couple of decades after Jesus' death. A good case can be made that a version of another early wisdom gospel, the Gospel of Thomas, was also composed in the middle of the first century, around the time of Q, or maybe a little later. This evidence leads to the conclusion that some of the earliest Christian gospels were gospels of wisdom, presenting Jesus as a teacher of wisdom. The sayings gospel Q and the Gospel of Thomas present Jesus of Nazareth as a Jewish sage, and they may well have gotten it, in large part, historically right.

As a Jewish teacher, Jesus announces the presence of the reign or kingdom of god, and he does so with aphorisms and stories (usually termed parables). Q 6:20–31 (from Luke's sermon on the plain and Matthew's sermon on the mount) illustrates how Jesus speaks in this sayings gospel:

> Blessings on you the poor,
>   for the kingdom of god is yours.
> Blessings on you who are hungry,
>   for you will eat well.
> Blessings on you who grieve,
>   for you will be comforted.
> Blessings on you
>   when they insult you
>   and oppress you
>   and tell all kinds of evil about you
>   because of the human child.
>   Rejoice and be glad,
>   for your reward is great in heaven.

---

6. On Q, see Mack, *The Lost Gospel,* and Robinson, Hoffman, and Kloppenborg, *The Critical Edition of Q.* Since Q material is preserved in Matthew and Luke, with variations, we sometimes refer to the Matthean and Lukan versions of Q. The usual means of referencing Q, also used here, employs the chapter and verse designations of Luke.

For this is how they oppressed the prophets
who came before you.

Love your enemies,
and pray for those who oppress you,
that you may be children of your father,
for he makes the sun rise on the evil and the good,
and makes it rain on the just and the unjust.

If someone slaps you on one cheek,
offer the other also.
If someone wants to sue you and take your shirt,
let the person have your coat also.
And if someone compels you to go one mile,
go with the person a second mile.
Give to one who begs from you,
and if someone borrows from you,
do not ask for it back.

And treat people the way you want people to treat you.

The texts that follow in this volume, especially the Gospel of Thomas, give more examples of aphorisms of Jesus. The Gospel of Thomas also presents a number of his stories, or parables, as do other texts in this volume, especially the Secret Book of James and the Book of Thomas.

Thus the sayings attributed to Jesus in Q reflect the Jewish wisdom tradition. But Q also reflects the Jewish tradition of personified wisdom, Sophia, who comes to expression through the sagacity of Jesus. According to the Lukan version of Q 11:49, the wisdom (Sophia) of god utters a saying about those who are sent forth; in the Matthean version it is Jesus who says this. The two texts seem to agree that divine wisdom speaks through Jesus, but this idea is expressed in two different ways. Again, according to the Lukan version of Q 7:35, Jesus refers to wisdom (personified) being vindicated by her children (John the baptizer and Jesus), but in the Matthean version, by her deeds. Once more Jesus and wisdom, Sophia, are closely connected to one another. This relationship between Jesus and wisdom continues in gnostic traditions, as can be seen in other texts within the present collection, for example, the Valentinian texts. John the baptizer likewise continues to play a significant role in other works included here (for example, Gospel of Thomas 46), and his place is particularly prominent in Mandaean texts.

THE GOSPELS OF THOMAS AND JOHN

In this first part of the present book, two early gospels with wisdom orientations are included: the Gospel of Thomas and the Gospel of John. Both present Jesus as a proclaimer of wisdom and knowledge. The Gospel of Thomas (like Q) has pithy sayings of Jesus, the Gospel of John (like many gnostic sources) offers mystical discourses of Jesus, but both stress the role of Jesus as one who discloses insight and knowledge. Although the Gospels of Thomas and John cannot be described as specifically gnostic without some qualification, both of these gospels employ themes that bring to mind gnostic motifs that are more fully developed elsewhere, and the Gospel of John was the favored canonical gospel for gnostic exegesis. The Gospels of Thomas and John may thus be described as representing incipient gnostic perspectives—but they do so in very different ways.

Jesus in the Gospel of Thomas utters life-giving words, promising that those who follow him, respond to his words, and find their true meaning will not taste death. Yet Thomas's Jesus is "just Jesus," as Stephen Patterson puts it.[7] Thomas's Jesus does not pull rank. He does not refer to himself (and he is not referred to by others) as the Christ or the messiah, he is not acclaimed master or lord, he is not announced as the incarnate and unique son of god, and when he refers to himself as the son of man (the human child) once in the gospel (saying 86), he does so in the generic sense of referring to any person or simply to himself. Further, if Thomas's Jesus is a human child, so are other people called human children in the Gospel of Thomas.

Jesus in Thomas is just Jesus, but his words are not just words. They are hidden words of wisdom from a living Jesus who lives on in his sayings—hidden sayings, secret sayings, with hidden meanings. According to the Gospel of Thomas, the interpretation of these wise but hidden sayings will bring knowledge and life. Saying 2 states, "Whoever discovers what these sayings mean will not taste death"; saying 3 goes on to declare, "When you know yourselves, then you will be known, and you will understand that you are children of the living father"; sayings 5 and 6 affirm, "There is nothing hidden that

---

7. Patterson, Bethge, and Robinson, *The Fifth Gospel*, p. 43.

will not be revealed." In its concern for hidden wisdom that is revealed and understood, the Gospel of Thomas displays an interest found in other traditions, especially other gnostic traditions. In the Book of Thomas and the Secret Book of James, for example, reference is also made to hidden sayings of Jesus and the interpretation of the sayings. In the Secret (or Hidden) Book of John, as elsewhere, the revealer indicates that questions will be answered and secrets will be revealed to the inquirers. In the Secret Book of John the secrets of wisdom in the world are said to be revealed, but this is personified wisdom, Sophia, whose story is told in mythical narrative and drama. The Secret Book of John ends with the revealer uttering a curse against anyone who betrays the mystery. The savior says, "I have finished everything for you in your hearing. I have told you everything, for you to record and communicate secretly to your spiritual friends. For this is the mystery of the unshakable race." In such ways is wisdom hidden and revealed in the Gospel of Thomas and the Secret Book of John.

Gospel of Thomas 50 is one of the most perplexing and perhaps one of the most gnostic of the hidden sayings of Jesus. It reflects early traditions about wisdom and the life of the soul (*psyche*), which must go through transitions and passages of life in order to attain its proper destiny. In the present volume, the Song of the Pearl and the Exegesis on the Soul provide versions of such a myth of the soul. In gnostic texts like the Secret Book of John, some of the same motifs are used to present a gnostic account of the story of the light and enlightened people, whose origin is in the divine light, who are created in the image of the divine, and who are given movement and destined for rest in the light. The format of Gospel of Thomas 50, with questions asked and answers given, brings to mind accounts, in other sources and especially gnostic sources, of heavenly powers interrogating the soul as it passes through the spheres of heaven. Of course, many of these ideas are also reminiscent of the creation story in the opening chapters of Genesis, in this case particularly the first creation story in Genesis 1:1–2:3. And these ideas are paralleled in the poem to the divine logos at the opening of the Gospel of John.

In the Gospel of John, in stark contrast to the Gospel of Thomas, Jesus is hardly "just Jesus." In John, Jesus is the Christ, the messiah, the son of god and son of man. He is addressed as rabbi and is called master or lord. Here Jesus is an exalted being, one with god the father, who walks around the world, incognito, as god in the flesh, and who speaks in a way that sounds like the divine talking, in "I am" utterances. There are many of these "I am" declarations throughout ancient religious literature, as well as in the gnostic texts published in the present volume—see Thunder, for example. In the Gospel of

John, John the baptizer, in contrast to Jesus, is nobody: he admits that he is neither the messiah nor Elijah (the prophet of the end time) nor another prophet. The author of the Gospel of John is clearly painting a polemical portrait of John the baptizer, in order to play down the significance of a figure whose role elsewhere, as we have seen, rivals that of Jesus. Among the Mandaeans, John the baptizer is said to be the guarantor of the true ways of *manda*, or gnosis, and Jesus is depicted as one who perverts the law and encourages sorcery and error by departing from John and his ways. The author of the Gospel of John also appears to paint a polemical portrait of another character in his gospel account, namely, Thomas, who becomes in John's gospel the quintessential skeptic, "doubting Thomas." That may be John's way of casting doubt upon the hero of the Gospel of Thomas and other texts, the twin who was responsible for safeguarding the wisdom and knowledge of Jesus.

The Gospel of John, unlike the Gospel of Thomas (and the sayings gospel Q), is a narrative gospel, with a narration of the life of Jesus. John begins his gospel story with the poem to the divine logos:

In the beginning was the word
and the word was with god,
and god was the word.
The word in the beginning was with god.
Through god everything was born
and without the word nothing was born.
What was born through the word was life
and the life was the light of all people
and the light in the darkness shone
and the darkness could not apprehend the light. (1:1-5)

All this echoes what is said of divine wisdom in Proverbs 8 and other texts (see above), but here the Johannine poem serves as a preamble to the story of Jesus. That story proceeds with miracles, called "signs" (Greek, *semeia*) in John, such as Jesus' changing water to wine at Cana.[8] The signs, like the sayings, have hidden meanings: Jesus explains this and other signs to Nikodemos (Nicodemus) in a long, rambling discourse that is characteristic of the Gospel of John—and some other gnostic texts. In his discourse Jesus distinguishes

---

8. This is originally the famous miracle of Dionysos, the Greek god of wine, whose power comes to expression in the transformation of water into wine.

between what is of flesh—like the water and the wine—and what is of spirit, what is earthly and what is heavenly:

> If I tell you of earthly things and you do not believe,
> how if I tell you of heavenly things will you believe? (3:12)

The real meaning of the signs, then, must be on the side of the spiritual and the heavenly. Later Jesus clarifies the meaning of water being changed into wine. The person of Jesus himself is the real, spiritual point of the sign, and Jesus says, with divine nuances,

> I am the true vine and my father is the gardener.

> I am the vine, you the branches.
> You who dwell in me as I in you
> bear much fruit,
> but without me you can do nothing. (15:1, 5)

According to John, then, Jesus the divine word in flesh discloses god:

> The word became flesh and lived among us.
> And we gazed on his glory,
> the glory of the only son of the father,
> who is filled with grace and truth. (1:14)

Jesus in John is a revealer who reveals what god's presence and glory mean:

> No one has ever seen god.
> Only the one born of god,
> who is in the heart of the father,
> has made him known. (1:18)

The story of Jesus in the Gospel of John culminates with the account of the crucifixion and the resurrection appearances of Jesus. This conclusion to the story of Jesus is somewhat like that of the synoptic gospels, which focus special attention on the death and resurrection of Jesus. This sort of conclusion is also similar to the proclamation of the messenger (or apostle) Paul, who maintains that the message of the cross and resurrection is central to the

Christian gospel. In 1 Corinthians Paul argues this point with vigor, and he does so in opposition to the Corinthian Christians, who champion wisdom and a gospel of wisdom; these wisdom Christians may even have used something like Gospel of Thomas 17 (see below, with the note). The Gospel of John, then, like the synoptic gospels and Paul, is quite unlike the sayings gospel Q and the Gospel of Thomas, which show little or no interest in the crucifixion of Jesus.[9]

John's account of the crucifixion of Jesus puts his own theological spin on the story. In the high priestly prayer in John 17 (which is neither high priestly nor a prayer, but instead a commentary on the crucifixion story), Jesus announces that the hour or time has come—the hour or time of his death. The hour of death, however, is not to be an hour of darkness, as in the synoptics, where darkness overshadows the crucifixion of Jesus. Rather, it is an hour of glory and of light. As Jesus says to god,

Father, the hour has come.
Glorify your son so that your son may glorify you.

I glorified you on earth
by completing the work you gave me to do.
And now glorify me, father, with yourself,
with the glory I had with you before the world was. (17:1, 4-5)

The scandal and the sting of the crucifixion are nearly gone in the Gospel of John. Jesus' death is glory, a homecoming, a return to god's heavenly presence above. The light that had fallen, like a shooting star, into the world of darkness, may now return back to god and the fullness (Greek *pleroma*, as in John 1:16) of light above. It is a story reminiscent of the personified wisdom, Hokhmah, Sophia. We shall see this story told about a variety of gnostic revealers and saviors, including Jesus, in the gnostic sacred literature included in this volume.

---

9. On the crucifixion of Jesus in gnostic sources, see particularly the Letter of Peter to Philip, the Gospel of Truth, the Gospel of Philip, the Secret Book of James, the Round Dance of the Cross, and the Second Treatise of the Great Seth; on the resurrection in gnostic sources, see particularly the Treatise on Resurrection.

1

The Gospel of Thomas

The Gospel of Thomas is a wisdom gospel. Like the sayings gospel Q, which most scholars now suggest was a source used in compiling the gospels of Matthew and Luke, the Gospel of Thomas portrays Jesus as one who disseminates life-giving wisdom through his sayings.

Unlike the New Testament gospels of Matthew, Mark, Luke, and John, and other, non-canonical gospels, the Gospel of Thomas contains almost no narrative. Jesus in Thomas performs no physical miracles, reveals no fulfillment of prophecy, announces no apocalyptic kingdom about to disrupt the world order, dies for no one's sins, and does not rise from the dead on Easter Sunday. His value, rather, lies in his enigmatic sayings, which are pregnant with possibility and power. "Whoever discovers what these sayings mean will not taste death," Jesus promises. That is to say, one who uncovers the interpretive keys to the meaning of these sayings thinks Jesus' thoughts after him and completes his sayings in new and sagacious ways. Such a one seeks and finds true wisdom and knowledge.

The editor of the gospel is said to be Judas Thomas, or Judas the twin, who is acclaimed by Syrian Christians as the twin brother of Jesus and the messenger (or apostle) to the Syrians. A version of this gospel may have been composed, most likely in Greek, as early as the middle of the first century, or somewhat later. A few scholars have suggested that the Gospel of Thomas may have been composed in Syriac, but that proposal has not proved to be convincing. The gospel may have been written in Syria, possibly at Edessa (modern Urfa), where the memory of Thomas was revered and where his bones were venerated. Many of the sayings in the Gospel of Thomas recall sayings of Jesus in the New Testament gospels, but many are previously unknown sayings or versions of sayings of Jesus. Some sayings may well derive ultimately from the historical Jesus. The Gospel of Thomas has attracted a great deal of popular interest and was portrayed as a significant and suppressed collection of sayings of Jesus in the film *Stigmata*.

The numbering of the sayings employed here (1–114) is a scholarly convention. The translation gives the Semitic forms of Semitic names, in order to highlight the Jewish identity of Jesus and his students and the Jewish context of the life of the historical Jesus. For example, the name Yeshua is used for Jesus; the other names are identified in the notes.

THE GOSPEL OF THOMAS[1]

These are the hidden sayings that the living Yeshua spoke and Yehuda Toma the twin recorded.[2]

(1) And he said,[3]
   Whoever discovers what these sayings mean[4]
   will not taste death.

(2) Yeshua said,
   Seek and do not stop seeking until you find.
   When you find, you will be troubled.

---

1. The Gospel of Thomas: Nag Hammadi library, Codex II,2, pp. 32,10 to 51,28, and in the Greek fragments in Oxyrhynchus Papyrus 1, 654 and 655; translated from the Coptic by Marvin Meyer. There are many parallels in the New Testament gospels to the sayings of Jesus in the Gospel of Thomas. The New Testament parallels are not listed in the notes, for reasons of economy of space, but the serious seeker will easily find them.
2. Instead of "hidden sayings," we may translate as "secret sayings," or "obscure sayings" (Coptic *enshaje ethep*, Greek Papyrus Oxyrhynchus 654 *hoi logoi hoi [apokryphoi]*). The Book of Thomas has a similar opening, and the Secret Book of James also calls itself a "secret book." Yeshua is Jesus (here and throughout), and Yehuda Toma is Judas Thomas. The "living Yeshua" is almost certainly not a reference to the resurrected Jesus as traditionally understood, but rather to Jesus who lives through his sayings.
3. The speaker is probably Jesus, otherwise Judas Thomas with an editorial remark.
4. Or, "the interpretation [Coptic *hermeneia*, from Greek] of these sayings."

When you are troubled,
you will marvel and rule over all.[5]

(3) Yeshua said,

If your leaders tell you, "Look, the kingdom is in heaven,"
then the birds of heaven will precede you.
If they say to you, "It's in the sea,"[6]
then the fish will precede you.
But the kingdom is inside you and it is outside you.
When you know yourselves,[7] then you will be known,
and you will understand that you are children of the living father.
But if you do not know yourselves,
then you dwell in poverty and you are poverty.

(4) Yeshua said,

A person old in days
will not hesitate to ask a little child
seven days old[8] about the place of life,
and the person will live.[9]
For many of the first will be last
and become a single one.

(5) Yeshua said,

Know what is in front of your face
and what is hidden from you will be disclosed.
There is nothing hidden that will not be revealed.[10]

(6) His students asked him and said to him,

Do you want us to fast?
How should we pray?

---

5. Greek Papyrus Oxyrhynchus 654 adds: "and having ruled, you will rest" (partially restored).
6. Greek Papyrus Oxyrhynchus 654 reads: "it is under the earth."
7. "Know yourself" (Greek *gnothi sauton*) was a famous maxim from the oracular center dedicated to Apollo at Delphi, Greece.
8. This probably indicates an uncircumcised boy (a Jewish boy was to be circumcised on the eighth day), or else a child of the Sabbath of the first week of creation.
9. Hippolytus of Rome cites a version of this saying from the Gospel of Thomas used among the Naassenes, in his *Refutation of All Heresies* 5.7.20: "One who seeks will find me in children from seven years, for there, hidden in the fourteenth age, I am revealed."
10. Greek Papyrus Oxyrhynchus 654 adds: "and nothing buried that will not be raised" (partially restored).

Should we give to charity?
What diet should we observe?[11]

Yeshua said,
Do not lie and do not do what you hate.[12]
All things are disclosed before heaven.
There is nothing hidden that will not be revealed,
nothing covered that will remain undisclosed.

(7) Yeshua said,
  Blessings on the lion if a human eats it,
  making the lion human.
  Foul is the human if a lion eats it,
  making the lion human.[13]

(8) And he said,
  Humankind is like a wise fisherman who cast his net into the sea
  and drew it up from the sea full of little fish.
  Among the fish he found a fine large fish.
  He threw all the little fish back into the sea
  and easily chose the large fish.
  Whoever has ears to hear should hear.

(9) Yeshua said,
  Look, the sower went out, took a handful of seeds,
  and scattered them.
  Some fell on the road
  and the birds came and pecked them up.
  Others fell on rock
  and they did not take root in the soil
  and did not produce heads of grain.
  Others fell on thorns
  and they choked the seeds
  and worms devoured them.

---

11. These questions seem to be answered in saying 14.
12. This is the negative formulation of the golden rule.
13. This obscure saying seems to appeal to the lion as a symbol of all that is passionate and bestial: the passions may either be consumed by a person or consume a person. The Secret Book of John portrays Yaldabaoth, the ruler of this world, as lionlike in appearance. On the saying in general, see Jackson, *The Lion Becomes Man.*

And others fell on good soil
and it brought forth a good crop,
yielding sixty per measure and one hundred twenty per measure.

(10) Yeshua said,
I have thrown fire upon the world,
and look, I am watching till it blazes.

(11) Yeshua said,
This heaven will pass away
and the one above it will pass away.
The dead are not alive
and the living will not die.
During the days when you ate what is dead
you made it alive.
When you are in the light, what will you do?
On the day when you were one
you became two.
But when you become two, what will you do?[14]

(12) The students said to Yeshua,
We know you will leave us.
Who will be our leader?

Yeshua said to them,
Wherever you are, seek out Yaakov the just.[15]
For his sake heaven and earth came into being.

(13) Yeshua said to his students,
Compare me to something
and tell me what I am like.

Shimon Kefa[16] said to him,
You are like a just messenger.

---

14. This saying consists of four riddles about life in this world and beyond. A different phrasing of the third riddle appears in the Naassene Sermon, in Hippolytus of Rome, *Refutation of All Heresies* 5.8.32: "If you ate dead things and made them living, what will you do if you eat living things?"
15. Yaakov the just (or the righteous) is James the just, the brother of Jesus and the leader of the church in Jerusalem until his death in 62 CE. He was given his nickname because of his reputation for piety and Torah observance. On James the just in Jerusalem, see the conclusion to the Secret Book of James.
16. Simon Peter.

Matai[17] said to him,
You are like a wise philosopher.

Toma[18] said to him,
Rabbi,[19] my mouth is utterly unable to say
what you are like.

Yeshua said,
I am not your rabbi.
Because you have drunk, you are intoxicated
from the bubbling spring I tended.[20]

And he took him and withdrew, and spoke three sayings[21] to him.

When Toma came back to his friends, they asked him,
What did Yeshua say to you?

Toma said to them,
If I tell you one of the sayings he spoke to me,
you will pick up rocks and stone me[22]
and fire will come out of the rocks and consume you.

(14) Yeshua said to them,
If you fast you will bring sin upon yourselves,
and if you pray you will be condemned,
and if you give to charity you will harm your spirits.[23]
When you go into any region and walk through the countryside,
and people receive you, eat what they serve you
and heal the sick among them.
What goes into your mouth will not defile you,
but what comes out of your mouth will defile you.

---

17. Matthew.
18. Thomas.
19. Or, "Teacher" (Coptic *sah*).
20. Jesus is the enlightened bartender who serves up wisdom. In general this saying resembles saying 108.
21. Or "three words" (Coptic *enshomt enshaje*). These three sayings or three words are not reported; the reader must discover the interpretation. On three such words, see also Kaulakau, Saulasau, Zeesar in the Naassene Sermon.
22. Within Judaism stoning was the punishment for blasphemy.
23. These statements seem to be answers to the questions in saying 6.

(15) Yeshua said,

> When you see one not born of woman,
> fall on your faces and worship.
> That is your father.

(16) Yeshua said,

> People may think I have come to impose peace upon the world.
> They do not know that I have come to impose conflicts upon the earth:
>   fire, sword, war.
> For there will be five in a house.
> There will be three against two and two against three,
> father against son and son against father,
> and they will stand alone.

(17) Yeshua said,

> I shall give you what no eye has seen, what no ear has heard,
> what no hand has touched, what has not arisen in the human heart.[24]

(18) The students said to Yeshua,

> Tell us how our end will be.

Yeshua said,

> Have you discovered the beginning and now are seeking the end?
> Where the beginning is, the end will be.
> Blessings on you who stand at the beginning.
> You will know the end and not taste death.

(19) Yeshua said,

> Blessings on you who came into being
> before coming into being.
> If you become my students and hear my sayings,
> these stones will serve you.
> For there are five trees in paradise for you.
> Summer or winter they do not change
> and their leaves do not fall.
> Whoever knows them will not taste death.[25]

---

24. Paul may cite this saying in 1 Corinthians 2:9 as a wisdom saying in use among enthusiasts in Corinth.

25. The five trees of paradise are also discussed in Manichaean texts and in the Islamic Mother of Books.

(20) The students said to Yeshua,
   Tell us what the kingdom of heaven is like.

   He said to them,
   It is like a mustard seed, the tiniest of seeds,[26]
   but when it falls on prepared soil,
   it produces a great plant
   and becomes a shelter for the birds of heaven.

(21) Miryam[27] said to Yeshua,
   What are your students like?

   He said,
   They are like little children living in a field that is not theirs.
   When the owners of the field come, they will say,
   "Give our field back to us."
   The children take off their clothes in front of them
   to give it back,
   and they return their field to them.
   So I say, if the owner of a house knows that a thief is coming,
   he will be on guard before the thief arrives
   and will not let the thief break into the house of his estate
   and steal his possessions.
   As for you, be on guard against the world.
   Arm yourselves with great strength,
   or the robbers will find a way to reach you,
   for the trouble you expect will come.
   Let someone among you understand.
   When the crop ripened,
   the reaper came quickly with sickle in hand
   and harvested it.
   Whoever has ears to hear should hear.

(22) Yeshua saw some babies nursing. He said to his students,
   These nursing babies
   are like those who enter the kingdom.

---

26. Or, "a mustard seed. It is the tiniest of seeds."
27. Mary.

They said to him,
Then shall we enter the kingdom as babies?

Yeshua said to them,
When you make the two into one,
and when you make the inner like the outer
and the outer like the inner
and the upper like the lower,
and when you make male and female into a single one,
so that the male will not be male nor the female be female,
when you make eyes in place of an eye,
a hand in place of a hand,
a foot in place of a foot,
an image in place of an image,
then you will enter the kingdom.[28]

(23) Yeshua said,
I shall choose you as one from a thousand
and as two from ten thousand
and they will stand as a single one.

(24) His students said,
Show us the place where you are.
We must seek it.

He said to them,
Whoever has ears should hear.
There is light within a person of light
and it shines on the whole world.
If it does not shine it is dark.[29]

(25) Yeshua said,
Love your brother like your soul.
Protect that person like the pupil of your eye.

(26) Yeshua said,
You see the speck in your brother's eye

---

28. This is a statement of human transformation. The transformation of genders also is treated in saying 114, but in somewhat different terms.
29. Instead of "it" in these clauses, we may also read "he."

but not the beam in your own eye.

When you take the beam out of your own eye,

then you will see clearly to take the speck out of your brother's eye.

(27) If you do not fast from the world, you will not find the kingdom.

If you do not observe the Shabbat as Shabbat,[30]

you will not see the father.

(28) Yeshua said,

I took my stand in the midst of the world,

and I appeared to them in flesh.

I found them all drunk

yet none of them thirsty.

My soul ached for the human children

because they are blind in their hearts

and do not see.

They came into the world empty

and seek to depart from the world empty.

But now they are drunk.

When they shake off their wine, they will repent.

(29) Yeshua said,

If the flesh came into being because of spirit,

it is a marvel,

but if spirit came into being because of body,

it is a marvel of marvels.

Yet I marvel at how this great wealth has come to dwell

in this poverty.

(30) Yeshua said,

Where there are three deities,

they are divine.

Where there are two or one,

I am with that one.[31]

---

30. Sabbath.

31. Greek Papyrus Oxyrhynchus 1 has been reconstructed to read: "Where there are three, they are without god, and where there is only one, I say, I am with that one." The Greek text then goes on to present part of saying 77.

(31) Yeshua said,

> A prophet is not accepted in the hometown.
> A doctor does not heal those who know the doctor.

(32) Yeshua said,

> A city built upon a high hill and fortified cannot fall,
> nor can it be hidden.

(33) Yeshua said,

> What you will hear in your ear
> in the other ear[32] proclaim from your rooftops.
> No one lights a lamp and puts it under a basket,
> nor in a hidden place.
> You put it on a stand
> so that all who come and go will see its light.

(34) Yeshua said,

> If a blind person leads a blind person,
> both will fall in a hole.

(35) Yeshua said,

> You cannot enter the house of the strong
> and take it by force without binding the owner's hands.
> Then you can loot the house.

(36) Yeshua said,

> From morning to evening and from evening to morning,
> do not worry about what you will wear.[33]

(37) His students said,

> When will you appear to us
> and when shall we see you?

---

32. "In the other ear" (Coptic *hem pkemaaje*) may be an instance of dittography (that is, inadvertently writing something twice), or the phrase may refer to another person's ear or perhaps even one's own "inner" ear.

33. Greek Papyrus Oxyrhynchus 655 reads: "Do not worry, from morning to evening nor from evening to morning, either about your food, what you will eat, or about your clothing, what you will wear. You are much better than the lilies, which do not card or spin. And since you have one change of clothing, . . . you . . . ? Who might add to your stature? That is the one who will give you your garment."

Yeshua said,
When you strip naked without being ashamed
and take your clothes and put them under your feet
like small children and trample them,
then you will see the child of the living one
and you will not be afraid.

(38) Yeshua said,
Often you wanted to hear these sayings I am telling you,
and you have no one else from whom to hear them.
There will be days when you will seek me
and you will not find me.

(39) Yeshua said,
The Pharisees and the scholars have taken the keys of knowledge
and have hidden them.
They have not entered,
nor have they allowed those who want to enter
to go inside.
You should be shrewd as snakes and innocent as doves.

(40) Yeshua said,
A grapevine has been planted far from the father.
Since it is not strong
it will be pulled up by the root and perish.

(41) Yeshua said,
Whoever has something in hand will be given more
and whoever has nothing will be deprived
of the paltry things possessed.

(42) Yeshua said,
Be passersby.[34]

(43) His students said to him,
Who are you to say these things to us?

---

34. Or, "Be wanderers," or, much less likely, "Come into being as you pass away" (Coptic *shope etetenerparage*). A parallel to this saying appears in an inscription from a mosque at Fatehpur Sikri, India: "Jesus said, 'This world is a bridge. Pass over it, but do not build your dwelling there.'"

Yeshua said,
From what I tell you, you do not know
who I am,
but you have become like the Jews.
They love the tree but hate its fruit
or love the fruit but hate the tree.

(44) Yeshua said,
Whoever blasphemes against the father
will be forgiven,
and whoever blasphemes against the son
will be forgiven,
but whoever blasphemes against the holy spirit will not be forgiven,
either on earth or in heaven.

(45) Yeshua said,
Grapes are not harvested from thorn trees,
nor are figs gathered from thistles.
They yield no fruit.
A good person brings forth good from the storehouse.
A bad person brings forth evil things
from the corrupt storehouse in the heart
and says evil things.
From the abundance of the heart
such a person brings forth evil.

(46) Yeshua said,
From Adam to Yohanan the baptizer,[35]
among those born of women,
no one of you is so much greater than Yohanan
that your eyes should not be averted.
But I have said that whoever among you becomes a child
will know the kingdom
and become greater than Yohanan.

(47) Yeshua said,
A person cannot mount two horses or bend two bows,

---

35. John the baptizer.

and a servant cannot serve two masters,
or the servant will honor one and offend the other.
No one who drinks aged wine
suddenly wants to drink new wine.
New wine is not poured into aged wineskins
or they may break,
and aged wine is not poured into a new wineskin
or it may spoil.
An old patch is not sewn onto a new garment
or it may tear.

(48) Yeshua said,
If two make peace with each other in one house,
they will tell the mountain, "Move,"
and the mountain will move.

(49) Yeshua said,
Blessings on you who are alone and chosen,
for you will find the kingdom.
You have come from it
and will return there again.

(50) Yeshua said,
If they say to you, "Where have you come from?"
say to them, "We have come from the light,
from the place where the light came into being by itself,
established itself, and appeared in their image."
If they say to you, "Is it you?"
say, "We are its children and the chosen of the living father."
If they ask you, "What is the evidence of your father in you?"
say to them, "It is motion and rest."[36]

(51) His students said to him,
When will the dead rest?
When will the new world come?

---

36. This saying recalls the accounts of the career of the soul or of the person in the Secret Book of John, the Song of the Pearl, and the Exegesis on the Soul.

He said to them,
What you look for has come
but you do not know it.

(52) His students said to him,
Twenty-four prophets have spoken in Israel
and they all spoke of you.[37]

He said to them,
You have disregarded the living one among you
and have spoken of the dead.

(53) His students said to him,
Is circumcision useful or not?

He said to them,
If it were useful, fathers would produce their children
already circumcised from their mothers.
But the true circumcision in spirit[38]
is altogether valuable.

(54) Yeshua said,
Blessings on you the poor,
for yours is the kingdom of heaven.

(55) Yeshua said,
Those who do not hate their father and mother
cannot be my students,
and those who do not hate their brothers and sisters
and bear the cross[39] as I do
will not be worthy of me.

(56) Yeshua said,
Whoever has come to know the world
has discovered a carcass,
and whoever has discovered a carcass,
of that person the world is not worthy.

---

37. Twenty-four is sometimes given as the number of books in the Hebrew Bible.
38. Paul also refers to spiritual circumcision in Romans 2:25–29 and elsewhere.
39. This is a common figure of speech for bearing up under burdens or difficulties.

(57) Yeshua said,

The father's kingdom is like someone with good seed.
His enemy came at night and sowed weeds among the good seed.
He did not let them pull up the weeds
but said to them,
"No, or you might go to pull up the weeds
and pull up the wheat along with them."
On harvest day the weeds will be conspicuous
and will be pulled up and burned.

(58) Yeshua said,

Blessings on the person who has labored[40]
and found life.

(59) Yeshua said,

Look to the living one as long as you live
or you may die and try to see the living one
and you will not be able to see.

(60) He saw a Samaritan carrying a lamb as he was going to the land
of Yehuda.[41]

He said to his students,
. . . that person . . .
around the lamb.[42]

They said to him,
So he may kill it
and eat it.

He said to them,
He will not eat it while it is alive
but only after he has killed it
and it has become a carcass.

---

40. Or, "Blessings on the person who has suffered."
41. This saying is partially restored. Instead of "He saw" (Coptic *afnau*), it is also possible to re-store to read "They saw" (Coptic *aunau*). The "land of Yehuda" is Judea.
42. Instead of ". . . that person . . . around the lamb," it is possible to read "That person is around the lamb," or "Why does that person carry around the lamb?" It may be possible to understand that the Samaritan was "trying to catch a lamb," and Jesus said, "That person is after the lamb."

They said,
Otherwise he cannot do it.

He said to them,
So with you. Seek a place of rest
or you may become a carcass and be eaten.

(61) Yeshua said,
Two will rest on a couch. One will die, one will live.

Salome said,
Who are you, mister? You have climbed on my couch
and eaten from my table as if you are from someone.[43]

Yeshua said to her,
I am the one who comes from what is whole.
I was given from the things of my father.

Salome said,
I am your student.

Yeshua said,
I say, if you are whole,[44] you will be filled with light,
but if divided, you will be filled with darkness.

(62) Yeshua said,
I disclose my mysteries to those who are worthy
of my mysteries.[45]
Do not let your left hand know
what your right hand is doing.

(63) Yeshua said,
There was a rich person who was very wealthy.
He said, "I shall invest my money so I may sow, reap, plant,
and fill my storehouses with produce.
Then I shall lack nothing."

---

43. The word translated "couch" (Coptic *cloc*) may also be translated "bed," but the saying probably refers to a couch used for dining. The clause "as if you are from someone" may derive from the phrase "as a stranger."
44. The Coptic text is emended slightly here.
45. Partially restored.

This is what he was thinking in his heart,
but that very night he died.
Whoever has ears should hear.

(64) Yeshua said,
A person was receiving guests. When he prepared the dinner
he sent his servant to invite the guests.
The servant went to the first and said,
"My master invites you."

That person said,
"Some merchants owe me money.
They are coming tonight.
I must go and give them instructions.
Please excuse me from dinner."

The servant went to another and said,
"My master invites you."

He said to the servant,
"I have bought a house
and I've been called away for a day.
I have no time."

The servant went to another and said,
"My master invites you."

He said to the servant,
"My friend is to be married
and I am to arrange the banquet.
I can't come. Please excuse me from dinner."

The servant went to another and said,
"My master invites you."

He said to the servant,
"I have bought an estate
and I am going to collect rent.
I shall not be able to come. Please excuse me."

The servant returned and said to his master,
"Those you invited to dinner have asked to be excused."

The master said to his servant,

"Go out into the streets and invite whomever you find for the dinner.
Buyers and merchants will not enter the places of my father."

(65) He said,

A ... person[46] owned a vineyard and rented it
to some farmers to work it
and from them he would collect its produce.
He sent his servant for the farmers to give him
the produce of the vineyard. They seized, beat,
and almost killed his servant, who returned
and told his master. His master said,
"Perhaps he did not know them." And he sent
another servant, but they beat him as well.
Then the master sent his son and said,
"Perhaps they will respect my son."
Since the farmers knew the son was the heir
of the vineyard, they seized him and killed him.
Whoever has ears should hear.

(66) Yeshua said,

Show me the stone that the builders rejected.
That is the cornerstone.

(67) Yeshua said,

One who knows all but lacks within
is utterly lacking.

(68) Yeshua said,

Blessings on you when you are hated and persecuted,
and no place will be found,
wherever you are persecuted.[47]

---

46. This may be restored to read "A good person" (Coptic *ourome enchre[sto]s*), or "A usurer," "A creditor" (Coptic *ourome enchre[ste]s*), with very different implications. In the first instance a good person may be interpreted as the victim of violent tenant farmers, in the second an abusive creditor may be understood as opposed by the victimized poor.

47. This saying may be understood to mean "you will find a place where you will not be persecuted," perhaps alluding to the flight of early Christians from Jerusalem to Pella in Transjordan at the time of the first-century revolt against the Romans.

(69) Yeshua said,
> Blessings on you who have been persecuted in your hearts.
> Only you truly know the father.
> Blessings on you who are hungry
> that the stomach of someone else in want may be filled.

(70) Yeshua said,
> If you bring forth what is within you, what you have will save you.
> If you have nothing within you,
> what you do not have within you will kill you.

(71) Yeshua said,
> I shall destroy this house
> and no one will be able to rebuild it.

(72) Someone said to him,
> Tell my brothers to divide my father's possessions with me.

> He said to the person,
> Mister, who made me a divider?

> He turned to his students and said to them,
> I am not a divider, am I?

(73) Yeshua said,
> The harvest is large but the workers are few.
> Beg the master to send out workers to the harvest.

(74) He said,[48]
> Master, there are many around the drinking trough
> but nothing in the well.[49]

(75) Yeshua said,
> There are many standing at the door
> but those who are alone will enter the wedding chamber.

(76) Yeshua said,
> The father's kingdom is like a merchant
> who owned a supply of merchandise and found a pearl.

---

48. Or, "Someone said" (Coptic *pejaf*). Sayings 73–75 most likely should be read as a small dialogue.
49. The word *well* is emended slightly. Instead of "nothing" it is also possible to read "no one" (Coptic *men laau*).

The merchant was prudent.
He sold his goods and bought the single pearl
for himself.
So with you. Seek his treasure that is unfailing
and enduring,
where no moth comes to devour and no worm destroys.

(77) Yeshua said,
I am the light over all things.
I am all.
From me all has come forth,
and to me all has reached.
Split a piece of wood.
I am there.
Lift up the stone
and you will find me there.[50]

(78) Yeshua said,
Why have you come out to the countryside?
To see a reed shaken by the wind?
Or to see a person dressed in soft clothes
like your rulers and your people of power?
They are dressed in soft clothes
and cannot understand truth.

(79) A woman in the crowd said to him,
Blessings on the womb that bore you
and the breasts that fed you.

He said to her,
Blessings on those who have heard the word of the father
and have truly kept it. Days will come when you will say,
"Blessings on the womb that has not conceived
and the breasts that have not given milk."

(80) Yeshua said,
Whoever has come to know the world
has discovered the body,

---

50. Greek Papyrus Oxyrhynchus 1 adds a version of this part of the saying after saying 30.

and whoever has discovered the body,
of that person the world is not worthy.

(81) Yeshua said,

Let a person of wealth rule,
and a person of power renounce it.

(82) Yeshua said,

Whoever is near me is near fire,
and whoever is far from me is far from the kingdom.[51]

(83) Yeshua said,

You see images,
but the light within them is hidden in the image
of the father's light.
He will be disclosed,
but his image is hidden by his light.

(84) Yeshua said,

When you see your likeness you are happy.
But when you see your images that came into being before you
and that neither die nor become visible,
how much you will bear!

(85) Yeshua said,

Adam came from great power and great wealth,
but he was not worthy of you.
Had he been worthy,
he would not have tasted death.

(86) Yeshua said,

Foxes have their dens[52] and birds have their nests,
but the human child[53] has no place to lay his head and rest.

---

51. A version of this saying has recently been discovered in a Coptic text (Berlin 22220) now referred to as the Gospel of the Savior: "If someone is near me, he will burn. I am the fire that blazes. Whoever is near me is near fire; whoever is far from me is far from life" (see Hedrick and Mirecki, *Gospel of the Savior*, pp. 40–41).

52. Partially restored.

53. This common phrase (here in Coptic *shere emprome,* from the Greek *huios tou anthropou*) often is translated "son of man" in other translations of Jewish and Christian texts. Sometimes it can mean a person, or it can be a way of referring to oneself, "I." Such seems to be the meaning here. At other times (as in the book of Daniel and other similar texts) it may have a more apocalyptic meaning.

(87) Yeshua said,

How miserable is the body that depends on a body,
and how miserable is the soul that depends on both.

(88) Yeshua said,

The messengers and the prophets will come to you
and give you what is yours.
You give them what you have and wonder,
"When will they come and take what is theirs?"

(89) Yeshua said,

Why do you wash the outside of the cup?
Don't you understand that the one who made the inside
also made the outside?

(90) Yeshua said,

Come to me, for my yoke is easy and my mastery gentle,
and you will find rest for yourselves.

(91) They said to him,

Tell us who you are so that we may believe in you.

He said to them,
You examine the face of heaven and earth
but you have not come to know the one who is in your presence,
and you do not know how to examine this moment.

(92) Yeshua said,

Seek and you will find.
In the past I did not tell you the things about which you asked me.
Now I am willing to tell you, but you do not seek them.

(93) Do not give what is holy to dogs.

They might throw them upon the manure pile.
Do not throw pearls to swine.
They might ... it. ...[54]

---

54. This clause cannot be restored with confidence. Layton, ed., *Nag Hammadi Codex II,2–7*, 1:87, notes the following attempts: "They might make mud of it," "They might grind it to bits," "They might bring it to naught."

(94) Yeshua said,
>One who seeks will find.
>For one who knocks it will be opened.

(95) Yeshua said,[55]
>If you have money, do not lend it at interest,
>but give it to someone
>from whom you will not get it back.

(96) Yeshua said,
>The father's kingdom is like a woman
>who took a little yeast, hid it in dough,
>and made large loaves of bread.
>Whoever has ears should hear.

(97) Yeshua said,
>The father's kingdom is like a woman
>who was carrying a jar full of meal.
>While she was walking along a distant road,
>the handle of the jar broke
>and the meal spilled behind her along the road.
>She did not know it.
>She noticed no problem.
>When she reached her house she put the jar down
>and found it empty.

(98) Yeshua said,
>The father's kingdom is like a person
>who wanted to put someone powerful to death.
>While at home he drew his sword
>and thrust it into the wall
>to find out whether his hand would go in.
>Then he killed the powerful person.

(99) The students said to him,
>Your brothers and your mother are standing outside.

---

55. Restored.

He said to them,
Those here who do the will of my father
are my brothers and my mother.
They will enter my father's kingdom.

(100) They showed Yeshua a gold coin and said to him,
Caesar's people demand taxes from us.

He said to them,
Give Caesar the things that are Caesar's,
give god the things that are god's,
and give me what is mine.

(101) Those who do not hate their father and mother as I do
cannot be my students,
and those who do not love their father and mother as I do
cannot be my students.
For my mother . . .
but my true mother gave me life.[56]

(102) Yeshua said,
Shame on the Pharisees.
They are like a dog sleeping in the cattle manger.
It does not eat or let the cattle eat.

(103) Yeshua said,
Blessings on you if you know where the robbers will enter
so you can wake up, rouse your estate,
and arm yourself before they break in.

(104) They said to Yeshua,
Come let us pray today and fast.

Yeshua said,
What sin have I committed
or how have I been undone?

---

56. This saying is partially restored. The clause "For my mother . . ." cannot be restored with confidence. One possibility is: "For my mother gave me falsehood" (Coptic *tamaau gar entas[ti naei empc]ol*; see Layton, ed., *Nag Hammadi Codex II,2–7*, 1:89). Another possibility: "For my mother brought me forth."

When the bridegroom leaves the wedding chamber,
then let the people fast and pray.

(105) Yeshua said,
   Whoever knows the father and the mother
   will be called the child of a whore.

(106) Yeshua said,
   When you make two into one,
   you will become human children.
   When you say, "Mountain, move,"
   the mountain will move.

(107) Yeshua said,
   The kingdom is like a shepherd who had
   a hundred sheep.
   One of them, the largest, went astray.
   He left the ninety-nine and looked for the one until he found it.
   After so much trouble he said to the sheep,
   "I love you more than the ninety-nine."

(108) Yeshua said,
   Whoever drinks from my mouth will become like me.
   I myself shall become that person,
   and the hidden things will be revealed to that one.[57]

(109) Yeshua said,
   The kingdom is like a person who had a treasure hidden in his field.
   He did not know it, and when he died, he left it to his son.
   The son did not know about it.
   He took over the field and sold it.
   The buyer was plowing and found the treasure,
   and began to lend money at interest to whomever he wished.

(110) Yeshua said,
   You who have found the world
   and become wealthy,
   renounce the world.

---

57. This saying recalls saying 13.

(111) Yeshua said,
> The heavens and earth will roll up in your presence
> and you who live from the living one will not see death.

> Doesn't Yeshua say this?
> Whoever has found oneself,
> of that person the world is not worthy.

(112) Yeshua said,
> Shame on the flesh that depends on the soul.
> Shame on the soul that depends on the flesh.

(113) His students said to him,
> When will the kingdom come?

> Yeshua said,
> It will not come because you are watching for it.
> No one will announce, "Look, here it is,"
> or "Look, there it is."
> The father's kingdom is spread out upon the earth
> and people do not see it.

(114) Shimon Kefa said to them,
> Miryam should leave us.
> Females are not worthy of life.

> Yeshua said,
> Look, I shall guide her to make her male,
> so she too may become a living spirit resembling you males.
> For every female who makes herself male
> will enter the kingdom of heaven.[58]

---

58. A somewhat different statement of gender transformation is given at saying 22.

2

The Gospel of John

The Gospel of John is the fourth gospel included in the New Testament, usually presented after Matthew, Mark, and Luke. Like the other New Testament gospels, the Gospel of John is a narrative gospel that offers a portrait of Jesus, whose life concludes with his crucifixion and resurrection from the dead. Yet this gospel differs remarkably in detail and message from the other, synoptic New Testament gospels.

Jesus, according to John, is an exalted being who is the incarnate son of god and is one with god. Jesus is the divine word or reason of god, the logos, who descends like a falling star from heaven, becomes flesh, and makes his home in this mortal realm below. As the word of god in human flesh, Jesus performs mighty deeds, called "signs" in John, which demonstrate his power and greatness. These signs most likely come from an earlier source, a gospel of signs, which meant to highlight the miracles of Jesus. In the Gospel of John these signs are interpreted in a more spiritual manner, as becomes clear in the story of Nicodemus. The signs also become the occasion for Jesus to utter long, mystical discourses in which he declares that he himself provides the real meaning for the signs. Thus Jesus in the Gospel of John commonly speaks in "I am" self-declarations, a form of speech reminiscent of the divine "I am" of Jewish tradition and of divine speech in general (note also the use of "I am" statements in gnostic texts, for example, Thunder). Finally, Jesus is glorified in his death and returns to the realm above to prepare a place for those who are to follow him.

These features of the portrait of Jesus in the Gospel of John are reminiscent of themes found in a number of gnostic sources. It is no wonder, then, that John is sometimes linked to gnostic religion, or that in its present form the Secret Book of John is also attributed to John, or that the Valentinian Herakleon composed a commentary on the Gospel of John, or that the Acts of John contains a Round Dance of the Cross with gnostic features, or that the Cathar Gospel of the Secret Supper is said to be narrated by John. Nor is it surprising that some scholars understand the Gospel of John to be a gnosticizing gospel or a gospel written within the context of gnostic themes.

The Gospel of John was composed in Greek, probably near the end of the first century. The references to followers of Jesus being evicted from the synagogue would suggest a date during the last decade or two of the first century. Like the Gospel of Thomas, the Gospel of John may also have been written somewhere in Syria. However, Thomas, the authoritative figure of the Gospel of Thomas, is subjected to a much more negative evaluation in the Gospel of John, where he is made to assume the infamous role of "doubting Thomas."

The translation given here presents three excerpts from the Gospel of John, chapters 1–3, 11–12, and 17–21. These excerpts are crucial for understanding how the author of the gospel portrays Jesus and what gnostics found attractive about that portrayal. This translation, like that of the Gospel of Thomas, gives Semitic forms of Semitic names, in order to emphasize the Jewish identity of Jesus and his students and the Jewish context of the life of Jesus. Thus the name Yeshua is used for Jesus and Yohanan for John. For an identification of other names, see the notes.

THE GOSPEL OF JOHN[1]

(Chapter 1)

IN THE BEGINNING WAS THE WORD

In the beginning was the word[2]
and the word was with god,

---

1. The Gospel of John: translated by Willis Barnstone from the Greek text of the New Testament.
2. The word (Greek *logos*), sometimes capitalized as "the Word," is immediately personified as "he." See parallel in Genesis 1:1. John 1:1–18 is a prologue and is often held to be a separate poem adapted for the gospel. *Logos* may be given multiple meanings: the word of god, the Greek principle of reason ordering the universe, and a kabbalistic principle of the primacy of creating words and letters of words, before god could speak the universe into being.

and the word was god.
He was in the beginning with god.
Through him everything came to be
and without the word nothing came to be.
What came to be in him was life
and life was the light of all people
and the light in the darkness shone
and the darkness could not apprehend the light.

YOHANAN CAME TO PROCLAIM LIGHT

There was a man sent from god.
His name was Yohanan.[3]
He came as a witness in testimony of the light
so that all might believe through him.
He was not the light,
but came to testify about the light.[4]
The light was the true light,
which illuminates every person
who comes into the world.

THE LIGHT WAS IN THE WORLD

He was in the world
and through him the world was born,
and the world did not know him.[5]
He went to his own
and his own did not receive him.[6]

---

3. John the baptizer.
4. John was not the light, meaning not Jesus the messiah, but the lamp carrying the light, defining the baptizer's testifying, prophetic, but secondary role to Jesus.
5. That is, Jesus.
6. The majority of Jews did not recognize Jesus as messiah when he came. Those Jews who did recognize Jesus, the early messianists, who broke off from mainstream Jewry, were the Christian Jews (followers of the messiah).

To all who received him
he gave power to become the children of god,
to those who believed in his name,
who were born not from blood
or from the will of the flesh
or from the will of a man,
but were born of god.

THE WORD BECAME FLESH

And the word became flesh
and lived among us.[7]
And we gazed on his glory,
the glory of the only son born of the father,
who is filled with grace and truth.

YOHANAN TESTIFIES ABOUT YESHUA

Yohanan testified about him and cried out, saying,
"He is the one of whom I said,
'One who will come after me was before me,'
because before me he was.
From his bounty we have all received grace upon grace,
and as the law was given through Moshe,[8]
grace and truth have come through Yeshua the Galilean.
No one has ever seen god.
Only the one born of god,[9]
who is in the heart of his father,
he has made him known."

---

7. God's word became human flesh in the person of Jesus.
8. Moses.
9. Other texts have "only son" (or "only begotten son").

YOHANAN DENIES BEING THE MESSIAH

And this is the testimony of Yohanan the baptizer when the Jews[10] sent priests and Levites from Yerushalayim[11] to ask him, "Who are you?"

And he confessed and made no denial, but confessed,

"I am not the Galilean."

They asked him, "What then? Are you Elijah?"

He said, "I am not."

"Are you the prophet?"

He answered, "No."

"Who are you? Give us an answer for those who sent us here. What do you say about yourself?"

He said,

"I am the voice of one crying in the desert.

'Make straight the way of the lord,'

as the prophet Isaiah said."[12]

Now, they had been sent by the Pharisees. They questioned him and said to him, "Why then do you baptize if you are not the Galilean or Elijah or the prophet?"

He answered them,

"I baptize in water.

Among you stands one you do not know,

one who will come after me,

whose sandal strap I am unworthy to loosen."

All this happened in Bethany across the Jordan, where Yohanan was baptizing.

---

10. All the people in these scenes are Jews. The appellation "Jew" here and in most places in John has two functions: to distinguish Jews who do not believe Jesus to be the son of god from those who do, and to cast hatred on and condemn the unbelievers to immediate and eternal punishment. The followers of Jesus were initially few in number among the many sects that made up the Jewish population. All thought themselves Jews, whether traditional Jews or Christian Jews. Therefore, naming the Jews as a hated community existing alongside Jesus and his followers almost certainly reflects the later, competitive period of nascent Christianity, when the Jews had expelled Christian Jews from the synagogues and when the traditional Jews, in turn, became the vilified enemy.

11. Jerusalem.

12. Isaiah 40:3.

THE LAMB OF GOD

The next day Yohanan saw Yeshua coming toward him and said,
"Look, the lamb of god who takes away the wrong of the world.
He is the one of whom I have said,
'A man is coming after me who was before me,'
because before me he was.
And I did not know him,
but so that he might be known in Israel
is why I came baptizing in water."

SPIRIT DESCENDING LIKE A DOVE

And Yohanan testified, saying,
"I saw the spirit descending like a dove from the sky
and it rested on him and I did not know him,
but the one who sent me to baptize in water said,
'The one on whom you see the spirit descend and rest,
he is the one baptizing in holy spirit.'
And I have seen and I have testified that he is the son of god."

WE HAVE FOUND THE MESSIAH

The next day Yohanan again was standing with two of his students. When he saw Yeshua walking by, he said, "Look, the lamb of god."
His two students heard him speaking and they followed Yeshua.
And Yeshua turned and saw them following him and said,
"What are you looking for?"
"Rabbi," which translated means teacher,[13] "where are you staying?"
He told them,
"Come and see."
So they came and saw where he was staying, and stayed with him that day. It was about four in the afternoon.

---

13. This clause and others like it are scribal asides that appear to be a later interpolation whose purpose is to persuade the reader that "rabbi" meant a teacher or scholar rather than a Jewish rabbi, whose profession was to lead a congregation and interpret Jewish law. *Rabbi* is from Hebrew for "my master, great one, teacher."

One of the two who heard Yohanan and followed him was Andreas, brother of Shimon Kefa.[14] First he found his own brother Shimon and told him,

> "We have found the messiah,"
> meaning the anointed.[15]

He led Shimon to Yeshua.

Looking at him Yeshua said,

> "You are Shimon, the son of Yohanan.
> You will be called Kefa, meaning 'rock.'"[16]

YOU ARE THE SON OF GOD

The next day Yeshua wished to go out to Galil.[17] He found Philippos[18] and said to him, "Follow me."

Now, Philippos was from Bethsaida, the city of Andreas and Kefa.[19] Philippos found Nathanael and said to him, "The one whom Moshe wrote about in Torah[20] and whom the prophets describe, we have found, Yeshua, son of Yosef,[21] from Nazareth."

And Nathanael said to him, "Can anything good come out of Nazareth?"

"Come and see!" Philippos replied.

Yeshua saw Nathanael coming to him and said of him, "Look, a true Jew, one in whom there is no cunning."

"How do you know me?" Nathanael said.

Yeshua answered,

> "Before Philippos called you,
> you were under the fig tree and I saw you."

Nathanael answered,

> "Rabbi, you are the son of god,
> you are the king of Israel."

---

14. Andrew and Simon Peter.

15. In Greek, *christos*.

16. Peter.

17. Galilee.

18. Philip.

19. Andrew and Peter.

20. "The law" in Hebrew is *Torah*. *Torah* most commonly means the five books of Moses as well as the entire Hebrew Bible.

21. Joseph.

Yeshua responded, saying,

"Because I told you I saw you under the fig tree,
do you believe?
You will see even greater things."

And he said to him,

"Truly, truly I say to you,
you will see the sky open
and angels of god ascending and descending
upon the earthly son."[22]

(Chapter 2)

WINE AND WATER AT A WEDDING

On the third day there was a wedding in Kana[23] in Galil, and Yeshua's mother was there. Yeshua and his students had also been invited to the wedding. And when the wine gave out, Yeshua's mother said to him, "They have no wine."

Yeshua said to her,

"What is that to me and you, woman?[24]
My hour has not yet come."

His mother said to the servants, "Do what he tells you."

Now, there were six waterpots of stone standing there for the Jewish custom of washing,[25] each holding two or three measures.[26]

Yeshua said to them,

"Fill the pots with water."

They filled them to the brim.

And he said to them,

"Now pour some of the water out
and take it to the master of the feast."

They took it.

---

22. Or "human son," "son of man," throughout the text.
23. Cana.
24. The gruff use of "woman," rather than "lady," is softened in many translations.
25. Washing hands in rite of purification.
26. Twenty or thirty gallons.

When the master of the feast tasted the water become wine, not knowing where it came from—though the servants knew, those who had drawn the water—he called the bridegroom and said to him, "Everybody serves the good wine first, and when the guests are drunk brings out the inferior kind. You have been saving the good wine till now."

Yeshua did this, the first of his miraculous signs in Kana in Galil, and he revealed his glory, and his students believed in him.

DAYS IN KEFAR-NAHUM WITH FAMILY AND STUDENTS

After this he went down to Kefar-Nahum[27] with his mother and brothers and students. They stayed there for a few days.

DRIVING VENDORS FROM THE TEMPLE

It was almost Pesach[28] of the Jews and Yeshua went up to Yerushalayim. In the temple he found the people selling oxen and sheep and doves, and the coin changers sitting there. He made a whip out of ropes and drove out all the animals, the sheep and the oxen. He also scattered the coins of the changers and knocked over their tables. To the dove sellers he said,

"Get these things out of here!
Do not make the house of my father
a house of business!"

His students remembered how it is written,

"Zeal for your house will consume me."[29]

Then the Jews said to him, "What sign can you show us for doing this?" Yeshua answered,

"Destroy this temple
and in three days I shall raise it up."

Then the Jews said, "This temple was built over forty-six years, and you will raise it up in three days?"

---

27. Capernaum.
28. Passover.
29. Psalm 69:9.

But he was speaking about the temple of his body. After he was raised from the dead, his students remembered what he said and they believed the scripture and the word that Yeshua said.

When he was in Yerushalayim during the Pesach suppers, many people believed in his name, seeing the wondrous signs he was doing. But Yeshua would not entrust himself to them, because he knew all people and because he had no need to have anyone testify about a person and he knew what was in a person.

(Chapter 3)

NIKODEMOS QUESTIONS YESHUA

Now, there was a Pharisee named Nikodemos,[30] a leader of the Jews. He came to Yeshua at night and said, "Rabbi, we know that you came as a teacher from god since no one can perform these wondrous signs if god were not with him.
Yeshua answered,
"Truly, truly I say to you,
unless you are born from above
you cannot see the kingdom of god."
"How can one be born when one is old?" he asked. "One cannot enter a mother's womb a second time and be born."
Yeshua answered,
"Truly, truly I say to you,
unless you are born from water and the wind of god[31]
you cannot enter the kingdom of god.
What is born from the flesh is flesh,
what is born from the wind is wind.
Do not wonder that I told you
you must be born again from above.
The wind blows where it wants to and you hear its sound,
but you cannot know where it comes from and where it goes.
So it is for everyone born from the wind of god."

---

30. Nicodemus.
31. Or "the spirit of god."

"How can these things happen?" Nikodemos asked.

Yeshua said to him,

> "You are the teacher of Israel and do you not know this?
> Truly, truly I say to you,
> we speak of what we know and we testify to what we have seen,
> yet you do not receive our testimony.
> If I tell you of earthly things and you do not believe,
> how if I tell you of heavenly things will you believe?
> And no one has gone up into the sky
> except the one who came down from the sky, the earthly son.
> And as Moshe raised up the snake in the desert,
> the earthly son must be raised up
> so that all who believe in him will have eternal life.

> "God loved the world so much that he gave his only son,
> so that all who believe in him might not be destroyed
> but have eternal life.
> For god did not send his son into the world
> to judge the world
> but so that through him the world might be saved.
> One who believes in him is not judged,
> but one who does not believe is judged already
> for not believing in the name of god's only son.
> And this is the judgment:
> that the light came into the world
> and people loved the darkness rather than the light,
> for their works were cunning.
> For all who do paltry things[32] hate the light
> and do not come toward the light
> so that their works will not be exposed.
> But those who do the truth come toward the light
> so that their works may shine as accomplished through god."[33]

---

32. The Greek means "slight" or "paltry" rather than "evil" or "wrong."

33. The gnostics made similar distinctions between darkness and light and emphasized light as spiritual knowledge and salvation.

YESHUA BAPTIZES IN YEHUDA

After this Yeshua and his students came into the land of Yehuda.[34] He stayed there with them and baptized.

Yohanan also was baptizing in Ainon near Salim, since there were many waters there, and the people came and were baptized. Yohanan had not yet been thrown into prison.

There was a dispute between Yohanan's students and a Jew[35] about ceremonial washing. They came toward Yohanan and said, "Rabbi, the one who was with you across the Jordan, to whom you testified, look, he is baptizing all who come to him."

Yohanan answered,

"No one can receive anything
unless it comes from heaven.
You are my witnesses that I have said,
'I am not the messiah
but I am sent before him.'

"He who has the bride is the groom.
The groom's friend who stands near and hears him
is filled with joy at the groom's voice.
So my happiness is completed.
He must increase and I be diminished.

"The one who comes from above is above all.
The one who is of the earth is of the earth
and speaks from the earth.
The one who comes from the sky is above all.
To what he has seen and heard he testifies,
yet his testimony no one receives.
Who receives his testimony proves that god is true.
Whom god sent speaks the words of god,
for the wind of spirit he gives out is beyond measure.
The father loves the son and has given all things into his hand.

---

34. Judea.
35. In this context a Jew means a person from Judea as opposed to another region of Israel.

Who believes in the son has eternal life,
but one who disbelieves the son will not see life.
The wrath of god remains upon him."

.   .   .   .

(Chapter 11)

THE RESURRECTION OF ELEAZAR

There was a man who was sick, Eleazar[36] from Bethany, from the village of
Miryam[37] and Martha her sister. It was Miryam who anointed the lord with oil
of myrrh and wiped his feet with her hair. Her brother Eleazar was sick. So the
sisters sent word to him, saying, "Lord, look, one whom you care for is sick."
        When Yeshua heard this, he said,

"This sickness is moving not to death
    but to the glory of god,
    so that through it the son of god
    may be glorified."

Now, Yeshua loved Martha and his sister and Eleazar. So when he heard
that he was sick, he remained in the place where he was for two days. After this
he said to his students,

"Let us go to Yehuda again."

His students said to him, "Rabbi, the Jews were just now trying to stone
you and are you going there again?"
        Yeshua replied,

"Are there not twelve hours in the day?
Whoever walks around in the day does not stumble
since one sees the light of this world.
Whoever walks around in the night does stumble
since the light is not in that person."

These things he said, and then he told them,

"Our friend Eleazar has fallen asleep,
but I am going there to awaken him."

---

36. Lazarus.
37. Mary.

So the students said, "Sir, if he has fallen asleep, he will be cured."[38]

Yeshua had spoken about his death, but they thought he was talking about restful sleep.

Then Yeshua told them plainly,

"Eleazar died, and I am happy for you
that I was not there so that you may believe.
But now let us go to him."

Toma,[39] who was called the twin, said to his fellow students, "Let us also go so that we may die with him."

When Yeshua arrived, he found that Eleazar had already been four days in the tomb. Now, Bethany was near Yerushalayim, about two miles away, and many of the Jews had come to console Martha and Miryam for their brother. When Martha heard that Yeshua was coming, she went out to meet him, but Miryam sat in her house. Then Martha said to Yeshua, "Sir, if you had been here my brother would not have died. Even now I know that whatever you ask god, god gives you."

Yeshua said to her,

"Your brother will rise again."

Martha said to him,

"I know he will rise in the resurrection on the last day."

Yeshua said to her,

"I am the resurrection and the life.
Those who believe in me even if they die
will live.
And everyone who lives and believes in me
will not die into eternity.
Do you believe this?"

She said to him,

"Yes, lord. I believe that you are the messiah,
the son of god, who is coming into this world."

After she said this, she left and called her sister Miryam, telling her secretly,

"The teacher is here and calls for you."

---

38. Or "he will be saved" or "preserved." Both cure and salvation are implicit.
39. Thomas.

When that woman heard, she got up quickly and came to him.

Now, Yeshua had not yet come into the village, and he was still at the place where Martha had met him.

The Jews who were with her in the house, consoling her, saw Miryam quickly get up and go out, and they followed her, thinking that she was going to the tomb to weep there. Miryam came to where Yeshua was, and seeing him she fell at his feet, saying to him, "Sir, if you had been here my brother would not have died."

When Yeshua saw her weeping and that the Jews who had come with her were weeping, he raged at his own spirit, harrowed himself, and said,

"Where have you laid him?"

They said to him, "Sir, come and see."

Yeshua wept.

Then the Jews were saying, "See how he loved him."

But some of them said, "Couldn't he who opened the eyes of the blind man have done something so this man wouldn't die?"

Yeshua again raged inwardly and went to the tomb.

It was a cave, and a stone was lying against it.

Yeshua said,

"Lift the stone."

The sister of the one who died, Martha, said to Yeshua,

"Lord, he already stinks. It's the fourth day."

Yeshua said to her,

"Did I not tell you that if you believed
you would see the glory of god?"

So they lifted the stone.

Yeshua lifted his eyes up and said,

"Father, I thank you for hearing me,
and I know that you always hear me
but because of the crowd that is around me
I spoke so they would believe you sent me."

After saying this, in a great voice he cried out,

"Eleazar, come out!"

The one who had died came out, bound feet and hands in grave clothes and his face wrapped around in a cloth.

Yeshua said to them,

"Untie him and let him go."

THE JEWS PLOT TO KILL YESHUA

Then many of the Jews who had come to Miryam and seen what he did believed in him. But some of them went away to the Pharisees and told them what Yeshua had done.

So the high priests and the Pharisees called a meeting of the Sanhedrin[40] and said, "What can we to do about this man who is performing so many miraculous signs? If we leave him like this, everyone will believe in him, and the Romans will come and take away our holy place and nation."

But one of them, Caiaphas, who was high priest for that year, said to them, "You know nothing. You haven't understood that it is better for one man to die for the sake of the people and not have the whole nation destroyed."

This he did not say on his own, but as high priest for that year he prophesied that Yeshua would die for the sake of the nation, and not only for the nation but so that he might bring together the scattered children of god.

From that day on they planned to kill him.

So Yeshua no longer walked openly among the Jews but went away from there to the country near the desert, to a city called Ephraim, and he stayed there with the students.

Now, the Pesach of the Jews was near, and many went up from the country to Yerushalayim before Pesach to purify themselves. They were looking for Yeshua and said to one another as they stood in the temple, "What do you think? That he won't come to the festival?"

But the high priests and the Pharisees had given orders that if anyone knew where he was, he should report it so they might seize him.

(Chapter 12)

MIRYAM ANOINTS YESHUA'S FEET

Six days before the Pesach, Yeshua came to Bethany where Eleazar was, whom he had raised from the dead. So they prepared a supper for him, and Martha

---

40. Council.

served, and Eleazar was one of those reclining at the table with him. Then Miryam took a pound of spikenard ointment, pure and precious, anointed the feet of Yeshua, and wiped his feet with her hair. And the house was full of the fragrance of the unguent.

Yehuda of Kerioth,[41] one of his students, who was about to betray him, said, "Why was this ointment not sold for three hundred denarii[42] and given to the poor?" But he said this not because he cared about the poor, but because he was a thief and he was the keeper of the money box and was removing what was dropped into it.

So Yeshua said,

"Let her be, so she may keep it for the day of my burial.
The poor you always have with you,
but me you do not always have."[43]

THE HIGH PRIESTS PLOT TO KILL ELEAZAR

Then a great crowd of Jews learned that he was there, and they came, not only because of Yeshua but also to see Eleazar, whom he had raised from the dead. But the high priests planned also to kill Eleazar since because of him many of the Jews were going away and believing in Yeshua.

YESHUA ENTERS YERUSHALAYIM

On the next day the great crowd that came to the festival heard that Yeshua was coming to Yerushalayim. They took palm branches and went out to meet him and, as in Psalms, they cried,

"Hosanna!
Blessings on him who comes in the name of the lord,
the king of Israel."[44]

And Yeshua found a young donkey and was seated on it just as it is written,

---

41. Judas Iscariot.
42. Three hundred denarii could be a year's wages.
43. Similar stories about anointing Jesus' body appear in Mark and Luke. In Mark, it is the house of Simon the leper, not Lazarus. The grumbling about the money wasted on anointing Jesus that might have gone to the poor is voiced by unnamed diners, not Judas. In Luke the scene is more erotic, there is also a Simon, the speech about the poor is almost the same, and Judas is not mentioned.
44. Psalm 118:25–26.

"Do not fear, daughter of Zion.
Look, your king is coming,
sitting on a foal of a donkey."[45]

His students did not understand these things at first, but when Yeshua was glorified, then they remembered that these things had been written about him and these things had been done for him.

The crowd that was with him when he raised Eleazar from the tomb bore witness to it all. That was why the crowd went to meet him, for they heard that he had performed the miraculous sign.

So the Pharisees said to one another, "You see, you can do nothing. Look, the world has gone over to him."

YESHUA FORETELLS HIS DEATH

Now, there were some Greek Jews[46] among those who went up to worship at the feast. They came to Philippos from Bethsaida of Galil and asked him, saying, "Sir, we wish to see Yeshua."

Philippos came and told Andreas.

Andreas and Philippos came and told Yeshua.

And Yeshua answered them, saying,

"The hour has come when the earthly son is glorified.[47]
Truly, truly I say to you,
unless a grain of wheat falling into the earth dies,
it remains alone.
But if it dies it brings forth a great harvest.[48]

"Whoever loves life will lose it,
and whoever hates life in this world
will keep it for life everlasting.

"Let anyone who serves me, follow me,
and where I am, there also will be my servant.
Whoever serves me, the father will honor.

---

45. Zechariah 9:9.
46. Ethnic Greeks who had converted to Judaism.
47. Glorification is the hour of his death, resurrection, and ascension.
48. "Harvest" is literally "fruit." It is often translated "harvest" or "crop," since here it refers specifically to the fruit of a wheat grain, which would be a harvest or crop.

"Now my soul is shaken
and what shall I say?
Father, save me from this hour?
But I came for this hour.
Father, glorify your name."
A voice came out of the sky,
"I have glorified it, and I will glorify it again."
Then the crowd standing there heard it. They said,
"It has thundered."
Others said,
"An angel has spoken to him."
Yeshua answered and said,
"Not because of me has this voice come
but because of you.
Now is the judgment of the world,
now the ruler of this world will be cast out.
And if I am raised above the earth
I will draw everyone to me."
This he said, signifying what kind of death he was to die.

The crowd answered him, "We heard from the law that the messiah remains forever. How can you say the earthly son must be raised? Who is this earthly son?"
Yeshua said to them,
"For a little time longer the light is with you.
Walk while you still have the light
so that the darkness may not overtake you.
And the one walking in the darkness
does not know where he is going.
While you have light, believe in the light
so you may be the children of light."

OF THE UNBELIEVERS

Yeshua said this and went away and went into hiding from them. Though he had performed so many miraculous signs before them, they did not believe in him so that the word spoken by Isaiah will be fulfilled:
"Lord, who has believed in our message?

And to whom was the arm of the lord revealed?"[49]
This is why they could not believe, because since Isaiah said elsewhere,

"He has blinded their eyes and hardened their heart
so that they might not see with their eyes
and understand with their heart and turn their mind around
so that I might heal them."[50]

Isaiah said these things because he saw his glory and he spoke about him. Still, even among the rulers many believed in him, but because of the Pharisees they did not admit it so that they would not be put out of the synagogue. They loved human glory more than the glory of god.

But Yeshua cried out and said,

"Who believes in me does not believe in me
but in the one who sent me.
As light into the world I have come
so that who believes in me not reside in darkness.
And who hears my words and does not keep them
I do not judge,
for I have come not to judge the world
but to save the world.

"Who rejects me and will not receive my words
has a judge waiting.
The word I spoke will judge him on the last day.
Because I spoke not from myself but from the one
who sent me,
the father has given me his commandment,
what I should say and how I should speak.
And I know his commandment is life everlasting.
So what I say,
as the father told me, I say it."

. . . .

---

49. Isaiah 53:1. See also Romans 10:16.
50. Isaiah 6:10. See also Matthew 13:15, Mark 4:12.

(Chapter 17)

YESHUA PRAYS TO THE FATHER

Yeshua said this, then raised his eyes to the sky and said,
    "Father, the hour has come.
    Glorify your son so that your son may glorify you,
    as you gave him authority over all flesh[51]
    so he may give life everlasting to all you have given him.

    "And this is the life everlasting
    so that they may know you, the only true god,
    and he whom you sent, Yeshua the anointed.[52]
    I glorified you on earth
    by completing the work you gave me to do.
    And now glorify me, father, with yourself,
    with the glory I had with you before the world was.

    "I made your name known to the people
    whom you gave me from the world.
    They were yours and you gave them to me
    and they have kept your word.
    Now they know that all you gave me comes from you.
    Because the words you gave me I gave them.
    And they accepted them,
    and they knew the truth that I came from you
    and believed that you sent me.

    I ask for their sake.
    I am asking not for the sake of the world
    but for the ones whom you gave me
    because they are yours.
    And all that is mine is yours and yours is mine
    and I am glorified in them.

    "And I am no longer in the world
    but they are in the world,

---

51. Here "all flesh" in a larger sense means "all people."
52. Or "the messiah."

and I am coming to you.
Holy father, keep them in your name,
which you gave me,
so they may be one as we are one.

"When I was with them,
through your name I kept those whom you gave me.
I guarded them and not one of them was lost
except the son of perdition
so that the scripture be fulfilled.

"Now I am coming to you
and these things I say in the world
so my elation be fulfilled in them.
I gave them your word and the world hated them
since they are not of the world
as I am not of the world.

"I do not ask you to take them from the world
but to keep them from the cunning one.[53]
They are not of this world as I am not of this world.
Sanctify them in the truth.
Your word is truth.
As you sent me into the world so I sent them
into the world.
And for them I sanctify myself
so they may also be sanctified in truth.

"I do not ask for them alone,
but for those believing in me through their word
that we may all be one
as you, father, are in me and I in you,
that the world may believe that you sent me.

"The glory you gave me I gave them
so they may be one as we are one,
I in them and you in me
so they may be made perfect as one,

---

53. Or "from the evil one," "from the devil."

so the world may know that you sent me
and loved them just as you loved me.

"Father, wherever I am I want the ones you gave me
also to be with me and see my glory,
which you gave me since you loved me
before the foundation of the world.

"Just father, the world did not know who you were,
but I knew you
and these ones knew that you had sent me.
I made your name known to them
and I shall make it known
so the love with which you loved me
may be in them and I in them."

(Chapter 18)

BETRAYAL AND CAPTURE OF YESHUA

After saying these words, Yeshua went out with his students across the ravine[54]
where there was a garden, which he and his students entered.

Now, Yehuda, who betrayed him, also knew the place, since Yeshua often
met there with his students. Then Yehuda got a band of soldiers and serving
men of the high priests and Pharisees, and went there with lamps and torches
and weapons.

Yeshua, who knew everything that was to happen to him, went out and said
to them,

"Who are you looking for?"
They answered him, "Yeshua the Nazarene."
He said to them,

"I am he."
And they stepped backward and fell to the ground.
So again he answered them,

"I told you that I am he.
If you are looking for me, let these men go."

---

54. The King James Version gives "brook Cedron." The valley lies east of Jerusalem, on the way
to the Mountain of Olives.

All this happened to fulfill the word he said, "I have not lost one of those you gave me."

Then Shimon Kefa had a knife and took it out and struck the slave of the high priest and cut off his right ear. The slave's name was Malchos.
But Yeshua said to Kefa,
"Put your knife back in its sheath.
Shall I not drink the cup the father gave me?"

Then the guard and the commander and servants of the Jews took Yeshua and bound him. And first they led him to Annas, who was the father-in-law of Caiaphas, the high priest for that year. Now, it was Caiaphas who advised the Jews that it is better for one man to die for the people.

KEFA DISOWNS YESHUA

Shimon Kefa and another student followed Yeshua. And that student, who was known to the high priest, went with Yeshua into the high priest's court. But Kefa stayed outside the door. So the other student, an acquaintance of the high priest, spoke to the doorkeeper and brought Kefa inside.
Then the girl who was at the door said to Kefa, "Aren't you one of that man's students?"
He said, "I am not."

Now, the slaves and assistants stood around a charcoal fire they had made, since it was cold and they were warming themselves. Kefa also was standing there with them, keeping warm.
Then the high priest questioned Yeshua about his students and about his teaching.
Yeshua replied to him,
"I have spoken openly to the world.
I always taught in a synagogue and in the temple
where all the Jews gather. And in secret
I spoke nothing. Why question me?
Ask those who heard what I said to them.
Look, they know what I said."
When he said this, one of the serving men slapped Yeshua and said, "Is that how you answer the high priest?"
Yeshua answered him,

"If I spoke wrong, testify to the wrong.
But if I spoke right, why do you beat me?"
Then Annas sent him bound to Caiaphas the high priest.

Shimon Kefa was standing and warming himself. So they said to him, "Aren't you also one of his students?"

He denied it and said, "I am not."

One of the high priest's slaves, a relative of the one whose ear Kefa cut off, said, "Didn't I see you in the garden with him?"

Again Kefa denied it and at once the cock crowed.

YESHUA GOES BEFORE PILATUS

They led Yeshua from Caiaphas to the Praetorium.[55] It was early morning. They didn't enter the Praetorium, so as to avoid defilement that might prevent them from eating the Pesach meals. So Pilatus[56] emerged and said to them, "What charge do you bring against this man?"

They answered him and said, "Unless he were doing wrong, we would not have turned him over to you."

Pilatus said to them, "Take him and judge him according to your law."

Then the Jews said to him, "It is not lawful for us to put anyone to death."

This happened to fulfill Yeshua's word when he foretold what kind of death he was to die.[57]

Then Pilatus again went into the Praetorium and called Yeshua and said to him, "Are you the king of the Jews?"

Yeshua answered,

"Are you speaking for yourself
or did others tell you about me?"

"Am I a Jew?" Pilatus answered. "Your people and the high priest handed you over to me. What did you do?"[58]

---

55. Governor's house.
56. Pilate.
57. This sentence, a commentary and interpretation interrupting the narration, may be a scribal interpolation and is usually placed in parentheses or brackets.
58. Pilate's essential question, "What did you do?," would suggest that Pilate was unaware of wrongdoing. Among historians there is a large consensus that Rome executed Jesus as a seditionist, as one opposed to Roman occupation. Without historical evidence, Pilate's question is not plausible. Its consequence is to accuse Jews of initiating Jesus' execution and to emphasize Rome's unwilling and marginal involvement in it.

Yeshua responded,
  "My kingdom is not of this world.
  If my kingdom were of this world
  my servants would have fought to keep me
  from being delivered to the Jews.[59]
  But now my kingdom is not here."
Then Pilatus said to him,
  "Then you are a king?"
Yeshua answered,
  "You say I am a king.
  For this I was born
  and for this I came into the world
  that I might testify to the truth.
  Everyone born of truth hears my voice."
Pilatus said to him, "What is truth?"

And after he said this, again he went out to the Jews and told them, "I find no fault in him. But you have this custom that I should release someone to you at Pesach. So do you want me to release the king of the Jews?"

They shouted back saying, "Not this man but Barabbas."

Now, Barabbas was a robber.

(Chapter 19)

PILATUS YIELDS TO THE JEWS AND ORDERS CRUCIFIXION

Then Pilatus took Yeshua and flogged him. And the soldiers wove a wreath out of thorns and put it on his head and threw a purple robe around him. And they went up to him and said, "Hail, king of the Jews!"

And they struck him in the face.

And Pilatus again went outside and said to them, "Look, I am bringing him out to you so you may know that I find no fault in him."

Then Yeshua came out, wearing the wreath of thorns and the purple robe.

---

59. Here the "we and them" reference to Jews means that the speaker and his supporters, incredibly, are not to be identified as Jews, according to this gospel.

And Pilatus said to them,

"Look at the man."

When the high priests and the serving men saw him, they shouted,

"Crucify, crucify!"

Pilatus said to them, "You take him and crucify him. I find no fault in him."

The Jews answered him, "We have a law and according to that law he should die, because he made himself son of god."

When Pilatus heard this word, he was more frightened. Again he went back into the Praetorium and said to Yeshua, "Where are you from?"

But Yeshua didn't answer him.

Then Pilatus told him, "You don't speak to me? Don't you know that I have the authority to free you and I have the authority to crucify you?"

Yeshua answered him,

"You would have no authority over me at all

were it not given to you from above.

Therefore the one who handed me over to you

has the greater sin."[60]

Thereupon Pilatus sought to release him, but the Jews cried out, saying, "If you free this man, you are not a friend of Caesar! Everyone who makes himself a king defies Caesar."

When Pilatus heard these words, he led Yeshua outside and sat on the judgment seat called Stone Pavement, but in Hebrew Gabbatha.

Now, it was Friday, the Preparation Day for Pesach, the sixth hour, which is noon. He said to the Jews, "Look, here is your king."

Then they shouted, "Take him away, take him away and crucify him!"

Pilatus said to them, "Shall I crucify your king?"

The high priest answered, "We have no king but Caesar."

So he gave him to them to be crucified.[61]

---

60. Jesus fully exonerates Pilate, who is acting not through his authority or free will, but by the authority given to him from the father. The Jews, however, have acted freely and therefore their sin is greater.

61. Robert J. Miller, in *The Complete Gospels*, offers the following comment: "The resulting implication that all the Jews/Judeans, or perhaps only some Jewish officials, crucified Jesus—as Pilate had suggested (v. 6)—is wholly inaccurate. In historical fact, whatever Pilate's view of Jesus' guilt, it was certainly he who saw to the execution (see v. 19); crucifixion was never practiced by Jews. The monstrous unreality of this half-verse, if it reads as intended, must be entirely a function of theological or political polemic" (p. 240).

YESHUA IS CRUCIFIED

They took Yeshua. Carrying the cross himself, he went to what was called the Place of the Skull, which in Hebrew is Golgotha, where they crucified him and two others, one on either side with Yeshua in the middle.

Pilatus wrote a placard and put it on the cross. It read,

Yeshua the Nazarene the King of the Jews.

Many Jews read the placard because the place where Yeshua was crucified was near the city. And it was written in Hebrew, Latin, and Greek. So the high priests of the Jews said to Pilatus, "Do not write, 'The King of the Jews,' but write what he said: 'I am king of the Jews.'"

Pilatus answered, "What I've written, I've written."

When the soldiers crucified Yeshua, they took his clothes and divided them in four parts, one part for each soldier. And they took his tunic too. Now, his tunic shirt was seamless, woven in one piece from the top straight down. So they said to each other, "Let's not tear it, but casts lots for it to see whose it will be. This was to fulfill the words of the scripture, saying,

"They divided my clothes among them
and for my clothes they cast lots."[62]

That is what the soldiers did.

But near the cross of Yeshua stood his mother and his mother's sister Miryam of Klopas and Miryam of Magdala.[63]

Then Yeshua, seeing his mother and the student he loved standing near, said to his mother,

"Woman, here is your son."[64]

Then he said to the student,

"Here is your mother."

And from that hour the student took her into his own.[65]

---

62. Psalm 22:18.
63. Mary Magdalene.
64. Literally, "Woman, look, your son," which is followed by "Look, your mother." In the synoptic gospels, Mary, Jesus' mother, does not appear. Here she appears briefly, but her name goes unmentioned. The other Marys appear by name.
65. Although "home" or "care" may be the implied translation, it says no more than "He took her into his own."

After this Yeshua, knowing that all had been done to fulfill the words of the scripture, said,

"I am thirsty."[66]

A jar filled with vinegar[67] was lying there. So they put a sponge soaked with the vinegar on a branch of hyssop and held it to his mouth.

Then when Yeshua had taken the wine, he said,

"It is ended."

And bowing his head, he gave up his spirit.[68]

THE FATE OF YESHUA'S BODY

Since it was Friday the Preparation Day, the Jews asked Pilatus that their legs be broken and they be taken away so that the bodies would not remain on the cross on Shabbat.[69] The soldiers came and broke the bones of the first man and then of the other one crucified with him. But when they came to Yeshua and saw that he was already dead, they did not break his legs. But one of the soldiers stabbed his side with his spear, and at once blood and water came out.

And the one who saw this has testified to it, and the testimony is true, and he knows he is speaking the truth so that you may also believe.[70]

These things happened to fulfill the scripture, "No bone of his will be broken."[71] And elsewhere it says, "They will look at him whom they stabbed."[72]

After these things Yosef of Arimathea,[73] being a student of Yeshua, but a secret one for fear of the Jews, asked Pilatus if he could take away Yeshua's body. Pilatus allowed it.

Then he came and took the body.

Nikodemos came too, the one who first came to him during the night, and he brought a mixture of myrrh and aloes, about a hundred pounds. So they took the body of Yeshua and wrapped it in aromatic spices in linen cloths, as is the burial custom of the Jews.

---

66. Psalm 22:15.

67. This could mean a cheap, sour wine.

68. Or "his breath."

69. Sabbath.

70. In this unusual insertion into the narration, the narrator notes the specific event of blood and water issuing from Jesus' side and concludes that the event has been witnessed, the testimony is true, and "you may also believe."

71. Psalm 34:20; Exodus 12:36; Numbers 9:12.

72. Zechariah 12:10.

73. Joseph of Arimathea.

Now, in the region where he was crucified there was a garden, and in the garden a new tomb in which no one had been placed. So because it was the Friday the Preparation Day of the Jews, and the tomb was near, in it they placed Yeshua.

(Chapter 20)

YESHUA APPEARS TO MIRYAM OF MAGDALA

On Sunday the first day of the week, Miryam of Magdala came to the tomb early while it was still dark and saw that the stone had been removed from the tomb. So she ran and came to Shimon Kefa and to the other student whom Yeshua loved and said to them,

"They took the lord from the tomb
and we don't know where they put him."

Then Kefa and the other student came out and went to the tomb. The two ran together, but the student ran faster than Kefa and reached the tomb first. And he stooped down and saw the linen cloths lying there, but didn't go in. Then Shimon Kefa came, following him, and he went into the tomb and saw the linen cloths lying there, but the kerchief which had been on his head was lying not next to the cloths but apart and folded up in its own place. And then the other student, who had come first to the tomb, saw and believed. They didn't yet know the scripture that he must rise from the dead.[74]

Then the students went off to their own places.

But Miryam stood by the tomb, weeping. Then as she was weeping, she stooped and looked into the tomb and saw two angels in white sitting there, one at the head and one at the feet where the body of Yeshua was laid.

And they said to her,

"Woman, why are you weeping?"

She said to them,

"They have taken my lord away
and I don't know where they put him."

---

74. There is a resurrection of the dead in Isaiah 26:19 and Daniel 12:2. The notion of resurrection of the dead and immortality of the soul is derived from Jewish apocalyptic literature and probably the influence of Plato, platonism, and contemporary Greco-Roman notions.

Saying this, she turned around and saw Yeshua standing there and didn't know it was Yeshua.

Yeshua said to her,

"Woman, why are you weeping?

Whom are you looking for?"

Thinking he was the gardener, she said to him,

"Sir, if you took him away,

tell me where you put him and I will take him."

Yeshua said to her,

"Miryam!"

She turned and said to him in Hebrew,

"Rabbouni!"

(which means teacher).

Yeshua said to her,

"Do not hold on to me,

since I have not yet gone up to the father.

But go to my brothers and tell them,

I am ascending to my father and your father

and my god and your god."

Miryam of Magdala went and announced to the students,

"I have seen the lord."

And she told them that he had said these things to her.

YESHUA APPEARS TO THE STUDENTS

So when it was early evening of that first day of the week and the doors of the house where the students met were locked for fear of the Jews, Yeshua came and stood in their midst and said to them,

"Peace to you."

And saying this, he showed his hands and his side to them.

The students were overjoyed when they saw the lord.

So Yeshua said to them again,

"Peace to you.

As the father sent me

so I send you."

And saying this, he breathed over them and said to them,

"Receive the holy spirit.

For any whose sins you forgive,
their sins are forgiven.
For any whose sins you do not release,
they are not released."[75]

DOUBTING TOMA IS CONVINCED

But Toma, who was one of the twelve, called the twin, was not with them when Yeshua came.

So the other students were saying to him,

"We have seen the lord."

But he said to them, "Unless I see the mark of the nails in his hands and I put my finger into the place of the nails and I put my hand into his side, I shall not believe."

After eight days the students were again in the house and Toma with them. Though the doors were shut, Yeshua stood in their midst and said,

"Peace to you."

Then he said to Toma,

"Bring your fingers here and see my hands,
and bring your hand and put it in my side,
and do not be without faith but of faith."

Toma answered, saying to him,

"My lord and my god."[76]

Yeshua said to him,

"Do you believe because you have seen me?
Blessings on those who have not seen and believe."

Yeshua performed many other signs before his students, which have not been written in this book. But these things were written that you may believe that Yeshua is the messiah the son of god, and that in believing you may have life in his name.[77]

---

75. This is John's version of the sending of the spirit to the church; see also the Pentecost account in Acts 2:1–41.
76. These words, "My lord and my god," are the common initial epithet in Hebrew prayer in addressing god: *Adonai elohim*.
77. Most scholars say that the gospel concludes here, and what follows is added by the presumed author or by another.

(Chapter 21)

YESHUA AT THE SEA OF TIBERIAS

After this, Yeshua again showed himself to the students at the Sea of Tiberias. And this is how he showed himself. Gathered together were Shimon Kefa and Toma called the twin and Nathanael from Kana in Galil and the sons of Zebedee and two other students.

Shimon Kefa said, "I'm going fishing."

They told him, "We're coming with you."

They went out and got into the boat, and all that night caught nothing.

At daybreak Yeshua was standing on the beach. But the students didn't realize that it was Yeshua.

Yeshua said to them,

"Children, have you any fish?"

"No," they answered him.

And he said to them,

"Cast the net in the waters to the right side
of the ship and you will find some."

So they cast, and they weren't strong enough to haul it back in because of the swarm of fish.

Then that student whom Yeshua loved[78] said to Kefa,

"It is the lord."

When Shimon Kefa heard it was the lord, he put on his outer garment, for he had stripped naked and thrown himself into the sea.

But the other students came in a small boat—they were not far from the land, about a hundred yards away—dragging the net full of fish.

When they came out on the shore, they saw a charcoal fire and a small fish placed on it, and bread.

Yeshua said to them,

"Now bring some of the fish you caught."

---

78. Apparently the unknown student, who ran faster to the empty tomb than Peter and believed what he saw. When fishing, the beloved student, not Peter, recognized Jesus on the shore. In the same supplement, however, Peter appears to be elevated to leadership by virtue of his foretold crucifixion in service of the church.

So Shimon Kefa went on board and dragged the net onto the land, filled with big fish, a hundred fifty-three of them, yet with so many the net didn't tear.

Yeshua said to them,

"Come have breakfast."

None of the students dared ask, "Who are you?," knowing that it was the lord.

Yeshua came and took the bread and gave it to them, and also the fish.

This was already the third time that Yeshua appeared to the students after he was raised from the dead.

YESHUA QUESTIONS SHIMON KEFA'S LOVE

So when they had breakfasted, Yeshua said to Shimon Kefa,

"Shimon son of Yohanan, do you love me
more than they do?"

Shimon said to him, "Yes, lord, you know that I love you."

Yeshua said to him,

"Feed my lambs."

He asked Shimon a second time,

"Shimon son of Yohanan, do you love me?"

Shimon said, "Yes, lord, you know that I love you."

He said to Shimon son of Yohanan for the third time,

"Do you love me?"

Kefa was hurt that he had asked him for the third time, "Do you love me?"
And he said to him, "Lord, you know all things, you know that I love you."[79]

Yeshua replies,

"Graze my sheep."

YESHUA FORETELLS SHIMON KEFA'S DEATH

And he said to him,

"Truly, truly I say to you,
when you were younger,
you fastened your own belt
and walked about where you wished.

---

79. Peter's threefold profession of love parallels his earlier threefold denial.

But when you grow old
you will stretch out your hands
and another will fasten your belt
and take you where you do not wish to go." [80]
This he said, signifying by what death he would glorify god.
After he said this, he told him,
"Follow me."

THE AUTHOR REVEALED

Kefa turned and saw the student whom Yeshua loved following them, the one who also lay next to his chest at the supper and who had said, "Who is betraying you?"

When Kefa saw him, he said to Yeshua, "Lord, what about him?"

Yeshua said to Kefa,
"If I want him to stay until I come,
what is that to you?
Follow me."

So word went out to the brothers that the student would not die. But Yeshua did not tell Kefa that the student would not die, but rather,
"If I want him to stay until I come,
what is that to you?"

This is the student who testifies to these things and who has written these things, and we know that his testimony is true.

And there are many other things that Yeshua did. If they were written down one by one, I think the world itself would not have room to hold the books that would be written.

---

80. This passage suggests Peter's later crucifixion in Rome, and while there is no information on how Peter got to Rome, there is archeological evidence of a shrine to Peter in an ancient cemetery under the basilica of Saint Peter in Rome.

PART TWO

Literature of Gnostic Wisdom

INTRODUCTION

MARVIN MEYER

The sacred literature of gnostic wisdom offers some of the most beautiful, enlightening, and disturbing mystical poetry and prose in all religious literature. The selection presented here consists of twenty-nine texts, some considered classics of gnostic spirituality, that represent varieties of gnostic religions in the Mediterranean region during the early centuries of the common era. Of the many texts that might have been included in this part of the volume, we have selected texts that are not only representative of major options in gnostic spirituality but also well preserved and attractive as literature. These texts illustrate early gnostic, Sethian, Valentinian, Syrian, and other varieties of gnostic religions, yet there are points of similarity and connection among them. All of the texts are concerned with wisdom and knowledge; many of them trace the fortunes (and misfortunes) of wisdom—personified as Hokhmah or Sophia—in the context of gnostic themes. Here, as in the wisdom literature discussed above, the figure of wisdom remains a focal point of attention, but now wisdom is radicalized, and reflects the very nature of gnosticism by embracing the tragedy and hope of the human experience. In these texts wisdom creates and reveals, falls and is restored, saves and is saved. And with divine wisdom, these texts proclaim, fallen human beings too are saved and restored.

THE BOOK OF BARUCH

The church fathers and heresiologists describe, in polemical terms, a number of figures whom they consider to be early gnostic teachers: Simon Magus, a first-century teacher from Samaria; Dositheos and Menander, also from Samaria; Cerinthos, Carpocrates, Saturnilus, Marcellina, and a few others. About these figures we know only what the heresiologists choose to tell us, and they choose to tell us little more than that these teachers proclaimed error and impiety.

About the writings of the gnostic teacher Justin, however, we know some-what more, thanks to Hippolytus of Rome. In his *Refutation of All Heresies,* Hippolytus cites and paraphrases a gnostic text composed by Justin, the Book of Baruch, although Hippolytus says it is the most abominable book he has read. From Hippolytus's citations we learn enough to reconstruct large frag-ments of Justin and his book. Kurt Rudolph describes the Book of Baruch as "one of the most original and probably also the oldest testimonies of Gnosis."[1] Strongly Jewish in its perspective, the book seems to propose a gnostic system that is one of the earliest representations of gnosis. Robert Grant calls it "an ex-ample of a gnosis that is almost purely Jewish,"[2] though in its present form, the book also incorporates references to Greco-Roman deities, as well as to Jesus.

The Book of Baruch presents a gnostic system with three principles, two that are male and one that is female. The most exalted manifestation of the di-vine is called the Good, a male power; he is also called Priapos, the Greco-Roman ithyphallic fertility god. The other powers take their names from Hebrew tradition, the male Elohim from the Hebrew word for "god" and the female Edem from the Hebrew for "earth."[3] The female principle Edem is reminiscent of wisdom, Sophia, and she has many characteristics in the Book of Baruch: she is earth; garden; Israel; creator of humans, beasts, and the soul; and a symbol of Eve, who is her creation and double.

The story of Baruch is a tale of the love of Elohim and Edem, heaven and earth, love that is expressed and is lost, with the author, Justin, employing themes from Genesis to tell his gnostic story of the fate of humanity and the emergence of evil in the world. Elohim, the heavenly father god and the cre-ator of the world, is the lover of Edem, the earthly mother goddess. From their impassioned sexual union come twenty-four angelic children, and the angels in turn create humankind and paradise. These twenty-four angels seem to an-ticipate the more developed portrayals of the realm of the divine fullness, or pleroma, in Sethian and Valentinian gnostic systems. Elohim breathes spirit (Greek *pneuma*) into Adam, and Edem breathes soul (Greek *psyche*). Baruch (Hebrew for "blessed") is the good tree of life and the chief paternal angel, and Naas (from *nahash*, Hebrew for "serpent")[4] is the evil tree of the knowledge of good and evil and the chief maternal angel.

---

1. Rudolph, *Gnosis,* 145.
2. Grant, *Gnosticism and Early Christianity,* 19.
3. The spelling Edem is used for Eden, as in the garden of Eden in Genesis, both in the Book of Baruch and in the Septuagint translation of Genesis—hence also in our translation here.
4. See the use of Naas among the Naassenes in this volume.

Elohim ascends to the Good in "the highest part of heaven" and becomes aware of "what eye has not seen or ear heard or what has not entered the human heart."[5] With this awareness of the grandeur of the divine, Elohim proposes that he destroy the world he made and take back his spirit imprisoned among people there, but the Good does not allow it. Instead, Elohim stays above, on high, and Edem, abandoned down below, brings all sorts of evil upon the spirit of Elohim within people.

The lovers' quarrel between Elohim and Edem continues through human history. Elohim sends the angel Baruch to "comfort the spirit living in all people." Baruch tries to solicit the aid of Moses, the Hebrew prophets, and even the prophet Herakles (Hercules), all in vain. Finally Elohim sends Baruch to Nazareth, and he "found Jesus, son of Joseph and Mary, feeding sheep, a boy of twelve, and he told him everything that had happened from the beginning, from Edem and Elohim and all that will be. He said, 'All the prophets before you were seduced, but Jesus, earthly son, try not to be seduced, and preach the word to people and tell them about the father and the Good, and ascend to the Good and sit with Elohim, father of us all.'" The story of the Book of Baruch concludes, according to the account in Hippolytus, with allegorical interpretations that connect portions of the gnostic story with Greco-Roman mythology.

SETHIAN LITERATURE

The name Sethian denotes a body of gnostic texts and myths that give prominence to Seth, the third son of Adam and Eve. Because a second divine entity, often named Barbelo, the divine forethought and revealer, also figures in these texts and myths, heresiologists nicknamed the gnostics who produced them Barbeloites and Barbelognostics, designations still used by modern scholars. Bentley Layton, as we noted in the general introduction to this volume, emphasizes that these religious figures called themselves gnostics, and he refers to their writings as "classic gnostic scriptures." In the sacred texts included here, the ancient authors refer to spiritually enlightened people like themselves as "the unshakable race of perfect humankind" or "the offspring (or seed) of Seth." Hence, for the sake of convenience we shall call these gnostics Sethians.

The Sethians understood themselves to be children of Adam and Eve, through Seth. Adam and Eve were the first parents, through whom the divine

---

5. See Gospel of Thomas 17.

light is communicated to enlightened gnostics. Genesis hints that Seth marked a new beginning for humanity after the violence that plagued the relationship of the brothers Cain and Abel. In Genesis 4, Cain is described as killing his brother Abel and being banished for his act of murder; in the Secret Book of John, Cain and Abel are said to have been fathered by the seductive first ruler Yaldabaoth, who defiled Eve sexually to get her pregnant. In Genesis 4:25, in the Septuagint, Seth is said to be *sperma heteron*, "another seed," in place of the dead Abel. The gnostics, in turn, described themselves as "another race," the offspring or seed of Seth. Another gnostic text, part of which is presented below, is mentioned by Porphyry as a gnostic text known to his teacher Plotinos, and is entitled Allogenes, "Foreigner," literally "One from Another Race."

The sacred literature of the Sethians features a mythological narrative that provides a reinterpretation of the opening chapters of Genesis. Several of the Sethian texts included here reflect features of this mythological narrative, but one of the most compelling of the presentations of the myth is to be found in the Secret Book of John. Although in its present form, in the versions of the Secret Book of John that have been preserved in the Nag Hammadi library and the Berlin Gnostic Codex 8502, the myth is recounted in a Christianized form, the literary evidence (more obvious in the Coptic) suggests that the myth derives from a hellenistic Jewish gnostic tradition that was in dialogue with Greek mythological and philosophical traditions, particularly Greek philosophical traditions going back to Plato.[6] This Hellenistic Jewish telling of the gnostic creation myth describes the origin, fall, and restoration of the light, the light within gnostics and the light within god. The cast of characters in the myth, some of whom are known from Genesis, appear within the Sethian texts given here. The original divine entity is the infinite One, the invisible spirit (revealed as the transcendent One in the Secret Book of John and the Vision of the Foreigner). From the One emanates the divine forethought Barbelo, and together the One and Barbelo produce a divine child, to form an exalted triad or trinity. With the divine in the fullness or pleroma of divinity are four luminaries, Harmozel, Oroiael, Daveithai, and Eleleth, along with Geradamas (Adam the stranger) and his son Seth. Mother Sophia—herself an eternal realm connected with Eleleth—miscalculates (her motives are described in different ways), and from her mistake comes her arrogant son, the demiurge and creator of the world named Yaldabaoth, Sakla, or Samael. At

---

6. Philo of Alexandria gives another example of Jewish interpretation of Genesis shaped by platonic concerns.

this point in the myth humans enter into the plot, especially Adam, Eve, Cain, Abel, Seth, and Seth's offspring, the gnostics themselves.

Of the gnostic texts included in this volume,[7] most of the texts designated as Sethian exhibit clear Sethian affinities. Thunder is less obviously Sethian (or gnostic, for that matter), but we classify it, tentatively, as a Sethian gnostic text (with Bentley Layton), for several reasons. First is its concern for wisdom and knowledge, and its resemblance to portions of the statement of divine transcendence at the beginning of the Secret Book of John. In Thunder, the "I am" self-declarations, with their paradoxical formulations, reveal a female deity who comes from above to the human realm. She is called life (as Eve is called "the mother of all living" in Genesis 3:20), and she is wisdom and knowledge, and thus she resembles the female deities who appear in a number of roles and accomplish a number of tasks in the Secret Book of John and other Sethian texts: forethought, wisdom, life (Eve), and especially after-thought (*epinoia*), which is specifically mentioned in Thunder.

The Letter of Peter to Philip incorporates various traditions into a text that resembles the New Testament or apocryphal Acts of the Apostles, but the rev-elation about the deficiency of divine light brought about by the fall of Sophia, though tersely presented, contains elements that bring to mind the Sophia myth of the Secret Book of John. In the Letter of Peter to Philip, like the Secret Book of John, the problem in the eternal realms stems from the mother, whose disobedience leads her to act independently of the father. She produces a child, an arrogant one, who steals power from his mother, establishes a bu-reaucracy of ignorant cosmic administrators, and collaborates in the creation of mortal human beings. This human creation is based, however, upon a mis-representation of the image of the divine that had appeared. For, in words that closely parallel Gospel of Thomas 72, the creator wished to make "an image in place of an image and a form in place of a form" (see also Genesis 1:26).

VALENTINIAN LITERATURE

One of the two great gnostic teachers of the second century whom we know by name is Valentinos. The other is Basilides, who was a contemporary of Valentinos but who is given little attention in this volume because he is known

---

7. Additional Sethian texts not included in this volume on account of their fragmentary charac-ter or their length include Melchizedek (Nag Hammadi Codex IX,1), the Thought of Norea (IX,2), Marsanes (X), perhaps Hypsiphrone (XI,4), and the untitled text from the Bruce Codex. Other mythological texts with some similarities to Sethian mythological texts include On the Origin of the World and the Paraphrase of Shem, both presented below.

only through fragments preserved in and discussions included in the heresiologists. Suffice it to say that Basilides was a successful early second-century
gnostic teacher in the cosmopolitan city of Alexandria, Egypt, and Valentinos
must have known of his teachings while he was there. Another well-known
teacher of the second century is Marcion, whom we discussed briefly in the
general introduction to this volume. On account of his theological dualism,
with its critical stance toward the Jewish god, the Hebrew Bible, and the world
in general, Marcion sometimes is called a gnostic, though we do not understand him to be an advocate of a religion of gnosis, as we noted above.

Valentinos was an Egyptian born in the Nile delta around the beginning of
the second century. A convert to Christianity, Valentinos was educated in
Alexandria, and he learned about Greek philosophy, Christian thinking (most
likely including that of Basilides), and hellenistic Jewish methods of reading
and interpreting the scriptures. He also seems to have been influenced by the
Sethian gnostics of his time. Bentley Layton supports this by citing Irenaeus's
observation: "Valentinos adapted the fundamental principles of the so-called
gnostic school of thought [Layton's classic gnostics] to his own kind of system."[8] Valentinos went on to Rome, where he was caught up in theological
and ecclesiastical affairs in the Christian community there. The heresiologist
Tertullian maintained that Valentinos hoped to become bishop of Rome—or,
we might say, his century's equivalent of the pope. Valentinos proved to be a
brilliant teacher, and among his followers several continued his gnostic
thought in their own literary works. This volume contains the best of their efforts. Of Valentinos's own writings little survives. Among the Valentinian texts
presented here only the mystical meditation entitled the Gospel of Truth may
have been composed by Valentinos himself.[9] Of the other literary works of
Valentinos, a fragment of a poem, "Summer Harvest," survives in the writings
of the heresiologist Hippolytus:

> Through spirit I see that all are suspended,
> through spirit I know that all are conveyed,
> flesh suspended from soul,
> soul depending on air,
> air suspended from atmosphere.

---

8. Irenaeus, *Against Heresies* 1.11.1.
9. Kurt Rudolph, incidentally, disagrees with this suggestion (*Gnosis,* 319).

From the depth come crops,
from the womb comes a child.[10]

Valentinian thought, as intimated in the poetic fragment from Valentinos, is based upon *bythos* or *bathos*, divine depth. In the words of the Gospel of Truth, the person of knowledge, the gnostic revealer, "has turned many from error. He went before them to their own places, from which they departed when they erred because of the depth of him who surrounds every place, whereas there is nothing which surrounds him." Again, later in the Gospel of Truth, "This is the perfection in the thought of the father and these are the words of his reflection. Each one of his words is the work of his will alone, in the revelation of his word. Since they were in the depth of his mind, the word, who was the first to come forth, caused them to appear, along with an intellect which speaks the unique word by means of a silent grace."

From depth emanates the pleroma of divinity, organized as (at least) fifteen pairs of beings, or couples, for a total of (at least) thirty eternal realms (aeons). All are suspended, all are held in the fullness of the divine, as the poem of Valentinos shows. While different names are assigned to the eternal realms in the different versions of the Valentinian scheme of things, the first two groups of four (tetrads) are most prominent. The resultant realm of eight (ogdoad), according to Irenaeus, looks like this:

depth	and	thought (*ennoia*)
		or grace
		or silence
mind (*nous*)	and	truth
or only child (*monogenes*)		
word (*logos*)	and	life (*zoe*)
human being	and	church

A number of these eternal realms resemble the eternal realms in the Secret Book of John and other Sethian texts, as does Sophia, the last of the Valentinian eternal realms. Through ignorance or error Sophia falls from grace and disturbs the divine order, and two other eternal realms, Christ and holy spirit,

---

10. Hippolytus, *Refutation of All Heresies* 6.37.7.

are brought forth to deal with the disturbance. Christ helps restore Sophia to the pleroma, but her desire is expelled outside the pleroma, and it becomes another Sophia, a lower wisdom called Achamoth (a name that resembles Hokhmah, the Hebrew word for "wisdom"—see the Gospel of Philip). Jesus the savior in turn is brought forth to heal Achamoth through knowledge, but her passions are also set aside, destined to be elements used for the creation of the cosmos. In Valentinian thought the mythic drama thus takes place at two levels, above and below, and the integrity of the divine fullness itself is protected by means of a limit or boundary (*horos*)—hence the need for Sophia above and Achamoth below, and Christ above and Jesus below. A mythic drama that takes place above and below also may be observed in the Secret Book of John and other Sethian texts, with forethought above and afterthought below, Geradamas above and Adam below, and heavenly Seth above and earthly Seth, and the Sethian gnostics, below. From these experiences of wisdom in Valentinian thought come three sorts of elemental stuff that characterize life, including human life, in the world: the material, the psychical, and the spiritual. Human beings, then, are divided into three groups in Valentinian thought: hylics—material people of flesh and blood who are unbelievers; psychics—psychical people, people with soul, who are ordinary Christians; and pneumatics—truly spiritual people, people with divine spirit, who are gnostics. These last are the Valentinians themselves.

All in all, Valentinian thought shows a complexity in its gnostic scheme that builds upon previous gnostic reflections, especially Sethian reflections, and incorporates Greek philosophical observations, especially platonic observations. There is variety in Valentinian expression—for example, scholars sometimes distinguish between a Western or Italic branch and an eastern branch—and there is subtlety and insight in the theological and exegetical formulations of Valentinian teachers.

While most of the texts included here are unquestionably Valentinian, the Secret Book of James and the Round Dance of the Cross are much less certainly so, as explained in the introductions to those texts.[11]

---

11. Other Valentinian texts and fragments of texts are also known, including fragments and discussions in the heresiologists, Excerpts of Theodotus, the Tripartite Tractate (Nag Hammadi Codex I,5), the Interpretation of Knowledge (XI,1), and a Valentinian Exposition (XI,2). The Testimony of Truth (IX,3) also has echoes as well as criticism of Valentinian thought and practice. Birger Pearson suggests the possibility that Julius Cassianus may have been the author of this text.

THOMAS AND OTHER SYRIAN LITERATURE

In addition to the Gospel of Thomas, which is included in Part One of this volume, three additional texts representing the tradition of Syrian spirituality in general and (in two instances, at least) Judas Thomas in particular are included in this part of the volume: the Songs of Solomon, the Song of the Pearl, and the Book of Thomas. None of these texts is unequivocally gnostic, but all proclaim a mystical wisdom and knowledge that illustrate the religious milieu of Syria and northern Mesopotamia during the early centuries of the common era. These texts also are documents that had a considerable influence on the development of religions, including gnostic religions. The great New Testament scholar Rudolf Bultmann used the Songs (or Odes) of Solomon to show what he considered to be the background of another document from Syria, the Gospel of John. Likewise, Thomas literature was known throughout the region and also in Egypt, and Thomas literature, particularly the Gospel of Thomas, appears to have shaped the thinking of Valentinian and Manichaean gnostics.

The Songs of Solomon comprise a hymnbook of poetic and mystical beauty. Scholars disagree about whether these songs originally functioned as a Jewish, Christian (or Jewish Christian), or gnostic hymnbook, but whatever might be the case, these poems are permeated with a profound concern for mystical wisdom and knowledge. Portions of the songs are excerpted in the gnostic text Pistis Sophia. Selections from Song 8 may show the mystical concerns of the Songs of Solomon:

Hear the word of truth and drink the knowledge
that I offer from my station.
Your flesh cannot know what I say to you,
nor your robes what I show you.
Keep my mystery. It harbors you.
Keep my faith. It harbors you.
Know my knowledge, you who know me in truth.

Love me gently, you who love.
I do not turn my face from my own.
I know them. Before they were, I knew them
and set my seal on their faces.
I fashioned their limbs and prepared my breasts for them,
for them to drink my holy milk and live on it.

The similarities of some of these expressions to the Gospel of Thomas are noteworthy (see, for instance, Gospel of Thomas 108).

According to Christian traditions, Judas Thomas the twin was the brother of Jesus, and in Syrian tradition he was thought to be the twin brother of Jesus. This concept of the twin also functions importantly in Manichaean sacred literature. The New Testament book of Jude is apparently attributed to this Judas, and in the Acts of Thomas, Judas Thomas is the apostolic missionary to northern Mesopotamia and India—hence the presence of the church of Saint Thomas in India to the present day. As the twin brother of Jesus, Judas Thomas was credited with special knowledge and insight, although not all Christians agreed with this positive assessment. In the Gospel of John, presented above, this evaluation of Judas Thomas as a person of knowledge, Thomas the "gnostic," is directly contradicted, and Thomas is portrayed as "doubting Thomas," Thomas the "agnostic."

In the Song of the Pearl and, less directly, in the Gospel of Thomas and the Book of Thomas, the story of the soul is depicted in mythic narrative. The mythic story of the soul was recounted throughout the literature of antiquity and late antiquity. It was told by storytellers, interpreted by philosophers, and incorporated into texts of gnostic wisdom. It is the story of Eros (or, Cupid, love) and Psyche (soul), told by Apuleius of Madaura in his romance entitled *Metamorphoses* (or *The Golden Ass*). The word *psyche* is feminine in gender in Greek, and the soul is often considered female in stories of the soul. In the Exegesis on the Soul, included here, the story of the soul is recounted in graphic form as the fall and restoration of the soul, who succumbs to bodily and sexual defilement and is restored to her former condition by her heavenly lover.

Simon Magus, the first-century teacher from Samaria claimed by the heresiologists to be the founder of the gnostic religions, seems to have acted out a myth of the soul not unlike that described in Exegesis on the Soul.[12] Simon himself apparently was called "the great power of god," an expression found in Acts 8:10,[13] and associated with a woman named Helena, whom he found working as a prostitute in Tyre and subsequently redeemed. He is said to have called her "first thought" (*ennoia*) and imagined her incarnating and reincarnating as thought or soul in one human body after another—Helen of

---

12. See Rudolph, *Gnosis*, 297–98.
13. This expression is also found in the title of a text from the Nag Hammadi library, the Concept of Our Great Power (VI,4).

Troy, for example—until he found and delivered her. Simon Magus is parodied as nothing but a cheap magician in the New Testament Acts of the Apostles 8 as well as the apocryphal Acts of Peter, which is the basis for the film *The Silver Chalice.*

The Song of the Pearl is part of the apocryphal Acts of Thomas, a Syrian text. In the Acts of Thomas the messenger Judas Thomas is described as praying and meditating in an Indian prison, and there he writes the Song of the Pearl as a poem on the soul. The poem relates a quest for a pearl, sleep and forgetfulness while on the quest, and a call to remembrance. The speaker recites:

> I remembered that I was a son of kings
> and my free soul longed for its own kind.
> I remembered the pearl
> for which I was sent down into Egypt,
> and I began to enchant
> the terrible and snorting serpent.
> I charmed him into sleep
> by calling the name of my father over him
> and of my mother, the queen of the east.
> I seized the pearl
> and turned to carry it to my father.

So ends, in enlightened discovery, the quest of the traveler, the quest of the soul. The traveler and the soul have sought and have found.

ADDITIONAL LITERATURE OF GNOSTIC WISDOM

Several additional texts, which seem to represent gnostic religious options but which cannot be classified along with Sethian, Valentinian, or Thomas and Syrian literature with any confidence, are included in this part of the volume. The Exegesis on the Soul, like the Song of the Pearl, narrates the story of the career of the soul, but the Exegesis on the Soul stresses the seductive nature of the body and sexuality in its account of the fall of the soul, and the liberation of the soul from the filthiness of bodily corruption in its account of the restoration of the soul. The gnostic text On the Origin of the World resembles the Reality of the Rulers in a number of ways, and it contains themes that recall Sethian, Valentinian, Manichaean, and other religious traditions. The

Paraphrase of Shem brings to mind, in its title, the text that Hippolytus of Rome in his account of the Sethians calls the Paraphrase of Seth, but its contents do not square well with his description of that text. Rather, the Paraphrase of Shem is a gnostic account of the creation of the world, with strongly sexual characteristics, in which Shem is the hero. The Second Treatise of the Great Seth appears to be Sethian only in title. This text is a gnostic meditation on the meaning of the life and death of Jesus and the relationship between gnostic and emerging orthodox Christians. The Gospel of Mary, a fragmentary gospel attributed to Mary (that is, Mary of Magdala), is a gnostic dialogue of Jesus with his students. The Naassene Sermon describes "serpentine" gnostics, who studied the mystery religions and drew gnostic conclusions. The sermon contains passages reminiscent of the Gospel of Thomas, including a provocative statement that proclaims the remarkable transformation of those who are spiritual and embrace knowledge: "This is the gate of heaven and the house of god, where the good god dwells alone, where no impure person enters, none psychical, none carnal. It is reserved for the spiritual alone, and those who come there must put on the wedding garments and all become bridegrooms, made masculine by the virgin spirit."

Such is the gnostic message of hope for the spiritual and the enlightened. They will come to the light, to god, and be transformed.

3

The Book of Baruch

Justin

The Book of Baruch, by Justin, is a Jewish gnostic myth, set in Eden, that exists today in a lightly Christianized and hellenized form. A sizable fragment of a lost larger scripture, Baruch is preserved only as a paraphrase in Hippolytus of Rome's *Refutation of All Heresies*. Who the author of the Book of Baruch is we cannot know. Hippolytus tells us little other than that he is a gnostic named Justin.

Baruch may be one of the earliest extant gnostic texts,[1] a missing gnostic link between Jewish monotheism and full-blown gnosticism. Elohim is still Elohim of Genesis 1:1, the essentially good creator god, but he is no longer the one almighty god, for now he reports to a deity above him, whose epithet is "the Good." Elohim is not devoid of frailties—he is a blundering lover in the garden of Eden—yet he is not the demonized demiurge that he will become in classical gnosticism. In normative gnostic scripture, the creator god of the Hebrew Bible will be declared guilty of having created humans on earth and having locked their divine particles of spiritual light inside the prison of material flesh. For that travesty, Elohim will be given dreadful epithets, while his present master,

---

1. Irenaeus declares the oldest gnostic scriptures to be the three doctrines of Simon Magus, Menander, and Saturninus, which are known through refutations of them. To these doctrines we should add the Samaritan Dositheos.

the Good, will, as the invisible source of spiritual light, acquire luminous names. For now, in this quintessential moment of gnostic development, we have the anomaly of familiar almighty Jewish Elohim being guided by his new gnostic master, the Good. The Book of Baruch, then, is our first clear paradigm of gnostic dualism in which worldly and heavenly authority is shared by two divinities, one of whom, Elohim, will eventually become nearly synonymous with Satan, and the other, the Good, will become the core of the pleroma, the gnostic fullness from which all spirit emanates and to which all light returns.

Early Jewish gnosticism is Jewish in speech and preoccupation. It still remembers its Hebrew names such as those of its leading figures Elohim and Edem (who is also called Israel), it concentrates on marriage and family, and the love scenes return to the erotic diction of the Song of Songs. Unlike other contemporary gnostic texts that are said to have had a Jewish Urtext, here the Jewish basis has not been excised. Robert W. Grant compares Baruch to "the mystical Judaism we find in the *Zohar,* where Yahweh is called the father and Elohim the mother."[2]

Jewish gnosticism is born in a first-century climate of diverse Jewish visions, ranging from those of utopian Essene communities in the desert to cosmopolitan Jews in Alexandria, such as the philosopher Philo, who is filled with Torah, neoplatonism, and strategies of mystical ascension. In the midst of all this religious ferment and the political realities of Roman occupation, the destruction of Jerusalem in 70 CE and the subsequent terrifying diaspora, Jewish gnosticism seems to gain strength as does the other new major Jewish sect, the messianists or Christians. The Christians offer faith in an earthly Jewish messiah who has become divine and identified with god, and who promises salvation after death—a matter of scant interest in the Hebrew Bible. By contrast, the gnostics will offer the promise of an interior light or breath, attainable during one's lifetime through the epiphany of gnosis. In Baruch, through the commands and actions of the Good, we see hints of a true paradise on earth and in heaven, which in its allegorical ending points to hope.

Yet the narration ends with Eden still a conflicted mess, lacking harmony or immediate resolution. There will be no peaceable kingdom on earth until the human and divine forces on earth resolve their discord by means of an as yet unavailable fully gnostic design. Everything in Baruch is transitional,

---

2. Grant, *Gnosticism and Early Christianity.*

including the Jews, who initially dominate and then share the stage with Christians and pagans. This fantastic, eclectic tale, speaking to diverse religious audiences of the period, initiates the gnostic drama that will persist on many sundry stages for the next thirteen or fourteen hundred years.[3]

The Book of Baruch has three principles: two male and one female. The two male principles are the Good and Elohim, the father of all, who is stationed below the Good. The transcendent Good as the highest divine manifestation clearly goes back to the good as the highest principle in platonic philosophy. The third figure is the female principle, Edem (earth) or Eden (garden), inferior to both, who is half woman and half beast. She participates in both upper and lower worlds. Humans are the fruit of the union of Elohim with Edem, from whom they receive spirit and soul respectively.[4]

Father Elohim represents spirit and breathes spirit (*pneuma*) into the first-born Adam, while mother Edem, representing soul and earth, breathes soul (*psyche*) into Adam. When Elohim dumps Edem in Eden and returns to his creator, the Good, Edem is jealous and revengeful. As the drama unfolds and Edem brings out her angels, including the serpent Naas (from *nahash*, Hebrew for "serpent"), to fight against what is left of Elohim's spirit on earth, Baruch, a top angel of the Good, sends a series of liberators—Moses, Herakles, prophets, and finally Jesus—to ensure redemption and return.

As the female principle, Edem in Baruch has many essences: she is garden; earth; Israel; creator of humans, beasts, and the soul; and a symbol of Eve, who is her creation and her double as the earth mother. Edem recalls the gnostic creator Sophia, thought and wisdom, who because of a disturbance and inadequacy in god was separated from the One, fell from the pleroma, and created the world. The Good is the entirely new personage in this triadic system of principles, and he is already a gnostic figure in name and transcendent powers. Elohim and Edem have a biblical past and a gnostic future. Elohim is still seen as a benign creator god and father, not the demiurge who imprisons particles of light in earthly bodies, yet he now must rise to heaven, report to the Good, and confess his error in thinking himself the lord. Then he is redeemed.

---

3. From the vantage of Jewish orthodoxy, the violation of monotheism has also begun in the dualistic reception of a Jew called Jesus not only as the *messiah*—who in Judaism is foreseen as a human leader anointed and sent by god—but as a messiah (Christ) celebrated as god himself or as god's son or equal, sitting beside god in heaven on the closest throne.

4. See Filoramo, *A History of Gnosticism*, p. 169.

As for Edem, she remains a Genesis sinner, though with greater powers than she had as biblical Eve. Indeed, Edem the mother shares with Elohim the father the deed of creating the earth. However, she has none of the heroic qualities of Eve of later gnosticism, who through her embodiment of knowledge offers salvific knowledge to humans during their residence on earth.

The story that sets the main characters in supernatural action is the romance between Elohim and Edem and the subsequent fallout of those disgruntled lovers. Their meeting is an idyllic tale of life among the angels, culminating in marriage. And before the lovers separate, they generate twenty-four angels. Twelve are paternal, twelve maternal, representing the good (male) and evil (female) sides of the cosmos. The third paternal angel is Baruch, and the third maternal angel is Naas, who, though male, fashions Edem's female strategies through his persuasions. They represent a dualistic good and evil, spirit and soul, the tree of life and the tree of knowledge. Elohim, the world creator, learns of his inferiority before the highest god, the Good, who is his lord to whom he ascends. But by abandoning and thereby enraging his wife, he allows evil to come into the earth and specifically into Edem (Eve) and Adam. In her revenge against Elohim's desertion, Edem uses her baleful angels to infect the spirit that Elohim has left behind with no protection, and that spirit becomes polluted with earthly soul.

Elohim is portrayed not as wicked but as a neglectful god who has loved, married, and abandoned his woman. Edem's wild flaws reflect a woman's scorn for her wayward spouse. Each responds to dramatic circumstance. Edem, seething against fickle Elohim, who has escaped into the sky to leave her alone, opposes the spirit he has breathed into earthly humans and uses Naas to destroy it. To counter Edem's fury, the Good sends Elohim's angel Baruch back down to oppose Naas and to save rather than punish Edem: despite her war against the father, the woman, mother of Adam and of wild beasts, may also be redeemed. To heal the rift and make redemption possible for those of soul, including Edem, the Good directs Elohim to bring his diverse prophets—a Jew, a Greek, and a Christian—back to the garden. These messengers, paying homage to each of the main religions of the day, are to combat evil and turn soul into spirit. In Justin's Baruch the author attempts ingenious solutions to resolve spiritual problems on earth. The angel Baruch turns to Moses, the prophets, and even Herakles, the Greek god of prodigious strength, whom he calls "a prophet from the uncircumcised." All fail in their mission. Edem's ally Naas outwits them one by one.

The next resource for Baruch is Jesus, whose entry is imperative for a gnostic teacher intent on converting Christians and pagans as well as Jews. When Jesus comes to earth, Naas brings out his usual tricks and applies them to him. Jesus resists. After having seduced all the earlier prophets, Naas is furious not to have defiled Jesus, and so he has him crucified. Jesus leaves his body to Edem by the tree (the Edenic tree and the cross) saying, "Woman, here is your son" (John 19:26). He delivers his spirit into the hand of the father (Luke 23:46). They all have failed, and even Jesus succeeds only in a limited way: he saves his own spirit, which is delivered, as in the gospels, to "the father," but he does not save the world or resolve the strife in paradise. Moreover, while he delivers his spirit on earth to the father Elohim, Jesus ascends (in his resurrection) not to the father but to the Good. He rises into what will be the gnostic fullness. Jesus does not have the last word as a salvific figure. In this episode there is a resemblance to the later Qur'an, where Jesus is one of the prophets but not the ultimate savior.

So the task of overcoming Naas and his evil continues. Now, almost as an explanatory afterthought (this concluding passage in Hippolytus is separated from the main text by writings that are not in Baruch), the angel Baruch sends down Priapos, the Greek phallic god of fertility, yet Naas persists. In a lovely and confused resolution, we again hear the voice of the Psalms, the gospels, and the Jewish prophets Isaiah and Hosea. Isaiah blames Israel (Edem) for not recognizing Elohim, and we seem to be back, in some unreflected, uncorrected, and muddling way to both the Hebrew Bible and the New Testament, where Edem as both the earlier Eve in Eden and as Israel and the Jews does not listen to lord Elohim. The final sermon ends with what at first appears to be an excursion elsewhere but in fact fits in perfectly with its extraordinary panreligious appeal: the Good is equated with Priapos, Elohim with Zeus, Edem with Danae. This inconclusive ending is appropriate for a fabled book whose message points to three moments of gnostic development: a Jewish past, an eclectic present, and a fully gnostic future.

Justin speaks for his day. In his syncretistic system, he includes fantastic borrowings from the main contemporary sources to persuade Jews, Christians, and Greeks to embrace this widely inclusive and developing gnostic speculation. Everyone is welcome: Elohim, Edem, Moses, Baruch, Jesus, Priapos, and Zeus. The Book of Baruch is thus a fusion of literary myths and religious systems of the first and second centuries, a coherent mythological romance held together by the spirit of knowledge.

THE BOOK OF BARUCH[5]

OATH OF SECRECY

If you would know what eye has not seen nor ear heard
and what has not arisen in the human heart,[6]
and who stands high above all good,
swear to keep the mystery of instruction secret.
Our father, who saw the good perfected in him,
has kept the mysteries of silence secret.
He has sworn and will not waver.[7]
Here is his oath:
"I swear by the one over all, which is the Good,
to keep these mysteries, to tell them to no one,
and not to go from the Good back to the creation."

When you take this oath, you enter the Good
and see what eye has not seen nor ear heard
and what has not arisen in the human heart.
You drink from the living water,
the washing, the spring of living water bubbling up.[8]
And there was a separation of waters from waters,[9]
and the waters below the firmament belong to the evil creation.
In them are washed those who are earthly and psychical.
The waters above the firmament belong to the Good
and are alive. The spiritual and the living are washed in them
as Elohim was after the washing. He did not waver.

---

5. The Book of Baruch: Book 5 of Hippolytus, *Refutation of All Heresies* (5.24.1 and 37.1–3; 5.26.1–37 and 27.4); translated from the Greek by Willis Barnstone.
6. Gospel of Thomas 17; 1 Corinthians 2:9.
7. Psalm 110:4.
8. John 4:10, 14.
9. Genesis 1:6.

THE MYTH OF THE CREATORS

There were three ungenerated principles
governing the cosmos: two male and one female.
One of the male principles is called the Good,
and it alone carries that epithet[10]
and knows everything ahead of time.
The other male principle is named father of all things
begotten in the world, has no forethought,
and he is unknown and invisible.
The female is angry.
She knows nothing ahead of time
and she has two minds and two bodies. As in Herodotos's myth,
she is a virgin above and a viper below.[11]
She is called both Edem and Israel.
These are the principles of the cosmos,
the roots and pools from which all sprang,
and nothing else was in the world.

When the father knowing nothing beforehand
saw that half-virgin Edem,[12] he burned for her,
and he the father is called Elohim,[13]
and Edem burned equally for Elohim. Their desire
drew them to a single union of love.
From this coupling the father seeded twelve angels
for himself through Edem.
The paternal angels are Michael, Amen, Baruch, Gabriel, Esaddaeus....[14]

---

10. See Luke 18:19.
11. Herodotos, 4.8–10. The ancient notion of a woman consisting of two parts, the virgin breasts above the waist and an animal temptation below, is contained in myths of the siren, a symbol in Homer's *Odyssey* of seduction and destruction.
12. *Edem* means "earth" and *Eden* means "paradise." Traditionally, *Eden* is said to be from the Hebrew *eden*, meaning "delight," or god's garden of delight. However, it is more probably related to a Sumerian word meaning "plain." The extant Greek text gives *edem*, as in the early Septuagint Greek translation.
13. Originally the Hebrew word for "gods," *Elohim* came to be normally translated "god" (singular) in Genesis 1:1, though elsewhere, as in the Psalms, it retains the plural notion of "gods."
14. Seven of the names of paternal angels are now lost.

The maternal angels are Babel, Achamoth, Naas, Bel, Belias, Satan,
Sael, Adonaios, Kauithan, Pharaoth, Karkamenos, and Lathen.
Of these twenty-four the paternal ones side
with the father and obey his will in everything,
and the maternal ones hear their mother, Edem.
Their common domain is paradise,
about which Moses tells us,
"God planted paradise east of Eden,"[15]
before the face of Edem, and therefore
she always looks at paradise, her angels.

The angels of paradise are allegorically called trees,
and the tree of life is the third paternal angel,
and his name is Baruch,
while the tree of the knowledge of good and evil
is the third maternal angel, and he is Naas.
Moses spoke these things covertly
because not everyone can hold the truth.

THE CREATION OF ADAM AND EVE

After paradise came into being through the love
of Elohim and Edem,
the angels of Elohim took some of the best earth
(not from the bestial, naked part of Edem
but from her upper, civilized regions)
and from that good earth they made man,[16]
but from the bestial land came wild beasts and creatures.

They made man a symbol of their union and love
and planted some of their powers in him.
Edem provided the soul and Elohim the spirit.
The man Adam was a seal and memory of their love,
an eternal symbol of the wedding of Edem and Elohim.
And, as Moses wrote, Eve was image and symbol,

---

15. Genesis 2:8. The relevant phrase in this verse may be translated "east of Eden" or "before Eden," as here in the Book of Baruch.
16. Genesis 2:7.

and the seal of Edem preserved forever.
Edem set the soul in Eve and Elohim the spirit.

And they were given commandments:
"Be fruitful and multiply and subdue the earth."[17]
Edem gave away all her power to Elohim,
like a marriage dowry, and till this day,
in imitation of that first marriage,
a woman comes to her husband with a dowry,
obeying a holy and hereditary law
that Edem carried out toward Elohim.[18]

THE ANGELS ARE DIVIDED

When, according to Moses, everything was created
including heaven and earth and all therein,
the twelve angels of the mother were divided
into four principles, and each quadrant is called
a river: Pishon, Gihon, Tigris, and Euphrates.
Huddled in these four parts, the twelve angels
circle around and govern the cosmos.
Their authority over the world comes from Edem.
They are not forever in the same region,
but as in a circular chorus they move
from place to place at fixed intervals and periods
according to their assignments.
When the angels of Pishon rule a region,
then famine, distress, and tribulation
foul that segment of the earth,
for their criterion for ruling is avarice.
And in all regions come bad times and disease
according to each power and nature.
There is a torrent of evil pouring out
like the rivers, and constantly around the world
Edem's will controls every quadrant.

---

17. Genesis 1:28.
18. See Genesis 2:24.

ELOHIM'S ASCENT

The necessity of evil has this circumstance:
when Elohim and Edem in mutual love made the cosmos,
Elohim chose to rise to the highest part of heaven
to see if their creation lacked any elements.
He took his angels with him and rose, as was his nature,
and he abandoned Edem below,
who being earth declined to follow her husband upward.
When Elohim reached the upper border of heaven,
he saw a light stronger than the sun he created,
and he said, "Open the gates for me to enter
and to acknowledge the lord.[19]
I had thought I was the lord!"

He heard a voice out of the light, saying,
"This is the lord's gate. The just pass through it."[20]
The gate was immediately opened,
and the father, without his angels, went into the Good
and saw what eye has not seen or ear heard
and what has not arisen in the human heart.
The Good said to him, "Sit down at my right hand."[21]
The father said to the Good,
"Let me destroy the cosmos I made.
My spirit is imprisoned among people.
I want to take it back."[22]

Then the Good told him, "Nothing which comes
from me can be evil. In your companion love
you and Edem made the world. Let Edem keep the creation
as long as she wishes, but you must stay with me."

EDEM'S RESPONSE

Then Edem knew she was abandoned by Elohim
and sorrowfully began to gather angels around her

19. Psalm 118:19.
20. Psalm 118:20.
21. Psalm 110:1.
22. Genesis 6:7.

and adorn herself brightly[23] to arouse his return.
But under the Good's control Elohim no longer
descended to Edem. Then Edem commanded Babel,
which here means the goddess Aphrodite,
to incite fornication and divorce among people,
so that as she was separated from Elohim
the spirit of Elohim in people might feel affliction
and be tormented and suffer like her, Edem,
his abandoned wife. And Edem gave grand authority
to Naas, her third angel, to torture the spirit
of Elohim in people with all possible tortures
so through that spirit Elohim might himself
be tortured—he who had abandoned Edem
in cold violation of their covenant.

ELOHIM SENDS DOWN HIS ANGEL BARUCH

When the father Elohim saw these things,
he sent down Baruch, his own third angel,
to comfort the spirit living in all people.
When Baruch came he stood among the angels
of Edem, in the midst of paradise.[24] Paradise
was the angels among whom he stood,
and he commanded the people "to eat from
every tree in paradise, except from the tree
of the knowledge of good and evil,"[25]
which tree is Naas.[26] They could obey
the other eleven angels of Edem,
for though they have passions they do not disobey
the commandment. But Naas disobeyed.
He approached Eve and seduced her
and debauched her, which is a transgression,
and he approached Adam and played with him
as a boy, which is a transgression.

---

23. See, perhaps, Genesis 2:1 (heaven and earth are finished in their full array).
24. Genesis 2:9.
25. Genesis 2:16, 17.
26. Note that Naas is both the tree of knowledge and (since his name derives from the Hebrew
nahash, "snake") the serpent of seduction to eat from the tree.

So adultery and pederasty were born.
Since then evil and good have ruled people.
It began from a single source. When the father
ascended to the Good, he showed the way
for those who wish to rise, and by leaving Edem
he began the evil for his spirit in people.

BARUCH SEARCHES FOR A SAVIOR

Baruch went to Moses and through him spoke
to the children of Israel to turn them back to the Good,
but Edem's third angel Naas barred his way.
Through the soul Edem gave him and Moses
and all people, Naas expunged Baruch's orders
and only Naas's commandments were heard,
and so soul was set against spirit
and spirit set against soul.
The soul is Edem while the spirit is Elohim,
and each is in both man and woman.

Then Baruch was sent down to the prophets
so that the spirit living in people might hear
and flee from Edem and her corrupt creation
as once father Elohim fled. But Naas, using
his old tactics, dragged the father's spirit down
into the soul of people he seduced, who scorned
Baruch's words in Elohim's commandments.

Then Baruch chose a prophet from the uncircumcised,
Herakles, and sent him to subdue the twelve angels
of Edem,[27] and free the father from the twelve evil
angels of the creation.[28] These are the twelve labors
in which Herakles contended, from first to last,
with the lion, the hydra, the boar, and the rest.
And they are names of nations given to them

---

27. The allusion is to the twelve labors that Herakles must perform in order to attain immortality.
28. This passage is translated by Robert Haardt as "the twelve angels of the Creation of Evil."

from the power of the maternal angels.
Just when he seemed victorious, Omphale,[29]
who is Babel or Aphrodite, attacked him
and seduced him and took away his strength
and Baruch's commandments ordered by Elohim,
and then she wrapped him in her own robe,
the power of Edem, the power from below.
Herakles' prophecies and work were nothing.

BARUCH FINDS JESUS

Finally, "in the days of king Herod,"[30]
Baruch was sent once more by Elohim
and he came to Nazareth and found Jesus,
son of Joseph and Mary, feeding sheep,
a boy of twelve,[31] and he told him everything
that had happened from the beginning,
from Edem and Elohim and all that will be.
He said, "All the prophets before you
were seduced, but Jesus, earthly son,
try not to be seduced, and preach the word
to people and tell them about the father
and the Good, and ascend to the Good
and sit with Elohim, father of us all."

JESUS' CRUCIFIXION AND ASCENT

And Jesus obeyed the angel. He said,
"Lord, I will do all things." He affirmed this.
Naas wanted to seduce him too, but he
could not. Jesus kept faith with Baruch.
Then Naas was enraged because he could not
seduce him, and he had him crucified.

---

29. Omphale is the queen of Lydia to whom Herakles was enslaved for a period of time, according to Greek mythology.
30. Luke 1:5.
31. Luke 2:42.

Jesus left his body to Edem by the tree
and ascended to the Good. He said to her,
"Woman, here is your son."[32] He left
his soul and earthly body, but his spirit
he placed in the hands of the father[33]
and then he ascended to the Good.

ALLEGORICAL INTERPRETATIONS

The Good is Priapos, who created before
anything was.[34] He is called Priapos
because he made everything. So in temples
everywhere he is honored by all creation.
On the roads he walks carrying fruit,
fruits of creation, whose cause he was,
since he created before anything was.

Now, when you hear that the swan lay on Leda
and produced a child from her,
the swan is Elohim and Leda is Edem.[35]

When they say that the eagle came upon Ganymede,
the eagle is Naas and Ganymede is Adam.[36]

When you hear one say that gold came upon Danae
and produced a child from her,
the gold is Elohim and Danae is Edem.[37]

In this way these tales are interpreted
comparing them to similar myths.

---

32. John 19:26.
33. Luke 23:46.
34. Priapos, the fertility god of the enormous phallus, is connected to all sorts of fruitfulness in Greek mythology.
35. Leda is the woman who in Greek mythology was ravished by Zeus, who took the form of a swan.
36. Ganymede is the Greek youth of great beauty who was kidnapped by an eagle to become a cupbearer to Zeus.
37. Zeus managed to rape Danae by becoming a shower of gold rain falling on her in her tower prison. She and her son Perseus escaped, floating on a raft to Seriphos. Here Elohim is compared to Zeus, the gold rain.

When the prophets say, "Hear, heaven,
and listen, earth, the lord has spoken,"[38]
the spirit of Elohim in people is heaven,
and soul living with the spirit in people is earth.
The lord is Baruch, and Israel Edem,
and Elohim's wife is called Edem and Israel.
"Israel did not know me."[39] And if she[40] had known
that I[41] am with the Good, she would not
have tortured the spirit that lives in people
because of the ignorance of the father.
When the prophet is said to take a woman
for himself to fornicate because "the earth has fornicated
behind the lord,"[42] even as Edem behind Elohim,
in these words the prophet clearly tells the whole mystery,
but because of Naas's wickedness he is unheard.

---

38. Isaiah 1:2.
39. Isaiah 1:3.
40. This is Edem, Israel.
41. This is Elohim.
42. Hosea 1:2.

4

The Secret Book
of John

The Secret Book (or Apocryphon) of John is a classic work of Sethian gnostic mythology. It presents an early and elegant version of the gnostic myth of creation. Versions of the myth articulated here will resurface throughout the texts that are included in this volume. The Secret Book of John was almost certainly widely distributed in its time: no fewer than four copies of it have survived, and Irenaeus of Lyon, in his tract *Against Heresies*, attempts to debunk certain "heretics," also called Barbelognostics or Barbeloites, whose system of thought resembles that of the Secret Book of John.

The Secret Book of John presents a mythological account of the creation, fall, and salvation of the world and the people within the world, featuring Sophia in the role of the wisdom of god. In its present form it is a Christian text consisting of discourses and disclosures of Jesus set within the framework of a dialogue between John and Jesus. The Secret Book of John thus stands within the Johannine tradition, the tradition of the Gospel of John and other texts attributed to John; the scholar Karen L. King has even suggested that Sethian gnostics have considered it to be Part Two of the gospel.[1] This Christian form of the text appears to be based on an earlier Jewish text that addressed

---

1. King, "The Apocryphon of John: Part II of the Gospel of John?"

the problem of evil and vindicated the goodness of god by interpreting the opening chapters of Genesis and other portions of the Hebrew Bible in an innovative and even shocking manner. In the hypothetical Jewish text the revealer and savior must have been the heavenly forethought of god, as is clear from the hymn of the savior that concludes the revelation in the longer version of the Secret Book of John. In the hymn of the savior, and elsewhere in the Secret Book of John, the revealer speaks in the first-person singular ("I"). In the earlier Jewish text, the revealer would have been Barbelo, the forethought of god, but in the present Christian version of the Secret Book of John, the revealer is Jesus.

The Secret Book of John explains the contrast between an absolutely excellent and all-transcendent One (or monad) and an absurd and fallen world by means of an intricate mythological account of a god who emanates, creates, falls, and finally is saved. It combines insights derived from Genesis with Greek philosophical and mythological themes to produce a dramatic story of salvation, a remarkable account of the evolution, and the devolution, of the invisible divine spirit.

Greek psychology and philosophy (platonism, for example) posited a system in which the mind is linked to the divine and the divine is said to be mind. Accordingly, the Secret Book of John employs a series of Greek terms related to the word mind (*nous*) in order to describe the career of the divine and the creation of the cosmos. The account describes the invisible spirit or mind extending itself through a thought (*ennoia*), a forethought (*pronoia*), until it achieves an enlightened state of mind (*nous*) and a spiritual fullness (*pleroma*). Alas, a loss of wisdom (*Sophia*) brings about mindlessness (*aponoia*); the restoration of wisdom is finally accomplished through the expression of divine afterthought (*epinoia*).

The following cast of principal characters emerges in the mythic account of the Secret Book of John:

The father of all, called the One, the invisible virgin spirit

The divine mother, forethought of all, Barbelo, called mother-father, first human, holy spirit, triple male

The divine child, the self-conceived, the anointed

The four heavenly luminaries, Harmozel, Oroiael, Daveithai, Eleleth

Afterthought, a heavenly aeon, sent as a revealer with connections to forethought, Sophia, and Eve

Geradamas ("Adam the stranger"), the heavenly human

Seth, heavenly son of Geradamas, whose offspring are the Sethian gnostics

Sophia, divine wisdom from among the aeons

Yaldabaoth, also called Sakla, Samael, child of Sophia, arrogant first ruler
and creator of this world Authorities, powers, archons, rulers, angels,
demons, lackeys of Yaldabaoth

Adam and Eve

Noah

Moses

Yahweh and Elohim, sons of Yaldabaoth and Eve, also called Cain and Abel

The savior, forethought or Jesus

John son of Zebedee, a student of Jesus and the supposed author or editor
of the Secret Book of John

The offspring or seed of Seth, the unshakable race, the Sethian gnostics

All this takes place, the Secret Book of John declares, "in order that when
the spirit comes down from the holy realms, it may raise up the seed and heal
it of what it lacks, that the entire realm of fullness may be holy and lacking in
nothing." Ultimately, then, god saves and is saved, and with god all those,
called the offspring of Seth, who participate in light and wisdom. Thus divine
wisdom, personified as Sophia, is finally vindicated, and the glorious fullness
of the divine is realized.

All four extant versions of the Secret Book of John are preserved in Coptic,
but a version of the Secret Book of John was most likely composed in Greek in
the second century or earlier. The text is now known in short and long versions; the long version is the one translated here.[2]

---

2. For another Sethian text in this volume that closely parallels the Secret Book of John, most
significantly in its revelation about the One, see the Vision of the Foreigner. Other mythological creation accounts with similarities to the Secret Book of John appear particularly in the
Sethian texts collected here, but also in On the Origin of the World and the Paraphrase of
Shem. Among heresiological works, see especially Irenaeus, on the Barbelognostics, or gnostics
of Barbelo, in *Against Heresies* 1.29.1–4.

THE SECRET BOOK OF JOHN[3]

The teaching of the savior, and the revelation of the mysteries and the things hidden in silence, things he taught his student John.

THE REVEALER APPEARS TO JOHN

One day when John the brother of James, the sons of Zebedee, went up to the temple, it happened that a Pharisee named Arimanios[4] came up to him and said to him, Where is your teacher, whom you followed?

John said to him, He has returned to the place from which he came.

The Pharisee said to him, This Nazarene has deceived you badly, filled your ears with lies, closed your minds, and turned you from the traditions of your parents.

When I, John, heard this, I turned away from the temple and went to a mountainous and barren place. I was distressed within, and I said,

How was the savior selected?

Why was he sent into the world by his father?

Who is his father who sent him?

To what kind of eternal realm shall we go?

And what was he saying when he told us,

This eternal realm to which you will go is modeled

after the incorruptible realm,

but he did not teach us what kind of realm that one is?[5]

At the moment I was thinking about this, look, the heavens opened, all creation under heaven lit up, and the world shook.[6] I was afraid, and look, I

---

3. The Secret Book of John: translated by Marvin Meyer, based largely on the Coptic text of Nag Hammadi Codex II,1, Coptic pages 1,1 to 32,9. The text of Nag Hammadi Codex IV,1, which also represents the long version, has been consulted, as have the texts representing the short version, Nag Hammadi Codex III,1, and Berlin Gnostic Codex [BG] 8502,2. A number of minor restorations have been incorporated into the translation, especially at the beginning of the text. Readings have been confirmed whenever possible by consulting the four Coptic texts of the Secret Book of John.
4. The name recalls the evil Zoroastrian deity Ahriman.
5. An eternal realm (or a realm) is an aeon, throughout the Secret Book of John. The list of questions summarizes what must be known about salvation. Here the list functions as a virtual table of contents for the text. Other gnostic texts also include such lists of questions, for example, the Letter of Peter to Philip, the Gospel of Truth, and the Book of Thomas.
6. The revelation is accompanied by apocalyptic phenomena: the heavens open and the world is illuminated and shaken.

saw within the light a child standing by me. As I was staring, it seemed to be an elderly person. Again it changed its appearance to be a youth. Not that there were several figures before me. Rather, there was a figure with several forms within the light. These forms appeared through each other, and the figure had three forms.

The figure said to me, John, John, why are you doubting? Why are you afraid? Are you not familiar with this figure? Then do not be fainthearted. I am with you always. I am the father, I am the mother, I am the child. I am the incorruptible and the undefiled one.[7] Now I have come to teach you what is, what was, and what is to come,[8] that you may understand what is invisible and what is visible; and to teach you about the unshakable race of perfect humankind.[9] So now, lift up your head that you may understand the things I shall tell you today, and that you may relate them to your spiritual friends, who are from the unshakable race of perfect humankind.

THE ONE

I asked if I might understand this, and it said to me, The One[10] is a sovereign that has nothing over it. It is god and father of all, the invisible one that is over all, that is incorruptible, that is pure light at which no eye can gaze.

The One is the invisible spirit. We should not think of it as a god or like a god. For it is greater than a god, because it has nothing over it and no lord above it.[11] It does not exist within anything inferior to it, since everything exists within it alone.[12] It is eternal, since it does not need anything. For it is absolutely complete. It has never lacked anything in order to be completed by it. Rather, it is always absolutely complete in light. The One is

illimitable, since there is nothing before it to limit it,

unfathomable, since there is nothing before it to fathom it,

immeasurable, since there was nothing before it to measure it,

---

7. The revelation opens with "I am" statements, used also in the Gospel of John, Thunder, the Round Dance of the Cross, and other texts.

8. Another list of questions.

9. This is a phrase used to described the gnostic group. These people cannot be shaken and do not waver in their quest for knowledge and truth.

10. Coptic *monas* (from Greek), "monad." The following lines offer a classic statement of divine transcendence formulated in terms of negation. This statement in the Secret Book of John is similar to the Vision of the Foreigner and reminiscent also of the *via negativa* of the Hindu Upanishads, with the insistence that the ultimate is *neti neti,* "not this, not that."

11. The One is beyond deity.

12. The One is beyond existence.

invisible, since nothing has seen it,

eternal, since it exists eternally,

unutterable, since nothing could comprehend it to utter it,

unnamable, since there is nothing before it to give it a name.

The One is the immeasurable light, pure, holy, immaculate. The One is unutterable and is perfect in incorruptibility. Not that it is part of perfection or blessedness or divinity: it is much greater.

The One is not corporeal and is not incorporeal.

The One is not large and is not small.

It is impossible to say,

"How much is it?

What kind is it?"

For no one can understand it.[13]

The One is not among the things that exist, but it is much greater. Not that it is greater.[14] Rather, as it is in itself, it is not a part of the eternal realms or of time. For whatever is part of a realm was once prepared by another. Time was not allotted to it, since it receives nothing from anyone: what would be received would be on loan. The one who is first does not need to receive anything from another. Such a one beholds itself in its light.

The One is majestic and has an immeasurable purity.

The One is a realm that gives a realm, life that gives life, a blessed one that gives blessedness, knowledge that gives knowledge, a good one that gives goodness, mercy that gives mercy and redemption, grace that gives grace.

Not as if the One possesses all this. Rather, it is that the One gives immeasurable and incomprehensible light.

What shall I tell you about it? Its eternal realm is incorruptible, at peace, dwelling in silence, at rest, before everything.[15]

It is the head of all realms, and it sustains them through its goodness.

We would not know what is ineffable, we would not understand what is immeasurable, were it not for what has come from the father. This is the one who has told these things to us alone.[16]

---

13. The One is beyond finite categories.
14. The text suggests that since no finite categories are appropriate to describe the infinite One, not even the term "greater" is appropriate, since it implies a comparison among finite entities.
15. The One, finally, is known in ineffable silence. The divine silence is a common theme in mystical traditions.
16. The one who has told these things is the father.

BARBELO APPEARS

Now, this father is the One who beholds himself in the light surrounding him, which is the spring of living water, and provides all the realms. He reflects on his image everywhere, sees it in the spring of the spirit, and becomes enamored of his luminous water, for his image is in the spring of pure luminous water surrounding him.[17]

The father's thought became a reality, and she who appeared in the presence of the father in shining light came forth. She is the first power who preceded everything and came forth from the father's mind as the forethought of all. Her light shines like the father's light; she, the perfect power, is the image of the perfect and invisible virgin spirit.[18]

She, the first power, the glory of Barbelo, the perfect glory among the realms, the glory of revelation, she glorified and praised the virgin spirit, for because of the spirit she had come forth.

She is the first thought, the image of the spirit. She became the universal womb, for she precedes everything,

the mother-father,[19]
the first human,
the holy spirit,
the triple male,[20]
the triple power,
the androgynous one with three names,
the eternal realm among the invisible beings,
the first to come forth.

---

17. The father gazes into the water and falls in love with his own image in a manner that calls to mind Narcissus in Greek mythology (see Ovid, *Metamorphoses* 3.402–510).

18. Through this love of the father for his own image the father's thought (Coptic *ennoia*, from Greek) emanated, and the first thought or forethought (Coptic *pronoia*, from Greek) comes from the mind of the father: the divine mother, Barbelo. The father thus produces an entity independently, without the aid of a lover. Other gods who are credited with acts of independent procreation include the Greek god Zeus, who produces Athena the daughter of Metis (wisdom or skill) from his head alongside the River (or Lake) Triton (see Hesiod, *Theogony* 886–900, 924–29), or the Egyptian god Atum, who mates with his hand and spits, that is, he produces the seed of life by means of masturbation. On Sophia conceiving independently, see below.

19. Coptic *metropator* (from Greek), probably a term for an androgynous parent.

20. This is a term of praise, in which maleness symbolizes all that is heavenly, like the divine father, and maleness is amplified by being male three times over. Even Barbelo can be a triple male! Similar themes occur in Gospel of Thomas 114, the Three Steles of Seth, and other texts.

Barbelo asked the invisible virgin spirit to give her foreknowledge, and the spirit consented. When the spirit consented, foreknowledge appeared and stood by forethought. This is the one who came from the thought of the invisible virgin spirit.[21] Foreknowledge glorified the spirit and the spirit's perfect power, Barbelo, for because of her, foreknowledge had come into being.

She asked again to be given incorruptibility, and the spirit consented. When the spirit consented, incorruptibility appeared and stood by thought and foreknowledge. Incorruptibility glorified the invisible one and Barbelo. Because of her they had come into being.

Barbelo asked to be given life eternal, and the invisible spirit consented. When the spirit consented, life eternal appeared, and they stood together and glorified the invisible spirit and Barbelo. Because of her they had come into being.

She asked again to be given truth, and the invisible spirit consented. Truth appeared, and they stood together and glorified the good invisible spirit and its Barbelo. Because of her they had come into being.

This is the father's realm of five. It is:

the first human, the image of the invisible spirit, that is, forethought, which is
     Barbelo, and thought,
along with foreknowledge,
incorruptibility,
life eternal,
truth.

This is the androgynous realm of five, which is the realm of ten, which is the father.[22]

BARBELO CONCEIVES

The father gazed into Barbelo, with the pure light surrounding the invisible spirit, and its radiance. Barbelo conceived from it, and it produced a spark of light similar to the blessed light but not as great. This was the only child of the mother-father that had come forth, its only offspring, the only child of the

---

21. The one who comes from the spirit's thought is most likely forethought, or possibly foreknowledge.

22. The five in Coptic is *pentas* (from Greek), "pentad" or "quintet." It consists of Barbelo and the four spiritual attributes Barbelo requested. Since they are androgynous, they can also be called the ten (Coptic *dekas*, from Greek). The five or the ten are the same as the father in emanation.

father, the pure light.[23] The invisible virgin spirit rejoiced over the light that was produced, that came forth first from the first power of the spirit's forethought, who is Barbelo. The spirit anointed it with its own goodness until it was perfect, with no lack of goodness, since it was anointed with the goodness of the invisible spirit. The child stood in the presence of the spirit as the spirit anointed the child. When the child received this from the spirit, at once it glorified the holy spirit and perfect forethought. Because of her it had come forth.[24]

The child asked to be given mind[25] as a companion to work with, and the spirit consented. When the invisible spirit consented, mind appeared and stood by the anointed, and glorified the spirit[26] and Barbelo.

All these beings came into existence in silence.

Mind wished to create something by means of the word of the invisible spirit.[27] Its will became a reality and appeared, with mind and the light, glorifying it. Word followed will. For the anointed, the self-conceived god,[28] created everything by the word. Life eternal, will, mind, and foreknowledge stood together and glorified the invisible spirit and Barbelo, for because of her they had come into being.

The holy spirit brought the self-conceived divine child of itself and Barbelo to perfection, so that the child might stand before the great, invisible virgin spirit as the self-conceived god, the anointed, who honored the spirit[29] with loud acclaim. The child came forth through forethought. The invisible virgin spirit set the true, self-conceived god over everything, and caused all authority and the truth within to be subject to it, so that the child might understand everything, the one called by a name greater than every name, for that name will be told to those who are worthy of it.

---

23. Spiritual intercourse between the father and Barbelo produces a child of light. In the long version of the Secret Book of John, the father is considered to be the active procreative force. In the version found in BG 8502 and Nag Hammadi Codex III, Barbelo is the one who gazes into the father or the pure light, and then she gives birth.

24. The text apparently maintains that the divine child is both good (Greek, *chrestos*) and anointed (Greek, *christos*).

25. *Nous* (from Greek; the Coptic *meeue* is also used).

26. Coptic, "it" or "him"; possibly "the anointed."

27. Here begins creation by the word, as in Genesis 1 and John 1, as well as in the Egyptian creation text called the Memphite cosmogony, in which Ptah is described as creating by means of the spoken word.

28. Coptic *autogenes* (from Greek).

29. Or "whom the spirit honored."

THE FOUR LUMINARIES

Now, from the light, which is the anointed, and from incorruptibility, by the grace of the spirit, the four luminaries that derive from the self-conceived god gazed out [30] in order to stand before it. The three beings are:

    will,

    thought,

    life.

The four powers are:

    understanding,

    grace,

    perception,

    thoughtfulness.

Grace dwells in the eternal realm of the luminary Harmozel, who is the first angel.[31] There are three other realms with this eternal realm:

    grace,

    truth,

    form.[32]

The second luminary is Oroiael, who has been appointed over the second eternal realm. There are three other realms with it:

    afterthought,[33]

    perception,

    memory.

The third luminary is Daveithai, who has been appointed over the third eternal realm. There are three other realms with it:

    understanding,

---

30. Or "appeared" (in BG 8502 and Nag Hammadi Codex III).

31. Or "and is the first angel."

32. The lists of heavenly beings and powers here and elsewhere are meant to indicate the glorious manifestations of the emerging fullness of the divine mind. Upon occasion the lists include duplicate names.

33. *Epinoia* (from Greek). In Greek mythology the Titans Prometheos ("forethought") and Epimetheos ("afterthought") create human beings, though Epimetheos does his job imperfectly. Prometheos, who is linked to Athena, makes the humans stand upright, after the manner of the gods, and he takes fire from the gods and brings it down to earth. He thus functions as a savior of humans, but he is punished for his actions by being chained to a pillar in the mountains, where a bird of prey continually eats his liver. Eventually Herakles frees him. Much of this recalls aspects of the plot in the Secret Book of John, particularly the roles of forethought (*pronoia*), afterthought (*epinoia*), and the demiurge.

love,

idea.

The fourth eternal realm has been set up for the fourth luminary, Eleleth. There are three other realms with it:

perfection,

peace,

Sophia.

These are the four luminaries that stand before the self-conceived god; these are the twelve eternal realms that stand before the child of the great self-conceived, the anointed,[34] by the will and grace of the invisible spirit. The twelve realms belong to the child of the self-conceived one, and everything was established by the will of the holy spirit through the self-conceived one.

GERADAMAS AND SETH

Now, from the foreknowledge of the perfect mind, through the expressed will of the invisible spirit and the will of the self-conceived one, came the perfect human, the first revelation, the truth. The virgin spirit named the human Geradamas[35] and appointed Geradamas to the first eternal realm with the great self-conceived, the anointed, by the first luminary, Harmozel. Its powers dwell with it. The invisible one gave Geradamas an unconquerable power of mind.

Geradamas spoke and glorified and praised the invisible spirit by saying,

"Because of you everything has come into being, and to you everything will return.

"I shall praise and glorify you, and the self-conceived, and the eternal realms,

the three—father, mother, child, the perfect power."

Geradamas appointed his son Seth to the second eternal realm, before the second luminary, Oroiael.

In the third eternal realm were stationed the offspring of Seth,[36] with the third luminary, Daveithai. The souls of the saints were stationed there.

---

34. Geradamas? Perhaps read "the great self-conceived child, the anointed." See also below.
35. Geradamas is the perfect human being, Adamas or Adam, in the divine realm, the father of Seth and the heavenly ancestor of humankind. The name probably derives from Hebrew, perhaps meaning Adam the stranger (so Howard M. Jackson and Birger A. Pearson), that is, Adam who is an alien in this world but is at home in the divine realm. For other suggestions for the meaning of Geradamas, see James E. Goehring in Pearson, ed., *Nag Hammadi Codex VII*, p. 388.
36. The phrase "the offspring of Seth," like "the unshakable race," designates the gnostic group.

In the fourth eternal realm were stationed the souls of those who were ignorant of the fullness. They did not repent immediately but held out for a while and repented later. They came to be with the fourth luminary, Eleleth, and they are creatures that glorify the invisible spirit.

THE FALL OF SOPHIA

Now, Sophia, who is the wisdom of afterthought and who constitutes an eternal realm, conceived of a thought from herself, with the conception of the invisible spirit and foreknowledge. She wanted to bring forth something like herself, without the consent of the spirit, who had not given approval, without her partner and without his consideration.[37] The male did not give approval. She did not find her partner, and she considered this without the spirit's consent and without the knowledge of her partner. Nonetheless, she gave birth. And because of the invincible power within her, her thought was not an idle thought. Something came out of her that was imperfect and different in appearance from her, for she had produced it without her partner. It did not resemble its mother and was misshapen.

When Sophia saw what her desire had produced, it changed into the figure of a snake with the face of a lion. Its eyes were like flashing bolts of lightning. She cast it away from her, outside that realm so that none of the immortals would see it. She had produced it ignorantly.

She surrounded it with a bright cloud and put a throne in the middle of the cloud so that no one would see it except the holy spirit, who is called the mother of the living. She named her offspring Yaldabaoth.

YALDABAOTH'S WORLD ORDER

Yaldabaoth is the first ruler, who took great power from his mother. Then he left her and moved away from the place where he was born. He took control

---

37. Sophia tries to imitate the original procreative act of the father. This account of Sophia bringing forth by herself seems to reflect ancient gynecological theories about women's bodies and reproduction. In Greek mythology the goddess Hera also imitates Zeus and brings forth a child by herself. According to one version of the myth, the child is the monster Typhon (*Homeric Hymn to Pythian Apollo* 300–62). According to another, it is the lame deity Hephaistos, whom Hera evicts from Olympus and sends down to the world below (Hesiod, *Theogony* 924–29). Hephaistos, the artisan among the gods, is represented in Egypt by his counterpart Khnum, a ram-headed creator who molds creatures on a potter's wheel. In the Secret Book of John all the evils and misfortunes of this world derive from Sophia's blunder.

and created for himself other realms with luminous fire, which still exists. He mated with the mindlessness[38] in him and produced authorities for himself:

The name of the first is Athoth, whom generations call the reaper.[39]

The second is Harmas, who is the jealous eye.

The third is Kalila-Oumbri.

The fourth is Yabel.

The fifth is Adonaios, who is called Sabaoth.

The sixth is Cain, whom generations of people call the sun.

The seventh is Abel.

The eighth is Abrisene.

The ninth is Yobel.

The tenth is Armoupieel.

The eleventh is Melcheir-Adonein.

The twelfth is Belias, who is over the depth of the underworld.[40]

Yaldabaoth stationed seven kings, one for each sphere of heaven, to reign over the seven heavens, and five to reign over the depth of the abyss.[41] He shared his fire with them, but he did not give away any of the power of the light that he had taken from his mother. For he is ignorant darkness.

When light mixed with darkness, it made the darkness shine. When darkness mixed with light, it dimmed the light and became neither light nor darkness, but rather gloom.

This gloomy ruler has three names: the first name is Yaldabaoth, the second is Sakla, the third is Samael.[42]

He is wicked in his mindlessness that is in him. He said, I am god and there is no other god but me,[43] since he did not know where his own strength had come from.

The rulers created seven powers for themselves, and the powers created six angels apiece, until there were 365 angels.[44] These are the names and the corresponding appearances:

---

38. Or "was amazed in the mindlessness." Yaldabaoth mating with his mindlessness (Coptic *aponoia*, from Greek) probably suggests that he masturbated.

39. The reading is tentative.

40. The twelve cosmic authorities probably correspond to the signs of the zodiac.

41. The seven kings probably correspond to the seven planetary spheres (for the Sun, the Moon, Mercury, Venus, Mars, Jupiter, and Saturn) described by ancient astronomers.

42. These names of the first ruler come from Aramaic, and probably mean, respectively, "child of (S)abaoth" (or "child of chaos"), "fool," and "blind god."

43. Isaiah 45:5–6, 21, 46:9.

44. The number of angels corresponds to the days in the solar year.

The first is Athoth and has the face of sheep.
The second is Eloaios and has the face of a donkey.
The third is Astaphaios and has the face of a hyena.
The fourth is Yao and has the face of a snake with seven heads.
The fifth is Sabaoth and has the face of a snake.
The sixth is Adonin and has the face of an ape.
The seventh is Sabbataios[45] and has a face of flaming fire.
This is the sevenfold nature of the week.[46]

Yaldabaoth has many faces, more than all of these, so that he could show whatever face he wanted when he was among the seraphim.[47] He shared his fire with them and lorded it over them because of the glorious power he had from his mother's light. That is why he called himself god and defied the place from which he came.

In his thought he united the seven powers with the authorities that were with him. When he spoke, it was done. He named each of the powers, beginning with the highest:
First is goodness, with the first power, Athoth.
Second is forethought, with the second power, Eloaios.
Third is divinity, with the third power, Astaphaios.
Fourth is lordship, with the fourth power, Yao.
Fifth is kingdom, with the fifth power, Sabaoth.
Sixth is jealousy, with the sixth power, Adonin.
Seventh is understanding, with the seventh power, Sabbataios.
Each has a sphere in its own realm.

They were named after the glory above for the destruction of the powers. While the names given them by their maker were powerful, the names given them after the glory above would bring about their destruction and loss of power. That is why they have two names.

Yaldabaoth organized everything after the pattern of the first realms that had come into being, so that he might create everything in an incorruptible form. Not that he had seen the incorruptible ones. Rather, the power that is in him, that he had taken from his mother, produced in him the pattern for the world order.

---

45. Others versions of the Secret Book of John cite the names Sabbadaios and Sabbede. Here and below the names vary in the manuscripts.
46. The seven powers correspond to the days of the week.
47. The seraphim are a class of angels, here angels of Yaldabaoth.

When he saw creation surrounding him, and the throng of angels around him who had come forth from him, he said to them, I am a jealous god and there is no other god beside me.[48]

But by announcing this, he suggested to the angels with him that there is another god. For if there were no other god, of whom would he be jealous?

SOPHIA REPENTS

Then the mother began to move around. She realized that she was lacking something when the brightness of her light diminished. She grew dim because her partner had not collaborated with her.

I[49] said, Master, what does it mean that she moved around?

The master laughed and said, Do not suppose that it is as Moses said, above the waters.[50] No, when she recognized the wickedness that had occurred and the robbery her son had committed, she repented. When she became forgetful in the darkness of ignorance, she began to be ashamed. She did not dare to return, but she was agitated. This agitation is the moving around.

The arrogant one took power from his mother. He was ignorant, for he thought no one existed except his mother alone. When he saw the throng of angels he had created, he exalted himself over them.

When the mother realized that the trappings[51] of darkness had come into being imperfectly, she understood that her partner had not collaborated with her. She repented with many tears. The whole realm of fullness heard her prayer of repentance and offered praise on her behalf to the invisible virgin spirit, and the spirit consented. When the invisible spirit consented, the holy spirit poured upon her some of the fullness of all. For her partner did not come to her on his own, but he came to her through the realm of fullness, so that he might restore what she lacked. She was taken up not to her own eternal realm, but to a position above her son. She was to remain in the ninth heaven until she restored what was lacking in herself.[52]

---

48. Isaiah 45:5–6, 21, 46:9.

49. John is speaking.

50. Genesis 1:2.

51. Or "aborted fetus," that is, Yaldabaoth.

52. Sophia dwells in the ninth sphere, above Yaldabaoth, who occupies the eighth sphere (sometimes called the ogdoad and identified as the sphere of the fixed stars). Yaldabaoth himself is thus positioned over the seven kings in their seven spheres (sometimes called the hebdomad; see above). See also the Hermetic Discourse on the Eighth and Ninth, and other gnostic texts.

THE HUMAN APPEARS

A voice called from the exalted heavenly realm,

> The human exists
> and the human child.

The first ruler, Yaldabaoth, heard the voice and thought it had come from his mother. He did not realize its source.

> The holy perfect mother-father,
> the complete forethought,
> the image of the invisible one,
> being the father of everything,
> through whom everything came into being,
> the first human—

this is the one who showed them, and appeared in human shape.

The entire realm of the first ruler quaked, and the foundations of the abyss shook. The bottom of the waters above the material world was lighted by this image that had appeared. When all the authorities and the first ruler stared at this appearance, they saw the whole bottom as it was illuminated. And through the light they saw the shape of the image in the water.[53]

THE CREATION OF ADAM

Yaldabaoth said to the authorities with him, Come, let us create a human being after the image of god and with a likeness to ourselves, so that this human image may give us light.[54]

They created through their respective powers, according to the features that were given to them. Each of the authorities contributed a psychical feature corresponding to the figure of the image they had seen. They created a being like the perfect first human and said, Let us call it Adam, that its name may give us power of light.[55]

---

53. Yaldabaoth and his authorities look at the waters above the earth, and from underneath they see the reflection of a human shape in the water. The heavenly human thus revealed is most likely Barbelo, who has a divine child, though we may also think of Geradamas and his heavenly son Seth.
54. Genesis 1:26. In the Secret Book of John a distinction is made between the image of god and the likeness of the creators.
55. Yaldabaoth and his authorities create a psychical man with a psychical body, that is, they create a soul-man, his body composed entirely of animating soul. His physical body of flesh and blood will be constructed later.

The powers began to create:

The first one, goodness, created a soul of bone.

The second, forethought, created a soul of sinew.

The third, divinity, created a soul of flesh.

The fourth, lordship, created a soul of marrow.

The fifth, kingdom, created a soul of blood.

The sixth, jealousy, created a soul of skin.

The seventh, understanding, created a soul of hair.

The throng of angels stood by and received these seven psychical substances from the authorities[56] in order to create a network of limbs and trunk, with all the parts properly arranged.

The first one, who is Raphao, began by creating the head,

Abron created the skull,[57]

Meniggesstroeth created the brain,

Asterechme the right eye,

Thaspomocha the left eye,

Yeronumos the right ear,

Bissoum the left ear,

Akioreim the nose,

Banen-Ephroum the lips,

Amen the teeth,

Ibikan the molars,

Basiliademe the tonsils,

Achcha the uvula,

Adaban the neck,

Chaaman the vertebrae,

Dearcho the throat,

Tebar the right shoulder,

N—— the left shoulder,

Mniarchon the right elbow,

——e the left elbow,

Abitrion the right underarm,

Euanthen the left underarm,

Krus the right hand,

---

56. Or "and these seven psychical substances were taken by the authorities."

57. Or "The first one began by creating the head, Eteraphaope-Abron created the skull."

Beluai the left hand,
Treneu the fingers of the right hand,
Balbel the fingers of the left hand,
Krima the fingernails,
Astrops the right breast,
Barroph the left breast,
Baoum the right shoulder joint,
Ararim the left shoulder joint,
Areche the belly,
Phthaue the navel,
Senaphim the abdomen,
Arachethopi the right ribs,
Zabedo the left ribs,
Barias the right hip,
Phnouth the left hip,
Abenlenarchei the marrow,
Chnoumeninorin the bones,
Gesole the stomach,
Agromauma the heart,
Bano the lungs,
Sostrapal the liver,
Anesimalar the spleen,
Thopithro the intestines,
Biblo the kidneys,
Roeror the sinews,
Taphreo the backbone,
Ipouspoboba the veins,
Bineborin the arteries,
Aatoimenpsephei the breaths in all the limbs,
Entholleia all the flesh,
Bedouk the right buttock,
Arabeei the left buttock,[58]
... the penis,
Eilo the testicles,
Sorma the genitals,

---

58. Uncertain.

Gormakaiochlabar the right thigh,
Nebrith the left thigh,
Pserem the muscles of the right leg,
Asaklas the muscle of the left,
Ormaoth the right leg,
Emenun the left leg,
Knux the right shin,
Tupelon the left shin,
Achiel the right ankle,
Phneme the left ankle,
Phiouthrom the right foot,
Boabel its toes,
Trachoun the left foot,
Phikna its toes,
Miamai the toenails,
Labernioum. . . .

Those who are appointed over all these are seven in number:
Athoth,
Armas,
Kalila,
Yabel,
Sabaoth,
Cain,
Abel.

Those who activate the limbs are, part by part:
the head, Diolimodraza,
the neck, Yammeax,
the right shoulder, Yakouib,
the left shoulder, Ouerton,
the right hand, Oudidi,
the left one, Arbao,
the fingers of the right hand, Lampno,
the fingers of the left hand, Leekaphar,
the right breast, Barbar,
the left breast, Imae,
the chest, Pisandraptes,
the right shoulder joint, Koade,

the left shoulder joint, Odeor,
the right ribs, Asphixix,
the left ribs, Sunogchouta,
the abdomen, Arouph,
the womb, Sabalo,
the right thigh, Charcharb,
the left thigh, Chthaon,
all the genitals, Bathinoth,
the right leg, Choux,
the left leg, Charcha,
the right shin, Aroer,
the left shin, Toechtha,
the right ankle, Aol,
the left ankle, Charaner,
the right foot, Bastan,
its toes, Archentechtha,
the left foot, Marephnounth,
its toes, Abrana.

Seven have been empowered over all these:
Michael,
Uriel,
Asmenedas,
Saphasatoel,
Aarmouriam,
Richram,
Amiorps.

Those who are over the senses are Archendekta,
the one who is over perception is Deitharbathas,
the one who is over imagination is Oummaa,
the one who is over arrangement is Aachiaram,
the one who is over all impulse to action is Riaramnacho.

The source of the demons that are in the entire body is divided into four:
heat,
cold,
wetness,
dryness.

The mother of them all is matter.

The one who is lord over heat is Phloxopha,
the one who is lord over cold is Oroorrothos,
the one who is lord over what is dry is Erimacho,
the one who is lord over wetness is Athuro.

The mother of all these, Onorthochras, stands in the midst of them, for she is unlimited and mingles with them all. She is matter, and by her they are nourished.

The four principal demons are:
Ephememphi, the demon of pleasure,
Yoko, the demon of desire,
Nenentophni, the demon of grief,
Blaomen, the demon of fear.
The mother of them all is Esthesis-Ouch-Epi-Ptoe.[59]

From the four demons have come passions:
From grief come jealousy, envy, pain, trouble, distress, hardheartedness, anxiety, sorrow, and others.
From pleasure comes an abundance of evil, vain conceit, and the like.
From desire come anger, wrath, bitterness, intense lust, greed, and the like.
From fear come terror, servility, anguish, and shame.
All these are like virtues and vices. The insight into their true nature is Anaro, who is head of the material soul, and it dwells with Esthesis-Z-Ouch-Epi-Ptoe.[60]

This is the number of angels. In all they number 365.[61] They all worked together until, limb by limb, the psychical and material body was completed. Now, there are others over the remaining passions, and I have not told you about them. If you want to know about them, the information is recorded in the Book of Zoroaster.[62]

---

59. "Sense-perception is not in an excited state" (from Greek), a philosophical saying (see Layton, *Gnostic Scriptures*, p. 43, who calls the saying "Stoic ethical jargon").
60. "The seven senses [?] are not in an excited state" (from Greek), another version of the philosophical saying cited in the preceding note.
61. The angels assembling the psychical body parts correspond to the days in the solar year, as above.
62. The precise identification of the Book of Zoroaster remains uncertain, but the title calls to mind a text from the Nag Hammadi library, Zostrianos, or else Porphyry's Life of Plotinos 16, where Porphyry refers to other texts written under the name of Zoroaster, including a book of Zoroaster.

ADAM RECEIVES SPIRIT AND LIFE

All the angels and demons worked together until they fashioned the psychical body. But for a long time their creation did not stir or move at all.

When the mother wanted to take back the power she had relinquished to the first ruler, she prayed to the most merciful mother-father of all. With a sacred command the mother-father sent five luminaries down to the place of the angels of the first ruler. They advised him so that they might recover the mother's power.

They said to Yaldabaoth, Breathe some of your spirit into the face of Adam, and then the body will arise.

He breathed his spirit into Adam.[63] The spirit is the power of his mother, but he did not realize this, because he lives in ignorance. The mother's power went out of Yaldabaoth and into the psychical body that had been made to be like the one who is from the beginning.

The body moved and became powerful.[64]And it was enlightened.

At once the rest of the powers became jealous. Although Adam had come into being through all of them, and they had given their power to this human, Adam was more intelligent than the creators and the first ruler. When they realized that Adam was enlightened, and could think more clearly than they, and was stripped of evil,[65] they took and threw Adam into the lowest part of the whole material realm.

The blessed, benevolent, merciful mother-father had compassion for the mother's power that had been removed from the first ruler. The rulers might be able to overpower the psychical, perceptible body once again. So with its benevolent spirit and great mercy the mother-father sent a helper to Adam, an enlightened afterthought who is from the mother-father and who was called life.[66] She helped the whole creature, laboring with it, restoring it to its fullness, teaching it about the descent of the seed, teaching it about the way of ascent, which is the way of descent.

Enlightened afterthought was hidden within Adam so that the rulers

---

63. Genesis 2:7.
64. Gospel of Thomas 50 also describes the primal movement of a person.
65. Perhaps parallel to Genesis 2:25.
66. Coptic *zoe* (from Greek). See Genesis 3:20: Eve is named Zoe in the Septuagint, the Greek translation of the Hebrew Bible.

might not recognize her, but that afterthought might be able to restore what the mother lacked.[67]

THE IMPRISONMENT OF HUMANITY

The human being Adam was revealed through the bright shadow within. And Adam's ability to think was greater than that of all the creators. When they looked up, they saw that Adam's ability to think was greater, and they devised a plan with the whole throng of rulers and angels. They took fire, earth, and water, and combined them with the four fiery winds.[68] They wrought them together and made a great commotion.[69]

The rulers brought Adam into the shadow of death so that they might produce a figure again, from earth, water, fire, and the spirit that comes from matter,[70] that is, from the ignorance of darkness, and desire, and their own false spirit. This is the cave for remodeling the body that these criminals put on the human, the fetter of forgetfulness.[71] Adam became a mortal being, the first to descend and the first to become estranged.

The enlightened afterthought within Adam, however, would rejuvenate Adam's mind.

The rulers took Adam and put Adam in paradise. They said, Eat, meaning, do so in a leisurely manner.[72] But in fact their pleasure is bitter and their beauty is perverse. Their pleasure is a trap, their trees are a sacrilege, their fruit is deadly poison, their promise is death.

They put their tree of life in the middle of paradise.[73]

I[74] shall teach you the secret of their life, the plan they devised together, the nature of their spirit: The root of their tree is bitter, its branches are death, its shadow is hatred, a trap is in its leaves, its blossom is bad ointment, its fruit is

---

67. Afterthought helps to restore the divine spirit or light that mother Sophia lost to Yaldabaoth.
68. Here fiery winds replace air as the fourth element.
69. The scene recalls a noisy workshop in which a statue or a fetter is being forged.
70. Here material spirit replaces air as the fourth element.
71. The description of a human being and a shadow in a cave may well derive from the allegory of the cave in Plato's *Republic*, Book 7. Further, the body as the prison or tomb of the soul is also a well-known platonic and Orphic teaching.
72. Genesis 2:16–17.
73. Literally, "the tree of their life" (in Nag Hammadi Codex II).
74. The savior, here Jesus, is speaking.

death, desire is its seed, it blossoms in darkness. The dwelling place of those who taste of it is the underworld, and darkness is their resting place.

But the rulers lingered in front of what they call the tree of the knowledge of good and evil, which is the enlightened afterthought,[75] so that Adam might not behold its fullness[76] and recognize his shameful nakedness.

But I[77] was the one who induced them to eat.

I[78] said to the savior, Master, was it not the snake that instructed Adam to eat?

The savior laughed and said, The snake instructed them to eat of the wickedness of sexual desire and destruction so that Adam might be of use to the snake. This is the one[79] who knew Adam was disobedient because of the enlightened afterthought within Adam, which made Adam stronger of mind than the first ruler. The first ruler wanted to recover the power that he himself had passed on to Adam. So he brought deep sleep upon Adam.

I said to the savior, What is this deep sleep?

The savior said, It is not as Moses wrote and you heard. He said in his first book, He put Adam to sleep.[80] Rather, this deep sleep was a loss of sense. Thus the first ruler said through the prophet, I shall make their minds sluggish, that they may neither understand nor discern.[81]

THE CREATION OF EVE

Enlightened afterthought hid herself within Adam. The first ruler wanted to take her from Adam's side, but enlightened afterthought cannot be apprehended. While darkness pursued her, it did not apprehend her. The first ruler removed part of Adam's power and created another figure in the form of a female, like the image of afterthought that had appeared to him. He put the part

---

75. Afterthought assumes the form of a tree, just as in Greek mythology Daphne changes into a laurel tree (see Ovid, *Metamorphoses* 1.452–562; also Reality of the Rulers and On the Origin of the World). Like Daphne, afterthought is not to be apprehended, according to a later passage in the Secret Book of John.

76. Or "his fullness."

77. The savior, here Jesus, is still speaking.

78. John is speaking.

79. Either the first ruler or the snake.

80. Genesis 2:21; Moses' first book is thought to be Genesis.

81. Isaiah 6:10.

he had taken from the power of the human being into the female creature. It did not happen, however, the way Moses said: Adam's rib.[82]

Adam saw the woman beside him. At once enlightened afterthought appeared and removed the veil that covered his mind. He sobered up from the drunkenness of darkness. He recognized his counterpart and said, This is now bone from my bones and flesh from my flesh.[83]

For this reason a man will leave his father and his mother and will join himself to his wife, and the two of them will become one flesh. For his partner will be sent to him, and he will leave his father and his mother.[84]

Our sister Sophia is the one who descended in an innocent manner to restore what she lacked. For this reason she was called life,[85] that is, the mother of the living, by the forethought of the sovereignty of heaven and by the afterthought that appeared to Adam.[86] Through her have the living tasted perfect knowledge.

As for me, I appeared in the form of an eagle[87] on the tree of knowledge, which is the afterthought of the pure enlightened forethought, that I might teach the human beings and awaken them from the depth of sleep. For the two of them were fallen and realized that they were naked.[88] Afterthought appeared to them as light and awakened their minds.

YALDABAOTH DEFILES EVE

When Yaldabaoth realized that the humans had withdrawn from him, he cursed his earth. He found the woman as she was preparing herself for her husband. He was master over her. And he did not know the mystery that had come into being through the sacred plan. The two of them were afraid to denounce Yaldabaoth. He displayed to his angels the ignorance within him. He threw the humans out of paradise and cloaked them in thick darkness.[89]

---

82. Genesis 2:21–22.
83. Genesis 2:23.
84. Genesis 2:24.
85. Zoe, Genesis 3:20.
86. A line is largely restored, from Nag Hammadi Codex IV.
87. The savior appears as a heavenly bird; the eagle is the bird of Zeus. Compare the Song of the Pearl, in which the royal letter flies as an eagle and becomes a voice of revelation.
88. Genesis 3:7, 10–11.
89. Genesis 3:22–24.

The first ruler saw the young woman standing next to Adam and noticed that the enlightened afterthought of life had appeared in her. Yet Yaldabaoth was full of ignorance. So when the forethought of all realized this, she dispatched emissaries, and they stole life[90] out of Eve.

The first ruler defiled Eve and produced in her two sons, a first and a second: Elohim and Yahweh.[91]

Elohim has the face of a bear,

Yahweh has the face of a cat.

One is just, the other is unjust.

He placed Yahweh over fire and wind,

he placed Elohim over water and earth.

He called them by the names Cain and Abel, with a view to deceive.[92]

To this day sexual intercourse has persisted because of the first ruler. He planted sexual desire in the woman who belongs to Adam. Through intercourse the first ruler produced duplicate bodies, and he blew some of his false spirit into them.

He placed these two rulers[93] over the elements so that they might rule over the cave.[94]

When Adam came to know the counterpart of his own foreknowledge, he produced a son like the human child. He called him Seth, after the manner of the heavenly race in the eternal realms.[95] Similarly, the mother sent down her spirit, which is like her and is a copy of what is in the realm of fullness, for she was going to prepare a dwelling place for the eternal realms that would come down.

The human beings were made to drink water of forgetfulness[96] by the first ruler, so that they might not know where they had come from. For a time the seed remained and helped so that when the spirit descends from the holy realms, it may raise up the seed and heal what it lacks, that the entire realm of fullness may be holy and lack nothing.

---

90. Zoe.

91. Coptic, *Eloim* and *Yawe,* two names of god in the Hebrew Bible. Elohim is a word that means "god" (literally "gods" since it is plural in form and ending), Yahweh is the name of god (based on the tetragrammaton, the ineffable four-letter name).

92. Genesis 4:1–2.

93. That is, Elohim and Yahweh.

94. Or "the tomb" (as above).

95. Genesis 4:25, 5:3.

96. The water of forgetfulness recalls the water of the River Lethe in the Greek conception of the underworld. If a thirsty soul drinks of the water of this river, it forgets about its previous lives and thus may be reincarnated in another body.

ON HUMAN DESTINY

I said to the savior, Master, will all the souls then be led safely into pure light?

He answered and said to me, These are great matters that have arisen in your mind, and it is difficult to explain them to anyone except those of the unshakable race.

Those upon whom the spirit of life will descend and whom the spirit will empower will be saved and become perfect and be worthy of greatness and be cleansed there of all evil and the anxieties of wickedness, since they are anxious for nothing except the incorruptible alone, and concerned with that from this moment on, without anger, jealousy, envy, desire, or greed for anything.

They are affected by nothing but being in the flesh alone, and they wear the flesh as they look forward to a time when they will be met by those who receive them. Such people are worthy of the incorruptible, eternal life and calling. They endure everything and bear everything so as to finish the contest and receive eternal life.

I said to him, Master, will the souls of people be rejected[97] who have not done these things, but upon whom the power and the spirit of life have descended?

He answered and said to me, If the spirit descends upon them, by all means they will be saved and transformed. Power will descend upon every person, for without it no one could stand.[98] After birth, if the spirit of life grows, and power comes and strengthens that soul, no one will be able to lead it astray with evil actions. But people upon whom the false spirit descends are misled by it and go astray.

I said, Master, where will their souls go when they leave their flesh?

He laughed and said to me, The soul in which there is more power than the contemptible spirit is strong. She escapes from evil, and through the intervention of the incorruptible one she is saved and is taken up to eternal rest.[99]

I said, Master, where will the souls go of people who have not known to whom they belong?

---

97. Or "be saved" (partially restored, from Nag Hammadi Codex IV).
98. This description of every person is like that of Adam moving and standing after receiving spirit from Yaldabaoth earlier in the Secret Book of John.
99. Feminine pronouns are used for the soul in the translation of this part of the Secret Book of John; the soul is commonly depicted as being female in Greek and gnostic literature. Compare the myth of Psyche (soul) and Eros (or Cupid, love) in Apuleius's *Metamorphoses*, Books 4–6, as well as the Exegesis on the Soul and On the Origin of the World.

He said to me, The contemptible spirit has grown stronger in such people while they were going astray. This spirit lays a heavy burden on the soul, leads her into evil, and hurls her down into forgetfulness. After the soul leaves the body, she is handed over to the authorities who have come into being through the ruler. They bind her with chains and throw her into prison.[100] They go around with her until she awakens from forgetfulness and acquires knowledge. This is how she attains perfection and is saved.

I said, Master, how can the soul become younger and return into its mother's womb,[101] or into the human[102]?

He was glad when I asked him about this, and he said to me, You are truly blessed, for you have understood. This soul will be made to follow another in whom the spirit of life dwells, and she is saved through that one. Then she will not be thrust into flesh again.

I said, Master, where will the souls go of people who had knowledge but turned away?

He said to me, They will be taken to the place where the angels of misery go, where there is no repentance. They will be kept there until the day when those who have blasphemed against the spirit will be tortured and punished eternally.

I said, Master, where did the contemptible spirit come from?

He said to me, The mother-father is great in mercy, the holy spirit, who in every way is compassionate, who sympathizes with you,[103] the afterthought of enlightened forethought. This one raised up the offspring of the perfect generation and raised their thought and the eternal light of the human. When the first ruler realized that these people were exalted above him and could think better than he, he wanted to grasp their thought. He did not know that they surpassed him in thought and that he would be unable to grasp them.

He devised a plan with his authorities, who are his powers. Together they fornicated with Sophia, and through them was produced bitter fate,[104] the final, fickle bondage. Fate is like this because the powers are fickle. To the present

---

100. The soul is thrown into another body and thus is reincarnated.

101. Literally "nature," Coptic *physis* (from Greek). Returning to the mother's womb is also a theme encountered in John 3.

102. The heavenly human.

103. "You" are apparently the human beings caught up in the machinations of the creator of this world, that is, the gnostics.

104. In the Greco-Roman world, fate (in Greek, *heimarmene,* as in the present text) was considered to be the overwhelming force of bondage that determines the destiny of all that is earthly and heavenly.

day fate is harder and stronger than what gods, angels, demons, and all the generations have encountered. For from fate have come all iniquity and injustice and blasphemy, the bondage of forgetfulness, and ignorance, and all burdensome orders, weighty sins, and great fears. Thus all of creation has been blinded so that none might know the god that is over them all. Because of the bondage of forgetfulness, their sins have been hidden. They have been bound with dimensions, times, and seasons, and fate is master of all.

The first ruler regretted everything that had happened through him. Once again he made a plan, to bring a flood upon the human creation.[105] The enlightened greatness of forethought, however, warned Noah. Noah announced this to all the offspring, the human children, but those who were strangers to him did not listen to him. If did not happen the way Moses said, They hid in an ark.[106] Rather, they hid in a particular place, not only Noah, but also many other people from the unshakable race. They entered that place and hid in a bright cloud. Noah knew about his supremacy. With him was the enlightened one who had enlightened them, since the first ruler had brought darkness upon the whole earth.

The first ruler formulated a plan with his powers. He sent his angels to the human daughters so they might take some of them and raise offspring for their pleasure.[107] At first they were unsuccessful. When they had proved unsuccessful, they met again and devised another plan. They created a contemptible spirit similar to the spirit that had descended, in order to adulterate souls through this spirit. The angels changed their appearance to look like the partners of these women and filled the women with the spirit of darkness that they had concocted, and with evil.

They brought gold, silver, gifts, copper, iron, metal, and all sorts of things. They brought great anxieties to the people who followed them, leading them astray with many deceptions. These people grew old without experiencing pleasure and died without finding truth or knowing the god of truth. In this way all creation was forever enslaved, from the beginning of the world until the present day.

The angels took women, and from the darkness they produced children similar to their spirit. They closed their minds and became stubborn through the stubbornness of the contemptible spirit until the present day.

---

105. The biblical story of the great flood is in Genesis 6:5–8:22.
106. Genesis 7:7.
107. See Genesis 6:1–4; 1 Enoch 6–11.

HYMN OF THE SAVIOR

Now I, the perfect forethought of all, transformed myself into my offspring. I existed first and went down every path.[108]

I am the abundance of light,

I am the remembrance of fullness.

I went into the realm of great darkness and continued until I entered the midst of the prison. The foundations of chaos shook, and I hid from them because of their evil, and they did not recognize me.

Again I returned, a second time, and went on. I had come from the inhabitants of light—I, the remembrance of forethought.

I entered the midst of darkness and the bowels of the underworld, turning to my task. The foundations of chaos shook as though to fall upon those who dwell in chaos and destroy them. Again I hurried back to the root of my light so they might not be destroyed before their time.

Again, a third time, I went forth—

I am the light dwelling in light,

I am the remembrance of forethought—

so that I might enter the midst of darkness and the bowels of the underworld. I brightened my face with light from the consummation of their realm and entered the midst of their prison, which is the prison of the body.

I said, Let whoever hears arise from deep sleep.[109]

A person wept and shed tears. Bitter tears the person wiped away, and said, Who is calling my name? From where has my hope come as I dwell in the bondage of prison?

I said,

I am the forethought of pure light,

I am the thought of the virgin spirit, who raises you to a place of honor.

Arise, remember that you have heard

and trace your root,

which is I, the compassionate.

---

108. The concluding hymn of the savior is found only in the longer version of the Secret Book of John (Nag Hammadi Codices II and IV). It reflects a hymn of heavenly forethought, the divine mother, as savior. In the present christianized version of the Secret Book of John the reader may understand the savior to be Jesus. Three descents of the savior are also described in the Sethian text Three Forms of First Thought, in this volume.

109. The call to awaken addresses a prototypal sleeper—any person who may awaken to knowledge and salvation.

Guard yourself against the angels of misery,
the demons of chaos and all who entrap you,
and beware of deep sleep
and the trap[110] in the bowels of the underworld.

I raised and sealed the person in luminous water with five seals, that death might not prevail over the person from that moment on.

CONCLUSION

Look, now I shall ascend to the perfect realm. I have finished everything for you in your hearing. I have told you everything for you to record and communicate secretly to your spiritual friends. This is the mystery of the unshakable race.

The savior communicated this to John for him to record and safeguard. He said to him, Cursed be anyone who will trade these things for a gift, for food, drink, clothes, or anything like this.

These things were communicated to John in a mystery, and at once the savior disappeared. Then John went to the other students and reported what the savior had told him.

Jesus the anointed

Amen[111]

---

110. Or "enclosure," even "garment."

111. The shorter versions of the Secret Book of John in BG 8502 and Nag Hammadi Codex III do not include this overtly Christian concluding statement.

5

The Reality of
the Rulers

The Reality of the Rulers, also called the Hypostasis (or Nature) of the Archons, was written in Greek, perhaps in Egypt, sometime before 350 CE, probably in the third century. It now exists as a Coptic text in the Nag Hammadi library. Like the Secret Book of John, it is a syncretic retelling of early Genesis myth, but this account is more abbreviated. The Secret Book of John, or a similar text with a more complete cosmogony, needs to be consulted to understand more fully the dramatic story that is told here.[1]

In the Reality of the Rulers the story begins with the words of the blind ruler Samael (the demiurge, later referred to as Sakla and Yaldabaoth), who arrogantly states that he is the one god. The story focuses on Eden (referred to only as "the garden"), then turns to the lands of death outside Eden where Adam, Eve, and their progeny live after their expulsion, and ends with Noah and the flood. Thereafter the text recounts Norea's narration and the angel Eleleth's description of a gnostic cosmogony and theogony. Eleleth, a luminary of Sethian fame, promises that death will be trampled, and the gnostics, the children of light, will be in the presence of the father of all, whom they will

---

1. For another text from the Nag Hammadi library that resembles the Reality of the Rulers in a number of significant respects, see On the Origin of the World, which is copied immediately after the Reality of the Rulers in Nag Hammadi Codex II.

praise in a single voice. These dramatic scenes present both biblical and gnostic figures: first of all the divine father and great invisible spirit, the divine aeon incorruptibility, and the divine child, with the heavenly luminaries, particularly Eleleth; next Adam and Eve in the garden, with a gnostic serpent and the rapacious rulers of this world; then Eve's children, including Norea, who battles the rulers; and finally Zoe (life), daughter of Sophia, who battles and punishes the demiurge himself.

As in the Secret Book of John, the arrogant ruler decides to create a material earth and fashion a human in the image of the high god, made from the earth. He does so, but the human is merely material and lies on the ground, incapable of rising. So the demiurge breathes life into him, but then he is only psychical, animated with a worldly soul from the world ruler. Finally the spirit comes to live in Adam, and he is able to rise. After he is placed in the garden and put to sleep, woman is taken from his side. She is spiritual (endowed with *pneuma*) and wakes him, saying, "Arise, Adam." When he sees her, he says, "You have given me life. You will be called 'mother of the living.'"

Then darkness enters. Dazzled by Eve's beauty, the rulers lust for her and try to rape her and sow seed in her. They pursue her, and like Daphne she turns into a tree, leaving a shadow of herself, which they rape foully. Here the text has assumed the Greco-Roman myth of Daphne and Apollo, with a new twist. Then the snake—which, in a remarkable revision of the Genesis account, is called the instructor, because it knows and teaches about knowledge—urges Eve to eat the fruit and obtain knowledge, whereupon begin the Genesis problems of shame, banishment, exile, and mortality.

The character who emerges as a new gnostic hero is Norea, Eve's virgin daughter. She successfully confronts both Noah and the rulers of darkness. She asks Noah to let her enter his ark, and when he refuses, she burns it. Norea (here also called Orea, perhaps "beautiful") thus assumes independence and great powers. When the rulers find her and desire her, she defies them and curses the arrogant god himself for his lechery, claiming her descent from the world above. She turns to the god of all to rescue her, and he sends down Eleleth, the great angel and luminary from the heavens. At her request he tells her about the world above, separated by a veil from the realms below. And so the narration moves to an accounting of the apocalyptic space of the gods.

This narration fuses Jewish biblical, hellenistic, Christian, and gnostic tales. The garden story resembles the rape of Eve by the rulers in the text On the Origin of the World. However, in the latter treatise the garden scene is more elaborately developed and central to the document. It also differs in essential details, for the rape is not an illusion but actually takes place in On the Origin of the World, by a gang of ruler angels, and the progeny is humankind. In the Reality of the Rulers, the rulers are real troublemakers who create but who will eventually perish in ignorance and darkness.

THE REALITY OF THE RULERS[2]

SAMAEL'S SIN

Because of the reality of the authorities,[3] inspired by the spirit of the father of truth, the great messenger[4] referring to the authorities of the darkness[5] told us that "our contest is not against flesh and blood, rather, the authorities of the universe and the spirits of wickedness."[6] I[7] have sent you this because you inquire about the reality of the authorities.

Their chief[8] is blind. Because of his power and his ignorance and his arrogance he said, with his power, "I am god; there is no other but me."[9]

When he said this, he sinned against all. This speech rose up to incorruptibility.[10] Then there was a voice that came forth from incorruptibility, saying, "You are wrong, Samael," that is, god of the blind.[11]

His thoughts became blind. And having expelled his power—that is, the blasphemy he had spoken—he pursued it down to chaos and the abyss, his mother, at the instigation of Pistis Sophia.[12] She[13] established each of his offspring in conformity with its power, after the pattern of the realms that are above, for by starting from the invisible world the visible world was invented.

---

2. Reality of the Rulers: Nag Hammadi Codex II,4, pp. 86,20 to 97,23; translated from the Coptic by Bentley Layton (Robinson, ed., *Nag Hammadi Library in English,* rev. ed., pp. 162–69); revised by Willis Barnstone and Marvin Meyer.
3. In the Reality of the Rulers the authorities are apparently the same as the rulers or archons.
4. The apostle Paul.
5. Colossians 1:13.
6. Ephesians 6:12.
7. The author of the text ("I"), who is otherwise unknown, promises to explain to the readers the reality (or nature, hypostasis) of the rulers of this world.
8. Samael, the demiurge.
9. Isaiah 45:5–6, 21, 46:9.
10. Incorruptibility is a divine female aeon related to Barbelo, divine forethought, in the Secret Book of John.
11. Or possibly "blind god."
12. Faith wisdom, a form of Sophia.
13. Pistis Sophia.

As incorruptibility looked down into the region of the waters, her image appeared in the waters, and the authorities of the darkness became enamored of her. But they could not lay hold of that image which had appeared to them in the waters, because of their weakness, since beings that merely have soul cannot lay hold of those that have spirit. For they[14] were from below, while it[15] was from above.[16]

THE CREATION OF ADAM AND EVE

This is the reason why incorruptibility looked down into the region, so that, by the father's will, she might bring all into union with the light.

The rulers laid plans and said, "Come, let us create a human that will be soil from the earth." They modeled their creature as one wholly of the earth.[17]

The rulers have bodies that are both female and male, and faces that are the faces of beasts. They took some soil from the earth and modeled their man, after their body and after the image of god that had appeared to them in the waters.[18]

They said, "Come, let us lay hold of it[19] by means of the form that we have modeled, so that it may see its male partner[20] and we may seize it with the form that we have modeled," not understanding the partner of god, because of their powerlessness. And he[21] breathed into his face, and the man came to have a soul[22] and remained on the ground many days. But they could not make him rise because of their powerlessness. Like storm winds they persisted in blowing,[23] that they might try to capture that image which had appeared to them in the waters. And they did not know the identity of its power.

Now, all these events came to pass by the will of the father of all. Afterward the spirit[24] saw the man of soul on the ground. The spirit came forth from the

---

14. The rulers or authorities.
15. The image of incorruptibility.
16. Here and throughout the text there are close parallels to Genesis. Only a few will be noted.
17. See Genesis 2:7.
18. The image of incorruptibility, above. This paragraph is partially restored.
19. The image.
20. Probably the male partner of incorruptibility, who is a female aeon.
21. Samael, the chief ruler.
22. This is the psychical human, the soul man, as in the Secret Book of John.
23. See Genesis 2:7.
24. The spirit is the female spiritual presence who is at work in the world and is reminiscent of afterthought in the Secret Book of John. She plays a key role throughout the Reality of the Rulers.

adamantine land.[25] It descended and came to dwell in him, and that man became a living soul.[26] And the spirit called his name Adam, since he was found moving upon the ground.

A voice came forth from incorruptibility for the assistance of Adam. The rulers gathered together all the animals of the earth and all the birds of heaven and brought them in to Adam to see what Adam would call them, that he might give a name to each of the birds and all the beasts.[27]

The rulers took Adam and put him in the garden, that he might cultivate it and keep watch over it. They issued a command to him, saying, "From every tree in the garden shall you eat, but from the tree of knowledge of good and evil don't eat, nor touch it. For the day you eat from it you will surely die."[28]

They said this to him, but they did not understand what they said.[29] Rather, by the father's will, they said this in such a way that he might in fact eat, and that Adam might not[30] regard them as would a man of an exclusively material nature.[31]

The rulers took counsel with one another and said, "Come, let us cause a deep sleep to fall on Adam."[32] And he slept. Now, the deep sleep that they caused to fall on him, and he slept, is ignorance. They opened his side, which was like a living woman.[33] And they built up his side with some flesh in place of her, and Adam came to be only with soul.

The woman of spirit[34] came to him and spoke with him, saying, "Rise, Adam." And when he saw her, he said, "It is you who have given me life. You will be called 'mother of the living.' For she is my mother. She is the physician, and the woman, and she has given birth."

---

25. The adamantine land is probably called adamantine because it is hard like steel in its heavenly character. Otherwise it may derive from the realm of heavenly Adamas or Geradamas (see the Secret Book of John).
26. Genesis 2:7, again.
27. Genesis 2:19.
28. Genesis 2:16–17.
29. Partially restored.
30. The word *not* has been mistakenly left out of the Coptic text.
31. That is, the father wanted Adam to have spiritual insight into the intentions of the rulers.
32. Genesis 2:21.
33. This sentence seems to suggest that one side of Adam, a female side, is removed; this is the spiritual side of Adam, the female spiritual presence.
34. She is the female spiritual presence—described like Eve in Genesis—while Adam is merely psychical again, endowed with soul but not with spirit.

ADAM AND EVE IN THE GARDEN

The authorities came up to their Adam. When they saw his female partner speaking with him, they became very excited and enamored of her. They said to one another, "Come, let us sow our seed in her," and they pursued her. And she laughed at them for their foolishness and blindness. In their clutches she became a tree and left before them her shadowy reflection resembling herself, and they defiled it foully. And they defiled the seal of her voice, so that by the form they had modeled, together with their own image, they made themselves liable to condemnation.[35]

Then the female spiritual presence came in the form of the snake, the instructor,[36] and it taught them,[37] saying, "What did he[38] say to you? Was it, 'From every tree in the garden shall you eat, but from the tree of recognizing evil and good do not eat'?"

The woman of flesh[39] said, "Not only did he say 'Don't eat,' but even 'Don't touch it. For the day you eat from it, you will surely die.'"

The snake, the instructor, said, "It is not the case that you will surely die, for out of jealousy he said this to you. Rather, your eyes will open and you will be like gods, recognizing evil and good." And the female instructing power was taken away from the snake, and she left it behind, merely a thing of the earth.[40]

And the woman of flesh took from the tree and ate, and she gave to her husband as well as herself, and those beings, who possessed only a soul,[41] ate. And their imperfection became apparent in their lack of knowledge. They recognized that they were naked of the spiritual, and they took fig leaves and bound them around themselves.

Then the chief ruler came, and he said, "Adam, where are you?"—for he did not understand what had happened.

---

35. This passage closely resembles the Greek myth of Daphne changing into a laurel tree. See also the Secret Book of John and On the Origin of the World for similar accounts. The meaning of the last sentence is obscure, but it seems to indicate that the rulers raped a shadow, perhaps an echo, perhaps the mouth of the woman of spirit after whom they lusted.
36. The female spiritual presence now appears in the serpent.
37. Adam and Eve.
38. Samael, the chief ruler.
39. Eve of flesh, without the female spiritual presence.
40. See Genesis 3:1–5.
41. They are merely psychical.

Adam said, "I heard your voice and was afraid because I was naked, and I hid."[42]

The ruler said, "Why did you hide, unless it is because you have eaten from the tree from which alone I commanded you not to eat? You have eaten!"

Adam said, "The woman you gave me gave me fruit and I ate." And the arrogant ruler cursed the woman.

The woman said, "The snake led me astray and I ate." They[43] turned to the snake and cursed its shadowy reflection, so it was powerless, and they did not comprehend that it was a form they themselves had modeled.[44] From that day, the snake came to be under the curse of the authorities. Until the perfect human[45] was to come, that curse fell on the snake.

They turned to their Adam and took him and expelled him from the garden along with his wife, for they[46] have no blessing, since they too are under the curse.

Moreover, they threw human beings into great distraction and into a life of toil, so that their human beings might be occupied by worldly affairs and might not have the opportunity of being devoted to the holy spirit.[47]

EVE BEARS CHILDREN

Now, afterward she[48] bore Cain, their son,[49] and Cain cultivated the land. Thereupon he[50] knew his wife. Again becoming pregnant, she bore Abel, and Abel was a herdsman of sheep. Cain brought in from the crops of his field, but Abel brought in an offering from among his lambs. God looked upon the votive offerings of Abel, but he did not accept the votive offerings of Cain. And fleshly Cain pursued Abel his brother.

God said to Cain, "Where is Abel your brother?"

---

42. Genesis 3:10.
43. The rulers, who curse the snake as their chief curses the woman.
44. The snake no longer has the spiritual presence and is only a shadow of its former self.
45. The perfect or all-powerful human, or man, is the human of perfect knowledge, like Seth and the offspring of Seth and even forethought as the first human in the Secret Book of John. See also the narration of Norea at the end of the Reality of the Rulers.
46. Apparently the rulers of this world.
47. See Genesis 3:14–19, with curses against the snake, the woman, and the man.
48. Eve.
49. Cain is the son of Eve and the rulers of this world; in the Secret Book of John, Cain and Abel both are sons of Eve and Yaldabaoth.
50. Adam.

He answered, saying, "Am I my brother's keeper?"

God said to Cain, "Listen! The voice of your brother's blood is crying up to me. You have sinned with your mouth. It will return to you: anyone who kills Cain will let loose seven vengeances, and you will exist groaning and trembling upon the earth."[51]

And Adam knew his partner Eve, and she became pregnant and bore Seth to Adam. And she said, "I have borne another man through god, in place of Abel."[52]

Again Eve became pregnant, and she bore Norea.[53] And she said, "He has produced for me a virgin as an assistance for many generations of human beings." She is the virgin whom the forces did not defile.

Then humankind began to multiply and improve.

THE FLOOD

The rulers took counsel with one another and said, "Come, let us cause a flood with our hands and obliterate all flesh, from man to beast."[54] But when the ruler of the forces[55] came to know of their decision, he said to Noah, "Make yourself an ark from wood that does not rot and hide in it, you and your children and the beasts and the birds of heaven from small to large—and set it upon Mount Sir."[56]

Then Orea[57] came to him, wanting to board the ark. When he would not let her, she blew upon the ark and caused it to be consumed by fire. Again he made the ark, for a second time.

---

51. On Cain and Abel see Genesis 4:1–16.

52. Seth is the hero for the Sethian gnostics. See Genesis 4:25–5:5.

53. Norea is a familiar figure, especially in Sethian literature; there is a tractate in Nag Hammadi Codex IX entitled the Thought of Norea. Sometimes she is related to Naamah (Genesis 4:22) in Jewish lore. Naamah plays around with the infamous sons of god (see Genesis 6:2), but Norea in the Reality of the Rulers is "the virgin whom the forces did not defile." Like wisdom (Sophia), Norea is saved and also saves. Books attributed to a figure like Norea may be referred to in On the Origin of the World.

54. Genesis 6–9.

55. This is Sabaoth, discussed later in the text, who is god of the forces. The name Sabaoth comes from the Hebrew word for "hosts" or "forces," particularly in the expression "Adonai Sabaoth," lord of hosts. Sabaoth plays a similar role in On the Origin of the World, where he is portrayed as rebelling against the rulers of this world and creating Jesus and the virgin of the holy spirit.

56. Mount Sir is a legendary site of wisdom and knowledge.

57. Here Orea, perhaps "beautiful"; usually Norea.

NOREA BATTLES THE RULERS

The rulers went to meet her, intending to lead her astray. Their supreme chief said to her, "Your mother Eve came to us."

But Norea turned to them and said to them, "It is you who are the rulers of the darkness; you are accursed. You did not know my mother. Instead it was your own female that you knew. For I am not your descendant. Rather, it is from the world above that I am come."

The arrogant ruler turned with all his might, and his countenance was like a blazing fire. He said to her presumptuously, "You must service us, as did also your mother Eve. . . ."[58]

But Norea turned with power and, in a loud voice, she cried out up to the holy one, the god of all, "Rescue me from the rulers of unrighteousness and save me from their clutches—at once!"

The great angel came down from the heavens and said to her, "Why are you crying up to god? Why do you act so boldly toward the holy spirit?"

Norea said, "Who are you?"

The rulers of unrighteousness had withdrawn from her. He said, "I am Eleleth, sagacity, the great angel who stands in the presence of the holy spirit. I have been sent to speak with you and save you from the grasp of the lawless. And I shall teach you about your root."[59]

THE REVELATION OF ELELETH

Now, as for that angel, I[60] cannot speak of his power. His appearance is like fine gold and his raiment is like snow. No, truly, my mouth cannot bear to speak of his power and the appearance of his face.

Eleleth, the great angel, spoke to me. "It is I," he said, "who am understanding. I am one of the four luminaries who stand in the presence of the great invisible spirit.[61] Do you think these rulers have any power over you? None of them can prevail against the root of truth, for on its account he[62] has

---

58. Part of this paragraph cannot be restored with confidence.
59. See also the reference to the root and tracing the root in the conclusion to the Secret Book of John.
60. Norea.
61. Eleleth is one of the four Sethian luminaries, with Harmozel, Oroiael, and Daveithai.
62. Perhaps the perfect human; see below.

appeared in the final ages, and these authorities will be restrained. And these authorities cannot defile you and that race,[63] for your abode is in incorruptibility, where the virgin spirit lives, who is superior to the authorities of chaos and to their universe."

But I[64] said, "Sir, teach me about these authorities. How did they come into being? By what genesis, and out of what material, and who created them and their power?"

The great angel Eleleth, understanding, spoke to me: "Incorruptibility inhabits limitless realms. Sophia, who is called Pistis,[65] wanted to create something, alone, without her partner, and what she created was celestial.

"A veil exists between the world above and the realms below, and shadow came into being beneath the veil.[66] That shadow became matter, and that shadow was projected apart. And what she had created came to be in matter, like an aborted fetus. It assumed a shape molded out of shadow, and became an arrogant beast resembling a lion. It was androgynous, as I have already said, because it derived from matter.[67]

"Opening his eyes he saw a vast quantity of endless matter, and he turned arrogant, saying, 'I am god, and there is no one but me.'[68]

"When he said this, he sinned against all. And a voice came from above the realm of absolute power, saying, 'You are wrong, Samael,' that is, god of the blind.[69]

"And he said, 'If any other thing exists before me, let it become visible to me!' Immediately Sophia pointed her finger and introduced light into matter, and she pursued it down to the region of chaos. And she returned up to her light. Once again darkness returned to matter.[70]

"This ruler, by being androgynous, made himself a vast realm, an endless precinct. And he contemplated creating offspring for himself, and created seven offspring, androgynous like their parent.

---

63. The unshakable race, the offspring of Seth.
64. Again, Norea.
65. Pistis Sophia, faith wisdom, as above.
66. The veil or curtain between heaven and earth keeps the light of heaven from shining upon the earth and produces a shadow. Similar ideas are found in Jewish thought, for example, in Philo of Alexandria. In a more general sense, see Psalm 104:2; Isaiah 40:22.
67. The arrogant demiurge is also lionlike in the Secret Book of John and elsewhere.
68. Isaiah 45:5–6, 21, 46:9.
69. Or possibly "blind god."
70. Partially restored; the meaning is uncertain. The basic sense is that Sophia brings light into the dark world of matter.

"And he said to his offspring, 'I am the god of all.'[71]

"Zoe[72] the daughter of Pistis Sophia shouted, saying to him, 'You are wrong, Sakla' (for which the alternate name is Yaldabaoth).[73] She breathed into his face, and her breath became a fiery angel for her; and that angel bound Yaldabaoth and cast him down into Tartaros, at the bottom of the abyss.[74]

"Now, when his offspring Sabaoth saw the strength of that angel, he repented and condemned his father and his mother matter.[75]

"He loathed her, but he sang songs of praise up to Sophia and her daughter Zoe. And Sophia and Zoe found him and put him in charge of the seventh heaven, below the veil between above and below. And he is called 'god of the forces, Sabaoth,'[76] since he is up above the forces of chaos, for Sophia placed him there.

"Now, when these events had come to pass, he made himself a huge four-faced chariot of cherubim and harps and lyres and an infinity of angels to act as ministers.[77]

"Sophia took her daughter Zoe and had her sit at his right to teach him about the things that exist in the eighth heaven,[78] and the angel of wrath she placed at his left. Since that day, his right has been called life, and the left has signified the unrighteousness of the realm of absolute power above. It was before your time that they came into being.

"Now, when Yaldabaoth saw him in this great splendor and at this height, he envied him, and the envy became something androgynous, and this was the origin of envy. And envy engendered death, and death engendered his offspring and gave each of them charge of its heaven. All the heavens of chaos became full of their multitudes.

"But it was by the will of the father of all that they all came into being, after the pattern of all the things above, so that the sum of chaos might be attained.[79]

---

71. On this arrogant claim see above.
72. Life.
73. On the names of the demiurge see the Secret Book of John, with the notes.
74. Tartaros is the underworld, the realm of the dead, hell.
75. Sabaoth is the son of Yaldabaoth his father and matter his mother.
76. On the meaning of the name Sabaoth, see note 55, above.
77. This chariot recalls the throne or chariot of god, the merkavah, in Ezekiel and Revelation.
78. The seventh and eighth heavens also appear in the Secret Book of John and the Hermetic Discourse on the Eighth and Ninth.
79. This may indicate that the sum total of all things is attained, from the top in heaven to the bottom in the realm of chaos, as here. Layton, Gnostic Scriptures, p. 75, suggests that this idea may come from a neoplatonic doctrine.

"There, I have taught you about the pattern of the rulers and the matter in which it was made visible, along with their parent and their universe."

EPILOGUE

But I[80]said, "Sir, am I also from their matter?"

"You,[81] together with your offspring, are from the primeval father. Their souls come from above, out of the incorruptible light.[82] Therefore, the authorities cannot approach them, since the spirit of truth resides in them, and all who have known this way exist deathless in the midst of dying people. Still, the offspring will not become known now. Instead, after three generations it will come to be known and free them from the bondage of the authorities' error."

Then I said, "Sir, how much longer?" He said to me, "Until the moment when the true human,[83] within a modeled form, reveals the existence of the spirit of truth that the father has sent.

"Then he will teach them about everything. And he will anoint them with the unction of life eternal, given him from the generation without a king.

"Then they will be free of blind thought. And they will trample on death, which comes from the authorities. And they will ascend into the limitless light where this offspring belongs.

"Then the authorities will relinquish their ages. And their angels will weep over their destruction, and their demons will lament their death.

"Then all the children of the light will truly know the truth and their root and the father of all and the holy spirit. They will all say with a single voice, 'The father's truth is just, and the child[84] presides over all.' And from everyone, till the ages of ages, 'Holy, holy, holy! Amen!'"[85]

---

80. Norea.
81. Eleleth is again speaking to Norea.
82. The wording here is similar to Gospel of Thomas 50 and other texts.
83. The true man, the perfect human, as above.
84. Or "son."
85. The trisagion, "Holy, holy, holy," is sung by those around the divine throne in Isaiah and Revelation.

6

The Revelation
of Adam

The Revelation (or Apocalypse) of Adam is a mythic narration poem attributed to Adam, who communicated it to his son Seth. Composed as early as the first or second century CE, this Jewish gnostic apocalypse (with apparently no Christian element in or amended to it) is recognized as a transition stage from Jewish apocalypse to gnostic apocalypse.[1]

In this apocalypse Adam reveals to his son Seth a history of human creation, before and after the fall, and a way to redemption through secret knowledge. The revelation occurs as a dream vision passed on by Adam, in his seven hundredth year, and on his deathbed, to Seth and his seed. It has the form of a historical testament. It moves from a period when Adam and his consort, Eve, were like eternal angels, existing above the creator god. Spiritual Eve imparted her knowledge of the eternal god to Adam, but that knowledge and the paradisal condition were lost when the demiurge took knowledge from them and instructed them only about "dead things." Then to wake Adam and Eve from dark ignorance and slavery, three persons (heavenly messengers) come to Adam and Eve and say, "Rise, Adam, from the sleep of death." They reveal to Adam hints of the great race that will come from the heavenly seed of Seth.

---

1. Some have seen the Revelation's third story of the origin of the illuminator as a story about Jesus, but Douglas M. Parrott considers the evidence and states, "It is difficult to see any compelling reason to identify this figure with Christ" (in Robinson, ed., *Nag Hammadi Library in English*, rev. ed., p. 278).

But there follows a series of contentions between Adam's descendent Noah and the creator, leading to the creator's attempt to destroy the peopled earth with water and fire. Noah makes a pact with the creator of this world, and he and his family are saved personally on earth. More significant, the angels of the great light save the people of knowledge, the Sethians, who live for six hundred years. And from Noah's seed, Shem, Ham, and Japheth, come the people of the world, the descendants of Shem and thirteen kingdoms from Ham and Japheth. The thirteenth kingdom consists of four hundred thousand people who will live with those who have the great eternal knowledge.

The Revelation of Adam seems to distinguish several groups of people on the earth, according to their degree of enlightenment:

The seed of Seth, the gnostics.

The descendants of Shem, perhaps the people of Israel,[2] who are mentioned only obscurely in the text.

The descendants of Ham and Japheth. These include not only the twelve
kingdoms that constitute the people of this world but also the four
hundred thousand, the thirteenth kingdom that sojourns with the
seed of Seth. These must form a special group, drawn from the
people of the world and associated with the gnostics of the seed
of Seth.[3]

Bentley Layton, acknowledging the difficulties faced in distinguishing the different groups of people in the Revelation of Adam, suggests that that text may intend to specify a division of human beings into three essential groups: the seed of Seth, the descendants of the sons of Noah, and the four hundred thousand. Such a threefold division, Layton concludes, may be reminiscent of the Valentinian tendency to divide people into three groups.[4]

Sakla the creator, in a way that may recall the destruction of Sodom and Gomorrah, brings apocalyptic catastrophes of fire, sulfur, and asphalt darkening the powers of the luminaries of the world, the sun and the moon. But now clouds of light called Abrasax, Sablo, and Gamaliel come down and transport the chosen above the realms and rulers, and they are saved and become like

---

2. Layton, *Gnostic Scriptures*, p. 52.
3. Here 400,000 is a symbolic number used to designate this group of people. In another apocalyptic text a similar use of a symbolic number for a group of people is to be noted in the 144,000 people to be saved according to the New Testament Apocalypse.
4. Layton, *Gnostic Scriptures*, p. 52.

angels. At this point the illuminator of knowledge passes by a third time, after flood and holocaust, performing signs to bring the seed of Noah redemption for their souls from the day of their death. "Those who reflect upon the knowledge of the eternal god in their hearts will not perish."

There now comes, almost as an intrusion, a long poem. The thirteen kingdoms utter marvelous tales of the origin and nature of the illuminator, the savior, who we understand is a manifestation linked to heavenly Seth. Each description is a minor apocalypse, each more fantastic. Each of the statements by these thirteen kingdoms ends with the statement "and in this way he came to the water." The water endings may be a baptismal rite, yet even the coming to the water is not an assurance of purification, for with desire and darkness those waters too can be polluted by the wicked. And it is the generation or race without a king over it—the Sethian gnostics—that has the true view of the origin of the illuminator. More Sethian insights into the true origin of the illumination may be gained from the fuller account in The Secret Book of John, especially the concluding hymn of the savior.

Near the end of the Revelation of Adam a paragraph celebrates the fate of the words of this revelation. Though unwritten, these words will be brought by angels to "a high mountain, upon a rock of truth," and they will be known as words of truth and incorruptibility. In this way the destiny of the words of Sethian revelation brings to mind traditions of gnostic revelatory steles and monuments on mountains or elsewhere, as in the Three Steles of Seth, the Gospel of the Egyptians, and the Discourse on the Eighth and Ninth.

THE REVELATION OF ADAM[5]

THE FALL OF ADAM AND EVE

The revelation[6] that Adam taught his son Seth in the seven hundredth year,[7] saying, Listen to my words, my son Seth. When god[8] created me out of the

---

5. The Revelation of Adam: Nag Hammadi Codex V, pp. 64,1 to 85,32;. translated from the Coptic by George W. MacRae (Robinson, ed., *Nag Hammadi Library in English*, rev. ed., 279-86); revised by Willis Barnstone.
6. Apocalypse.
7. The seven hundredth year is the year of Adam's death according to the version of Genesis in the Septuagint.
8. The creator of this world, called Sakla elsewhere in the text.

earth along with your mother Eve, I went about with her in a glory that she saw in the eternal realm from which we came. She taught me knowledge of the eternal god. And we resembled the great eternal angels, for we were higher than the god who created us and the powers with him, whom we did not know.

God, the ruler of the realms[9] and the powers, divided us in wrath, and then we became two beings.[10] And the glory in our hearts left us, me and your mother Eve, along with the first knowledge that breathed in us. And glory fled from us and entered another great realm. Your mother Eve and I didn't come from this realm. But knowledge entered into the seed of great eternal beings. For this reason I myself have called you by the name of that person who is the seed of the great generation[11] or its predecessor.[12] After those days the eternal knowledge of the god of truth withdrew from me and your mother Eve. Then we learned about the inanimate as we did about human beings. We recognized the god who created us. We were not strangers to his powers. And we served him in fear and slavery. After these events our hearts darkened, and I slept in my heart's darkened thought.

ADAM AND EVE ARE AWAKENED

And I saw three persons before me whose likeness I was unable to recognize. They were not from the powers of the god who created us.[13] They surpassed glory, saying to me, "Rise, Adam, from the sleep of death, and hear about the eternal being and the seed of that person to whom life has come, who came from you and from Eve, your wife."

When I heard these words from the great persons standing before me, Eve and I sighed in our hearts. And the lord, the god who created us, stood before us. He said, "Adam, why were you both sighing in your hearts? Don't you know that I am the god who created you? I breathed into you a spirit of life as a living soul."[14] Darkness came over our eyes.

---

9. The aeons, in this case the aeons in this world below.

10. Again, aeons. This describes the splitting of the androgynous primal human into male and female beings.

11. Or "race," throughout the text.

12. Seth son of Adam is named after the eternal, heavenly Seth in the realm of the divine fullness.

13. The three persons appearing to Adam are like the threefold figure appearing to John at the opening of the Secret Book of John.

14. Genesis 2:7.

Then the god who created us created a son from himself and Eve, your mother....[15] I knew a sweet desire for your mother. And the vigor of our eternal knowledge was destroyed in us, and weakness pursued us. The days of our life were few. I knew that I had come under the authority of death.

Now, my son Seth, I will reveal what those whom I saw revealed to me. After I went through the period of this generation and the years of the generation were over....

NOAH AND THE FLOOD

For rain showers of god almighty[16] will pour down so that he can destroy all flesh from the earth, using what is around them, along with people from the seed of those who received the life of knowledge. That life of knowledge came from your mother Eve and me.[17] They were strangers to him. Afterward great angels come on high clouds, who take those people where the spirit of life lives.... The whole multitude of flesh will be left behind in the waters.

God will rest from his wrath. And he casts his power on the waters, and gives power to his[18] sons and their wives by means of the ark along with the animals, whichever he pleased, and the birds of heaven, which he called and released upon the earth. And god says to Noah, whom generations call Deucalion,[19] "Look, I have protected you in the ark along with your wife and your sons and their wives and their animals and the birds of heaven, which you called and released upon the earth.... So I give the earth to you, to you and your sons. In kingly fashion you will rule over it, you and your sons. And you will have no seed from the people who do not stand in my presence in another glory."

Some[20] become like the cloud of great light, and those people come who are sent out from the knowledge of the great eternal realms and the angels.[21] They stand before Noah and the realms.[22]

---

15. Cain, as in the Reality of the Rulers; in the Secret Book of John, Cain and Abel both are sons of Eve and the demiurge.

16. Again, the creator of this world.

17. The descendants of Seth; see Genesis 6–9.

18. Most likely Noah's.

19. Deucalion is the Greek hero of the flood, who survived the deluge brought by Zeus.

20. Probably the descendants of Seth.

21. Again, probably the descendants of Seth. The translation may also mean that some will come "who have been cast forth" from knowledge; that is, they may be outcasts from divine knowledge, and thus descendants of Cain.

22. Probably the lower aeons.

And god says to Noah, "Why have you strayed from what I told you? You have created another generation so you can scorn my power." And Noah says, "I testify before your might that the generation of these people didn't come from me or my sons. . . ."[23]

And . . . those people[24] are brought into their proper land and a holy dwelling will be built for them. And they are called by that name[25] and live there six hundred years in knowledge of incorruptibility.[26] Angels of the great light live with them. No foul deed resides in their hearts, but only the knowledge of god.

Then Noah divides the whole earth among his sons, Ham and Japheth and Shem. He says to them, "My sons, hear me. Look, I have divided the earth among you. But serve him in fear and slavery all the days of your life. You children must not go away from the face of god almighty. . . ."

. . . the son of Noah[27] says, "You and your power will be pleased with my seed. Seal it with your strong hand of fear and command, and then the whole seed that came from me will not turn from you and god almighty, but they will serve in humility and fear of what they know."

THE FOUR HUNDRED THOUSAND

Then others from the seed of Ham and Japheth come, four hundred thousand, and enter another land and stay with those people who came from the great eternal knowledge.[28] The shadow of their power protects those with them from everything evil and every filthy desire.

Then the seed of Ham and Japheth forms twelve kingdoms,[29] and their other seed enters into the kingdom of other people.[30]

. . . they take counsel . . . aeons . . . that are dead . . . the great aeons of incorruptibility.[31] And they go to their god Sakla.[32] They go in to the powers, accusing the great ones who are in their glory.

---

23. They seem to have come from Seth.
24. The descendants of Seth.
25. The name of Seth.
26. Incorruptibility plays a significant role within the divine realm in Sethian texts, as in the Secret Book of John.
27. Shem.
28. From the descendants of Ham and Japheth four hundred thousand will sojourn with the descendants of Seth.
29. Or "dominions."
30. These are the thirteen kingdoms.
31. These lines cannot be reconstructed with confidence.
32. Sakla, which means "fool" in Aramaic, is a name of given to the creator of this world.

They say to Sakla, "What is the power of these people who stood in your presence, who were taken from the seed of Ham and Japheth, who number four hundred thousand?[33] They were received into another realm from which they came, and they overturned all the glory of your power and the dominion of your hand. The seed of Noah through his sons has done your will, and so have all the powers in the realms over which your might rules. Both those people and those who reside in their glory have not done your will. But they have turned aside your whole throng."

FIRE AND SULFUR AND ASPHALT

Then the god of the realms gives them some of those who serve him. . . . They come on that land where the great ones are who have not been defiled, nor will they be defiled by any desire. For their souls did not come from a defiled hand, but from an eternal angel's great command.

Then fire and sulfur and asphalt are cast upon those people, and fire and blinding mist come over those realms, and the eyes of the powers of the luminaries[34] are darkened, and the inhabitants of the realms cannot see in those days.[35]

And great clouds of light descend, and other clouds of light come down on them from the great eternal realms. Abrasax and Sablo and Gamaliel[36] descend and bring those people out of the fire and the wrath, and take them above the eternal realms and the rulers of the powers, and take them away . . . there with the holy angels and the eternal beings. The people will be like those angels, for they are not strangers to them. But they work with the imperishable seed.

---

33. The 400,000 constitute a thirteenth kingdom.

34. The sun and moon are the two eyes illuminating the world.

35. This description most likely recalls the fire cast upon Sodom and Gomorrah according to the book of Genesis, or it may recall something like the eruption of Vesuvius and the destruction of Pompeii. In any case, the language is apocalyptic: the fabric of the cosmos is being destroyed by the fire and the wrath.

36. These are powers of the eternal realms; see also the Baptismal Ceremony of the Gospel of the Egyptians. The Three Forms of First Thought preserves the names Kamaliel and Samblo as servants of the luminaries. The name Abrasax is a common name of power in a variety of textual traditions. Reading the Greek letters as numbers (the art of gematria), the name Abrasax totals 365. Abrasax frequently designates the Jewish god.

THE ILLUMINATOR OF KNOWLEDGE

Once again, for the third time,[37] the illuminator of knowledge passes by in great glory to leave some of the seed of Noah and the sons of Ham and Japheth—to leave fruit-bearing trees for himself.[38] And he redeems their souls from the day of death. The whole creation that came from the dead earth will be under the authority of death. But those who reflect on the knowledge of the eternal god in their hearts will not perish. They have not received spirit from this kingdom[39] but from something eternal, angelic. . . . The illuminator will come. . . Seth. And he will perform signs and wonders to scorn the powers and their ruler.

Then the god of the powers[40] is disturbed and says, "What is the power of this person who is higher than we are?"[41] Then he brings a great wrath against that person. And glory withdraws and lives in holy houses it has chosen for itself. The powers do not see it with their eyes, nor do they see the illuminator. They punish the flesh of the one over whom the holy spirit has come.[42]

THE ORIGIN OF THE ILLUMINATOR

Then the angels and all the generations of the powers will use the name in error, asking, "Where did this come from?" or "Where did the words of deception, which all the powers have failed to realize, come from?"[43]

Now, the first kingdom says of the illuminator that he came from . . . a spirit . . . to heaven. He was nourished in the heavens. He received the glory of that one and the power. He came to the bosom of his mother, and in this way he came to the water.

And the second kingdom says of him that he came from a great prophet. And a bird came, took the child who was born, and brought him onto a high

---

37. The three descents of the illuminator are featured in the concluding hymn of the savior in the Secret Book of John. Here the illuminator comes a third time, after the flood and the fire.
38. Fruit-bearing trees may be a metaphor for fruitful, productive people. The topic of fruitful people comes up again at the end of the Revelation of Adam.
39. Or "from this kingdom alone."
40. Again, the creator of this world, Sakla.
41. That is, the illuminator.
42. The illuminator will be persecuted. Here some see the crucifixion of Jesus as a manifestation of Seth.
43. The text now encapsulates legends about the origin of the illuminator from each of the thirteen kingdoms. Each dominion of the world has its own story about the origin of the savior.

mountain. And he was nourished by the bird of heaven. An angel came forth there. He said to him, "Rise! God has given you glory." He received glory and strength, and in this way he came to the water.

The third kingdom says of him that he came from a virgin womb.[44] He was cast out of his city, he and his mother; he was brought to a desert place. He was nourished there. He came and received glory and power, and in this way he came to the water.

The fourth kingdom says of him that he came from a virgin. . . . Solomon sought her, he and Phersalo and Sauel and his armies, which had been sent out. Solomon himself sent his army of demons to seek out the virgin. [45] And they did not find the one whom they sought, but the virgin who was given to them. It was she whom they fetched. Solomon took her. The virgin became pregnant and gave birth to the child there. She nourished him on a border of the desert. When he was nourished, he received glory and power from the seed from which he was conceived, and in this way he came to the water.

And the fifth kingdom says of him that he came from a drop from heaven. He was thrown into the sea. The abyss received him, gave birth to him, and brought him to heaven. He received glory and power, and in this way he came to the water.

And the sixth kingdom says that one . . . came down to the realm that is below in order to gather flowers. She became pregnant from the desire of the flowers. She gave birth to him in that place. The angels of the flower garden nourished him. He received glory and power there, and in this way he came to the water.

And the seventh kingdom says of him that he is a drop and came from heaven to earth. Dragons brought him down to caves, and he became a child. A spirit came over him and raised him to the place from where the drop had come. He received glory and power there, and in this way he came to the water.

And the eighth kingdom says of him that a cloud came over the earth and enveloped a rock. He came from it.[46] The angels above the cloud nourished him. He received glory and power there, and in this way he came to the water.

And the ninth kingdom says of him that from the nine muses one separated. She came to a high mountain and spent some time seated there, so that she desired her own body in order to become androgynous. She fulfilled her desire and became pregnant from her desire. He was born. The angels who

---

44. Jesus?
45. King Solomon commonly was thought to have harnessed the power of the demons.
46. In the ancient world the deity Mithras was thought to have been born from rock.

were over the desire nourished him. And he received glory there and power, and in this way he came to the water.

The tenth kingdom says of him that his god loved a cloud of desire. He fathered him in his hand and cast upon the cloud above him some of the drop, and he was born.[47] He received glory and power there, and in this way he came to the water.

And the eleventh kingdom says of him that the father desired his own daughter. She was pregnant from her father. She cast her child[48] . . . tomb out in the desert. The angel nourished him there, and in this way he came to the water.

The twelfth kingdom says of him that he came from two luminaries.[49] He was nourished there. He received glory and power, and in this way he came to the water.

And the thirteenth kingdom[50] says of him that every birth of their ruler is a word. And this word received a mandate there.[51] He received glory and power, and in this way he came to the water, that the desire of those powers might be satisfied.

But the generation without a king[52] says that god[53] chose him from all the eternal realms. He caused knowledge of the one of truth, who is undefiled, to reside in him. He said, "Out of a foreign air, from a huge eternal realm, the great illuminator appeared. And he made the generation of those people whom he had chosen for himself shine, so that they should shine on the whole eternal realm."

PEOPLE ACKNOWLEDGE THEIR ERROR

The seed,[54] those who will receive his name upon the water and that of them all, will fight against the power. And a cloud of darkness will come upon them.

---

47. That is, god masturbated.
48. Restored.
49. The sun and the moon.
50. After the twelve kingdoms, this is the kingdom of the 400,000 noted above.
51. This phrase may relate to the familiar unfolding of the word or logos as part of the creative act, with "mandate" referring to divine command or authority. This account is reminiscent of the logos hymn at the beginning of the Gospel of John.
52. These are the seed of Seth, the Sethian gnostics, who have the true view of the origin of the illuminator. This view, given briefly here, may be compared with fuller accounts of the origin of the illuminator elsewhere, for example, in the Secret Book of John.
53. This is the exalted, true god.
54. That is, the seed of Seth.

Then the peoples[55] will cry out with a great voice, saying, "Blessings on the soul of those people because they have known god with a knowledge of the truth. They shall live forever, because they have not been corrupted by their desire, along with the angels, nor have they performed the works of the powers, but they have stood in his presence in a knowledge of god like light that has come forth from fire and blood.

"But we have done every deed of the powers foolishly. We have boasted in the transgression of all our works. We have cried against the god of truth because all his work . . . is eternal. These are against[56] our spirits. For now we know that our souls will die in death."

Then a voice came to them. Micheus and Michar and Mnesinous, who are over the holy baptism and the living water,[57] were saying, "Why were you crying out against the living god with lawless voices and tongues without law over them, and souls full of blood and foul deeds? You are full of works that are not of the truth, yet your ways are full of joy and rejoicing. Having defiled the water of life, you have drawn it within the will of the powers to whom you have been given to serve them.

"And your thought is not like that of those people whom you persecute. . . . Their fruit does not wither. But they will be known up to the great eternal realms, because the words they have kept, of the god of the eternal realms, were not committed to the book, nor were they written. Angelic beings will bring them, whom all the generations of people will not know. For they will be on a high mountain, upon a rock of truth. Therefore they will be called words of incorruptibility and truth, for those who know the eternal god in wisdom of knowledge and teaching of angels forever, for he knows all things."

These are the revelations that Adam made known to Seth his son. And his son taught his seed about them. This is the hidden knowledge of Adam, which he gave to Seth, which is the holy baptism of those who know the eternal knowledge through those born of the word and the imperishable illuminators, who came from the holy seed: Yesseus Mazareus Yessedekeus, the living, water.[58]

---

55. The people of the world praise the seed of Seth and decry their own actions.
56. The reading remains somewhat uncertain.
57. In Sethian tradition the triad of Micheus, Michar, and Mnesinous is connected to baptism, as, for example, in the Baptismal Ceremony of the Gospel of the Egyptians, included in this volume.
58. On Yesseus Mazareus Yessedekeus, also connected to baptism in Sethian tradition, see the Baptismal Ceremony of the Gospel of the Egyptians.

7

Three Forms of
First Thought

T he Three Forms of First Thought, or the Trimorphic Protennoia,
is a Sethian tractate that reached its present form around 200 CE.
It features a divine triad of father, mother, and child (or son), who
each descend as first thought, Protennoia. First thought's descents from the
pleroma to earth are also symbolized as voice, speech, and word.

The profound poetry of Three Forms of First Thought shares with most
gnostic scripture an exuberant gift for mythopoetic language. In its lexicon
and three stages, Three Forms of First Thought resembles the Secret Book of
John, probably written about the same time: both apocalyptic treatises offer a
philosophical meditation on the formation and history of the universe.

In the Secret Book of John there is a triple descent of the redeemer—from
the riches of light in the heavenly pleroma; to the second period in darkness,
chaos, and the prison of the body; to the third phase, where, being the pure
light in light, the redeemer speaks to the redeemable and pronounces a wak-
ening call for their deliverance. In its revelation of the creation, fall, and salvation of the world and its people, the Secret Book of John resembles the Three
Forms of First Thought's discourse by the personified Protennoia in her three
revelatory descents as heavenly redeemer. Protennoia's ultimate purpose is to
combat the darkness that earth's inhabitants have fallen under as a result of
the plots of their chief creator, the boasting demiurge, and offer the children
of light hope of redemption.

Protennoia, first thought, is female. But she lives in the light, who is the father of all, and in her is also the divine child, the son of god. So the book begins, "I am first thought, the thought that is in light. I am movement that is in all, she in whom the realm of all takes its stand." The figures and attributes manifest a complex variety from the very first statements of the text. First thought is also the eternal being of Barbelo. As a woman and female principle she evokes Sophia, wisdom in her earlier descent with all her creation. She also corresponds to the son in the form of the logos, the savior. This mingled scheme of references, ecstatically uttered, and its continued mingling, from the very first lines of Jewish, gnostic, and Christian elements, leads John Turner to state,

> *Trimorphic Protennoia* has undergone at least three states of composition. First, there was the original triad of the aretalogical self-predications ["I am" statements] of Protennoia as Voice, Speech, and Word that were probably built up out of the Jewish wisdom tradition and maybe out of *The Apocryphon of John*'s similar Pronoia aretalogy itself sometime during the first century c.e.; there is little here that seems specifically gnostic or Christian or Sethian or Barbeloite. Second, this was supplemented . . . by various narrative doctrinal passages based upon traditional Barbeloite theogonical materials [about the emergence of the divine realm]. . . . After circulation as a mildly Christian Barbeloite text in this form, the third and last stage of composition seems to have involved a deliberately polemical incorporation of Christian, specifically Johannine Christian, materials into the aretalogical portion of the third subtractate.[1]

Initially, the voice of first thought descends as a light force into darkness and shapes the fallen in their world of error and mortality. They have experienced the destructions brought on by the chief creator of the earth (who is the demiurge, called variously Sakla, Samael, and Yaldabaoth). The victims of the creator listen to the mother, who offers the mystery hidden from the eternal beings, which is embedded in the formation of language itself. She tells them,

---

1. In Robinson, ed., *Nag Hammadi Library in English,* pp. 512–13.

I am the womb that gives shape to all by bearing light shining in splendor. I am the coming eternal realm. I am the fulfillment of all. . . . I cast the voice's speech into the ears of those who know me. I invite you into the high, perfect light.

She offers hope to save the children of light on the earth, telling them they will be as they were when they were light.

In the second descent, the speech of first thought gives spirit and breath to the fallen. And in the third, the word or logos of thought descends in human form and restores the fallen to light, a feat accomplished by means of the baptismal rite of the five seals. The human form may be Christ the anointed, who is mentioned a few times, reflecting the tractate's light christianization, which, though at moments polemical, seems to lack conviction. This is not fundamentally a Christian treatise. Nonetheless, it still merits comparison with the opening hymn to the word or logos in the Gospel of John.

The discourse ends with a gnostic baptismal rite leading to the five seals that contain the light of ineffable knowledge. In the last line we learn that the author of this sacred scripture is the father of perfect knowledge.

THREE FORMS OF FIRST THOUGHT[2]

THE WORD OF FIRST THOUGHT: THE FIRST DESCENT

I am first thought,[3] the thought that is in light. I am movement that is in all, she in whom the realm of all takes its stand, the firstborn among those who came into being, she who exists before all. She is called by three names,[4] although she exists alone, since she is perfect. I am invisible within the thought

---

2. Three Forms of First Thought: Nag Hammadi Codex XIII,1, pp. 35,1 to 50,24; translated from the Coptic by John D. Turner (Robinson, ed., *Nag Hammadi Library in English*, rev. ed., pp. 513–22); revised by Willis Barnstone. The translation includes a number of textual restorations.
3. Protennoia resembles forethought, Pronoia, elsewhere in Sethian texts.
4. This statement recalls forethought, or Barbelo, as the triple male and the triple power in the Secret Book of John and elsewhere.

of the invisible one.[5] I am revealed in the immeasurable, ineffable things. I am intangible, dwelling in the intangible. I move in every creature.

I am the life of my afterthought[6] that is within every power and every eternal movement, and in invisible lights, and within the powers and angels and demons and every soul in Tartaros,[7] and in every material soul. I live in those who came into being. I move in everyone and I enter them. I walk upright, and those who sleep I awaken. And I am the sight of those who dwell in sleep.

I am the invisible one in all. I counsel those who are hidden, since I know the whole realm of all that exists in it. I am numberless beyond everyone. I am immeasurable, ineffable, yet whenever I wish, I shall reveal myself. I am the head of all. I am before all, and I am all, since I am in everyone.[8]

I am a voice speaking softly. I am from the beginning. I am in the silence that surrounds every one of them. And the hidden voice is in me, in intangible, immeasurable thought, in the immeasurable silence.[9]

I descended into the underworld and shone down on the darkness. I poured water. I am hidden in radiant waters. I gradually dawn on all by my thought. I am weighed down with the voice. Through me knowledge comes. I am in the ineffable and unknowable. I am perception and knowledge, uttering a voice by means of thought. I am the real voice. I cry out in everyone, and they recognize it, since a seed lives in them. I am the father's thought, and through me came the voice: the knowledge of everlasting things. I am as thought for all. I am joined to unknowable and intangible thought. I revealed myself in all who know me, for I joined everyone in hidden thought and exalted voice, and in a voice from the invisible thought.

It is immeasurable, since it is in the immeasurable one. It is a mystery, unrestrained by the intangible. It is invisible to all who are visible in the realm of all. It is light in light.[10]

We also have left the visible world since we are saved by hidden wisdom

---

5. This invisible one seems to be the invisible spirit, the father of the pleroma.
6. *Epinoia* (from Greek).
7. Tartaros is the underworld, the realm of the dead, hell.
8. These statements of self-predication are reminiscent of the opening of the Secret Book of John.
9. This description is similar to the description of word, and silence, in the Secret Book of John.
10. Other Sethian texts, such as the Secret Book of John and the Vision of the Foreigner, have similar statements of divine transcendence.

mediated by the ineffable, immeasurable voice. And the one who is hidden within us pays a tribute of fruit to the water of life.[11]

The son is perfect in every respect. He is the word who originated through that voice,[12] who came from on high, who has within him the name, who is light. The son revealed the everlasting, and all the unknown was known. He revealed what is hard to interpret and what is secret, and he preached to those who live in silence with first thought, and he revealed himself to those who are in darkness, and he clarified himself to those in the abyss.[13] To those in the hidden treasuries he told ineffable mysteries, and he taught unspeakable doctrines to all those who became children of the light.[14]

Now the voice that came from my thought exists as three permanences: the father, the mother, the son. The voice is perceptible speech containing a word rich in every glory. It has three masculinities, three powers, and three names. They are in the manner of the triad of three [shapes],[15] which are quadrangles, secretly in silence of the ineffable one.

He alone came into being as the anointed.[16] I anointed him with goodness as the glory of the invisible spirit. I established these three alone in glory over the eternal realms in living water: glory surrounding him who first appeared to the light of the exalted aeons and realms. He persists in light. And he stood in a light surrounding him who is the eye of light gloriously shining on me. He gave aeons for the father of all aeons, I the thought of the father, first thought,[17] Barbelo,[18] the perfect glory and the immeasurable invisible hidden one. I am the image of the invisible spirit. Through me all took shape. I am the mother as well as the light whom she appointed as virgin, she who is called Meirothea,[19] the intangible womb, the unrestrained and immeasurable voice.

Then the perfect son revealed himself to his aeons who came through him. He revealed, glorified, and enthroned them, and stood in the glory made for himself. They blessed the perfect son, the anointed,[20] the god who came into

---

11. The water of life may be baptismal water.
12. Here word (logos) is linked to voice.
13. Darkness and the abyss are terms describing the world of matter here below.
14. The children of the light are Sethian gnostics.
15. Quadrangles are drawn in the Coptic text for "shapes."
16. Christ.
17. Protennoia, again.
18. Barbelo is the name of the divine mother in Sethian literature.
19. This name or epithet for the divine is also used in the Three Steles of Seth. Suggestions for its meaning vary.
20. Christ, again.

being by himself. And they gave glory, saying, "He is! He is! God's son! God's son! He is! The being of eternal beings! He sees the eternal beings that he conceived. For you have conceived by your own desire! So we glorify you: MA! MO! You are O, O, O. You are A. You are being![21] The eternal realm of the eternal realms! The eternal realm he gave!"

Then the god who was conceived[22] gave the eternal realms a power of life for them to rely on, and he established them. The first eternal realm he established over the first—Armedon, Nousanios, Harmozel;[23] the second he established over the second eternal realm—Phaionios, Ainios, Oroiael; the third over the third eternal realm— Mellephaneus, Loios, Daveithai; the fourth over the fourth: Mousanios, Amethes, Eleleth. Now, those eternal realms are the ones conceived by the god who was conceived—the anointed—and these eternal realms received and gave glory. They were the first to appear, exalted in their thought, and each eternal realm gave ten thousand glories in great unsearchable lights, and as one they blessed the perfect son, the god who was conceived.

Then came a word from the great light Eleleth, and said, "I am king! Who is of chaos and who is of the underworld?" And suddenly his light appeared, shining forth, given afterthought. The powers of the powers asked nothing of him. Suddenly there appeared the great demon who rules over the lowest part of the underworld and chaos. He has no form or perfection. Rather, he has the form of the glory of those conceived in darkness. Now, he is called Sakla, Samael, Yaldabaoth, he who took power, who stole it away from innocent Sophia. Originally he overpowered her; she is the light's afterthought who descended, from whom the great demon came from the beginning.[24]

The afterthought of light knew the great demon had begged Eleleth for another order, though he was lower than afterthought, and she said, "Give me another order so that you may be a place for me to live, so I will not fall into endless disorder." And the order of the entire house of glory agreed with her word. She was blessed, and the higher order yielded to her.

---

21. The Coptic text has *ma mo o o o ei a ei on ei,* which might be understood as glossolalia. For the translation given here, which assumes that the Coptic reproduces Greek, see Layton, *Gnostic Scriptures,* p. 92. In the translation O is omega and A is alpha.
22. The son, the anointed.
23. The last luminaries of the triads here—Harmozel, Oroiael, Daveithai, and Eleleth—are the same four luminaries listed in the Secret Book of John. There each is listed with personified spiritual characteristics; here the other names may be epithets or other powers.
24. On the names and the diabolical ploys of the demiurge, see the Secret Book of John.

Now the great demon began to make aeons in the likeness of the real eternal realms, except that he produced them out of his own power.

I too revealed my voice secretly, saying, "Stop, stop, you who walk on matter. Look, I am coming down to the world of mortals for my portion that was there from the time when the innocent Sophia was conquered. She descended so that I might counter their plan, which was determined by the one who reveals himself through her." Everyone in the house of the ignorant light was disturbed, and the abyss trembled.

The chief creator[25] of ignorance reigned over chaos and the underworld and produced a human being in my likeness. But he didn't know that his creation would be a decree of his annulment, nor did he recognize the power in him.

But now I have come down and reached chaos. I was there with my own. I am hidden in them, empowering them, and giving them shape. From the first day until the day I grant enormous power to those who are mine, I will reveal myself to those who have heard my mysteries, the children of light.

I am their father, and I shall tell you an utterly ineffable and unspeakable mystery: I tore off from you the bonds and broke the chains of the underworld demons, the same restraints that bound me. I overthrew the high walls of darkness, and I broke the secure gates of those pitiless ones and smashed their bars. And I spoke of the evil force and the one who beats and harms you, the tyrant, the adversary, the king, and the real enemy. I informed all who are mine, who are children of light, how to nullify the enemies, be free of bonds, and return to where they first were.

I am the first who descended for my portion of what was left behind: the spirit in the soul, which came from the water of life and the immersion of the mysteries. I spoke and the archons and authorities spoke. I went under their language and spoke my mysteries to my own—a hidden mystery—and the bonds and eternal oblivion were nullified. And I bore fruit in them, the thought of the unchanging eternal realm, and my house, and their father. And I went down to those who were mine from the first, and reached them and broke the first strands that enslaved them. Then everyone in me shone, and I made a pattern for those lights that are ineffably in me. Amen.[26]

---

25. Greek *archigenitor,* here and elsewhere in the text.
26. This concludes the first descent of the light. On the three descents of the light, see the concluding hymn of the savior in the Secret Book of John.

ON DESTINY: THE SECOND DESCENT

I am the voice that appeared through my thought. I am one joined to another.[27] I am called the thought of the invisible one. Because I am called the unchanging speech, I am called she who is joined to another.[28]

I am alone and undefiled. I am the mother of the voice, speaking in many ways, completing all. Knowledge is in me, a knowledge of things everlasting. I speak in every creature, and I was known by all. I lift up the speech of the voice to the ears of those who have known me, the children of light.

Now, I have come the second time in the likeness of a female and have spoken with them. And I shall tell them of the coming end of this realm and teach them of the beginning of the eternal realm to come, the one without change, the one in which our appearance will be changed. We shall be purified in those eternal realms from which I revealed myself in the thought of the likeness of my masculinity. I settled among those who are worthy in the thought of my changeless eternal realm.

I shall tell you a mystery of this realm and of its forces.[29] Birth cries out; hour gives birth to hour, and day gives birth to day. Months reveal months, time follows time. This realm was completed in this fashion, and as quickly, it is thought, as a finger releases a finger and a joint separates from a joint. When the great authorities knew that the time of fulfillment had appeared—just as the time of the birth pangs came, the time of destruction approached—the elements trembled, and the foundations of the underworld and the ceilings of chaos shook, and a great fire shone in their midst, and rocks and earth were shaken like a reed by the wind.

And a great thunder disturbed the allotments of fate and those who apportion the houses.[30] The thrones of the powers were disturbed because they were overturned, and their king was afraid. And those who follow fate paid their allotment of visits to the path, and said to the powers, "What is this disturbance and this shaking we have felt through the voice of exalted speech? And our entire world has been shaken, the entire circuit of our path of ascent

---

27. Or "syzygetic," a term indicating heavenly conjunction or spiritual marriage.
28. Or "syzygetic," once again.
29. This section gives an apocalyptic vision of the end times, from a Sethian perspective.
30. The houses of the heavens in astronomy. This section reflects upon the planets and their heavenly circuits.

has been destroyed, and our way up to the chief creator of our birth[31] no longer exists for us."

Then the powers answered, saying, "We too are at a loss about it because we did not know what caused it. But get up and let's go to the chief creator and ask him." And the powers gathered and went up to the chief creator. They said to him, "What kind of boasting is this? Didn't we hear you say, 'I am god, and I am your father and it is I who produced you, and there is no other god but me'?[32] Now look, the aeon's voice of invisible speech has appeared. We don't recognize the voice, nor to whom we belong, for the voice that we heard is foreign and its origin unknown. It came and terrified and weakened our arms. So let's weep and mourn bitterly! And let us fly away before we are forcibly imprisoned and taken down to the bowels of the underworld. Already the slackening of our bondage is near, and time is short, and the days are brief, and our time fulfilled. The weeping of our destruction is near and we may be taken to the place we recognize. The tree from which we grew has fruit of ignorance. Death is in its leaves, and darkness under the shadow of its boughs. In deceit and lust we harvested the tree through which ignorant chaos became our home. For look, even the chief creator of our birth, about whom we boast, did not know this speech."

O children of thought, hear me, hear the speech of the mother of your mercy. You have earned the right to own the mystery hidden from eternity. Now accept it. And the end of this realm and of the life of injustice is near, and the beginning of the coming eternal realm dawns and will never change.

I am androgynous. I am mother and father. I copulate with myself. I copulate with myself and with those who love me, and through me alone all are standing firm. I am the womb that gives shape to all by bearing light shining in splendor. I am the coming eternal realm. I am the fulfillment of all, Meirothea[33] the glory of the mother. I cast the voice's speech into the ears of those who know me.

I invite you into the high perfect light. When you enter light, you will be glorified by those who give glory, and those who enthrone will enthrone you. You will receive robes from those who give robes, the baptizers will baptize

---

31. The demiurge.
32. Isaiah 45:5–6, 21, 46:9.
33. On Meirothea, see above.

you, and you will become exceedingly glorious, the way you first were when you were light.

I hid in everyone and revealed myself in them, and every mind seeking me longed for me, for I gave shape to the full realm when it had no form. I transformed their forms into other forms until the time when form is given to everyone. The voice came through me. I created breath in my people. And I cast the eternally holy spirit into them, and I ascended and entered my light. I got on my branch and sat among the children of holy light. And I withdrew to where they lived. Amen.

THE WORD OF APPEARANCE:
THE THIRD DESCENT

I am the word in the ineffable voice. I am in undefiled light, and thought came clearly through the great speech of the mother, though a male offspring is my foundation. Speech exists from the beginning in the foundations of the full realm.

But a light hides in silence, and it was first to appear. Whereas the mother alone exists as silence, I alone am the ineffable, incorruptible, immeasurable, and inconceivable word. The word is hidden light bearing fruit of life, pouring living water from the invisible, unpolluted, immeasurable spring. The source is the inimitable voice of the mother's glory, the glory of god's offspring, the male virgin in hidden intellect, silence hidden from everyone, inimitable, immeasurable light, the full source and root of the whole eternal realm. It is the foundation of every movement of the eternal realms that are of mighty glory. It is the base of every foundation, the breath of powers. It is the eye of the three permanences, which are a voice in thought. It is a word in speech. It was sent to illumine those in darkness.

Look, I will reveal my mysteries because you are my brothers and sisters,[34] and you will know them. I told them about my mysteries that exist in the ineffable, inexpressible eternal realms. I taught them the mysteries through the voice of perfect intellect, and I became a foundation for all and I strengthened them.

The second time I came as my voice's speech. I shaped those who took shape before their completion.

---

34. Or "fellow brothers," here and below.

The third time I revealed myself in their tents as the word.[35] I revealed myself in the likeness of their shape. I wore everyone's garment. I hid in them, and they didn't know who strengthens me. For I am in all dominions and powers and among angels and in every movement in matter. I hid in them until I revealed myself to my brothers and sisters. None of the powers knew me, though I work in them. They thought they created everything, because they are ignorant. They didn't know the root and source of their growth.

I am light illumining all. I am light happy in my brothers and sisters. I came down to the world of mortals because of the spirit in what descended and came from the innocent Sophia. I came and delivered . . . and went . . . that which he once had. I gave him some of the living water, which strips him of chaos in uttermost darkness, in the whole abyss, which is corporeal and psychical thought. All these I put on. And I stripped him of inferior thought and clothed him in shining light: knowledge of the thought of fatherhood.

I delivered him to those who give robes—Yammon, Elasso, Amenai[36]—and they covered him with a robe from the robes of the light; I delivered him to the baptizers and they baptized him—Micheus, Michar, Mnesinous[37]—and they immersed him in the spring of the water of life. I delivered him to those who enthrone—Bariel, Nouthan, Sabenai—and they enthroned him from the throne of glory. I delivered him to those who glorify—Ariom, Elien, Phariel—and they glorified him with the glory of the fatherhood. And those who snatch away, snatched away—Kamaliel . . . Samblo, the servants of the great holy luminaries—and they took him into the place of the light of his fatherhood. And he received the five seals[38] from the light of the mother, first thought,[39] and it was granted him to partake of the mystery of knowledge, and he became a light in light.

So, now . . . I was in them, in each one's form. The rulers thought I was their anointed.[40] Actually, I dwell in everyone. Indeed, within those in whom I revealed myself as light, I eluded the rulers. I am their beloved, for in that place I clothed myself as the son of the chief creator, and I was like him until the end of his regime, which is the ignorance of chaos. And among the angels I

---

35. Their tents are bodies. The image of the word revealed in tents is used in John 1. On this entire paragraph, see the hymn to the word in the Gospel of John.
36. This paragraph contains multiple images of Sethian baptism.
37. On Micheus, Michar, and Mnesinous, see the Revelation of Adam and other Sethian texts.
38. The five seals are connected to baptism in Sethian literature.
39. Protennoia.
40. Christ.

revealed myself in their likeness, and among the powers as if I were one of them, but among the human children[41] as if I were a human child,[42] even though I am father of everyone.

I hid in them all until I revealed myself among my members, which are mine, and I taught them about the ineffable ordinances, and about the brothers and sisters. But they are inexpressible to every sovereignty and every ruling power except to the children of light, decreed by the father. These are the glories that are higher than every glory, that is, the five seals, complete by virtue of intellect. One who possesses the five seals with these names has stripped off the garments of ignorance and put on shining light. And nothing will appear to one who belongs to the powers of the rulers. In them darkness will dissolve and ignorance die. And thought of the scattered creature will have a single appearance, and dark chaos will dissolve . . . until I reveal myself to my brothers and sisters and gather all my brothers and sisters in my eternal kingdom. I proclaimed the ineffable five seals to them so that I might live in them and they in me.

I wore Jesus.[43] I carried him from the cursed wood and set him in his father's house. And those who guard their houses didn't recognize me. My seed and I are unrestrained. My seed is mine. I shall place it in holy light in intangible silence. Amen.[44]

41. Or "earthly children," "sons of man."
42. Or "earthly son," "son of man."
43. Wearing Jesus as a garment suggests the incarnation of Jesus. This is the manifestation of the Sethian savior in Christian garb.
44. Following the title, the manuscript adds here, "A sacred scripture written by the father with perfect knowledge."

8

The Three Steles of Seth

Like other Sethian texts, the Three Steles of Seth is a text featuring the salvation of the offspring of Seth. The Three Steles praise each member of the divine family in turn: the invisible father (addressed, as in the Secret Book of John, as the One [or monad], the five, the ineffable); his counterpart, Barbelo; and the self-conceived child. The Jewish historian Josephus recounts a story of how the descendants of Seth preserved the wisdom of Adam, Eve, and Seth by inscribing it on two steles of brick and stone, in order to preserve it through hell and high water. This legend becomes the occasion for explaining the origin of the present text, in which the original two steles may have become three to allow for praise to the threefold nature of the divine family. A similar legend may suggest that Hermetic texts were also preserved on steles and thus were communicated to later generations. This legend is recounted in the Discourse on the Eighth and Ninth.

The Three Steles of Seth claims to be the original set of divine hymns of praise formulated through heavenly Seth and his father, Geradamas, and recovered as a latter-day collection of hymns. Reading them, it is easy to imagine the gnostic Sethian community at worship, offering hymns of praise to the divine family. The text concludes with instructions for the use of the hymns: they are to be used in a liturgy of ecstatic ascent—inviting the worshiper to approach god, see god, and learn "about things infinite"—and return from ascent.

The contents of the hymns recall other texts written in the spirit of Seth, such as the Secret Book of John, the Vision of the Foreigner, the Sermon of Zostrianos, and Marsanes.[1] The Three Steles of Seth reflects Jewish and neoplatonic philosophical ideas, the latter particularly in the numerous references to the neoplatonic triad of existence, life, and mind.

The Three Steles of Seth was likely composed in Greek. The date and place of composition are unknown, though Alexandria, Egypt, is as likely a place of composition as any other that has been proposed. Since the neoplatonic philosopher Plotinos taught a course against the gnostics in 265–66 CE, and his student Porphyry mentions Zostrianos, the Foreigner (Allogenes), and other gnostic works, the first half of the third century has been proposed as a plausible time of composition.

THE THREE STELES OF SETH[2]

The revelation of Dositheos[3] about the three steles of Seth,[4] father of the living and unshakable race.[5] He remembered what he saw, understood, and read, and gave it to the chosen, just as it was written there.

Often I have joined in glorifying with the powers, and I was considered worthy by the immeasurable majesties.

The steles are as follows:

THE FIRST STELE OF SETH

I praise you, father Geradamas,[6]
I, your son Emmacha Seth,[7]

---

1. Marsanes, which is the single text preserved in Nag Hammadi Codex X, is very fragmentary and not included in this volume.
2. The Three Steles of Seth: Nag Hammadi Codex VII,5, pp. 118,10 to 127,27; translated from the Coptic by Marvin Meyer.
3. Dositheos was a Samaritan religious leader and the teacher of Simon Magus. Simon Magus is discussed in Acts of the Apostles 8 and elsewhere in early Christian literature.
4. Or "three pillars of Seth." Steles are monuments, well known in the Middle East, typically with significant public inscriptions.
5. This phrase describes the gnostics, who cannot be shaken and do not waver in their commitments.
6. As in the Secret Book of John, Geradamas is the perfect exalted human, heavenly Adamas or Adam, the father of Seth.
7. The meaning of Emmacha is unknown. Elsewhere in gnostic literature featuring Seth reference is also made to Emmacha Seth (in Zostrianos) or Eli Eli Machar Machar Seth (in the Baptismal Ceremony of the Gospel of the Egyptians).

whom you produced without generation
for the praise of our god.
I am your son
and you are my mind, O my father.
I have sown and produced,
but you have seen the majesties
and have stood endlessly.
I praise you, father.
Praise me, father.
Because of you I am,
because of god you are,
because of you I am with him.
You are light and you see light.
You have revealed light.
You are a Mirotheas,
you are my Mirotheos.[8]
I praise you as god,
I praise your divinity.
Great is the good one, self-conceived,[9] who stood,
the god who was first to stand.
You came in goodness,
you appeared
and you revealed goodness.
I shall speak your name,
you are a primary name.
You are unborn,
you have appeared to reveal the eternal.
You are who is,
so you have revealed those who really are.
You are uttered by a voice,
but by mind you are glorified.
You are powerful everywhere
so the world of senses also knows you,
because of you and your seed.
You are merciful

---

8. Forms of this name or epithet for the divine are also used in the Three Forms of First Thought.
9. Coptic *autogenes* (from Greek).

and from another race,[10]
and it is placed over another race.[11]
Now, you are from another race,
and it is placed over another race.
You are from another race,
you are different.
You are merciful,
you are eternal.
You are placed over a race,
you made all these increase
because of my seed,
and you know it is placed in generation.[12]
But they are from other races,
they are different.
They are placed over other races,
they are placed in life.
You are a Mirotheos.
I praise its power given to me.

You who made the masculinities
that really are three times male,[13]
who were divided into five,[14]
who were given to us in triple power,
who were conceived without generation,
who came forth from the superior

---

10. Coptic *kegenos,* a term similar to Allogenes. Geradamas is Adam the stranger or foreigner from the heavenly realm, and Sethians are said to belong to another race, the unshakable race of perfect humankind.

11. The references here and in the following lines to "another race" indicate the divine realm of the pleroma above, as well as the people of Seth here below. Heavenly Geradamas is from the divine fullness above, and his seed, particularly heavenly Seth, is over the gnostic race of Sethians. In the Secret Book of John, Geradamas places his son Seth in a position of power in the second aeon of the divine pleroma, with the luminary Oroiael, and the offspring of Seth are in the third aeon, with the luminary Daveithai. The Sethian gnostics here below in turn trace their origin from the offspring of Seth above.

12. The seed of Seth is "mortalized," placed in the realm of earthly procreation, in the Sethian gnostics present in this world.

13. That is, triple male, a term of praise in which maleness symbolizes what is heavenly. This term is used in the Secret Book of John and elsewhere.

14. In the Secret Book of John, the father's realm of five consists of Barbelo and the four spiritual attributes requested by Barbelo. Elsewhere the five can indicate other divine attributes or emanations, or even five seals, as at the end of the Secret Book of John.

and for the inferior entered the midst,
you are a parent through a parent,
a word from a command.
We praise you, triple male,
you have unified all through them all,
you have empowered us.
You came into being from One,[15]
from One you left.
You have come to One.
You have saved,
you have saved,
you have saved us,
you who are crowned and crown.
We praise you eternally,
we praise you,
we who are saved,
who are perfect beings,
who are perfect because of you,
who have become perfect with you.
You who are complete,
who complete,
who are perfect through all these,
who are everywhere similar,
triple male,
you have stood,
you were first to stand.
You have been divided everywhere,
you have remained one.
Whomever you wished
you have saved,
and you wish
that all who are worthy be saved.
You are perfect,
you are perfect,
you are perfect.

---

15. In the Three Steles of Seth the One is referred to in Coptic as *oua* (masculine) and *ouei* (feminine), and as *monas* (from Greek), here and below.

THE SECOND STELE OF SETH

Great is the first eternal realm,
male virgin Barbelo,[16]
the first glory of the invisible father.
You who are called perfect
first saw
that the one who really preexists
is not.[17]
From that one and through it
you have come into being first and forever,
you who are nonexistent from One, the indivisible, triple power.
You are a triple power,
you are a great One from a pure One.
You are a superior One,
first shadow of the holy father,
light from light.
We praise you,
maker of perfection,
donor of eternal realms.
You saw that those who are eternal
are from a shadow.
You have conferred multiplicity,
you have found and remained One,
while still conferring multiplicity through division.[18]
You are a threefold replication,
truly you are replicated three times.
You are One, of the One,
and you are from its shadow.
You are hidden,
you are a world of knowledge,
you know that those who are of the One are from shadow.

---

16. Barbelo is the divine mother, the first emanation or thought of the invisible father.
17. The divine is beyond existence.
18. These lines describe the mystery of how in a sense the One may also be three, how the singular may also be plural. Here the issue is in large part a neoplatonic, philosophical issue. In other times and places the issue becomes a Christian issue, in trinitarian discussions.

And they are yours in your heart.
Because of them you made the eternal be,
you made divinity live,
you made knowledge good,
in blessedness you made the shadows flowing from the One.
You made one in understanding;
you made another in creation.
You made the equal and the unequal,
the similar and the different.
You have empowered in generation and formation,
by that which is, to others . . .
. . . and generation.
You have given these strength,
hidden in the heart,
and you came forth to them and from them.
You are divided among them
and become a great male first-appearing mind.

Father god,
divine child,
maker of multiplicity,
in dividing all those who really are,[19]
you revealed to them all a word.
You possess them all without birth,
eternally, imperishably.
Because of you salvation has come to us,
from you comes salvation.
You are wisdom,[20]
you are knowledge,
you are truth.
Because of you is life,
from you life.
Because of you is mind,
from you mind.
You are mind,

---

19. Or "all those who really exist."
20. Sophia.

you are a world of truth.
You are a triple power,
you are a threefold replication,
truly you are replicated three times,
the eternal realm of eternal realms.
You alone see purely the first, undying, unborn ones
and the first divisions, as you were divided.
Unify us as you were unified.
Teach us what you see.
Give us strength so we may be saved to eternal life.
We are a shadow of you . . .
as you are a shadow of that first preexistent one.
Hear us first.
We are eternal.
Hear us as perfect beings.
You are the eternal realm of eternal realms,
the all-perfect one, who is established.
You have heard,
you have heard.
You have saved,
you have saved.
We give thanks,
we praise always,
we shall glorify you.

THE THIRD STELE OF SETH

We rejoice
we rejoice
we rejoice.
We saw
we saw
we saw what really preexists,
that it really is
and is the first eternal one.
You, unborn,
from you come the eternal ones
and eternal realms,

the all-perfect ones, who are established,
and the perfect beings.
We praise you, nonbeing,
reality before realities,
first being before beings,
father of divinity and life,
creator of mind,
donor of goodness,
donor of blessedness.
We all praise you,
you who know,
with glorifying praise,
you, because of whom all these are . . .
who know yourself through yourself alone.
There is nothing active prior to you.
You are spirit, alone and living.
You know the One,
that we cannot speak of this One,
which is yours everywhere.
Your light enlightens us.
Command us to see you
so we may be saved.
Knowledge of you is our salvation.
Command!
If you command,
we have been saved.

Truly we are saved
We have seen you through mind.
You are all these
and save them all,
you who will not be saved   ·
nor have been saved by them.
You have commanded us.
You are One,
you are One,
as one might tell you,
you are One.

You are a single, living spirit.
How shall we give you a name?[21]
We have none.
You are their existence,
you are their life,
you are their mind.[22]
In you they rejoice.
You ordered them saved
through your word . . .
the single glory, at the fore,
O hidden one, blessed Senaon, who conceived himself,[23]
Asineus
Mephneus
Optaon
Elemaon, the great power
Emouniar
Nibareus
Kandephoros
Aphredon
Deiphaneus
you who are my Armedon
you generator of powers
Thalanatheus
Antitheus.
You are in you,
you are before you,
and after you none have come to act.
How shall we praise you?
We cannot,
but we thank you,
we who are inferior.
For you commanded us,

---

21. The One, as in the Secret Book of John, is ineffable and transcends every finite name.
22. That is, you are existence, life, mind—the neoplatonic triad.
23. The section of the hymn that follows contains a series of spiritual or mystical names of the divine; Asineus and Mephneus are partially restored. Such spiritual names are also used in the hymns in Zostrianos and the Foreigner (Allogenes).

you who are our superior,
to glorify you
as best we can.
We praise you because we are saved
and we always glorify you.
Now we shall glorify you
that we be saved to eternal salvation.
We have praised you
for we can.
We have been saved.
You always wished
us to do it.
We have done it. . . .

Whoever remembers these[24] and always glorifies will be perfect among the perfect and free of suffering beyond all things. They all praise these, individually and collectively, and afterward they will be silent.

As assigned, they ascend. After silence, they descend from the third. They praise the second, and afterward the first. The way of ascent is the way of descent.[25]

So understand, as those who are alive, that you have succeeded. You have taught yourselves about things infinite. Marvel at the truth within them, and at the revelation.[26]

---

24. That is, "these steles."
25. This paragraph gives instructions for the order of the hymns, with intervening silence, in the liturgy of ecstatic ascent and descent.
26. After a concluding title, the manuscript adds a scribal note that refers either to the Three Steles of Seth or the codex in general: "This text belongs to the fatherhood; it is the son who wrote it. Bless me, father. I bless you, father, in peace. Amen."

9

The Vision of
the Foreigner

The Foreigner (or Allogenes) is another Sethian text of gnostic wisdom, of which the Vision is a part. In this text Allogenes the foreigner has a visionary experience of the divine, and at the end of the text (not included here) it is said that he writes it down in the document for his child Messos. The neoplatonist author Porphyry maintains that Plotinos opposed gnostics who used revelations by Allogenes and Messos, among others, and the present text may be one of the works referred to by Porphyry. The role of Allogenes as foreigner or one from another race suggests that the visionary protagonist of this text may be Seth—described in Genesis as "another seed" in place of the dead Abel—or a follower of Seth, or every person, every gnostic who follows the enlightened way of Sethian knowledge.

In the section of the text translated here, the foreigner has a vision of the divine that recalls the Secret Book of John and other Sethian literature. Earlier in the text the foreigner has been instructed in the proper method of meditation, and now the foreigner employs this method in the visionary experience. The visionary experience is understood not as an ascent upward through stages of enlightenment but rather as an inner experience of deeper and deeper insight. The foreigner thus envisions within self aspects of the divine, in silence, as a part of the inner journey.

But the revelatory vision of god within is hardly the end of the experience. The nature of the divine is explained, in more philosophical terms, by the powers of the luminaries, who use language closely connected to that of the opening portion of the Secret Book of John to explain the unexplainable and communicate what cannot be put into words. Whatever the divine is, it is not this, it is not that. "It is not something that exists, which people can understand, but something greater, which no one can understand."

The Foreigner is a Coptic text in the Nag Hammadi library, and like other texts in the Nag Hammadi library, it was most likely composed in Greek. Karen L. King suggests a date of composition in the first quarter of the third century to correspond with the likelihood that Plotinos knew of the text. She also suggests, more tentatively, that the text may have been written in Egypt, possibly in Alexandria.[1]

VISION OF THE FOREIGNER[2]

Through a primary revelation of the first one,[3] which is unknown to all, I saw the god that is greater than perfection, and the triple power[4] that exists in all. I was seeking the ineffable, unknowable god, of which people are ignorant even if they understand it at all, the mediation of the triple power, which is located in stillness and silence and is unknowable.

When I was empowered by these things, the powers of the luminaries[5] said to me, You have done enough to hinder the inactivity that is in you by seeking what is incomprehensible. Rather, hear about it, as is possible, through a primary revelation and a revelation.[6]

Does it[7] exist through its own being, or does it exist and will it come further into being? Does it act? Does it know? Is it alive? For it has no mind, no life, nothing real—and nothing unreal, incomprehensibly. Does it come from what it has? No, there is nothing at all left over, as if it causes something to be undertaken, or it purifies something, or it receives or gives something. Nor is

---

1. King, *Revelation of the Unknowable God,* pp. 60-61.
2. Vision of the Foreigner: Nag Hammadi Codex XI,3, pp. 61,8 to 64,1; translated from the Coptic by Marvin Meyer.
3. The invisible spirit.
4. Forethought, or Barbelo.
5. In Sethian texts the luminaries are Harmozel, Oroiael, Daveithai, and Eleleth.
6. The primary revelation seems to be a visual disclosure, the revelation an oral disclosure.
7. That is, the invisible spirit. Much of what follows in the Vision of the Foreigner resembles the opening portion of the Secret Book of John.

it limited by its own desire or by giving or by receiving from another. Its desire is not from itself, nor does desire come to it from anything else, yet it does not give anything of itself, or it would be limited. Thus it has no need of mind or life or anything, for it is greater than all in its ultimacy and incomprehensibility, in nonexistent reality. It has silence and stillness not to be limited by the unlimited.

It is not divinity or blessedness or perfection; rather, it is something unknowable. Not that it has this, but it is greater than blessedness and divinity and perfection. It is not perfect, but greater. It is not infinite or limited by another, but greater. It is not corporeal and is not incorporeal. It is not large and it is not small. It is not quantifiable, not a created thing. It is not something that exists, which people can understand, but something greater, which no one can understand. It is a first revelation and knowledge of itself, since it alone understands itself. For it is not among the things that exist, but is greater among what is greater. And it is like what it has and unlike what it has. It is not part of an eternal realm nor time, and it receives nothing from anyone. It is not limited, nor does it limit, nor is it illimitable.

It is self-knowledge, since it is unknowable, and it is greater than what is good in its unknowability, having blessedness and perfection and silence—not blessedness or perfection or stillness, but something that is, that no one can understand, being at rest.

10

The Sermon of Zostrianos

T his concluding portion of the long Sethian text Zostrianos provides a fine example of a gnostic sermon. The figure named Zostrianos was said to have been an older relative (perhaps a grandfather or uncle) of the Persian religious teacher Zoroaster, or Zarathustra, the founder of the Zoroastrian religion. Zoroaster himself is mentioned, along with Zostrianos, in the set of cryptographic titles and descriptions after the conclusion of the text. Revelations by Zostrianos and Zoroaster are also referred to by Porphyry in his *Life of Plotinos* as texts known to neoplatonists, and Porphyry claims that Plotinos's student Amelios wrote as many as forty volumes refuting the book of Zostrianos.

Although the text of Zostrianos is poorly preserved and in fragmentary condition, parts of the text are quite legible, including the beginning, where the author, writing in the name of Zostrianos, recounts his call. Once he was in the desert, meditating on deep questions, when he grew profoundly depressed, to the point of contemplating suicide. Suddenly an angel appears to him, "the angel of the knowledge of the eternal light," and this angel guides Zostrianos in an out-of-the-body journey up through the heavenly realms. As he ascends, Zostrianos is baptized at the various stages of ascent into the knowledge of the divine. After a series of revelatory experiences, in which Zostrianos learns about the meaning of the universe and the divine realms, which are populated with the usual Sethian characters, Zostrianos returns down to this world and his body. Now enlightened, Zostrianos preaches the impassioned gnostic sermon given here, in order to awaken lost people to saving knowledge.

The text of Zostrianos survives in Coptic in the Nag Hammadi library. It was composed in Greek some time before it became known, in the latter half of the third century, to Plotinos and his students. Despite the suggestion that the text tells the story of the Persian sage Zostrianos, the text is a pseudonymous composition, and its actual place of composition is unknown.

THE SERMON OF ZOSTRIANOS[1]

A lost crowd I[2] awakened, saying,
You who are alive, holy offspring of Seth,[3]
understand this. Do not turn a deaf ear to me.
Awaken your divinity to divinity
and strengthen your undefiled chosen souls.
Observe the constant change that is here
and seek the unchanging state of being unborn.
The father of all these beings invites you.
When you are being rebuked and maltreated,
he will not forsake you.
Do not wash yourselves[4] with death,
nor rely on those who are inferior
as if they were superior.
Flee from the madness and the fetter of femaleness
and choose the salvation of maleness.[5]

---

1. The Sermon of Zostrianos: Nag Hammadi Codex VIII,1, pp. 130,14 to 132,5; translated from the Coptic by Marvin Meyer.
2. The speaker is thought to be Zostrianos, now back in the body and enlightened after his heavenly trip.
3. This phrase designates the Sethian gnostics.
4. Or "baptize yourselves."
5. Femaleness may symbolize this world, maleness the world above, in Zostrianos and other texts, for example, Gospel of Thomas 114.

You have come not to suffer
but to break your fetters.
Break free, and what has bound you will be broken.
Save yourselves so that part[6] may be saved.
The good father has sent you the savior
and has strengthened you.
Why are you waiting? Seek when you are sought.
When you are invited, listen, for the time is short.
Do not be led astray.
Great is the eternal realm of the eternal realms
of the living,
but great also is the punishment of the unconvinced.
Many fetters and punishers surround you.
Get away quickly before destruction overtakes you.
Look to the light, fly from the darkness.
Do not be led astray to destruction.

---

6. That is, the soul or spiritual part of a person.

11

The Baptismal Ceremony of the Gospel of the Egyptians

The Gospel of the Egyptians, or, more accurately, the Holy Book of the Great Invisible Spirit, is a Sethian text that includes a baptismal ceremony showing, in part, how a Sethian gnostic baptism might have been celebrated. Sethian and other gnostic texts refer to baptism and the importance of baptism. In the Secret Book of John, for example, the awakened person is raised and sealed "in luminous water with five seals, that death might not prevail over the person from that moment on." Another Sethian text, the Three Forms of First Thought, describes gnostic baptism in a series of ceremonial acts: stripping off the darkness, dressing in a robe of light, being baptized or washed in the water of life, and being enthroned, glorified, raised, and sealed with five seals. The point of baptism, the Three Forms of First Thought suggests, is knowledge and enlightenment.

The Baptismal Ceremony of the Gospel of the Egyptians opens with a list of the dignitaries who stand in attendance during the baptismal ceremony.

The list includes figures well known from Sethian lore, for example, the four luminaries Harmozel, Oroiael, Daveithai, and Eleleth. The last such figure is Yoel, who is stationed over the name of the one baptizing "with the holy, incorruptible baptism that surpasses heaven." The balance of the Baptismal Ceremony of the Gospel of the Egyptians consists mainly of a hymn that is apparently uttered by the person being baptized. The hymn is an ecstatic statement of confession and praise, and it incorporates, after the manner of some other gnostic texts and magical texts of ritual power, the chanting of the (Greek) vowels. However this baptismal ceremony was enacted (or understood on a metaphoric level, rather than literally enacted), baptism is here portrayed as an ecstatic celebration. As the text puts it, those baptized "have been instructed and have understood, and they will not taste death."

The Gospel of the Egyptians was composed in Greek, but the circumstances of composition are unknown. The text is now represented in two Coptic versions in the Nag Hammadi library.

THE BAPTISMAL CEREMONY OF THE GOSPEL OF THE EGYPTIANS[1]

Through forethought Seth established what is holy and the baptism that surpasses the heavens—through what is holy, through what is incorruptible, and through Jesus,[2] who has been conceived by a living word[3] and with whom great Seth has been clothed. He has nailed down the powers of the thirteen realms and neutralized them; through him they are brought in and taken out. And they are equipped with armor of the knowledge of truth, with incorruptible, invincible power.

---

1. The Baptismal Ceremony of the Gospel of the Egyptians: Nag Hammadi Codex IV,2, pp. 75,24 to 80,15; translated by Marvin Meyer. The text is preserved in Nag Hammadi Codex III,2 and Codex IV,2: this translation is based mainly on the version found in Nag Hammadi Codex IV, though the Codex III version has also been consulted and used for lines of the ceremony not found in Codex IV.
2. Or "the living Jesus" (more clearly in Nag Hammadi Codex III). This phrase also occurs in the prologue of the Gospel of Thomas.
3. If "Jesus" is read as "the living Jesus," above, then "living word" may be read simply as "word."

THE HEAVENLY ATTENDANTS

These have been revealed[4] as dignitaries standing in attendance:
    Yesseus Mazareus Yessedekeus, the living water,
    the great commanders, great Jacob,[5] Theopemptos, and Isaouel,
    one stationed over grace, Mep——el,[6]
    those stationed over the springs of truth, Micheus, Michar, and
        Mnesinous,
    one stationed over the baptism of the living, the purifier Sesengen-
        barpharanges,[7]
    those stationed over the gates of the waters of life, Miseus and Michar,
    those stationed over the ascent, Seldao and Elainos,
    those receiving the holy race and the incorruptible, mighty people of
        great Seth,
    the ministers of the four luminaries, great Gamaliel, great Gabriel,
        great Samblo, and great Abrasax,[8]
    those stationed over sunrise, Olses, Hymneus, and Heurumaious,
    those stationed over the entrance into the state of rest of eternal life,
        Phritanis, Mixanther, and Michanor,
    the guardians of chosen[9] souls, Akraman and Strempsouchos,
    the great power Telmachael Telmachael Eli Eli Machar Machar Seth,
    the great one, invisible, incorruptible, unnamable, who is in spirit and
        silence,
    the great luminary, Harmozel, where there is the living self-conceived
        god in truth, with whom is the incorruptible human Adamas,
    second, Oroiael, where there is great Seth and Jesus of life, who has
        come and crucified what is under the law,
    third, Daveithai, where the children of great Seth are at rest,
    fourth, Eleleth, where the souls of the children are at rest,[10]

---

4. Possibly "revealed to me."
5. Coptic Yakob (Yakobos) in Nag Hammadi Codex III (from Greek) can be Jacob or James. James is also discussed in Gospel of Thomas 12 and the Secret Book of James.
6. This name cannot be completely restored.
7. This name is commonly found in Greek and Coptic magical texts of ritual power, and probably derives from Aramaic.
8. The name Abrasax is a common name of power; see the Revelation of Adam, note 37.
9. The reading in Nag Hammadi Codex III; Codex IV reads "slain."
10. The four names in these lines are the names of the luminaries.

fifth, Yoel, stationed over the name of the one who will be ordained to
baptize with the holy, incorruptible baptism that surpasses heaven.

But from now on, through the holy, incorruptible Poimael,[11] for those
worthy of baptisms of renunciation and the ineffable seals of their baptism,
they have known those who receive them, as they have been instructed and
have understood, and they will not taste death.

BAPTISMAL CEREMONIAL HYMN

Yesseus
EOEOUOOUA
in truth truly
Yesseus Mazareus Yessedekeus
living water
child of the child
name of all glories
in truth truly
eternal being
I I I I
E E E E
E E E E
O O O O
U U U U
O O O O
A A A A,
in truth truly
E I A A A A O O O O[12]
being who sees the eternal realms
in truth truly
A
E E
E E E

---

11. This name resembles the name Poimandres in Hermetic literature.

12. Perhaps (from Greek), "You are alpha (four times), omega (four times)." Because alpha and omega are, respectively, the first and last letters of the Greek alphabet, they can symbolize the first and the last, the beginning and the end, as in Revelation 1:8, 21:6, 22:13, and other texts. See Layton, *Gnostic Scriptures*, p. 118.

I I I I
U U U U U U
O O O O O O O[13]
being who exists forever
in truth truly
I E A A I O[14]
in the heart
being
U[15]
forever and ever
you are what you are
you are who you are.

This great name of yours is upon me,
You, self-conceived,
lacking nothing,
being independent,
invisible to all except me,
invisible to all.
Who comprehends you in speech or praise?
Having known you,
I now have mingled with your constancy.
I have armed myself,
and have put on armor of grace and light
and have become bright.
The mother[16] was there for the lovely beauty of grace.
So I stretch out my two hands.
I am formed in the circle of the riches of light
in my chest,

---

13. The (Greek) vowels in sequence; five omicrons are expected after I I I I, in order to maintain the sequence (one alpha, two epsilons, etc.). In texts of ritual power such vowels may be arranged for visual effectiveness, in this case perhaps in the form of a pyramid.
14. Böhlig and Wisse, eds., *Nag Hammadi Codices III,2 and IV,2*, p. 201, suggest that these enigmatic lines, beginning here and extending to the end of the stanza, may be translated as follows: "Jesus, you eternal realm (aeon), who are in the heart, eternal one, son forever and ever, you are what you are, you are who you are."
15. Upsilon.
16. Forethought, Barbelo; forethought is referred to at the beginning of the baptismal ceremony and throughout Sethian literature.

giving form to the many beings produced in light beyond reproach.
In truth I shall declare your glory,
I have comprehended you—
yours,[17] Jesus;
look,
eternal O[18]
eternal E[19]
Jesus
O eternal realm, eternal realm,
god of silence,
I honor you completely.
You are my place of rest,
child,
E S E S[20]
the E[21]
formless one existing among formless ones,
raising the person by whom you will purify me into your life,
according to your imperishable name.
So the sweet smell of life lies in me.
I have mixed it with water as a model for all the rulers,
that I may live with you in the peace of saints,
you who are forever
in truth truly.

---

17. Coptic *sou* (from Greek) may be so translated, or it may be left as glossolalia, "SOU."
18. Omega.
19. Epsilon. The numerical value of the letter epsilon is five; this may recall the realm of five in the Secret Book of John.
20. The meaning of these letters, if there is a rational meaning, is unknown. Böhlig and Wisse, eds., *Nag Hammadi Codices III,2 and IV,2*, p. 204, speculate that the letters could designate the heavenly figure Esephech, but this identification remains uncertain.
21. Epsilon, as above.

12

Thunder

T hunder (or Thunder: Perfect Mind) is a sacred text of paradox and antithesis, with few obvious characteristics of Jewish, Christian, or gnostic themes. However, gnostic ideas such as liberation from the material world, a pantheistic deity that permeates matter and life, and the promise of salvation of return distinguish it from traditional religious poems. Hence we may recognize gnostic and even Sethian themes in Thunder. The speaker is a woman, and while there are diverse views on her identity—appropriate in a riddle poem—we favor those who find in her a concealed Sophia, after her fall, carrying her spark into the world of body, what Bentley Layton calls "a manifestation of wisdom and Barbelo in gnostic myth."[1] However, her mystery is that one cannot know for certain who she is and whom she represents. In being that mystery she transcends sects.

George W. MacRae discerns the formal qualities and the transcendence of this poem:

> While the Jewish wisdom literature and the Isis aretalogies provide texts which are parallel in tone and style, the particular significance of the self-proclamations of *Thunder, Perfect Mind* may be found in their antithetical character. Antithesis and paradox may be used to proclaim the absolute transcendence of the

---

1. Layton, *Gnostic Scriptures*, p. 77.

224

revealer, whose greatness is incomprehensible and whose being is unfathomable.[2]

Thunder is a universal poem, a shout that is at once unique and yet has parallels in world literature ancient and modern. Commentators on Thunder have looked to Sanskrit, Egyptian, and Jewish religious literature to find equivalents for its pervasive use of oxymoron, antithesis, and paradox. However, it is not necessary to confine oneself to religious sources for precedents, since these rhetorical tropes are standard in classical and later literature, and their enunciation in the terms we still use today was established by Greek grammarians in hellenistic Alexandria on the basis of examples drawn from Greek poetry, from Sappho to Pindar. The author of Thunder wrote in Greek, and his poem follows the prosody of Greek verse. As an obscure imitator of Greek and Hebrew expression, the author reproduced the forms and breath of Pindar and the verbal élan of the biblical prophets.

Thunder is a strange book whose voice is that of a powerful, confessional Sophia figure who takes on the world with extraordinary vigor and piercing candor. She is not an aloof prophet or a cloistered sibyl, but an assertive woman engaged in all strata of human society. In the course of Thunder, the woman relentlessly contradicts herself: "What you see outdoors you see within you," or "I am speech undecipherable," or "I am below and they come up to me." And she shows no remorse for her dissenting ways. Although the author's sex is unknown, the female voice in the text speaks for herself, and as such is an early instance of complete female empowerment, without apology or compromise. She speaks a metaphysical tour de force, a sermon singing the self in which the woman is the universal paradigm. Her presence adds evidence to Elaine Pagels's persuasive assertion of women's freer role in gnosticism, which she documents in *The Gnostic Gospels*. What can be said with certainty is that the woman of Thunder represents a great woman's voice in antiquity.

The woman in Thunder prepares her "interior bread and mind." She has no shame in being seen anywhere provided that she follows her spiritual convictions, even if "cast down on the earth" and "lying on animal dung." She sternly abuses and demeans herself yet affirms herself. She is the disgraced and

---

2. In Robinson, ed., *The Nag Hammadi Library in English*, 1st ed., p. 271.

the grand being. She is whore and holy. Throwing us off stride, she claims to be the mother of her father. Finally, in her tractate of paradox, she reassures by announcing that she is the knowledge of her search. And crucially she of the perfect mind tells of the good reward for turning to her sumptuous spirit: "There they will find me and live, and they will not die again."

The paradoxical self-declaration of the speaker as wife and virgin, mother and daughter, and midwife, is paralleled in the text On the Origin of the World.

THUNDER[3]

I was sent out from the power
    and have come to you who study me
    and am found by you who seek me.
Look at me, you who study me,
    and you who hear, hear me.
You waiting for me, take me into yourselves.
Don't banish me from your vision.
Don't let hatred enter your voice against me
    or let anger enter your hearing.
In no place, in no time, be unknowing of me.
Be alert. Don't be ignorant of me.[4]

I am the first and the last.
I am the honored and scorned.
I am the whore and holy.
I am the wife and the virgin.
I am the mother and daughter.
I am the members of my mother
    and the barren one with many sons.
I have had a grand wedding
    and have not found a husband.
I am a midwife and do not give birth.

---

3. Thunder: Nag Hammadi Codex VI,2, pp. 13,1 to 21,32; translated from the Coptic by George W. MacRae in Robinson, ed., *Nag Hammadi Library in English,* rev. ed., pp. 297–303; revised in verse by Willis Barnstone.
4. Much of this language recalls the role of wisdom in Jewish wisdom literature.

I am the solace of my labor pains.
I am bride and groom,
    and my husband produced me.
I am the mother of my father
    and sister of my husband,
    and he is my offspring.
I am a slave of him who prepared me
    and ruler of my offspring.
He produced me earlier yet on my birthday.
He is my offspring to come,
    and from him is my power.
I am the staff of his power in his youth
    and he the rod of my old age,
    and whatever he wants happens to me.[5]
I am a silence incomprehensible
    and an idea remembered often.
I am the voice whose sound is manifold
    and word whose appearance is multiple.
I am the utterance of my name.

Why do you who hate me love me
    and hate those who love me?
You who deny me confess me,
    and you who confess me deny me.
You who tell the truth about me lie about me,
    and you who lie tell the truth.
You who know me,
    be ignorant of me, and those who have not known me,
    let them know me.

I am knowledge and ignorance.
I am shame and fearlessness.
I am shameless and ashamed.
I am strength and fear.
I am war and peace.
Hear what I say.
I am the disgraced and the grand being.

---

5. These paradoxical lines are paralleled in On the Origin of the World.

Consider my poverty and wealth.
Don't be arrogant when I am cast down on the earth,
   and you will find me in those who are to come.
Don't stare at me lying on a dung heap.
Don't run off and cast me away.
In the kingdoms you will find me.
Don't stare when I am cast with the disgraced
    in the most sordid places
    or laugh at me.
Don't throw me out among those violently slaughtered.
I am compassionate and cruel.

Be careful.
Don't hate my obedience
   or love my self-control.
When I am weak, don't forsake me
   or fear my power.
Why do you despise my fear
   and curse my pride?
I am a woman existing in every fear
   and in my strength when I tremble.
I am a woman, weak,
   and carefree in a pleasant place.
I am senseless and wise.

Why have you hated me in your counsels?
I will be silent among the silent
   and appear and speak.
Greeks, why do you hate me?
Because I am a barbarian among the barbarians?
I am the wisdom of Greeks and knowledge of barbarians.
I am the judgment of Greeks and barbarians.
My image is great in Egypt, and I have no image among the barbarians.
I am hated everywhere and loved everywhere.
I am called life[6] and you have called me death.

---

6. Zoe, Greek for "life," is the name for Eve in Genesis. She plays a leading role in the Secret Book of John and elsewhere.

I am called law and you have called me lawlessness.
I am one you pursued and seized.[7]
I am one you scattered and gathered together.
I am one before whom you are ashamed,
    and to me you are shameless.
I am the woman who attends no festival
    and whose festivals are many.
I am godless and one whose god is great.
I am one you studied and you scorn me.
I am unlettered and you learn from me.
I am one you despise and you study me.
I am one you hide from and you appear to me.
When you hide I show.
When you appear I hide. . . .

Take me into understanding from grief,
    and take me from understanding and grief.
Receive me into yourselves from other places
    ugly and destroyed.
And steal from the good even in their ugliness.
Out of shame take me to yourselves shamelessly.
Without shame and with shame, rebuke what is mine
    in you
    and come to me, you who know me
    and you who know my members,
    and make great ones among small first creatures.
Come to childhood
    and don't despise it, because it is small and tiny.
Don't turn away the great in parts from the small,
    for the small is known from the great.
Why do you curse and honor me?
You wound me and have mercy.
Don't separate me from the first you have known.
Don't cast out or turn away,
    turn away and not know. . . .

---

7. Eve is often described as being seized or raped in gnostic literature.

I know the first ones,
and those after them know me.
I am perfect mind and rest. . . .
I am the knowledge of my search,
the finding of those who look for me,
the command of those who ask about me,
the power of powers
in my knowledge of angels sent at my word,
and of gods in their seasons sent by my counsel,
and of spirits of all who exist with me
and of women who live in me.

I am one who is honored, praised, and scornfully despised.
I am peace, and war has come because of me.
I am alien[8] and citizen.
I am the substance and one without substance.

Those unconnected to me are unfamiliar with me,
and those in my substance know me.
Those close to me are ignorant of me,
and those far away have known me.
On the day I am close to you, you are far,
and on the day I am far, I am close to you.

I am . . . within.
I am . . . of natures.
I am . . . of created spirits,
the request of souls.
I am control and the uncontrollable.
I am union and dissolution.
I abide and dissolve.
I am below and they come up to me.
I am judgment and acquittal.
I am sinless,
and the root of sin comes from me.
I am lust outwardly, yet within me is control.

---

8. The reference to the alien recalls the Foreigner (Allogenes) and the concept of the alien or
stranger elsewhere in gnostic literature; see the Vision of the Foreigner in this volume.

I am hearing for all, and my speech is indecipherable.
I am an unspeaking mute
   and enormous in my many words.

Hear me in gentleness and discover me in roughness.
I am the woman crying out
   and cast upon the face of the earth.
I prepare bread and my mind within.
I am the knowledge of my name.
I am the one who cries out
   and I listen.
I appear . . . walk in . . . I am . . . the defense.
I am called truth and iniquity. . . .

You honor me and whisper against me.
You, the vanquished, judge those who vanquish you
   before they judge you,
      because in you the judge and partiality exist.
If you are condemned by one, who will acquit you?
If acquitted by him, who will arrest you?
What is in you is outside,
   and one who fashions you on the outside
   shapes you inside.[9]
   What you see outside you see within you.[10]
It is visible and your garment.
Hear me, hearers,
   and find out about my words, you who know me.
I am the hearing all can reach;
I am speech undecipherable.
I am the name of the sound
   and the sound of the name.
I am the sign of the letter
   and the designation of the division.
I . . . light . . . great power . . . will not move the name . . .
to the one who created me.

---

9. This statement is similar to Gospel of Thomas 22, 89.
10. This statement recalls Gospel of Thomas 3, on the kingdom, and the Gospel of Mary, on the human child.

I will speak his name.

Look at his words and all the writings completed.
Be alert, hearers and angels and those sent
    and you spirits arisen from the dead.
I alone exist and have no one to judge me.
Many pleasures exist in many sins,
    uncontrolled passions and disgraceful desires
    and brief pleasures
    embraced by people until they sober up
    and float up to their place of rest.
There they will find me and live, and they will not die again.

13

The Letter of Peter to Philip

The Letter of Peter to Philip is a short text that relates traditions about the Christian messengers (or apostles) and incorporates other revelatory materials in order to proclaim a message of gnostic wisdom. In the text, as in other Christian traditions, Peter is the leader of the messengers, and his letter to Philip underscores his authority. Here Philip is portrayed with features both of Philip the student in the New Testament gospels and of Philip the evangelist in the Acts of the Apostles.

The Letter of Peter to Philip calls to mind the New Testament Acts of the Apostles and the apocryphal Acts of the Apostles. In the present text, too, Peter and the other messengers are eating, talking, praying, going to temple, and teaching and healing together in the period following the suffering and death of Jesus. At the end of the present text, they disperse to preach and, perhaps, to write the four gospels.

As they gather together, Jesus appears as light and voice, and he answers their questions with enlightened knowledge. The revelation about the deficiency of the aeons, though abbreviated, summarizes the story of the fall of the mother as told in dramatic detail in the Secret Book of John. In the abbreviated story in the Letter of Peter to Philip the names are not given, and the anonymity of the characters in the drama is maintained. The revelation about the fullness of the divine rehearses themes much like those in the hymn to the word in the Gospel of John: the savior is the incarnate deity who travels incognito through this world and speaks with those who will listen. In particular there is one who listens, a prototypal listener, who was lacking but now is filled. Peter's sermon on the suffering of Jesus and of Christians is especially appropriate for the community of the Letter of Peter to Philip. This is an embattled group, which is fighting against the rulers. It is to struggling believers that Jesus is made to offer peace, and to promise joy, grace, and power.

The Letter of Peter to Philip was probably composed in Greek, most likely sometime in the second or third century, but at present exists only in Coptic. Where it was composed is unknown.

THE LETTER OF PETER TO PHILIP[1]

Peter,[2] messenger[3] of Jesus the anointed,[4] to Philip,[5] our beloved brother and our fellow messenger, and the brothers who are with you: greetings.

I want you to understand, our brother, that we received orders from our lord, the savior of the whole world, that we should come together to teach and preach concerning the salvation that was promised us by our lord Jesus the anointed. But you were separated from us, and you did not wish us to come together and learn how to orient ourselves that we might tell the good news.[6] So would it be agreeable to you, our brother, to come according to the orders of our god Jesus?

When Philip received and read this, he went to Peter, rejoicing with gladness.

Then Peter gathered the others. They went to the mountain called Olivet, where they used to gather with the blessed anointed one when he was in the body.

---

1. The Letter of Peter to Philip: Nag Hammadi Codex VIII,2, pp. 132,10 to 140,27; translated from the Coptic by Marvin Meyer. Another Coptic copy of this text has been announced by James M. Robinson and Stephen Emmel, but at present it remains unavailable.
2. As in the New Testament Acts of the Apostles, Peter is a leader of the messengers (or apostles).
3. Apostle.
4. Christ.
5. This portrait of Philip has features both of Philip the disciple in the New Testament gospels and of Philip the evangelist in the Acts of the Apostles.
6. That is, the gospel.

When the messengers came together and fell on their knees, they prayed in this way, saying,

Father, father, father of the light,
you who possess the incorruptions, hear us,
just as you have taken pleasure
in your holy child Jesus the anointed.
For he has become for us a luminary[7] in the darkness.
Yes, hear us.

And they resumed again and prayed, saying,

Child of life, child of immortality,
you who are in the light,
child, deathless anointed, our redeemer,
give us strength,
because they are searching for us to kill us.

Then a great light appeared, and the mountain shone from the vision of the one who appeared. And a voice called out to them, saying, "Listen to my words that I may speak to you. Why are you looking for me? I am Jesus the anointed, who is with you forever."

The messengers answered and said, "Lord, we would like to understand the deficiency of the realms[8] and their fullness. And how are we detained in this dwelling place? How have we come to this place? In what way shall we leave? How do we possess the authority of boldness? Why do the powers fight against us?"[9]

Then a voice called to them from the light, saying, "You bear witness that I have said all these things to you. But because of your unbelief I shall speak again.

THE DEFICIENCY OF THE AEONS

"To begin with, concerning the deficiency of the aeons, this is the deficiency. When the disobedience and the foolishness of the mother[10] appeared, without

---

7. Or "light, illuminator."
8. Aeons.
9. For other examples of such a list of questions, see the Secret Book of John, the Gospel of Truth, and the Book of Thomas.
10. The mother recalls mother Sophia and mother Eve in the Secret Book of John, Genesis, and other texts.

the command of the majesty of the father, she wanted to set up eternal realms. When she spoke, the arrogant one[11] followed. But when she left behind a portion, the arrogant one grabbed it, and it became a deficiency. This is the deficiency of the aeons.

"When the arrogant one took a portion, he sowed it. He placed powers and authorities over it, and he confined it within the mortal realms. All the powers of the world rejoiced that they had been brought forth. But they do not know the preexistent father, since they are strangers to him. Rather, he was given power, and they served him and praised him.

"But the arrogant one grew proud because of the praise of the powers. He was jealous and wanted to make an image in place of an image and a form in place of a form.[12] He assigned the powers within his authority to mold mortal bodies. And they came into being from a misrepresentation of the appearance.[13]

THE FULLNESS

"Concerning the fullness, it is I.[14] I was sent down in the body for the seed that had fallen away. And I came down to their mortal model. But they did not recognize me, thinking I was a mortal. I spoke with the one who is mine, and the one who is mine listened to me just as you also who have listened to me today. And I gave him authority to enter into the inheritance of his fatherhood. And I took him ... filled ... through his salvation. Since he was deficiency, he became fullness.

"Concerning the fact that you are being detained, it is because you are mine. When you strip yourselves of what is corruptible, you will become luminaries[15] in the midst of mortals.

"Concerning the fact that you will fight against the powers, it is because they do not have rest like you, since they do not want you saved."

---

11. Coptic *authades* (from Greek). The arrogance of the creator of this world is amply demonstrated in the Secret Book of John.

12. On the jealousy of the creator of this world, see the Secret Book of John ("I am a jealous god"). On "an image in place of an image and a form in place of a form," see Gospel of Thomas 22.

13. This description brings to mind the vision of the image of the human in the water in the Secret Book of John.

14. On this entire passage about the fullness see John 1.

15. Or "lights, illuminators."

FIGHTING THE RULERS

The messengers worshiped again, saying, "Lord, tell us, how shall we fight against the rulers, since the rulers are over us?"

A voice called out to them from the appearance, saying, "You must fight against them like this, for the rulers fight against the inner person. You must fight against them like this: come together and teach salvation in the world with a promise. And arm yourselves with my father's power, and express your prayer, and surely the father will help you, as he helped you by sending me.[16] Do not be afraid. I am with you forever, as I already said to you when I was in the body."[17]

Then came lightning and thunder from heaven, and what appeared to them there was taken up to heaven.

THE MESSENGERS RETURN TO JERUSALEM

The messengers thanked the lord with every praise, and they returned to Jerusalem.

Now, as they were going up, they spoke with each other on the way about the light that had appeared. And a statement was made about the lord. It was said, "If even our lord suffered, how much more are we to suffer?"

Peter answered, saying, "He suffered for us, and we must also suffer for our smallness."[18]

Then a voice called to them, saying, "I often told you that you must suffer. You must be brought to synagogues and governors so that you will suffer. But the one who will not suffer will not ... my father. ..."

And the messengers rejoiced greatly, and they went up to Jerusalem. They went up to the temple and taught salvation in the name of the lord Jesus the anointed. And they healed a crowd.

---

16. The battle is essentially spiritual. A spiritual battle is also described in Ephesians 6:10–20.
17. Partially restored; see Frederik Wisse in Sieber, ed., *Nag Hammadi Codex VIII*, 245.
18. Or "pettiness." Here smallness or pettiness is synonymous with deficiency. Jesus suffered because of human beings, and human beings suffer because of their own deficiencies, traceable to the transgression of the mother.

PETER PREACHES

Now, Peter opened his mouth and said to his students,[19] "When our lord Jesus was in the body, he revealed everything to us. He came down. My brothers, listen to my voice."

And he was filled with holy spirit and spoke in this way: "Our luminary[20] Jesus came down and was crucified. He wore a crown of thorns, was clothed in a purple robe, crucified upon a cross, and buried in a tomb. And he rose from the dead.

"My brothers, Jesus is a stranger to this suffering. But we are the ones who have suffered through the mother's transgression.[21] And for this reason he did everything like us. The lord Jesus, child of the father's immeasurable glory, is the author of our life.

"My brothers, let us not listen to these lawless ones and walk. . . ."

THE MESSENGERS DISPERSE TO PREACH

Peter assembled the others and said, "Our lord Jesus the anointed, author of our rest, give us a spirit of understanding, so we also may perform great deeds."

Then Peter and the other messengers saw and were filled with holy spirit. And each one performed healings. And they left to preach the lord Jesus.[22]

They gathered with their companions and greeted them, saying, "Amen."

Then Jesus appeared, saying to them, "Peace be with all of you and everyone who believes in my name. When you go, you will have joy and grace and power. Do not be afraid. Look, I am with you forever."

The messengers parted from each other with four words,[23] to preach. And they went in the power of Jesus, in peace.

---

19. Or "his fellow students." Either Peter has his own students, or he and the others together are students of Jesus.

20. Or "light, illuminator."

21. Sophia or Eve.

22. These lines are similar to the scene in which holy spirit is imparted in John 20; also see the Pentecost story in Acts of the Apostles 2.

23. Literally, "into four words," perhaps "with four messages" or "in four directions." This may be a reference to four gospels for the whole world. The point of the passage seems to be that the messengers are to preach a universal message of power.

14

The Gospel of Truth

The Gospel of Truth, a work of consummate artistry, is an early discourse on Christian gnostic mysticism and remains a key philosophical and literary document in the history of Valentinian gnostic speculation. Incorporating much of the technical language of Valentinian gnosticism, the Gospel of Truth presents its ideas in a nontechnical way as the proclamation of the meaning of Jesus for Valentinian Christians. This is a pivotal work, reinterpreting Jewish apocalyptic Christianity as Jewish gnostic Christianity. A deeply gnostic tractate, seminally influenced by Johannine literature, the Gospel of Truth maps a way of knowing the father through the word of gnosis, which is mystical knowledge.

Written in Greek in the mid-second century, between about 140 and 180 CE, the Gospel of Truth was found among the documents at Nag Hammadi in Egypt and exists in its totality in Coptic translation. In addition, Irenaeus refers to a Gospel of Truth read among Valentinians in his tract *Against Heresies* 3.11.9.

Scholars have advanced arguments for assigning the work to Valentinos himself, rather than to one of his students. Valentinos, a mediator between gnosticized and traditional Christianity, was born in Alexandria and from about 135 practiced his gnostic interpretation of Christianity in Rome. Although Valentinians were attacked by traditional Christians for their mythic theology as early as 160, they did not initially separate on their own from Christians, and some held ecclesiastical ranks in the Roman church. They called themselves the students of Christ, were largely from the middle and lower classes, and resembled other Christians in many respects.

The Valentinians met privately and later in churches, as students guided by scholars. Many of their leaders' were women, for whom gnostic Christianity held out positions as leaders and teachers not available in the official church. The Valentinians saw their mythic theologies as allegorical commentaries on the Hebrew Bible and Christian scripture, but their opponents saw them as extravagant heresies. In Valentinian gnosticism Christ and the word (logos) are eternal beings (aeons), and Jesus is brought forth to bring salvation and enlightenment here below. This recalls the logos made flesh in the Gospel of John. But beyond some common interpretations of the life of Christ, their beliefs and documents clashed. One cannot read the Valentinian documents without concluding that gnosticism was different, and not just allegorically, from mainstream Christianity. The Valentinians offered a whole new scheme of salvation through knowledge, and an unknowable father in the heavenly realm of light, which is the pleroma or fullness. Traditional Christians were right to suspect otherness in the Valentinians.

The Gospel of Truth begins with a Jewish-Christian enunciation of joy in the good news of the gospel, which brings hope to those who would seek the father. The following lines describe the generation of ignorance and error, which derives ultimately from the father. Here ignorance, terror, and error reside in the pleroma, which resides in the father. It is clear that this represents a crisis in the pleroma, site of the thirty aeons of light, but the text suggests that the father is neither responsible for this error nor diminished in his powers. In the contrast, the paradox, between the error in the pleroma and the goodness of the father we have perhaps the most fascinating aspect of this sermon of truth. Somehow, from the very realm of the good father, error comes. Herein lies the mystery, for gnostics, of the goodness of the divine and the reality of evil in the world.

This section ends with the appearance and death of Jesus the anointed, whose fate at the hands of "error" is described in an amazing passage that in a few words sets Jewish-Christian orthodoxy apart from gnosticism:

> He was nailed to a tree. He became a fruit of the knowledge of the father. He did not, however, destroy them because they ate of it. He rather caused those who ate of it to be joyful because of this discovery.

This passage reverses the fundamental biblical notion that knowledge is sin. It dissolves the original stricture against obtaining knowledge by eating of its fruit, for which disobedience came a punishment of shame, sensuality, and death. Rather, here in the Gospel of Truth the fruit of knowledge is a discovery bringing joy. It signifies that one finds god in oneself, that the fog of error and terror is gone, and that the nightmare of darkness is exchanged for an eternal heavenly day. Therein is stated the essence of gnosis: the word of knowledge redeems rather than kills.

There follows an idealized, moving portrait of the son, of whom the father is not jealous, and who utters no threat of gnashing teeth or hell and brimstone to fellow Jews who do not accept that he is the messiah. In addition to being a quiet guide of sheep gone astray, the implied Jesus also teaches a portrait of the father's face. We soon realize that the father, not the son, is the center of the sermon, and he is personified and endowed with utter sweetness.

The return of the awakened ones is then described in the superb poetry of gnosticism:

> Until the moment when they who are passing through all these things . . . awaken, they see nothing because the dreams were nothing. It is thus that they who cast ignorance from them like sleep do not consider it to be anything, nor regard its properties to be something real, but they renounce them like a dream in the night and they consider the knowledge of the father to be the dawn. It is thus that each has acted, as if asleep, during the time of ignorance, and thus a person comes to understand, as if awakening. And happy is one who comes to himself and awakens. Indeed, blessings on one who has opened the eyes of the blind.

God's face is sweet and his will is good. God gives his aroma to the light, which the spirit smells. God's presence is deeply joyous and sensual: "He brought the warm fullness of love, so that the cold may not return, but the unity of the perfect thought may prevail." The agent of human return is the son. The father exists in the saved and they exist in the father. Such is the place of the blessed: "They are in that true and eternal life and speak of the perfect light filled with the seed of the father, and which is in his heart and in the fullness."

The Gospel of Truth is an exhortation of truth, a sermon of hope. We hear again and again the cheerful, intellectual message of knowledge that dissolves darkness:

> What, then, is that which he wants such a one to think? "I am like the shadows and phantoms of the night." When morning comes, this one knows that the fear that had been experienced was nothing.

THE GOSPEL OF TRUTH[1]

JOY TO THOSE WHO KNOW THE FATHER

The gospel of truth is joy for those who have received from the father of truth the grace of knowing him by the power of the word,[2] who has come from the fullness[3] and who is in the thought and the mind of the father. This is the one who is called the savior, since that is the name of the work that he must do for the redemption of those who have not known the father. For the name of the gospel is the revelation of hope, since that is the discovery of those who seek him, because the realm of all sought him from whom it came. You see, all was inside of him, that illimitable, inconceivable one, who is better than every thought.

IGNORANCE OF THE FATHER BRINGS ERROR

This ignorance of the father brought about terror and fear.[4] And terror became dense like a fog, so no one was able to see. Because of this, error[5] became strong. But she worked on her material substance[6] vainly, because she did not know the truth. She assumed a fashioned figure while she was preparing, in power and in beauty, the substitute for truth.

This, then, was not a humiliation for the illimitable, inconceivable one. For they were as nothing, this terror and this forgetfulness and this figure of falsehood, whereas established truth is unchanging, unperturbed, and completely beautiful.

For this reason, do not take error too seriously.

Since error had no root, she was in a fog regarding the father. She was preparing works and forgetfulnesses and fears in order, by these means, to

---

1. The Gospel of Truth: Nag Hammadi Codex I, pp. 16,31 to 43,24, along with passages from Nag Hammadi Codex XII; translated by Robert M. Grant (*Gnosticism*, 146–61) and by Harold W. Attridge and George W. Mac Rae (Robinson, ed., *Nag Hammadi Library in English*, rev. ed., 40–51); revised by Willis Barnstone and Marvin Meyer.
2. See John 1:1.
3. *Pleroma*, here and elsewhere in the text.
4. It is ignorance rather than sin that is the source of human problems, such as terror and fear.
5. Error is personified and is feminine in gender. The role of error may be compared to that of wisdom, Sophia, or even Yaldabaoth the demiurge.
6. The material world.

beguile those of the middle[7] and to make them captive. The forgetfulness of error was not revealed. It did not become light beside the father. Forgetfulness did not exist with the father, although it existed because of him.[8] What exists in him is knowledge, which was revealed so that forgetfulness might be destroyed and that the father might be known. Since forgetfulness existed because the father was not known, if the father comes to be known, from that moment on forgetfulness will cease to exist.

JESUS IS THE FRUIT OF KNOWLEDGE

That is the gospel of him whom they seek, which he has revealed to the perfect through the mercies of the father as the hidden mystery, Jesus the anointed.[9] Through him he enlightened those who were in darkness because of forgetfulness. He enlightened them and gave them a path. And that path is the truth that he taught them.[10] For this reason error was angry with him, so she persecuted him. She was distressed by him, and she was made powerless. He was nailed to a tree.[11] He became a fruit of the knowledge of the father. He did not, however, destroy them because they ate of it. He rather caused those who ate of it to be joyful because of this discovery.

And as for him, he found them in himself, and they found him in themselves, that illimitable, inconceivable one, that perfect father who made all, in whom the realm of all is, and whom the realm of all lacks, since he retained in himself their perfection, which he had not given to all.[12] The father was not jealous. What jealousy, indeed, is there between him and his members? For, even if the eternal being had received their[13] perfection, they would not have been able to approach the perfection of the father, because he retained their perfection in himself, giving it to them as a way to return to him and as a knowledge unique in perfection. He is the one who set all in order and in

---

7. Possibly psychical people who, as ordinary Christians, linger in the world between the spiritual and the physical.

8. Or "if it existed, then (it existed) because of him." Bentley Layton, *Gnostic Scriptures*, 254, translates this difficult passage as follows: "and surely then not because of him!"

9. Christ.

10. See John 14:6.

11. This reference to the tree recalls both the cross on which Christ was crucified and the tree of the knowledge of good and evil (in Genesis 2:17 and gnostic texts).

12. Here and elsewhere in this and other gnostic texts, all (or, the all) can refer to the realm of all the powers, the pleroma.

13. That is, the members'.

whom all existed and whom all lacked. As one of whom some have no knowledge, he wants them to know him and love him. What did they lack, if not the knowledge of the father?[14]

JESUS AS QUIET GUIDE

Jesus became a guide, quiet and at leisure. In the middle of a school he came and spoke the word, as a teacher. Those who were wise in their own estimation came to put him to the test. But he discredited them as empty-headed people. They hated him because they really were not wise. After all these came also the little children, those who possess the knowledge of the father. When they became strong they were taught the aspects of the father's face. They came to know and they were known. They were glorified and they gave glory.

THE LIVING BOOK IN THE HEART OF THE LITTLE CHILDREN

In their heart, the living book of the living was manifest, the book that was written in the thought and in the mind of the father and, from before the foundation of all, is in that incomprehensible part of him.[15]

This is the book that no one found possible to take, since it was reserved for him who will take it and be slain. No one could appear among those who believed in salvation as long as that book had not appeared. For this reason, the compassionate, faithful Jesus was patient in his sufferings until he took that book, since he knew that his death meant life for many.[16] Just as in the case of a will that has not yet been opened, the fortune of the deceased master of the house is hidden, so also in the case of all that had been hidden as long as the father of all was invisible and unique in himself, in whom every space has its source. For this reason Jesus appeared. He put on that book. He was nailed to a cross. He affixed the edict of the father to the cross.

Oh, such great teaching! He abases himself even unto death, though he is clothed in eternal life. Having divested himself of these perishable rags,[17] he

---

14. This lack is the lack of absolute perfection and transcendence found only in the perfect father, who makes it known by revealing it.
15. In the book of life the knowledge of the father is revealed.
16. See Hebrews 2:17; Mark 10:45; 1 Timothy 2:6.
17. The body.

clothed himself in incorruptibility, which no one could possibly take from him. Having entered into the empty territory of fears, he passed before those who were stripped by forgetfulness, being both knowledge and perfection, proclaiming the things that are in the heart of the father, so that he became the wisdom of those who have received instruction. But those who are to be taught, the living who are inscribed in the book of the living, learn for themselves, receiving instructions from the father, turning to him again.[18]

Since the perfection of all is in the father, it is necessary for all to ascend to him. Therefore, if one has knowledge, he gets what belongs to him and draws it to himself. For one who is ignorant is deficient, and it is a great deficiency, since he lacks that which will make him perfect. Since the perfection of all is in the father, it is necessary for all to ascend to him and for each one to get the things that are his. He wrote these things first, having prepared them to be given to those who came from him.

THE FATHER CALLING THOSE WHO HAVE KNOWLEDGE

Those whose names he knew first were called last, so that the one who has knowledge is one whose name the father has pronounced.[19] For one whose name has not been spoken is ignorant. Indeed, how shall one hear if a name has not been uttered? For whoever remains ignorant until the end is a creature of forgetfulness and will perish with it. If this is not so, why have these wretches no name, why have they no voice? Hence, whoever has knowledge is from above. If called, that person hears, replies, and turns toward him who called. That person ascends to him and knows how he is called. Having knowledge, that person does the will of him who called. That person desires to please him, finds rest,[20] and receives a certain name. Those who thus are going to have knowledge know whence they came and whither they are going. They know it as someone who, having become intoxicated, has turned from his drunkenness and, having come to himself, has restored what is his own.[21]

---

18. According to the Gospel of Truth, the death of Jesus reveals the truth of the father. It does not save from sin.

19. The call of the father, the utterance of the name of a person, brings knowledge and salvation.

20. For gnostics rest is bliss, especially the final bliss of the union of self with the divine, as in Gospel of Thomas 2 (Greek version), the Secret Book of John, and throughout the Gospel of Truth.

21. Returning to sobriety from drunkenness is a common gnostic image for returning to knowledge from ignorance.

He has turned many from error. He went before them to their own places, from which they departed when they erred because of the depth[22] of him who surrounds every place, whereas there is nothing that surrounds him. It was a great wonder that they were in the father without knowing him and that they were able to leave on their own, since they were not able to contain him and know him in whom they were, for indeed his will had not come forth from him. For he revealed it as a knowledge with which all its emanations agree, namely, the knowledge of the living book that he revealed to the eternal beings at last as his letters, displaying to them that these are not merely vowels or consonants, so that one may read them and think of something void of meaning. On the contrary, they are letters that convey the truth. They are pronounced only when they are known. Each letter is a perfect truth like a perfect book, for they are letters written by the hand of the unity, since the father wrote them for the eternal beings, so that they by means of his letters might come to know the father. [23]

THE FATHER'S SON IS JESUS OF UTMOST SWEETNESS

His wisdom contemplates the word,
his teaching expresses it,
his knowledge has revealed it,
his honor is a crown upon it,
his joy agrees with it,
his glory has exalted it,
his image has revealed it,
his rest has received it,
his love has embodied it,
his trust has embraced it.

Thus the word of the father goes forth into all, being the fruit of his heart and expression of his will. It supports all. It chooses them and also takes the character of all and purifies them, causing them to return to the father, to the

---

22. "Depth" refers to the divine depth, the first aeon, from which the pleroma emanates, in Valentinian thought.
23. The living book of the father communicates eternal truth. Truth is also an aeon in the Valentinian pleroma.

mother, Jesus of the utmost sweetness.[24] The father opens his bosom, and his bosom is the holy spirit. He reveals his hidden self, which is his son, so that through the compassion of the father the eternal beings may know him, end their wearying search for the father, and rest themselves in him, knowing that this is rest. After he had filled what was incomplete, he did away with its form. The form of that which was incomplete is the world, which it served.

For where there is envy and strife, there is an incompleteness;[25] but where there is unity, there is completeness. Since this incompleteness came about because they did not know the father, from the moment when they know the father, incompleteness will cease to exist. As one's ignorance disappears when one gains knowledge, and as darkness disappears when light appears, so also incompleteness is eliminated by completeness. Certainly, from that moment on, form is no longer manifest but will be dissolved in fusion with unity. Now their works lie scattered. In time unity will make the spaces complete. By means of unity each one will understand himself. By means of knowledge one will purify himself from multiplicity into unity, devouring matter within himself like fire and darkness by light, death by life.

BREAKING DEFECTIVE DISHES WHEN MOVING

Certainly, if these things have happened to each one of us, it is fitting for us, surely, to think about all so that the house may be holy and silent for unity. Like people who have moved from a house, if they have some dishes around that are not good, they are broken. Nevertheless, the householder does not suffer a loss but rejoices, for in the place of these defective dishes there are those that are completely perfect. For this is the judgment that has come from above and that has judged every person, a drawn two-edged sword cutting on this side and that.[26] When the word appeared, who is in the heart of those who pronounce it—it was not merely a sound but has become a body—a great disturbance occurred among the dishes, for some were emptied, others filled; some were provided for, others were removed; some were purified, still others were broken. All the spaces were shaken and disturbed for they had no composure nor stability. Error was disturbed, not knowing what she should do.

---

24. See 1 Peter 2:2–3.
25. Or "lack," "deficiency." What is incomplete is often specified, in gnostic thought, as the antithesis of fullness (the pleroma).
26. Descriptions of two-edged swords occur in Philo of Alexandria and the New Testament.

She was troubled, she lamented, she was beside herself because she did not know anything. When knowledge, which is the abolishment of error, approached her with all her emanations, error was empty, since there was nothing in her. Truth appeared; all its emanations recognized it. They greeted the father in truth with a power which is complete and which joins them with the father.

TRUTH IS THE MOUTH OF THE FATHER

Each one loves truth because truth is the mouth of the father. His tongue is the holy spirit. Whoever touches truth touches the mouth of the father by his tongue at the time when one will receive the holy spirit.

This is the manifestation of the father and his revelation to his eternal beings. He revealed what is hidden in him and explained it. For who is it who exists if it is not the father himself? All the spaces are his emanations. They knew that they stem from him as children from a perfect man. They knew that they had not yet received form, nor had they yet received a name, every one of which the father produces. If they at that time receive the form of his knowledge, though they are truly in him, they do not know him.[27] But the father is perfect. He knows every space that is within him. If he pleases,[28] he reveals anyone whom he desires by giving him a form and by giving him a name; and he does give a name and cause to come into being. Those who do not yet exist are ignorant of him who created them. I do not say, then, that those who do not yet exist are nothing.[29] But they are in him who will desire that they exist when he pleases, like an event that is going to happen. On the one hand, he knows, before anything is revealed, what he will produce. On the other hand, the fruit that has not yet been revealed does not know anything nor is anything either. Thus each space that, on its part, is in the father comes from the existent one, who, on his part, has established it from the nonexistent. For whoever has no root has no fruit, but although thinking, "I have come into being," that one will perish. For this reason, whoever does not exist at all will never exist.

---

27. Layton, *Gnostic Scriptures*, 258, punctuates differently. Thus the text could read as follows: "It is when they receive the form of his knowledge that the father produces them. Otherwise, though they are within him, they do not know him."

28. Or "If he wills."

29. That is, they have potential if not actual existence. Here the author of the text, perhaps Valentinos, is writing in the first person singular.

WAKING UP AND COMING TO KNOWLEDGE

What, then, is that which he[30] wants such a one to think? "I am like the shadows and phantoms of the night." When morning comes,[31] this one knows that the fear that had been experienced was nothing.

Thus they were ignorant of the father; he is the one whom they did not see. Since there had been fear and confusion and a lack of confidence and double-mindedness and division, there were many illusions that were conceived by them,[32] as well as empty ignorance—as if they were fast asleep and found themselves a prey to troubled dreams.[33]

Either they are fleeing somewhere, or they lack strength to escape when pursued. They are involved in inflicting blows, or they themselves receive bruises. They are falling from high places, or they fly through the air with no wings at all. Other times, it is as if certain people were trying to kill them, even though there is no one pursuing them; or they themselves are killing those beside them, and they are stained by their blood. Until the moment when they who are passing through all these things—I mean they who have experienced all these confusions—awaken, they see nothing because the dreams were nothing. It is thus that they who cast ignorance from them like sleep do not consider it to be anything, nor regard its properties to be something real, but they renounce them like a dream in the night and they consider the knowledge of the father to be the dawn.[34] It is thus that each one has acted, as if asleep, during the time of ignorance, and thus a person comes to understand, as if awakening. And happy is the one who comes to himself and awakens. Indeed, blessings on one who has opened the eyes of the blind.[35]

The spirit came to this person in haste when the person was awakened. Having given its hand to the one lying prone on the ground, it placed him firmly on his feet, for he had not yet stood up.[36] This gave them the means of knowing the knowledge of the father and the revelation of his son. For when

---

30. The father.
31. Or "When the light shines," that is, the light of enlightenment, revelation, and knowledge.
32. Or "done by them."
33. Descriptions of the troubled dreams and nightmares follow.
34. This is how one awakens to gnosis.
35. Matthew 11:5; Luke 7:21–22; John 9: 11:37. Here the imagery suggests coming to clarity of vision regarding the father.
36. This description resembles gnostic stories (for example, in the Secret Book of John) of Adam lying on the ground and being raised onto his feet by means of divine breath.

they saw it and listened to it, he permitted them to take a taste of and to smell and to grasp the beloved son.

THE SON REVEALS THE WORD OF THE FATHER

The son[37] appeared, informing them of the father, the illimitable one. He inspired them with that which is in the mind, while doing his will. Many received the light and turned toward him. But material people[38] were alien to him and did not discern his appearance nor recognize him. For he came in the likeness of flesh and nothing blocked his way because what is incorruptible is irresistible.[39] Moreover, while saying new things, speaking about what is in the heart of the father, he proclaimed the faultless word. Light spoke through his mouth, and his voice brought forth life. He gave them thought and understanding and mercy and salvation, and the spirit of strength derived from the infinity and sweetness of the father. He caused punishments and scourgings to cease, for it was they that caused many in need of mercy to stray from him in error and in chains—and he mightily destroyed them and derided them with knowledge. He became a path for those who went astray and knowledge for those who were ignorant, a discovery for those who sought, and a support for those who tremble, a purity for those who were defiled.

THE SON IS THE SHEPHERD OF
THE ONE LOST SHEEP

He is the shepherd who left behind the ninety-nine sheep that had not strayed and went in search of that one which was lost.[40] He rejoiced when he had found it. For ninety-nine is a number expressed with the left hand. The moment he finds the one, however, the whole number is transferred to the right hand.[41] Thus it is with him who lacks the one, that is, the entire right hand, which attracts that in which it is deficient, seizes it from the left side, and

---

37. This is the beloved son, as mediator.
38. Possibly material or earthly people, who, according to Valentinian thought, derive from and belong to the world of matter.
39. The portrayal of the beloved son in this paragraph resembles the portrayal of the logos incarnate in Jesus according to the Gospel of John, especially chapter 1.
40. Matthew 18:12–14; Luke 15:4–7; Gospel of Thomas 107.
41. In the Roman system of counting on the fingers, the numbers one to ninety-nine were counted on the left hand, and the number one hundred entailed switching to the right. In Valentinian thought those of the right are psychical, people of soul, and those of the left are material, people of flesh.

transfers it to the right. In this way, then, the number becomes one hundred. This is the symbol of the sound of the numbers. It is the father.[42]

He labored even on the Sabbath for the sheep that he found fallen into the pit. He saved the life of that sheep, bringing it up from the pit that you may understand fully what that Sabbath is, you who are the children of the understanding of the heart.[43] It is a day in which it is not fitting that salvation be idle, so that you may speak of that heavenly day that has no night and of the sun that does not set because it is perfect. Say then in your heart that you are this perfect day and that in you lives the light that does not fail.

PUTTING KNOWLEDGE INTO PRACTICE

Speak concerning the truth to those who seek it and of knowledge to those who, in their error, have committed sins.[44] Make sure-footed those who stumble, and stretch forth your hands to the sick. Nourish the hungry, and set at ease those who are troubled. Raise up and awaken those who sleep. You are this understanding that seizes you.[45] If the strong follow this course, they are even stronger. Turn your attention to yourselves. Do not be concerned with other things, namely, that which you have cast forth from yourselves, that which you have dismissed. Do not return to them to eat them. Do not be moth-eaten. Do not be worm-eaten, for you have already shaken it off. Do not be a place of the devil, for you have already destroyed him. Do not strengthen your last obstacles, because that is reprehensible. For the lawless one is nothing. He harms himself more than the law. For that one does his works because he is a lawless person. But this one, because he is a righteous person, does his works among others. Do the will of the father, then, for you are from him.

THE SWEETNESS OF THE FATHER

For the father is sweet and his will is good. He knows the things that are yours, so that you may rest yourselves in them. For by the fruits one knows the things

---

42. Bentley Layton takes the reference to the father with the next clause: "It is the father who labored even on the Sabbath" (*Gnostic Scriptures*, 260).
43. Or "you who possess full understanding," but the metaphor has more levels and is poetic.
44. The words of exhortation in this paragraph recall similar words throughout early Christian (and other) literature. The helpfulness that is called for may be understood in a literal or a metaphorical way. For example, the hunger to be satisfied may be physical hunger or spiritual hunger.
45. Or, more abstractly, "encourages."

that are yours,[46] that they are the children of the father, and one knows his aroma, that you originate from the grace of his countenance. For this reason, the father loves his aroma; and it manifests itself in every place; and when it is mixed with matter, he gives his aroma to the light; and into his rest he causes it to ascend in every form and in every sound. For it is not ears that smell the aroma, but it is the spirit that possesses the sense of smell and draws it for itself to itself and sinks into the aroma of the father. Thus the spirit cares for it and takes it to the place from which it has come, the first aroma, which has grown cold. It is in a psychical form, resembling cold water[47] that has sunk into soil that is not hard, of which those who see it think, "It is earth." Afterward, it evaporates if a breath of wind draws it, and it becomes warm. The cold aromas, then, are from division. For this reason, faith came and destroyed division and brought the warm fullness of love, so that the cold may not return, but the unity of perfect thought may prevail.[48]

THE FATHER RESTORES DEFICIENCY WITH FULLNESS

This is the word of the gospel about finding the fullness for those who wait for the salvation that comes from above. When their hope, for which they are waiting, is waiting—they whose likeness is the light in which there is no shadow—then at that time the fullness is about to come. The deficiency of matter, however, is not because of the infinity of the father, who came to give time to deficiency. In fact, it is not right to say that the incorruptible one will come in this manner. The depth of the father is profound, and the thought of error is not with him. It is a matter of falling down and a matter of being readily set upright at the discovery of the one who has come to what he would bring back.[49]

This bringing back is called repentance. For this reason, incorruption has breathed. It followed one who has sinned, in order that he may find rest. Forgiveness is that which remains for the light in the deficiency, the word of the fullness. For the doctor hurries to the place where there is sickness, because

---

46. Matthew 7:16; 12:33; Luke 6:44.
47. The author is employing a pun (in Greek) by comparing *psyche* (soul, psychical form) and *psychos* (cold).
48. The sweetness of the father, having grown cold, is restored to the warmth of love.
49. The translation is difficult here, but it seems to mean that repentance is the discovery of what may be brought back to heal a person, namely, knowledge.

that is the doctor's wish. The sick person is in a deficient condition but does not hide, because the doctor possesses what the patient lacks. In this manner the deficiency is filled by the fullness, which has no deficiency, and which was given in order to fill the one deficient, so that the person may receive grace. For while deficient, this person had no grace. Because of this a diminishing occurred where there is no grace. When the diminished part was restored, the person in need revealed himself as fullness. This is what it means to find the light of truth that has shone toward the person: it is unchangeable.

ANOINTING THE CHOSEN WITH THE FATHER'S MERCY

For this reason they who have been troubled speak about Christ[50] in their midst so that they may receive restoration and he may anoint them with the ointment. The ointment is the pity of the father, who will have mercy on them. But those whom he has anointed are those who are perfect. For filled vessels are usually coated with sealing wax.[51] But when the coating is ruined, the vessel may leak, and the cause of its defect is the lack of coating. For then a breath of wind and the power that it has can make it evaporate. But from the jar that is without defect no seal is removed, nor does it leak. But what it lacks is filled again by the perfect father.

The father is good. He knows his plantings because he is the one who has planted them in his paradise. And his paradise is his place of rest.

THE FATHER IS BEGINNING AND END

Paradise is the perfection in the thought of the father, and the plants are the words of his reflection. Each one of his words is the work of his will alone, in the revelation of his word. Since they were in the depth of his mind, the word,[52] who was the first to come forth, caused them to appear, along with an intellect that speaks the unique word by means of a silent grace. It was called thought, since they were in it before becoming manifest.[53] It happened, then,

---

50. The anointed.
51. The suggestion of this translation comes from Layton, *Gnostic Scriptures*, 262.
52. *Logos.*
53. This meditation rehearses details of the emergence of the pleroma from the divine depth in Valentinian thought. Depth and thought are the first two Valentinian aeons; thought is also called grace and silence.

that the word was the first to come forth at the moment pleasing to the will of him who desired it; and it is in the will that the father is at rest and with which he is pleased. Nothing happens without him, nor does anything occur without the will of the father. But his will is incomprehensible. His will is his footstep,[54] but no one can know it, nor is it possible for them to concentrate on it in order to possess it. But that which he wishes takes place at the moment he wishes it—even if the view does not please people before god: it is the father's will. For the father knows the beginning of them all as well as their end. For when their end arrives, he will greet them. The end, you see, is the recognition of him who is hidden, that is, the father, from whom the beginning came forth and to whom will return all who have come from him. For they were made manifest for the glory and the joy of his name.

THE SON IS THE NAME AND REVELATION OF THE FATHER

The name of the father is the son. It is he who, in the beginning, gave a name to him who came from him, while he remained the same, and he conceived him as a son. He gave him his name, which belonged to him—he, the father, who possesses everything that exists around him. He possesses the name; he has the son. It is possible for the son to be seen. The name, however, is invisible, for it alone is the mystery of the invisible about to come to ears completely filled with it through the father's agency. Moreover, as for the father, his name is not pronounced but is revealed through a son. Thus, then, the name is great.[55]

Who, then, has been able to pronounce a name for him, this great name, except him alone to whom the name belongs and the children of the name, in whom the name of the father is at rest, and who themselves in turn are at rest in his name, since the father has no beginning?[56] It is he alone who conceived it for himself as a name, in the beginning before he had created the eternal beings, that the name of the father should be supreme over them—that is, the true name, which is secure by his authority and by his perfect power. For the name is not drawn from lexicons, nor is his name derived from common name-giving. It is invisible. The father alone gave the son a name, because he alone saw him and because he alone was capable of giving him a name. For

---

54. "Footstep" here carries the sense of identifying him, marking him.
55. The name of the father is invisible, ineffable.
56. In the sense that the father has always been.

he who does not exist has no name. For what name would one give him who did not exist? Nevertheless, he who exists exists also with his name, and he alone knows it, and to him alone the father gave a name. He is the father, his name is the son. He did not, therefore, keep it secretly hidden, but it came into existence, and the son himself disclosed the name. The name, then, is that of the father, just as the name of the father is the beloved son. For otherwise, where would he find a name except from the father? But someone will probably say to a friend, "Who would give a name to someone who existed before himself, as if, indeed, children did not receive their name from one of those who gave them birth?"

Above all, then, it is fitting for us to think this point over: what is the name? This is the true name, the name that came from the father, for it is he who owns the name. He did not, you see, get the name on loan, as in the case of others, who receive names that are made up. This is the proper name. There is no one else to whom he has given it. It remained unnamed, unuttered, till the moment when he who is perfect pronounced it himself; and it was he alone who was able to pronounce his name and to see it. When it pleased the father, then, that his son should be his pronounced name, and when he who has come from the depth disclosed this name, he divulged what was hidden, because he knew that the father was absolute goodness. For this reason, indeed, the father brought this particular one forth, that he might speak concerning the realm and his place of rest from which he had come forth, and that he might glorify the fullness, the greatness of his name and the sweetness of the father.

THE PLACE OF THE BLESSED

Each one will speak concerning the place from which they have come forth, and to the region from which they received their essential being they will hasten to return once again and receive from that place, the place where they stood before, and they will taste of that place, be nourished, and grow. And their own place of rest is their fullness.[57] All the emanations from the father, therefore, are fullnesses, and all his emanations have their roots in the one who caused them all to grow from himself. He assigned their destinies. They, then, became manifest individually that they might be perfected in their own thought, for that place to which they extend their thought is their root, which

---

57. Or, "And his own place of rest is his fullness," with reference to the father.

lifts them upward through all heights to the father. They reach his head, which is rest for them, and they remain there near to it as though to say that they have touched his face by means of embraces. But they do not make this plain. For neither have they exalted themselves nor have they diminished the glory of the father, nor have they thought of him as small, nor bitter, nor angry, but as absolutely good, unperturbed, sweet, knowing all the spaces before they came into existence and having no need of instruction.

Such are they who possess from above something of this immeasurable greatness, as they strain toward that unique and perfect One who exists there for them.[58] And they do not go down to Hades.[59] They have neither envy nor moaning, nor is death in them. But they rest in him who rests, without wearying themselves or becoming confused about truth. But they, indeed, are the truth, and the father is in them, and they are in the father, since they are perfect, inseparable from him who is truly good. They lack nothing in any way, but they are given rest and are refreshed by the spirit. And they listen to their root; they are busy with concerns in which one will find his root, and one will suffer no loss to his soul.[60]

Such is the place of the blessed; this is their place. As for the others, then, may they know, in their place, that it does not suit me, after having been in the place of rest, to say anything more.[61] It is there I shall dwell in order to devote myself, at all times, to the father of all and the true friends,[62] those upon whom the love of the father is lavished, and in whose midst nothing of him is lacking. It is they who manifest themselves truly, since they are in that true and eternal life and speak of the perfect light filled with the seed of the father, which is in his heart and in the fullness, while his spirit rejoices in it and glorifies him in whom it was, because the father is good. And his children are perfect and worthy of his name, because he is the father. Children of this kind are those whom he loves.[63]

---

58. Or "who is a mother to them."
59. They do not die.
60. The root of salvation is also discussed in other gnostic texts, including the hymn of the savior at the conclusion of the Secret Book of John.
61. The author has already realized something of the bliss of the place of rest.
62. Literally, "true brothers."
63. These are the Valentinians. The references to the blessed of the father, the true friends (or brothers), the seed of the father, designate in a particular way the spiritual people.

15

The Gospel of Philip

The Gospel of Philip is not a traditional gospel with good news on the life and death of Jesus; rather, it is an anthology of Christian gnostic aphorisms, parables, narrative dialogues, and sayings of Jesus, which have the quality of gnomic poetry:

Winter is the world, summer the other realm.
It is wrong to pray in winter.

The pieces, strung together as a sacramental catechesis, are short, and they may be taken from larger texts that have not survived. Separations in the texts vary according to scholarly edition, but they are, by content, largely self-evident. The book is pseudepigraphically attributed to the messenger Philip, who is mentioned by name only once, and this is certainly not a work in any way connected with Philip. Here, as in other apocryphal works, it is Philip who informs us that Joseph was the carpenter who made the cross on which his son Jesus was hung.

Unlike many gnostic texts, this eclectic book contains patches of gnostic tale, but it does not tell or invent any extensive myth. Although it contains no single long poem or narration, the work has, despite its eccentric order, a cumulative strength of insight, wit, and aphoristic incision. It is strongest when it brings image, message, and metaphysical tinkering together in short, accomplished pieces as in this baptismal catechism:

> God is a dyer.
> Good dyes, true dyes, dissolve into things
> dyed in them.
> So too for things god has dyed.
> His dyes are imperishable because of their colors.
> What god dips he dips in water.

Only at the end are some themes developed at length.

The Gospel of Philip contains a gnostic exegesis of some New Testament passages; deals with Valentinian notions of life, death, and resurrection, and flesh and spirit; and centers on one side of Christian tradition, the sacraments. The sacraments include baptism, chrism (a form of anointing with olive oil), the eucharist, redemption, and the bridal chamber. Originally Adam and Eve were joined as an androgynous figure, the text points out. Problems of sexuality and other sicknesses came about when this union was broken. With Christ's aid, the reunion takes place in the bridal chamber. This reunion is a precursor to the later union when the spirit returns to the heavenly realm. The notion of a chaste union in the bed, when one is clothed in protective light of the spirit, goes through many poems:

> The rulers do not see you
> who wear the perfect light,
> and they cannot seize you.
> You put on the light
> in the mystery of union.

Other themes concern free men and virgins, slaves, defiled women, animals in human form, conversion, and agriculture. As in the canonical gospels, the parable themes embrace sowing, reaping, and the seasons. Nonetheless, gnosis is always apparent, as are other favored gnostic ideas of light and darkness, names of earthly and heavenly things, the word, the mischief of the rulers (archons), and reversal of traditional ideas about resurrection and even "my father" in the Lord's Prayer. With a heterodoxy of view typical of gnostic reinterpretations of Christianity, the text frequently surprises, as in lines such as "god is a man-eater" or "Jesus came to crucify the world."

Probably written in the third century, in Greek and possibly in Syria, the Gospel of Philip exists in Coptic translation in the Nag Hammadi library.

THE GOSPEL OF PHILIP[1]

CONVERTS

A Jew[2] makes a Jew whom we call a convert.[3]
A convert makes no convert.
Some are and make others like them,
while others simply are.

SLAVES

A slave longs for freedom
and doesn't hope to own a master's estate.

A child claims the father's legacy,
but those who inherit the dead are dead.

Heirs to the living are alive
and are heirs to life and death.

The dead are heirs to nothing.
How can the dead inherit?

Yet if the dead inherits the living,
the living won't die and the dead will survive.

GENTILES, JEWS, CHRISTIANS

A gentile doesn't die, never
having been alive to die.

---

1. The Gospel of Philip: Nag Hammadi Codex II,3, pp. 51,29 to 86,19; translated by Wesley W. Isenberg, "Gospel of Philip" (Robinson, ed., *Nag Hammadi Library in English*, rev. ed., 141–60); revised in verse by Willis Barnstone.
2. Or "Hebrew," here and below.
3. Or "proselyte."

You who find truth are alive;
another may die, being alive.

Since Christ came the world was made,
cities adorned, and the dead buried.

When we were Jews we were orphans
with only a mother.

When we turned Christian we had a father
and a mother.[4]

SOWING IN SEASON

Those who sow in winter reap in summer.
Let us sow in the world to reap in summer.

Winter is the world, summer the other realm.[5]
It is wrong to pray in winter.[6]

From winter comes summer.
If you reap in winter you will not reap.

You will pull up young plants.
At the wrong season no crop is yours.

Even on the days of the Sabbath
the field is barren.

CHRIST AND THE SOUL

Christ came to buy. He rescued and redeemed,
redeeming aliens. He made strangers his own.[7]
He brought his own and made promises,
construing a strategy, and gave his life
when he appeared and when the world began.

---

4. For parallels to this passage see Gospel of Thomas 101, 105.
5. Aeon.
6. For parallels to this passage see Gospel of Thomas 6, 14.
7. Aliens and strangers are commonly discussed in gnostic texts, and a Sethian gnostic text is entitled the Foreigner (Allogenes).

Then he came and took back what he promised,
which fell into the hands of thieves. They captured it,
but he rescued it back. Then he redeemed
both the good and evil people in the world.

LIGHT AND DARKNESS

Light and darkness, life and death, on the right and left,
these are children, they are inseparably together.
But the good are not good, the wicked not wicked,
life not life, death not death.
Each element fades to an original source.
But those who live above the world cannot fade.
They are eternal.

NAMES

The names of earthly things are illusory.
We stray from the real to the unreal.
If you hear the word "god," you miss the real
and hear the unreal.[8]
Father, son, holy spirit, life, light, resurrection, church.
These words are not real. They are unreal
but refer to the real, and are heard in the world.
They fool us. If those names were in the eternal realm,
they would never be heard on earth.
They were not assigned to us here.
Their end dwells in the eternal realm.

THE NAME NOT UTTERED

Only one name is not uttered in the world:
the name the father gave the son.[9]

---

8. The word *god* as unreal recalls the discussion of reality and the transcendent One in the Secret Book of John and the Vision of the Foreigner.
9. The son as the name of the father is also discussed in the Gospel of Truth.

Above the name of all others is the father's name.
The son would not be father without wearing
the father's name.
Those with his name know it but do not speak it.
Those without his name do not think it.

TRUTH MADE NAMES

Truth made names in the world,
and without them we can't think.
Truth is one and is many,
teaching one thing through the many.

RULERS

The rulers[10] wanted to fool us,
since they saw we were connected with the good.
They took the names of the good
and gave them to the not good
so with names they could trick
and rope us to the not good.
As though doing us a favor,
they took names from the not good
and placed them on the good.
They knew what they were doing.
They wanted to grab those of us who were free
and make us eternal slaves.

FORCES

There are forces that don't want us to be saved.
They act for their own sake. . . .
If we are saved there will be no sacrifices,
no animals offered to the forces.
Yes, they made sacrifices to the animals.

---

10. Archons.

They were alive when they offered them,
and then they died.
They offered us dead to god,
and we lived.

ONCE THERE WAS NO BREAD

Before Christ came there was no bread in the world,
just as paradise, with its Adam, had many trees
for nourishing animals but no wheat for humans.
Once we nourished ourselves like animals,
but when the perfect Christ came,
he carried bread down from heaven
so we could eat like humans.[11]

RULERS AND THE HOLY SPIRIT

The rulers thought they had done everything
alone, but in secret
the holy spirit on her own accomplished it all.

SOWING TRUTH

Truth from the beginning is sown everywhere.
Many see it sown. Few see it reaped.

MARY AND THE HOLY SPIRIT

Some say the holy spirit inseminated Mary.
They are wrong and don't know what they are saying.
When did a woman ever get a woman pregnant?[12]
Mary is a virgin and no powers dirtied her.

---

11. On Christ bringing bread from heaven in the Gospel of Philip, see manna and Christ as bread from heaven in John 6.

12. The spirit is considered feminine in Semitic sources, and in texts such as Gospel of Thomas 101, the Secret Book of James, and especially the Gospel of the Hebrews, in which Jesus refers to his mother the holy spirit.

She is a great repugnance to the Jews
who are apostolic, who are the messengers.
No powers dirtied the virgin.
They dirtied themselves.

THE LORD'S FATHER

The lord would never say, "My father who is in heaven"[13]
unless he had another father elsewhere.
He would have simply said, "My father."

POSSESSIONS

The lord said to the students,
"From every house you are in, take out possessions,
but take things into the father's house
and do not steal what is inside and run off."

JESUS IS A HIDDEN NAME

Jesus is a hidden name, Christ is an open one.
So Jesus is not a word in any tongue but a name
they call him.
In Syriac the Christ is *messias,* in Greek he is *christos.*
All languages have their own way of calling him.
Nazarene is the revealed name for what is secret.

WHAT IS CHRIST?

In himself Christ has everything, be it human
or angel or mystery and the father.

THE LORD ASCENDING

Some say the lord died first and then ascended.
They are wrong. He rose first and then he died.

---

13. Matthew 6:9.

Unless you are first resurrected, you will not die.
As god lives, you would already be dead.[14]

PENNY AND SOUL

No one would hide a beautiful and valuable object
under a lovely cover, but often vast monies are held
in a bag worth only a penny.
Consider the soul. It is a precious spirit and it came
in a contemptible body.[15]

SOME ARE AFRAID

Some are afraid that they will ascend from death naked,
and they want to climb back to life in their flesh.[16]
They are unaware that those who wear their flesh are naked,
and those who strip are not naked.
"Flesh and blood cannot inherit the kingdom of god."[17]
What will we not inherit? The flesh we wear on us.
But what then will we inherit as our own ?
The body of Jesus and his blood. And Jesus said,
"Whoever will not eat my flesh and drink my blood
has no life within him."[18] What does he mean?
His flesh is the word and blood the holy spirit.
Who has received these has food and drink and clothing.
I condemn those who say the flesh won't rise.
Then both are wrong. You say the flesh won't ascend.
Tell me, what will rise so I can honor you?
You say spirit in the flesh and light in the flesh.
What is the flesh?
You say there is nothing outside the flesh.
Then rise in the flesh, since everything exists in it.

---

14. Resurrection is fully discussed in the Valentinian Treatise on Resurrection.
15. A similar contrast between soul or spirit and body occurs in Gospel of Thomas 29.
16. The question of whether the dead are naked or clothed is also discussed in 2 Corinthians 5:1–10.
17. 1 Corinthians 15:50.
18. John 6:53.

In this world those wearing garments are better than garments.
In heaven the garments are better than the wearers.

THROUGH WATER AND FIRE

Through water and fire this wide realm is purified,
and the visible cleaned by the visible,
and the hidden by the hidden,
but there are elements concealed in the visible.
There is water within water
and fire in the oil of chrism.

JESUS TRICKED EVERYONE

Jesus tricked everyone. He did not appear as he was
but in a way not to be seen.
Yet he appeared to all of them.

To the great he appeared as great,
to the small as small. To angels he appeared as an angel,
and to humans as a human.
And he hid his word from everyone.
Some looked at him and thought they saw themselves.

When before his students he appeared gloriously
on the mountain, he was not small.
No, he became great, and he made his students grow
so they would know his immensity.[19]

UNION WITH ANGELS

On the day of thanksgiving prayer he said,[20]
"You who have joined perfect light with holy spirit,
join the angels with us as a single image."

---

19. On the glory of Jesus on the mountain, see accounts of the transfiguration appearance and glorious resurrection appearances in the gospels and other early Christian literature.
20. Perhaps Jesus is speaking here, or perhaps Philip.

THE LAMB

Don't hate the lamb.
Without the lamb you can't see the king.[21]

MEETING THE KING

You don't meet the king
if you are naked.

CONCEIVING WITH A KISS

The heavenly man has more children
than a man on earth. If the offspring of Adam
are many and die,
how many more are the offspring of perfect beings
who do not die and are born each second?
The father makes a child.
The child cannot make a son. He has not the power
to make children. One recently born is not a parent.
The son has brothers and sisters, not children.
In this world there is a natural order to birth,
and one is nourished by ordinary means.
We are nourished by the promise of heaven,
from the mouth of the word.
If the word emanated from the mouth, it is perfect.
By a kiss the perfect conceive and give birth.
That is why we kiss.
From the grace in others we conceive.

THREE MARYS

Three Marys walked with the lord:
His mother, his sister, and Mary of Magdala,
his companion.[22]

---

21. Or "door," "gate," as in sheepfold door or heaven.
22. On the love between Jesus and Mary of Magdala, see "Wisdom, Mother of the Angels" later
in the Gospel of Philip, as well as the Gospel of Mary.

His sister and mother and companion
were Mary.

THE HOLY SPIRIT

Father and son are single names.
Holy spirit is a double name and everywhere:
above and below, hidden and revealed.
The holy spirit lives in the revealed.
It is concealed below. It is above.

BLINDERS

Even evil powers serve the saints.
The holy spirit blinds the powers
who suppose they are treating a simple man
when they are treating saints.

ASK YOUR MOTHER

A student once asked the lord for something
from the world, and he said, "Ask your mother,
and she will give you something
from another realm."

SOPHIA AND SALT

The messengers said to the students,
"Let our offering all be for obtaining salt."
Salt is what they called Sophia.
Without salt no offering is acceptable.[23]
But Sophia is barren. She has no child,
and so she is called a trace of salt.
Yet wherever others are will be the holy spirit.[24]
Her children are many.

---

23. On salt and offering, see Leviticus 2:13; Mark 9:49 (variant reading: "every sacrifice will be salted with salt"); Colossians 4:6.
24. Partially restored.

FATHER AND CHILD

What a father has belongs to his child,
but not while the child is still little.
When the child is grown, however,
then the father turns over all he possesses.

THE LOST

Those who have gone astray are those born
of the spirit. And they are usually lost
because of the spirit. So from one single breath
of spirit the fire blazes and is blackened.

WISDOM AND THE WISDOM OF DEATH

Echamoth is one thing and Echmoth another.
Echamoth is simply wisdom,[25]
but Echmoth is the wisdom of death,
who is the one who knows death,
who is called little wisdom.[26]

DOMESTIC ANIMALS AND BEASTS

Domestic animals may be the bull and the donkey
and other species.
Others are wild and live in the deserts.
A man plows the field with a domestic animal,
and from the fruit of his labor
he feeds himself and the animals, tame or wild.
Compare the perfect human.
Through submissive powers he plows
and prepares for everything to come into being.
So his world holds together, good or evil, the right and the left.
The holy spirit shepherds everyone and rules all the powers,

---

25. Echamoth is Achamoth, lower wisdom in Valentinian thought.
26. *Echmoth* means "like death" in Hebrew and Aramaic.

those tame and wild and running loose.
He gathers them and shuts them in
so, like it or not, they cannot escape.

CAIN

The one who has been created[27] is beautiful,
and you would expect his sons to be noble creations.[28]
If one was not created but engendered,
you would find his seed was noble,
but now he was created and he engendered.
Is this nobility? Adultery came into being,
then murder. One[29] was engendered in adultery,
since he was the child of the serpent.[30]
So like his father he too became a murderer and killed his brother.
Every sexual act between unlike persons is adultery.

GOD IS A DYER

God is a dyer.[31]
The good dyes, true dyes, dissolve into things
dyed in them.
So too for things god has dyed.
His dyes are imperishable because of their colors.
What god dips he dips in water.

SEEING

It is impossible to see anything in the real realm
unless you become it.
Not so in the world. You see the sun without being the sun,

---

27. Adam, or else a more general statement about anyone.
28. Bentley Layton suggests that the negative has been omitted here, and that the sentence should read "his sons are not noble creations" (*Gnostic Scriptures,* 336).
29. Cain.
30. On the description of the origin of Cain, see the accounts of the seduction of Eve by Yaldabaoth in the Secret Book of John and the rape of Eve in the Reality of the Rulers.
31. The Gospel of Philip has more on dyeing below; see "The Lord in the Dye Works of Levi."

see sky and earth but are not them.
This is the truth of the world.
In the other truth you are what you see.
If you see spirit, you are spirit.
If you look at the anointed, you are the anointed.
If you see the father, you will be father.
In this world you see everything but yourself,
but there, you look at yourself and are what you see.

FAITH AND LOVE

Faith receives, love gives.
No one receives without faith.
No one gives without love.
To receive, believe; to love, give.
If you give without love,
no one derives a thing from what is given.
Whoever has not accepted the lord
is still a Jew.[32]

NAMES OF JESUS

The messengers[33] who were before us had these names
for him: Jesus, the Nazorean, messiah,
that is, Jesus, the Nazorean, the Christ.
The last name is Christ,
the first is Jesus,
the middle name is the Nazarene.
Messiah has two meanings, both "Christ" and "measured."
Jesus in Hebrew is "redemption."
Nazara is "truth."
Christ has been measured.
The Nazarene and Jesus are they who have been measured.

---

32. Compare this section's treatment of faith and love to 1 Corinthians 13 and the Secret Book of James.
33. Apostles.

PEARL IN THE MUD

If a pearl is thrown into mud, it loses no value,
and if rubbed with balsam oil, it gains no value.
It always is precious in its owner's eyes.[34]
Wherever they are, the children of god
are precious in the eyes of the father.

JEW, ROMAN, GREEK, CHRISTIAN

If you say, "I am a Jew," no one will be moved.
If you say, "I am a Roman," no one will be upset.
If you say, "I am Greek, a barbarian, a slave, a freeman,"
no one will be troubled.
But if you say, "I am a Christian," they will tremble.
I wish I had that title. The world
will not endure it when hearing the name.[35]

GOD IS A MAN-EATER

God is a man-eater. So people are sacrificed to him.
Before humans were sacrificed, it was animals,
because those they were eaten by were not gods.

GLASS AND EARTH

Glass decanters and earthenware jugs are both made with fire.
When a glass decanter breaks, it is redone,
since it was made through a breath.
When earthenware jugs break, they are destroyed,
since they were born without a breath.

DONKEY AND MILLSTONE

A donkey turning a millstone walked a hundred miles.
When it was set loose, it found itself in the same place.

---

34. See Gospel of Thomas 93 (and New Testament parallels).
35. Partially restored.

Some people travel long but go nowhere.
At twilight they have seen no cities or villages,
no human constructions or phenomena of nature,
no powers or angels.
These miserable ones have labored in vain.

THE EUCHARIST IS JESUS

The eucharist is Jesus. In Syriac it is called *pharisatha*,
which is "one who is spread out,"
since Jesus came to crucify the world.[36]

THE LORD IN THE DYE WORKS OF LEVI

The lord went into the dye works of Levi
and took seventy-two different colors and threw them
into a vat. He drew them out perfectly white.
He said, "In this way the earthly son has come as a dyer."[37]

WISDOM, MOTHER OF THE ANGELS

Wisdom, who is called "barren," is mother of the angels.
The companion is Mary of Magdala. Jesus loved her
more than his students. He kissed her often
on her face, more than all his students,
and they said, "Why do you love her more than us?"[38]
The savior answered, saying to them,
"Why do I not love you like her? If a blind man
and one who sees are together in darkness,
they are the same.
When light comes, the one who sees will see light.
The blind man stays in darkness."

---

36. The meaning of the Syriac word is actually "broken bread."
37. Stories of Jesus in a dyehouse are also told in the Arabic Infancy Gospel, a version of the Infancy Gospel of Thomas, and an Islamic text. Seventy-two (or seventy) is a traditional number of nations in the world.
38. On Jesus and Mary of Magdala, see "Three Marys," earlier in the Gospel of Philip, and the Gospel of Mary.

BEING

The lord said, "Blessings on you
who were before you came into being.
Whoever is, was, and will be."[39]

HUMANS AND ANIMALS

The superiority of humans is not obvious to the eye
but lies in what is hidden.
Consequently they have mastery over animals
who are stronger and larger in ways apparent
and hidden. So the animals survive.
When humans withdraw, the animals slay and devour
each other, because they do not find food.
Now they have food because humans plow the soil.

WATER AND MYSTERY

If you go down into the water and come up,
receiving nothing, and say, "I am a Christian,"
you have borrowed the name at interest.
But if you receive the holy spirit,
you have the name as a gift. And a gift
you do not pay back.
But if you have borrowed at interest,
you must pay. So it works
when you have passed through mystery.

MARRIAGE

Great is the mystery of marriage! Without it,
the world would not be.
The existence of the world depends
on marriage.

---

39. See Gospel of Thomas 19.

Think of sex. It possesses deep powers,
though its image is filthy.

BRIDAL CHAMBER AND ANDROGYNY

Among the forms of unclean spirits are male
and female ones. Males have sex with souls
who inhabit a female shape,
and females mingle promiscuously with souls
in a male form. No one escapes those spirits:
they seize you, unless you take on the power
of male or female, of groom and bride.
This power resides in the mirrored bridal chamber.
When wanton women see a man sitting alone,
the man is overcome. They fondle him
and pollute him. When wanton men see
a beautiful woman sitting alone, they overcome her,
and she is violated and polluted.
But when spirits see a man and his wife sitting together,
the female spirits cannot enter the male, nor the male
the woman. When the image and angel are joined,
none can force themselves on the man and woman.

LEAVING THE WORLD

When you leave the world, nothing can stop you
because you were in the world. You are above desire
and fear. You are master of envy. If someone does not
leave the world, the forces grab and choke him.
How can one escape those great grasping rulers?
How can one hide from them? Some say,
"We were faithful," to escape the filthy spirits and demons.
But if they had the holy spirit, nothing filthy
would cleave to them. Have no fear of the flesh.
Don't love it. If you are fearful, it will gain mastery
over you. If you love the flesh,
it will swallow and paralyze you.

IN THIS WORLD OR THE RESURRECTION

Either someone will be in this world
or in the resurrection or in the middle place.
God forbid that I be found in the middle!
In this world there is good and evil.
Its good is not good, and evil not evil.
But there is evil after this world
that is truly evil—which is called the middle.[40]
The middle is death.
While we are in this world it is best to acquire resurrection
for ourselves[41]
so when we strip off the flesh we may rest
and not walk in the middle.
Many go astray on the way.

WILL AND SIN

It is good to leave the world before one has sinned.
Some have neither the will nor the ability to act.
Others, even if they have the will, are better off
if they do not act, for the act of the will makes them sinners.
But even if they have no will to act,
justice may be concealed from them,
whether they have the will or not.
Will, not action, is always primary.

HELL

A messenger in a vision saw people
locked up in a house of fire and bound with fiery chains,
lying in a flaming ointment.
He asked them, "Why can't they be saved?"
"We did not desire it," they told the messenger,

---

40. The middle realm as the world between the spiritual realm above and the physical world below is also treated in other gnostic texts, including the Gospel of Truth.
41. Resurrection is discussed in the Treatise on Resurrection.

"but we got this place of punishment.
It is the outer darkness, and we are in it."[42]

KINDS OF FIRE

Soul and spirit came into being from water and fire.
From water and fire and light came the attendant
in the bridal chamber.
Fire is chrism. Light is fire. I am not referring to flame,
which has no form, but to another kind of fire,
whose appearance is white,
which is luminous and beautiful
and gives beauty.

TRUTH AND NAKEDNESS

Truth didn't come into the world naked
but in types and images. Truth is received only
that way. There is rebirth and its image.
They must be reborn through image.
What is the resurrection?
Image must rise again through image.
The bridegroom and image enter through image
into truth, which is restoration. It is right
that those who don't have it take on the name
of the father and son and the holy spirit.
But they have not done so on their own.
If you do not take on the names for yourself,
the name "Christian" will be taken from you.
You receive them in the oil of the chrism,
the aromatic unction of the power of the cross.
The messengers called this power "the right and left."
You are no longer a Christian but Christ.[43]

---

42. Partially restored; this description of hell is similar to the vision of hell in the Book of Thomas.
43. See Gospel of Thomas 108, on becoming Christ.

FIVE SACRAMENTS

The lord did everything through mystery:
baptism and a chrism and a eucharist
and a redemption and a bridal chamber.

THINGS BELOW LIKE THINGS ABOVE

The lord said, "I came to make things below
like things above, and the outside like the inside.
I came to join them in one place."[44]
He revealed who he is through types and images.
Those who say, "There is a heavenly person
and one even higher," are wrong.[45]
Who is seen in heaven is the heavenly person,
who is called "the one below,"
and the one to whom the hidden belongs
is called "higher."
It is best to say "inner" and "outer" and "what is beyond the outer."
So the lord called destruction "the outer darkness."[46]
There is nothing beyond.
He said, "My father who is in secret."
He said, "Go into the chamber and shut the door behind you,
and pray to your father who is in secret,"[47]
the one who is innermost.
But what is within them all is the fullness.[48]
Beyond it there is nothing inside.
This is the place they call "the uppermost."

PLACES OF THE SPIRIT

Before Christ, some came from a realm
they could not reenter,

---

44. See Gospel of Thomas 22, on the inner and the outer.
45. Here the text recommends the language of inner transcendence rather than that of heavenly transcendence.
46. Matthew 8:12, 22:13, 25:30.
47.Matthew 6:6.
48. Pleroma.

and they went where they could not come out.
Then Christ came.
Those who went in he took out.
Those who went out he took in.

EVE IN ADAM

When Eve was in Adam there was no death.[49]
When she was cut from him,
death came into being.
If he enters what he was and takes her in him fully,
death will disappear.[50]

CRUCIFIXION

"My god, my god, O lord, why have you abandoned me?"[51]
He said these words on the cross.
But not from that place. He was already gone. . . .

RISING FROM THE DEAD

The lord rose from the dead.
He became as he was,
but now his body was perfect.
He possessed flesh,
but this was true flesh.
Our flesh isn't true.
Ours is only an image of the true.[52]

BEDROOM

Animals don't have a bridal bedroom,
nor do slaves or dirtied women.
Bedrooms are for free men and virgins.

---

49. This is the original androgynous state.
50. This is the return to (androgynous) unity, a theme emphasized in the Gospel of Thomas.
51. Matthew 27:46; Mark 15:34; both quote Psalm 22:1.
52. Partially restored.

BORN AGAIN

Through the holy spirit we are again engendered,[53]
but conceived through Christ.
We are anointed in the spirit.
When we were conceived we were united.
No one will be able to look at oneself
either in water or in a mirror without light,
nor see in light without water or mirror.
So it is fitting to baptize in light and water.
Now the light is the chrism.

THREE BUILDINGS IN JERUSALEM

There were three buildings in Jerusalem,[54]
one facing west called "the holy,"
another facing south called "the holy of the holy."
The third facing east was called "the holy of the holies,"
where only the high priest enters.
Baptism is the holy building.
Redemption is the holy of the holy.
The holy of the holies is the bridal chamber.
Baptism includes resurrection and redemption.
Redemption happens in the bridal chamber,
but the bridal chamber is part of something
superior to it and the others
because you will find nothing like it.
Those familiar with it are those who pray
in spirit and in truth[55]
for they do not pray in Jerusalem.
There are some who pray in Jerusalem,
awaiting the kingdom of heaven,
called the holy of the holies.
Before the veil was rent we had no bridal chamber

---

53. Or "born again."
54. The Jewish temple, which here is interpreted allegorically.
55. See John 4:23.

but the image of the bridal chamber above.
So its veil was torn from top to bottom.[56]
It was right for some below to ascend.

GARMENT OF LIGHT

The rulers do not see you
who wear the perfect light,
and they cannot seize you.
You put on the light
in the mystery of union.

REUNION IN THE BEDROOM

If the woman and man had not come apart,
they would not know death.[57]
Christ came to repair the split, there from the beginning,
and join the two and give them life
who had died because of separation.
Now the woman and man are one in the chamber
with the bed, and those so joined will not come apart again.
Eve and Adam separated because when they joined
it was not in the chamber with the bed.

ADAM'S SOUL

The soul of Adam came into being through
a breath blowing into him.[58] Breath is spirit.
The element given him is his mother.
Soul became spirit. When he was joined to spirit,
he spoke words incomprehensible to the powers.

---

56. These observations are based on accounts of the rending of the temple veil at the time of the crucifixion of Jesus (Matthew 27:51; Mark 15:38; also Luke 23:45; Hebrews 10:19–20).
57. This is similar to the saying above, in "Eve in Adam," about Adam and Eve in original union, resultant disunion, and final reunion.
58. On the breath blowing into Adam, see Genesis 2:7, a verse variously interpreted in gnostic literature.

They envied him, excluded from the union of the spirit.
Their exclusion spurred them into fashioning the bridal chamber
where lovers would come and be defiled.[59]

JESUS AT THE JORDAN

Jesus appeared at the Jordan River with the fullness of the kingdom
     of heaven.
He was born before there was birth.
He was anointed once and was anointed anew.
He who was redeemed redeemed the world.

MYSTERY

It is good to speak of mystery,
especially because the father of all
joined with the virgin who came down,
and on that day a fire shone over him.
He came to the bridal chamber.
So on that very day his body came into being.
And on that day he left the chamber with the splendor
of what passed between the bride and bridegroom.
Through this force Jesus did everything.
It is good for each of his students
to go into the chamber and rest.

VIRGIN BIRTHS

Adam came into being from two virgins:
from the spirit and from the virgin earth,
and Christ was born of a virgin to heal the initial fall.

TWO TREES OF PARADISE

Two trees are growing in paradise.[60]
One bears animals, the other bears people.

---

59. Partially restored.
60. On the trees of paradise, see Genesis 2:9 and following, along with gnostic interpretations.

Adam ate from the tree that bore animals
and became an animal and brought forth animals,
and so Adam's children worship animals.
The tree whose fruit Adam ate is the tree of knowledge.
So his sins increased. If he had eaten fruit
from the tree of life, the one bearing people,
the gods would worship man and woman,
for in the beginning god created man and woman.
Now they create god. In the world
humans make gods and worship their creation.
It would be better if the gods worshiped them![61]

A MAN AND HIS CHILDREN

A man does what he has the skills to do.
He has the ability to make children.
He does it easily in a few seconds.
His accomplishment shows in his children.
They are the image.
He was also made after the image,
doing things with his physical strength
and producing his children with ease.

SLAVES AND THE FREE

In this world the slaves serve the free.
In the kingdom of heaven the free will serve the slaves,
and the attendants of the bridal chamber
will minister to the wedding guests.
The attendants of the bridal chamber have one name, rest,
and need take no other form because they meditate
and comprehend by insight.
They are many, since they do not store their treasures
in things below, despicable things, but in unknown glory.[62]

---

61. Partially restored.
62. Partially restored. Matthew 6:19–21 also deals with treasures on earth and in heaven.

INTO THE WATER

It was necessary for Jesus to descend into the water
so that he could perfect and consecrate it.
So also they who have received baptism in his name may be perfect.
He said, "It is right in this way to perfect all that is just."[63]

BAPTISM

When you say you will die first and then rise,
you are wrong. If you are not resurrected in life,
you will receive nothing when you are dead.
Great is baptism. Enter the water and live.

JOSEPH AND THE WOODEN CROSS

Philip the messenger[64] said,
"Joseph the carpenter planted a garden of paradise
because he needed wood for his trade.
He made the cross from the trees he planted,
and his seed hung from what he planted.
His seed was Jesus, and the plant was the cross."
The tree of life in the middle of that garden
of paradise is an olive tree, and from the olive tree
comes chrism, and from that oil
comes the resurrection.

THE WORLD EATS BODIES

The world eats bodies,
and everything eaten in the world dies.
Truth eats life,
but no one fed on truth will find death.[65]
Jesus came and he carried food,

---

63. Partially restored. Matthew 3:15 is cited here.
64. Apostle.
65. Compare, perhaps, Gospel of Thomas 11, on the living who will not die.

giving life to whoever wanted it
so they might not die.

ADAM IN PARADISE

God planted a garden, and humans were placed
in the garden. They lived among many trees
with the blessing and in the image of god.
The things in it I will eat as I wish.
Here in this garden they will tell me,
"Eat this or do not eat that, just as you wish."
Here I will eat all things,
where the tree of knowledge is.[66]
That tree killed Adam,
but here the tree of knowledge made us alive.
The law was the tree.
It has the power to give knowledge of good and evil.
It did not remove me from evil
or set me among the good.
It created death for those who ate it. When they said,
"Eat this or do not eat that," death began.

SUPERIORITY OF CHRISM TO BAPTISM

The *chrism* is superior to baptism.
From the word chrism we have been called Christians,
and surely not from the word *baptism*.
And because of the chrism Christ has his name.
The father anointed the son,
and the son anointed the messengers,
and the messengers anointed us.
Who has been anointed possesses everything:
resurrection, light, cross, holy spirit.
The father gave him this in the bridal chamber.
He merely accepted the gift.

---

66. Partially restored.

The father was in the son and the son in the father.
This is the kingdom of heaven.

LAUGHING CHRIST

The lord said it perfectly:
"Some have entered the kingdom of heaven laughing,
and they have come out laughing."
They do not remain there:
one because he is not a Christian,
another because he laments his later acts.
As soon as Christ went down into the water
he came out laughing at everything in this world,
not because he thought it a trifle, but out of contempt.[67]
Whoever wants to enter the kingdom of heaven will do so.
Whoever despises everything of this world, scorns it as a trifle,
will emerge laughing.
So with the bread and the cup and the oil,
for above is one superior to all these.[68]

CREATION

The world came into being through error.
The agent who made it[69]
wanted it to be imperishable and immortal.
He failed. He came up with less than his desire.
The world was never incorruptible,
nor was its maker. Things are not imperishable,
but children are. Nothing can endure
that is not first a child. Whoever cannot receive
surely will be unable to give.

CUP OF PRAYER

The cup of prayer holds wine and water.
It is appointed for the blood for which thanks is given.

---

67. On the laughing Christ see the Second Treatise of the Great Seth and the Round Dance of the Cross.
68. Partially restored.
69. The creator of the world, the demiurge.

It is filled with holy spirit
and is of the perfect human.
When we drink, we drink the perfect human.

LIVING WATER

The living water is a body.
We must put on the living human.
When you go into the water, you strip naked
and put on the living human.

A HORSE SIRES A HORSE

A horse sires a horse, a human gives birth to a human,
a god engenders a god.
Compare the bridegroom and the bride.
Their children were born in the chamber.
No Jew was ever born to Greek parents
as long as the world has existed.
And as Christians, we do not descend from the Jews.
There was another people.
These blessed ones were the chosen ones,
the chosen people of the living god;
and then the true man, the earthly son,
and the seed of the earthly son.[70]
In the world these are the true people.
They are the attendants of the bridal chamber.[71]

POWER AND WEAKNESS

In this world, power and weakness mingle
when man and woman have sex.
Joining is different in the eternal realm,
though we use the same names to speak of it.
There are names beyond the ordinary ones
and stronger than showy brute strength.

---

70. Or "human son," "son of man."
71. Partially restored.

Yet all is the same, and this is incomprehensible
to hearts of flesh.

KNOWLEDGE OF SELF

Should you who possess everything not know yourself?[72]
If you do not know yourself,
you will not enjoy what you own.
But know yourself
and what you have enjoy.

GARMENT OF LIGHT

The perfect human can neither be restrained nor seen.
If they see him, they can stop him,
so there is no way to grace but to put on
the perfect light and become perfect.
All who put on that garment will enter the kingdom.
This is the perfect light.
We must become perfect before leaving this world.
Who is rich and has not thrown it off
will not share in the kingdom
but will go as imperfect into the middle.
Only Jesus knows where that will end.[73]

THE HOLY PERSON

The priest is fully holy, including his body.
Does one take bread and make it holy?
Or the cup or anything drunk?
Are they sanctified?[74]
If so, why not the body too?

---

72. This set of reflections upon knowing or not knowing oneself recalls the Delphic maxim
"Know yourself," as well as Gospel of Thomas 3.
73. Partially restored.
74. These are eucharistic themes.

BAPTISM AND DEATH

By perfecting the water of baptism,
Jesus emptied it of death.
We go into the water but not into death,
so we are not poured out into the wind of the world.[75]
Whenever that wind blows, winter comes.
When the holy spirit breathes, summer blows in.

KNOWLEDGE AND LOVE

Whoever has knowledge of the truth is a free being,
but the free human doesn't sin.
"Whoever sins is the slave of sin."[76]
Truth is the mother, knowledge the father.
Those who think that sinning does not apply to them
are called free by the world.
Knowledge of the truth can make one arrogant,
giving meaning to the words "being free."
It makes them feel superior to the world.
But love builds up.[77]
Who is really free through knowledge
is a slave because of love for those
who have not yet attained the freedom of knowledge.
Knowledge makes them capable of freedom.
Love never calls something its own,
yet it too may possess the same thing.
Love never says, "This is mine," or "That is mine,"
but "All these are yours."

SPIRITUAL FRAGRANCE

Spiritual love is wine and fragrance.
Those nearby also enjoy it

---

75. These are baptismal themes.
76. John 8:34.
77. 1 Corinthians 8:1.

from those who are anointed.
But if the anointed withdraw and leave,
then those unanointed, who are hanging around,
remain in their bad odor.
The Samaritan gave nothing but wine and oil to the wounded.[78]
Only the ointment. It healed the wounds,
for "love covers a multitude of sins."[79]

CHILDREN AND ADULTERY

The children a woman gives birth to
resemble the man who loves her.
If her husband loves her,
then they are like her husband.
If affections comes from an adulterer,
then the children are like him.
Often, if a woman sleeps with her husband
out of need, while her heart is with the adulterer
with whom she also has sex,
her child will look like the adulterer.
You who live together with the son of god,
love not the world but the lord,
so your children will look not like the world
but like the lord.

SEX AND SPIRIT

Humans have sex with humans, horses with horses,
donkeys with donkeys.
Those of one sort usually linger with those like them.
So spirit mingles with spirit
and thought consorts with thought
and light shares light.
If you are born a person, a person will love you.

---

78. Luke 10:33–35 describes the actions of the good Samaritan.
79. 1 Peter 4:8.

If you become a spirit, a spirit will join with you.
If you become thought, thought will mingle with you.
If you become light, light will share you.
If you are of those from above,
one of those from above will rest in you.
If you become a horse or a donkey or bull or dog or sheep
or another animal that is wild or tame,
then neither a person nor spirit nor thought nor light
can love you.
None of those from above or within can rest in you,
and you have no part in them.

SLAVES AND FREEDOM

Those who are enslaved against their will
can be free.
Those who are freed by favor of a master
but have sold themselves into slavery
can no longer be free.

FARMING

Farming in this world demands four elements.
A harvest is collected and taken into the barn
as a result of water, earth, wind, and light.
God's farming also has four elements:
faith, hope, love, and knowledge.[80]
Faith is our earth in which we take root.
Hope is the water through which we are nourished.
Love is the wind through which we grow.
Knowledge is the light through which we ripen.
Grace exists in four ways:
earthborn, heavenly, from highest heaven,
and living in truth.[81]

---

80. On these elements see 1 Corinthians 13 and the Secret Book of James.
81. Partially restored.

BLESSINGS ON ONE WHO NEVER HARMS A SOUL

Blessings on one who never harms a soul.
That person is Jesus Christ.
He came to the whole earth and distressed no one.
Blessings on one like him, the perfect person.
This is the word.
Tell us about the word, since it is hard to define.
How shall we be able to accomplish such a feat?
How will he comfort everyone?
Especially, it is improper to cause anyone distress,
whether that person be great or small,
infidel or believer.
It is improper to comfort only those who enjoy good deeds.

Some find it useful to comfort one who is lucky.
You who do good deeds cannot comfort them,
for it goes against your will.
You cannot cause them distress, since you are not afflicting them.
Yet you who are lucky in life sometimes cause distress
unintentionally.
but the source is not you but the other person's wickedness.
Whoever has the qualities of the perfect human
is happy in the good.
Yet some are enormously put out by these distinctions.

A HOUSEHOLDER WITH EVERYTHING

There was a householder who had every possible thing,[82]
be it son or slave or cattle or dog or pig or wheat
or barley or chaff or grass or castor oil or meat or acorn.
He was sensible and knew what each one's food was.
He served children bread and meat.
He served slaves castor oil and meal.

---

82. This story or parable of the householder, known only in the Gospel of Philip, is given an allegorical interpretation.

He threw barley and chaff and grass to the cattle.
He threw bones to the dogs,
and to pigs he threw acorns and scraps of bread.

Compare the student of god.
If you are sensible, you understand the nature of learning.
Bodily forms will not deceive you,
since you will look at the condition of each person's soul
and speak with that form.
There are many animals on earth in human form.
When you identify them,
then you throw acorns to swine,
barley and chaff and grass to cattle,
and bones to the dogs.
To slaves you will give only what is preliminary,
but to children you give what is complete.

THE EARTHLY SON AND HIS SON

There is the earthly son, and there is the son
of the earthly son.
The lord is the earthly son,[83]
and the son of the earthly son is he who is created
through the earthly son.
The earthly son received the capacity to create from god.
He also had the ability to engender.
He who has the ability to create is a creature.
He who has the ability to engender is an offspring.
But he who creates cannot engender.
He who engenders also has the power to create.
Now they say, "He who creates engenders,"
but his so-called offspring is merely a creature;
therefore his children are not offspring but creatures.
He who creates works openly and is visible.
He who engenders does so in private. . . .

---

83. That is, Christ as the human son or son of man.

MYSTERY OF UNDEFILED MARRIAGE

No one can know when the husband and wife have sex
except those two.
Marriage in the world is a mystery for those who are married.
If there is a hidden defilement in the marriage,
how much greater is the true mystery of the undefiled marriage!
It is not fleshly but pure.
It belongs not to desire but to the will.
It belongs not to the darkness of the night
but to the day and the light.
If a marriage is open to the public,
it has become prostitution,
and the bride plays the harlot
not only when impregnated by another man
but even if she slips out of her bedroom and is seen.
Let her show herself only to her father and her mother
and to the friend and attendants of the bridegroom.
They are permitted to enter every day into the bridal chamber.
But let the others yearn just to listen to her voice
and to enjoy her fragrant ointments,
and let them feed on the crumbs falling from the table,
like dogs.
Bridegrooms and brides belong to the bridal chamber.
No one shall be able to see the bridegroom or bride
unless one becomes a bridegroom or bride.

ABRAHAM'S CIRCUMCISION

When Abraham rejoiced in seeing what he was to see,
he circumcised the flesh of his foreskin,
teaching us that it is proper to destroy the flesh.

HIDDEN PARTS ARE UPRIGHT

As long as they are hidden, most things in the world
are upright and live.

If they are revealed they die,
as is clear by the example of the visible person:
as long as the intestines are hidden, a person is alive.
When the intestines are exposed and come out,
the person will die.
So also with a tree.
While its root is hidden, it sprouts and grows.
If its root is exposed, the tree dries up.
So it is with every birth that is in the world,
not only with the revealed but also the hidden.
As long as the root of wickedness is hidden, it is powerful.
But when it is recognized, it is dissolved.
When it is revealed, it perishes.
That is why the word says,
"Even now the ax lies set against the root of the trees."[84]
It will not merely cut—what is cut sprouts again—
but the ax penetrates deeply until it brings up the root.

ROOT OF EVIL

Jesus pulled out the root of the whole place
while others did it only partially.
As for us, let each one dig down after the root of evil
that is within us
and pluck it out of our heart from the root.
It will be uprooted if we recognize it.
But if we are ignorant of it, it takes root in us
and produces fruit in our heart. It masters us.
We are its slaves. It takes us captive
to make us do what we do not want;
and what we do want we do not do.
It is powerful because we have not recognized it.
While it exists it is active.

---

84. Matthew 3:10.

IGNORANCE

Ignorance is the mother of all evil.
Ignorance will eventuate in death,
because those who come from ignorance
neither were nor are nor will be.
But those who are in the truth will be perfect
when all the truth is revealed.
For truth is like ignorance: while hidden it rests in itself,
but when revealed and recognized,
it is praised in that it is stronger than ignorance and error.
It gives freedom. The word said,
"If you know the truth, the truth will make you free."[85]
Ignorance is a slave,
knowledge is freedom.
If we know the truth, we shall find the fruits of the truth
within us.
If we join it, it will fulfill us.

THE STRONG AND WEAK,
THE MANIFEST AND HIDDEN

Now we have the manifest things of creation.
We say, "The strong are they who are held in high regard,
and the obscure are the weak who are despised."
Contrast the manifest things of truth:
they are weak and despised, whereas the hidden things are strong
and held in high regard.
The mysteries of truth are revealed,
though, in type and image.[86]
The bridal chamber remains hidden.
It is the holy in the holy.
The veil at first concealed how god controls creation,
but when the veil is torn and things inside are revealed,

---

85. John 8:32.
86. This fits in with the Alexandrian gnostic invention of hermeneutics, an allegorical way of interpreting scripture.

this house will be left desolate,
or rather it will be destroyed.
But the whole inferior godhead will not flee from these places
into the holies of the holies,
for it cannot mix with the pure light and the perfect fullness.
Rather, it will be under the wings of the cross and under its arms.
This ark will be the salvation of people
when the floodwater surges over them. [87]

SECRET OF THE TRUTH

If some belong to the order of the priesthood,
they will be able to go within the veil with the high priest.
So the veil was not torn at the top,
since it would have been open only to those above.
Nor was it torn at the bottom,
since it would have been revealed only to those below.
But it was rent from top to bottom.[88]
Those above opened to us who are below,
that we may go in to the secret of the truth.
The truth is what is held in high regard, since it is strong.
But we shall go in there by means of lowly types
and forms of weakness.
They are lowly when compared with the perfect glory.
There is glory that surpasses glory.
There is power that surpasses power.
Therefore, the perfect things have opened to us
together with the hidden things of truth.
The holies of the holies has been revealed,
and the bridal chamber has invited us in.

THE PERFECT LIGHT

As long as the seed is hidden, wickedness is ineffectual,
but it has not yet been removed from the midst of the seed

---

87. These lines reflect on the crucifixion and the great flood.
88. Again, observations based on the rending of the temple veil at the time of the crucifixion.

of the holy spirit.

Everyone is a slave of evil.

But when the seed is revealed, the perfect light will flow out on
  everyone.

And all those who are in the light will receive the chrism.

Then the slaves will be free and the captives ransomed.

"Every plant that my heavenly father has not planted will be
  uprooted."[89]

Those who are separated will be joined and filled.

Everyone who enters the bridal chamber will kindle the light,

for it burns just as in marriages performed,

though they happen at night.

That fire burns only at night and is put out.

Yet the mysteries of this marriage are perfected

rather in the day and the light.

Neither that day nor its light ever sets.

If you become an attendant of the bridal chamber,

you will receive the light.

If you do not receive it while in those places,

you cannot receive it in the other place.

You who receive the light will not be seen nor detained.

And no one will be able to torment you

even while you live in the world.

And when you leave the world

you have already received the truth in the images.

The world has become the eternal realm,[90]

because the eternal realm is fullness for you.

This is the way it is. It is revealed to you alone,

not hidden in the darkness and the night

but in a perfect day and a holy light.

---

89. Matthew 15:13.
90. Or "aeon."

16

Letter to Flora

Ptolemy

Ptolemy was Valentinos's disciple and apparently succeeded him in the school sometime after 160. He was called the greatest systematic theologian of the school. He was also an allegorical exegete of the Gospel of John. Ptolemy's letter is addressed to "dear sister Flora," Flora presumably being an educated Christian woman who will receive the theologian's lessons on questions of Mosaic law. After the salutation, however, there is no indication that Flora is a real person. She may represent the Christian church in Rome or simply individual Christian readers who may be persuaded by the broader speculation of a Valentinian gnostic.

The letter speaks, especially at the beginning, as a fellow Christian making distinctions between the validity of the law in the Hebrew Bible—originally designed for the Jews, who could not abide by pure law—and the New Testament. Eventually the path of instruction leads to a strong endorsement of the gnostic perfect god over his biblical adversary, who is the maker of the universe and the demiurge. The savior came to earth, it becomes clear, to complete his spiritual regeneration. He was not a messenger of the creator god but an emanation of the father of all. Throughout the persuasive letter, however, the author presents Valentinian gnostic ideas as completely concordant with Christianity.

Ptolemy tells Flora that the law in the five books of Moses has three parts by three authors. There is the pure law of god in the form of the ten commandments (which the savior came to fulfill, not to destroy); Moses' own additions to the law; and the additions by the elders. The latter two parts were mixed with impure and evil law, which was a compromise necessary to control the people before the advent of New Testament rigor. These lapses in law were made with regard to "hard-hearted divorce," revenge killing, and all other injustices. For his part, the savior Jesus altered the commands on offerings, circumcision, fasting, and the Passover unleavened bread. The new law takes commands to a spiritual level. Following Paul, one should have circumcision not of the flesh but of the spiritual heart.

Ptolemy's exegesis of Christian law was certainly already clear in Paul's changes and the New Testament itself, but now it is presented in a way to show that pure law derives not from the perfect god but from the demiurge, the creator god of the Bible. The god of the Bible, however, is presented not entirely as a narrow, angry god of the Jews, but as a middle deity between the perfect, ungenerated god and the devil. That god of the law, who is still in the Christian province, is the arbitrator of justice, which depends on him. But he is inferior to the perfect god, as his justice is lower. His world is corruption, darkness, and the material, while the god of all is incorruption and self-existent light. Finally, the savior is with the perfect god. We read, "The substance of the latter [the god of all] produced a double power, while the savior is an image of the greater one."

At the conclusion, the writer of the didactic letter returns to the reader, telling her personally, "These points will be of great benefit to you in the future, if like fair and good ground you have received fertile seeds and go on to show forth their fruit." The Letter to Flora is a letter to convert. It speaks for the power of Valentinian thought to address significant issues, concerning god and law, in a creative and thoughtful manner.

LETTER TO FLORA[1]

RECASTING OF THE MOSAIC LAW

The law ordained through Moses, my dear sister Flora, has not been understood by many persons, who have accurate knowledge neither of him who

---

1. Ptolemy's Letter to Flora survives in Greek as a quotation from a work by the heresiologist Epiphanius of Salamis in his *Panarion* (33.3–7); translated by Grant, *Gnosticism,* pp. 184–90; adapted by Willis Barnstone.

ordained it nor of its commandments. I think that this will be perfectly clear to you when you have learned the contradictory opinions about it.

Some say that it is legislation given by god the father of all; others, taking the contrary course, maintain stubbornly that it was ordained by the opposite, the devil who causes destruction, just as they attribute the fashioning of the world to him, saying that he is the father and maker of this universe. Both are completely in error; they refute each other, and neither has reached the truth of the matter.For it is evident that the law was not ordained by the perfect god the father, for it is secondary, being imperfect and in need of completion by another, containing commandments alien to the nature and thought of such a god. On the other hand, one cannot impute the law to the injustice of the adversary,[2] for it is opposed to injustice. Such persons do not comprehend what was said by the savior. "For a house or city divided against itself cannot stand," declared our savior.[3]

Furthermore, the messenger[4] says that the creation of the world is due to him, for "everything was made through him and apart from him nothing was made."[5] Thus he takes away in advance the baseless wisdom of the false accusers and shows that the creation is due not to a god who corrupts but to the one who is just and hates evil. Only unintelligent people have this idea, people who do not recognize the providence of the creator and have blinded not only the eye of the soul but also the eye of the body.

From what has been said, it is evident that these persons entirely miss the truth; each of the two groups has experienced this, the first because they do not know the god of justice, the second because they do not know the father of all, who was revealed by him alone who came and who knew him.

It remains for us who have been counted worthy of the knowledge of both of these to provide you with an accurate explanation of the nature of the law and of the legislator by whom it was ordained. We shall draw the proofs of what we say from the words of the savior, which alone can lead us without error to the comprehension of reality.

THE THREEFOLD SOURCES OF THE LAW

First, you must learn that the entire law contained in the Pentateuch of Moses was not ordained by one legislator, I mean, not by god alone; some

---

2. Satan.
3. Matthew 12:25.
4. Or "apostle," here probably John.
5. John 1:3.

commandments are Moses', and some were given by men. The words of the savior teach us this triple division. The first part must be attributed to god himself and his legislating, the second to Moses—not in the sense that god legislates through him, but in the sense that Moses gave some legislation under the influence of his own ideas—and the third to the elders of the people, who seem to have ordained some commandments of their own at the beginning. You will now learn how the truth of this theory is proved by the words of the savior.

In some discussion with those who disputed with the savior about divorce, which was permitted in the law, he said, "Because of your hard-heartedness Moses permitted a man to divorce his wife; from the beginning it was not so; for god made this marriage, and what the lord joined together, man must not separate."[6] In this way he shows that there is a law of god, which prohibits the divorce of a wife from her husband, and another law, that of Moses, which permits the breaking of this yoke because of hard-heartedness. In fact, Moses lays down legislation contrary to that of god; for joining is contrary to not joining. But if we examine the intention of Moses in giving this legislation, it will be seen that he did not give it arbitrarily or of his own accord, but by necessity because of the weakness of those for whom the legislation was given. Since they were unable to keep the intention of god, according to which it was not lawful for them to reject their wives, with whom some of them disliked to live, and therefore were in danger of turning to greater injustice and thence to destruction, Moses wanted to remove the cause of dislike, which was placing them in jeopardy of destruction. There-fore because of the critical circumstances, choosing a lesser evil in place of a greater, he ordained, of his own accord, a second law, that of divorce, so that if they could not observe the first, they might keep this and not turn to unjust and evil actions, through which complete destruction would be the result for them. This was his intention when he gave legislation contrary to that of god. Therefore it is indisputable that here the law of Moses is different from the law of god, even if we have demonstrated the fact from only one example.

The savior also makes plain the fact that some traditions of the elders are interwoven with the law. "For god said," he states, "'Honor your father and your mother, that it may be well with you.' But you have declared," he says, ad-dressing the elders, "that what help you might have received from me is a gift

---

6. Matthew 19:8, 6.

to god; and you have nullified the law of god through the tradition of your elders."[7] Isaiah also proclaimed this, saying, "This people honors me with their
lips, but their heart is far from me, teaching precepts that are the commandments of men."[8]

THE TRIPARTITE LAW OF GOD

Therefore it is obvious that the whole law is divided into three parts; we find
in it the legislation of Moses, of the elders, and of god himself. This division of
the entire law, as made by us, has brought to light what is true in it. This part,
the law of god himself, is in turn divided into three parts: the pure legislation
not mixed with evil, which is properly called law, which the savior came not to
destroy but to complete[9]—for what he completed was not alien to him but
needed completion, for it did not possess perfection—next, the legislation interwoven with inferiority and injustice, which the savior destroyed because it
was alien to his nature; and finally, the legislation that is exemplary and symbolic, an image of what is spiritual and transcendent, which the savior transferred from the perceptible and phenomenal to the spiritual and invisible.

The law of god, pure and not mixed with inferiority, is the decalogue, those
ten sayings engraved on two tables, forbidding things not to be done and en-
joining things to be done. These contain pure but imperfect legislation and required the completion made by the savior. There is also the law interwoven
with injustice, laid down for vengeance and the requital of previous injuries,
ordaining that an eye should be cut out for an eye and a tooth for a tooth, and
that a murder should be avenged by a murder. The person who is the second
one to be unjust is no less unjust than the first; he simply changes the order of
events while performing the same action. Admittedly, this commandment was
a just one and still is just, because of the weakness of those for whom the legislation was made so that they would not transgress the pure law. But it is alien
to the nature and goodness of the father of all. No doubt it was appropriate to
the circumstances, or even necessary. For he who does not want one murder
committed, saying, "You shall not kill," commands a murder to be repaid by
another murder, and so he has given a second law, which enjoins two murders

---

7. Matthew 15:4–9. Ptolemy here cites Matthew's (and Jesus') discussion of whether there are
occasions when one need not honor father and mother.
8. Isaiah 29:13.
9. Matthew 5:17.

although he had forbidden one. This fact proves that he was unsuspectingly the victim of necessity. This is why, when his son came, he destroyed this part of the law while admitting that it came from god. He counts this part of the law as in the old religion, not only in other passages but also where he said, "God said, 'He who curses father or mother shall surely die.'"[10]

Finally, there is the exemplary part, ordained in the image of spiritual and transcendent matters; I mean the part dealing with offerings and circumcision and the Sabbath and fasting and Passover and unleavened bread and other similar matters. Since all these things are images and symbols, when the truth was made manifest they were translated to another meaning. In their phenomenal appearance and their literal application they were destroyed, but in their spiritual meaning they were restored; the names remained the same, but the content was changed. Thus the savior commanded us to make offerings not of irrational animals or of incense of this worldly sort, but of spiritual praise and glorification and thanksgiving and of sharing and well-doing with our neighbors. He wanted us to be circumcised, not in regard to our physical foreskin but in regard to our spiritual heart; to keep the Sabbath, for he wishes us to be idle in regard to evil works; to fast, not in physical fasting but in spiritual, in which there is abstinence from everything evil.[11] Among us external fasting is also observed, since it can be advantageous to the soul if it is done reasonably, not for imitating others or from habit or because of a special day appointed for this purpose. It is also observed so that those who are not yet able to keep the true fast may have a reminder of it from the external fast. Similarly, Paul the messenger shows that the Passover and the unleavened bread are images when he says, "Christ our Passover has been sacrificed, in order that you may be unleavened bread, not containing leaven"—by leaven he here means evil—"but may be a new batch of dough."[12]

Thus the law of god itself is obviously divided into three parts. The first was completed by the savior, for the commandments, You shall not kill, you shall not commit adultery, you shall not swear falsely, are included in the forbidding of anger, desire, and swearing. The second part was entirely destroyed. For an eye for an eye and a tooth for a tooth, interwoven with injustice and itself a work of injustice, was destroyed by the savior through its opposite.

---

10. Matthew 15:4, citing Exodus 21:17; Leviticus 20:9.
11. On a spiritual understanding of circumcision, see Romans 2:25–29 and Gospel of Thomas 53; on that of Sabbath observance and fasting, see Gospel of Thomas 27.
12. 1 Corinthians 5:7.

Opposites cancel out. "For I say to you, do not resist one who is evil, but if anyone strikes you, turn the other cheek."[13] Finally, there is the part translated and changed from the literal to the spiritual, this symbolic legislation which is an image of transcendent things. For the images and symbols that represent other things were good as long as the truth had not come; but since the truth has come, we must perform the actions of the truth, not those of the image.

The students of the savior and the messenger Paul showed that this theory is true, speaking of the part dealing with images, as we have already said, in mentioning the Passover for us and the unleavened bread; of the law interwoven with injustice when he says that "the law of commandments in ordinances was destroyed"[14]; and of that not mixed with anything inferior when he says that "the law is holy, and the commandment is holy and just and good."[15]

I think I have shown you sufficiently, as well as one can in brief compass, the addition of human legislation in the law and the triple division of the law of god itself.

THE LAW IS BY THE DEMIURGE

It remains for us to say who this god is who ordained the law; but I think this too has been shown you in what we have already said, if you have listened to it attentively. For if the law was not ordained by the perfect god himself, as we have already taught you, nor by the devil, a statement one cannot possibly make, the legislator must be someone other than these two. In fact, he is the demiurge and maker of this universe and everything in it; and because he is essentially different from these two and is between them, he is rightly described as intermediate.

And if the perfect god is good by nature, as in fact he is, for our savior declared that there is only a single good god, his father whom he manifested;[16] and if the one who is of the opposite nature is evil and wicked, characterized by injustice; then the one situated between the two, neither good nor evil and unjust, can properly be called just, since he is the arbitrator of the justice that depends on him. On the one hand, this god will be inferior to the perfect god

---

13. Matthew 5:39.
14. Ephesians 2:15.
15. Romans 7:12.
16. See Matthew 19:17, on one good god.

and lower than his justice, since he is generated and not ungenerated; there is only one ungenerated father, from whom are all things,[17] since all things depend on him in their own ways. On the other hand, he will be greater and more powerful than the adversary, by nature, because he has a substance and nature different from the substance of either of them. The substance of the adversary is corruption and darkness, for he is material and complex, while the substance of the ungenerated father of all is incorruption and self-existent light, simple and homogeneous. The substance of the latter produced a double power, while the savior is an image of the greater one.

Do not let this trouble you for the present in your desire to learn how from one first principle of all, simple, and acknowledged by us and believed by us, ungenerated and incorruptible and good, were constituted these natures of corruption and the middle, which are of different substances, although it is characteristic of the good to generate and produce things that are like itself and have the same substance. For, if god permit, you will later learn about their origin and generation, when you are judged worthy of the apostolic tradition that we too have received by succession. We too are able to prove all our points by the teaching of the savior.

In making these brief statements to you, my sister Flora, I have not grown weary; and while I have treated the subject with brevity, I have also discussed it sufficiently. These points will be of great benefit to you in the future, if like fair and good ground you have received fertile seeds and go on to show forth their fruit.

---

17. 1 Corinthians 8:6 describes the one divine father with the same acclamation ("from whom are all things").

17

Commentary on the Gospel of John

Herakleon

H erakleon's Commentary on the Gospel of John is the first substantive exegesis, Christian or gnostic, that we have of a canonical gospel. Herakleon (also spelled Heracleon) lived at the end of the second century and probably into the third; he was a disciple of Valentinos. Spread throughout the Roman Empire, east and west, Valentinian gnosticism initially sought not to separate from Christianity but to become the true Christian way; for that reason, Herakleon's exegesis was directed specifically to Christians. But Christian authority viewed gnosticism as an impossible and dangerous heresy and refused to compromise. Refuted by Origen in great detail, Herakleon's analyses and allegorical interpretations were nevertheless so important that they served as a model for the famous theologian's own exegetical methods: Origen, too, became famous for his exegesis of the Gospel of John. In this respect he was like other major theologians, such as Clement of Alexandria, who were profoundly imbued with the thought and reasoning of their opponents.

Herakleon's purpose in explaining the inner meaning of John was to bring the Christian reader to a decisively new interpretation of the gospel and the meaning of the role of the savior. In his exegesis, the familiar vocabulary and concepts of the gnostics appear: aeons, pleroma, demiurge, and the father of truth. Yet even here he refrains, probably because of the intended audience, from going into the esoteric mythopoetic structure of the Valentinian cosmos, with its tales of Sophia and other principle eternal beings (aeons) in the fullness (pleroma).

Herakleon focuses both on the nature of the savior and on those who have accepted and denied him. Jesus is accepted as the anointed (Christ, messiah) by some Jews, whom we now call Christians, and not by other Jews. He informs us that the Jews of the New Testament (by this he is excluding Jesus' followers and Jesus himself) are even seen as not descended from the patriarch Abraham but as descendants of the devil, and he cites John 8:44, "You are from your father the devil." "They are neither children of Abraham nor children of god, because they do not love Jesus." They are from the demiurge, the biblical creator god.

At this point he moves into the crucial area of Christian and Christian-gnostic thought and confusion—who is this Jesus? The orthodox views of the church father Justin (or Justin Martyr, as he is conventionally known) that "Jesus Christ alone really was born as the son of god"[1] and of Irenaeus that "god was made man"[2] contrast with the gnostic view that Christ was not a human. In her *Johannine Gospel in Gnostic Exegesis,* Elaine Pagels compares Christian belief and gnostic heterdoxy:

> Heracleon claims, for example, that those who insist that Jesus, a man who lived "in the flesh," is "Christ" fail to distinguish between literal and symbolic truth. Those who write accounts of the revelation as alleged biographies of "Jesus of Nazareth"—or even of Jesus as messiah—focus on mere historical "externals" and miss the inner truth they signify.[3]

Herakleon saw the view of an earthly Jesus as an error of the flesh in which undenied historical data pass for spiritual truth when such events have been really just earthly reflections of a divine reality whose appearance of corporality was pure illusion. The word was not made real flesh in the instance of Jesus Christ. The word was made image, a simulacrum of the flesh.

---

1. Justin, *First Apology* 21.
2. Irenaeus, *Against Heresies* 3.2.1.
3. Pagels, *Johannine Gospels in Gnostic Exegesis,* 13.

In his commentary, which moves through the pages toward more purely Valentinian speculation, Herakleon speaks of the three levels of people: the material (or hylic, earthly), the psychical (with soul, *psyche*), and the spiritual (or pneumatic, with spirit, *pneuma*) and their special apprehension of reality. The material people worship the demiurge, who made the earth and flesh; the psychical people also worship the demiurge and god as Jesus in the flesh. They all miss what the spiritual people apprehend, which is the higher father of truth, or whatever of the many names the transcendent gnostic deity is given. In disputing the nature of reality that the other Christians perceive, Herakleon is not suggesting that Jesus did not exist or that the events recounted in the gospels were false. They did take place, yet their meaning is not the apparent historical meaning but an image of the inner meaning, of a higher reality. Through knowledge, the spiritual one comes upon and participates in that higher reality, which is the gnostic deity. Sometimes the elect are unaware of their spiritual, pneumatic level and can falter: the gnostics tended to ascribe such ignorance to error rather than moral sin. The true gnostics understand the symbolic meaning of the images in the world, and turn inward to look for the indescribable and secret forces of the divine.

COMMENTARY ON JOHN[4]

(1) John 1:3
> Through the word everything came to be,
> and without the word nothing came to be.

Everything is the world and what is in the world, but the aeon and what is in the aeon was not born through the word. Nothing is what is in the world and the creation. Who provided the cause of the generation of the world to the demiurge was the word, who is not the one from or by whom but through whom the world was generated. The word did not create as if he were given energy by another, but while he was providing energy, another, the demiurge, created. In that sense the world was generated through the word.

---

4. Herakleon's Commentary on John; translated from the Greek by Willis Barnstone.

(2) John 1:4

> In him was life.

"In him" refers to spiritual people, for he[5] first formed them in accordance with their generation, making what has been seeded by another, and making its form, illumination, and own outline.

(3) John 1:18

> No one has ever seen god.
> Only the one born of god,
> who is in the heart of his father,
> he has made him known.

This passage was said not by the baptizer[6] but by the student John.

(4) John 1:21

> They asked him, "What then? Are you Elijah?"
> He said, "I am not."
> "Are you the prophet?"
> He answered, "No."

John acknowledges that he was not the Christ or a prophet or Elijah.

(5) John 1:23

> I am the voice of one crying in the desert.

The word is the savior. The voice that was in the desert is symbolized through John. And its echo is the whole prophetic order. The voice that is closely related to the word, to reason, becomes the word, just as woman is transformed into man. And for the echo there will be a transformation into voice, replacing the student with the voice that changes into the word. The slave changes from echo into voice. When the savior calls John a prophet and Elijah,[7] he does not designate his nature but his attributes. But when he calls him greater than the prophets and among those born of women,[8] he is characterizing John himself. When John is asked about himself, he does not speak

---

5. The word.
6. John the baptizer.
7. See Matthew 11:9, 14.
8. See Matthew 11:10–11.

of his attributes. Attributes can be clothing, things other than himself. When he was asked about his clothing, whether he was his clothing, would he have answered yes?

John 1:19
> The Jews sent priests and Levites from Jerusalem to ask him,
>> "Who are you?"

It was the duty of these persons to investigate and ask about these matters, since they were devoted to god. John also was of the tribe of Levi. They asked him if he was a prophet, since they wished to learn about it. "Greater than prophets"[9] and "among those born of women"[10] was prophesied by Isaiah, so none of the earlier prophets was considered worthy of this honor by god.

(6) John 1:25
> Why then do you baptize if you are not the Christ or Elijah
>> or the prophet?

Only Christ and Elijah and the prophets should baptize. The Pharisees asked the question out of malice, not from a desire to learn.

(7) John 1:26
> I baptize in water.

John answers those sent by Pharisees not with respect to their question but on his own terms.

(8) John 1:26
> Among you stands one you do not know.

This signifies that he is already present, here in the world and among people, and he is already manifest to everyone.

John 1:27
> One who will come after me,
>> whose sandal strap I am unworthy to loosen.

---

9. Matthew 11:10.
10. Matthew 11:11.

John is the precursor of Christ. With these words the baptizer acknowledges that he is not worthy of even the least honorable service to Christ. "I am unworthy" signifies that he came down from the greatness because of me and he assumed flesh as a sandal. I cannot account for or describe or explain the dispensation of this flesh. The world is the sandal. The demiurge of the world,[11] who is inferior to Christ, acknowledges these facts in this passage.

(9) John 1:28
   All this happened in Bethany across the Jordan.

[Origen preferred reading Bethabara to Bethany.]

(10) John 1:29
   Look, the lamb of god who takes away the wrong of the world.

As a prophet John said "lamb of god." As more than a prophet,[12] he also said "who takes away the wrong of the world." The first expression refers to Christ's body, the second one to him who was in the body. As the lamb is imperfect in the genus of sheep, so the body is imperfect compared to him who inhabits the body. If he had wished to ascribe perfection to the body, he would have spoken of a ram that was to be sacrificed.

(11) John 2:12
   After this he went down to Capernaum.

Here too the passage signifies the beginning of another dispensation, since "he went down" was not spoken without purpose. Capernaum means both the ends of the world and the material things to which he descended. Because to him this was an alien place, nothing is noted as having been done or said there.

(12) John 2:13
   It was almost the Passover of the Jews.

The great feast was a symbol of the passion of the savior, when the sheep not only was slain but, when eaten, gave rest. When sacrificed, it meant the passion of the savior in the world. When eaten, it meant rest, which lies in marriage.

---

11. That is, allegorically, John.
12. See Matthew 11:9.

(13) John 2:13–15
> Jesus went up to Jerusalem. In the temple he found the
> people selling oxen and sheep and doves, and the coin
> changers sitting there. He made a whip out of ropes and
> drove out all the animals, the sheep and the oxen.

The ascent to Jerusalem signifies the ascent of the lord from material things to the psychical place, which is an image of Jerusalem.[13] He found them in the innermost holy place, not in the temple courtyard, so one might think that a simple calling, even when not from the spirit, is helped by the lord. The holy place is the holy of holies in which only the high priest enters,[14] and where the spiritual people come. But the court of the temple, where the Levites also are, is a symbol of the psychical people outside the pleroma, who are found to be in salvation. Those who are there in the holy space selling oxen and sheep and doves, and the money changers sitting there, are those who offer nothing freely but look at the coming of strangers to the temple as an occasion for trade and gain, and because of their profit and love of money supply the sacrifices for worshiping god. The whip that Jesus made of small cords is an image of power and energy of the holy spirit, blowing away the wicked. The whip and the linen[15] and the winding sheet[16] and other such things are also an image of the power and energy of the holy spirit. The whip was tied on wood, and this wood was a symbol of the cross. On this wood the gambling merchants and wickedness[17] were nailed and destroyed. The whip was made of these two substances. Jesus did not make it of dead leather, since he wished to build the church no longer as a den of thieves and merchants but as a house of his father.

(14) John 2:17
> Zeal for your house will consume me.

These words were spoken from the mouth of those powers cast out and consumed by the savior.

---

13. Here the entry of Jesus into the temple is interpreted as the ascent from the material and the attainment of salvation. The three Valentinian divisions of humanity are assumed. Thus Capernaum symbolizes the material, Jerusalem the psychical, and the holy of holies the spiritual.
14. See Hebrews 9:7.
15. See Revelation 15:6.
16. See Matthew 27:59.
17. See Colossians 2:14.

(15) John 2:19

> Destroy this temple
> and in three days I shall raise it up.

In three full days, not on the third day, which is the day of the resurrection of the church.

(16) John 2:20

> This temple was built over forty-six years, and you will
>   raise it up in three days?

Solomon's constructing the temple in forty-six years is an image of the savior. The number six refers to matter, that is, what is fashioned, while forty, the uncombined realm of four,[18] refers to god's breathing in[19] and the seed in that breathing in.[20]

(17) John 4:12

> You are not greater than our father Jacob,
> who gave us the well and who himself drank
> and whose sons and cattle drank?

That well signified weak, temporary, and deficient life and its glory. It was limited to being worldly. This is proved by the fact that Jacob's cattle drank from it. But the water that the savior gave is of his spirit and power. "You will not be thirsty forevermore," for his life is eternal and will never perish like the first water from the well. It is permanent. The grace and gift of our savior are not taken away or consumed or defiled by whoever shares in them. But the first life is perishable. "Water springing into eternal life" refers to those who receive life supplied abundantly from above and who pour out what has been given them for the eternal life of others. The Samaritan woman revealed uncritical faith, alien to her nature, when she did not waiver about what was said to her. "Give me this water so I won't be thirsty." She hated the shallows pierced by the word and that place of so-called living water.

(18) John 4:16

> Go and call your husband and come back here.

---

18. Or, "tetrad," a group of four aeons in the Valentinian concept of the pleroma.
19. On god breathing the breath of life into the nostrils of the first human, see Genesis 2:7.
20. The seed in the divine in-breathing refers to the spiritual people.

What this means is obvious. This is the Samaritan woman's mingling with the pleroma. Coming with her husband to the savior, she might receive from him power, union, and mingling with pleroma. He was not speaking to her about an earthly husband and telling her to call him, because he knew that she didn't have a lawful husband. The savior said to her, "Call your husband and come back here," meaning her fellow or husband[21] from the pleroma. As for what was meant allegorically, she did not know her own husband. Simply put, she was ashamed to admit that she had an adulterer, not a husband. "You are right to say, I have no husband," since in the world the Samaritan woman had no husband, for her husband was in the aeon. The six husbands signify all the material evil to which she was bound and with which she consorted when she was irrationally debauched, insulted, refused, and abandoned by them.

(19) John 4:19–20

> Sir, I see that you are a prophet.
> Our parents worshiped on this mountain.

The Samaritan properly acknowledged what was said to her. Typically only a prophet knows all such things. She acted as appropriate to her ways, neither lying nor openly acknowledging her immorality. Certain that he was a prophet, she asked him about it while she revealed the cause of her sexual activity. Because of her ignorance of god she had neglected his worship and all that was necessary in her life. She would not have come to the well outside the city unless she had desired to learn how, and for whom, and by worshiping god she might escape from her sexual acts. So she said, "Our parents worshiped on this mountain."

(20) John 4:21

> Believe me, woman, the hour is coming
> when not on this mountain
> nor in Jerusalem will you worship the father.

Earlier Jesus did not say, "Believe me, woman." But now he commands her to believe. The mountain signifies the devil or his world, since the devil was one part of the whole of matter, and the whole world is a mountain of evil, a deserted habitat of beasts, which all Jews who lived according to the law and all

---

21. In Greek, *syzygos*, "partner," "companion."

the gentiles worship. Jerusalem is the creation or the creator, whom Jews worship. In another sense the mountain is the creation, which the gentiles worship. But you as spiritual people will worship neither the creation nor the demiurge, but the father of truth. And he accepts her as one already faithful and who will be numbered among the worshipers in truth.

(21) John 4:22

You worship what you do not know.

These are the Jews and gentiles. As Peter teaches, "We must not worship in the Greek manner, accepting the works of matter and worshiping wood and stone, or in the Jewish manner worship the divine. They, thinking that they alone know god, do not know him, and worship angels and the month and the moon."[22]

(22) John 4:22

We worship what we know
since salvation is from the Jews.

"We" signifies the one who is in the aeon and those who have come from him. They knew the one they worship as they worship in truth. "Salvation is from the Jews," because he was born in Judea, but not among them, "since he was not pleased with all of them,"[23] and because from that group of people came salvation and the word to the world. In terms of what was meant allegorically, salvation came from the Jews because they are regarded as images of beings in the pleroma. Earlier worshipers worshiped him who was not father, but of flesh and error. They worshiped the creation, not the true creator, who is Christ, since "through him everything came to be and without the word nothing came to be."

(23) John 4:23

God is spirit,
and those worshiping must worship him
in spirit and truth.

Lost in the deep matter of error is what is related to the father, which is sought after so that the father may be worshiped by those who are related to him.

---

22. Preaching of Peter (*Kerygma Petrou*), cited in Clement of Alexandria, Miscellanies (Stromateis) 4.39–41.
23. 1 Corinthians 10:5.

(24) John 4:23

> God is spirit,
> and those worshiping must worship him
> in spirit and truth.

Unpolluted and pure and invisible is his divine nature. And to be worthy of him who is worshiped one must worship in a spiritual, not a fleshly, way. For those who are of the same nature as the father are spirit and worship in truth and not in error, just as Paul teaches when he calls this worship a "spiritual service."[24]

(25) John 4:25

> I know a messiah is coming,
> who is called the anointed.

The church expected Christ and believed that he alone would know all things.

(26) John 4:26

> I am he,
> talking to you.

Since the Samaritan woman was convinced that Christ would proclaim everything to her when he came, he said, "Know that I who speak to you am the one you expected." And when he acknowledged himself as the expected one who had come, "his students came to him," since because of them he had come to Samaria.

(27) John 4:28

> Then the woman left her water pot.

The water pot that can receive life is the condition and thought of the power contained in the savior. She left it with him, which is to say, she had such a vessel with the savior, a vessel in which she had come to get living water, and she returned to the world, proclaiming the coming of the Christ to the calling. For through the spirit and by the spirit the soul is taken to the savior. "They went out of the town and came toward him." This means they went out of the town, that is, their former worldly way of life, and through faith came to the savior.

---

24. Romans 12:1.

(28) John 4:31

> Meanwhile, the students were saying,
> "Rabbi, eat."

They wanted to share with him something of what they had bought in Samaria.

(29) John 4:32

> I have a meat to eat that you do not know.

[Herakleon does not comment on this passage.]

(30) John 4:33

> Then the students said to each other, "Could someone have brought him something to eat?"

The students understood on a low level and imitated the Samaritan woman, who said, "Sir, you have no bucket and the well is deep."[25]

(31) John 4:32

> My meat is to do the will of him
> who sent me and to complete his work.

The savior told his students that this was what he said to the woman, calling the will of the father his meat. This was his food and rest and power. The father's will for people is to know the father and be saved. This was the savior's work, for which reason he was sent into Samaria, that is, into the world.

(32) John 4:35

> Four more months and then comes the harvest?

He speaks of the harvest of the fruit as if it had fixed four-month intervals, and yet the harvest he was speaking of was already there. The harvest is of souls of believers. They are already ripe and ready for harvest, and ready to carry into the barn,[26] through faith into rest, as many as are ready. But not all are ready. Some are, some will be, others are still being sown.

---

25. John 4:11.
26. Matthew 13:30.

(33) Matthew 9:37

> The harvest is abundant but the field workers are few.

This line refers to those ready for the harvest and for gathering into the barn, to go through faith into rest, and be prepared for salvation and receiving the word.

(34) John 4:36

> The reaper is taking his wages.

This is said because the savior calls himself a reaper. And the wages of our lord are the salvation and restoration of those reaped, which means, his rest upon them. "And gathering the grain for eternal life" means either that what is gathered is the fruit of eternal life or that it is itself eternal life.

(35) John 4:37

> So sower and reaper alike may be happy.

The sower is happy because he sows, and because he is already gathering part of his seeds. Likewise, the reaper is happy because he is reaping. The first began by sowing, the second by reaping. Both could not begin with the same task, since sowing is first and reaping afterward. When the sower stops sowing, the reaper is still reaping. But for the moment both do their own work and share a common joy when they consider the perfection of the seeds. "One sows, another reaps." The earthly son[27] above the place[28] sows.[29] The savior, who is also the earthly son, reaps and sends the angels down as reapers known through the students,[30] each for his own soul.

(36) John 4:38

> Others worked and you entered their work.

These seeds were sown neither through nor by them. Those who worked are the angels of the dispensation, through whom as mediators the seeds were sown and nourished. The work of sowers and reapers is not the same, for the former in cold and rain work and dig up the earth and sow, and through the winter

---

27. Or "human son," "son of man."
28. The place probably refers to the place of god, as a circumlocution for god.
29. See Matthew 13:37.
30. See Matthew 13:39.

look after it, hoeing and weeding. The latter, who enter a prepared harvest, reap the harvests with happiness.

(37) John 4:39
> And many Samaritans from the city believed in him,
> because of what the woman said when she testified.

Out of that town or city, meaning out of the world. Through the woman's report, that is, through the spiritual church. "Many" because there are many psychical people, but the imperishable nature of the election is one and uniform and unique.

(38) John 4:42
> He stayed there two days.

He stayed with them and not in them, and for two days, either to signify the present aeon and the future one in marriage, or the time before his passion and that after the passion, which he spent with them. After converting many more to faith through his own word, he left them.

(39) John 4:42
> It is no longer because of your talk that we believe.

This passage should say, "It is no longer only because of your talk."

John 4:42
> We ourselves have heard and we know that he is truly
> the savior of the world.

At first people are led by others to believe in the savior, but when they read his words, they no longer believe because of human testimony alone but because of the truth.

(40) John 4:46–47
> There was a certain prince whose son was sick in
> Capernaum. When he heard that Jesus had come from
> Judea into Galilee, he went to him and asked him to
> come down and heal his son, for he was near death.

The prince or royal officer is the demiurge, since he reigned over those under him. But because his dominion is small and temporary, he is called a prince, like some petty king set over a small kingdom by a universal king. His son in

Capernaum, in the lower part of the middle area by the sea, refers to what adjoins matter. In other words, the man belonging to him was sick not with respect to nature but in his ignorance and sins. "From Judea to Galilee" means from the Judea above. The phrase "he was near death" refutes the doctrines of those who say that the soul is immortal. Soul and body are destroyed in Gehenna.[31] The soul is not immortal but only has a disposition to salvation. It is the perishable that robes itself in imperishability, and the mortal that robes itself in immortality, when its death was swallowed in victory.[32] "Unless you see signs and wonders you will not believe"[33] was correctly spoken to a person who had the nature to be persuaded through works and through sense perception, not to believe a word. "Descend before my child dies," because the end of law was death.[34] The law kills through sins. Before death finally came into being in accordance with sins, the father asks the only savior to help the son, whose nature is to do this. "Go, your son lives,"[35] the savior said modestly, since he didn't say, "Let him live," or show that he himself had given him life. Having gone down to the sick man and healed him of the disease, that is, of his sins, and having made him alive through remission, he said, "Your son lives." "The man believed" because the demiurge can easily believe that the savior is able to heal even when he is not present. The prince's slaves[36] are the angels of the demiurge, proclaiming, "Your son lives," because he is behaving correctly, no longer doing what is wrong. Therefore the slaves proclaimed to the prince the news about his son's salvation, because the angels are the first to observe the actions of men on earth and to see if they have lived well and sincerely since the savior's sojourn on earth. "The seventh hour" refers to the nature of the man healed. "And he believed and along with all his household" refers to the angelic order and men related to him. It is a question whether some angels, those who descended upon the daughters of men,[37] will be saved. The destruction of people by the demiurge is made clear by the sentence "The children of the kingdom will go out into the outer darkness."[38] About them Isaiah prophesied, "I produced and raised sons, but they set me aside." He calls them "alien sons and a wicked and lawless seed and a vineyard producing thorns."[39]

---

31. See Matthew 10:28.
32. See 1 Corinthians 15:53–55.
33. John 4:48.
34. See Romans 7:13.
35. John 4:50.
36. John 4:51.
37. See Genesis 6:2.
38. Matthew 8:12.
39. Isaiah 1:2, 4; 5:1.

(41) John 8:21

> Where I am going you cannot come.

How have they come to be in imperishability when they remain in ignorance and disbelief and sins?

(42) John 8:22

> Will he kill himself? because he said, "Where I am
>   going you cannot come."

In their wicked thoughts the Jews said these things and declared themselves greater than the savior and thought that they would go to god for eternal rest but the savior would slay himself and go to corruption and death, where they thought they would not go. The Jews thought the savior said, "When I have slain myself, I shall go to corruption, where you cannot come."

(43) John 8:37

> My word has no place in you.

The word has no place because others are unsuited for it either by substance or inclination.

(44) John 8:44

> You are from your father the devil.

This passage accounts for their inability[40] to hear the word of Jesus or to understand his speech. It means "of the substance of the devil." It makes their nature evident to them and convicts them in advance. They are neither children of Abraham nor children of god, because they do not love Jesus.

(45) John 8:44

> You are from your father the devil.

The word was spoken to those who were of the substance of the devil.

(46) John 8.44

> And you want to do the desires of your father.

---

40. The Jews' inability.

The devil has no will. He has desires. These things were spoken not to those who are by nature children of the devil, the people of the earth, but to the psychical people, who are children of the devil by adoption. Some of them who are this way by nature can become children of god by adoption. From having loved the desires of the devil and carrying them out these people become children of the devil, though they are not so by nature. The name "children" must be understood in three ways. First, by nature, second by inclination, third by merit. "By nature" means what is generated by some generator, which may be called a child; "by inclination," when one does someone else's will by one's own inclination and is called the child of the one whose will one does; and "by merit," in the way that some are called children of Gehenna and of darkness and of lawlessness,[41] and offspring of snakes and vipers,[42] for those parents generate nothing by their own nature. They are ruinous and consume those who are cast into them. Jesus calls them children of the devil, not because the devil generates offspring, but because by doing the works of the devil they became like him.

(47) John 8:44

> From the beginning he was a murderer,
> and he does not stand in the truth,
> because there is no truth in him.
> When he lies he speaks from himself,
> since he is a liar and the father of lies.

His nature is not of the truth but of its opposite, which is error and ignorance. Therefore one cannot stand in truth nor have truth in oneself. One has lies as one's own nature, being by nature unable ever to speak truth. Not only is that person a liar, but so too his father, which is also his nature, since he originated from error and lies.

(48) John 8:50

> There is one who seeks it, and he is the judge.

The one who seeks and judges is the one who avenges me, the servant commissioned for this, the one who does not bear the sword in vain.[43] The judge

---

41. See Matthew 23:15, 33.
42. See Matthew 3:7.
43. See Romans 13:4.

and punisher is Moses, who is also the legislator. How does he say that all judgment was given to him?[44] He speaks correctly, for the judge who does his will judges as a servant. Such is what happens among people.[45]

(49) Matthew 3:11

John said,

"I baptize you in water for repentance,

but after me will come one stronger than I,

and I am not fit to carry his sandals.

He will baptize you in the holy spirit and fire."

He baptized no one in fire. However, some understand fire to be in the ears of those who are sealed in baptism and so have heard the apostolic preaching.

(50) Matthew 10:32-33

Anyone who confesses me[46] before others,

I will confess before my father in heaven,

and whoever denies me before others,

I will deny before my father in heaven.

One type of confession is made by faith and behavior, another by voice. The confession by voice also takes place before authorities. The crowds consider this the only confession. They are wrong because hypocrites can also make this confession. This word will not be found universally, since not all those who are saved made the confession by voice. Among the exceptions are Matthew, Philip, Thomas, Levi, and many others. The confession by voice is not universal but particular. What he mentions here is universal, the one by works and actions corresponding to faith in him. This confession is followed by the particular one before authorities, if necessary and reason requires it. This one also confesses by voice, if that person has previously confessed by disposition.

And he correctly said "in me" of those who confess, and "me" of those who deny. For the latter deny him, even if they do not confess by action. The only ones who confess in him are those who live in confession and action related to

---

44. See John 5:27.

45. Or, "Such is the role of human beings before God."

46. Literally, "confesses in me."

him. He confesses in them, since he is wrapped up in them and contained by them. Therefore they never deny him. But those who are not in him deny him. He did not say, "Whoever will deny in me," but "me." No one who is in him ever denies him. "Before others" refers to both the saved and the gentiles, and in like fashion, to their behavior before the former and to their voice before the latter.

18

The Treatise on Resurrection

The question of resurrection was a controversial one within Jewish and Christian circles in the world of antiquity and late antiquity; the issue of the survival of the soul and the possibility of reincarnation were discussed extensively by Greek philosophers as well. Resurrection, reincarnation, and survival after death remain hot points of discussion to the present day. The Valentinian Treatise on Resurrection offers a spiritual understanding of resurrection that picks up ideas from Paul's letters (see 1 Corinthians 15, for example) but parts company with Paul and his followers on several significant matters. The author of the treatise, rejecting a literal interpretation of the resurrection in favor of a spiritual understanding, emphasizes that the spiritual resurrection is no illusion. It is real and it is true, more real and true, in fact, than the material world. The author cites Paul approvingly as "the messenger" (or apostle), and states with Paul, "We suffered with him [that is, Jesus], we arose with him, and we went to heaven with him." The author of the Treatise on Resurrection understands that suffering and death actually occur in this material world, and the author proposes, in contrast to Paul's more apocalyptic view, that resurrection is actually the transcending of the material world through the liberation of the spirit. Referring to the Valentinian threefold division of humanity into the spiritual (or pneumatic), the psychical, and the fleshly or material (or hylic), author writes, "This is the spiritual resurrection [or resurrection of the spirit], which swallows up the [resurrection of the] soul and [the resurrection of] the flesh." So it was with Jesus, so it is with all of us.

Further, the Treatise on Resurrection proclaims that the resurrection is not reserved for some future time but is a spiritual transition that has already begun: "already you have the resurrection." Like Hymenaeus and Philetus according to 2 Timothy 2:18, the author of this text announces the resurrection as a present reality and thus adheres to a realized eschatology. With a formulation reminiscent of Hindu and other statements, the Treatise on Resurrection affirms that one may call the world of matter illusion, but the world of spirit, and the resurrection of the spirit, is truth.

The Treatise on Resurrection is found in the Nag Hammadi library. It was composed in Greek by an unknown author who presents the treatise in the form of a letter to a certain Rheginos. The circumstances of composition are unknown.

THE TREATISE ON RESURRECTION[1]

My son Rheginos,[2] some people want to become learned. That is their purpose when they begin to solve unsolved problems. If they succeed, they are proud. But I do not think they have stood in the word of truth. Rather, they seek their own rest, which we have received from our savior and our lord, the Christ. We received rest when we came to know the truth and rested on it.

Since your pleasant question concerns what is the truth about the resurrection, I am writing you today to tell you. Many do not believe in it, but a few find it. So let us see.

HOW GOD BECAME A HUMAN SON

How did the lord proclaim things while he was in flesh and after he had revealed himself to be the son of god? He lived in this world that you live in,

---

1. The Treatise on Resurrection: Nag Hammadi Codex I,4, pp. 43,25 to 50,18; translated by Malcolm L. Peel (Attridge, ed., *Nag Hammadi Codex I*, 1.123–57, 2.137–215; Robinson, ed., *Nag Hammadi Library in English*, rev. ed., 54–57), and Bentley Layton (*The Gnostic Scriptures*, 320–24), revised by Willis Barnstone.
2. The recipient of the letter is known only from this text.

speaking about the law of nature, which I call death. And more, Rheginos, the son of god became a human son. He embraced both qualities, possessing humanity and divinity so he could, by being the son of god, conquer death, and, by being the human son, restore the pleroma.[3] At the beginning he was above as a seed of truth, which was before the cosmos came into being.[4] In the cosmic structure many dominions and divinities have come into being.

TRUTH AS THE AGENT

I know that I am presenting the problem in difficult words, but there is nothing in the word of truth that is difficult. After the solution appeared,[5] to ensure that nothing be hidden and everything be openly revealed, there are two essentials: the destruction of evil and the revelation of the elect. This solution entails the emanation of truth and spirit, and of grace bestowed by truth.

THE SAVIOR SWALLOWED DEATH

The savior swallowed death. You must know this. He laid aside the perishable world and made himself into an imperishable aeon, raised himself up, and swallowed the visible with the invisible. Thereby he gave us our immortality. Then, as the messenger Paul[6] said of him, "We suffered with him, we rose with him, and we entered heaven with him."[7] Now, since we are seen in this world, we wear it like a garment. From the savior we radiate beams, and we are held in his arms until our own sunset, our death in this life. We are drawn to heaven by him, like beams, by the sun, and nothing holds us down. This is the resurrection of the spirit, which swallows up the soul and the flesh.[8]

---

3. Or "fullness," here and throughout the text. The restoration of the pleroma is the ultimate salvation of the light when it returns to the divine fullness, the fundamental act of Valentinian salvation.

4. Jesus is understood to be both human and divine, but his origin is from the divine realm above.

5. This is the appearance of the savior.

6. The apostle Paul.

7. See Romans 8:17, Ephesians 2:4–6, Colossians 2:12, 3:1–3.

8. The spirit, soul, and flesh represent the Valentinian hierarchy of the pneumatic, psychic, and hylic. Here the spiritual resurrection consumes, or supersedes, the resurrection of soul and flesh.

WITH FAITH RISE

If you cannot believe, you cannot be persuaded. My son, these matters belong to the domain of faith, and not to persuasive argument, in asserting that the dead will rise. Among the philosophers in the world there may be one who believes.[9] Certainly that philosopher will rise. And let that philosopher here on earth not believe that he is returning to the self by himself, and because of faith. We have known the human son, and we believe that he rose from among the dead. We say of him, "He is the destroyer of death."

The goal as well as its believers is great. And the thinking mind of believers will not disappear, nor will the mind of those who know. We are chosen for salvation and redemption, since from the beginning we were predestined not to fall into the folly of the ignorant. We shall enter into the wisdom of those who have known the truth. Those who have wakened to the truth cannot abandon it. The system of the pleroma is strong. A small part of it is what broke loose to make up the world. What encompasses everything, the realm of all, did not come into being. It was. So never doubt the resurrection, my son Rheginos.

FATE OF THE FLESH AND OF THE SPIRIT

If you did not exist in flesh, you took on flesh when you entered the world. Why is it, then, that you will you not take your flesh with you when you rise into the aeon? What is better than flesh is what animates.[10] What came into being because of you,[11] is it not yours? Doesn't it exist with you? But while you are in the world, what are you missing? That is precisely what you have attempted to learn.

After the birth of the body comes old age, and you exist in corruption. But what you lack is a gain. You will not give up the better part when you leave. The inferior part suffers, but it finds grace.[12] Nothing redeems us from this

---

9. The author of the text incorporates sentiments critical of philosophers.
10. What animates is the soul.
11. What came into being because of a person is the flesh.
12. The meaning here is uncertain. Perhaps the better, spiritual self finds grace by being liberated from the body. Perhaps the inferior body is favored, either because it lives at all, or because features of its existence somehow continue on.

world, but we are members of the realm of all and are saved.[13] We have received salvation from start to finish. Let us think in this way, let us comprehend in this way.

WHAT IS THE RESURRECTION?

Some ask whether one will be saved immediately, if the body is left behind. Let no one doubt. The visible parts of the body that are dead will not be saved. Only the living parts that exist inside will rise. What is the resurrection? It is the revelation of those who have risen. If you remember reading in the gospel that Elijah appeared and Moses with him,[14] do not suppose that the resurrection is an illusion. It is no illusion. It is truth. It is more proper to say that the world is illusion, rather than the resurrection that is because of our lord the savior, Jesus the Christ.

THE TRUTH OF RESURRECTION

What am I telling you now? The living will die.
How do they live in illusion?
The rich become poor and kings are overthrown.
All changes. The world is an illusion.
Why do I seem to shout?
The resurrection has nothing of this character.
It is truth standing firm. It is revelation of what is,
and the transformation of things,
and a transition into freshness.
Incorruptibility floods over corruption.
Light rivers down upon the darkness, swallowing obscurity.
The pleroma fills the hollow.
These are the symbols and images of resurrection.
They establish its goodness.

---

13. People, as spiritual beings, are saved as members of the realm of fullness.
14. This reference is to the accounts of the transfiguration in Matthew 17:1–8, Mark 9:2–8, and Luke 9:28–36.

RESURRECTION IS HERE

O Rheginos, do not lose yourself in details, nor live obeying the flesh for the sake of harmony. Flee from being scattered and being in bondage, and then you already have resurrection.[15] If you know what in yourself will die,[16] though you have lived many years, why not look at yourself and see yourself risen now? You have the resurrection, yet you go on as if you are to die when it is only the part destined to die that is moribund. Why do I put up with your poor training? Everyone finds a way, and there are many ways, to be released from this element and not to roam aimlessly in error, all with the end of recovering what one was at the beginning.

GOOD-BYE

These words I have received from the generosity of my lord, Jesus the Christ. I have taught you and your brothers and sisters, who are my children, about them, and have omitted nothing that may strengthen you. If there is anything among these written words that is obscure, ask and I will explain.

Do not be worried about consulting anyone in your circle who can help. Many await what I have written to you. I say peace and grace be among them.

I greet you and whoever loves you with the love of family.

---

15. See 2 Timothy 2:18.
16. This expression recalls the Delphic maxim, "Know yourself," Gospel of Thomas 3, and other texts.

19

The Prayer of the
Messenger Paul

The Prayer of the Messenger Paul is a lovely prayer, with apparent Valentinian features. For Valentinians Paul was a special messenger, and they maintained that Paul was the teacher of Theudas and Theudas the teacher of Valentinos. The prayer opens with a meditation on intimacy with god, who is the mind, treasure, fullness, and rest for the one praying: "My redeemer, redeem me, I am yours. I came from you." The prayer then requests authority, that the body may be healed, the soul redeemed, and the mind granted "the fullness of grace." Lastly, the prayer asks for enlightenment in words that recall Gospel of Thomas 17 and 1 Corinthians 2:6, and it closes with a doxology and a final amen. The reference in the last section of the prayer to "the animate god [or the psychical god]," as well as the "eyes of angels" and the "ears of rulers [or archons]," is reminiscent of Valentinian and other gnostic texts.

The Prayer of the Messenger Paul is also the first text of Nag Hammadi Codex I, which may well be a Valentinian book. It was copied onto the front flyleaf of the codex, probably after the scribe had copied the rest of the texts in that codex. The prayer was composed in Greek, but precisely when, where, and by whom remains unknown. It is attributed to Paul, pseudonymously, in the title at the end of the text.

PRAYER OF THE MESSENGER PAUL[1]

Grant me your mercy.[2]
My redeemer, redeem me,
for I am yours.
I came from you.
You are my mind:
give me birth.
You are my treasure:
open for me.
You are my fullness:
accept me.
You are my rest:
give me unlimited perfection.

I pray to you,
you who exist and preexisted,
in the name exalted above every name,[3]
through Jesus the anointed,
lord of lords,
king of the eternal realms.
Give me your gifts, with no regret,
through the human child,
the spirit,
the advocate of truth.
Give me authority, I beg of you,
give healing for my body, as I beg you,

---

1. The Prayer of the Messenger Paul: Nag Hammadi Codex I (I,1, pp. 1-B, 10), translated from the Coptic by Marvin Meyer. For an additional example of gnostic prayer, see the Hermetic Prayer of Thanksgiving; also see the Three Steles of Seth.
2. Two or three lines of the Coptic text are missing at the very beginning of the prayer, and the first line here is partially restored. The missing line just before may read something like the following: "Fill me with your light."
3. Philippians 2:9.

through the preacher of the gospel,[4]
and redeem my enlightened soul forever, and my spirit,
and disclose to my mind the firstborn of the fullness of grace.

Grant what eyes of angels have not seen,
what ears of rulers have not heard,
and what has not arisen in the hearts of people,[5]
who became angelic,
and after the image of the animate god[6]
when it was formed in the beginning.
I have the faith of hope.
And bestow upon me
your beloved, chosen, blessed majesty,
you who are the firstborn, the first-conceived,
and the wonderful mystery of your house.
For yours is the power and the glory and the praise and the greatness,
forever and ever.
Amen.

---

4. Perhaps Paul, or Jesus.
5. Gospel of Thomas 17; 1 Corinthians 2:6.
6. Or, "the psychical god," that is, the creator of this world and people in this world, as described in other gnostic texts.

20

Valentinian Liturgical Readings

The Valentinian Liturgical Readings illustrate a Valentinian gnostic understanding of the sacraments of anointing (chrism), baptism, and the eucharist. These readings appear in the Nag Hammadi library after a Valentinian Exposition, which Elaine Pagels interprets as a catechism for gnostic initiates.[1] The instruction provided in the Valentinian Exposition, though in fragmentary condition, addresses controversial and disputed issues regarding the father of all and silence, the role of the limit or boundary for the divine realm, and the actions and motivations of Sophia.

Once the gnostic initiates had been appropriately instructed, we may assume, they would have been able to participate in the rituals of anointing, baptism, and the eucharist, using the liturgical readings included here. These emphasize empowerment and enlightenment. In the reading on anointing the gnostics seek power over evil; in the first reading on baptism they celebrate their exodus from the world into the eternal realm; in the second reading on baptism they announce their transition from the physical realm to the spiritual realm. Some of the readings conclude with a doxology and Amen.

---

1. In Robinson, ed., *Nag Hammadi Library in English*, 481–82.

VALENTINIAN LITURGICAL READINGS

ON ANOINTING[2]

It is fitting for you at this time
to send your son Jesus the anointed
and anoint us,
so we can trample on snakes
and the heads of scorpions
and all the power of the devil,[3]
since he is the shepherd of the seed.
Through him we have known you.
And we glorify you:
Glory be to you,
the father in the son,
the father in the son,
the father in the holy church,
and in the holy angels.
From now on he abides forever
in the perpetuity of the eternal realms,
forever,
until the untraceable eternal realms
of the eternal realms.
Amen.

---

2. The Valentinian Liturgical Readings: Nag Hammadi Codex XI, pp. 40,1 to 44,37, translated by John D. Turner in Charles W. Hedrick, ed., *Nag Hammadi Codices XI, XII and XIII* (Leiden & New York: E. J. Brill, 1990), pp. 142–51; revised in verse by Willis Barnstone and Marvin Meyer. Reprinted by permission of Brill Academic Publishers. The selections are in a very fragmentary state, and we have arranged the fragments and presented the legible words in such a way as to allow for an appreciation of something of their poetic quality.
3. Luke 10:19; see also Mark 16:18 (longer ending of Mark); Acts 28:3–6. Snake-handling religions in the present day also handle serpents.

ON BAPTISM (A)

This is the fullness of the summary of knowledge,
the summary revealed to us
by our lord Jesus the anointed,
the only son.
These are the sure and necessary things,
so that we may walk in them.
They are of the first baptism . . .
The first baptism is the forgiveness of sins . . .
you . . . your sins
a pattern . . . of the anointed,
which is the equal . . . within him
Jesus
The first baptism is the forgiveness of sins.
It delivers us from them
into those of the right,[4]
into the incorruptibility that is the Jordan.
But that place is of the world.
So we have been sent out of the world
into the eternal realm.
For the interpretation of John[5] is the eternal realm,
while the interpretation of the Jordan
is the descent that is the upward progression,[6]
our exodus from the world
into the eternal realm.

ON BAPTISM (B)

From the world into the Jordan,
and from the world's blindness into the sight of god,
from the carnal into the spiritual,

---

4. In Valentinian thought those of the right are psychical people, as opposed to those of the left, who are material people.
5. John the baptizer.
6. The upward progression is the ascent to the pleroma, or fullness.

from the physical into the angelic,
from the created into the fullness,
from the world into the eternal realm,
from enslavements into sonship,
from entanglements into one another,
from the desert into our estate,
from the cold into the hot. . . .
Thus we were brought from seminal bodies
into bodies with a perfect form.
Indeed, I[7] entered by way of example
the remnant for which the anointed rescued us
in the fellowship of his spirit.
And he produced us who are in him,
and from now on the souls will be perfect spirits.
Now what is granted to us by the first baptism
is invisible . . . and is his . . . since . . . he speaks about them.

ON THE EUCHARIST (A)

We thank you
and celebrate the eucharist, father,
remembering your son
Jesus the anointed
come . . . invisible . . . your son . . . his love
to knowledge . . . they do your will
through the name of Jesus the anointed,
and will do your will
now and always.
They are complete
in every spiritual gift
and every purity.
Glory be to you
through your son
and your child Jesus the anointed,

---

7. "I" may be the person reciting the liturgy.

now and always.
Amen.

ON THE EUCHARIST (B)

The word . . . the holy one is . . . food and drink
son, since you . . . food . . . to us . . . in the life
he does not boast . . . that is . . . the church
you are pure . . . you are the lord.
Whenever you die purely,
you will be pure
so as to have him . . .
everyone who will guide him
to food and drink.
Glory be to you forever. Amen.

21

The Secret Book of James

The Secret Book (or Apocryphon) of James is a text presented, rather like the Letter of Peter to Philip, within the frame of an introductory letter, as a secret book with sayings of Jesus that his followers remembered. According to the text, this is the second such secret book that James sent. The letter of James is addressed to someone whose name is preserved imperfectly in the papyrus, with only the final three letters (in Coptic, or Greek) visible: ——thos. Some scholars have suggested that the name of the recipient of the letter may be restored to designate Cerinthos, a Christian teacher who flourished in the early second century and who proclaimed a christology similar to the view of Jesus in the Secret Book of James.

In the body of the Secret Book of James are sayings of Jesus presented, expanded, and interpreted in the context of questions and comments by the students of Jesus, particularly James and Peter. The sayings include statements of good fortune and woe, parables and stories, and discourses on being "filled," lacking, and suffering. Many of these sayings are unknown elsewhere; some may contain elements and themes that recall the historical Jesus. Some of these sayings reflect on themes familiar from gnostic sources: fullness and deficiency, the life of the spirit, self-knowledge. At one point Jesus says, "This is also how you can acquire the kingdom of heaven for yourselves. Unless you acquire it through knowledge, you will not be able to find it." Some of the sayings seem deliberately obscure and enigmatic as they play with contradictions and paradoxes of the human condition.

The Secret Book of James is a Coptic text in Nag Hammadi Codex I, a codex that contains several Valentinian texts. This has led some scholars to consider the Secret Book of James to be a gnostic and perhaps a Valentinian document. It contains themes that are typical of gnostic texts—knowledge, self-knowledge, fullness, deficiency, and the like. Further, the discussion of people being of three parts—body, soul, and spirit—is reminiscent of the threefold division of elemental stuff and of people in Valentinian thought.

The Secret Book of James was probably written in the first half of the second century; portions of the text may well be even older. The text was most likely composed in Greek, though it claims to have been written in Hebrew. The place of composition is unknown. The reference to burial "in the sand" could suggest that the author was writing in Egypt, but the reference may well be corrupt and in need of emendation (see the notes).

THE SECRET BOOK OF JAMES[1]

James[2] writes to ——thos.[3]
 Peace be with you from peace,
 love from love,
 grace from grace,
 faith from faith,
 life from holy life.[4]

JAMES'S SECRET BOOKS

You have asked me to send you a secret book revealed to Peter and me by the master, and I could not turn you down, nor could I speak to you, so I have

---

1. The Secret Book of James: Nag Hammadi library, Codex I,2, pp. 1,1 to 16,30, translated by Marvin Meyer.
2. This is apparently James the just, the brother of Jesus and leader of the church in Jerusalem (see Gospel of Thomas 12), though here James is also made part of the apostolic circle of the twelve.
3. The salutation of the letter is in large part restored. Some scholars restore the name of the recipient to read Cerinthos, a well-known early Christian teacher.
4. These lines are partially restored.

written it in Hebrew[5] and have sent it to you, and to you alone. But since you are a minister of the salvation of the saints, try to be careful not to reveal to many people this book that the savior did not want to reveal even to all of us, his twelve students. Nonetheless, those who will be saved through the faith of this treatise will be blessed.

Ten months ago I sent you another secret book[6] that the savior revealed to me. Think of that book as revealed to me, James. But this one. . . .[7]

JESUS ADDRESSES PETER AND JAMES

Now, the twelve students were all sitting together, recalling what the savior had said to each of them, whether in a hidden or an open manner, and organizing it in books.[8] I was writing what is in my book. Look, the savior appeared, after he had left us, while we were watching for him.

Five hundred fifty days[9] after he rose from the dead, we said to him, "Did you depart and leave us?"

Jesus said, "No, but I shall return to the place from which I came. If you want to come with me, come."

They all answered and said, "If you order us, we shall come."

He said, "I tell you the truth, no one will ever enter the kingdom of heaven because I ordered it, but rather because you yourselves are filled. Leave James and Peter to me that I may fill them."

When he called the two of them, he took them aside and commanded the rest to keep doing what they were doing.

The savior said, "You have been treated kindly,

---

5. The Coptic here includes *hebraiois* (from Greek, with the Greek case ending remaining). No such Hebrew text is known.

6. No additional secret book of James has been identified.

7. Several lines cannot be readily restored. One attempt is made by Dankwart Kirchner, "The Apocryphon of James," in Schneemelcher, ed., *New Testament Apocrypha,* 1.291: "[Regarding] this one, however, since I have not yet fully comprehended it, and since it was revealed for you as well, and for those who belong to you, exert yourself, and search after its doctrine. In this way you will attain salvation. After all this you shall reveal it as well."

8. The openings of the Gospel of Thomas and the Book of Thomas also contain comments on composing books with hidden sayings.

9. Other texts, including gnostic texts, suggest similarly long periods of time for appearances of Jesus, for example eighteen months (540 days), or 545 days (eighteen months plus five intercalary days?), or even twelve years. On eighteen days or months, see "Be Eager for the Word," below in the Secret Book of James.

... have not understood.[10]

Do you not want to be filled?

Your hearts are drunk.

Do you not want to be sober?

You ought to be ashamed.

"From now on, awake or asleep, remember that you have seen the human son[11] and have spoken with him and have listened to him.

"Shame on those who have seen the human son.

"Blessings will be on you who have not seen him, or associated with him, or spoken with him, or listened to anything from him. Yours is life.[12]

"Understand that he healed you when you were sick, that you might reign.

"Shame on those who have found relief from their sickness, for they will relapse into sickness.

"Blessings on you who have not been sick, and have known relief before getting sick. The kingdom of god is yours.

"So I tell you: Be filled and leave no space in you empty, or he who is coming will mock you."

BEING FILLED AND LACKING

Then Peter answered, "Look, three times you have told us, 'Be filled,' but we are filled."

The savior answered and said, "For this reason I have told you, 'Be filled,' that you may not lack. Those who lack will not be saved. To be filled is good and to lack is bad. Yet since it is also good for you to lack but bad for you to be filled, whoever is filled also lacks. One who lacks is not filled in the way another who lacks is filled, but whoever is filled is brought to an appropriate end. So you should lack when you can fill yourselves and be filled when you lack,

---

10. Several lines cannot be restored with confidence. A tentative attempt is made by Dankwart Kirchner, "The Apocryphon of James," in Schneemelcher, ed., *New Testament Apocrypha*, 1.297: "You have been treated kindly through the father, that you may receive my words. If the rest of the students as well have written my words in their books as if they had understood, beware! For they have exerted themselves without understanding. They have heard just like fools, and just like the deaf they have not understood.

11. Or "earthly son," "son of man."

12. On being blessed but not seeing, see "Know Yourself," later in the Secret Book of James, and John 20:29.

that you may be able to fill yourselves more. Be filled with spirit but lack in reason, for reason is of the soul. It is soul."[13]

BELIEVE IN MY CROSS

I answered and said to him, "Master, we can obey you if you wish, for we have forsaken our fathers and our mothers and our villages, and followed you. Give us the means not to be tempted by the evil devil."

The master answered and said, "What good is it to you if you do the father's will but you are not given your part of his bounty when you are tempted by Satan? But if you are oppressed by Satan and persecuted and do the father's will, I say he will love you, make you my equal, and consider you beloved through his forethought,[14] and by your own choice. Won't you stop loving the flesh and fearing suffering? Don't you know that you have not yet been abused, unjustly accused, locked up in prison, unlawfully condemned, crucified without reason,[15] or buried in the sand[16] as I myself was by the evil one? Do you dare to spare the flesh, O you for whom the spirit is a wall surrounding you? If you consider how long the world has existed before you and how long it will exist after you, you will see that your life is but a day and your sufferings an hour. The good will not enter the world. Disdain death, then, and care about life. Remember my cross and my death, and you will live."

I answered and said to him, "Master, do not mention to us the cross and death, for they are far from you."

The master answered and said, "I tell you the truth, none will be saved unless they believe in my cross, for the kingdom of god belongs to those who have believed in my cross. Be seekers of death, then, like the dead who seek life, for what they seek becomes apparent to them. And what is there to cause them concern? As for you, when you search out death, it will teach you about being chosen. I tell you the truth: No one afraid of death will be saved, for the

---

13. The beginning of this paragraph incorporates minor restorations, and the entirety of this paragraph is difficult to translate. A significant distinction is made between the spirit *(pneuma)* and the soul *(psyche)*, as in Valentinian texts.
14. *Pronoia* (from Greek), as in the Secret Book of John and other texts.
15. The text is emended here. The manuscript reads "with reason."
16. Burial in the sand is characteristic of Egypt. Some scholars would emend the text to read "in shame."

kingdom of death[17] belongs to those who are put to death.[18] Become better than I. Be like the child of the holy spirit."[19]

BE EAGER FOR THE WORD

Then I asked him, "Master, can we prophesy to those who ask us to prophesy to them? There are many who bring a request to us and look to us to hear our pronouncement."

The master answered and said, "Do you not know that the head of prophecy was cut off with John?"[20]

But I said, "Master, is it not impossible to remove the head of prophecy?"

The master said to me, "When you realize what 'head' means, and that prophecy comes from the head, then understand the meaning of 'its head was removed.'

"First I spoke with you in parables, and you did not understand. Now I am speaking with you openly, and you do not grasp it. Nevertheless, you were for me a parable among parables and a disclosure among things revealed.

"Be eager to be saved without being urged. Rather, be fervent on your own and, if possible, outdo even me, for this is how the father will love you.

"Come to hate hypocrisy and evil intention. Intention produces hypocrisy, and hypocrisy is far from truth.

"Do not let the kingdom of heaven wither away. It is like a palm shoot whose dates dropped around it. It produced buds, and after they grew, its productivity dried up. This is also what happened with fruit that came from this single root. After it was harvested, fruit was obtained by many. It certainly was good. Is it not possible to produce the new growth now, and for you to find it?[21]

"Since I was glorified like this once before, why do you hold me back when I am eager to go? After my labor[22] you have made me stay with you another

---

17. Or possibly emend to read "the kingdom of god," reading *noute* instead of *mou*.
18. Or "who put themselves to death," as with people coming forward voluntarily for martyrdom.
19. The child of god, where the holy spirit may be understood to be god the mother. See Gospel of Thomas 101; also the Gospel of Philip.
20. John the baptizer; see Gospel of Thomas 46.
21. This parable of the date palm shoot remains difficult to translate, and the translation given here is somewhat tentative. The reference to "it" in the last sentence must be a reference to the kingdom.
22. Or "suffering."

eighteen days[23] because of the parables. For some people it was enough to listen to the teaching and understand 'The Shepherds,' 'The Seed,' 'The Building,' 'The Lamps of the Young Women,' 'The Wage of the Workers,' and 'The Silver Coins and the Woman.'[24]

"Be eager for the word. The first aspect of the word is faith, the second is love, the third is works, and from these comes life.

"The word is like a grain of wheat. When someone sowed it, he had faith in it, and when it sprouted, he loved it, because he saw many grains instead of just one. And after he worked, he was saved because he prepared it as food and he still kept some out to sow.

"This is also how you can acquire the kingdom of heaven for yourselves. Unless you acquire it through knowledge,[25] you will not be able to find it."

UNDERSTAND THE LIGHT

"So I say to you, be sober. Do not go astray. And often have I said to you all together, and also to you alone, James, be saved. I have commanded you to follow me, and I have taught you how to speak before the rulers.

"See that I have come down and have spoken and have exerted myself and have won my crown when I saved you. I came down to live with you, so you might also live with me. And when I found that your houses had no roofs, I lived in houses that could receive me when I came down.

"Trust me, my brothers. Understand what the great light is. The father does not need me. A father does not need a son, but it is the son who needs the father. To him I am going, for the father of the son is not in need of you.

"Listen to the word, understand knowledge, love life, and no one will persecute you and no one will oppress you other than you yourselves."

SHAME ON YOU, BLESSINGS ON YOU

"You wretches! You losers! You pretenders to truth! You falsifiers of knowledge! You sinners against the spirit! Do you still dare to listen when from the beginning you should have been speaking? Do you still dare to sleep when

---

23. Or perhaps emend to read "eighteen months" (see note 9 above).
24. These are titles of or references to parables.
25. Gnosis, here and below.

from the beginning you should have been awake so that the kingdom of heaven might receive you? I tell you the truth, it is easier for a holy person to sink into defilement, and for an enlightened person to sink into darkness, than for you to reign—or not to reign.[26]

"I remember your tears, your mourning, and your grief. They are far from us. You who are outside the father's inheritance, weep when you should, mourn, and preach what is good. As is proper, the son is ascending.

"I tell you the truth, if I had been sent to those who would listen to me and had spoken with them, I would never have come down to earth. Now be ashamed.

"Look, I shall be leaving you and go away. I do not want to stay with you any longer just as you yourselves have not wanted this. Follow me quickly. I tell you, for you I came down. You are loved ones. You will bring life to many people. Invoke the father, pray to god frequently, and he will be generous with you.

"Blessings on one who has seen you with him when he is proclaimed among the angels and glorified among the saints. Yours is life. Rejoice and be glad as children of god. Observe his will that you may be saved. Accept correction from me and save yourselves. I am mediating for you with the father, and he will forgive you many things."

FEW FIND THE KINGDOM OF HEAVEN

When we heard this, we were delighted. We had become gloomy because of what we[27] said earlier. But when he saw us happy, he said,

"Shame on you who are in need of an advocate.

"Shame on you who stand in need of grace.

"Blessings will be on those who have spoken out and acquired grace for themselves.

"Compare yourselves to foreigners. How are they viewed in your city? Why are you anxious to banish yourselves on your own and distance yourselves from your city? Why abandon your dwelling on your own and make it available for those who want to live in it? O you exiles and runaways, shame on you. You will be captured.

---

26. Literally, "or not to do so."
27. Perhaps emend to read "he."

"Or maybe you think that the father is a lover of people, or that he is won over by prayers, or that he is gracious to one because of another, or that he tolerates whoever is seeking?

"He[28] knows about desire and what the flesh needs. Does it not desire the soul? The body does not sin apart from the soul just as the soul is not saved apart from the spirit. But if the soul is saved from evil and the spirit too is saved, the body becomes sinless. The spirit animates the soul but the body kills it. The soul kills itself.[29]

"I tell you the truth, he will never forgive the sin of the soul or the guilt of the flesh, for none of those who have worn the flesh will be saved. Do you think that many have found the kingdom of heaven?

"Blessings on one who has seen oneself as a fourth one in heaven."[30]

KNOW YOURSELVES

When we heard this, we became sad. But when he saw that we were sad, he said, "I say this to you that you may know yourselves.[31]

"The kingdom of heaven is like a head of grain that sprouted in a field. And when it was ripe, it scattered its seed, and again it filled the field with heads of grain for another year. So with you, be eager to harvest for yourselves a head of the grain of life that you may be filled with the kingdom.

"And as long as I am with you, pay attention to me and trust in me, but when I am far from you, remember me. And remember me because I was with you and you did not know me.

"Blessings will be on those who have known me.

"Shame on those who have heard and have not believed.

"Blessings will be on those who have not seen but yet have believed.

"And once again I appeal to you. I am disclosed to you as I am building a house useful to you when you find shelter in it, and it will support[32] your neighbors' house when theirs threatens to collapse.

---

28. That is, "the father."
29. In this paragraph it is assumed that a person is composed of a body of flesh, an animating soul, and a vivifying spirit, as in Valentinian sources. To indulge the flesh and the soul is to court death, but to live a life of spirit is to realize life for the whole person.
30. This may be a way of stating that few are saved, and it may be an indication of one who is alone with god the father, mother, and child.
31. "Know yourself" was a maxim from the oracular center dedicated to Apollo at Delphi, Greece. See also Gospel of Thomas 3.
32. Or "stand alongside."

"I tell you the truth, shame on those for whom I was sent down here.

"Blessings will be on those who are going up to the father.

"Again I warn you, you who are. Be like those who are not, that you may be with those who are not.[33]

"Do not let the kingdom of heaven become a desert within you. Do not be proud because of the light that enlightens. Rather, act toward yourselves as I myself have toward you. I have put myself under a curse for you to save you."

THE LAST WORD

Peter responded to these comments and said, "Sometimes you urge us on toward the kingdom of heaven, but at other times you turn us away, master. Sometimes you encourage us, draw us toward faith, and promise us life, but at other times you drive us away from the kingdom of heaven."

The master answered and said to us, "I have offered you faith many times—and have revealed myself to you, James—and you have not known me. Now I see you often rejoicing. And although you are delighted about the promise of life, you are sad and gloomy when you are taught about the kingdom.

"Nevertheless, you, through faith and knowledge, have received life. So disregard rejection when you hear it, but when you hear about the promise, be joyful all the more.

"I tell you the truth, whoever will receive life and believe in the kingdom will never leave it, not even if the father wants to banish him.

"This is all I shall tell you at this time. Now I shall ascend to the place from which I have come. When I was eager to go, you have driven me off, and instead of accompanying me, you have chased me away.

"Be attentive to the glory that awaits me, and when you have opened your hearts, listen to the hymns that await me up in heaven. Today I must take my place at the right hand of my father.

"I have spoken my last word to you; I shall depart from you, for a chariot of spirit[34] has carried me up, and from now on I shall strip that I may be clothed.[35]

---

33. On existing and not existing, see the opening portion of the Secret Book of John, the Three Steles of Seth, and the Vision of the Foreigner.

34. On Jesus riding a chariot into heaven, see the accounts of Elijah and Enoch traveling into heaven in 2 Kings 2 and 1 Enoch 70, as well as various figures ascending to heaven in chariots on Roman commemorative coins.

35. Stripping and clothing refers to shedding the flesh as a garment and sometimes, as here, putting on a new and glorious heavenly garment.

"Pay attention: Blessings on those who have proclaimed the son before he came down, so that, when I did come, I might ascend.

"Blessings three times over on those who were proclaimed by the son before they came into being, so that you might share with them."

THE MESSENGERS DISPERSE

When he said this, he left. We knelt down, Peter and I, and gave thanks and sent our hearts up to heaven. We heard with our ears and saw with our eyes the noise of wars, a trumpet blast, and great turmoil.[36]

When we passed beyond that place, we sent our minds up further. We saw with our eyes and heard with our ears hymns, angelic praises and angelic rejoicing. Heavenly majesties were singing hymns, and we rejoiced too.

Again after this we wished to send our spirits up to the majesty. When we ascended, we were not allowed to see or hear anything. The other students called to us and asked us, "What did you hear from the teacher? What did he tell you? Where did he go?"

We answered them, "He ascended. He gave us his right hand, and promised all of us life. He showed us children coming after us, having commanded us to love them, since we are to be saved for their sakes."

When they heard this, they believed the revelation, but they were angry about those who would be born. Not wishing to give them reason to take offense, I sent each of them to a different location. I myself went up to Jerusalem, praying that I might acquire a share with the loved ones who are to come.[37]

I pray that the beginning may come from you.[38] This is how I can be saved. They will be enlightened through me, by my faith, and through another's that is better than mine. I wish mine to be the lesser.

Do your best to be like them, and pray that you may acquire a share with them. Beyond what I have said, the savior did not disclose any revelation to us on their behalf. We proclaim a share with those for whom the message was proclaimed, those whom the lord has made his children.

---

36. Apocalyptic images accompany the spiritual ascent to heaven.

37. This paragraph describes the dispersal of the messengers (or apostles) to spread the message of Jesus throughout the world. A similar scene occurs at the conclusion of the Letter of Peter to Philip. James is based in Jerusalem, as the leader of the church there. The "loved ones who are to come" are future believers, like the very people reading the Secret Book of James. They are the children coming after James and Peter, and it is for their sakes that the revelation is given.

38. The "you" to whom the book is addressed, "——thos," possibly Cerinthos.

22

The Round Dance of the Cross

Imbedded in the Acts of John is a famous song, with instructions for liturgical dance to accompany the hymn, here called the Round Dance of the Cross. This hymn has long attracted the attention of a variety of creative people. The novelist Marguerite Yourcenar wrote about it in *L'oeuvre au noir* (translated as *The Abyss*), the composer Gustav Holst set it to music as *The Hymn of Jesus,* and the film director Luis Buñuel incorporated a version of it in his film *La voie lactée* (The Milky Way). The Round Dance of the Cross is followed in the Acts of John by the Revelation of the Mystery of the Cross (not translated here). Both have a distinctive character and a gnostic—even a Valentinian—flavor.

The Round Dance of the Cross employs themes familiar from the tradition of John and the Gospel of John (for example, Jesus is the word of god who recounts the mystery of suffering) within a hymn that is performed by Jesus and his followers. The hymn illustrates features familiar from gnostic texts; some scholars believe it may constitute a gnostic ritual in song and dance. The verses sung by Jesus the leader include self-declarations, some of which recall the riddlelike and paradoxical declarations of Thunder. The chorus of followers responds to the leader's verses antiphonally by singing "Amen" and dance in a circle around him. Jesus' assertion that he will both save and be saved parallels the roles of god and the revealer in other gnostic texts in which god and the savior give and receive salvation. Echoes of Valentinian thought may be heard in references to grace, word, the realm of eight, wisdom, and knowledge.

The textual history of the Acts of John is complex, but it is commonly assumed by scholars that the Acts of John was composed in the second half of the second century, or maybe, some would say, a little later. It was likely composed, at least in large part, in Greek, though some portions may derive from Syriac. Syria is the probable place of composition.

THE ROUND DANCE OF THE CROSS[1]

Jesus told us to form a circle and hold each other's hands, and he himself stood in the middle, and said, "Respond to me with 'Amen.'"[2]

THE SONG

So he began by singing a hymn and declaring,
 "Glory to you, father."
And we circled around him and responded to him,
 "Amen."
 "Glory to you, word. Glory to you, grace."
 "Amen."
 "Glory to you, spirit. Glory to you, holy one. Glory to your glory."
 "Amen."
 "We praise you, father. We give thanks to you, light, in whom no
  darkness is."
 "Amen."
 "Why we give thanks, I declare:
 I will be saved and I will save."
 "Amen."

---

1. The Round Dance of the Cross: translated from the Greek by Marvin Meyer.
2. The Round Dance of the Cross is said to have been taught by Jesus to his students just before his crucifixion. The paragraph that precedes this opening in the Acts of John explains the suggested circumstances for the Round Dance of the Cross in strongly polemical terms, referring to "lawless Jews" inspired by the serpent.

"I will be released and I will release."

"Amen."

"I will be wounded and I will wound."

"Amen."

"I will be born and I will bear."

"Amen."

"I will eat and I will be eaten."

"Amen."

"I will hear and I will be heard."

"Amen."

"I will be kept in mind, being all mind."

"Amen."

"I will be washed and I will wash."

"Amen."

GRACE DANCES[3]

"I will play the flute. Dance, everyone."

"Amen."

"I will mourn. Lament, everyone."

"Amen."

"A realm of eight[4] sings with us."

"Amen."

"The twelfth number[5] dances on high."

"Amen."

"The whole universe takes part in dancing."

"Amen."

"Whoever does not dance does not know what happens."

"Amen."

"I will flee and I will stay."

"Amen."

---

3. Instructions for liturgical dance, included in the text.

4. This may refer to the realm of eight (ogdoad) in Valentinian thought. The realm of eight recalls the seven planetary spheres, plus the eighth sphere (of the stars) beyond these cosmic powers. The eighth sphere is sometimes thought to be the abode of the ruler of the cosmos and at other times is considered a higher level for spiritual advancement and perfection. See the Secret Book of John and the Hermetic Discourse on the Eighth and Ninth.

5. The twelfth number recalls the twelve signs of the zodiac.

"I will adorn and I will be adorned."

"Amen."

"I will be united and I will unite."

"Amen."

"I have no house and I have houses."

"Amen."

"I have no place and I have places."

"Amen."

"I have no temple and I have temples."

"Amen."

"I am a lamp to you who see me."

"Amen."

"I am a mirror to you who perceive me."

"Amen."

"I am a door to you who knock on me."

"Amen."

"I am a way to you, you passerby."[6]

"Amen."

UNDERSTANDING THE SONG

"If you respond to my dance, see yourself in me as I speak, and if you have seen what I do, keep silent about my mysteries. You who dance, understand what I do, for yours is this human passion I am to suffer. You could by no means have comprehended what you suffer unless I had been sent as the word to you by the father. You who have seen what I suffer have seen me as suffering, and when you have seen it, you have not stood firm but were completely moved. You were moved to become wise, and you have me for support. Rest in me. Who I am you will know when I depart. What now I am seen to be I am not. You will see when you come. If you knew how to suffer, you would have been able not to suffer. Learn about suffering, and you will be able not to suffer. What you do not know I myself shall teach you. I am your god, not the traitor's. I want holy souls to be in harmony with me. Know the word of wisdom. Say again with me,

---

6. See Gospel of Thomas 42.

Glory to you, father.
Glory to you, word.
Glory to you, spirit.
Amen.

"If you want to know what I was, once I mocked everything with the word, and I was not put to shame[7] at all. I leaped. But understand everything, and when you have understood, declare,

Glory to you, father.
Amen.

---

7. Or, "mocked."

23

The Songs of Solomon

T he Songs of Solomon (or Odes of Solomon) is one of the great
wisdom poetry anthologies of antiquity. No more lyrically powerful and imaginative collection of poems exists in ancient religions.
Their eclectic outsider's vision, the outrageously imaginative symbolism, the
conversation with the soul and the divine, the passionate embrace of love, and
the separation, search, and encounter with deity—all of these aspects make it
a major volume of religious poetry: a book of light, knowledge, and the enlightened voice.

Until 1909 only five odes from this very important hymnbook were
known. They appeared in the Pistis Sophia, a gnostic text preserved in Coptic. Then, in 1909, the archaeologist and Syriac scholar J. Rendel Harris discovered a four-hundred-year-old Syriac text of the collection. The original
language of the songs was probably Greek, although some scholars argue for
a Syriac original. Harris conjectured a Jewish-Christian origin from the first
century CE. Others suggest a Jewish original with a Christian redaction. Walter Bauer offers a third possibility, that the songs constitute a second-century
gnostic hymnbook.

Scholars disagree over how gnostic the Songs of Solomon really are. Many
scholars, from Harris and Gunkel to Bultmann, Jonas, Grant, and Rudolph,
take the songs to be gnostic, but others, such as Charlesworth, Chadwick,
Burkitt, Braun, and Worrell, do not see them as fully gnostic. In his book *The*

Odes of Solomon, James Charlesworth argues that these songs are not gnostic but a mystical Jewish-Christian hymnbook, "a tributary to Gnosticism which flows from Jewish apocalyptic mysticism."[1] Whatever the origin and degree of gnosticism, in their present form it is clear that the Songs of Solomon are based on Jewish sacred song tradition as exemplified in the Psalms and Song of Songs, that many of them have been subjected to a Christian overlay, and that their gnostic references are more significant than their mere inclusion in the Pistis Sophia. Harris also points out many quotations of the songs in the works of the early fathers of the church.

The songs were of particular interest because of their christology, that is, the use of Christ as a speaker in the songs, and for their deep dependence on the Gospel of John, which is typical of many gnostic texts. Frequently, the structure of a song consists of a prologue on the part of the singer, then an oracular statement *ex ore Christi,* and finally a doxology in which the congregation is to participate.[2] In his study of the Songs of Solomon, Gerald Blaszcak notes that they are composed largely in the first person singular as "individual confession songs."[3]

Many of these songs are hauntingly beautiful. The images soar. The diction is rich with surprising references, such as "milk from the lord," which apologists, dismayed by the female imagery for the divine, explain away as odd symbolism. Here are songs as poetic, profound, and astonishing as the most compelling songs and psalms of the Hebrew Bible. So we read: "The dew of the lord rinsed me with silence and a cloud of peace rose over my head" (Song 35); or, with typical chariot imagery of Jewish mysticism: "I went up to the light of truth as into a chariot and truth took me across canyons and ravines" (Song 38). The beautiful imagery encompasses Christian vocabulary as well: "My heart was cloven and there appeared a flower, and grace sprang up" (Song 11). The thought of all three prevailing traditions, Jewish, Christian, and gnostic, is suggested in Song 7: "The father of knowledge is the word of knowledge. He who created wisdom is wiser than his works."

---

1. Charlesworth, *Odes of Solomon,* p. 190.
2. Each song ends with "hallelujah," a stock response by the listener or congregation and probably a scribal addition. The tag is here omitted as unnecessary and distracting from the content and beauty of the poem.
3. Blaszczak, *A Formcritical Study of Selected Odes of Solomon,* p. 76.

SONGS OF SOLOMON[4]

Song 1

> You the lord are mingled in my hair like a crown,
> and I shall never be without you.
> This crown of truth was woven for me
> and makes your branches blossom in me.
> The crown is not dry and sterile.
> You live and blossom across my head.
> Your fruit is full, perfect, and mingled with salvation.

Song 3[5]

> I clothe his limbs and hang from them;
> I hang from his limbs. He loves me.
> How would I know how to love the lord
> if he didn't love me?
> And who can tell us about love?
> Only one who is loved knows.
> I love the beloved and my soul loves him,
> and I am where he reposes
> and will be no stranger, for he is not petty.
> He is my high merciful lord.
> I have gone to merge in him.
> The lover has found his beloved,
> and to love the son I become the son.

> Who joins the eternal? The eternal,
> and who delights in the living one lives.
> Such is the lord's spirit.
> It doesn't lie. It teaches us ways. Be wise,
> understand, and keep your eyes open.

---

4. The Songs of Solomon; translated by Willis Barnstone.
5. Song 2 is missing.

Song 4

    O my god, no one can seize your holy place
    nor alter it, for no one has such power.
    You designed your sanctuary before you drew the world.
    What is older will not be undone by the younger.
    You gave your heart to your believers, O lord,
    and will not stumble or be fruitless.

    One hour of your faith is more precious than all days and years.
    Who can feel pain by wearing your grace?
    Your seal is known. Creatures know it.
    Archangels are robed in it.
    You gave your fellowship. Not you, but we, were in need.
    Distill your dews upon us.
    Open your rich fountains and let milk and honey pour out.
    You hold back nothing that you promise
    and know the ends and give freely
    so you might withdraw and give us again.
    You know all, god, and from the beginning fix order.
    And you, O lord, make all things.

Song 5

    I thank you, O lord, because I love you.
    O highest one, do not abandon me,
    for you are my hope.
    Your grace I have received freely and live on it.
    My persecutors will come, but let them not see me.

    Let a cloud of darkness fall on their eyes
    and thick gloom darken them.
    Let light be gone and I be invisible
    so they will not come to seize me.
    Let their counsel be thick darkness
    and their cunning turn on their own heads,
    for their counsel is sham.

    The lord is my hope; I will not fear.
    He is a garland on my head. I will not move into sorrows.

Should everything tremble, I will stand firm.
If all visible things perish, I will not die,
for the lord is with me and I am with him.

Song 6

As a hand moves over a harp and strings speak,
so the spirit of the lord speaks in my members
and I speak through his love,
for he destroys what is foreign and bitter.
So he was from the beginning and so he will contend to the end.
No one can remain his adversary or resist him.
The lord multiplies his knowledge.
He is zealous to inform us, and he gives through grace.
Through his name we apprehend praise,
and our spirits praise his holy spirit.

A stream erupts into a wide and endless river
that floods and, breaking, carries away the temple.
Ordinary men, and even those whose art is to stem
rough waters, cannot hold it back,
and the river covers the face of the whole earth.
The river fills everything,
and the thirsty of the earth drink and satisfy thirst.
The drink comes from the highest one.

Blessings on the ministers of that drink,
who guard his waters that assuage dry lips and raise the fainted.
Souls about to depart, his waters rescue from death
and straighten crooked limbs.
They strengthen our feebleness and feed our eyes with light.
Those who know the river of the lord live through it forever.

Song 7

As anger moves over evil, so joy moves over the beloved
and floods us with her fruit.
My joy is the lord, and I move toward him.

The way is excellent. My helper is the lord,
who in candor lets me know him intimately.
His kindness has humbled his magnitude.
He became like me so I might receive him.
He thought like me so I could become him,
and I do not tremble when I look at him,
for he is gracious to me.
He assumed my nature so I could learn from him.
He assumed my form so I would not turn away.
The father of knowledge is learning's word.
He who created wisdom is wiser than his works.
He who created me knew how to attend me
when I came into being.

From his abundant grace he has found mercy for me
and lets me request and receive his sacrifice.
He is incorruptible,
the perfection of the worlds, and our father.
He lets himself be seen in his works
and be recognized as their creator,
and none will think his works are self-made.
Over what he has done, from the beginning
and to the end, is the gaze of his light.

He was resting in his son and found pleasure in his son,
and through his salvation the lord possessed all things.
The highest one will be known in his saints,
sung in songs of the coming of the lord
and those who sing may go forth to meet him
and find him with joy and a harp of many tunes.
Seers will go before him and be seen
and praise the lord for his love. He is near and sees.
Hatred will leave the earth, jealousies drown,
and ignorance be eroded,
for knowledge of the lord has come.

Let singers sing the grace of the high lord.
Let them sing. Let their hearts be like day,
their harmonies like the lord's excellent beauty.

Let there be nothing without his life,
his knowledge, or his speech.
The lord has given tongue to his creation.
He opens the lips of our mouth to praise him.
Confess his powers and release his grace.

Song 8

Open your hearts to the exultation of the lord,
and float your love from your heart to your lips in a holy life.
Carry fruit to the lord.
Talk and look into his light.
You who sank low, stand up and hold your shoulders erect.
You who were silent, speak.
Your mouth has been opened.
You were despised. Now feel uplifted.
Your goodness is high.
The lord's right hand is with you,
and he will help you,
and before wars rage through the lands,
for you he prepares peace.

RESPONSE

Hear the word of truth and drink the knowledge
that I offer from my station.
Your flesh cannot know what I say to you,
nor your robes what I show you.
Keep my mystery. It harbors you.
Keep my faith. It harbors you.
Know my knowledge, you who know me in truth.

Love me gently, you who love.
I do not turn my face from my own.
I know them. Before they were, I knew them
and set my seal on their faces.
I fashioned their limbs and prepared my breasts for them,
for them to drink my holy milk and live on it.
I took pleasure in them and see no shame in them.

Through my handiwork they are and feel
the enormity of my thought.

Who can stand against my handiwork?
Who is not its subject?
I willed and fashioned my mind and heart;
they are mine, and with my own hand I created them.
My goodness goes before them, and they will not lack my name.
I am with them.

RESPONSE 2

Pray and grow, survive in the love of the lord.
You are loved in the loved one.
You survive in him who lives.
You are saved in him who was saved.
In all ages you will be found incorruptible
through the name of your father.

Song 9

Open your ears and I shall speak to you.
Give me your soul that I may give you mine.
Here is the lord's word and his desires,
and his holy thought about the messiah.
In the will of the lord is your life.

His purpose is your eternal life.
Your perfection is incorruptible.
Be rich in god the father
and receive the purpose of the high one.
In his grace be strong and redeemed.
I tell you, and the holy ones will know peace,
and if you hear you will not fall into war.
Who knows him will not perish.
Who receives him will not be confused.
His eternal crown is truth,
and those who wear it on their heads are blessed.
It is made of precious stones,
and wars were fought over the crown,

which goodness seized and gave to you.
Wear the crown in a covenant with the lord.

All who have conquered will be inscribed in his book.
Their book is a triumph and is yours.
Victory sees you foremost and wills you saved.

Song 10

The lord has changed my mouth by his word
and opened my heart by his light.
He causes his eternal life to inhabit me
and lets me speak the fruit of his peace
to convert souls who would come to him,
and he leads captives into freedom.

RESPONSE

I took courage, rose strong, and captured the world,
yet my captivity lies in the high one's glory
and lies in god my father.
The gentiles who were scattered abroad are gathered together,
and I am not polluted by my love for them.
They praise me in high holy places,
and seas of light enter their heart as they become forever my people.

Song 11

My heart was cloven and there appeared a flower,
and grace sprang up
and fruit from the lord,
for the highest one split me with his holy spirit,
exposed my love for him
and filled me with his love.

His splitting of my heart was my salvation,
and I followed the way of his peace,
the way of truth.
From the beginning to the end
I received his knowledge
and sat on the rock of truth where he placed me.

Speaking waters came near my lip
from the vast fountain of the lord,
and I drank
and was drunk with the living waters
that never die,
and my drunkenness gave me knowledge.

I threw off vanity and turned to my god,
and his bounty made me rich.
I threw off the madness of the earth;
I stripped that madness from me
and cast it away,

and the lord renewed me
in his raiment
and held me in his light.
From above he gave me uncorrupt ease,
and I was like land deep and happy in its orchards,
and the lord was sun on the face of the land.

My eyes were clear,
dew was on my face,
and my nostrils enjoyed the aroma of the lord.
He took me to paradise,
where I knew joy
and worshiped his glory.

Blessings on those who are planted in your land, in paradise,
who grow in the growth of your trees
and change from gloom into light.
Your servants are lovely.
They do good;
they abjure evil and turn to your pleasantness.

They are free of the bitterness of trees
ancient in their land. You are everywhere,
always before your servants.
There is much space in paradise
but no wasteland. All is fruit.
Glory, lord, and eternal joy in paradise.

Song 12

He filled me with words of truth that I may speak the same.
Like flows of waters, truth flows from my mouth,
and my lips reveal its harvest.
It gives me the gold of knowledge,
for the mouth of the lord is the true word
and the door of his light.
The highest one gave the words to his worlds,
which interpret his beauty,
recite his praise, confess his thought
as heralds of his mind and instructors of his deeds.

The quickness of his words is unsayable,
and like his statement it is sharp.
Its course knows no end and never fails.
It stands. Its descent and ways are incomprehensible.
Like his work is its end,
which is the light and dawn of thought.
Through it worlds converse and the silent acquire speech.
From it came love and concord and candor,
and the word penetrated them and knew him who made it.
They came into concord.

The mouth of the highest one spoke to them,
and that word made him clear.
The dwelling place of the word is you,
and its truth is love.
Blessings on you who by it have learned everything
and have known the lord in his truth.

Song 13

Look, the lord is our mirror.
Open your eyes and see your eyes in him.
And learn the way of your face
and praise his spirit.
Wipe the makeup from your face
and love his holiness. Dress in him.
Then at all times, dressed in him,
you will be stainless.

Song 14

> As the eyes of a son to his father,
> so my eyes turn to you always, O lord.
> You are my consolation and happiness.
> Don't turn your mercy from me, O lord,
> nor withhold your kindness,
> but stretch out your right hand
> and guide me until the end of time.
>
> Care for me, save me from evil,
> and let your gentleness and love be with me.
> Teach me to sing truth that I may engender fruit in you.
> Open the harp of your holy spirit
> so I may praise you with all its notes.
> From your sea of mercy, help me in my hour of need.

Song 15

> As the sun is joy to those who seek daybreak,
> my joy is the lord.
> He is my sun, and his rays have lifted me up
> and chased all darkness from my face.
> I have acquired eyes and heard his truth.
> I have acquired knowledge, and he has made me happy.
> I left the way of error, went to him, and he saved me.
> According to his bounty, he gave me;
> according to his beauty, he made me.
> I found purity through his name.
> I shed corruption through his grace.
> Death has died before my countenance.
> Hell is abolished by my word.
> A deathless life appears in the land of the lord,
> known to those with belief, and lasts unceasingly.

Song 16

> As the work of the farmer is the plow
> and the helmsman the guidance of the ship,
> my work is a song to the lord.
> My art and occupation are in singing his good name.

His love feeds my heart.
His sweet foods reach my lips.
In my mouth his spirit talks of his glory and beauty,
labor of his hands, the craft of his fingers,
mercy of infinite horizon, the power of his word.
The lord's word finds the invisible and reveals his thought.

Our eye sees his labor, our ears hear his mind.
He spread out the earth and placed the waters in the sea.
He measured the firmament and fixed the stars.
He created and rested.
Created things follow a pattern. They know no rest.
Throngs of people follow his word.

The gold coin of light is the sun.
The gold coin of darkness is the night.
He made the sun to clarify the day
but evening blurs the face of the earth.
Their alternation speaks the beauty of god.
And nothing exists without the lord.
He was before anything was. With his word,
his thought, and his heart he made our worlds.
To his name glory and honor.

Song 17

I was crowned by god, by a crown alive.
My lord justified me. He is my sure salvation.
He freed me from myself and condemnation.
The chain fell from my wrists.
I took on the face and ways of a new person,
walked in him, and was redeemed.
The thought of truth drove me.
I walked to it and didn't wander off.
Those who saw me were amazed,
supposing me to be a strange person.
He who knew me and brought me up
is the mountain of perfection.
He glorified me by kindness
and raised my thought to truth, showing me his way.

I opened closed doors, shattered bars of iron.
My shackles melted. Nothing appeared closed
because I opened the door to everything.
I freed slaves, left no one in bonds.
I spread my knowledge and love
and sowed my fruits in hearts, transforming them.
I blessed them. They lived.
I gathered and saved them.
They became the limbs of my body and I their mind.
Glory to the mind, you my lord and messiah.

Song 18

My heart was raised and magnified in the love of the highest one.
I wanted to celebrate his name.
My arms and legs were made powerful
that they might not fall from his power.
He healed my bodily sickness.
His will was firm as his kingdom.

O lord, that I may help the weak,
let me keep your word. For their sake,
don't deny me your perfection.
Let the luminary not be conquered by darkness.
Let truth not fear the hands of falsehood.

Appoint me to victory. Your right hand is salvation.
Receive and preserve us who greet
temptation. In your mouth there is no falsehood,
no death, my god.
Your will is perfection.

Vanity you don't know, nor does it know you.
Error you don't know, not does it know you.
Ignorance appeared like the dust and scum of the sea.
The vain thought error great and pregnant with child.
The wise understood
and meditated unpolluted in their meditations.
They shared the mind of the lord.
They laughed at those in error.

They spoke truth breathed into them from the highest one.
His name is great and beautiful.

Song 19

A cup of milk was offered,
and I drank its sweetness as the delight of the lord.
The son is the cup,
and he who was milked is the father.
His milk should not drip out wastefully.
The holy ghost opened the father's raiment
and mingled the milk from the father's two breasts
and gave that mingling to the world,
which was unknowing.
Those who drink
are near his right hand.
The spirit opened the virgin's womb,
and she received the milk.
The virgin became a mother
of enormous mercy.
She labored but not in pain
and bore a son.
No midwife came.
She bore him as if she were a man,
openly, with dignity, with kindness.
She loved him and swaddled him
and disclosed his majesty.

Song 20

I am a priest of the lord and serve him as priest.
I offer him the offering of his thought.
His thought is not like the world,
not of the flesh
or of those who serve in the flesh.
The lord offers his goodness, his stainless heart and lips,
his inner world that is faultless.
Let hearts not oppress hearts, nor souls harm souls.

Don't bribe a stranger, because that stranger is you.
Don't trick your neighbor.
Don't take the clothing from him that hides his nakedness,
but dress in the grace of the lord generously
and walk in paradise
and from his tree make a garland[6] for your head.
Loop it around your hair. Be happy and rest in his rest.
His glory will go before you.
You will inhabit his kindness and grace
and be fat in truth[7]
with the praise of his holiness.
Praise and honor his name.

Song 21

I raised my arms high to the grace of the lord,
for he cast off my bonds.
My helper had raised me to his grace and salvation.
I discarded darkness
and dressed in the clothing of light.
My soul acquired a body free from sorrow,
free from torture and mutilation.
The lord's thought restored me.
I fed on his incorruptible fellowship.
In the light he raised me.
I went to him, near him,
praising and shouting his name.
He made my heart flood into my mouth.
He made it shine on my lips.
On my face the exultation of the lord grew.
My praise exploded.

---

6. Harris and Mingana give "garland," Charlesworth "crown." "Garland" carries out the
metaphor into the next line.
7. "Fat in truth" is Harris and Mingana's version, "anointed in truth" is Charlesworth's. Harris
and Mingana cite Isaiah 58: "and he shall satisfy thy soul with fatness."

Song 22

You who bring me down from on high
and bring me up from the regions below,
who gather what is on the earth
and hurl at me,
who scatter my enemies,
who gave me mastery of binding ropes
for me to loosen them
and with my hands have overthrown the dragon
with seven heads
and inserted myself in his roots to destroy his seed,

you were here and helped me,
and everywhere your name circled me.
Your right hand destroyed his wicked poison.
Your hand smoothed the way for those who believe in you
and chose them from their graves,
separating them from the dead,
and you took dead bones and covered them with bodies.
They were motionless,
and you gave them the energy of life.

Your way and your face were stainless.
To corruption you brought your world cleaned and refreshed.
The foundation is your rock on which you built your kingdom
where the holy live.

Song 23

The holy are happy. Who but they alone will wear joy?
The elect wear grace.
And who will be arrayed in grace
but those who from the beginning have believed?
The elect wear love.
And who will be arrayed in love
but those who from the beginning have believed?

Walk in the knowledge of the lord,
and you will know the grace of the lord of generosity,

his exultation, and the perfection of his gnosis.
His thought was a letter,
and his will descended from the skies,
shot like an arrow violently released from its bow.
Many hands rushed to the letter
to catch it, take it, and read it,
yet it slipped from their fingers,
and they were terrified of it and its seal.
They couldn't loosen the seal,
for the power of the seal was greater than they.
Others saw the letter and chased it,
wondering where it would land
and who might read it, who might hear it.

But a wheel caught the letter
and rolled over it, and it stuck there,
and it was a sign of the kingdom and realm.
Everything moving near the wheel
the wheel cut down,
and it destroyed a multitude of enemies
and bridged rivers and crossed over and uprooted forests,
leaving a huge ditch.
As if a body were on the wheel, a head turned
down to the feet. The wheel turned on the feet
and on whatever struck it.

The letter commanded over all districts,
and there appeared a head. It became
the son of truth from the father on high, who possessed all,
and the thought of many became nothing,
and the apostates and seducers grew brave yet fled,
and tormentors were blotted out.
The letter became a great tablet,
a volume written by the finger of god.
On it was the name of the father and the son
and the holy spirit,
and their word of dominion forever.

Song 24

> The dove flew over the head of the messiah,
> who was her head, and she sang over him
> and her voice was heard.
> The inhabitants were terrified
> and travelers shuddered.
> Birds took flight
> and all creeping things died in their holes.
> Abysses opened and closed.
> Like women in labor they were seeking god.
> They had no food.
> No one belonged to them.
> The abysses sank and were sealed by the lord,
> and the people perished
> in their own thought ancient and new.
> Everyone was imperfect and died.
> They could say nothing.
> The lord destroyed the imagination
> of all who didn't have his truth.
> They were weak in wisdom
> and were rejected. They lacked his truth.
> The lord disclosed his way
> and sprang his grace in alien lands.
> Those who understand know holiness.

Song 25

> I was rescued from my chains
> and fled to you, my god.
> You are the right hand of my salvation
> and my helper.
> You held back those who rose against me
> and the disappeared.
> Your face was with me.
> I was saved by your grace.
> But in the eyes of many I was abhorred and excluded.
> In their eyes I was lead.

I assumed strength from you
and drank your help.
You placed a lamp at my right hand and at my left.
In me nothing is not bright.
Your spirit covered me,
and I took off my robe of skin.
Your right hand raised me
and removed my sickness.
I grew strong in your truth,
holy in your goodness.
My enemies feared me.
I was of the lord by the name of the lord,
and justified by his gentleness.
His rest goes on forever.

Song 26

I poured praise on the lord.
I am his.
I recite his holy poem.
My heart is with him.
His harp is in my hand,
and the poems of his rest will not be silent.
I cry to him from my whole heart,
praise and exalt him with my limbs.
From the east and far into the west
is his praise.
From the south and far into the north
confession is his.
And from the top of hills to the greatest peaks
is his perfection.

Who can write the poems of the lord,
or who can read them?
Who can train the soul for life to save the soul?
Who can rest high in the firmament
so that the mouth speaks?
Who can decipher the wonders of the lord?

The interpreter perishes, the interpreted stops.
It is enough to know and to rest and rest.
The motionless singers stand before a great river
with a huge fountain
flowing to those who seek the poem of the lord.

Song 27

I extend my hands and hallow my lord.
The expansion of my hands is his sign,
and my expansion is the erected wood.

Song 28

Like the wings of the doves over their infant doves
whose mouths lift to their mothers' mouths,
so are the wings of the spirit over my heart.
My heart is happy and leaps
like the infant who moves happy in her mother's womb.
I believed. I was peaceful.
My faith was in him whom I trusted.
He hugely blessed me.
My mind is with him.
No sword nor scimitar divides us:
I prepared before destruction came.
I am in his arms that do not know death.
Deathless life hugged and kissed me.
That spirit is in me; it cannot die. It lives.

RESPONSE

They marveled at me because I was persecuted.
They supposed me swallowed up.
To them I seemed lost.
My oppression was my salvation.
They scorned me because in me was no anger.
Because I did good I was hated.
They surrounded me like mad dogs
who stupidly attack their masters.

Their thought is corrupt, their mind perverted.
I carried water in my right hand.
With sweetness I endured the bitter.
I didn't perish. I wasn't their brother.
My birth was other.
They sought my death. They failed.
I was older than their memory.
They cast lots against me. They failed.
Those who came later
tried to destroy the memory of him before them.
No one foretells the thought from the one in the sky.
His heart surpasses wisdom.

Song 29

The lord is my hope. With him I shall not be lost,
and through his praise he made me,
and through his goodness he gave me common objects,
and through his beauty he set me on high.
He led me out of the depths of Sheol[8]
and saved me from the mouth of death.
I laid my enemies low,
and he justified me through his grace.
I believed in him. I believed in the messiah,
and he came to me and showed me his sign
and led me by the way of his light.

He also gave me the rod of his power
to subdue the dreams of others, to bring down the mighty,
to make war through his word
and find victory through his power.
By his word the lord overthrew my enemy,
who was like stubble blown away in the wind.
I praise him on high who exalts me, his servant.
He has exalted the son of his handmaid.

---

8. Hell.

Song 30

> Drink deeply from the living fountain of the lord.
> It is yours.
> Come, all who are thirsty, and drink,
> and rest by the fountain of the lord.
> How beautiful and pure.
> It eases the soul.
> That water is sweeter than honey.
> The combs of bees are nothing beside it.
> It flows from the lips of the lord.
> Its name is from the lord's heart.
> It is invisible but has no borders
> and was unknown until it was set in our midst.
> They who drink are blessed and are eased.

Song 31

> Chasms vanished before the lord,
> and darkness fades with his appearance.
> Error wandered and disappeared because of him.
> Contempt found no path and was submerged in the truth of the lord.
> He opened his mouth and spoke grace and happiness.
> He sang a new poem to his name
> and raised his voice to the firmament
> and offered him children in his hands.
> By the ways his father gave to him,
> his face was justified.

RESPONSE

Come, you who have suffered, and be happy.
Possess your souls through grace.
Accept deathless life.
They condemned me when I stood on my feet,
I who was guiltless.
They divvied the spoil though nothing was theirs. I endured, held my peace,
silent so they couldn't get to me.
I was a firm rock pounded by waves, braving the blows.

I bore their bitterness with humility
to redeem and instruct my people.
I couldn't forget my word to the patriarchs,
to whom I had promised salvation of their seed.

Song 32

To the blessed, happiness lives in the heart,
and his light resides in them.
The word comes out of self-created truth.
He is strong from the holy force up in the skies
and forever unshaken.

Song 33

Grace raced away from the corrupter,
then turned her back on him to denounce him.
He left utter havoc around him
and spoiled his constructions.
He stood on a summit and screamed
from one end of the earth to the other,
drawing near those who obeyed.
He did not seem evil,
but a perfect virgin stood near and cried out:
"Sons and daughters, come back.
Leave the corrupter.
Come to me. I will enter you
and lead you out of devastation.
I will make you wise in the way of truth.
Do not destroy yourself.
Do not perish. Hear me and be saved.
I tell you of god's grace.
By me you will be redeemed and blessed.
I am your judge.
You who help me will not be injured.
You will possess purity in a fresh world.
My chosen ones stroll in me.
I shall inform you who seek me.
I shall make you trust my name.

Song 34

> The simple heart finds no bad way,
> good thought finds no wounds.
> Deep in the illuminated mind is no storm.
> Surrounded on every side by the beauty of the open country,
> who is not free of doubt?
> Below is like above. Everything is above.
> Below is nothing,
> but the ignorant think they see.
> Now you know grace and salvation.
> Believe and live and be saved.

Song 35

> The dew of the lord rinsed me with silence,
> and a cloud of peace rose over my head,
> guarding me.
> It became my salvation.
> Everybody quivered in horror.
> They issued smoke and judgment,
> but I was silent, near my lord,
> who was more than shadow, more than foundation.
>
> He carried me like a child by its mother.
> He gave me milk, his dew,
> and I grew in his bounty
> and rested in his perfection.
> I spread my hands out
> as my soul pointed to the firmament,
> and I slipped upward to him
> who redeemed me.

Song 36

> I found rest in the spirit of the lord,
> who raised me
> and had me stand on my feet in the high terrains
> of the lord,
> before his perfection, before his glory,
> while I praised him in my poems.

RESPONSE

Soul led me before the face of the lord.
Through the earthly son
I was named the light, the child of god.
I was the most glorified of the glorious,
greatest of the great.
Like the great lofty one, she the soul made me
like his freshness. He renewed me.
From his perfection he anointed me,
and I became equal to those near him.
My mouth was open like a dew cloud,
my heart gushed with goodness,
my way to him was peace,
and I joined the soul of his providence.

Song 37

I extended my hand to the lord
and to his skies raised my voice.
I spoke through the lips of my heart,
and he heard me when my voice went to him.
His word came to me with the fruit of my labor.
I found ease through the grace of the lord.

Song 38

I went up to the light of truth
as into a chariot,
and truth took me across canyons and ravines
and preserved me against waves smashing the cliffs.
She was my haven and salvation
and left me in the arms of immortal life.
She went with me, soothed me, kept me from error.
She was and is the light of truth.

Song 39

Mammoth rivers are the force of the lord.
They wash away those who despise him.

They entangle their paths and destroy their crossings.
They carry away their bodies
and burn their souls.
They are faster than lightning. Quicker.

Yet those who walk stainlessly on rivers
will not be hurt.
Those who walk without blame on them
need not cringe.
Their sign is the lord.
The sign is the way for those who cross in the name
of the lord.

Dress in the name of the high one and know him
and cross unworried. The rivers obey you.
The lord bridges waters with his word
as he walked and crossed on them with his feet.
His feet are firm on the water and do not sink.
They are a fixed beam of wood fashioned of truth.
Wave rise on both sides. The lord messiah stands.
His footsteps are not washed away.
They do not perish.
A way exists for those who cross after him,
for those on his path of faith and who love his name.

Song 40

As honey drips from the combs of bees
and milk flows from the woman who loves her child,
so my hope goes to you, my god.

As a fountain bursts with water
my heart bursts with praise for the lord
through my lips.

My tongue is sweet from his conversation,
my limbs fattened by the sweetness of his poems.
My face joys in his exultation.

My spirit exults in his love.
My soul shines in him.
Who is afraid finds safety in him

and redemption is certain in him,
and possession of eternal life.
Those who are in him cannot be stained.

Song 41

All who see me will be astonished,
for I am an alien among you.

The father of truth remembered me.
He possessed me from the beginning.

Through his riches and thought in his heart
he engendered me.

His word is our way.
The savior makes us alive and doesn't forget our souls.

The humbled
are exalted in him.

The son of the highest one
appeared in the father's perfection.

Light found daybreak in the word
that was earlier his.

The messiah is one,
known before the foundation of the world.

He saves souls in his truth and name.
Let us sing to the lord. We love him.

Song 42

I stretched out my hands and came near my lord.
It is my sign, stretching my hands as if spread on a tree.
That was my way up to the good one.
I became useless to those who didn't seize me.
I hid from those who don't love me
but am with them who love me.
My persecutors died.

They sought me because I am alive.
I rose up and am with them
and speak through their mouths.
They despised their persecutors.
I locked them in the yoke of love.

Like the groom over the bride,
so is my love over those who believe in me.
They thought me rejected, destroyed. I wasn't.
Hell saw me and was miserable.
Death cast me up along with others.
I have been gall and bitterness to death.
I went down with it to the uttermost depth,
and it released my feet and head,
for it couldn't endure my face.

I made a congregation of living men among its dead
and spoke to them with living lips.
My word wasn't empty.
The dead ran toward me, screaming,
"Son of god, pity us. Be kind
and bring us out of the bonds of darkness.
Open the door into your being.
We perceive our death has not touched you.
Save us, redeemer."
I heard their voice and stored their faith in my heart.
I set my name upon their heads.
They are free men and mine.

24

The Song of the Pearl

The Song of the Pearl is a narrative poem about a prince's quest for a pearl. Presented in the Acts of Thomas as a hymn uttered by Thomas, The Song of the Pearl is also a gnostic tale of salvation, of sleeping in error and awakening to light, of quest not only for the pearl but for the benefit of possessing the pearl: a return to the light.

What is the pearl? As one of the alternative titles of the poem, "The Hymn of the Soul," suggests, the pearl may esoterically be the soul. Or the pearl may be gnosis, the awakening, and the knowledge that the soul must have to move to the next level of being. Bentley Layton suggests that the prince and his quest may be the soul and its journey, the poem a tale of "the soul's entry into bodily incarnation and its eventual disengagement from the body."[1] The soul on entering matter becomes inert, but once in possession of its pearl of knowledge it will waken into wisdom and reunion with "the first principle." Günther Bornkamm believes the young prince and savior to be Mani himself, the founder of Manichaeism. The mysteries of interpretation fortunately are not fixed and apparent. Were the symbolic figures—a road, a coat, a serpent, a pearl, a wandering prince—easily decodable, the poem might be merely didactic. But the narrative is shot through with mysterious changes, dramatic turns and transformations that may be interpreted as theology only at risk of error.

---

1. Layton, *Gnostic Scriptures*, p. 366.

Having discounted absolute interpretation, we perceive some clues. On the surface the poem is simply an adventure. Yet everywhere in it are clues of other meanings. After all, serpents who sleep with pearls in their possession cannot but have an allegorical dimension. These symbols were used in Mandaean traditional tales as well as in such gnostic works as the Pistis Sophia. Scholarship suggests that the main characters—the father, mother, and prince—form a gnostic trinity, equivalent to the Christian trinitarian formula. They may represent the father of truth, the mother of wisdom, and the son. The son, who is redeemer and savior, is not Christ, however, or at least not primarily Christ. Hans Jonas identifies him with the Manichaean pre-cosmic human. The son has a double or twin role, for he appears to be both savior and the soul that he saves; he saves and must himself be saved. So too the pearl, which at first appears to be a symbol of the soul, is also the deity who saves the soul. The notion of the double is typically gnostic: the role of Thomas as twin in the Gospel of Thomas and the Book of Thomas is but one example. As Jonas points out, "the interchangeability of the subject and object of the mission, of savior and soul, Prince and Pearl, is the key to the true meaning of the poem, and to the gnostic eschatology in general."[2]

Other symbols in the poem are doubled as well. The prince's garment of glory, which is his spiritual body, he has taken off and left behind in order to assume the unclean robe of the world, which is obviously the unclean physical body. But the garment of glory also operates as an independent being, reminding him of his duty to return. So too the letter, on which is written the call of redemption, flies down like an eagle from heaven and becomes a messenger of light, in a way that recalls the heavenly letter of the Songs of Solomon. On the way the letter, the word, seems to take on a woman's voice. Whoever the author and whatever the background, that poem's creator revels in games of spiritual ambiguity, skirting confusion as it deepens into swift spectacle. The prince has left the east, the land of light and origin, to go down to Egypt, which stands traditionally for the body, for material things, for darkness and error. It is the kingdom of death, which is exemplified by the tomb culture and underground cult of the dead. Likewise, the serpent is the realm of darkness and ignorance, in dark waters on the earth below the sea.

In this fable of redemption, as Hans Jonas points out, the savior himself must be saved—or rather, must save himself. We see the dramatic way in

---

2. Jonas, *Gnostic Religion*, p. 127.

which the savior turns human, forgets who he is, and falls into the sleep of earthly things. Ultimately his parents, the father of truth and mother of wisdom, do not abandon him. They send messages. He wakes from the prison of earthly things, steals the pearl, and returns to his royal parents with the promise of rising to his true parents of the spirit.

Whether this popular tale is an old Mesopotamian legend or a Jewish or Christian story that has undergone a gnostic overlay, in the form in which it survives it is a poetic culmination of gnostic principles, conveyed with a minimum of cosmogony and deific mischief. It has the stanzaic form of Jewish poetry, without rhyme or fixed meter, where prosody is based largely on parallelistic couplets. The Song of the Pearl appears as a supplement to the apocryphal Greek Acts of Thomas. One version is in Greek and another slightly different version in Syriac. Its date of composition, Bentley Layton suggests, points to the Parthian dynasty of Persia (247 BCE–224 CE); or, if composed in Edessa when the city was under Parthian control, before 165 CE.

THE SONG OF THE PEARL[3]

DRESSING FOR THE JOURNEY

> When I was a little child living
> in my father's palace in his kingdom,
> happy in the glories and riches
> of my family that nurtured me,
> my parents gave me supplies
> and sent me out on a mission
> from our home in the east.
> From their treasure house
> they made up a cargo for me.
> It was big though light enough
> so I could carry it myself,
> holding gold from the highest houses

---

3. The Song of the Pearl: translated by Han J. W. Drijvers (Schneemelcher, ed., *New Testament Apocrypha*, vol. 2, 380–85), Robert M. Grant (*Gnosticism*, pp. 116–22), and Bentley Layton (*The Gnostic Scriptures: A New Translation with Annotations and Introductions*, pp. 371–75); translated by Willis Barnstone.

and silver of Gazzak the Great
and rubies of India
and opals from the land of Kushan,[4]
and they girded me with adamant
that can crush iron.
They took off my bright robe of glory,
which they had made for me out of love,
and took away my purple toga,
which was woven to fit my stature.
They made a covenant with me
and wrote it in my heart so I would not forget:
"When you go down into Egypt
and bring back the one pearl
that lies in the middle of the sea
and is guarded by the snorting serpent,
you will again put on your robe of glory
and your toga over it,
and with your brother, our next in rank,
you will be heir in our kingdom."

THE DRAGON AND THE DEEP SLEEP

I left the east and traveled down
to Egypt with my two royal guides,
since the way was dangerous and harsh
and I was very young to walk alone.
I crossed the borders of Maishan,[5]
the gathering place of merchants of the east,
came into the land of the Babylonians,[6]
and entered the walls of Sarbug.
When I went down into Egypt
my companions left me.
I went straight to the serpent

4. Kushan may be Kashan or Kosan, north of Isfahan, in Parthian Iran.
5. Bentley Layton suggests that Maishan may refer to "Mesene or Characene at the head of the Persian Gulf" (*Gnostic Scriptures*, p. 372).
6. Not Babylon by the Euphrates but the Roman fortress city in present-day Old Cairo.

and settled close by him in an inn,
waiting for him to sleep
so I could take my pearl from him.
Since I was alone
I was a stranger to others in the inn,
yet I saw one of my own people there,
a nobleman from the east,
young, handsome, lovable,
a son of kings—an anointed one,
and he came and was close to me.
And I made him my confidante
with whom I shared my mission.
I warned him against the Egyptians
and of contact with the unclean ones.
Then I put on a robe like theirs,
lest they suspect me as an outsider
who had come to steal the pearl,
lest they arouse the serpent against me.
Somehow they learned I was not
their countryman, dealt with me cunningly,
and gave me their food to eat.
I fell into a deep sleep.
I forgot that I was a son of kings
and served their king.
I forgot the pearl
for which my parents had sent me.
Through the heaviness of their food
I fell into a deep sleep.

"REMEMBER THE PEARL"

When all these things happened
my parents knew and grieved for me.
It was proclaimed in our kingdom
that all should come to our gate.
And the kings and princes of Parthia
and all the nobles of the east
wove a plan on my behalf
so I would not be left in Egypt.

And they wrote me a letter
and every noble signed it with his name:
"From your father, the king of kings,
and your mother, the mistress of the east,
and from your brother, our next in rank,
and to you, our son in Egypt, peace!
Awake and rise from your sleep
and hear the words of our letter!
Remember that you are a son of kings
and see the slavery of your life.
Remember the pearl
for which you were sent into Egypt!
Remember your robe of glory
and your splendid mantle, which you may wear
when your name is called in the book of life,
when it is read in the book of heroes,
when you and your brother inherit our kingdom."

THE BIRD OF SPEECH

And serving as messenger,
the letter was a letter sealed by the king
with his right hand
against the evil children of Babylon
and the savage demons of the Sarbug labyrinth.
It rose up in the form of an eagle,
the king of all winged fowl;
it flew and alighted beside me
and became speech.
At its voice and the sound of its rustling
I awoke and rose from my sleep.
I took it, kissed it, broke its seal, and read.
And the words written on my heart
were in the letter for me to read.
I remembered that I was the son of kings
and my free soul longed for its own kind.
I remembered the pearl
for which I was send down into Egypt,
and I began to enchant

the terrible and snorting serpent.
I charmed him into sleep
by calling the name of my father over him
and of my mother, the queen of the east.
I seized the pearl
and turned to carry it to my father.
Those filthy and impure garments
I stripped off, leaving them in the fields,
and went straight on my way
into the light of our homeland in the east.

THE LETTER'S VOICE

On my way the letter that awakened me
was lying like a woman on the road.[7]
And as she had awakened me with her voice
so she guided me with her light
as if she were an oracle.
She was written on Chinese silk
and shone before me in her own form.
Her voice soothed my fear
and its love urged me on.
I hurried past the labyrinth walls of Sarbug
and Babylon on the left
and came to Maishan, the haven of merchants,
perched over the coast of the sea.
My robe of glory that I had taken off
and the toga over it were sent by my parents
from the heights of Hyrcania.
They were in the hands of treasurers
to whom they were committed
because of their faith,
and I had forgotten the robe's splendor,
for as a child I had left it
in my father's house.

---

7. This understanding is based on the Greek version. In the Syriac version the letter, personified, simply speaks forth with its own voice.

THE GARMENT OF GNOSIS

As I gazed on it, suddenly the garment
like a mirror reflected me,
and I saw myself apart
as two entities in one form.
The treasurers had brought me one robe,
yet in two halves I saw one shape
with one kingly seal.
They gave me wealth,
and the bright embroidered robe
was colored with gold and beryls,
with rubies and opals,
and sardonyxes of many colors
were fastened to it in its high home.
All its seams were fastened
with stones of adamant,
and the image of the king of kings
was embroidered on it
as it rippled with sapphires
of many colors.
I saw it quiver all over,
moving with gnosis, in a pulsing knowledge,
and as it prepared to speak
it moved toward me,
murmuring the sound of its songs.
It descended and said,
"I am the one who acted for him.
For him I was brought up in my father's house.
I saw myself growing in stature
in harmony with his labors."

THE TOGA AND THE PEARL

With regal movements
the robe was spreading toward me,
urging me to take it,
and love urged me to receive it,

and I stretched forth and received it
and put on the beauty of its hues.
I cast my toga of brilliant colors
all around me.
Therein I clothed myself and ascended
to the gate of salutation and adoration.
I bowed my head and adored
the majesty of my father, who sent it to me.
I had fulfilled his commands
and he fulfilled what he had promised.
At the gate of his princes
I mingled with his nobles.
He was happy through me and received me,
and I was with him in his kingdom,
and his slaves praised him resoundingly.
He promised me that I would journey soon
with him to the gate of the king of kings,
and with my gifts and my pearl
I would appear with him before our king.

25

The Book of Thomas

The Book of Thomas is a text that claims to have been written in conjunction with Judas Thomas, the twin brother of Jesus and the apostolic hero of Syrian Christians. Like the Gospel of Thomas, the Book of Thomas is identified at the opening of the document as a sayings collection: "The hidden sayings that the savior spoke to Judas Thomas." The editor of the collection is identified as a certain Mathaias, whose name is similar to that of the messenger (or apostle) and gospel-writer Matthew (Matthaios) and the replacement apostle Matthias (Acts 1:26), but whose precise identity remains uncertain.

Appended at the end of the document are the words "the Book of Thomas the Contender Writing to the Perfect." Traditionally this inscription has been taken at face value, but some scholars have suggested that it may be read as two titles of the text, "The Book of Thomas," and "The Contender Writing to the Perfect," and that these two titles may reflect the composite nature of the text. After all, the text contains sayings of Jesus and a dialogue between Jesus and Thomas, along with a sermon by Jesus on sinners who face judgment. Hans-Martin Schenke argues that the contender designated in the second title is none other than the patriarch Jacob, the most famous contender in the Jewish tradition. Hence, Schenke maintains, behind the present Book of Thomas may be a Jewish source in the form of a letter said to be authored by Jacob the contender.

Within the Book of Thomas the utterances of Jesus sometimes recall sayings and themes in the Gospel of Thomas. Here Jesus comments on Judas the twin, on knowledge of self, on what is hidden and what is visible, on the desires of the flesh, and on wisdom and foolishness. In the middle of the text, and at the very end, Jesus states that one should seek (or pray) and find and rest, as in Gospel of Thomas 2. Like the Book of Thomas in general, the sermon of Jesus recommends an ascetic way of life, and as such it is profoundly concerned about the life and the sins of the flesh. In its presentation the sermon echoes ancient descriptions of the underworld and punishments for the wicked and anticipates later portrayals of judgment in Dante's *Inferno* and even Jonathan Edwards's sermon "Sinners in the Hands of an Angry God."

The Book of Thomas survives in Coptic in the Nag Hammadi library. Like the Gospel of Thomas, the Book of Thomas probably was composed in Greek, in Syria, where Thomas was revered. John Turner proposes that at least part of the Book of Thomas should be dated to the first part of the third century, that is, after the Gospel of Thomas and before the Acts of Thomas.

THE BOOK OF THOMAS[1]

The hidden sayings that the savior spoke to Judas Thomas, which I, Mathaias, in turn recorded.[2] I was walking, listening to them speak with each other.

JESUS TALKS TO HIS BROTHER THOMAS

The savior said, "Brother Thomas, while you are still in the world, listen to me and I shall reveal to you what you have thought about in your heart.

"Now, since it is said that you are my twin and my true friend, examine yourself and understand who you are, how you exist, and how you will come to be.[3] Since you are to be called my brother, it is not fitting for you to be ignorant of yourself. And I know that you have understood, for already you have understood that I am the knowledge of truth. So while you are walking with me, though you are ignorant, already you have obtained knowledge, and

---

1. The Book of Thomas: Nag Hammadi library, Codex II,7, pp. 138,1 to 145,19; translated by Marvin Meyer. Several passages are partially restored; see Hans-Martin Schenke and Einar Thomassen, "The Book of Thomas," in Schneemelcher, ed., *New Testament Apocrypha*, 1.232-47.
2. In the opening of the Gospel of Thomas, Judas Thomas is thought to be the twin brother of Jesus; the name of Mathaias resembles that of the original messenger Matthew and the replacement messenger Matthias, but his identity is unclear.
3. Similar lists of questions may be found in the Secret Book of John, the Letter of Peter to Philip, and the Gospel of Truth.

you will be called one who knows himself.[4] For someone who has not known self has known nothing, but someone who has known self already has acquired knowledge about the depth of the universe. So then, my brother Thomas, you have seen what is hidden from people, what they stumble against in their ignorance."

THE HIDDEN AND THE VISIBLE

Thomas said to the master, "For this reason I beg you to tell me what I ask before your ascension. When I hear from you about the hidden, I can speak of it. And clearly it is hard to bring truth to people."

The savior answered and said, "If what is visible to you is obscure to you, how can you comprehend what is invisible? If deeds of truth visible in the world are hard for you to carry out, how will you do invisible things of exalted greatness and fullness?[5] How can you be called workers? You are beginners and have not attained the greatness of perfection."

Thomas answered and said to the savior, "Tell us about these things that you say are not visible but are hidden from us."

The savior said, "All bodies have come into being in the same irrational way that animals are produced, and so they are visible, as creatures lusting after creatures. Those that are above, however, do not exist like those that are visible. Rather, they live[6] from their own root, and it is their crops that nourish them. These visible bodies feed on creatures that are like them, and so the bodies are subject to change. Now, whatever is subject to change will perish and be lost, and henceforth has no hope of life, because this body is an animal body. Just as animal bodies perish, so also will these figures perish. Is it[7] not from copulation like that of the animals? If it too is from copulation, how will it give birth to anything different from them? So then you are children until you become perfect."

Thomas answered, "So I say to you, master, those who speak about what is invisible and difficult to explain are like people who shoot their arrows at a target during the night. Of course, they shoot their arrows as any people do,

---

4. This recalls the Delphic maxim "Know yourself" and Gospel of Thomas 3.
5. This contrast between the visible and the invisible is a contrast between the lower world of body, change, perishability, and animal nature and the higher world of soul, constancy, immortality, and spiritual nature. This discussion resembles the discussion of the soul in Plato's *Phaedo*.
6. Coptic e[u]onh. Or, "they are visible" (Coptic e[uou]onh). The previous lines are partially restored.
7. The body.

since they are shooting at the target, but it is not visible. When light comes, however, and banishes darkness, then the accomplishment of each person will be clear. And you, our light, bring enlightenment, master."

Jesus said, "Light is in light."

Thomas spoke and said, "Master, why does this visible light shining for people rise and set?"[8]

The savior said, "O blessed Thomas, surely this visible light has shone for you, not to keep you here, but so you can leave. And when all the chosen ones lay down their animal nature, then this light will withdraw up to its being, and its being will welcome it to itself, because the light is a good helper."

WISDOM AND FOOLISHNESS

Then the savior continued and said, "Oh, unsearchable love of light! Oh, bitterness of the fire! You blaze in the bodies of people, and in the marrow of their bones, blazing in them night and day, burning their limbs and making their minds drunk and their souls deranged. You dominate males and females day and night, you move and arouse them secretly and visibly. When the males are aroused, they are attracted to the females and the females to the males. So it is said that everyone who seeks truth from true wisdom[9] will fashion wings to fly, fleeing from the passion that burns human spirits. And one will fashion wings to flee from every visible spirit."

Thomas answered, saying, "Master, this is precisely what I ask you. I understand that what you say is beneficial to us."

Again the savior answered and said, "This is why we must speak to you, because this teaching is for those who are perfect. If you wish to become perfect, keep these sayings. If not, the name for you is 'ignorant,' since an intelligent person cannot associate with a fool. The intelligent person is perfect in all wisdom. To the fool, however, good and evil are one and the same. The wise person will be nourished by truth and will be like a tree growing by the stream of water.[10] Some people have wings but rush toward visible things that are far from truth. The fire that guides them gives them an illusion of truth. And it will shine on them with a perishable beauty, and will imprison them in dark delight and capture them in sweet-smelling pleasure. And it will blind them with insatiable desire, inflame their souls, and be like a stake jammed into

---

8. That is, the sun.
9. Sophia. The previous lines are partially restored.
10. Psalm 1:3.

their heart that can never be removed. It leads them according to its own wish, like a bit in the mouth.[11]

"It has bound them with its chains and tied all their limbs with the bitterness of the bondage of desire for those visible things that perish and change and fluctuate impulsively. They have always been drawn downward. When they are slain, they are drawn to all the animals of corruption."

Thomas answered and said, "It is clear and has been said that many are . . . those who do not know . . . soul."

The savior answered and said, "Blessings on the wise person who has sought truth and, when it has been found, has rested upon it for ever and has not been afraid of those who wish to trouble him."[12]

OUR OWN AND THE OTHERS

Thomas answered and said, "Master, is it good for us to rest among our own?"

The savior said, "Yes, it is useful, and it is good for you, since the things visible among people will pass away. For the vessel of their flesh will pass away, and when it disintegrates, it will remain in visible things, among things that can be seen. The visible fire hurts them, because of the love of faith they once had. They will be gathered back to the visible realm.[13] Moreover, among the invisible, those who can see will perish, without the first love, in their concern for this life and the burning of the fire. There is only a little time before what is visible will pass away. Then shapeless phantoms will come and stay forever in tombs on corpses, in pain and destruction of soul."[14]

Thomas answered and said, "What can we say in the face of these things?[15] What shall we say to the blind? What teaching shall we give these miserable mortals who say, 'We have come to do good and not to curse,' and will say further, 'If we were not born in the flesh, we would not know iniquity'?"

The savior said, "To tell the truth, do not think of these as human beings, but as animals. As animals devour each other, so also people like this devour each other. They are deprived of the kingdom.[16] They love the delight of fire

---

11. On the imprisonment of these people see the discussion in Plato's *Phaedo*, especially *Phaedo* 81C–82A, 83DE.

12. See Gospel of Thomas 2.

13. This passage refers to the death and decay of the body (the vessel of flesh), and the punishment and reincarnation of ignorant people.

14. On phantoms see the similar discussion in Plato's *Phaedo* 81C–E.

15. Or "these people."

16. The word "kingdom" is partially restored.

and are slaves of death and rush to deeds of corruption. They fulfill their parents' desire. They will be cast down into the abyss and be afflicted by the compulsion of the bitterness of their evil nature. They will be whipped to drive them down to a place they do not know, and they will leave their limbs behind, not with fortitude but with despair. And they rejoice in the fire, they love madness and derangement, because they are fools. They rush after this derangement, not realizing their madness but thinking they are wise. They . . . their body . . . their hearts turning to themselves and their thoughts being on their affairs. But fire will consume them."[17]

Thomas answered and said, "Master, what can one cast down to them do? I am very concerned about them, for many oppose them."

The savior answered and said, "How does it look to you?"

Judas, who is called Thomas, said, "Master, you should speak and I should listen."

The savior answered, "Listen to what I tell you and believe the truth. What sows and what is sown will pass away in their fire, in fire and water, and will be hidden in tombs of darkness. And after a long time the fruit of evil trees will appear and be punished and slain in the mouths of animals and people through the agency of the rains, the winds, the air, and the light shining above."[18]

Thomas answered, "You have certainly convinced us, master. We perceive in our hearts, it is clearly so, and your word is not meager. But these sayings that you tell us are laughable and ridiculous to the world, since they are not understood. How can we go forth and preach them when we are not respected in the world?"

JESUS PREACHES ABOUT JUDGMENT

The savior answered and said, "I tell you the truth, whoever listens to your word and turns away or sneers at it or smirks at these things, that person will be handed over to the ruler who is on high, who rules as king over all the powers, and the ruler will make him turn away and cast him down from on high into the abyss, and he will be imprisoned in a cramped, dark place. So he cannot turn or move because of the great depth of Tartaros[19] and the

---

17. Partially restored.

18. On this description of what sows and is sown, note Plato's *Phaedo* 83DE, and other descriptions comparing the life cycles of plants and humans.

19. The underworld, the realm of the dead, hell. Here the description of the underworld contains features typical of other descriptions in Hesiod, Plato, Christian apocalypses, and even Dante.

burdensome bitterness of Hades. Whoever relies on what is brought to him . . . will not be forgiven his madness, but will be judged. Whoever has persecuted you will be handed over to the angel Tartarouchos,[20] who has flaming fire that pursues them, and fiery whips that spew forth sparks into the face of one who is pursued. If he flees to the west, he finds fire. If he turns south, he finds it there as well. If he turns north, the threat of erupting fire meets him again. Nor can he find the way to the east, to flee there and be saved, for he did not find it while embodied so as to find it on the day of judgment."

SHAME ON YOU

Then the savior continued and said, "Shame on you, godless people, who have no hope, who are secure in things that will not happen.

"Shame on you who hope in the flesh and in the prison that will perish.[21] How long will you sleep and think that what is imperishable will also perish? Your hope is based upon the world, and your god is this present life. You are destroying your souls.

"Shame on you with the fire that burns within you. It is insatiable.

"Shame on you because of the wheel that turns in your minds.

"Shame on you because of the smoldering in you. It will devour your flesh visibly, tear your souls secretly, and prepare you for each other.

"Shame on you, prisoners, for you are bound in caves. You laugh, you rejoice in mad laughter. You do not perceive your destruction. Neither do you perceive your plight, nor have you understood that you are in darkness and death. Rather, you are drunk with fire and full of bitterness. Your hearts are deranged because of the smoldering that is within you, and you delight in your enemies' poison and blows. Darkness has risen in you like light, for you have surrendered your freedom to slavery. You have darkened your hearts. You have given in to foolishness, and you have filled your minds with the smoke of the fire within. And your light has been hidden by the dark cloud. You love the garment[22] that you wear, although it is filthy, and you are gripped by nonexistent hope. You have believed in what you do not know. You all live in bondage

---

20. Tartarouchos is the angel or power who controls Tartaros.
21. The body is the perishable prison of the soul in Platonic and Orphic thought. Note also, below, the prisoners bound in caves, and the Secret Book of John, on the physical body as a cave (and the allegory of the cave in Plato's *Republic*).
22. The garment being worn is the body, which can be put on or taken off like an article of clothing.

but pride yourselves in your freedom. You have baptized your souls in the water of darkness. You have pursued your own wishes.[23]

"Shame on you who are in error, not seeing that the light of the sun, which judges the universe and looks down on the universe, will encircle everything to make slaves of the enemies. Nor do you perceive how the moon looks down night and day, seeing the bodies of your slaughters.

"Shame on you who love intercourse and filthy association with the female.

"Shame on you because of the powers of your bodies, for they will mistreat you.

"Shame on you because of the actions of the evil demons.

"Shame on you who entice your limbs with fire. Who will sprinkle a restful dew on you, to extinguish the many fires within you, and your burning? Who will shine the sun on you, to dispel darkness in you, and hide darkness and filthy water?

"The sun and the moon will give a fragrant aroma to you and the air, the spirit, the earth, and the water.[24] If the sun does not shine upon these bodies, they will rot and perish just like weed or grass. If the sun shines on it, it grows strong and chokes the grapevine. But if the grapevine becomes strong and casts its shadow over the weeds and all the rest of the brush growing with it, and spreads and fills out, it alone inherits the land where it grows, and dominates wherever it has cast its shadow. So when it grows, it dominates the whole land, and it is productive for its master and pleases him greatly. He would have labored painfully to pull out weeds, but the grapevine by itself has disposed of them and choked them, and they have died and have become like earth."

Then Jesus continued and said to them, "Shame on you, for you have not accepted the teaching, and those who wish to accept it will suffer when they preach. You will persecute them, but you will rush into your own traps. You will cast them down to the lions and put them to death, daily, but they will rise from death."[25]

---

23. These lines are partially restored.
24. These are the four elements, with spirit replacing fire, since fire is characteristic of passion, lust, and destruction in the Book of Thomas.
25. These lines are partially restored.

BLESSINGS ON YOU

"Blessings on you who understand beforehand temptations and flee from things that are alien.

"Blessings on you who are mocked and are not respected because of your master's love for you.

"Blessings on you who weep and are oppressed by those who have no hope, for you will be released from all bondage.

"Watch and pray that you may not come to be in the flesh, but that you may leave the bondage of the bitterness of this life. And when you pray, you will find rest, for you have left pain and reproach behind. When you leave the pains and the passions of the body, you will receive rest from the good one. You will reign with the king, you united with him and he with you, from now on and forever. Amen."[26]

---

26. This concluding paragraph is similar in wording to Gospel of Thomas 2.

26

The Exegesis on the Soul

The Exegesis on the Soul is a history of the soul, of her fall into the world, her corruption there in the body of a woman hounded by lecherous men, and the ways of her virtuous return, through repentance, to heaven. As in other tractates, such as Herakleon's Commentary on the Gospel of John, the notion of allegorical interpretation of scripture is central, a practice that orthodox Christians essentially adopted from the gnostics while repudiating their thought. Here the interpretation extends to the Hebrew prophets and Homer. Not only are these interpreted in ways that support a gnostic system, but the texts themselves, at least in our Coptic version, also appear in versions differing markedly from standard texts in ways that confirm a gnostic slant. The author's sources were probably the anthologies of the day.

The soul in Greek is Psyche. She is understood to be feminine in name and nature, and great stories are told about her in Greco-Roman literature. Here in the Exegesis on the Soul she is presented as originally androgynous when she was a virgin and with her father. When she fell into the earthly world she lost her virginity to lovers and bandits, who deceived her as she deceived herself. In her first fallen state, though the details are not transparent, the womb, which appears to be the womb of the soul, is external, like male genitalia. Captive to her body and to men who abuse her through physical pleasure and then abandon her, she asks the father to have mercy on her. The father turns the womb of her soul inward. Thereby she is stronger to protect herself against wanton carnal lovers. And he sends a bridegroom from heaven, her brother, to have chaste sex with her and produce good, rather than demented, children. Her chaste lovemaking in the bridal chamber is a form of purification and rebirth, which is equivalent to deliverance, resurrection, and ascension to heaven.

The story is fantastic and told like an ancient novella. It has been compared to Jewish writings from the Bible and the apocrypha, since the soul, the heroine, is presented as a woman. So it follows the scheme of redemption of such sinners as Ruth, Tamar, Rahab, and Bathsheba. Centering on women's redemption was also typical of other Jewish literature of the time, including documents recounting the experience of the soul in the Essene texts found at Qumran. The diverse influences in the exegesis—Jewish, Christian, Greco-Roman, gnostic—reveal a syncretistic context for composition. From this sophisticated mélange came this flagrantly sexual and heavenly erotic gnostic scripture.

THE EXEGESIS ON THE SOUL[1]

VIRGINITY AND DEFILEMENT

Sages gave the soul a feminine name. In nature she is also feminine. She even has a womb.

While she was alone with her father, she was a virgin and in an androgynous form. When she fell down into a body and entered this life, then she fell into the hands of thieves. Wanton men passed her from one to the other, used her, some by force, others by seducing her with a gift. They defiled her and took her virginity from her.

In her body she became a whore and gave herself to everyone, seeing each one she hugged as a husband. After she let herself be taken by lecherous, unfaithful adulterers, she sighed deeply and repented. But even when she turned her face from the adulterers, she ran to others, and they compelled her to live with them and make love with them on their beds as if they were her masters. Then, out of shame, she no longer dared leave them, while they double-

1. Exegesis on the Soul: Nag Hammadi library, Codex II,6, pp. 127,18 to 137,27; translated by William C. Robinson Jr. (Robinson, *Nag Hammadi Library in English*, pp. 192–98); revised by Willis Barnstone and Marvin Meyer.

crossed her, pretending to be faithful, true husbands, as if they respected her. After all these acts, they took off, abandoning her.

She became a poor desolate widow, helpless. In her affliction she had no food. From them she had gathered nothing but the defilements when they coupled with her. Her offspring from the adulterers are mute, blind, and sickly. They are disturbed. But when her father who is above looked down on her and saw her sighing, suffering and in disgrace, and repenting of her prostitution, then she began to call on him for help with all her heart, saying, "Save me, my father. Look, I will report to you, for I left my house and fled from my woman's quarters. Restore me to yourself."

When he saw her in this state, he thought her worthy of his mercy. She had many afflictions for having abandoned her house.

THE PROSTITUTION OF THE SOUL

Concerning the prostitution of the soul, the holy spirit prophesies in diverse places. The prophet Jeremiah said,[2]

> If a man divorces his wife, and she leaves him and takes another man, can she ever go back to him? Has such a woman not utterly defiled herself? "You have whored with many shepherds and you returned to me," said the lord. "Lift up your eyes and see where you went whoring. Were you not sitting in the streets defiling the land with your whoring and vices? And you took many shepherds for a way of stumbling. You were shameless with everyone. You did not call on me as a companion or father or author of your virginity."

It is also written in the prophet Hosea,[3]

> Come, go before the law with your mother, for she is not to be my wife nor I her husband. I shall remove her whoring from my presence and her adultery from between her breasts. I shall make her naked as on the day she was born, and desolate like a

---

2. Jeremiah 3:1–4. The version in Coptic of this and the following biblical passages, having gone through Hebrew and Greek, has changed substantially through the layers of transmission. Throughout this text, the biblical and Homeric quotations have not been altered here to reflect the source texts, since doing so would undermine the author's exegetical purpose.
3. Hosea 2:2–7.

waterless land. I shall make her childless and long for children. I shall show her children no pity, for they are children of prostitution, their mother having whored and shamed her children. She said, "I shall be a whore to my lovers. They gave me my bread and water and garments and clothes and wine and oil and everything I needed." Look, I shall shut them up so that she will not be able to chase after her adulterers. When she seeks them and doesn't find them, she will say, "I will go back to my former husband, for then I was happier than now."

Again in Ezekiel he said,[4]

It happened that after much depravity, the lord said, "You built yourself a brothel and made yourself a beautiful place in the streets. You built whorehouses in every alley and you wasted your beauty, you spread your legs in every alley, and multiplied your acts of prostitution. You were a whore for the sons of Egypt, those who are your neighbors, men great of flesh."

But what does "the sons of Egypt, men great of flesh" signify, if not the domain of the flesh and the perceptible realm and the affairs of the earth by which the soul is defiled here, receiving bread from them as well as wine, oil, clothing, and the other external nonsense surrounding the body—whose things she thinks she needs?

But as to this whoring, the messengers of the savior commanded,[5] "Guard and purify yourself against it," and not just the body's prostitution but especially the soul's. That is why the messengers write to the churches of god that such whoring might not go on here.

Yet the greatest struggle is the prostitution of the soul. From it comes the prostitution of the body. So Paul, writing to the Corinthians, said,[6]

I wrote in my letter, "Do not associate with whores," meaning not the whores of the world or the greedy or thieves or idol worshipers, since then you would have to leave the world.

Here he is speaking spiritually:[7]

---

4. Ezekiel 16:23–26.
5. See Acts 15:20, 29, 21:25; 1 Thessalonians 4:3; 1 Corinthians 6:18; 2 Corinthians 7:1.
6. 1 Corinthians 5:9.
7. Ephesians 6:12.

Our struggle is not against flesh and blood—as he said—but against the world rulers of this darkness and the spirits of evil.

BAPTISM OF THE SOUL

As long as the soul goes on running around everywhere sleeping with whomever she meets and defiling herself, she will suffer her deserved punishment. But when she perceives the troubles she is in, weeps before the father, and repents, then the father will pity her and make her womb turn from the external and turn inward again, and she will recover her proper character. It is not like this for a woman. The body's womb is inside the body like the other internal organs, but the soul's womb is turned to the outside like the male genitalia, which are external.

Therefore, when the womb of the soul, by the father's will, turns itself inward, she is baptized and immediately cleansed of external pollution forced upon her, just as dirty clothing is soaked in water and stirred until the dirt is removed and it is clean. So the cleansing of the soul is to recover the freshness of her former nature and to become as she was.

That is her baptism.

Then she will begin to rage at herself like a woman in labor, writhing and screaming in the hour of delivery. But since she is female, she is powerless by herself to inseminate a child. So the father sent her from heaven her man, her brother, the firstborn. The bridegroom came down to the bride. She gave up her former whoring and cleansed herself of the pollution of adulterers, and she was renewed to be a bride. She cleansed herself in the bridal chamber. She filled it with perfume and sat there waiting for the true groom. She no longer goes about the marketplace, copulating with whomever she desires, but she waits for him, saying, "When will he come?" And she feared him, not knowing what he looked like. She no longer remembers, since she fell from her father's house long ago.

She dreamed of him, by the father's will, like a woman in love with a man.

THE MARRIAGE

Then, by the will of the father, the bridegroom came down to her in the bridal chamber, which had been prepared. And he decorated the chamber.

This marriage is not like carnal marriage, in which those who make love with each other become satiated in their lovemaking. And as if it were a burden, they leave behind the annoyance of physical desire. They turn their faces from each other. In this marriage once they join they become a single life. As the prophet said about the first man and woman,[8]

They will become a single flesh.

They were originally joined to each other when they were with the father, before the woman led the man astray, who is her brother. This marriage brings them together again, and the soul joins her true love and real master, as the scriptures tell us[9]:

The woman's master is her husband.

Then gradually she recognized him and was again happy, weeping before him as she remembered the disgrace of her former widowhood. She adorned herself abundantly so he might be pleased to stay with her.

And the prophet said in the Psalms,[10]

Hear, my daughter, and see me and bend your ear, and forget
your people and your father's house, for the king has desired
your beauty, and he is your lord.

He has her turn her face from her people and the gang of her adulterers with whom she had mingled, to devote herself now to her king, her real lord, and to forget the house of the earthly father with whom things were bad for her, and remember her father in heaven. So Abraham was told,[11]

Leave your country and kin and your father's house.

REGENERATION OF THE SOUL

When the soul had adorned herself again in her beauty, she enjoyed her beloved. He also loved her. And when they made love, she got from him the seed which is the life-giving spirit. By him she has good children and brings them up. Such is the great and perfect marvel of birth. This marriage is made perfect by the will of the father.

Now, it is right that the soul be regenerated and be as she formerly was. The soul stirred. Her divine nature and her rejuvenation came from her father so she might return to where she was before. This is resurrection from the dead.

---

8. Genesis 2:24.
9. See Genesis 3:16; 1 Corinthians 11:1; Ephesians 5:23.
10. Psalm 45:10–11.
11. Genesis 12:1.

This is ransom from captivity. This is the ascent to heaven. This is the ascent to the father. As the prophet said,[12]

> Praise the lord, O my soul and all within me, praise his holy name. O my soul, praise god, who forgave all your sins, who healed all your sicknesses, who ransomed your life from death, who crowned you with mercy, who satisfies your longing for good things. Your youth will be renewed like the eagle's.

When she becomes young again she will rise, praising the father and her brother who rescued her. Through rebirth the soul will be saved. And salvation will not be because of rote phrases or professional skills or learned books. Rather, it will come from the grace and gift of the merciful god. Such is the heavenly way. So the savior cries out,[13]

> No one can come unless my father draws him and brings him to me. I myself will raise him on the last day.

PRAYING FROM THE SOUL

So it is right to pray to the father and to call on him with our soul—not externally with our lips but with the spirit, which is inside and comes from the depths, sighing, repenting for the life we led, confessing sins, recognizing the deception we were in as shallow; perceiving the empty zeal; weeping over how we lived in darkness and in the wave; mourning for what we were so that he might pity us; hating ourselves for what we still are.

The savior said,[14]

> Blessings on those who mourn, for they will be pitied. Blessings on the hungry, for they will be filled.

And he said,[15]

> If one does not hate one's own soul, one cannot follow me.

The beginning of salvation is repentance. So it says,[16]

> Before Jesus came John, preaching the baptism of repentance.

---

12. Psalm 103:1–5.
13. John 6:44.
14. Matthew 5:4, 6; Luke 6:21.
15. Luke 14:26.
16. Acts 13:24.

And repentance occurs in distress and sorrow. The father is good and loves humankind, and hears the soul that calls him and sends her the light of salvation. Through the spirit to the prophet he says,[17]

> Say to the children of my people, "If your sins extend from earth to heaven, if they become red like scarlet and blacker than sackcloth, and if you return to me with all your soul and say to me, 'My father,' I will care for you as for a holy people."

Again elsewhere,[18]

> So the lord, the holy one of Israel, says, "If you return and sigh, then you will be saved and will know where you were when you trusted what is shallow."

And again,[19]

> Jerusalem wept profusely, saying, "Pity me." He will have pity at the sound of your lamentation. And when he saw, he cared for you. And the lord will give you the bread of affliction and water of oppression. From now on those who deceive will not go near you. Your eye will spot those who would deceive you.

THE REPENTANCE OF ODYSSEUS AND HELEN

So it is right to pray to god night and day, extending our hands toward him as do people sailing in the middle of the sea. They pray to god with all their heart and without hypocrisy. Those who pray hypocritically fool only themselves. Yes, it is to know who is worthy of salvation that god examines our inner selves and the bottom of our heart. No one is worthy of salvation who still loves the place of deception. So the poet writes,[20]

> Odysseus sat on the island weeping and grieving and turning his face from the words of Calypso and from her tricks, while longing to see his village and smoke coming forth from it. Had he not

---

17. See 1 Clement 8:3.
18. Isaiah 30:15.
19. Isaiah 30:19–20.
20. Homer, *Odyssey* 1.48–59. The quotations from Homer are not exact quotations from a specific passage but a hodgepodge summary from diverse places, altered both for sermonizing purposes and by the process of translation.

received help from heaven, he would not have been able to return to his village.

Again Helen says,[21]

My heart turned away from myself. I want to return to my own house.

She sighed, saying,[22]

Aphrodite deceived me and brought me out of my village. My only daughter I left behind me as well as my good, understanding, and handsome husband.

When the soul leaves her perfect husband because of the treachery of Aphrodite, who exists here in the act of conception, then the soul will suffer harm. But if she sighs and repents, she will be restored to her house.

THE REPENTANCE OF ISRAEL

Israel surely would not have been visited by god and brought out of the land of Egypt and the house of bondage if it had not sighed to god and wept about its oppressive labors. Again in the Psalms it is written,[23]

I was greatly troubled in my groaning. I will bathe my bed and my cover each night with my tears. I have become old in the midst of all my enemies. Depart from me, all you who work at lawlessness, for look, the lord has heard the cry of my weeping and the lord has heard my prayer.

If we repent, truly god will heed us, he who is long-suffering and abundantly merciful, to whom be glory forever and ever.

Amen.

---

21. *Odyssey* 4.260–61.
22. *Odyssey* 4.261–64.
23. Psalm 6:6–9.

27

On the Origin
of the World

O n the Origin of the World is a gnostic treatise that offers explanations of key gnostic themes, particularly themes having to do with first things, last things, and hidden things.

On the Origin of the World appears in the Nag Hammadi library, Codex II, immediately after the Sethian text Reality of the Rulers, the text it most closely resembles. The parallels between the two texts are extensive. On the Origin of the World reflects many of the Sethian gnostic themes found in other Sethian texts as well, but the present text is not easily classified as Sethian. Sometimes it seems Sethian, sometimes Valentinian, sometimes Manichaean. It always is, in some sense, gnostic.

On the Origin of the World opens with a philosophical issue that sounds disarmingly modern in its formulation: What, if anything, existed prior to the original chaos, the primal ooze, the beginning as described in Genesis 1 and other ancient Middle Eastern creation myths? On the Origin of the World seeks to demonstrate that before chaos was the root of chaos, the infinite.

The plot that unfolds in the text features the creative and salvific roles of Sophia and her mother, Pistis (faith). The daughter is also called Sophia Zoe (life) or simply Zoe, the mother Pistis Sophia. From Pistis Sophia, in a manner recalling childbirth, emerges the demiurge Yaldabaoth, who is expelled, the text emphasizes, like an aborted fetus (as in an interpretation of the Secret Book of John). He establishes his kingdom of chaos, complete with the powers of the world, and brags that he is god alone. Of course he is wrong, and one of his sons, Sabaoth by name, is exalted above him with Sophia in the seventh heaven, where he proceeds to create an assembly of angels, a firstborn named Israel, and Jesus the anointed. Father Yaldabaoth, in turn, counters by creating death. Thus unfolds the gloomy process of mortal dissolution in the cosmos, of life leading inexorably to death.

This story, familiar from other gnostic accounts of the creation of the world and people in the world, is told with reference to the opening chapters of Genesis from the Hebrew Bible. In a manner that recalls the Secret Book of John and the three divisions of humankind in Valentinian texts, Adam is understood in three ways, as spiritual Adam, psychical Adam, and earthly Adam. Also inserted into the account are asides on Eros, the Greek god of love, along with Psyche (soul), lover of Eros, and Egyptian phoenixes, water animals, and bulls, and all of these are part of the gnostic cosmology. Innocent spirits come to awaken people to gnosis, as does Jesus, so that finally the powers of the present age will collapse, and light and life will triumph. As the text concludes, "it is necessary that everyone enter the place from which he has come. For each one by his deeds and his gnosis will reveal his nature."

On the Origin of the World is untitled in the manuscripts that have survived, but the present descriptive title is often used. The text was almost certainly written in Greek before being translated into Coptic. Hans-Gebhard Bethge suggests, "The work was probably composed in Alexandria at the end of the third century A.D. or beginning of the fourth."[1] The text is in a learned, even scholarly style and contains etymological and bibliographical references. Most of the works cited in the text are unknown to us. Exceptions to this may include books of Noraia (or Oraia), which may refer to the Thought of Norea in the Nag Hammadi library, Codex IX,2, and the Archangelic Book of the Prophet Moses, which may refer to a text from the Greek magical papyri.

---

1. Hans-Gebhard Bethge in Layton, *Nag Hammadi Codex II,2–7*, 2.12.

ON THE ORIGIN
OF THE WORLD[2]

BEFORE THE BEGINNING

Since everyone—the gods of the world and people—says that nothing existed prior to chaos, I shall demonstrate that they all are mistaken, since they do not know the origin of chaos and its root. Here is the demonstration.

How agreeable it is to all people to say that chaos is darkness! But actually chaos comes from a shadow that has been called darkness. The shadow comes from something existing from the beginning. So it is obvious that something in the beginning existed before chaos came into being, and that chaos came after what was in the beginning.[3]

Now let us consider the facts of the matter, and in particular what was in the beginning, from which chaos came. In this way the truth will be clearly demonstrated.

BIRTH OF SOPHIA AND THE FORCES OF
DARKNESS

After the nature of the immortals was completed out of the infinite one,[4] then a likeness called Sophia[5] flowed out of Pistis,[6] with the wish[7] that something should come into being like the light that first existed. Immediately her wish appeared as a heavenly likeness with an incomprehensible greatness. This

---

2. On the Origin of the World is preserved in Nag Hammadi library, Codex II,5 pp. 97,24 to 127,17. A portion of the text is also preserved in the Oeyen fragments (British Library Oriental Manuscript 4927[1]) and in a fragment of Nag Hammadi library, Codex XIII. On the Origin of the World has been translated by Hans-Gebhard Bethge and Orval S. Wintermute (Robinson, *Nag Hammadi Library in English*, 1st ed., 161–79), and by Hans-Gebhard Bethge, Bentley Layton, and the Societas Coptica Hierosolymitana (Robinson, *Nag Hammadi Library in English*, rev. ed., 170–89); revised by Willis Barnstone and Marvin Meyer.

3. In other words, something existed before the primordial chaos (see Genesis 1:1–2). That is the infinite one, the source of all.

4. The infinite one recalls the One (monad) in the Secret Book of John and other gnostic texts.

5. Wisdom, also known as Sophia Zoe, wisdom life, the daughter of Pistis Sophia.

6. Faith, also known as Pistis Sophia, faith wisdom, the mother of Sophia Zoe.

7. The wish is most likely that of Sophia, the likeness that appeared.

came between the immortals and those who came into being after them, like what is above. It was a veil separating people from the things above.[8]

Now, the eternal realm of truth has no shadow within it because the immeasurable light is everywhere within it. Outside it, however, is a shadow, and it was called darkness.[9] From it appeared a power over the darkness. And the powers that came into being afterward called the shadow the limitless chaos. From it every kind of deity was brought forth, one after another, along with the whole place. Consequently, the shadow too is subsequent to what was in the beginning. The shadow appeared in the abyss, which is derived from Pistis, whom we have mentioned.

The shadow perceived that there was one stronger than it.[10] It was jealous, and when it became self-impregnated, it immediately bore envy. Since that day the principle of envy has appeared in all of the aeons and their worlds. But envy was found to be an aborted fetus without any spirit in it. It became like the shadows in a great watery substance.

Then the bitter wrath that came into being from the shadow was cast into a region of chaos. Since that day a watery substance has appeared. What was enclosed in the shadow flowed forth, appearing in chaos. Just as all the useless afterbirth of one who bears a little child falls, likewise the matter that came into being from the shadow was cast aside. Matter did not come out of chaos, but it was in chaos, existing in a part of it.

YALDABAOTH ESTABLISHES HIS RULE

Now, after these things happened, Pistis came and appeared over the matter of chaos, which was cast off like an aborted fetus, since there was no spirit in it. For all of that is a boundless darkness and water of unfathomable depth. And when Pistis saw what came into being from her deficiency, she was disturbed. And the disturbance appeared as something frightful, and it fled to her in the chaos. She turned to it and breathed into its face in the abyss, which is beneath all of the heavens.

---

8. A similar veil is mentioned in the Gospel of Philip, and limit (*horos*) functions as a cosmic boundary in Valentinian thought in general. The concept of the region of the middle, between the immortal and mortal realms, is also common in gnostic texts.

9. The infinite is all light, and outside is shadow, darkness.

10. This account resembles features of the story of the fall of Sophia and the birth of the demiurge in other gnostic accounts.

Now, when Pistis Sophia wanted to cause the thing that had no spirit to be formed into a likeness and rule over matter and over all its powers,[11] a ruler first appeared out of the waters, lionlike in appearance, androgynous, with great authority within himself but ignorant of whence he came into being.[12]

When Pistis Sophia saw him moving in the depth of the waters, she said to him, "Youth, pass over here," which is interpreted as "Yaldabaoth."[13] Since that day, the first principle of the word that referred to the gods and angels and people has appeared. And the gods and angels and people constitute that which came into being by means of the word. Moreover, the ruler Yaldabaoth is ignorant of the power of Pistis. He did not see her face, but he saw in the water the likeness that spoke with him. And from that voice he called himself Yaldabaoth. But the perfect ones call him Ariael because he was like a lion.[14] And after he came to possess authority over matter, Pistis Sophia withdrew up to her light.

YALDABAOTH CREATES HEAVEN AND EARTH AND BEARS THREE SONS

When the ruler saw his greatness, he saw only himself; he saw nothing else, except water and darkness. Then he thought that he alone existed. His thought was made complete by means of the word, and it appeared as a spirit moving to and fro over the waters.[15] And when that spirit appeared, the ruler separated the watery substance to one region and the dry substance to another region. From matter he created a dwelling place for himself and called it heaven. And from matter the ruler created a footstool and called it earth.

Afterward the ruler thought, according to his nature, and he created an androgynous being by means of the word. He opened his mouth and cooed to him. When his eyes were opened, he saw his father and said to him, "Eee." So his father called him Yao.[16] Again he created the second son and cooed to him. He opened his eyes and said to his father, "Eh." So his father called him Eloai.[17]

---

11. Or "her powers."

12. This is the inopportune birth of the creator of the world, Yaldabaoth.

13. On the names of the creator, see the Secret Book of John and the Reality of the Rulers (with the notes) in this volume.

14. In Hebrew the name Ariel is commonly taken to mean "lion of god."

15. Here and throughout the text are parallels to the opening chapters of Genesis, as well as to the Reality of the Rulers. Only a few will be noted.

16. A form of the ineffable divine name Yahweh. In Greek Yao is spelled Iao, hence the baby-talk "Eee."

17. A name that resembles the Hebrew for god, El or Elohim.

Again he created the third son and cooed to him. He opened his eyes and said to his father, "Asss." So his father called him Astaphaios. These are the three sons of their father.

THE SEVEN HEAVENS OF CHAOS

Seven appeared in chaos as androgynous beings. They have their masculine name and their feminine name. The feminine name of Yaldabaoth is fore-thought[18] Sambathas,[19] which is the week.[20] His son is called Yao, and his feminine name is lordship. Sabaoth's[21] feminine name is divinity. Adonaios's feminine name is kingship. Eloaios's feminine name is envy. Oraios's feminine name is wealth. Astaphaios's feminine name is Sophia. These are the seven powers of the seven heavens of chaos. And they came into being as androgynous beings according to the immortal pattern that existed before them and in accord with the will of Pistis, so that the likeness of what existed from the first might rule until the end.

You will find the function of these names and the power of the males in the Archangelic Book of Moses the Prophet.[22] But the feminine names are in the First Book of Noraia.[23]

Now since the chief creator[24] Yaldabaoth had great authority, he created for each of his sons, by means of the word, beautiful heavens as dwelling places, and for each heaven great glories, seven times exquisite. Each one has within his heaven thrones, dwelling places, and temples, as well as chariots and spiritual virgins and their glories, looking up to an invisible realm, and also armies of divine, lordly, angelic, and archangelic powers, myriads without number, in order to serve.

The report concerning these you will find accurately in the First Account of Noraia.

Now, they were completed in this way up to the sixth heaven, the one belonging to Sophia. And the heaven and its earth were disrupted by the troublemaker, who was beneath all of them. The six heavens trembled, for the

18. Pronoia.
19. The name Sambathas resembles the Hebrew Shabbat or Sabbath.
20. This is the realm of seven, the hebdomad, the astronomical realm of the planets.
21. Sabaoth resembles the Hebrew for "hosts," as in "lord of hosts."
22. A text with this name is known from the Greek magical papyri.
23. This text recalls the Thought of Norea, Nag Hammadi library, Codex IX,2. Also note the discussion of Norea in the Reality of the Rulers.
24. Greek *archigenitor*, here and throughout.

powers of chaos knew[25] who it was who disturbed the heaven beneath them. And when Pistis knew of the harm caused by the troublemaker, she blew her breath, and she bound him and cast him down to Tartaros.[26]

THE BOASTING OF YALDABAOTH

Since that day, the heaven has been consolidated along with its earth by means of Sophia, the daughter of Yaldabaoth, who is beneath them all.[27] After the heavens and their powers and all of their government set themselves aright, the chief creator exalted himself and was glorified by the whole army of angels. And all the gods and their angels gave him praise and glory.

And he rejoiced in his heart, and he boasted continually, saying to them, "I do not need anything. I am god and there is no other god but me."[28] But when he said these things, he sinned against all of the immortal imperishable ones, and they kept their eyes on him.

Moreover, when Pistis saw the impiety of the chief ruler, she was angry. Without being seen, she said, "You're wrong, Samael," that is, "blind god."[29] "An enlightened, immortal human exists before you and will appear within your fashioned bodies.[30] The human will trample upon you as potter's clay is trampled. And you will go with those who are yours down to your mother, the abyss. For in the consummation of your works, all of the deficiency that appeared in the truth will be dissolved. It will cease, and it will be like something that never existed."

After Pistis said these things, she revealed the likeness of her greatness in the waters. And so she withdrew up to her light.

SABAOTH WORSHIPS PISTIS

When Sabaoth, the son of Yaldabaoth, heard the voice of Pistis, he worshiped her. He condemned his father and mother.[31] on account of the word of

---

25. Or emend to "knew not."

26. The underworld, the realm of the dead, hell.

27. This is the lower Sophia, one of the seven offspring of Yaldabaoth (see above).

28. Isaiah 45:5–6, 21; 46:9.

29. Samael also figures prominently in the Secret Book of John and the Reality of the Rulers.

30. The immortal human recalls the first human, or Geradamas (heavenly Adam), in the Secret Book of John and elsewhere.

31. Partially restored; see Hans-Martin Schenke in Layton, *Nag Hammadi Codex II,2–7,* 2.42.

Pistis. He glorified her because she informed them of an immortal human and the light of the human. Then Pistis Sophia stretched forth her finger and poured upon him light from her light for a condemnation of his father. When Sabaoth received light, he received great authority against all of the powers of chaos. Since that day he has been called "the lord of the powers."[32] He hated his father, the darkness, and his mother, the abyss. He loathed his sister, the thought of the chief creator, the one who moves to and fro over the water.

On account of his light, all of the authorities of chaos were jealous of him. And when they were disturbed, they made a great war in the seven heavens. Then when Pistis Sophia saw the war, she sent seven archangels from her light to Sabaoth. They snatched him away up to the seventh heaven.[33] They took their stand before him as servants. Furthermore, she sent him three other archangels and established the kingdom for him above everyone so that he might dwell above the twelve gods of chaos.

When Sabaoth received the place of rest because of his repentance, Pistis also gave him her daughter, Zoe,[34] with great authority, so that she might inform him about everything that exists in the eighth heaven. And since he had authority, he first created a dwelling place for himself. It is huge, magnificent, seven times as great as all those that exist in the seven heavens.

Then in front of his dwelling place he created a great throne on a chariot with four faces, called cherubim.[35] And the cherubim throne has eight shapes on each side of the four corners—forms of lions and bulls and humans and eagles—so that all of the forms total sixty-four forms. And seven archangels stand before him. He is the eighth, having authority. All of the forms total seventy-two. For from this chariot the seventy-two gods took shape; they took shape so that they might rule over the seventy-two languages of the nations.[36] And by that throne he created other dragon-shaped angels called seraphim, who glorify him continually.

---

32. Or "lord of hosts," for Yahweh Sabaoth.
33. Sabaoth assumes a place above his father, Yaldabaoth, in the seventh heaven.
34. Life, exalted Eve.
35. The Hebrew word *cherubim* designates angels who are around the throne-chariot of god (often called the *merkavah*).
36. Seventy-two is a traditional number of nations in the world.

SABAOTH CREATES AN ASSEMBLY WITH JESUS AND THE VIRGIN

Afterward he created an angelic assembly[37]—thousands, myriads without number belong to it—that was like the assembly in the eighth heaven,[38] and a first-born called Israel, that is, the one who sees god, and also another called Jesus Christ, who is like the savior above in the eighth heaven and who sits at his right upon an excellent throne. But at his left the virgin of the holy spirit sits upon a throne praising him. And the seven virgins stand before her, with thirty lyres and harps and trumpets in their hands, glorifying him.[39] And all of the armies of angels glorify him and praise him. But he sits on a throne concealed by a great light-cloud. And there was no one with him in the cloud except Sophia, the daughter of Pistis, teaching him about all those that exist in the eighth heaven, so that the likeness of those might be created, in order that his kingdom might continue until the consummation of the heavens of chaos and their powers.

Now, Pistis Sophia separated him from the darkness and summoned him to her right, but the chief creator she put at her left. Since that day right has been called justice, but left has been called injustice. Moreover, because of this they all received a realm in the assembly of justice, and injustice is set over all their creations.[40]

YALDABAOTH RETALIATES BY CREATING DEATH

When the chief creator of chaos saw his son Sabaoth, and that the glory in which he dwells is more exquisite than all the authorities of chaos, he was jealous of him. And when he was angry, he conceived death from his own death.[41] It was set up over the sixth heaven; Sabaoth had been snatched away from there. And thus the number of the six authorities of chaos was completed.

---

37. Or "congregation," "church," here and below.
38. The eighth heaven is the realm of light above and is commonly identified with the astronomical realm of the stars (the ogdoad).
39. Possibly emend to read "while thirty others, with lyres and harps and trumpets in their hands, glorify him."
40. The meaning of this sentence is unclear. Possibly read the last clause as "where they all stand upon their foundations" (Layton, *Nag Hammadi Codex II,2-7*, 2.47).
41. Death is a son of Yaldabaoth to replace Sabaoth.

Then, since death was androgynous, he mixed with his nature and conceived seven androgynous children.[42] These are the names of the males: envy, wrath, weeping, sighing, mourning, lamenting, tearful groaning. And these are the names of the females: wrath, grief, lust, sighing, cursing, bitterness, quarrelsomeness. They had intercourse with one another, and each one conceived seven, so that the children total forty-nine androgynous demons.

Their names and their functions you will find in the Book of Solomon.[43]

In the presence of these, Zoe, who dwells with Sabaoth, created seven good androgynous powers.[44] These are the names of the males: not-jealous, blessed, joyful, true, not-envious, beloved, trustworthy. And these are the names of the females: peace, gladness, rejoicing, blessedness, truth, love, faith. And many good and guileless spirits come from these.

Their accomplishments and their functions you will find in the Configurations of the Fate of Heaven beneath the Twelve.[45]

YALDABAOTH REALIZES HIS MISTAKE

But when the chief creator saw the likeness of Pistis in the waters,[46] he grieved, especially when he heard her voice, which was like the first voice that called to him out of the water. When he knew that this was the one who named him, he groaned and was ashamed on account of his transgression. And when he actually knew that an enlightened, immortal human existed before him, he was greatly disturbed, because previously he had said to all the gods and their angels, "I am god and there is no other god but me."

For he had been afraid that they might know that another existed before him and condemn him. But he, like a fool, despised the condemnation and acted recklessly, and said, "If something exists before me, let it appear so that we might see its light." And immediately, look, light came out of the eighth heaven above and passed through all the heavens of the earth.

When the chief creator saw that the light was beautiful as it shone forth, he was amazed and very much ashamed. When the light appeared, a human

---

42. Death is the source of much of the grief in the world.
43. The precise identity of this source is unknown. Several known texts are attributed to Solomon, such as the Testament of Solomon, with its discussion of how Solomon built the temple with the help of the demons.
44. Zoe (life) counters. She is the source of much of the good in the world.
45. This source is unknown.
46. On the image or likeness of god in the waters, see Genesis 1:26 and gnostic interpretations.

likeness, which was very wonderful, was revealed within it; and no one saw it except the chief creator alone and the forethought[47] who was with him. But its light appeared to all the powers of the heavens. Therefore they were all disturbed by it.

ADAM OF LIGHT SHINES FORTH

Then when forethought saw the messenger,[48] she became enamored of him, but he hated her because she was in darkness. Moreover, she desired to embrace him, but she was not able. When she was unable to quench her love, she poured out her light upon the earth. From that day, that messenger was called Adam of light, which is interpreted the enlightened man of blood.[49] And the earth upon which the light spread was called[50] holy Adamas, which is interpreted as "the holy steel-like earth." At that time, all the authorities began to honor the blood of the virgin, and the earth was purified because of the blood of the virgin. But especially the water was purified by the likeness of Pistis Sophia, who appeared to the chief creator in the waters. Rightly, then, has it been said, "through the waters."[51] Since the holy water gives life to everything, it purifies it too.

EROS AND PSYCHE

Out of this first blood Eros appeared, being androgynous. His masculine nature is Himeros, because he is fire from the light.[52] His feminine nature is that of a soul of blood and is derived from the substance of forethought. He is very handsome in his beauty, having more loveliness than all the creatures of chaos. Then when all the gods and their angels saw Eros, they became enamored of him. But when he appeared among all of them, he made them inflamed. Just as many lamps are kindled from a single lamp and the light shines but the lamp is not diminished, so also Eros was scattered in all the creatures of chaos but was not diminished. Just as Eros appeared out of the

---

47. Pronoia.
48. Or "angel."
49. This etymology may relate the name Adam to the Hebrew word *dam*, "blood."
50. Partially emended. Without emendation, the passage reads, "the earth spread over him."
51. This reference to the waters recalls Genesis 1:26 and gnostic interpretations of the appearance of the divine through the waters.
52. Eros is the Greek god of love, and Himeros is the related god of desire.

midpoint between light and darkness, and in the midst of the angels and people the intercourse of Eros was consummated, so too the first sensual pleasure sprouted upon the earth.

The woman followed the earth, and marriage followed the woman, and reproduction followed marriage, and death followed reproduction.

After Eros, the grapevine sprouted up from the blood that was shed upon the earth. Therefore those who drink the vine acquire the desire for intercourse.[53] After the grapevine, a fig tree and a pomegranate tree sprouted up from the earth, together with the rest of the trees, according to their kind, their seed deriving from the seed of the authorities and their angels.

THE CREATION OF PARADISE

Then justice created the beautiful paradise. It is outside the circuit of the moon and the circuit of the sun in the luxuriant earth, which is in the east in the midst of stones. And desire is in the midst of trees, since they are beautiful and appealing. And the tree of immortal life, as it was revealed by the will of god, is in the north of paradise to give life to the immortal saints, who will come out of the fashioned bodies of poverty in the consummation of the age. Now, the color of the tree of life is like the sun, and its branches are beautiful. Its leaves are like those of the cypress, and its fruit is like clusters of white grapes. Its height rises up to heaven. And next to it is the tree of knowledge, possessing the power of god. Its glory is like the moon shining forth brilliantly, and its branches are beautiful. Its leaves are like fig leaves, and its fruit is like good, delicious dates. And this tree is in the north of paradise to raise up the souls from the stupor of the demons, so they might come to the tree of life and eat its fruit and condemn the authorities and their angels.

The effect of this tree is described in the Holy Book as follows: [54]

> You are the tree of knowledge, which is in paradise, from which the first man ate and which opened his mind, so that he loved his female partner, and condemned other alien likenesses, and loathed them.

---

53. Greek literature has discussions of the connection between Eros and Dionysos, that is, between love and wine, as in Achilles Tatius, *The Adventures of Leucippe and Clitophon.*
54. The source of this quotation is unknown.

Now, after this there sprouted up the olive tree, which was to purify kings and chief priests of justice, who will appear in the last days. The olive tree appeared in the light of the first Adam for the sake of the anointing that they will receive.

THE CREATION OF PLANTS, ANIMALS, AND HEAVENLY ORBS

But the first Psyche[55] loved Eros, who was with her, and poured her blood upon him and upon the earth. Then from that blood the first rose sprouted upon the earth out of the thorn bush, for a joy in the light that was to appear in the bramble. After this the beautiful, fragrant flowers sprouted up from the earth according to their kind from the blood of each of the virgins of the daughters of forethought. When they had become enamored of Eros, they poured out their blood upon him and upon the earth. After these things every herb sprouted up in the earth according to its kind, having the seed of the authorities and their angels. After these things the authorities created from the waters all species of beasts and reptiles and birds according to their kind, having the seed of the authorities and their angels.

But before all these things, when Adam of light appeared on the first day, he remained upon the earth about two days. He left the lower forethought in heaven and began to ascend to his light. And immediately darkness came upon the whole world. Now, when Sophia, who is in the lower heaven,[56] wanted to receive authority from Pistis, she created great luminaries and all the stars, and put them in the heaven to shine upon the earth and to perfect chronological signs and seasons and years and months and days and nights and seconds, and so on. And thus everything up in the sky was ordered.

Now, when Adam of light wanted to enter his light, that is, the eighth heaven, he was unable because of the poverty that had mixed with his light. Then he created a great eternal realm for himself; in that eternal realm he created six realms and their worlds, six in number, which are seven times better than the heavens of chaos and their worlds. But all these realms and their worlds exist within the infinite region that is between the eighth and chaos beneath it, and they are reckoned with the world that belongs to the poverty.

---

55. Soul. The story of the soul (Psyche) and Eros (love) is told in the literature of antiquity and late antiquity. For gnostic versions of the myth of the soul, see the Song of the Pearl and the Exegesis on the Soul in this volume.
56. The lower Sophia.

If you wish to know the arrangement of these, you will find it written in the Seventh Cosmos of Hieralias the Prophet.[57]

THE CREATION OF HUMANKIND

Before Adam of light withdrew in the chaos, the authorities saw him. They laughed at the chief creator because he lied, saying, "I am god and there is no other god but me." When they came to him, they said, "Is this not the god who ruined our work?" He answered and said, "Yes, but if you wish that he not be able to ruin our work, come, let's create a human being from the earth according to the image of our body and according to the likeness of this being,[58] to serve us, so that whenever this being sees his likeness, he may become enamored of it. Then he will no longer ruin our work, but we shall make those who are born from the light our servants through all the time of this age."

Now, all this came to pass according to the forethought of Pistis in order that humankind might appear after this likeness and condemn them on account of their fashioned bodies. And their fashioned bodies became fences for the light.[59]

Then the authorities received knowledge necessary to create people. Sophia Zoe, who is with Sabaoth, anticipated them and laughed at their decision because they were blind—in ignorance they created him against themselves. They do not know what they do. Because of this she anticipated them. She created her human being first in order that he might tell their fashioned body how to scorn them and thus to escape them.

Now, the birth of the instructor occurred in this way.[60] When Sophia let a drop of light fall, it floated on the water. Immediately a human being appeared, being androgynous. She molded that drop first as a female body. Afterward she molded it, with the body, in the likeness of the mother who appeared, and she finished it in twelve months. An androgynous human being was conceived, whom the Greeks call Hermaphrodite,[61] while the Jews call his mother Eve of life, that is, the instructor of life. Her child is the creature who is lord. Afterward, the authorities called it the beast in order to lead their fashioned bodies astray. The meaning of the beast is the instructor, for it was

---

57. Another unknown source.
58. Adam of light.
59. That is, the light is trapped within human bodies.
60. As in the Reality of the Rulers, the snake in paradise is the instructor of Adam and Eve.
61. That is, an androgynous, male-female being.

found to be wiser than all beings. Moreover, Eve is the first virgin who gave birth without a man. She is the one who functioned as her own midwife.

SONG OF EVE

On account of this it is said concerning her that she said,

> I am part of my mother, and I am the mother.
> I am the wife, I am the virgin.
> I am pregnant. I am the midwife.
> I am the one who comforts during labor pains.
> My husband produced me, and I am his mother,
> and he is my father and my lord.
> He is my potency; what he desires he speaks with reason.
> I am becoming, but I have borne a lordly man.[62]

Now these things were revealed by the will of Sabaoth and his Christ to the souls who will come to the fashioned bodies of the authorities.[63] Concerning these the holy voice said, "Multiply and flourish to rule over all the creatures."[64] And these are the ones who are taken captive by the chief creator according to their destinies, and thus they were locked in the prisons of the fashioned bodies until the consummation of the age.

THE COSMIC RULERS MOLD ADAM

At that time the chief creator then expressed his opinion about humankind to those who were with him. Then each of them cast his seed[65] into the midst of the navel of the earth. Since that day, the seven rulers have formed humankind with his body like their body, but his likeness is like the human who appeared to them. His fashioned body came into being one part at a time, and their chief created the brain and nervous system. Afterward the person appeared like the one before him.[66] He became a person with soul,[67] and he was called Adam, that is, father, after the name of the one who was before him.

---

62. The song of Eve resembles lines from the Sethian text Thunder in this volume.
63. This sentence is rearranged and restored.
64. Genesis 1:28.
65. Or "semen," here and below.
66. The meaning is uncertain. Perhaps the sentence means to indicate that the earthly Adam resembles Adam of light.
67. That is, a psychical person.

Now, after Adam was made, he[68] left him as a lifeless vessel, since he had taken form like an aborted fetus, with no spirit in him. Regarding this, when the chief ruler remembered the word of Pistis, he was afraid that the true human might come into his fashioned body and rule over it. Because of this, he left this fashioned body forty days without soul. And he withdrew and left him.

But on the fortieth day Sophia Zoe sent her breath into Adam, who was without soul. He began to move upon the earth, but he could not stand up.[69] Now, when the seven rulers came and saw him, they were very much disturbed. They walked up to him and seized him, and the chief ruler said to the breath within him, "Who are you? And from where have you come here?" It answered and said, "I came through the power of the human for the destruction of your work." When they heard, they glorified him because he gave them rest from their fear and concern. Then they called that day the day of rest,[70] because they rested themselves from their troubles. And when they saw that Adam could not stand up, they rejoiced. They took him and left him in paradise and withdrew up to their heavens.

EVE GIVES ADAM LIFE

After the day of rest, Sophia sent Zoe, her daughter, who is called Eve, as an instructor to raise up Adam, in whom there was no soul, so that those whom he would produce might become vessels of the light. When Eve saw her male partner cast down, she pitied him, and she said, "Adam, live! Rise up on the earth!" Immediately her word became an accomplished deed. For when Adam rose up, immediately he opened his eyes. When he saw her, he said, "You will be called the mother of the living, because you are the one who gave me life."[71]

THE COSMIC RULERS RAPE THE EARTHLY EVE

Then the authorities were informed that their fashioned body was alive, and had risen, and they were very much disturbed. They sent seven archangels to see what had happened. They came to Adam, and when they saw Eve speaking

---

68. The chief creator.
69. Adam is described in a similar state in the Secret Book of John and the Reality of the Rulers.
70. The Sabbath day.
71. Genesis 3:20.

with him, they said to one another, "What is this enlightened woman? For truly she resembles the likeness that appeared to us in the light. Now come, let us seize her and cast our seed into her, so that when she is polluted she will not be able to ascend to her light, but those whom she bears will serve us. But let us not tell Adam, because he is not from us. Rather, let us bring a stupor upon him, and suggest to him in his sleep that she came into being from his rib, so that the woman may serve and he may rule over her."[72]

Then Eve, since she existed as a power, laughed at their false intention. She darkened their eyes and secretly left her likeness there with Adam. She entered the tree of knowledge and remained there. They pursued her, and she revealed to them that she had entered the tree and had become the tree. And when the blind ones fell into a great fear, they ran away.[73]

Afterward, when they sobered up from the stupor, they came to Adam. And when they saw the likeness of that woman with him, they were troubled, thinking that this was the true Eve. And they acted recklessly, and came to her and seized her and cast their seed upon her. They did it deceitfully, defiling her not only naturally but also abominably, first defiling the seal of her voice, which had spoken with them, saying, "What is it that exists before you?" They meant to defile those who might say at the consummation of the age that they had been born of a true human by means of the word. And they were deceived, not knowing that they had defiled their own body. It was the likeness that the authorities and their angels defiled in every way.

EVE BEARS THE CHILDREN OF THE COSMIC POWERS

First Eve conceived Abel from the first ruler; and she bore the rest of the sons from the seven authorities and their angels. Now, all this came to pass according to the forethought of the chief creator, so that the first mother might bear within herself every seed, mixed and joined together with the fate of the world and its configurations and justice. A plan came into being because of Eve, so that the fashioned bodies of the authorities might become fences for the light. Then the light will condemn them through their fashioned bodies.

The first Adam of light is spiritual and appeared on the first day. The second Adam is a person with soul and appeared on the sixth day, called

---

72. Genesis 2:21–22.

73. Eve's becoming a tree resembles the myth of Daphne changing into a laurel tree. See also the Secret Book of John and the Reality of the Rulers.

Aphrodite.[74] The third Adam is earthly, that is, a man of law, who appeared on the eighth day, after the rest of poverty, which is called Sunday. Now, the progeny of the earthly Adam multiplied and was completed and produced within itself all the technical skill of the Adam with soul. But all were in ignorance.

THE TREES OF PARADISE AND THE BEAST

Next, let me continue. When the rulers saw him and the woman who was with him erring in ignorance like beasts, they rejoiced greatly. When they learned that an immortal human was not going to pass them by, but that they would even have to fear the woman who had turned into a tree, they were troubled and said, "Is this, perhaps, the true human, who blinded us and taught us about this defiled woman who is like him, that we might be conquered?"

Then the seven took counsel. They came to Adam and Eve timidly, and they said to him, "The fruit of every tree created for you in paradise may be eaten, but beware, don't eat from the tree of knowledge. If you do eat, you will die."[75] After they gave them a great fright, they withdrew up to their authorities.

Then came the one who is wiser than all creatures, who was called the beast. When he saw the likeness of their mother, Eve, he said to her, "What is it that god said to you? 'Don't eat from the tree of knowledge'?" She said, "He said not only 'Don't eat from it' but also 'Don't touch it, lest you die.'" He said to her, "Don't be afraid! You certainly shall not die. For he knows that when you eat from it your mind will be sobered and you will become like gods, knowing the difference between evil and good people. For he said this to you because he is jealous, so that you would not eat from it."[76]

Now, Eve believed the words of the instructor. She looked at the tree and saw that it was beautiful and appealing, and she desired it. She took some of its fruit and ate, and she gave to her husband also, and he ate too. Then their minds opened. For when they ate, the light of knowledge shone for them. When they put on shame, they knew that they were naked with regard to knowledge. When they sobered up, they saw that they were naked, and they became enamored of one another. When they saw that their makers had beastly forms, they loathed them. They understood a great deal.

---

74. Or "Hermaphrodite."
75. Genesis 2:16–17.
76. Genesis 3:1–5. In the present text the serpent is the gnostic hero, since it understands knowledge and the tree of knowledge.

HAVE YOU EATEN FROM THE TREE?

Then when the rulers knew that Adam and Eve had transgressed their commandment, they entered paradise and came to Adam and Eve in an earthquake and a great threat, to see the result of the help that was given.[77] Then Adam and Eve were very much disturbed and hid under the trees in paradise. The rulers did not know where they were and said, "Adam, where are you?" He said, "I am here. But because of fear of you I hid after I became ashamed." But they said to him, in ignorance, "Who is the one who spoke to you of the shame that you put on—unless you ate from the tree?" He said, "The woman whom you gave me, she is the one who gave to me, and I ate." Then they said to that woman, "What is this you have done?" She answered and said, "The instructor is the one who incited me, and I ate." Then the rulers came to the instructor. Their eyes were blinded by him so they were not able to do anything to him. They merely cursed him, since they were powerless. Afterward they came to the woman, and they cursed her and her offspring. After the woman they cursed Adam and the earth and the fruit because of him. And everything that they created they cursed. There is no blessing from them. Good cannot come from evil.

Since that day the authorities knew that truly there was something stronger than they. They would not have known except that their commandment was broken. They brought a great envy into the world only because of the immortal human.[78]

Now, when the rulers saw that their Adam had acquired a different knowledge, they wanted to test him. They gathered all the domestic animals and wild beasts of the earth and the birds of the heaven, and brought them to Adam to see what he would call them. When he saw them, he gave names to their creatures. They were troubled because Adam had sobered up from all ignorance.[79] They gathered together and took counsel and said, "Look, Adam has become like one of us, so that he understands the difference between light and darkness. Now perhaps he will be deceived as with the tree of knowledge and will come to the tree of life and eat from it and become immortal and rule and condemn us and regard us and all our glory as folly. And then he will pass judgment on us and the world. Come, let's cast him out of

---

77. This is the help offered by the instructor, the serpent, which resulted in knowledge.
78. See Genesis 3:6–19.
79. Or "all the trials."

paradise down to the earth, the place from where he was taken, so that he will no longer be able to know anything better than we can." And so they cast Adam and his wife out of paradise.

And what they had done did not satisfy them. Rather, they were still afraid. They came to the tree of life and they set great terrors around it, fiery living beings called cherubim; and they left a flaming sword in the midst, turning continually with a great terror, so that no one from among earthly beings might ever enter that place.[80]

After these things, when the rulers had become jealous of Adam, they wanted to diminish the human lifetimes, but they were unable because of fate, which was established since the beginning. For their lifetimes were determined: for each of the people one thousand years according to the circuit of the luminaries. But although the rulers were not able to do this, each of the evildoers took away ten years. So all of the remaining time amounts to nine hundred thirty years, and these are spent in grief and weakness and in evil distractions. Thus life has gone, from that day until the consummation of the age.[81]

PHOENIXES, WATER ANIMALS, BULLS OF EGYPT

Then when Sophia Zoe saw that the rulers of darkness cursed her companions, she was angry. And when she came out of the first heaven with every power, she chased the rulers from their heavens, and she cast them down to the sinful world, that they might dwell there as evil demons upon the earth. She sent the bird that was in paradise so that, until the consummation of the age, it might spend the thousand years in the rulers' world: a vital living being with soul, called the phoenix, which kills itself and reanimates itself for a witness to their judgment, because they dealt unjustly with Adam and his race.

There are three human beings and their descendants in the world until the consummation of the age: the spiritual and the psychical and the earthly. This is like the three kinds of phoenixes of paradise: the first is immortal; the second attains one thousand years; as for the third, it is written in the Holy Book that it is consumed. Likewise three baptisms exist: the first is spiritual, the second is by fire, the third is by water.

---

80. See Genesis 3:21–24.
81. As a punishment for enlightenment, the length of human life is diminished by the rulers of this world.

Just as the phoenix appears as a witness for the angels, so too the water serpents[82] in Egypt have become a witness to those who go down for the baptism of a true person. The two bulls in Egypt,[83] insofar as they indicate the sun and the moon as a mystery, exist for a witness to Sabaoth, that Sophia of the world has been exalted above the sun and the moon, from the day when she created them and sealed her heaven until the consummation of the age. And the worm that is brought forth from the phoenix is also a human being. It is written of it, "The just will sprout like the phoenix."[84] The phoenix first appears alive, and dies, and rises again, as a sign of what appears at the consummation of the age. These great signs appeared only in Egypt, not in other lands, signifying that it is like the paradise of god.

ERROR AND IGNORANCE
ENTER HUMAN HISTORY

Let us come back to the rulers of whom we spoke, that we might present an explanation of them. For when the seven rulers were cast from their heavens down upon the earth, they created for themselves angels, many demonic angels, to serve them. But these demons taught humankind many errors with magic and potions and idolatry, and shedding of blood, and altars, and temples, and sacrifices, and libations to all the demons of the earth, having as their co-worker fate,[85] who came into being according to the agreement by the gods of injustice and justice. And thus when the world came into being, it wandered astray in distraction throughout all time. For all the people who are on the earth served the demons from the creation until the consummation of the age—both the angels of justice and the people of injustice. Thus the world came to be in distraction and ignorance and stupor. They all erred, until the appearance of the true human.

Enough for you to this point. Next we shall consider our world so that we might complete the discussion of its structure and its government in a precise manner. Then it will be clear how belief in hidden things, which have been apparent from the foundation to the consummation of the age, came about.

---

82. Water *hydria* (Coptic, Greek), perhaps crocodiles, water serpents, or otters. See Layton, *Nag Hammadi Codex II,2-7,* 2.81.
83. The two bulls in Egypt are most likely Apis and Mnevis.
84. Psalm 91:13 in the Septuagint.
85. Greek *heimarmene.*

THE BLESSED INNOCENT SPIRITS

Now I come to the main points about immortal humankind. I shall explain why the beings belonging to the immortal human are here. When a multitude of people came into being through Adam, who was fashioned, and from matter, and when the world was filled, the rulers reigned over it, that is to say, they held it in ignorance. What is the cause? It is this. Since the immortal father knows that deficiency of truth came into being among the eternal realms and their worlds, when he wanted to bring to naught the rulers of destruction by means of their fashioned creatures, he sent your likenesses, namely, the blessed little guileless spirits, down to the world of destruction.[86] They are not strangers to knowledge. For all knowledge is in an angel who appears before them, who stands in front of the father and is not powerless to give them knowledge. Immediately, whenever they appear in the world of destruction, they will first reveal the pattern of incorruptibility for condemnation of the rulers and their powers. Moreover, when the blessed ones appeared in the fashioned bodies of the authorities, they were envied. And because of envy, the authorities mixed their seed with them to defile them, but they were not able. Moreover, when the blessed ones appeared in their light, they appeared distinctively. And each one of them from their land revealed their knowledge to the assembly[87] that appeared in the fashioned bodies of destruction. The assembly was found to have every seed because of the seed of the authorities that was mixed with it. Then the savior made all of them one.[88] And the spirits of these appeared, being superior and blessed but varying in election, and many others are kingless and superior to everyone who was before them. Consequently, four races exist. There are three that belong to the kings of the eighth heaven. But the fourth race is kingless and perfect, above them all. For these will enter into the holy place of their father, and they will reside in rest, and eternal, ineffable glory, and ceaseless joy. They are already kings, immortal within the mortal realm. They will pass judgment on the gods of chaos and their powers.

---

86. These are spirits of light sent from the realm of light to enlighten gnostics in this world. They appear as revealers, in flesh.
87. Or "church," here and below.
88. Partially restored.

JESUS THE LOGOS

Now, the word,[89] who is more exalted than anyone, was sent for this work only, to announce what is unknown. He said, "There is nothing hidden that will not appear, and what was unknown will be known."[90] Now these were sent so they might reveal what is hidden and expose the seven authorities of chaos and their impiety. And they were condemned to be killed. So when all the perfect ones appeared in the fashioned bodies of the rulers and revealed incomparable truth, they put to shame every wisdom of the gods, and their fate was discovered to be condemnable, their power dried up, their dominion was destroyed, and their forethought and their glory became empty.

THE CONSUMMATION OF THE AGE
AND THE APOCALYPSE

Before the consummation of the age, the whole place will be shaken by great thunder.[91] Then the rulers will lament, crying out on account of their death. The angels will mourn for their human beings, and the demons will weep for their times and seasons, and their people will mourn and cry out on account of their death. Then the age will begin, and they will be disturbed. Their kings will be drunk from the flaming sword and will make war against one another, so that the earth will be drunk from the blood that is poured out. And the seas will be troubled by that war. Then the sun will darken and the moon will lose its light. The stars of the heaven will disregard their course, and great thunder will come out of great power that is above all the powers of chaos, the place where the firmament of the woman[92] is situated. When she has created the first work, she will take off her wise flame of afterthought and will put on irrational wrath. Then she will drive out the gods of chaos, whom she had created together with the chief creator. She will cast them down to the abyss. They will be wiped out by their own injustice. For they will become like the mountains that blaze out fire,[93] and they will consume one another until they are destroyed by their chief creator. When he destroys

---

89. Logos.
90. Matthew 10:26; Mark 4:22; Luke 8:17; 12:2; Gospel of Thomas 5, 6.
91. Apocalyptic signs precede the consummation of the age.
92. Pistis Sophia.
93. Volcanoes.

them, he will turn against himself and destroy himself until he ceases to be. And their heavens will fall upon one another and their powers will burn. Their realms will also be overthrown. And the chief creator's heaven will fall and split in two. Likewise, his stars in their sphere will fall down to the earth, and the earth will not be able to support them.[94] They will fall down to the abyss, and the abyss will be overthrown.

THE LIGHT IS SAVED AND GNOSTICS RETURN HOME

The light will cover the darkness and obliterate it. It will become like something that never existed. And the source of the darkness will be dissolved. The deficiency will be plucked out at its root and thrown down to the darkness. And the light will withdraw up to its root, and the glory of the unconceived will appear, and it will fill all the eternal realms, when the prophetic utterances and the writings of those who are rulers[95] are revealed and are fulfilled by those who are called perfect. Those who were not perfected in the unconceived father will receive their glories in their realms and in the kingdoms of immortals. But they will not ever enter the kingless realm.[96]

For it is necessary that everyone enter the place from which he has come. Each one by his deeds and his gnosis will reveal his nature.

---

94. Partly restored.
95. The prophets and writings may designate books of the Hebrew Bible.
96. In the end, light will obliterate darkness, the aeons will be filled with light, and the glory of the unconceived will be perfected. The text suggests that many, if not all, will be saved, though there are different levels of final bliss.

28

The Paraphrase of Shem

The Paraphrase of Shem is a difficult, confusing, and fascinating gnostic text about the origin of the world and the salvation of the people of Shem in the world. The document defies any obvious classification: though gnostic, it shares few features with other Sethian literature and may be closer, in some respects, to Manichaean literature and Manichaean themes. The title relates both to the entire text and to a later specific portion of the text that refers to itself as a paraphrase and explains names used in a litany. The title is similar to the Paraphrase of Seth mentioned by Hippolytus of Rome,[1] and the two texts share certain features, such as the conviction that everything originates from three primal powers. As Hippolytus presents the Paraphrase of Seth, however, it is a clearly Christian text that has more differences than similarities with the present text.

In the Paraphrase of Shem the father of the gnostics is not Seth, as among Sethian gnostics, but another figure with a significant role in the early chapters of Genesis, Shem (spelled Seem in the text). Here Shem receives a revelation from the savior and revealer, Derdekeas, whose name may derive from the Aramaic for "male child."[2] According to the Paraphrase of Shem, in the

---

1. *Refutation of All Heresies* 5.19–22.
2. See Frederik Wisse, "The Paraphrase of Shem (VII,1)," in Pearson, *Nag Hammadi Codex VII*, p. 16, and Stroumsa, *Another Seed: Studies in Gnostic Mythology,* p. 79.

beginning there is the light above, the darkness below, and the spirit in between. This view of the origin of the world probably comes from the opening verses of Genesis 1, with its introduction of the light, the darkness of the watery chaos, and the spirit (or wind) of god moving over the watery darkness. In the present text the darkness becomes active and emerges as a threat to the integrity of the spirit and the mind. The actions of the darkness are described in sexually graphic terms, so that the creation of the world of nature is depicted as an orgy of cosmic sexuality. Derdekeas, as the child and emissary of the light, intervenes in these affairs, but the opposition continues against the spirit and the mind and the people of Shem, the gnostics. The forces of darkness send a flood and try to destroy the people of Sodom, who are here seen as gnostics. Through it all, however, with the help of Derdekeas, the people of Shem persevere. As Derdekeas says to Shem at the close of the text, "go in grace and continue in faith upon the earth. For every power of light and fire will be completed by me because of you."

The Paraphrase of Shem is one of the Coptic texts from the Nag Hammadi library. It was composed in Greek, and the existing Coptic version presents significant problems of understanding.

THE PARAPHRASE OF SHEM[3]

ABOUT THE UNCONCEIVED

The paraphrase about the unconceived spirit; what Derdekeas revealed to me, Shem, according to the will of the majesty.[4]

SHEM HAS A VISION

My thought, which was in my body, snatched me away from my race. It took me up to the top of the world, which is close to the light that shone upon the

---

3. The Paraphrase of Shem: Nag Hammadi library, Codex VII,1, pp. 1,1 to 49,9; translated by Frederik Wisse, "The Paraphrase of Shem," in Birger Pearson, ed. *Nag Hammadi Codex VII.* Nag Hammadi and Manichean Studies 30 (Leiden & New York: E. J. Brill, 1996), pp. 25–127, English version on odd-numbered pages only; revised by Willis Barnstone. Reprinted by permission of Brill Academic Publishers.
4. Such lines constitute opening titles (incipits) describing the contents of the text.

whole area there. I saw no earthly likeness, but there was light.[5] And my thought separated from the body of darkness as though in sleep.

DERDEKEAS TELLS SHEM ABOUT THE POWERS OF THE UNIVERSE

I heard a voice saying to me, "Shem, since you are from an unmixed power and you are the first being upon the earth, hear and understand what I shall say to you first concerning the great powers who were in existence in the beginning before I appeared. There was light and darkness, and there was spirit between them.[6] Since your root fell into forgetfulness—that which was the unconceived spirit—I reveal to you the truth about the powers.[7] The light was thought, full of attentiveness and reason; they were united into one form. And the darkness was wind in waters. He possessed the mind wrapped in chaotic fire. And the spirit between them was a gentle, humble light. These are the three roots. They reigned each in themselves, alone. And they covered each other, each one with its power.

"But the light, since he possessed great power, knew the abasement of the darkness and his disorder, namely, that the root was not straight. The crookedness of the darkness was lack of perception, namely, the illusion that there is no one above him.[8] And as long as he was able to restrain his evil, he was covered with the water. And he stirred. And the spirit was frightened by the sound.[9] He lifted himself up to his station, and he saw a great, dark water. And he was nauseated. The thought of the spirit stared down; he saw the infinite light. But he was overlooked by the putrid root. And by the will of the great light the dark water separated. The darkness came up wrapped in vile

---

5. Shem ecstatically ascends to the light above for a revelation from Derdekeas. The light, also called here the majesty, is the primal power above. It may also be linked to the sun above.
6. Shem and his offspring derive from the spirit that is between the light and the darkness. The three primal powers are termed roots; similar terminology occurs in Manichaean literature.
7. This is the common gnostic problem, forgetfulness, which necessitates knowledge and remembrance.
8. This lack of perception recalls the ignorance and illusion of the demiurge in the Secret Book of John and other gnostic texts in this volume.
9. See Genesis 1:2. When the darkness moves, the spirit takes notice and the quietness is disturbed.

ignorance, and this was in order that the mind might separate from him, because he prided himself in it.[10]

DARKNESS SEES THE SPIRIT

"When the darkness stirred, the light of the spirit appeared to him. When he saw it he was astonished. He did not know that another power was above him. And when he saw that his likeness was dark compared with the spirit, he felt hurt. And in his pain he lifted up, above the height of the members of darkness, his mind, which was the eye of the bitterness of evil. He caused his mind to take shape in a member of the portions of the spirit, thinking that, by staring down at his evil, he would be able to equal the spirit.[11] But he was not able, for he wanted to do an impossible thing, and it did not take place. But in order that the mind of darkness, which is the eye of the bitterness of evil, might not be destroyed, since he was made partially similar, he arose and shone with a fiery light upon all of Hades,[12] that the equality of the faultless light might become apparent. For the spirit benefited from every form of darkness because he appeared in his majesty.

"And the exalted, infinite light appeared, for he was very joyful. He wished to reveal himself to the spirit. And the likeness of the exalted light appeared to the unconceived spirit. I appeared.[13] I am the son of the incorruptible, infinite light. I appeared in the likeness of the spirit, for I am the ray of the universal light. And his appearance to me was in order that the mind of darkness might not remain in Hades. For the darkness made himself like his mind in a portion of the members. When I, O Shem, appeared in the likeness, so that the darkness might become dark to himself, according to the will of the majesty, and so that the darkness might become devoid of every aspect of the power that he

---

10. Salvation in this text entails the freeing of the mind from the confines of darkness. In other gnostic creation texts it is explicitly said that the power below, for example, Yaldabaoth, takes something from the divine light above, and that divine light falls into darkness. The same sort of usurpation of light may be assumed here.

11. This difficult section of the text seems to assume that light from the spirit is lost in the realm of darkness. Later in the text we are told that the light of the spirit is separated from the spirit and eventually saved from darkness.

12. Darkness makes its home in Hades.

13. This is Derdekeas, the child of the light above, a ray of light shining down from above.

possessed, the mind drew the chaotic fire, with which it was covered, from the midst of the darkness and the water. And from the darkness the water became a cloud, and from the cloud the womb took shape.[14] The chaotic fire, which was a deviation, went there.

DARKNESS EJACULATES MIND INTO THE WOMB OF NATURE

"And when the darkness saw the womb, he became unchaste. And when he had aroused the water, he rubbed the womb.[15] His mind dissolved down to the depths of nature. It mingled with the power of the bitterness of darkness. And the womb's eye[16] ruptured at the wickedness in order that she might not again bring forth the mind. For it was a seed of nature from the dark root. And when nature had taken to herself the mind by means of the dark power, every likeness took shape in her. And when the darkness had acquired the likeness of the mind, it resembled the spirit. For nature rose up to expel it; she was powerless against it, since she did not have a form from the darkness. For she brought it forth in the cloud. And the cloud shone. A mind appeared in it like a frightful, harmful fire. The mind collided against the unconceived spirit, since it possessed a likeness from him, in order that nature might become empty of the chaotic fire.

And immediately nature was divided into four parts. They became clouds that varied in their appearance. They were called hymen, afterbirth, power, and water.[17] And the hymen and the afterbirth and the power were chaotic fires. And the mind was drawn from the midst of the darkness and the water— since the mind was in the midst of nature and the dark power—in order that the harmful waters might not cling to it. Because of this, nature was divided, according to my will, in order that the mind may return to its power, which the dark root, mixed with the mind, had taken from it. And the dark root appeared in the womb. At the division of nature the dark root separated from the

---

14. The womb, or female sexual nature, may be seen as the female counterpart of the male darkness, and so darkness becomes sexually active.

15. Rubbing is a colorful image to refer to sexual intercourse here and elsewhere in the text.

16. Or "outside," of the womb or of nature.

17. These are the inflamed manifestations of the female sexual nature. The myth of the soul in the Exegesis on the Soul, and the overall description of humanity in the Secret Book of John, both in this volume, include similar reflections on the mind trapped in sexuality.

dark power, which it possessed from the mind. The mind went into the midst of the power—this was the middle region of nature.[18]

THE LIGHT OF THE SPIRIT IS IN THE CONFINES OF NATURE

"The spirit of light, when the mind burdened him, was astonished. And the force of his astonishment cast off the burden. And it returned to its heat. It put on the light of the spirit. And when nature moved away from the power of the light of the spirit, the burden returned. And the astonishment of the light again cast off the burden. It stuck to the cloud of the hymen.[19] And all the clouds of darkness cried out, they who had separated from Hades, because of the alien power.

"This is the spirit of light who has come in them. And by the will of the majesty the spirit gazed up at the infinite light, that his light may be pitied and the likeness may be brought up from Hades. And when the spirit had looked, I flowed out—I, the son of the majesty—like a wave of light and like a whirl-wind of the immortal spirit. And I blew from the cloud of the hymen upon the astonishment of the unconceived spirit. The cloud separated and cast light upon the clouds. These separated so that the spirit might return. Because of this the mind took shape. Its rest was shattered. For the hymen of nature was a cloud that cannot be grasped; it is a great fire. Similarly, the afterbirth of nature is the cloud of silence; it is an august fire. And the power that was mixed with the mind—it, too, was a cloud of nature that was joined with the dark-ness that had aroused nature to unchastity. And the dark water was a frightful cloud. And the root of nature, which was below, was crooked, since it is bur-densome and harmful. The root was blind to the bound light, which was un-fathomable because it had many appearances.

DERDEKEAS APPEALS ON BEHALF OF THE SPIRIT

"I had pity on the light of the spirit that the mind had received. I returned to my position to pray to the exalted, infinite light that the power of the spirit

---

18. Through the intercourse of darkness and nature, mind enters into nature, producing aston-ishment in the light from the spirit that is there.
19. The image of light hidden in a cloud also appears as Yaldabaoth in the Secret Book of John.

might increase there and might be filled without dark defilement. And reverently I said, You are the root of the light. Your hidden form has appeared, O exalted, infinite one. May the whole power of the spirit spread and may it be filled with its light, O infinite light. Then he will not be able to join with the unconceived spirit, and the power of the astonishment will not be able to mix with nature. According to the will of the majesty, my prayer was accepted.[20]

"And the voice of the word was heard saying through the majesty of the unconceived spirit, 'Look, the power has been completed. The one who was revealed by me appeared in the spirit.'

"Again I shall appear. I am Derdekeas, the son of the incorruptible, infinite light.

"The light of the infinite spirit came down to feeble nature for a short time until all the impurity of nature became void, and in order that the darkness of nature might be exposed. I put on my garment, which is the garment of the light of the majesty—which I am.[21] I came in the appearance of the spirit to consider the whole light, which was in the depths of the darkness, according to the will of the majesty, in order that the spirit by means of the word might be filled with his light independently of the power of the infinite light. And at my wish the spirit arose by his own power. His greatness was granted to him that he might be filled with his whole light and depart from the whole burden of the darkness. For what was behind was a dark fire that blew and pressed on the spirit. And the spirit rejoiced because he was protected from the frightful water. But his light was not equal to the majesty. What he was granted by the infinite light was given so that in all his members he might appear as a single image of light. And when the spirit arose above the water, his dark likeness became apparent. And the spirit honored the exalted light: 'Surely you alone are the infinite one, because you are above every unconceived thing, for you have protected me from the darkness. And at your wish I arose above the power of darkness.'

"And that nothing might be hidden from you, Shem, the thought, which the spirit from the greatness had contemplated, came into being, since the darkness was not able to restrain his evil. But when the thought appeared, the three roots became known as they were from the beginning. If the darkness had been able to restrain his evil, the mind would not have separated from him, and another power would not have appeared.

---

20. Derdekeas prays to the light above for the salvation of the spirit, and the prayer is heard.
21. Derdekeas dresses in the light of the divine in order to save and enlighten the spirit.

DERDEKEAS BRIGHTENS THE
LIGHT OF THE SPIRIT

"But from the time it appeared I was seen, the son of the majesty, that the light of the spirit might not become faint, and that nature might not reign over it, because it gazed at me.

"And by the will of the greatness my equality was revealed, that what is of the power might become apparent. You are the great power that came into being, and I am the perfect light that is above the spirit and the darkness, the one who puts to shame the darkness for the intercourse of impure rubbing. For through the division of nature the majesty wished to be covered with honor up to the height of the thought of the spirit. And the spirit received rest in his power. For the image of the light is inseparable from the unconceived spirit. And the lawgivers did not name him after all the clouds of nature, nor is it possible to name him. For every likeness into which nature had divided is a power of the chaotic fire, which is the material seed. The one who took to himself the power of the darkness imprisoned it in the midst of its members. And by the will of the majesty, in order that the mind and the whole light of the spirit might be protected from every burden and from the toil of nature, a voice came forth from the spirit to the cloud of the hymen. And the light of the astonishment began to rejoice with the voice that was granted to him. And the great spirit of light was in the cloud of the hymen. He honored the infinite light and the universal likeness, who I am, the son of the majesty, saying, 'Anasses Duses,[22] you are the infinite light who was given by the will of the majesty to establish every light of the spirit upon the place, and to separate the mind from the darkness. For it was not right for the light of the spirit to remain in Hades. For at your wish the spirit arose to behold your greatness.'

DERDEKEAS DISTURBS THE POWERS OF NATURE

"For I said these things to you, Shem, that you might know that my likeness, the son of the majesty, is from my infinite thought, since I am for him a universal likeness that does not lie, and I am above every truth and am the origin of the word. His appearance is in my beautiful garment of light, which is the

---

22. This name is known only from this text. It probably derives from Greek words for "rising" (or "east") and "setting" (or "west"), to indicate the rising and setting of the light (see Michel Roberge, *La Paraphrase de Jem*, p. 139).

voice of the immeasurable thought. We are that single, sole light that came into being. He appeared in another root in order that the power of the spirit might be raised from feeble nature. For by the will of the great light I came forth from the exalted spirit down to the cloud of the hymen without my universal garment.

"And the word took me to himself, from the spirit, in the first cloud of the hymen of nature. And I put on this of which the majesty and the unconceived spirit made me worthy. And the threefold unity of my garment appeared in the cloud, by the will of the majesty, in a single form. And my likeness was covered with the light of my garment. And the cloud was disturbed, and it was not able to tolerate my likeness. It shed the first power, which it had taken from the spirit—that which shone on him from the beginning, before I appeared in the word to the spirit. The cloud would not have been able to tolerate both of them. And the light that came forth from the cloud passed through silence until it came into the middle region. And by the will of the majesty, the light mixed with him, that is, the spirit that exists in silence, which had been separated from the spirit of light. It was separated from the light by the cloud of silence. The cloud was disturbed. It was he who gave rest to the flame of fire. He humbled the dark womb that she might not reveal other seed from the darkness. He kept them back in the middle region of nature in their position, which was in the cloud. They were troubled because they did not know where they were. For still they do not possess the universal understanding of the spirit.

"And when I prayed to the majesty, toward the infinite light, that the chaotic power of the spirit might go to and fro, and the dark womb might be barren, and that my likeness might appear in the cloud of the hymen, as if I were wrapped in the light of the spirit that went before me, and by the will of the majesty and through the prayer, I came in the cloud in order that through my garment—which was from the power of the spirit—the pleroma of the word might bring power to the members who possessed it in the darkness. For because of them I appeared in this insignificant place. For I am a helper of everyone who has been given a name. When I appeared in the cloud, the light of the spirit began to save itself from the frightful water, and from the clouds of fire that had been separated from dark nature. And I gave them eternal honor that they might not again engage in the impure rubbing.

"And the light that was in the hymen was disturbed by my power, and it passed through my middle region. It was filled with the universal thought. And through the word of the light of the spirit it returned to its rest. It received form in its root and shone without deficiency. And the light that had come forth with it from silence went in the middle region and returned to the place. And the cloud shone. And from it came an unquenchable fire. And the portion that separated from the astonishment put on forgetfulness.[23] It was deceived by the fire of darkness. And the shock of its astonishment cast off the burden of the cloud. It was evil, since it was unclean. And the fire mixed with the water so that the waters might become harmful.

"Nature, which had been disturbed, immediately arose from the idle waters. For her ascent was shameful. And nature took to herself the power of fire. She became strong because of the light of the spirit that was in nature. Her likeness appeared in the water in the form of a frightful beast with many faces, which is crooked below. A light went down to chaos filled with mist and dust, in order to harm nature. And the light of astonishment in the middle region came to it after he cast off the burden of the darkness.[24] He rejoiced when the spirit arose. For he looked from the clouds down at the dark waters upon the light that was in the depths of nature.

"So I appeared that I might get an opportunity to go down to the nether world, to the light of the spirit that was burdened, that I might protect him from the evil of the burden. And through his looking down at the dark region the light once more came up, that the womb might again come up from the water. The womb came up by my will. Guilefully, the eye opened. And the light, which had appeared in the middle region and which had separated from the astonishment, rested and shone upon her. And the womb saw things she had not seen before, and she rejoiced joyfully in the light, although this one that appeared in the middle region, in her wickedness, is not hers. When the light shone upon her, and the womb saw things she had not seen, and she was brought down to the water, she was thinking that she had reached the power of light. And she did not know that her root was made idle by the likeness of the light, and that it was to the root that he had run.

THE LIGHT PRAYS FOR MERCY

"The light was astonished, the one that was in the middle region and that was beginning and end. Therefore his thought gazed directly up at the exalted

---

23. A portion of the light trapped in the darkness, the portion from astonishment of spirit, needs to be saved. Pneumatic people like the people of Shem trace their salvation to spirit.
24. This light is trapped in the middle region, the region of the sexual power of nature. The concept of the middle region is common in gnostic texts.

light. And he called out and said, 'Lord, have mercy on me, for my light and my effort went astray. For if your goodness does not establish me, I do not know where I am.' And when the majesty had heard him, he had mercy on him.[25]

"And I appeared in the cloud of the hymen, in silence, without my holy garment. With my will I honored my garment, which has three forms in the cloud of the hymen. And the light that was in silence, the one from the rejoicing power, contained me. I wore it.[26] And its two parts appeared in a single form. Its other parts did not appear on account of the fire. I became unable to speak in the cloud of the hymen, for its fire was frightful, lifting itself up without diminishing. And so that my greatness and the word might appear, I placed likewise my other garment in the cloud of silence. I went into the middle region and put on the light that was in it, that was sunk in forgetfulness and that was separated from the spirit of astonishment, for he had cast off the burden. At my wish, nothing mortal appeared to him, but they were all immortal things that the spirit granted to him. And he said in the mind of the light, 'AI EIS AI OU PHAR DOU IA EI OU,[27] I have come in great rest in order that he may give rest to my light in his root, and may bring it out of harmful nature.'

DERDEKEAS DONS A FIERY GARMENT AND HAS SEX WITH NATURE

"Then, by the will of the majesty, I took off my garment of light. I put on another garment of fire, which has no form, which is from the mind of the power, which was separated, and which was prepared for me, according to my will, in the middle region.[28] For the middle region covered it with a dark power that I might come and put it on. I went down to chaos to save the whole light from it. For without the power of darkness I could not oppose nature. When I came into nature she was not able to tolerate my power. But I rested myself upon her staring eye, which was a light from the spirit. For it had been prepared for me as a garment and rest by the spirit. Through me, he opened his eyes down to Hades. He granted nature his voice for a time.

---

25. The light trapped in the sexual power of nature prays to the divine for help.
26. Derdekeas dresses up again and prepares to liberate the light.
27. This is glossolalia, ecstatic speech, the language of the heavenly realm.
28. Now Derdekeas dons another garment, a garment of fire, probably sexual fire, in order to have sex with female nature and thereby liberate the light.

"And my garment of fire, according to the will of the majesty, went down to what is strong, and to the unclean portion of nature that the power of darkness was covering. And my garment rubbed nature in her covering.[29] And her unclean femininity was strong. And the wrathful womb came up and made the mind dry, resembling a fish that has a drop of fire and a power of fire. And when nature had cast off the mind, she was troubled and wept.[30] When she was hurt and in her tears, she cast off the power of the spirit and remained as I am. I put on the light of the spirit and rested with my garment on account of the sight of the fish. And that the deeds of nature might be condemned, since she is blind, manifold animals came out of her, in accordance with the number of the fleeting winds.[31] All of them came into being in Hades, searching for the light of the mind that took shape. They were not able to stand up against it. I rejoiced over their ignorance.

DERDEKEAS FOOLS NATURE, AND CREATION BEGINS

"They found me, the son of the majesty, in front of the womb that has many forms. I put on the beast and laid before her a great request that heaven and earth might come into being, so that the whole light might rise up.[32] For in no other way could the power of the spirit be saved from bondage except that I appear to her in animal form. Therefore she was gracious to me as if I were her son. And on account of my request, nature arose, since she possesses the power of the spirit and the darkness and the fire. For she had taken off her forms. When she had cast it off, she blew upon the water.[33] The heaven was created. And from the foam of heaven the earth came into being. And at my wish it brought forth all kinds of food in accordance with the number of the beasts. And it brought forth dew from the winds on account of you and those who will be conceived the second time upon the earth. For the earth possessed a power of chaotic fire. Therefore it brought forth every seed. And when the

---

29. Another description of sexual intercourse.
30. Nature has an orgasm and ejects mind.
31. Nature produces bestial offspring, reminiscent of Sophia's bestial child Yaldabaoth in the Secret Book of John.
32. Derdekeas puts on a bestial form, an animal form, and thus tricks nature into thinking that he is her son.
33. Nature begins to create the world. Heaven and earth are created, and food is produced for all the animals of nature. Nature blowing upon the water may be a parallel to Genesis 1:2.

heaven and the earth were created, my garment of fire arose in the midst of the cloud of nature and shone upon the whole world until nature became dry. The darkness that was the earth's garment was cast into the harmful waters. The middle region was cleansed from the darkness. But the womb grieved because of what had happened. She perceived, in her parts, water like a mirror. When she perceived it, she wondered how it had come into being. Therefore she remained a widow. It also was astonished that it was not in her. For still the forms possessed a power of fire and light. The power remained, that it might be in nature until all the powers are taken away from her. For just as the light of the spirit was completed in three clouds, it is necessary also that the power that is in Hades be completed at the appointed time. For, because of the grace of the majesty, I came forth to her from the water for the second time. For my face pleased her. Her face also was glad.

DERDEKEAS COMMANDS NATURE TO GIVE BIRTH

"And I said to her, 'May seed and power come forth from you upon the earth.'[34] And she obeyed the will of the spirit that she might be brought to naught. And when her forms returned, they rubbed their tongues with each other and copulated; they produced winds and demons and the power that is from the fire and the darkness and the spirit.[35] But the form that remained alone cast the beast from herself. She did not have intercourse, but she was the one who rubbed herself alone. And she brought forth a wind that possessed a power from the fire and the darkness and the spirit.[36]

"And in order that the demons also might become devoid of the power that they possessed through the impure intercourse, a womb was with the winds resembling water. And an unclean penis was with the demons in accordance with the example of the darkness, and in the way he rubbed with the womb from the beginning. And after the forms of nature had been together, they separated from each other. They cast off the power, being astonished about the deceit that had happened to them. They grieved with an eternal grief. They covered themselves with their power.

---

34. Nature is to give birth, again, to forms of herself.
35. More sex transpires, and female minds and male demons are produced.
36. A portion of nature masturbates and produces a powerful wind.

"And when I had put them to shame, I arose with my garment in the power—which is above the beast, which is a light—in order that I might make nature desolate. The mind that had appeared in the nature of darkness, and that was the eye of darkness, at my wish reigned over the winds and the demons.[37] And I gave him a likeness of fire, light, and attentiveness, and a share of guileless reason. Therefore he was given of the greatness in order to be strong in his power, independent of the power, independent of the light of the spirit and intercourse of darkness, in order that, at the end of time, when nature will be destroyed, he may rest in the honored place. For he will be found faithful, since he has loathed the unchastity of nature with the darkness. The strong power of the mind came into being from the mind and the unconceived spirit. But the winds, which are demons from water and fire and darkness and light, had intercourse unto perdition. And through this intercourse the winds received in their womb foam from the penis of the demons. They conceived a power in their womb. From the breathing, the wombs of the winds girded each other until the times of the birth came. They went down to the water. And the power was delivered, through the breathing that causes the birth, in the midst of the rubbing. And every form of the birth received shape in it. When the times of the birth were near, all the winds were gathered from the water that is near the earth. They gave birth to all kinds of unchastity. And the place where the wind alone went was permeated with unchastity. Barren wives came from it and sterile husbands. For just as they are born, so they bear.[38]

DEMONS BRING THE FLOOD AND THE TOWER OF BABEL

"Because of you,[39] the image of the spirit appeared in the earth and the water. For you are like the light. You possess a share of the winds and the demons and a thought from the light of the power of the astonishment. For everything that he brought forth from the womb upon the earth was not a good thing for her, but it was her groan and her pain, because of the image that appeared in you from the spirit. For you are exalted in your heart. And it is a blessing, Shem, if

---

37. At last mind is freed from the power of darkness and reigns over the winds and demons.
38. The winds and the demons have sex, and the winds give birth to all sorts of unclean things; one wind masturbates and produces barren women and sterile men.
39. That is, for the sake of the people or race of Shem, the gnostics.

a portion is given to someone and he departs from the soul to go to the thought of the light. For the soul is a burden to the darkness, and those who know where the root of the soul came from will be able to grope after nature also. For the soul is a work of unchastity and an object of scorn to the thought of light. For I am the one who revealed concerning all that is unconceived.

"And so that the sin of nature might be filled, I made the womb, which was disturbed, pleasant—the blind wisdom—that I might be able to bring it to naught.[40] And at my wish, he plotted with the water of darkness and also the darkness, that they might wound every form of your heart. For by the will of the light of the spirit they surrounded you; they bound you in faith.[41] And so that his mind might become idle, he sent a demon, that the plan of her wicked-ness might be proclaimed. And he caused a flood,[42] and he destroyed your race, to take the light and to take away from faith. But I proclaimed quickly by the mouth of the demon that a tower come to be up to the particle of light, which was left in the demons and their race—which was water—that the demon might be protected from the turbulent chaos. And the womb planned these things according to my will, that she might pour forth completely. A tower came to be through the demons.[43] The darkness was disturbed by his loss. He loosened the muscles of the womb. And the demon who was going to enter the tower was protected so that the races might continue and might ac-quire coherence through him. For he possesses power from every form.

"Return henceforth, O Shem, and rejoice greatly over your race and faith, for without body and necessity it is protected from every body of darkness, bearing witness to the holy things of the greatness that were revealed to them in their thought by my will. And they shall rest in the unconceived spirit without grief. But you, Shem, because of this, you remained in the body out-side the cloud of light, that you might remain with faith.[44] And faith will come to you. Her thought will be taken and given to you with a conscious-ness of light. I told you these things for the benefit of your race from the cloud of light. And likewise, what I shall say to you concerning everything, I

---

40. The meaning of this sentence is unclear. It may recall, vaguely, the disturbance and agita-tion of Sophia, or wisdom, and the resolution of her disturbance.

41. In Greek faith is Pistis, as in Pistis Sophia. Faith may be personified and given the name Pis-tis throughout the Paraphrase of Shem.

42. The great flood of Genesis 6–9.

43. The tower of Babel of Genesis 11:1–9.

44. Shem and his fellow gnostics remain embodied in order to communicate the revelation and the knowledge.

shall reveal to you completely, that you may reveal it to those who will be upon the earth the second time.

A DISTURBANCE UNDOES
THE POWER OF NATURE

"O Shem, the disturbance that occurred at my wish happened so that nature might become empty.[45] For the wrath of the darkness subsided. O Shem, the mouth of darkness was shut. No longer does the light that shone for the world appear in it, according to my will. And when nature had said that its wish was fulfilled, then every form was engulfed by the waters in prideful ignorance. Nature turned her dark vagina and cast from her the power of fire, which was in her from the beginning through the rubbing of the darkness. It lifted itself up and shone upon the whole world instead of the righteous one. And all her forms sent forth a power like a flame of fire up to heaven as a help to the corrupted light, which had lifted itself up. For they were members of the chaotic fire. And she did not know that she had harmed herself. When she cast forth the power, the power that she possessed, she cast it forth from the genitals. The demon, who is a deceiver, stirred up the womb in every form.

"And in her ignorance, as if she were doing a great thing, she granted the demons and the winds a star each. For without wind and star nothing happens upon the earth. For every power is filled by them after they were released from the darkness and the fire and the power and the light. For in the place where their darkness and their fire were mixed with each other, beasts were brought forth. And in the place of the darkness and the fire, and the power of the mind, and the light, human beings came into existence. Being from the spirit, the thought of the light, my eye, does not exist in every person. For before the flood came from the winds and the demons, rain came to people. But then, in order that the power that is in the tower might be brought forth and might rest upon the earth, nature, which had been disturbed, wanted to harm the seed that will be upon the earth after the flood. Demons were sent to them, and a deviation of the winds, and a burden of the angels, and a fear of the prophet, a condemnation of speech, that I may teach you, O Shem, from what blindness your race is protected. When I have revealed to you all that has been

---

45. Everything happens according to the will and word of the divine, for the undoing of nature and the glorification of the light.

spoken, then the righteous one will shine upon the world with my garment. And night and day will be separated.[46] For I shall hasten down to the world to take the light of that place, the one that faith possesses. And I shall appear to those who will acquire the thought of the light of the spirit. For because of them my majesty appeared.

SODOM, CITY OF GNOSIS, IS UNJUSTLY BURNED

"When he will have appeared, O Shem, upon the earth, in the place that will be called Sodom, then safeguard the insight that I shall give you.[47] For those whose heart was pure will congregate to you, because of the word that you will reveal. For when you appear in the world, dark nature will shake against you, together with the winds and a demon, that they may destroy the insight. But you, proclaim quickly to the Sodomites your universal teaching, for they are your members. For the demon of human form will part from that place by my will, since he is ignorant. He will guard this utterance. But the Sodomites, according to the will of the majesty, will bear witness to the universal testimony. They will rest with a pure conscience in the place of their repose, which is the unconceived spirit. And as these things will happen, Sodom will be burned unjustly by a base nature. For the evil will not cease in order that your majesty may reveal that place.

"Then the demon will depart with faith. And then he will appear in the four regions of the world. And when faith appears in the last likeness, then will her appearance become manifest. For the firstborn is the demon who appeared in the union of nature with many faces, that faith might appear in him.[48] For when he appears in the world, evil passions will arise, and earthquakes, and wars, and famines, and blasphemies. For because of him the whole world will be disturbed. He will seek the power of faith and light; he will not find it. For at that time the other demon will appear upon the river to baptize with an imperfect baptism, and to trouble the world with a bondage

---

46. See Genesis 1:14–19.

47. The story of Sodom, which here is given a positive spin, is also told in Genesis 14 and 18–19. Here the Sodomites are described as fellow gnostics with Shem and his race.

48. The identity of this demon is unknown. It is explained here in the context of faith, and earthquakes, wars, famines, and blasphemies come through him. The whole world is disturbed on account of him. Frederik Wisse indicates that this demon may be Jesus (in Pearson, *Nag Hammadi Codex VII*, p. 86).

of water.[49] But it is necessary for me to appear in the members of the thought of faith to reveal the great things of my power. I shall separate it from the demon, who is Soldas.[50] And the light that he possesses from the spirit I shall mix with my invincible garment, as well as him whom I shall reveal in the darkness for your sake and for the sake of your race, which will be protected from the evil darkness.

THE LITANY

"Know, O Shem,[51]
that without Elorchaios and Amoias
and Strophaias and Chelkeak
and Chelkea and Elaios,
no one will be able to pass by
this wicked region.
For this is my testimony,
that through it I have been victorious over
the wicked region.
And I have taken the light of the spirit
from the frightful water.
For when the appointed days of the demon—
he who will baptize erringly—
draw near, then I shall appear
in the baptism of the demon
to reveal with the mouth of faith
a testimony to those who belong to her.
I testify of you, spark, unquenchable,
Osei, the elect of the light, the eye of heaven,
and faith, the first and the last,
and Sophia, and Saphaia, and Saphaina,
and the righteous spark,

---

49. The identity of this other demon is also unknown, but it may be John the baptizer; see Wisse, in Pearson, *Nag Hammadi Codex VII*, p. 88.
50. This may be Jesus or John the baptizer.
51. This is the beginning of the litany or testimony or memorial of Derdekeas for Shem. Some of the names in the litany are explained in the paraphrase that follows.

and the impure light.
And you, east, and west, and north, and south,
upper air and lower air,
and all the powers and authorities,
you are in creation.
And you, Moluchtha and Soch,
are from every work
and every impure effort of nature.

"Then I shall come through the demon down to the water. And whirlpools of water and flames of fire will rise up against me. Then I shall come up from the water, having put on the light of faith and the unquenchable fire, that through my help the power of the spirit may cross over, she who has been cast in the world by the winds and the demons and the stars. And in them every unchastity will be filled.

"Finally, O Shem, consider yourself pleasing in the thought of the light. Do not let your thought have dealings with the fire and the body of darkness, which was an unclean work. These things that I teach you are right.

THE PARAPHRASE

"This is the paraphrase[52]: For you did not remember that it is from the firmament that your race has been protected. Elorchaios is the name of the great light, the place from which I have come, the word that has no equal. And the likeness is my honored garment. And Derdekeas is the name[53] of his word in the voice of the light. And Strophaia is the blessed glance, which is the spirit. And Chelkeach is my garment, who has come from the astonishment, who was in the cloud of the hymen that appeared as a cloud with three forms. And Chelkea is my garment that has two forms, he who was in the cloud of silence. And Chelke is my garment that was given him from every region; it was given him in a single form from the greatness, and he was in the cloud of the middle region. And the star of the light that was mentioned is my invincible garment, which I wore in Hades; this, the star of the light, is the mercy that surpasses the

---

52. This is the specific paraphrase itself. This paraphrase explains names in the litany or testimony or memorial in the overall context of aspects of the story of creation in the Paraphrase of Shem.
53. Partially restored.

thought and the testimony of those who bear witness. And the testimony was mentioned: the first and the last, faith, the mind of the wind of darkness. And Sophaia and Saphaina are in the cloud of those who have been separated from the chaotic fire. And the righteous spark is the cloud of light that has shone in your midst. For in the cloud of light my garment will go down to chaos. But the impure light, a power, appeared in the darkness and belongs to dark nature. And the upper air and the lower air, and the powers and the authorities, the demons and the stars, these possessed a particle of fire and a light from the spirit. And Moluchthas is a wind, for without it nothing is brought forth upon the earth. He has a likeness of a serpent and a unicorn. His protrusions are manifold wings. And the remainder is the womb that has been disturbed.[54]

THE BLESSING OF SHEM AND THE PEOPLE OF SPIRIT

"You are blessed, Shem, for your race[55] has been protected from the dark wind, which is many-faced. And they will bear witness to the universal testimony and to the impure rubbing of nature. And they will become higher of mind by remembering the light.

"O Shem, no one who wears the body will be able to complete these things. But through remembrance he will be able to grasp them, in order that, when his mind separates from the body, these things may then be revealed to him. They have been revealed to your race. O Shem, it is difficult for someone wearing a body to complete these things, as I said to you. And it is a small number that will complete them, those who possess the particle of the mind and the thought of the light of the spirit.[56] They will keep their mind from the impure rubbing. For many in the race of nature will seek the security of the power. They will not find it, nor will they be able to do the will of faith. For they are seed of the universal darkness. They will be found in much suffering. The winds and the demons will hate them. And the bondage of the body is severe. For where the winds, and the stars, and the demons are cast out from the power of the spirit, there repentance and testimony come upon them, and mercy will lead them to the unconceived spirit. And those who are repentant will find rest

54. This is the end of the paraphrase itself.
55. The gnostics.
56. This section describes the differing fates of different sorts of people—people of spirit, people of faith, people of flesh.

in the consummation and faith, in the place of the hymen. This is the faith that will fill the place that has been left empty. But those who do not share in the spirit of light and in faith will dissolve in the darkness, the place where repentance did not come.

"It is I who opened the eternal gates that were shut from the beginning. To those who long for the best of life, and those who are worthy of rest, he revealed them. I granted perception to those who perceive. I disclosed to them all the thoughts and the teaching of the righteous ones. And I did not become their enemy at all. But when I had endured the wrath of the world, I was victorious. There was not one of them who knew me. The gates of fire and endless smoke opened against me. All the winds rose up against me. The thunderings and the lightning flashes for a time will rise up against me. And they will bring their wrath upon me. And on account of me, with regard to the flesh, they will rule over them according to their race.

IMPURE BAPTISM LEADS TO BONDAGE

"And many who wear erring flesh will go down to the harmful waters through the winds and the demons. And they are bound by the water.[57] And the water will heal with a futile remedy. It will lead astray, and it will bind the world. And those who do the will of nature . . . two times in the day of the water and the forms of nature. And it will not be granted them, when faith disturbs them to take to herself the righteous one.

"O Shem, it is necessary that the thought be called by the word so the bondage of the power of the spirit may be saved from the frightful water. And it is blessedness if it is granted someone to contemplate what is exalted, and to know the exalted time and the bondage. For the water is an insignificant body. And people are not released because they are bound in the water, just as from the beginning the light of the spirit was bound.

"O Shem, they are deceived by manifold demons, thinking that through baptism with the uncleanness of water, which is dark, feeble, idle, and disturbing, the water will take away sins. And they do not know that from the water to

---

57. The text is highly critical of baptism with water, a criticism that may be directed toward the emerging orthodox church and its reliance upon baptism. For baptism in gnostic texts, with a more or less spiritualized understanding, see the Baptismal Ceremony of the Gospel of the Egyptians, the Gospel of Philip, and the Valentinian Liturgical Readings, among other texts in this volume.

the water there is bondage, error, unchastity, envy, murder, adultery, false witness, heresies, robberies, lusts, babblings, wrath, bitterness. . . . Therefore, there are many deaths that burden their thoughts. For I foretell it to those who have understanding. They will refrain from the impure baptism. And those who have understanding from the light of the spirit will not have dealings with the impure rubbing. And their heart will not grow faint, nor will they curse, nor will they give honor to the water. Where the curse is, there is the deficiency. And the blindness is where the honor is. For if they mix with the evil ones, they become empty in the dark water. Where the water has been mentioned, there is nature, and the oath, and the lie, and the loss. For only in the unconceived spirit, where the exalted light rested, has the water not been mentioned, nor can it be mentioned.

"For this is my appearance: when I have completed the times that are assigned to me upon the earth, then I will cast from me my garment of fire. And my unequalled garment will shine forth upon me, and all my other garments that I put on in all the clouds that were from the astonishment of the spirit. For the air will tear my garment. My garment will shine, and it will divide all the clouds up to the root of the light. Rest is the mind and my garment. And my remaining garments, those on the left and those on the right, will shine on the back in order that the image of the light may appear. For in the last day my garments that I put on in the three clouds will rest in their root, that is, in the unconceived spirit, since they are without fault, through the division of the clouds.

Therefore I have appeared, faultless, on account of the clouds, because they are unequal, that the wickedness of nature might be ended. For she wished at that time to snare me. She was about to restrain Soldas, who is the dark flame, who was set on high, on the tree of error, that it might snare me. She took care of her faith, being vainglorious.[58]

REBOUEL IS BEHEADED

"And at that time the light was about to separate from the darkness, and a voice was heard in the world, saying, 'Blessings on the eye that has seen you

---

58. Partially restored; "tree" may also be understood as "cross," hence "cross of error." The tree or cross may do the snaring. Michel Roberge understands all this as an unsuccessful attempt on the part of nature to attack the savior Derdekeas; she was unsuccessful, and crucified Jesus ("Soldas") instead. Also see Wisse, in Pearson, *Nag Hammadi Codex VII*, p. 107.

and the mind that has supported your majesty at my desire.'[59] It will be said by the exalted one, 'Blessings on Rebouel among every race of people, for it is you alone who have seen.'[60] And she will listen. And they will behead the woman who has the perception, whom you will reveal upon the earth. And according to my will, she will bear witness, and she will cease from every vain effort of nature and chaos. For the woman whom they will behead at that time is the support of the power of the demon who will baptize the seed of darkness in severity, that the seed may mix with unchastity. He begot a woman. She was called Rebouel.

"See, O Shem, how all the things I have said to you have been fulfilled. . . . And the things that you lack, according to my will, will appear to you at that place upon the earth, that you may reveal them as they are. Do not let your thought have dealings with the body. For I have said these things to you, through the voice of the fire, for I entered through the midst of the clouds. And I spoke according to the language of each one. This is my language that I spoke to you.[61] And it will be taken from you. And you will speak with the voice of the world upon the earth.[62] And it will appear to you with that appearance and voice, and all that I have said to you. Henceforth proceed with faith to shine in the depths of the world."

SHEM RETURNS FROM HIS ECSTATIC JOURNEY

And I, Shem, awoke as if from a deep sleep. I marveled when I received the power of the light and his whole thought. And I proceeded with faith to shine with me. And the righteous one followed us with my invincible garment. And all that he had told me would happen upon the earth happened. Nature was handed over to faith, that faith might overturn her and that nature might stand in the darkness. She produced a turning motion while wandering night and day, not getting rest with the souls. These things completed her deeds.

---

59. This vaguely recalls Luke 10:23.
60. Michel Roberge understands the account of Rebouel to be an allegory on the crucifixion and baptism: "Just as Rebouel is declared blessed in her beheading, so the noetics [people of mind] should not hesitate to separate from the Great Church, which practices baptism, and enter the community of those who possess gnosis" (in Robinson, *Nag Hammadi Library in English*, rev. ed., p. 341).
61. This must be a language of light, of heaven, not an earthly language.
62. This must be Shem's earthly language.

Then I rejoiced in the thought of the light. I came forth from the darkness and walked in faith where the forms of nature are, up to the top of the earth, to the things that are prepared. Your faith is upon the earth the whole day. For all night and day she surrounds nature to take to herself the righteous one. For nature is burdened, and she is troubled. For none will be able to open the forms of the womb except the mind alone who was entrusted with their likeness. For frightful is their likeness of the two forms of nature, the one that is blind.

But they who have a free conscience remove themselves from the babbling of nature. For they will bear witness to the universal testimony; they will strip off the burden of darkness; they will put on the word of the light; and they will not be kept back in the insignificant place. And what they possess from the power of the mind they will give to faith. They will be accepted without grief. And the chaotic fire that they possess they will leave in the middle region of nature. And they will be received by my garments, which are in the clouds. It is they who guide their members. They will rest in the spirit without suffering. And because of this, the appointed term of faith appeared upon the earth for a short time, until the darkness is taken away from her, and her testimony is revealed that was revealed by me. They, who will prove to be from her root, will strip off the darkness and the chaotic fire. They will put on the light of the mind and bear witness. For all that I have said must happen.

THE FINAL DESOLATION

After I cease to be upon the earth and withdraw up to my rest, a great, evil error will come upon the world, and many evils in accordance with the number of the forms of nature. Evil times will come.[63] And when the era of nature is approaching destruction, darkness will come upon the earth. The number[64] will be small. And a demon will come up from the power who has a likeness of fire. He will divide the heaven, and he will rest in the depth of the east. For the whole world will quake. And the deceived world will be thrown into confusion. Many places will be flooded because of envy of the winds and the demons who have a name that is senseless: Phorbea, Chloerga.

---

63. This section of the text has Shem explain the end of the world in apocalyptic terms somewhat reminiscent of the book of Revelation and other apocalyptic literature.
64. Probably the number of days.

They are the ones who govern the world with their teaching. And they lead astray many hearts because of their disorder and their unchastity. Many places will be sprinkled with blood. And five races by themselves will eat their sons. The regions of the south will receive the word of the light. But they who are from the error of the world and from the east. . . .[65] A demon will come forth from the belly of the serpent. He was in hiding in a desolate place. He will perform many wonders. Many will loathe him. A wind will come forth from his mouth with a female likeness. Her name will be called Abalphe. He will reign over the world from the east to the west.

Then nature will have a final opportunity. And the stars will cease from the sky. The mouth of error will be opened that the evil darkness may become idle and silent. And in the last day the forms of nature will be destroyed with the winds and all their demons; they will become a dark lump, just as they were from the beginning.[66] And the sweet waters that were burdened by the demons will perish. For where the power of the spirit has gone, there are my sweet waters. The other works of nature will not be manifest. They will mix with the infinite waters of darkness. And all her forms will cease from the middle region.

SHEM ASCENDS, IN MIND, AND RECITES THE LITANY

I, Shem, have completed these things. And my mind began to separate from the body of darkness.[67] My time was completed. And my mind put on the immortal testimony. And I said,

"I declare your testimony,[68]
which you have revealed to me:
Elorchaios,
and you, Amoiaias,
and you, Sederkeas,

---

65. Perhaps read "will not."
66. This eschatological concept of the lump also occurs in Manichaean literature.
67. Shem begins his spiritual ascent out of his body.
68. Shem recites (more or less) the litany given by Derdekeas earlier in the text. The scribe seems inadvertently to have copied several lines of the litany twice (a scribal error known as dittography). This repetition is not reflected in the present translation.

and your guilelessness, Strophaias,
and you, Chelkeak,
and you, Chelkea,
 and Chelke and Elaios,
you are the immortal testimony.
I testify to you,
spark, the unquenchable one,
who is an eye of heaven and a voice of light,
and Sophaia, and Saphaia, and Saphaina,
and the righteous spark,
and faith, the first and the last,
and the upper air and the lower air,
and all the powers and the authorities
that are in the world.
And you, impure light,
and you also, east, and west, and south, and north,
 you are the zones of the inhabited world.
And you also, Moluchtha and Essoch,
you are the root of evil
and every work and impure effort of nature."

These are the things that I completed while bearing witness. I am Shem. On the day that I was to come forth from the body, when my thought remained in the body, I awoke as if from a deep sleep. And when I arose as it were from the burden of my body, I said, "Just as nature became old, so is it also in the day of human beings. Blessings on those who knew, when they slept, in what power their thought rested."

And when the Pleiades separated, I saw clouds, which I shall pass by. For the cloud of the spirit is like a pure beryl. And the cloud of the hymen is like a shining emerald. And the cloud of silence is like a flourishing amaranth. And the cloud of the middle region is like a pure jacinth.

"And when the righteous one appeared in nature,[69] then, when nature was angry, she felt hurt, and she granted to Morphaia to visit heaven. The righteous one visits during twelve periods that he may visit them during one period, so that his time may be completed quickly and nature may become idle.

---

69. Here, abruptly, Derdekeas seems to be speaking once again.

GO IN GRACE AND FAITH

"Blessings on those who guard themselves against the heritage of death, which is the burdensome water of darkness. For it will not be possible to conquer them in a few moments, since they hasten to come forth from the error of the world. And if they are conquered, they will be kept back from them and be tormented in the darkness until the time of the consummation.[70] When the consummation has come and nature has been destroyed, then their thoughts will separate from the darkness. Nature has burdened them for a short time. And they will be in the ineffable light of the unconceived spirit without a form. And thus is the mind, as I have said from the first.

"Henceforth, O Shem, go in grace and continue in faith upon the earth. For every power of light and fire will be completed by me because of you. For without you they will not be revealed until you speak of them openly. When you cease to be upon the earth, they will be given to the worthy ones. And apart from this proclamation, let them speak about you upon the earth, since they will take the carefree and agreeable land."

---

70. On being kept back, Frederik Wisse refers to the role of purgatory (in Pearson, *Nag Hammadi Codex VII*, p. 125).

29

The Second Treatise of the Great Seth

The work entitled Second Treatise of the Great Seth is a fascinating gnostic text with a most peculiar title. It is called the second treatise (*logos*), but it is not really a treatise, and we know of no first treatise; and it is attributed to Seth, whose name occurs nowhere in the document itself. (If Jesus is assumed to be a manifestation of Seth, that might begin to help explain the title of the text.) The Second Treatise of the Great Seth is a gnostic meditation, presented as a revelation of Christ, on the meaning of the life and particularly the death of Jesus the anointed, and the relationship between gnostic believers and the emerging orthodox church.

The meditation has Jesus tell the story of his career: his beginnings in the divine assembly, his descent into this world and adoption of a body, his dealings with the cosmic rulers of this world, his crucifixion—or what seemed to be his crucifixion—and finally his ascent back home to the divine fullness. As in the Coptic Revelation of Peter, the Nag Hammadi text that follows the Second Treatise of the Great Seth in Codex VII, the heavenly Christ's death is said to have never happened. Jesus was thought by some to have suffered and died, but the rulers got the wrong man. The Second Treatise of the Great Seth says (rather like Basilides, according to Irenaeus of Lyon) that Simon of Cyrene (who in Mark 15:21, Matthew 27:32, and Luke 23:26 is enlisted to help Jesus carry the cross) was involved in events leading up to the crucifixion, and that another—perhaps Simon, perhaps the body that Jesus adopted—

was crucified, while Jesus stood above it all, laughing at the ignorance and foolishness of the rulers. (Similar interpretations may be found in the Qur'an and other Islamic accounts of the death or apparent death of 'Isa, that is, Jesus.) The present text also polemicizes against "those who think that they are advancing the name of Christ" but end up persecuting the gnostics, who, Jesus says, "have been liberated by me." These hostile people in the emerging orthodox church, the text claims, are confused in their christology, and they proclaim "a doctrine of a dead man," according to which they believe, quite mistakenly, that they should worship, follow, and imitate a dead, crucified Christ. Unlike the gnostics, Jesus observes, they do not have "the knowledge of the greatness that it is from above and from a fountain of truth."

The Second Treatise of the Great Seth is another text from the Nag Hammadi library, and like other texts in the collection it was composed in Greek. Gregory Riley suggests a date of composition in the second half of the second century, in part on the basis of the characterization of the opponents in the emerging orthodox church as small (or, few, of little account) and ignorant (or uninstructed). He guesses that Alexandria may be a possible place of composition. The Second Treatise of the Great Seth does not give a systematic treatment of its gnostic themes, but some ideas of Sethian and Valentinian character may be identified. Many of the characters in the Second Treatise of the Great Seth are also presented in the Secret Book of John and other gnostic texts in this volume.

THE SECOND TREATISE OF THE GREAT SETH[1]

I AM IN YOU AND YOU IN ME

The perfect majesty is at rest in the ineffable light, in the truth of the mother[2] of all these, and all of you that attain to me, to me alone who am perfect,

---

1. The Second Treatise of the Great Seth: Nag Hammadi library, Codex VII,2, pp. 49,10 to 70,12; translated by Roger A. Bullard and Joseph A. Gibbons in Robinson, *Nag Hammadi Library in English*, rev. ed., pp. 363–71; modified in consultation with the translation by Gregory Riley in Pearson, *Nag Hammadi Codex VII*, pp. 129–99 and revised by Willis Barnstone.
2. Gregory Riley translates this as "the truth, the mother" (personified truth is then understood to be the mother), on the basis of the assumed Greek original (in Pearson, *Nag Hammadi Codex VII*, pp. 146–47).

because of the word. For I exist with all the greatness of the spirit, which is a friend to us and our kindred alike. Since I brought forth a word to the glory of our father, through his goodness, as well as an imperishable thought, that is, the word within him, it is slavery that we should die with Christ,[3] with imperishable and undefiled thought. This is an incomprehensible marvel, the writing of the ineffable water, which is the word from us: I am in you and you are in me, just as the father is in you in innocence.[4]

I COME FROM ABOVE AND AM INCARNATED

Let us gather an assembly together. Let us visit that creation of his. Let us send someone forth in it, so that he may visit the thoughts[5] in the regions below. And I said these things to the whole multitude of the great assembly of the rejoicing majesty. The whole house of the father of truth rejoiced that I am the one who is from them. I reflected upon the thoughts that came out of the undefiled spirit about the descent upon the water, that is, the regions below. And they all had a single mind, since it is from one source. They ordered me, and because I was willing, I came forth to reveal the glory to my kindred and my fellow spirits.

For those who were in the world had been prepared by the will of our sister Sophia—she who is a whore[6]—because of her innocence that has not been uttered. And she did not ask anything from the realm of all, nor from the greatness of the assembly, nor from the pleroma, when she previously came forth to prepare lodgings and places for the son of light and the fellow workers. She took materials from the elements below to build bodily dwellings from them. But having come into being in an empty glory, they ended in destruction in the dwellings in which they were. Since they were prepared by Sophia, they stand ready to receive the life-giving word of the ineffable One[7] and the greatness of the assembly of all those who persevere and those who are in me.

---

3. This statement reflects the Pauline and Christian doctrines of dying with Christ, for example, in baptism. Here dying with Christ is not treated in so favorable a manner.
4. See John 17:21–23.
5. Greek *ennoia*, here and below.
6. Sophia as whore recalls the actions and descriptions of Sophia in the Secret Book of John, Helena as the first thought of the gnostic teacher Simon Magus, the soul in the Exegesis on the Soul, and Derdekeas as the sexual partner of nature in the Paraphrase of Shem.
7. Monad.

I visited a bodily dwelling.[8] I cast out the one who was in it first, and I went in. And the whole multitude of the rulers became troubled. And all the matter of the rulers as well as all the powers born of the earth were shaken when they saw the likeness of the image, since it was mixed. And I was the one who was in the image, not resembling him who was in the body first. For he was an earthly man, but I, I am from above the heavens. I did not refuse them even to become Christ, but I did not reveal myself to them in the love that was coming forth from me. I revealed that I am a stranger to the regions below.

THE RULERS ARE DISTURBED

There was a great disturbance in the whole earthly area, with confusion and flight, as well as in the plan of the rulers. And some were persuaded, when they saw the wonders that were being accomplished by me. And all those fled, those of the race that descended from the one who fled from the throne to the Sophia of hope, since she had earlier given the sign concerning us and all the ones with me—those of the race of Adonaios.[9] Others also fled, as though sent from the world ruler[10] and those with him, and brought every kind of punishment upon me. And there was a flight of their mind about what they would counsel concerning me, thinking that their own greatness is all, and speaking false witness, moreover, against the human and the whole greatness of the assembly.[11] It was not possible for them to know who is the father of truth, the human of greatness. They took the name because of contact with ignorance—which is a burning and a vessel created to destroy Adam, whom they had made, in order to cover up those who are theirs in the same way. But they, the rulers, of the place of Yaldabaoth, reveal the realm of the angels, which human beings were seeking because they did not know the human of truth. For Adam, whom they had formed, appeared to them. And a fearful disturbance came about throughout their entire dwelling, lest the angels surrounding them rebel. For on account of those who were offering praise I died, but not really, because their archangel was vacuous.

---

8. The heavenly Christ takes a body and assumes bodily form.

9. Adonaios is one of the rulers in the cosmic bureaucracy, sometimes also called Sabaoth, who is closely linked to Yaldabaoth. Elsewhere Sabaoth, or Adonaios, rebels against his father Yaldabaoth and turns to Sophia.

10. Greek *cosmocrator*, here and below.

11. The human is a name of a divine being, sometimes the divine mother or the heavenly Adam, in gnostic texts. The image of the heavenly human is the pattern for the creation of earthly humankind.

THE WORLD RULER TRIES TO KILL ME

And then a voice of the world ruler came to the angels: "I am god and there is no other god but me."[12] But I laughed joyfully when I examined his conceit.[13] But he went on to say, "Who is the human?" And the entire host of his angels who had seen Adam and his dwelling were laughing at his smallness. And thus did their thought come to be removed outside the majesty of the heavens, away from the human of truth, whose name they saw, since he is in a small dwelling place. They are foolish and senseless in their empty thought, namely, their laughter, and it was contagion for them.

The whole greatness of the fatherhood of the spirit was at rest in its places. And I was with him, since I have a thought of a single emanation from the eternal ones and the unknowable ones, undefiled and immeasurable. I placed the small thought in the world, having disturbed them and frightened the whole multitude of the angels and their ruler. And I was visiting them all with fire and flame because of my thought. And everything pertaining to them was brought about because of me. And there came about a disturbance and a fight around the seraphim and cherubim, since their glory will fade, and there was confusion around Adonaios on both sides and around their dwelling, up to the world ruler and the one who said, "Let us seize him." Others again said, "The plan will certainly not materialize." For Adonaios knows me because of hope. And I was in the mouths of lions. And as for the plan that they devised about me to release their error and their senselessness, I did not succumb to them as they had planned. And I was not afflicted at all. Those who were there punished me, yet I did not die in reality but in appearance, in order that I not be put to shame by them because these are my kinsfolk. I removed the shame from me, and I did not become fainthearted in the face of what happened to me at their hands. I was about to succumb to fear, and I suffered merely according to their sight and thought so that no word might ever be found to speak about them. For my death, which they think happened, happened to them in their error and blindness, since they nailed their man unto their death.[14] Their thoughts did not see me, for they were deaf and blind. But in doing these things, they condemn themselves. Yes, they

---

12. Isaiah 45:5–6, 21; 46:9. In the Secret Book of John and elsewhere the same arrogant claim is made by Yaldabaoth.
13. The image of the laughing Jesus that appears here and below also appears in the Gospel of Philip and the Round Dance of the Cross, both in this volume.
14. It is unclear who is crucified here: Simon of Cyrene or the body that Jesus adopted.

saw me; they punished me. It was another, their father, who drank the gall and the vinegar; it was not I. They struck me with the reed; it was another, Simon, who bore the cross on his shoulder. It was another upon whom they placed the crown of thorns.[15] But I was rejoicing in the height over all the wealth of the rulers and the offspring of their error, of their empty glory. And I was laughing at their ignorance.

JESUS DESCENDS INCOGNITO AND LIBERATES THE GNOSTICS

And I subjected all their powers. For as I came downward, no one saw me. For I was altering my shapes, changing from form to form. And so when I was at their gates I assumed their likeness.[16] For I passed them by quietly, and I was viewing the places, and I was neither afraid nor ashamed, for I was undefiled. And I was speaking with them, mingling with them through those who are mine, and trampling on those who are harsh to them with zeal, and quenching the flame. And I was doing all these things because of my desire to accomplish what I desired by the will of the father above.

And the son of the majesty, who was hidden in the region below, we brought to the height where I am with all these aeons, which no one has seen or known, where the wedding of the wedding robe is, the new one and not the old, which does not perish. For it is a new and perfect bridal chamber of the heavens, and I have revealed that there are three ways, which are an undefiled mystery in a spirit of this aeon, which does not perish, nor is it fragmentary, nor able to be spoken of; rather, it is undivided, universal, and permanent. For the soul, the one from the height, will not speak about the error that is here, nor transfer from these aeons, since it will be transferred when it becomes free and endowed with nobility in the world, standing before the father without weariness and fear, always mixed with the mind[17] of power and of form. They will see me from every side without hatred. For since they see me, they are being seen and are mixed with them. Since they did not put me to

---

15. As noted in the introduction to this text, Simon of Cyrene takes the place of Jesus during events leading up to the crucifixion in the Second Treatise of the Great Seth, as in the thought of Basilides.

16. These are the heavenly gates, guarded by cosmic powers, that must be passed by the person descending from above or ascending to the divine.

17. Greek *nous*.

shame, they were not put to shame. Since they were not afraid before me, they will pass by every gate without fear and will be perfected in the third glory.[18]

It was my cross that the world did not accept, my apparent exaltation, my third baptism in a revealed image.[19] When they had fled from the fire of the seven authorities, and the sun of the powers of the rulers set, darkness overtook them. And the world became poor. After they bound him with many restraints, they nailed him to the cross, and they fastened him with four nails of brass.[20] The veil of his temple he tore with his hands. There was a trembling that overcame the chaos of the earth, for the souls that were in the sleep below were released, and they arose. They walked about boldly, having shed jealousy of ignorance and unlearnedness beside the dead tombs; having put on the new human; having come to know that perfect blessed one of the eternal and incomprehensible father and the infinite light, which is I.[21] When I came to my own and united them with myself, there was no need for many words, for our thought was with their thought. Therefore they knew what I was saying, for we took counsel about the destruction of the rulers. And therefore I did the will of the father, who is I.

After we left from our home and came down to this world and came into being in the world in bodies, we were hated and persecuted, not only by those who are ignorant[22] but also by those who think that they are advancing the name of Christ, since they were unknowingly empty, not knowing who they are, like dumb animals.[23] They persecuted those who have been liberated by me,[24] since they hate them—those who, should they shut their mouth, would weep with a profitless groaning because they did not fully know me. Instead, they served two masters, even a multitude.[25] But you will become victorious

---

18. The chosen ones must pass through the heavenly gates mentioned earlier in the text.

19. Gregory Riley suggests that the three baptisms of Jesus are birth, baptism in water, and here, crucifixion, that is, baptism in blood (in Pearson, *Nag Hammadi Codex VII*, p. 171).

20. This is the apparent crucifixion of Jesus, when another is crucified instead.

21. See Matthew 27:51–53, with the tearing of the temple curtain, the earthquake, and the raising of dead bodies.

22. These may be ordinary unbelievers, plain folks who are material people of body and flesh only. The description of the kinds of people in this text resembles the Valentinian threefold designation of people of body, soul, and spirit (hylics, psychics, and pneumatics).

23. These are ordinary Christians, leaders or members of the emerging orthodox church—in Valentinian terms, people of soul.

24. These are the gnostics, the free spirits—in Valentinian terms, people of spirit.

25. See Matthew 6:24. Jesus here seems to maintain that these ordinary Christians serve Christ and the ruler of the world, Yaldabaoth.

in everything, in war and battles, jealous division and wrath. In the upright-
ness of our love we are innocent, pure, and good, since we have the mind of
the father in an ineffable mystery.

THE IGNORANT RULERS AND
THE PERFECT ONES

For it was ludicrous. It is I who bear witness that it was ludicrous, since the
rulers do not know that this is an ineffable union of undefiled truth, as exists
among the children of light, of which they made an imitation, having proclaimed a doctrine of a dead man and lies so as to resemble the freedom and
purity of the perfect assembly, and having joined themselves in their doctrine
to fear and slavery, worldly cares, and abandoned worship, being small and ignorant, since they do not contain the nobility of the truth. For they hate the
one in whom they are and love the one in whom they are not. For they did not
know the knowledge of the greatness that it is from above and from a fountain
of truth and not from slavery and jealousy, fear, and love of worldly matter.
For that which is not theirs and that which is theirs they use fearlessly and
freely. They do not desire because they have authority, and they have a law
from themselves over whatever they will wish.[26]

But those who have not are poor, that is, those who possess nothing, and
yet they desire something. And they lead astray those who, through them, have
become like those who possess the truth of their freedom, so as to bring us
under a yoke and constraint of care and fear. This person is in slavery. And one
who is brought by constraint of force and threat has been guarded by god. But
the entire nobility of the fatherhood is not guarded, since he guards what is his
own by himself, without word and constraint. He is united with his will, he
who belongs only to the thought of the fatherhood, to make it perfect and ineffable through the living water, to be with you mutually in wisdom, not only
in word of hearing but in deed and fulfilled word. For the perfect ones are
worthy to be established in this way and to be united with me, in order that
they may not share in any enmity, in a good friendship. I accomplish everything through the good one, for this is the union of the truth, that they should
have no adversary. But everyone who brings division—and such a one will

---

26. Ordinary Christians still observe the law, for example, the Torah and ten commandments
within the Torah.

learn no wisdom at all, because he brings division and is not a friend—is hostile to them all. But one who lives in harmony and friendship of brotherly love, naturally and not artificially, completely and not partially, this person is truly the desire of the father. This is the universal one and perfect love.

THE COUNTERFEIT FATHERS

For Adam was a laughingstock,[27] since he was made a counterfeit type of man by the realm of seven,[28] as if he had become stronger than my brothers and me. We are innocent with respect to him, since we have not sinned. And Abraham and Isaac and Jacob were a laughingstock, since they, the counterfeit fathers, were given a name by the realm of seven, as if he had become stronger than my brothers and me. We are innocent with respect to him, since we have not sinned. David was a laughingstock in that his son was named the human son, having been influenced by the realm of seven, as if he had become stronger than the fellow members of my race and me. But we are innocent with respect to him; we have not sinned. Solomon was a laughingstock, since he thought that he was Christ,[29] having become vain through the realm of seven, as if he had become stronger than my brothers and me. But we are innocent with respect to him. I have not sinned. The twelve prophets were laughingstocks, since they have come forth as imitations of the true prophets. They came into being as counterfeits through the realm of seven, as if he had become stronger than my brothers and me. But we are innocent with respect to it, since we have not sinned. Moses, a faithful servant,[30] was a laughingstock, having been named the friend,[31] since they perversely bore witness concerning him, who never knew me. Neither he nor those before him, from Adam to Moses and John the baptizer, none of them knew me or my brothers.

For they had a doctrine of angels to observe dietary laws and bitter slavery, since they never knew truth, nor will they know it. For there is a great deception upon their soul making it impossible for them ever to find a mind of

---

27. All the heroes of the Jews are laughingstocks, because they are lackeys of the ruler of the world, Yaldabaoth.
28. Or hebdomad, the realm of the planets. Here the realm of seven is closely connected to the ruler of the world, Yaldabaoth.
29. Or messiah, anointed one, as kings are anointed.
30. See Numbers 12:7; Hebrews 3:5.
31. See Isaiah 41:8; James 2:23.

freedom in order to know him, until they come to know the human son. Now, concerning my father, I am he whom the world did not know, and because of this, the world rose up against my brothers and me. But we are innocent with respect to it; we have not sinned.

For the ruler was a laughingstock because he said, "I am god, and there is none greater than I. I alone am the father, the lord, and there is no other god but me. I am a jealous god, who brings the sins of the fathers upon the children for three and four generations."[32] As if he had become stronger than my brothers and me! But we are innocent with respect to him, in that we have not sinned, since we mastered his teaching. Thus he is in an empty glory and does not agree with our father. And so through our fellowship we overcame his teaching, since he was vain in an empty glory. And he does not agree with our father, for he was a laughingstock with judgment and false prophecy.

O you who do not see, who do not see your blindness, that this is who was not known. They have never known him, nor have they known about him. They did not listen to a reliable report. Therefore they proceeded in a judgment of error, and they raised their defiled and murderous hands against him as if they were beating the air. And the senseless and blind ones are always senseless, always being slaves of law and earthly fear.

I AM CHRIST, THE HUMAN SON

I am Christ, the human son, the one from you who is in you. I am despised for your sake, in order that you yourselves may forget what is subject to change. And do not become female,[33] lest you give birth to evil and its brothers: jealousy and division, anger and wrath, fear and a divided heart, and empty, nonexistent desire. But I am an ineffable mystery to you.

Then before the foundation of the world, when the whole multitude of the assembly came together upon the places of the realm of eight,[34] when they had taken counsel, they married spiritually, which is in union. And thus he was perfected in the ineffable places by a living word, and the undefiled wedding was consummated through the mediation of Jesus, who inhabits

---

32. See Isaiah 45:5–6, 21; 46:9; also Exodus 20:5; Isaiah 44:6; the Secret Book of John and other gnostic texts.
33. Femaleness may symbolize this world, maleness the world above, as in Gospel of Thomas 114 and the Sermon of Zostrianos.
34. Or ogdoad, the realm of the stars.

them all and possesses them, who abides in an undivided power of love. And turning, he appears to himself as the One of all these, a thought and a father, since he is one. And he stands over against them all, since he as a whole came forth alone. And he is life, since he came from the father of ineffable and perfect truth,[35] the father of those who are there, the union of peace and a friend of good things, and life eternal and undefiled joy, in a great harmony of life and faith, through eternal life of fatherhood and motherhood and sisterhood and rational wisdom. They had agreed with the mind, who stretches out and will stretch out in joyful union and is trustworthy and faithfully listens. And this is in fatherhood and motherhood and rational brotherhood and wisdom. And this is a wedding of truth, and a repose of incorruption, in a spirit of truth, in every mind, and a perfect light in an unnameable mystery. But this is not, nor will it happen among us, in any region or place in division and breach of peace, but it is in union and a banquet of love, all being perfected in the one who is.

It also happened in the places under heaven for their reconciliation. Those who knew me in salvation and undividedness, and those who existed for the glory of the father and the truth, having been separated, blended into the One through the living word. And I am in the spirit and the truth of the motherhood, since unity was there, just as I was among those who are united in the friendship of friends forever. They know neither hostility at all, nor evil, but are united by my knowledge in word and peace, which exists in perfection with everyone and in them all. And those who assumed the form of my type will assume the form of my word. Indeed, these will come forth in light forever, and in friendship with each other in the spirit, since they have known in every respect and indivisibly that the one who is, is one. And all of these are one. And thus they will learn about the One, as well as the assembly and those dwelling in it. For the father of all of these exists, being immeasurable and immutable: mind and word and division and envy and fire. And he is entirely one, being all with them all in a single doctrine, because all these are from a single spirit. O unseeing ones, why did you not know the mystery rightly?

But the rulers around Yaldabaoth were disobedient because of the thought who went down to him from her sister Sophia. They made for themselves a union with those who were with them in a mixture of a fiery cloud, which was their envy, and the rest, who were brought forth by their creatures, as if they

---

35. See John 14:6.

had bruised the noble pleasure of the assembly. And therefore they revealed a mixture of ignorance in a counterfeit image of fire and earth and a murderer, since they are small and untaught, without knowledge, having dared these things, but not having understood that light has fellowship with light, and darkness with darkness, and the corruptible with the perishable, and the imperishable with the incorruptible.

REST WITH ME FOREVER

Now, these things I have presented to you—I, Jesus Christ, the human son, who is exalted above the heavens—O perfect and incorruptible ones, because of the incorruptible and perfect and ineffable mystery. But they think that we decreed them before the foundation of the world in order that when we emerge from the places of the world, we may present there the symbols of incorruption from the spiritual union with knowledge. You do not know this because the fleshly cloud overshadows you. But I alone am the friend of Sophia.[36] I have been in the bosom of the father from the beginning,[37] in the place of the children of the truth and the greatness. Rest then with me, my fellow spirits and my brothers and sisters, forever.

---

36. Or "the friend of wisdom."
37. See John 1:18.

30

The Gospel of Mary

T he Gospel of Mary is a gospel written in the name of Mary of Magdala, a follower of Jesus according to a number of early Christian texts and his dear companion according to the Gospel of Philip. In the Gospel of Mary she is said to be loved by Jesus more than the other followers, but Peter and Andrew wonder whether she can be taken seriously as a female teacher of revelatory wisdom. This dispute between Mary and the male followers of Jesus reflects the argument between gnostics and representatives of the emerging orthodox church about whether women can teach in church and whether private revelatory teachings can have the same authority as the official teachings of the priests and bishops.

After six missing pages, the Gospel of Mary introduces Jesus speaking about sin, and Jesus proclaims that sin is not an ethical problem but rather a cosmological problem, as Karen L. King puts it.[1] Sin is the material mixing improperly with the spiritual. Thereafter Mary recounts a vision of the soul's ascent beyond four cosmic powers (perhaps the four elements), in a passage that unfortunately is largely missing from the manuscript. After a hostile encounter between Mary and the male followers of Jesus, Levi intercedes, inviting all the followers of Jesus to put on the perfect person and go out to preach, without establishing any additional rules or laws. And, the Gospel of Mary concludes, that is what they did.

---

1. Karen L. King, "The Gospel of Mary," in Robinson, *Nag Hammadi Library in English*, rev. ed., p. 523.

The Gospel of Mary was composed in Greek, probably in the second century. Two fragments of the text have survived in Greek. The rest of the surviving text is preserved in Coptic in the Berlin Gnostic Codex.

THE GOSPEL OF MARY[2]

STUDENTS SPEAK WITH THE SAVIOR

"Will matter be destroyed or not?"

The savior said, "All natures, all formed things, all creatures exist in and with one another and will be resolved into their own roots. The nature of matter is resolved into its nature alone. Whoever has ears to hear should hear."

Peter said to him, "Since you have explained everything to us, tell us also, what is the sin of the world?"

The savior said, "There is no sin, but you create sin when you mingle as in adultery, which is called sin.[3] That is why the good came to be with you, to enter the essence of each nature, and to restore it to its root." He continued, "That is why you become sick and die, for you love what deceives you.[4] Whoever understands should understand.

"Matter gave birth to a passion that has nothing like it and came from what is contrary to nature. Then there arises a disturbance in the whole body. That is why I said to you, 'Be of good courage,'[5] and if you are discouraged, still take courage in the diverse forms of nature. Whoever has ears to hear should hear."

When the blessed one said these things, he greeted all of them, saying, "Peace be with you.[6] Receive my peace. Be careful that no one leads you astray

---

2. The Gospel of Mary: Berlin Gnostic Codex 8502,1, pp. 7,1 to 19,5; translated by E. R. Hardy in Grant, *Gnosticism: An Anthology*, pp. 65–68, George W. MacRae and R. McL. Wilson in Parrott, *Nag Hammadi Codices V, 2–5 and VI with Papyrus Berolinensis 8502, 1 and 4*, pp. 453–71, and Karen L. King, MacRae, and Wilson in Robinson, *Nag Hammadi Library in English*, rev. ed., pp. 523–27; adapted by Willis Barnstone and Marvin Meyer.

3. On adultery as improper mingling with the world, see Herakleon's Commentary on the Gospel of John 18, and the Exegesis on the Soul.

4. This discussion of sin recalls that of Paul in Romans 7. The clause "for you love what deceives you" is from the reconstruction in the translation of Karen King in *The Complete Gospels*, p. 355.

5. See Luke 24:38; John 14:27.

6. See John 14:27; 20:19, 21, 26.

with 'Come over here!' or 'Go there!' The human child is within you.[7] Follow him! Those who seek him will find him. Go then and preach the gospel of the kingdom. Do not follow any other words than these that I have commanded, and do not establish laws, as the lawgiver did, so that you will not be bound by them."

When he said this, he left.

MARY CONSOLES THE STUDENTS, BUT PETER CHALLENGES HER

The students were grieved. They wept profoundly, saying, "How can we go to the gentiles and preach the gospel of the kingdom of the human child? If they did not spare him, will we be spared?"

Then Mary stood up, greeted them all, and said to her brothers, "Do not weep and do not grieve or be irresolute, for his grace will be fully with you and will protect you. Rather, let us praise his greatness. He prepared us and made us truly human."

When Mary said this, she turned their hearts to the good, and they began to discuss the words of the savior.

Peter said to Mary, "Sister, we know that the savior loved you more than other women. Tell us the words of the savior that you remember, which you know and we do not. We have not heard them."

Mary answered, saying, "What is hidden from you I will reveal to you."

She began to speak these words, saying, "I saw the lord in a vision and I said to him, 'Lord, I saw you today in a vision.'

"He answered and said to me, 'Blessings on you, since you did not waver at the sight of me. Where the mind is, there is the treasure.'[8]

"I said to him, 'Lord, how does a person see a vision, through the soul or through the spirit?'

"The savior answered, saying, 'A person sees neither through the soul nor the spirit. The mind, which lives between the two, sees the vision. . . .'"

---

7. See Luke 17:21; Gospel of Thomas 113. "Human child" may also be translated "human son" or "son of man," here and below.
8. See Matthew 6:21.

MARY RECOUNTS HER VISION OF THE SOUL'S ASCENT BEYOND THE POWERS

. . . .

"Desire said,[9] 'I did not see you descending, but now I see you ascending. Why are you lying, since you belong to me?'

"The soul answered and said, 'I saw you, but you did not see me or know me. You perceived the garment I was wearing,[10] but you did not recognize me.'

"After the soul said this, she left, rejoicing greatly.

"The soul approached the third power, called ignorance. The power questioned the soul, saying, 'Where are you going? You are bound by wickedness, you are bound, so do not pass judgment.'

"The soul said, 'Why do you pass judgment on me, though I have not passed judgment? I was bound, but I have not bound. I was not recognized, but I have recognized that all is to be dissolved, both what is earthly and what is heavenly.'

"When the soul overcame the third power, she ascended and saw the fourth power. It took seven forms:

The first form is darkness,

the second, desire,

the third, ignorance,

the fourth, death wish,

the fifth, fleshly kingdom,

the sixth, foolish fleshly wisdom,

the seventh, angry person's wisdom.

These are the seven powers of wrath.

"The powers asked the soul, 'Where are you coming from, slayer of humans, and where are you going, conqueror of space?'

"The soul answered and said, 'What binds me is slain, what surrounds me is destroyed, my desire is gone, ignorance is dead. In a world I was freed through another world, and in an image I was freed through a heavenly image.

---

9. Pages 11–14 are missing from the Coptic text of the Gospel of Mary. Mary's vision of the soul's ascent beyond the cosmic powers seems to have included four stages of ascent, perhaps to describe the soul's liberation from the four elements of the material world. The name of the first power, missing in the text, may well have been darkness (see the list of forms of the fourth power below). The other powers are desire, ignorance, and a deadly composite power of wrath. The soul is successful in her ascent from this world of matter and body, and she is free at last.

10. The garment of the body.

This is the fetter of forgetfulness that exists in the world of time. From now on I shall rest, through time, age, and aeon, in silence.'"

PETER AND ANDREW DOUBT MARY'S WORD

When Mary said this, she fell silent, since the savior had spoken to her of all these things. But Andrew answered, saying to the brothers, "Say what you think about what she said. I do not believe that the savior said this. These teachings are of strange ideas."

Peter also opposed her about all this. He asked the others about the savior, "Did he really speak to a woman secretly, without our knowledge, and not openly? Are we to turn and all listen to her? Did he prefer her to us?" [11]

LEVI COMES TO MARY'S DEFENSE

Then Mary wept and said to Peter, "My brother, Peter, what do you think? Do you think I concocted this in my heart or I am lying about the savior?"

Levi answered, saying to Peter, "Peter, you are always angry. Now I see you contending against this woman as if against an adversary. If the savior made her worthy, who are you to reject her? Surely the savior knows her very well. That is why he loved her more than us. We should be ashamed and put on the perfect person [12] and be with him as he commanded us, and we should preach the gospel, without making any rule or law other than what the savior said."

When Levi said these things, they began to go out to proclaim and to preach.

---

11. On the hostility of Peter against Mary, see Gospel of Thomas 114, as well as another gnostic text, not included in this volume, entitled Pistis Sophia.
12. See "Living Water" in the Gospel of Philip.

31

The Naassene Sermon

In his *Refutation of All Heresies,* the Christian heresiologist Hippolytus of Rome describes certain second-century gnostics, termed Naassenes, from the Hebrew word *nahash,* "serpent." Such serpentine terminology recalls Justin's Book of Baruch, earlier in this volume, and the gnostics called Ophites or Ophians, that is, "snake people," who are sometimes linked with Sethians. Like many gnostics, the Naassenes apparently sought spiritual truths from a variety of sources. Hippolytus claims that they were especially attracted to the mystery religions of antiquity and late antiquity, which typically stressed mystical experience in the context of a dying and rising deity and which the Naassenes interpreted in such a way as to elucidate their own beliefs. These were alternative forms of religion in a post-Olympian world. When the Olympian gods and goddesses no longer captured the hearts and minds of people, many turned for their religious experience to the mysteries of Demeter and Kore; or Dionysos; or the Great Mother and Attis, the Phrygian fertility god; or Isis and Osiris; or Mithras—or Jesus Christ, whom people like Clement of Alexandria understood to be a deity of Christian mysteries.

The Naassenes, according to Hippolytus, attended the mystery celebrations—for example, the mysteries of the Great Mother and Attis—to gain insights into religious knowledge and life. In presenting materials on the Naassenes, Hippolytus cites hymns to Attis and a Naassene sermon that explains how themes from the mysteries contribute to their understanding of their own religion of gnosis. As Hippolytus portrays the Naassenes, he notes two sayings (one of which, he explicitly says, comes from the Gospel of

Thomas) that constitute alternative versions of Gospel of Thomas 4 and 11; the parallel to Gospel of Thomas 11 is in the translation below. Many of the explanations in the sermon are based on suggested—and forced—proof texts and etymologies in the text.

The two hymns and the sermon given here are taken from Hippolytus's *Refutation of All Heresies* 5.6.3–11.1 (see also 10.9.1–3). Another hymn is quoted at *Refutation of All Heresies* 5.9.9:

> I shall sing of Attis, son of Rhea,
> not with the clang of bells nor with the flute,
> nor with the bellowing of the Kouretes of Ida,
> but I shall tune it to the muse of Phoebus's lyre.
> All hail, all hail—as Pan, as Bacchus,
> as shepherd of the shining stars.

THE NAASSENE SERMON[1]

SONG TO ATTIS

> Whether you are the offspring of Kronos,[2]
> or the blessed child of Zeus[3] or great Rhea,[4]
> hail to you, Attis,[5] at whose name Rhea looks down.
> Assyrians call you thrice-lamented Adonis;[6]

---

1. The Naassene Sermon and two hymns: from Hippolytus, *Refutation of All Heresies* 5.6.3–11.1 (M. Marcovich, ed., *Hippolyti refutationis omnium haeresium librorum decem quae supersunt,* Patristische Texte und Studien 25); translated by Robert M. Grant in *Gnosticism: An Anthology,* pp. 105–15). Naassene song also translated by J. F. Henry in Haardt, ed., *Gnosis: Character and Testimony,* pp. 99–100); revised in verse and prose by Willis Barnstone. Grant's convention of placing the song to Attis before the sermon commenting on it is followed here. Of the long discussion on the Naassenes, we reproduce, with Grant, Hippolytus's *Refutation of All Heresies* 5.9.8; 5.7.3–8; 5.8.1–5; 5.8.9–9.6; 5.10.2.
2. Kronos is a Greek god, the ruler of the Titans and father of Zeus.
3. Zeus is the Greek father god and the ruler of the Olympian deities.
4. Rhea is a Greek goddess, the wife of Kronos and mother of Zeus.
5. Attis is a Phrygian eunuch, the lover of the Great Mother, who mirrors the interests of the dying and rising deities.
6. Adonis, the lover of Aphrodite, is a youth whose name means "lord" in Semitic languages and who dies and rises.

all Egypt, Osiris;[7]
Greek wisdom, the heavenly crescent moon;
Samothracians, venerable Adamas;[8]
people of Haimos, corybant;[9]
Phrygians, sometimes Papas,[10]
sometimes corpse or god or sterile
or goatherd or harvested green sheaf
or flute player whom the fertile almond brought forth.

SERMON

The Greeks say that earth first brought forth a human, bearing a good gift, who wished to become the mother not of insensible plants or of irrational animals but of a tame animal loved by god.

The Assyrians claim that among them was born Oannes the fish eater.[11] The Chaldaeans mention Adam and say that this person was the only one whom the earth produced. He lay without breath and motionless and immovable like a statue. He was an image of that human above, Adamas, and was made by many powers.

The great human from above, from whom he and "every family existing on earth and in the heavens"[12] is derived, had to be completely submissive. Therefore he was given a soul,[13] so that through the soul the enslaved creature of the great and most excellent and perfect human might suffer and be punished.

They also ask what the soul is and where it originates and what its nature is, since it enters human beings and, by its movement, enslaves and punishes the creature of the perfect being on earth. They inquire not from the scriptures but from mystical doctrines.

If you say that everything originated from one principle, you are wrong, but if you say it came from three, you are right and can prove the whole matter.

---

7. Osiris is an Egyptian god of moisture, kingship, and the underworld, and the husband of Isis. He also dies and yet lives on as king of the underworld.
8. Adamas is the primal human.
9. A corybant (or korybant) is an ecstatic celebrant sometimes linked to the Great Mother of Phrygia. Haimos is the name of a river in Thrace.
10. Papas is a name connected to Attis, possibly related to Papa.
11. Oannes is the Mesopotamian god of wisdom and is part man and part fish.
12. Ephesians 3:15.
13. The animating, as opposed to immortal, soul.

There is one blessed nature of the blessed Adam above, who is Adamas. There is one mortal nature below. And there is one kingless race that has ascended above where are the sought-after Miriam, the grand wise man Jethro and Zipporah the seer,[14] and Moses, whose origin is not in Egypt because he had sons in Midian.

The poets also knew this.

"All things were divided in three, and each received his lot of honor."[15] The great things must be expressed, but expressed by everyone in every possible way so "that hearing they may not hear and seeing may not see."[16] If the great things had not been expressed, the universe could not have come into existence. These are three supremely important words: Kaulakau, Saulasau, and Zeesar[17]—Kaulakau, the one above Adamas; Saulasau, the mortal below; and Zeesar, the Jordan that flows upward.

This is the male and female person who is in all, whom the ignorant call three-bodied Geryon as if his name meant "flowing from the earth."[18] The Greeks generally call him "the heavenly horn of the moon," because he has mixed and combined everything with everything else. "For all things came into existence through him, and apart from him nothing came into existence. What came into existence in him is life."[19] "Life" is the ineffable race of perfect human beings unknown to previous generations. "Nothing" that "came into existence . . . apart from him" is the world proper, and the world proper came into existence apart from him, and was made by the third and fourth gods.

ATTIS

This is the great and ineffable mystery of the Samothracians that only those of us who are perfect are allowed to know. In their mysteries the Samothracians have the explicit tradition that Adam is the archetypal human. In the temple of the Samothracians are two statues of naked men, with both hands raised toward heaven and with their male members erect like the statue of

---

14. Miriam, Jethro, and Zipporah were, respectively, Moses' sister and his Midianite father-in-law and wife.
15. Homer, *Iliad* 15.189.
16. Matthew 13:13; Mark 4:12; Luke 8:10; John 12:40, all citing Isaiah 6:9–10.
17. Three words derived from the Hebrew of Isaiah 28:10.
18. Greek *ge-rheon*.
19. John 1:3–4.

Hermes in Cyllene.[20] These statues are images of the first man and of the regenerated spiritual man who in every respect possesses the same nature as the first one.

This is what the savior meant when he said, "Unless you drink my blood and eat my flesh, you will not enter the kingdom of heaven.[21] But if you drink the cup which I drink[22] you cannot enter where I go."[23] For he knew the nature of each of his students, and he knew that each had to find his proper nature. He chose twelve students from the twelve tribes, and through them he spoke to every tribe. But not everyone hears the preaching of the twelve students, and if they do hear, they cannot accept them. For what is not according to nature is unnatural for them.[24]

CORYBANT

This human is called corybant by the Thracians who live by the Haimos River, and the Phrygians give him a similar name, because from the top of the head[25] and from the unimprinted brain he begins his descent and passes through all the elements of the lower parts. We do not know how and in what way he comes down. This is the meaning of "we heard his voice but we did not see his appearance."[26] One hears his voice when he has been separated and imprinted, but no one knows what form he takes when he comes down from above, from the unimprinted one. It is in the earthly creature, but no one knows it. This is the "god who dwells in the flood waters," according to the psalm book, and who mumbles and cries out "from many waters."[27] The "many waters" is the manifold race of people from which he shouts and cries to the unimprinted human, saying, "Save my only daughter from the lions."[28] To him was said, "You are my child, Israel. Do not fear. If you go through rivers, they will not engulf you, and if you go through fire it will not burn you."[29] Rivers are the

20. Hermes is the Greek messenger god and, as Hermes Trismegistos, the god of Hermetic religion.
21. John 6:53.
22. Mark 10:38.
23. John 8:21.
24. This relates to the ancient discussion of *physis,* nature.
25. Greek *koryphe.*
26. Deuteronomy 4:12.
27. Psalm 29:3.
28. Psalm 22:21–22.
29. Isaiah 41:8; 43:2.

moist matter of generation; fire is the impulse and desire for generation: "You are mine, do not fear." And again, "If a mother forgets to pity her children or to suckle them, I too will forget you," Adamas tells those who belong to him, "but if a woman forgets these things, I will not forget you. I have painted you on my hands."[30]

And concerning his ascent, which is the regeneration by which he becomes spiritual and not carnal, scripture says,

> Let your rulers lift up the gates,
> and be lifted up, eternal gates,
> and the king of glory will enter.[31]

This is the wonder of wonders, for "who is this king of glory?"[32] "A worm and no man, the reproach of a man and the one rejected by the people."[33] "This is the king of glory, the one mighty in war."[34] "War" means the war in the body, for the creature was formed out of conflicting elements. As it is written, "Remember the war"—which takes place in the body.[35] Jacob saw this entrance and this gate when he went into Mesopotamia, when he passed from childhood to youth and manhood. Mesopotamia is the course of the great ocean, flowing from the midst of the perfect human. And he marveled at the heavenly gate, saying, "How fearful is this place. It is no other than the house of god, and this is the gate of heaven."[36] For this reason Jesus says, " I am the true gate."[37] He who speaks in this way is the perfect being, imprinted from above from the unimprinted one. The perfect being cannot be saved unless he is regenerated and enters through this gate.

PAPAS

The same human is also called Papas by the Phrygians because he stopped everything[38] that was in a disorderly and confused motion before his appearance.

---

30. Isaiah 49:15.
31. Psalm 24:7, 9.
32. Psalm 24:10.
33. Psalm 22:7.
34. Psalm 24:10, 8.
35. Job 41:8.
36. Genesis 28:17.
37. John 10:9.
38. Greek *epausen panta*.

The name Papas belongs to everyone "in heaven, on earth, and under the earth."[39] This is true when they say, "Stop, stop"[40] the discord of the universe and make "peace for those far off," who are the material and earthly beings, and bring "peace to those near,"[41] who are spiritual and intelligent and perfect.

FROM CORPSE TO GOD

The Phrygians also call him corpse, because he is buried in the body as in a sepulcher and tomb. This is the meaning of "You are whitened tombs, full of dead men's bones within, since there is no living man among you,"[42] and again, "the dead will come forth from the sepulchers,"[43] from the earthly bodies, being regenerated as spiritual beings, not carnal. This is the resurrection that takes place through the gate of the heavens. All those who do not enter through it remain dead.

The Phrygians call him god when he has been transformed. He becomes god when he rises from the dead and through such a gate enters into heaven. The messenger Paul knew this gate. He half opened it in a mystery and said that he had been seized by an angel and "taken to the second and third heaven, to paradise itself," where he saw what he saw, and "heard ineffable words that a man is not allowed to relate."[44] These are the ineffable mysteries of which all people speak, "which we speak in words taught not by human wisdom but by the spirit, by explaining spiritual matters to the spiritual. The psychical people do not accept what belongs to the spirit of god. To them it is nonsense."[45]

These are the ineffable mysteries of the spirit, which we alone know. The savior said of them, "No one can come to me unless my heavenly father draws him."[46] But it is exceedingly difficult to receive and to absorb this great and ineffable mystery. And again, the savior said, "Not everyone who says to me, lord, lord, will enter into the kingdom of heaven, but one who does the will of

39. Philippians 2:10.
40. Greek *paue, paue.*
41. Ephesians 2:17.
42. Matthew 23:27.
43. John 5:28–29?
44. 2 Corinthians 12:2–4.
45. 1 Corinthians 2:13–14.
46. John 6:44.

my father in heaven."[47] And to show that doers, not only hearers, must enter the kingdom of heaven, he said again, "The tax collectors and prostitutes precede you into the kingdom of heaven."[48] Tax collectors[49] are those who receive duties[50] on everything, and we are the tax collectors "to whom the taxes of the aeons have come."[51] The taxes or perfections are the seeds sown in the universe by the unimprinted one. Through them the whole universe is completed.[52] Through them it began to come into existence. This is the meaning of the saying, "The sower went out to sow, and some seed fell by the way and were trodden down. Others fell on rocky ground and sprang up and, because they had no depth, withered and died. And others fell on beautiful and good ground and produced fruit—one into a hundred, another into sixty, another into thirty. Whoever has ears to hear should hear."[53] This signifies that no one has been a hearer of these mysteries except the perfect gnostics alone. This is the beautiful and good that Moses mentions, "I will lead you into a beautiful and good land, into a land flowing with milk and honey."[54] Honey and milk are what the perfect ones taste to become kingless and to share in the pleroma. The pleroma is that through which all created beings come into existence and are completed from the uncreated.

STERILE

The Phrygians also give him the name sterile. He is sterile when he is fleshly and performs the "lust of the flesh."[55] This is what is meant by "every tree that does not bring forth good fruit is cut down and cast into fire."[56] The fruits are only the rational, the living people, who enter through the third gate. They say, "If you ate dead things and made them living, what will you do if you eat living things?"[57] What they call "living" are rational principles

---

47. Matthew 7:21.
48. Matthew 21:31.
49. Greek *telonai.*
50. Greek *tele,* meaning "duties," "taxes," "fulfillment."
51. 1 Corinthians 10:11. The Greek for "taxes" may be translated "fulfillment"; the Greek for "aeons" may be translated "ages."
52. Greek *synteleitai,* "is completed," from the same root as *tele.*
53. Matthew 13:3–9; Mark 4:3–9; Luke 8:5–8; Gospel of Thomas 9.
54. Deuteronomy 31:20.
55. Galatians 5:16.
56. Matthew 3:10; 7:19; Luke 3:9.
57. Gospel of Thomas 11.

and intelligences and human beings, pearls that the unimprinted one has cast as fruits into the creation. This is the meaning of "Do not cast what is holy to the dogs, or pearls to swine."[58] The work of swine and dogs is the intercourse of woman with man.

GOATHERD

The Phrygians also call him goatherd,[59] not because he feeds goats, as the psychical people call them, but because he is ever turning,[60] always turning and circulating and impressing the whole universe with turning motion. For to turn[61] is to circulate and alter matters. That is why the two centers of the heaven are called poles. And the poet also said,

> An old man, wave dwelling, frequently comes around here,
> deathless Proteus, the Egyptian.[62]

Poleitai does not mean that he is sold but that he turns about and goes around. Furthermore, cities[63] in which we live are so called because we turn and circulate[64] in them. So the Phrygians call *aipolos* the one who always turns things in every direction and transfers them to his own domain.

FERTILE

The Phrygians also call him fertile, because "the children of the deserted woman are more than those of the one who has a husband."[65] They are those who are reborn immortal and endure forever, even though few of them are born. All carnal beings are perishable, even though very many of them are born. That is why "Rachel wept for her children and did not want to be comforted for them, for she knew that they were no longer."[66] Jeremiah too mourns for the Jerusalem below, not the city in Phoenicia, but the perishable

---

58. Matthew 7:6.
59. Greek *aipolos*.
60. Greek *aeipolos*.
61. Greek *polein*.
62. Homer, *Odyssey* 4.384–85. The Greek for "comes" is *poleitai*.
63. Greek *poleis*.
64. Greek *poloumen*.
65. Isaiah 54:1, also cited in Galatians 4:27.
66. Jeremiah 31:15, also cited in Matthew 2:18.

generation below. Jeremiah knew the perfect human who is regenerated "from water and spirit,"[67] not the carnal one. It was Jeremiah who said, "He is human, and who will know him?"[68] This shows how deep and difficult it is to comprehend the knowledge of the perfect being. The knowledge of the human being is the beginning of perfection, while finished perfection is the knowledge of god.

HARVESTED GREEN SHEAF

The Phrygians also call him the harvested green sheaf. According to them the Athenians give him the same name when they hold Eleusinian initiations and silently show the initiates the great, wondrous, and perfect mystery of the harvested sheaf. For the Athenians this sheaf is the perfect torch, which comes from the unimprinted one. So the hierophant declares that he is not castrated like Attis, but has become a eunuch by means of hemlock and has given up all carnal generation. By night in Eleusis in full light he performs the vital and ineffable mystery and cries out, "Brimo has borne a holy child, Brimos!" This signifies that the powerful woman has borne a powerful child. Holy is the spiritual generation, and heavenly and high. One born into it is powerful. This mystery is called Eleusis, and it occurs at the sanctuary[69] of Demeter. It is Eleusis because we the spiritual have come from above, floating down from Adamas;[70] *anaktoreion* is from "ascending above."[71] This is what the Eleusinian initiates call the great mysteries. It is law that those who are initiated into the lesser mysteries should later be initiated into the great ones. For greater lots acquire greater parts.[72] The lesser mysteries are those of Persephone below. Concerning these mysteries and the way that leads there, "broad and spacious,"[73] and taking the destroyed ones to Persephone, the poet said,

> Beneath her is a horrible pathway, hollow and muddy.
> It is excellent to lead to the lovely grove of Aphrodite
> who is much honored.[74]

---

67. John 3:5.
68. Jeremiah 17:9.
69. Greek *anaktoreion.*
70. In Greek *eleusesthai* means "come."
71. Greek *anelthein ano.*
72. Heraclitus, fragment 25.
73. Matthew 7:13.
74. Parmenides, fragment 20.

These are the lesser mysteries of carnal generation. After initiation into them, people should end the lesser and be initiated into the great and heavenly ones. Those who acquire lots connected with the latter will receive greater parts.

This is the gate of heaven and the house of god, where the good god dwells alone, where no impure person enters, none psychical, none carnal. It is reserved for the spiritual people alone, and those who come there must put on the wedding garments and all become bridegrooms, made male by the virginal spirit.[75] She is the virgin who is pregnant and conceives and bears a son,[76] a son who is not psychical or corporeal but is the blessed aeon of aeons. Concerning these matters the savior expressly said, "Narrow and strait is the way that leads to life, and there are few who enter it. But broad and spacious is the way that leads to destruction, and there are many who enter through it."[77]

ALMOND AND FLUTE PLAYER

The Phrygians also say that the father of all is an almond,[78] not the tree, but that preexistent almond that has within itself the perfect fruit, palpitating and moving in its interior. It tore open its own womb and brought forth its invisible and unnamable and ineffable child, of whom we are speaking. To tear open[79] is to tear open and cut through, just as physicians call scarifications[80] the incisions that they make in inflamed bodies or in those that contain some tumor. So the Phrygians call almond the being from which the invisible one came forth and was begotten, and "through whom everything came into existence and apart from him the nonexistent was made."[81] The being so born is called flute player, because what was born is a harmonious breath or spirit. "God is a spirit. Therefore the true worshipers will worship neither on this mountain nor in Jerusalem, but in spirit."[82] The worship of the perfect ones is spiritual, not carnal. The spirit is there where the father and the son are named, the son born of the father. He is the many-named one, many-eyed, incomprehensible, toward which every nature strives, and each in its own way.

---

75. See Gospel of Thomas 114.
76. Isaiah 7:14.
77. Matthew 7:13–14.
78. Greek amygdalos.
79. Greek amyxai.
80. Greek amychas.
81. John 1:3.
82. John 4:21, 23–24.

He is the expressed word of god, which is the word of declaration of the great power.[83] So the word is sealed and hidden and veiled, lying in the dwelling on which the root of all is founded, the root of aeons, powers, thoughts, gods, angels, envoy spirits—existent and nonexistent, generated and ungenerated, incomprehensible and comprehensible, years, months, days, hours, and an indivisible point from which the smallest being will come forth, part by part, to grow. The nonexistent, underived, indivisible point will, by its own thought, become an incomprehensible greatness. This is the kingdom of heaven, the grain of mustard seed, the indivisible point existing in the body, which no one but the spiritual ones alone know. This is the meaning of the words, "there are no words or language, whose voices are not heard."[84]

NAASSENE SONG

The law of cosmic genesis was the firstborn mind,
and after the firstborn came confused chaos.
The third place in this law fell to the soul
who was clad only in the shape of a red deer in a watery form,
and she is worn away in the slavery of death.

Sometimes she gains mastery and glimpses light,
or she plunges into evil misery and weeps.
Sometimes she is mourned and is happy,
or she weeps and is condemned.
Then she is judged and finally dies.
Sometimes she is misled down a labyrinth of evils,
trapped in a corner and with no way out.

Jesus said, Look, father, she is wandering the earth
and evil is trying to catch her.
She is wandering far from your breath.
She is trying to flee bitter chaos and knows no escape.

---

83. Compare the Great Declaration (or Great Exposition, *Apophasis megale*), a work attributed to Simon Magus.
84. Psalm 19:3.

O father, send me to her.
I will descend, carrying the seals.
I will wander through all the aeons and uncover all mysteries.
I will disclose the forms of the gods.
And I will teach the secrets of the holy way,
whose name is gnosis.

PART THREE

Hermetic Literature

INTRODUCTION

WILLIS BARNSTONE

The Greco-Roman way of gnosis is found in the hermetic tractates attributed to Hermes Trismegistos. These extraordinary writings, from the middle of the first through the end of the third centuries, make up a collection known as the Corpus Hermeticum or the Hermetica. They often deal with the occult sciences—alchemy, astrology, magic, and spiritual information—and reflect a hellenistic breakdown blurring science and religion.

These writings are known as "hermetic" because of their patron and author, Hermes Trismegistos, Hermes the thrice-greatest, the Greek incarnation of his Egyptian counterpart, the god Thoth. The images of Thoth and Hermes merge. Thoth was creator and orderer of the universe; god of magic, wisdom, and knowledge; inventor of writing; scribe of the gods and author of all scriptures; lord of the moon; and also giver of the first word, the logos. Both he and Hermes were believed to be master magicians of great sophistication. Thoth gave Isis knowledge how to realize the resurrection of her son Osiris, which served as a model for the later myth of Jesus' resurrection. Hermes was the intellectual, the patron of the arts, and the speaker in platonic dialogues that voice his philosophy and spiritual flight.

The extant texts of Hermes Trismegistos are seventeen Greek treatises of the Corpus Hermeticum, diverse fragments in the anthology of Ioannes Stobaios, a Latin translation of Asklepios found in the works of Apuleius, and texts from Codex VI of the Nag Hammadi library. They may point to a single person as editor, collector, or author of some of the major works, including Poimandres. More likely, however, these sacred works are pseudepigraphic, with no possible identifiable author. In the Hermetica, the dialogue is lively, profound, even ordinary in its speech. But there is no scent of an actual Philo or Plotinos behind the anonymous speeches, or even of a shadowy Pseudo-Dionysios (incorrectly connected with Dionysios the Areopagite), all of whose works bespeak the presence of a single author. On the contrary, these hermetic writings have the character of sacred scripture of unknown authorship typically ascribed falsely to a patriarchal figure or god—Thoth and Hermes—all of which confirms that the great name was chosen to help the work find entry into a sacred canon. These nominal uncertainties, however, in no way diminish the texts. The Greek epics—the Bible of classical religion—are not dulled because the twentieth century has questioned their traditional authorship. In the end, the author of major religious works has historically blurred into a tradition, not a named person. Such has been the fate of the sayings of Lao-tzu, Buddha, and probably Jesus in, for instance, the Gospel of Thomas. Such anonymity has been the interesting fate of the thrice-greatest Hermes.

THE HERMETIC MIX

Into the hermetic mix goes the rich influx of eastern religious elements, mystery religions, and the neopythagorean and neoplatonic philosophies of late hellenistic times. Much of the work is gnostic in character. The Corpus Hermeticum coincides with classical Christian gnostic texts not in Yahweh and Jesus, the central characters of the Bible; not in their transcendental tales or in the myths or even in the diction. These schools meet in the common centrality of gnosis, which is knowledge of the soul. Through gnosis, revealed in the self, one finds the divine. Through gnosis the spirit or soul ascends united to the divine. The Alexandrian platonists—Philo, a Jew, and Plotinos, an Egyptian pagan, both writing in Greek—contributed hugely to the gnostic pot, even when, in the instance of Plotinos, he wrote against the gnostics. The similarities of Plotinian mystical union with the soul's sun and the gnostic knowledge of the divine spark inside, ascending to the sky of inner light, easily belie the Egyptian philosopher's refutation of the gnostics. Even the metaphors "soul sun" and "divine spark inside" are almost identical in rhetorical phrase and philosophical meaning.

The jewel of the hermetic tradition is Poimandres. Poimandres means "shepherd of man" in Greek, or possibly "knowledge of the sun god Ra" in Coptic. Although the author (or authors) of Poimandres, probably composed and compiled at the end of the second century CE, is aware of Judaism and

Christianity, this syncretic work remains basically pagan, deriving from Egyptian platonism and contemporary Alexandrian theologies.

THE LEGACY OF HERMES TRISMEGISTOS

By ancient tradition, confirmed by Lactantius in the fourth century, these ecstatic tracts derive from the occult books of an ancient Egyptian sage who lived shortly after Moses. The word *hermetic* also carries an exotic lexical life of its own. Since Hermes is commonly seen as the Greek incarnation of Thoth and is identified with his attributes, those mysterious, hermetic writings of the Corpus Hermeticum became seen as the work of a secret Egyptian seer, a notion persisting from before Augustine, who took this to be a fact, and down to Giordano Bruno in the Renaissance.

The mystery surrounding this Egyptian seer or thrice-greatest Hermes contributed to his long afterlife in religion and literature and in scientific tracts on astrology, medicine, and alchemy, in Greek, Latin, Arabic, Italian, French, and English from antiquity to our own times. Hermes, after leaving the darkness of the physical universe where he has been trapped in nature, ascends through seven levels of spirituality to the realm of light and to immersion in the androgynous parent of all, a divine hermaphrodite (Hermes merged with Aphrodite). There he becomes god. Hermes' figure of Poimandres, through gnosis, presages the paths of later mystics, who partake in similar techniques and experiences but who are not seen as gnostics. Like Philo's ladders of spiritual ascent, these non-gnostic paths include Pseudo-Dionysios's diving gloom and ray of blackness, and John of the Cross's paradoxical ways of oblivion in which, like the gnostics, he dies from ordinary time, moves from sensations of the body into the soul, to vision in darkness, which is illumination, and to union, which is an ineffable ecstasy and another oblivion. The hermetic writings have suited a fusion of writers looking elsewhere (the literal sense of ecstasy, from *ex-histanai*, "stand out of place"), including William Blake and his mentor Thomas Taylor, who first introduced Blake to the neoplatonists and to the hermetic texts. In H.D.'s epic *Trilogy*, written in London during World War II, the second book, *Tribute to the Angels*, begins with an invocation to Thoth / Hermes / Mercury, the "angel" about whom the remainder of the book revolves:

Hermes Trismegistus
is patron of alchemists;

his province is thought,
inventive, artful and curious;
his metal is quicksilver,
his clients, orators, thieves and poets.[1]

In other gnostic works the soul (*psyche*) is of a lower order than spirit
(*pneuma*), and soul is associated with earthbound entities, particularly with
the biblical creator god. But in Poimandres, soul rather than spirit designates
the highest divine quality of *anthropos*, or earthly man: both *nous* and *psyche*
refer to this higher meaning. As in other gnostic texts, primal or first man (or
human) descends through the cosmos to the earth, where he mingles with
darkness and matter; that is, he becomes trapped in nature. To be free of that
darkness, he must abhor the senses, the body, all matter. After death, the
soul's ascent back through the sphere is a privilege of the select. After first
man's cosmic fall, a human being returns to become one with god. Hans
Jonas points out that the myth of cosmic return after death was transformed
in neoplatonic and Judeo-Christian mysticism into a technique of spiritual
ascent while alive and in the body. We see this phenomenon, of course, in
Plotinos, the last original neoplatonist, and in the practices of shamans and
mystics, east and west, whose principal aim is ecstatic transcendence. Jonas
summarizes brilliantly:

> In a later stage of "gnostic" development (though no longer
> passing under the name of Gnosticism) the external topology
> of the ascent through the spheres, with the successive divesting
> of the soul of its worldly envelopments and the regaining of its
> original acosmic nature, could be "internalized" and find its ana-
> logue in a psychological technique of inner transformations by
> which the self, *while still in the body*, might attain the Absolute as
> an immanent, if temporary, condition. An ascending scale of
> mental states replaces the stations of the mythical itinerary: the
> dynamics of progressive spiritual self-transformations, the spa-
> tial thrust through the heavenly spheres. Thus could transcen-
> dence itself be turned into immanence, the whole process
> become spiritualized and put within the power and the orbit of

---

1. H.D., *Trilogy*, vol. 2, *Tribute to the Angels*, 63.

the subject. With this transposition of a mythological scheme into the inwardness of the person, with the translation of its objective stages into subjective phases of self-performable experience whose culmination has the form of ecstasis, gnostic myth has passed into mysticism (Neoplatonic and monastic), and in this new medium it lives on long after the disappearance of the original mythological beliefs.[2]

The writings attributed to Hermes Trismegistos, and of Plotinos and Pseudo-Dionysios, have been a prime source for the occult as well as for orthodox religious mysticism in the Western world. Plotinos was a historical Greek from Egypt; Dionysius a Christian, probably a fifth-century Syrian monk; while Hermes Trismegistos has the aura of a mysterious visionary, a lunatic in the eyes of skeptics, a demigod to the faithful. All these human and divine attributes are intriguing and peculiar, since, in all probability, he was nobody at all; that is, he was a resonant name to replace a major hellenistic religious tradition.

The lessons in that tradition are universal. We are lone figures alienated on the earth from others, from sectarian and secular groups, even from our souls. Through gnosis, however, one's solitude becomes the springboard to a greater companionship, for a vision of and union with a spirit, which, depending on system and translation of terms, is god, or the one, or nothing or all.

---

2. Jonas, *The Gnostic Religion*, 165–66.

32

Poimandres

Of all hermetic texts surviving from Alexandria, Poimandres is the prime source of gnostic speculation. The speaker in the Socratic dialogue, Poimandres, proposes a severely dualistic view of life in which the body represents everything dark, deceptive, temporal, and mortal while the mind (*nous*) represents light, truth, timelessness, and eternal salvation. The purpose of life is to free the soul from the prison of the body through gnosis and to return to the heavenly realm of light. So one leaves the physical universe by embarking on a celestial journey, through seven levels of spirituality, until one comes to the father of all. Then "he enters the eighth sphere of the fixed star" and becomes god. It is notable that for the hermeticists, god, despite the title "*father* of all," is androgynous and contains both sexes. In the Revelation of Asklepios,[1] a hermetic text not included in this volume, god is defined as bisexual.

Poimandres has three sections. The first section, which tells of the creation of the world and human life, is a hermetic cosmogony and anthropogony, revealed to the speaker as a visionary experience. Part two recounts the soul's escape from the world and its ascent to heaven and mystical union with god; the final part contains instructions for proselytizing the gospel of gnosis. The work ends with a prayer.

---

1. The Revelation of Asklepios is a Hermetic dialogue between Hermes and Asklepios. It exists in Latin translation from a lost Greek original, dated in the second century, entitled Perfect Teaching (*Logos teleios*). In it Hermes Trismegistos speaks of piety as knowledge and impiety as ignorance and equates sexual with mystical knowledge. A portion of the text is also present in Coptic translation in Codex VI of the Nag Hammadi library.

Poimandres serves as a rather severe mentor to the speaker in the dialogue, explaining, reproaching, ordering redemption. We soon understand that Poimandres is the *nous,* the highest godhead. The creations or divine emanations of the father of all are the logos, the mind-demiurge (who in turn creates the planetary system and the physical world in which people are trapped), and anthropos (human being). The human appears in god's image, since it is an androgynous generative principle and contains a divine soul, a spark of light.

In Poimandres we have perhaps the earliest full and detailed instructions in the mystical experience of darkness and purification from matter, ascent to the light, and entry into a oneness with god; this map of spiritual ecstasy was to be imitated, or reproduced in other forms, in innumerable works thereafter.

POIMANDRES[2]

POIMANDRES APPEARS

Once when I began to think about the things that are, and my thoughts soared exceedingly high, and my bodily senses were held down by sleep like people weighed down by overeating and weariness, I thought I saw a being of vast and boundless magnitude coming toward me, who called me by name, and said, "What do you wish to hear and see, to learn and know?"

"Who are you?" I said.

"I am Poimandres," he said, "the mind[3] of absolute power. I know what you want and I am with you everywhere."

"I want to learn about the things that are, their nature, and to know god," I replied. "How I want to hear!"

He said, "Keep in mind what you wish to learn and I will teach you."

THE VISION OF CREATION

With these words he changed his form, and in a flash everything opened before me and I saw an unbounded vista. All was light, a soothing and happy light. And as I gazed I was entranced. But soon a stark and terrifying darkness descended gradually like a coiled snake, and I saw the darkness turn into a

---

2. Poimandres: translated from the Greek by Willis Barnstone.
3. *Nous.*

watery substance,[4] unspeakably agitated, giving off smoke as from fire, emitting an indescribable sound of lamentation. And after that an inarticulate cry like the voice of fire.

Out of the light a holy word[5] descended upon the watery substance, and I thought this word the voice of light; and unmingled fire leapt out of the watery substance and soared upward. The fire was quick and violent, and the air, being light, followed the breath[6] as it rose from earth and water to the fire, so that the breath seemed suspended from the fire. But the earth and water remained intermingled, and the earth could not be seen apart from the water. All these elements were kept in audible motion by the breath of the word hovering above them.

POIMANDRES IS LIGHT AND MIND

Then Poimandres asked me, "Do you understand what that vision means?"

"I will understand," I said.

"I am that light," he said, "and I am the mind, the first god, who existed before the watery substance appeared out of the darkness. And the luminous word that issued from the mind is the son of god."

"In what way?"

"Understand that what sees and hears inside you is the word of the lord, its son, but the mind is god the father. And they are not divided one from the other, for they are united by life."

"Thank you," I said.

"But think about the light, and understand it."

WHERE EVERYTHING COMES FROM

Having said this, he gazed intently at me for a long time, and I trembled at his aspect. When I raised my head I saw in my mind the light, consisting of innumerable powers, which had become a limitless cosmos, and the fire, contained by a mighty power, was held in place. This is what I saw and understood from the words of Poimandres.

---

4. Or "nature" (Greek, *physis*).
5. Logos.
6. Greek *pneuma*, "spirit" or "breath."

I was amazed, and he spoke to me again. "You have seen in your mind the archetypal form, infinite and prior to the beginning."

"But where do the elements of nature come from?" I asked.

"From god's will, which received the word, and saw and imitated the beautiful world. The watery substance of nature received the word and made itself into an orderly world from its diverse elements, and a brood of living creatures came forth.

ANOTHER MIND, THE DEMIURGE

"And the first mind, being both male and female, both life and light, conceived through the word another mind, the demiurge, and this second mind of fire and breath fashioned seven rulers, who encompass within their orbits the world perceived by the senses. Their government is called destiny.[7]

"Suddenly, the word of god leaped out of the downward-moving elements of nature to the pure body of heaven and was united with the mind of the demiurge. For the word was of one substance with the mind. And the lower elements of nature were left wordless,[8] that is, without reason, and became mere matter.

"Now the demiurge-mind worked together with the word to encompass the spheres of the rulers and to whirl them with thunderous speed, with no fixed beginning or determined end, since their revolutions begin where they end. And according to the mind's will, the lower elements of nature became animals devoid of reason, for they did not have the word. And the air brought forth winged creatures, and the water brought forth fish, and by then earth and water were separated from each other according to the will of the mind. And earth brought forth four-footed creatures and creeping things and wild and tame beasts.

MIND, FATHER OF ALL, GIVES BIRTH
TO A PRIMAL HUMAN

"But mind, the father of all, who is life and light, gave birth to a human being like himself. And he loved him as his own child, for he was very beautiful,

---

7. Greek, *heimarmene.*
8. Greek, *alogos.*
9. Greek, *anthropos.*

bearing the likeness of his father. And god was very pleased with his own beauty in the primal person[9] and delivered to him all that he had created.

"And the primal person took station in the highest sphere of heaven and observed the things made by its author, his brother the demiurge, who ruled over the region of fire. Now that the human had seen those things made in fire, he wished to create things of his own. And his father permitted him to do so. And since the rulers loved him too, each gave him a share of his own nature.

"When the human learned their characteristics, he wished to break through the bounding orbits of the rulers and to share the power of him who rules over the fire.

THE HUMAN DESCENDS INTO THE WORLD OF NATURE

"Then the primal person, who possessed all authority over the world of mortal creatures and irrational animals, leaned down through the harmony[10] and, having broken the vault, showed lower nature the beautiful form of god. When nature saw the beautiful form of god, it smiled on the human with love, for it had seen the wondrous beauty of the human reflected in the water and its shadow on the earth. And the human too, on seeing this form, a form similar to his own reflected in the water, loved it and wanted to live in it. And his wish was immediately realized, and he began to inhabit a form devoid of reason. And nature received its loved one, embraced him, and they mingled, for they were lovers.

HUMANKIND IS MORTAL AND IMMORTAL

"And this is why the human, of all creatures on the earth, is twofold: mortal in his body but immortal through the eternal human. Though he is immortal and has power over all things, he also suffers mortality, since he is subject to destiny. Though above the world of the spheres, he is a slave of destiny. Though he is male and female,[11] being born of a father who contains male and female, and is sleepless as his father is sleepless, he is vanquished by love and oblivion."

---

10. This is the world of the spheres.
11. That is, androgynous.

SEVEN EARTHLY HUMANS ARE BORN

And after this I said, "O mind, tell me the rest. I too love your teaching."

And Poimandres answered, "Here is the mystery that has been hidden until this day. Nature, intimately mingled with the primal person, produced a most wondrous miracle. The human had in himself the world of spheres of the seven rulers, which, as I told you, was made of fire and air. Nature immediately made seven humans corresponding to the natures of the seven rulers, and they were androgynous and sublime."

Then I said, "O Poimandres, a powerful desire has seized me and I want to hear more. Do not stop."

"Silence," Poimandres replied. "I have not yet finished with the first discourse."

"See, I am silent," I said.

"These seven humans were born as follows: nature brought forth their bodies. Earth was the female element, water the generative male element; from fire came their nature, from ether their spirit.[12] Nature brought forth their bodies in human likeness. And humankind, which was formed of life and light, became soul[13] and mind:[14] soul from life and mind from light. And all creatures in the world of senses remained that way until the end of an era.

MALE AND FEMALE ARE CREATED

"Now I will tell you what you long to hear. When that era was completed, the bond uniting all things was loosened by god's will. All living creatures, being androgynous, were suddenly divided into two, and the primal person became at once male and female. God immediately spoke a holy word: 'Increase and multiply, all you creatures and creations. And let humankind, being with a mind, recognize itself as immortal and know that the cause of death is eros.'[15]

"And when god said this, his providence,[16] by means of destiny and the world of spheres, brought male and female into union and established generations. And all creatures multiplied according to their kind. And whoever

---

12. Greek, *pneuma.*
13. Greek, *psyche.*
14. Greek, *nous.*
15. Genesis 1:22.
16. Greek, *pronoia,* elsewhere translated as "forethought."

recognized himself attained that good that is supreme, while whoever was led astray by desire, by love for the body, will wander in the darkness of the world of senses and suffer death."

LIFE AND DEATH

"But what kind of sin do the ignorant commit that they should be deprived of immortality?" I asked.

"You do not seem to have thought about what I told you. Did I not tell you to pay attention?"

"I understand and remember, and at the same time I thank you."

"If you understand, tell me why those who are ignorant deserve death."

"Because the material body has its source in the abhorrent darkness, from which came the watery substance of which the body is composed in the sensible world, and from this body death slakes its thirst."

"You have understood correctly. But why is it, as the word of god has it, that whoever recognizes and knows himself enters into the good?"[17]

I answered, "Because the father of all consists of light and life, and from him human beings were born."

"You are right. Light and life are god and father, out of which humans came. And if you learn that you are also made of light and life, you will return to light and life." These things Poimandres said.

THE PLACE OF THE MIND AMONG
THE GODLY AND GODLESS

"But tell me," I said, "how I shall come into life, for god told me, 'Let the thinking person know himself.' Don't all people have a mind?"

"Do not speak that way, for I, mind, am present to the holy and good and pure and merciful, and my presence is a help to them, and all at once they recognize everything and win the mercy of loving god, and thank him and praise him and sing hymns to him, and turn to him with devotion. And before they abandon the body to death, they loathe the bodily senses, since they know how they work. I, the mind, will not allow the workings of the body to attain their purpose. As a guardian of the gates, I bar the way to evil and shameful energies. I cut off their strategies.

---

17. This recalls the Delphic maxim "Know yourself," used here and in other gnostic texts.

"And I am far removed from those who are foolish and evil and sly and envious and covetous and murderous and godless. I yield place to the avenging demon[18] who visits such a person with the sharpness of fire, piercing his senses and driving him to further lawlessness so that he may incur greater punishment. Never ceasing his dark struggle, and giving in to boundless appetite, he inflicts upon himself greater torment and hotter fire."

THE ASCENT OF THE SOUL THROUGH SEVEN ZONES

"Mind, you have instructed me well in all things. But tell me more about the ascent. How shall I come to life?"

At this Poimandres said, "First, with the dissolution of your material body, you yield your character to the demon. Your image vanishes. The bodily senses return to their own sources, becoming part of the cosmos, and, combined in new ways, do other work. And anger and desire enter thoughtless nature.

"And then man rises into the harmony, the world of the spheres. In the first zone he leaves behind the force to grow and decrease, in the second the machinations of evil, in the third the guile of lust, in the fourth his domineering arrogance, in the fifth his unholy daring and rashness, in the sixth his striving for wealth by evil means, and in the seventh zone the malicious lie: all rendered powerless.

ENTERING THE EIGHTH AND BECOMING DIVINE

"Then, stripped naked by the force of the harmony, he enters the eighth sphere of the fixed stars,[19] and possessing his own energy he remains there with others, singing hymns to the father. And the others are happy at his coming. Resembling those who live there, he hears the powers who have their place in the substance of the eighth sphere and who sing to god with a special voice. They move in order up to the father. They surrender to the powers, and become the powers, and are in god. This is the good, the aim of those who have gnosis: to become god.

"Why then do you hesitate? Now that you have received everything from me, why not make yourself a guide to the worthy so that people may be saved

---

18. Greek, *daimon.*
19. The ogdoad. See also the hermetic Discourse on the Eighth and Ninth.

by god through you?" And, having said these things, Poimandres before my eyes mingled with the powers.

GOING FORTH TO PREACH

I thanked and blessed the father of all, and was sent forth, empowered and instructed concerning the nature of all and with a supreme vision. And I began to preach to the people of beauty, of piety and gnosis: "O people born of the earth, given over to drunkenness and sleep and ignorance of god, end your drunkenness and unreasoning sleep."

When they heard this, they gathered around me. I said, "Why have you accepted death when you have been given the power to enjoy immortality? Change your ways, you who walk with error and keep company with ignorance. Free yourself of darkness and seize the light. Abandon corruption and receive immortality."

And some of them mocked me and left me, for they had given themselves to death. But others begged me to teach them, and they threw themselves at my feet. I raised them up and became a guide to people, teaching them the word and how they might be saved. And I sowed words of wisdom in them, and they were nourished with ambrosial water. When evening came and the rays of sun began to fade, I called on them to thank god. And when they completed the thanksgiving, each sought his or her own bed.[20]

I recorded the beneficence of Poimandres, and how my hopes had been fulfilled. For the body's sleep became the soul's awakening, the closing of my eyes the true vision, my silence pregnant with the good, and my words the expression of good things. And all this happened to me, since I had received it from my mind, that is, from Poimandres, the word and mind of absolute sovereignty. I became god-inspired, god-minded, and came with the truth.

PRAISE TO GOD THE FATHER

So with all my soul and strength I praise god the father:

Holy is god the father of all, who precedes all beginnings.
Holy is god, whose will is accomplished by his own powers.

---

20. Such giving of thanks is also to be found in the Prayer of Thanksgiving, below.

Holy is god, who wishes to be known and is known to those
   who are his own.
You are holy, who by your word made all things that are.
You are holy, who have become the image of all nature.
You are holy, who are not formed by nature.
You are holy, who are stronger than all domination.
You are holy, who are greater than all eminence.
You are holy, who are superior to all praise.

Accept the pure offering of words from a soul and heart that rise to you, unnamable, ineffable, whom only silence calls!

I beg you, let me not be removed from gnosis, which is our nature. Fill me with strength, and with your grace let me bring light to those of my race who are in ignorance, to my brothers and sisters, sons and daughters. Therefore I believe and bear witness. I go to life and to light.

Father, bless you. Your child wishes to share the holy salvation you confer through your total authority.

33

The Discourse on the Eighth and Ninth

The hermetic Discourse on the Eighth and Ninth is a dialogue between a teacher, Hermes Trismegistos, and an unnamed student about the ascent to the higher stages of spiritual enlightenment, the eighth and the ninth. Such an ascent is also described in the preceding text, Poimandres. The present text assumes the astronomical system of late antiquity that describes the heavens as consisting of seven spheres surrounding the earth and housing the sun, moon, and planets (Mercury, Venus, Mars, Jupiter, Saturn). Beyond these spheres lies the divine. The eighth realm, astronomers thought, is the realm of the fixed stars, and the ninth realm is exalted beyond that. These realms are also depicted in the Secret Book of John, with the seven cosmic kings stationed in seven spheres of heaven, through the power of Yaldabaoth, and Sophia stationed in the ninth realm, above Yaldabaoth. According to the Discourse on the Eighth and Ninth, the student of knowledge has already advanced through the lower stages of spiritual enlightenment. The student prays, perhaps with the teacher, "Lord, grant us wisdom from your power that reaches us, that we may relate to ourselves the vision of the eighth and the ninth. Already we have advanced to the seventh, since we are pious and abide in your law." Further, the student mentions books that have been studied for their wisdom and understanding.

The student's visionary ascent to the eighth and the ninth entails singing a hymn in silence and being united with the mind of all. The souls and the angels who inhabit the eighth likewise sing a hymn in silence, for they also offer praise to the mind of all, which dwells in the ninth. This mind is recognized through the mystical guidance of Hermes Trismegistos, who himself announces, "I am mind, and I see another mind, one that moves the soul." And the student declares, "I am the instrument of your spirit, mind is your plectrum, and your guidance makes music with us. I see myself! I have been strengthened by you, for your love has reached us." The result of this enlightenment is wisdom, praise, ecstasy. In a way that recalls the Three Steles of Seth, the Discourse on the Eighth and Ninth includes instructions for preserving the text on turquoise steles.

The Discourse on the Eighth and Ninth survives in Coptic in the Nag Hammadi library. Its title is supplied from the contents of the text. It was probably composed in Greek, very likely in Egypt, considering the references to turquoise steles with hieroglyphic characters to be placed at the temple at Diospolis (Magna or Parva) in Upper Egypt, and deities with faces of animals. Some scholars suggest a date of composition in the second century CE, on account of similarities with the middle platonic philosopher Albinus.

THE DISCOURSE ON THE EIGHTH AND NINTH[1]

"My father, yesterday you promised me you would take[2] my mind to the eighth heavenly sphere and after that you would take me to the ninth. You said this is the sequence of the tradition."

---

1. The Discourse on the Eighth and the Ninth: Nag Hammadi Library, Codex VI,6 (pp. 52,1 to 63,32); translated by Marvin Meyer.
2. Partially restored.

"Yes, my child,[3] this is the sequence, but the promise was made about human nature. I said to you when I first made the promise, 'If you remember each of the stages.' After I received the spirit through the power, I established the action for you. Clearly understanding dwells within you. In me it is as if the power were pregnant, for when I conceived from the spring that flows to me, I gave birth."

"Father, you have spoken every word rightly to me, but I am amazed at what you say. You said, 'The power in me.'"

He said, "I gave birth to it as children are born."

"Then, father, I have many siblings if I am to be counted among the generations."

"Right, child. This good thing is counted . . . always. So, child, you must know your siblings and honor them rightly, since they have come from the very same father. For each of the generations have I addressed. I have named them, since they are offspring like these children."

"Then, father, do they have a day?"[4]

"Child, they are spiritual, for they exist as forces that nurture other souls. That is why I say they are immortal."

"Your word is true. From now on it cannot be refuted. Father, begin the discourse on the eighth and the ninth, and count me also with my siblings."

"Let us pray, child, to the father of the universe, with your siblings, who are my children, that the father may grant the spirit of eloquence."

"How do they pray, father, when they are united with the generations? Father, I want to obey."

". . . It is right for you to remember the progress you have experienced as wisdom in the books.[5] Child, recall your early childhood. You have posed, as children do, senseless and foolish questions."

"Father, I have experienced progress and foreknowledge from the books, and they are greater than what is lacking—these matters are my first concern."

"Child, when you understand the truth of your statement, you will find your siblings, who are my children, praying with you."

"Father, I understand nothing else than the beauty I have experienced in the books."

---

3. Literally, "my son" (Coptic *pashere*), throughout the text.
4. This may refer to a birthday; some scholars understand the Coptic words (*hoou emmau*) to refer to mothers, hence the alternate translation "do they have mothers also?"
5. This describes the instruction with books in the lower stages of spiritual enlightenment.

"This is what you call the beauty of the soul—the edification you have experienced in stages. May the understanding come to you, and you will teach."

"I have understood, father, each of the books, and especially. . . ."

"Child, . . . in praises from those who raise them."

"Father, I shall receive from you the power of the discourse you will utter. As it was spoken to the two of us, let us pray, father."

"Child, it is fitting for us to pray to god with all our mind and all our heart and our soul, and to ask god that the gift of the eighth reach us, and that each receive from god what belongs to god. Your job is to understand, mine is to be able to utter the discourse from the spring that flows to me."

PRAYER FOR THE ASCENT TO THE EIGHTH AND THE NINTH

"Let us pray, father:

I call upon you,
who rules over the kingdom of power,
whose word is an offspring of light,
whose words are immortal,
eternal, immutable,
whose will produces life for the semblances everywhere,
whose nature gives form to substance,
by whom the souls of the eighth and the angels are moved . . . ,
whose word reaches all who exist,
whose forethought reaches everyone here,
who produces everyone,
who has divided the eternal realm among spirits,[6]
who has created everything,
who, being self within self, supports everything,
being perfect,
the invisible god one speaks to, in silence,
whose image is moved when it is ordered,
and it is ordered,
mighty one in power,

---

6. Partially restored.

who is exalted above majesty,
who is superior to the honored ones,
ZOXATHAZO
A
OO EE
OOO EEE
OOOO EE
OOOOOO OOOOO
OOOOOO UUUUUU
OOOOOOOOOOOOOOO
ZOZAZOTH[7]
Lord, grant us wisdom from your power that reaches us,
that we may relate to ourselves the vision of the eighth and the ninth.
Already we have advanced to the seventh,
since we are faithful
and abide in your law.
Your will we fulfill always,
we have walked in your way
and have renounced . . .
so your vision may come.
Lord, grant us truth in the image.
Grant that through spirit we may see
the form of the image that lacks nothing
and accept the reflection of the fullness
from us through our praise.
And recognize the spirit within us.
From you the universe received soul.
From you, one unconceived,
one that has been conceived came into being.
The birth of the self-conceived is through you,
the birth of all conceived things that exist.
Accept these spiritual offerings from us,
which we direct to you
with all our heart and soul and strength.
Save what is within us,
and grant us immortal wisdom."

---

7. This is glossolalia, speaking in tongues, speaking in ecstasy.

VISION OF THE EIGHTH AND THE NINTH

"Child, let us embrace with love.[8] Be happy. Already the power, light, is coming
to us from them. I see, I see ineffable depths. How shall I tell you, child? . . .[9]
How shall I tell you about the universe? I am mind,[10] and I see another mind,
one that moves the soul. I see the one that moves me from pure forgetfulness.
You have given me power. I see myself. I want to speak. Fear seizes me. I have
found the beginning of the power above all powers, without beginning. I see a
spring bubbling with life. I have said, child, that I am mind. I have seen. Speech
cannot reveal this. For all of the eighth, child, and the souls in it, and the angels,[11] sing a song in silence.[12] I, mind, understand."

"How does one sing a song through silence?"

"Can no one speak to you?"

"I am silent, father. I want to sing a song to you while I am silent."

"Sing it. I am mind."

"I understand mind, Hermes. You cannot be known, since you stay in
yourself. I am happy, father. I see you laughing. The universe is happy. No
creature will lack your life, for you are the lord of the inhabitants everywhere.
Your forethought keeps watch. I call you father, eternal realm of eternal realms,
great divine spirit, who through spirit sends moisture on everyone.[13] What do
you tell me, father Hermes?"

"Child, I say nothing about this. It is right before god for us to be silent
about what is hidden."

"Trismegistos, don't let my soul be deprived of the great, divine vision.
Everything is possible for you as master of the universe."

"Praise again, child, and sing while you are silent. Ask what you want in
silence."

When he finished praising, he called out, "Father Trismegistos, what shall
I say? We have received this light, and I myself see this same vision in you. I

---

8. Or "in truth" (Coptic *hen oume*).
9. Jean Pierre Mahé, *Hermès en Haute-Egypte*, restores this; possibly read "We have begun to
behold these places, at once."
10. Partially restored; see, below, the same statement: "I am mind."
11. The souls and the angels are thought to dwell in the eighth.
12. Silence commonly expresses divine transcendence in gnostic and mystical texts. See, for example, the Secret Book of John: "Its eternal realm is imperishable, at peace, dwelling in silence,
at rest, before everything."
13. Or "sends rain on everyone." The text also refers to "a spring bubbling with life," and other
gnostic texts likewise mention water, including living water.

see the eighth, and the souls in it, and the angels singing a song to the ninth[14] and its powers. I see the one with the power of them all, creating those in the spirit."

"From now on it is good for us to remain silent, with head bowed.[15] From now on do not speak about the vision. It is fitting to sing a song to the father till the day of leaving the body."

"What you sing, father, I also want to sing."

"I am singing a song in myself. While you rest, praise. You have found what you seek."

"But is it right, father, for me to praise when my heart is filled?"

"What is right is for you to sing praise to god so it may be written in this imperishable book."

"I shall offer up the praise in my heart as I invoke the end of the universe and the beginning of the beginning, the god of the human quest, the immortal discovery, the producer of light and truth, the sower of reason, the love of immortal life. No hidden word can speak of you, lord. My mind wants to sing a song to you every day. I am the instrument of your spirit, mind is your plectrum, and your guidance makes music with us. I see myself. I have been strengthened by you, for your love has reached us."

"Yes, my child."

"O grace! After this, I thank you with my song. You gave me life when you made me wise. I praise you. I invoke your name hidden in me,

A
O EE
O EEE
OOO III
OOOO OOOOO
OOOOO UUUUUU
OOOOOOOOOO
OOOOOOOOOO.[16]

You exist with spirit. I sing to you in a devout manner."

---

14. Mind dwells in the ninth.
15. Literally, "leaning forward." The translators for *Nag Hammadi Codices V, 2–5 and VI*, p. 363, suggest "in a reverent posture," while Jean Pierre Mahé and Karl-Wolfgang Tröger translate "hastily."
16. More glossolalia.

INSTRUCTIONS FOR THE
PRESERVATION OF THE TEXT

"Child, copy this book for the temple at Diospolis[17] in hieroglyphic characters, and call it the Eighth Reveals the Ninth."

"I shall do it, father,[18] as you command."

"Child,[19] copy the contents of the book on turquoise steles.[20] Child, it is fitting to copy this book on turquoise steles in hieroglyphic characters, for mind itself has become the supervisor of these things. So I command that this discourse be carved into stone and that you put it in my sanctuary.[21] Eight guards watch over it with . . . the sun: the males on the right have faces of frogs, and the females on the left have faces of cats.[22] Put a square milkstone at the base of the turquoise tablets, and copy the name on the azure stone tablet in hieroglyphic characters. Child, you must do this when I[23] am in Virgo, and the sun is in the first half of the day, and fifteen degrees have passed by me."

"Father, all you say I shall gladly do."

"Write an oath in the book, so that those who read the book may not use the wording for malicious purposes or to subvert fate. Rather, they should submit to the law of god and not transgress whatsoever, but in purity ask god for wisdom and knowledge. And whoever will not be conceived in the beginning by god develops through the general and instructional discourses. Such a person will not be able to read what is written in this book, even though the person's conscience is pure within and the person does nothing shameful and does not go along with it. Rather, such a person progresses by stages and advances in the way of immortality, and so advances in the understanding of the eighth that reveals the ninth."

"I shall do it, father."

"This is the oath: I adjure you who will read this holy book, by heaven and earth and fire and water and seven rulers of substance and the creative spirit in them and the god not conceived and the self-conceived one and the one

---

17. Diospolis Magna is Thebes (Luxor), Diospolis Parva is Heou (near Nag Hammadi).
18. This is emended; the Coptic text reads "son."
19. This is emended; the Coptic text reads "Father."
20. The Three Steles of Seth also assumes such monuments.
21. The meaning is uncertain (Coptic *ouope*).
22. Egyptian deities often are depicted with faces of animals.
23. That is, Hermes, the planet Mercury.

who has been conceived, that you guard what Hermes has communicated. God will be at one with those who keep the oath and everyone we have named, but wrath will come upon each of those who violate the oath. This is the perfect one who is, child."

34

The Prayer of Thanksgiving

The hermetic Prayer of Thanksgiving is preserved in three versions: the Coptic version from the Nag Hammadi library, a Greek version from Papyrus Mimaut, and a Latin version from the Latin tractate Asclepius. It was probably originally composed in Greek. The Coptic version appears immediately after the Discourse on the Eighth and Ninth in Nag Hammadi Codex VI, in a fine state of preservation. The introduction to the Prayer of Thanksgiving implies that it was spoken by the teacher and the student of the preceding discourse. In the prayer the worshipers give thanks for having been made divine through knowledge and for having received the enlightenment that comes from hermetic knowledge and understanding: "If the instruction is sweet and simple, it grants us mind, word, and knowledge: mind, that we may understand you; word, that we may interpret you; knowledge, that we may know you." The prayer closes with a petition that the knowledge and the life of knowledge continue on and on. After the prayer, the text reports that those who prayed together embraced (with a kiss?) and shared a vegetarian meal.

THE PRAYER OF THANKSGIVING[1]

This is the prayer they[2] offered:

   We thank you,

   every soul and heart reaches out to you,

   O name free of trouble,

   honored with the designation god,

   praised with the designation father.

   To all and all things come fatherly kindness and affection and love.

   And if the instruction is sweet and simple,[3]

   it grants us mind, word, and knowledge:

   mind, that we may understand you,

   word, that we may interpret you,

   knowledge, that we may know you.

   We are happy,

   enlightened by your knowledge.

   We are happy.

   You have taught us about yourself.

   We are happy.

   While we were still in the body

   you have made us divine through your knowledge.

   The thanksgiving of those approaching you is only this:

   that we know you.

   We have known you,

   light of mind.

   Life of life,

   we have known you.

---

1. The Prayer of Thanksgiving: Nag Hammadi Codex VI,7 (pp. 63,33 to 65,7); translated from the Coptic by Marvin Meyer.

2. In the present context, those offering the prayer must be the teacher and the student of the Discourse on the Eighth and Ninth.

3. Here the Greek reads: "To all and all things you have shown fatherly kindness, affection, love, and even sweeter action" (the verb "come" in the English translation given here is only implied in the Coptic text).

Womb of every creature,
we have known you.
Womb pregnant with the nature of the father,
we have known you.
Eternal constancy of the father who conceives,
so have we worshiped your goodness.
We ask one favor:
we wish to be sustained in knowledge.[4]
We desire one protection:
that we not stumble in this life.

When they prayed and said these things, they embraced[5] and went to eat their sacred bloodless[6] food.

---

4. Or, reading with the Greek and Latin versions, "your knowledge."
5. Perhaps a ritual embrace or kiss.
6. Vegetarian food.

PART FOUR

Mandaean Literature

INTRODUCTION

NATHANIEL DEUTSCH

In the marshes of southern Iraq and Iran, in the cities of Baghdad and Basra, and increasingly in locales like suburban New Jersey, live the Mandaeans, the only surviving gnostic community from antiquity. These fascinating and tenacious people have maintained their traditions for nearly two thousand years, long after their better known gnostic "cousins" fell into obscurity. Although they have always been a relatively small community, the Mandaeans have produced an extremely rich body of rituals and texts written in Mandaic, an eastern dialect of Aramaic. Many of these traditions are unique, while others have parallels in gnosticism, Judaism, Christianity, and Islam, as well as in ancient Mesopotamian religions. Because of their geographical isolation, their traditional wariness toward outsiders, and the linguistic and interpretive challenges posed by their literature, the Mandaeans have remained a mystery to all but a few scholars of religion. In recent years the Mandaean community has begun to remove its veils of seclusion. At the same time, a small but growing number of dedicated researchers has initiated a renaissance of interest in Mandaean studies.

ORIGINS AND HISTORY

The origins of Mandaeism, like other branches of gnosticism, have long been debated. Mandaean literature and oral traditions preserve a number of intriguing references to the roots of the community. These combine mythological, biblical, and historical elements. Like all gnostics, the Mandaeans trace their ultimate ancestry to the world of light (in Mandaic, *alma dnhura,* an analogue to the pleroma). The Mandaean anthropogony echoes both rabbinic and gnostic accounts. Ptahil, the demiurge, creates the earthly Adam, who remains inanimate until the soul of his heavenly prototype, called Adakas (a

527

contraction of Adam Kasya, "hidden Adam"), is brought into his inert body from the world of light. In another version of the myth, Ptahil first creates Adam and then, "according to the likeness of Adam," he creates Eve (in Mandaic, Hawwa, whose heavenly counterpart is Anana dNhura or "cloud of light"). Both figures are immobile until Ptahil obtains a spirit (*mana*) from his father, Abathur, and places it into the couple. After this incarnation, the savior figure Manda dHayye ("knowledge of life") comes to Adam and Eve, instructing them in the knowledge (*manda,* similar to gnosis) of their true home in the world of light and the ritual means of returning there.

Mandaeans, whose very name means "knowers" or "gnostics," view Adam and Eve as their ancestors in two ways. First, they serve as the archetypal Mandaeans insofar as they are mired in ignorance until a messenger from the world of light reveals their true, divine nature—a more straightforward version of the gnostic allegory of the pearl in the mud. Second, the Mandaeans consider themselves to be the physical descendents of Adam and Eve.

In addition to shedding light on the Mandaeans' self-conception, these anthropogonic traditions illumine other important aspects of the religion. First, Mandaeans share with other gnostics a complex and ambivalent attitude toward the Hebrew Bible. On the one hand, they reject the canonical character of the Bible and substitute their own sacred texts. On the other hand, as in the above example, they liberally incorporate biblical stories into their own mythological narratives. In many cases, Mandaeans employ what scholars of gnosticism have called inverse exegesis, namely, offering interpretations that directly contradict the standard Jewish or Christian interpretations of the same biblical texts.

Second, these anthropogonic myths reveal the Mandaean affinity for what may be called "doubling": the view that heavenly beings and realities have counterparts in the physical world. Hence both Adam and Eve are images of heavenly prototypes. Related to this tendency is the Mandaean belief that Adam's body is a microcosm of the universe. Finally, the Mandaean version of the primal or cosmic Adam myth also hints at the great importance of rituals in returning the exiled soul to the world of light. Like Adam and Eve, the Mandaeans' own salvation depends not only on revelations from heavenly light messengers such as Manda dHayye but also on their own correct performance of rituals, most notably baptism (*masbuta*) in living waters (*mia hiyya*).

Another important set of Mandaean myths reflects the highly ambivalent relationship of Mandaeism to Judaism. In oral traditions, the Mandaeans imply that they were present in Egypt with the Israelites and at the biblical

Exodus. The Mandaeans identify with the Egyptians, however, instead of the Israelites. Indeed, there is an annual ritual meal dedicated to the Egyptians who perished in the Sea of Reeds while pursuing the Israelites. The Mandaeans claim that Moses (whom they call Musa) quarreled with their ancestors in Egypt. Instead of serving the true god, Moses worshiped the evil deity Adonai (that is, the biblical god, whom the Mandaeans also identify with the sun).

Although these stories suggest a desire to differentiate the Mandaeans from the biblical Israelites, they also reveal a kind of kinship, at least in terms of historical consciousness. Equally provocative is a text that depicts Judaism as a stage that must be "cast off" before becoming Mandaean. The same text, known as the Scroll of Exalted Kingship, connects the Mandaic term for Jewish people, or *iahutaiia,* with another word meaning "abortion" or "miscarriage," a midrashic type of pun that implies that Judaism is an incompletely developed religion in comparison with Mandaeism.

The most explicitly historical account of the group's origins, a document called the *Haran gawaita,* also suggests a link to Judaism. According to the *Haran gawaita,* a community of Mandaeans once lived in Jerusalem, where they were persecuted by the Jewish people. In response to this pressure, the text claims, the Mandaeans emigrated to the east, eventually settling in present day Iran and Iraq. Elements of the text, including a reference to a certain king Ardban (perhaps the Parthian ruler Artaban III, IV, or V), indicate a first or second century CE date for the events described. Finally, another story that takes place in Jerusalem tells of a Jewish girl named Miriai, who converted to Mandaeism after receiving a revelation from the savior figure Anosh. Miriai became the ancestor of 365 disciples, whose death at the hands of the Jewish people incited Anosh to destroy the city of Jerusalem and slay the Jewish community.

These and other complex stories allude to an intimate if highly ambivalent relationship between Mandaeism and Judaism. This relationship is also attested to by a host of similar (and in some cases identical) beliefs in angels, a number of striking and important parallels between Mandaeism and Jewish mysticism, and a shared history in Babylonia, where the two communities spoke similar dialects of Aramaic and had extensive contact over the centuries.

A different theory of origins was offered by the Portuguese Christians who came into contact with the Mandaeans in the sixteenth century. Although they were not the first European Christians to encounter the Mandaeans (an Italian Dominican monk reported a meeting in 1290), the

Portuguese were the first to establish an extensive and lengthy relationship. Based on the Mandaeans' baptismal practices and their veneration of John the baptizer, the Portuguese decided that the Mandaeans were a long lost Christian group. During the same period, the Portuguese came into contact with Indian Christians in Goa who traced their origins to Saint Thomas. Initially, the Portuguese linked the Mandaeans to the missionary efforts of John the evangelist in Mesopotamia. Later, however, they speculated that the Mandaeans were founded by John the baptizer in the area of the Jordan River before migrating to the east. For centuries thereafter, the Mandaeans were known in Europe as the "Christians of Saint John" (*Christiani di San Giovanni*).

Yet while the Mandaeans themselves venerated John the baptizer, they never depict him as their founder. Moreover, Mandaean texts condemn Jesus as a "false messiah" and a "liar" who perverted John the baptizer's teachings. Their extremely negative attitude to Jesus contrasts sharply with his positive image in many western gnostic texts and in Manichaeism, where Jesus is viewed as one of the revealer figures. Mandaean literature also polemicizes against Christian practices, most notably celibacy of the clergy, which Mandaeans view as an abomination. Thus the identification of the Mandaeans as a Christian sect must ultimately be rejected, even though the two religions share a number of significant parallels; for example, they both treat Sunday (in Mandaic, *habshaba*) as the sabbath.

Since the nineteenth century, Western scholars have taken up the question of Mandaean origins. While some have placed the group's roots in the early Islamic period, many more have speculated that the Mandaeans are pre-Christian and may have even influenced canonical Christian texts such as the Gospel of John. Other scholars have argued that the Mandaeans originated as a sectarian Jewish or Jewish-Christian group in Palestine, emerging in the fertile religious milieu that produced the Dead Sea Scrolls as well as a host of baptismal groups. Still others have argued that a non-Jewish western gnostic group may have migrated to Mesopotamia, where its members adopted and transformed indigenous religious traditions.

Earlier speculation that Mandaeism developed out of Manichaeism has been definitively refuted by the Coptic Manichaean songs (or psalms) of Thomas, discovered in Egypt and dated to the fourth century CE (see "The Coptic Manichaean Songbook" in Part Five). The songs of Thomas are close adaptations of Mandaean liturgical texts and suggest that Thomas (a student of Mani) was influenced by older Mandaean traditions while living in Mesopotamia, before Mani sent him to Egypt to preach. At the same time, the

hypothesis that Mani was born into a Mandaean community has also been refuted, in this case, by the Cologne Mani Codex, which indicates that Mani was
raised among the Jewish-Christian sect of the Elkesaites (see the introduction
to Part Five).

In dating the origins and development of Mandaeism, scholars have employed a number of approaches. Although the earliest extant manuscripts are
late (from about the sixteenth century), bowls and lead amulets used for
magic are much earlier, with one such amulet dated to the second or third
century CE. Comparisons of the Mandaic alphabet with other scripts, such as
Nabataean and Elymaean, have also shed light on where and when the group
developed. Another criterion for dating is the presence of Arabic terms in
Mandaean texts (for example, the name Allah for the highest god), thereby
suggesting a post-Islamic context for particular textual recensions. Recently,
attention has been focused on the colophons appended to practically all of the
Mandaean scrolls. These colophons contain scribal genealogies, in some cases
dating back for centuries, as well as historically valuable information on geography, politics, and relations within the community. The oldest of these genealogies may date back to 270 CE, making it one of the earliest extant sources
on the Mandaeans.

MYTHOLOGY

Mandaeism possesses an incredibly rich mythology, which—to borrow a
gnostic phrase—provides knowledge of "whence we have come and whither
we are going." Perhaps even more than their gnostic relatives, the Mandaeans
employ myth as the chief vehicle for articulating and transmitting their
worldview and ritual practices. Therefore, in order to understand Mandaean
theology, cosmology, anthropology, and ritual we must turn to myths. Like the
rabbinic midrash they frequently resemble, these are typically nonsystematic
in their presentation. While this does not diminish the myths' profundity or
cultural significance, it nevertheless presents an interpretive challenge to the
uninitiated. Additional features of many Mandaean mythological texts are the
highly original geometrical illustrations that accompany them.

Mandaean mythology evinces a dualistic worldview in which the world of
light (*alma dnhura*) opposes the world of darkness (*alma dshuka*) from the
beginning. As in other gnostic mythologies, a theogonic process of emanation
precedes a cosmogonic fall or rupture. The first god, known by a number of
names including the "great life" (*hiia raba*) and "lord of greatness" (*mara*

drabuta), emanates the second life, third life, and fourth life, who are also known by the names Yoshamin, Abathur, and Ptahil, respectively. Along with a host of lesser light beings, they occupy a realm (frequently called the "house of life") of heavenly waters or "Jordans." The light beings (*'utria* or uthras) who inhabit this realm of fullness are depicted as celestial priests whose rituals serve as the model for those performed by the Mandaean priests in the earthly "Jordans" of Mesopotamia.

Opposing this realm of light and water is the world of darkness, which originally consists of the "black waters." According to one tradition, the "king of darkness" (*malka dhshuka*) emerges from the waters in an act of self-production and then proceeds to create a host of demons, liliths, vampires, and other beasts. He himself is an androgyne with the head of a lion, the body of a dragon, the wings of an eagle, the back of a tortoise, and the hands and feet of a monster, a description that recalls some of the archons in the Secret Book of John.

In a different Mandaean tradition, which parallels the gnostic Sophia myth, a female figure named Ruha initially dwells in the world of light, until she "falls" and gives birth to the lord of darkness (also known as Ur, a dragon). Together they create a host of evil beings, including the seven planets and the twelve signs of the zodiac. Although Mandaeans condemn the powers of the zodiac, they also employ elements of Babylonian astrological magic in certain texts (for example, *Sfar malwashia*) and rites. As in Judaism, therefore, official condemnation of magic exists side by side with the proliferation of magical texts, amulets, and practices.

The creation of the physical world (*tibil*) also echoes the Sophia myth. In this case, however, a male figure (the third life, also called Abathur and Bhaq Ziwa) gazes into the black waters and declares, "I shall call forth a world." He then orders the demiurge Ptahil, called Gabriel in some sources, to create the world. After fashioning the earth with the help of the evil powers, Ptahil creates the bodies of Adam and Eve, a process discussed above. As punishment for the creation of the world, both Ptahil and Abathur are exiled from the world of light. Ptahil is put in stocks and Abathur is enthroned at the entrance of the world of light, where he weighs the souls and decides which ones are worthy to enter.

Complicating this picture is the fact that each of the fallen light beings, as well as the earth itself, possesses an ideal image or *dmuta* in the world of light. This fascinating and sophisticated ontological category prevents Mandaean dualism from becoming a static system of polar opposites. Instead, figures such as Abathur and Ruha continue to have a mirror image in the world of light, even after they have fallen from grace. Because of this dual quality, they are able to function as mediators and, as we will see shortly, always possess the potential for redemption.

Much of Mandaean literature is devoted to the ongoing struggle between the forces of light and darkness. These mytho-historical narratives frequently incorporate stories from the Hebrew Bible and the New Testament. More often than not, however, biblical episodes are turned on their head (thus Moses is a prophet of the evil god Adonai; Jesus is a false messiah and liar). Only the Mandaeans know the true nature of the world, and they alone are capable of escaping or, to put it more accurately, returning to the world of light.

Mandaean soteriology focuses on individual and collective salvation (in Mandaic, *purqana*) alike. Every Mandaean possesses a soul (*nishimta* or *mana*) from the world of light, as well as a spirit (*ruha*). At the time of death, the soul ascends through seven or eight "watchhouses" (*mattarta*) until it arrives at the throne of Abathur, who weighs the soul in his scales. If found worthy, the soul is joined with the spirit and helped across the celestial waters (*hafiqia mia*) by a messenger of light, and is thus returned to the house of life, where it receives a garment and a wreath. If found unworthy, the soul is relegated to a watchhouse or purgatory appropriate to its sin. For example, Jesus the "magician" occupies a watchhouse with other men and women who practiced celibacy, while a different watchhouse contains individuals who fasted and practiced self-mortification. On the final "day of judgment" (*yoma rba ddina*), the imprisoned souls will be cast into the fiery "sea of the end" (*yama dsuf*). Meanwhile, the fallen light beings, including Yoshamin, Abathur, Ptahil, and the female figure Ruha (like her counterpart, the spirit, *ruha*), will be rehabilitated and reintegrated into the world of light.

RITUAL AND ETHICS

Although there are many Mandaean rituals, the two most important are baptism (*masbuta*) and the mass for the dead (*masiqta*), of which several types exist. Baptism occurs every Sunday and can be performed only in an earthly Jordan or "living water" (a river, stream, or pool that contains flowing water). It represents a reenactment of Adam's baptism at the hands of the heavenly figure Hibil (Abel) and mirrors the baptisms performed by the celestial priests in the world of light. The ritual involves multiple immersions, blessings, and liturgical recitations, concluding with a handclasp (*kushta*) between the layperson and the priest. Preparations for the *masiqta,* as well as the rite itself, are highly complex and cannot be described in detail here. The ceremony occurs in a cult hut (*mandi*) built near a river or stream. Important elements include the priestly recitation of hymns, the sacrifice of a dove (which symbolizes the spirit), and the ritual preparation of small unleavened loaves called *fatiria,* as well as other foodstuffs. The purpose of the *masiqta* is to unite soul and spirit and help them enter the world of light.

There are three classes of Mandaean priests, the *tarmide* ("disciples" or "students"), the more lofty *ganzibre* ("treasurers"), and the *rish ama* ("head of the people"). Members of the priesthood are called Nasoreans, a name that once applied to all Mandaeans. Priests wear white garments mirroring those worn by beings in the world of light. Today all priests are male, but there is evidence of female priests in the past. Mandaean priests must be physically and ritually pure. They cannot be eunuchs or circumcised, must be married, and must avoid pollution through contact with improperly slaughtered meat, stagnant water, or menstruating women. The Mandaean valorization of marriage and procreation contrasts sharply with certain western gnostic sources, which portray sexual intercourse as a curse of the demiurge. In Mandaean mythology, sexual desire and pregnancy are given to humankind by the savior figure Hibil (Abel). While priests are held to a higher standard of ritual purity, all Mandaeans are expected to adhere to a rigorous ethical standard, which encourages the giving of alms (*zidqa*) and condemns the use of weapons.

RECENT HISTORY AND TODAY

In the aftermath of the Muslim conquest, Mandaeans were identified with the Sabians, a "people of the book" ('*ahl al-kitab*) mentioned three times in the Qur'an. Beginning in the ninth century, however, a pagan group in Mesopotamia known as the Harranians adopted the title Sabians in an effort to gain protection under Islamic law. From this point on, Muslim authorities frequently conflated the Mandaeans with the "Sabians of Harran" and condemned them as star worshipers. Over the centuries this identification has led to periodic persecutions of the Mandaeans. In response, the Mandaeans have vehemently denied the charges of idolatry and defended their status as a protected people.

At present, the status of the Mandaeans in Iraq and Iran is not entirely clear. The long conflict between the two countries, the Gulf War, the Iraq War of 2003, and other tumultuous events in the region have had a major impact on the environment and peoples of southern Iraq and Iran, including the Mandaeans. At a recent gathering of Mandaeans and scholars at Harvard University, leaders of the Mandaean community in Iran estimated the population of Mandaeans in Iraq as seventy-five thousand and in Iran as thirty-five thousand. The Mandaeans of Iran maintain schools where children learn Mandaic, and the number of Mandaic speakers appears to be greater there than in Iraq, although any precise comparison is currently impossible.

Turmoil in the Persian Gulf region has created a growing Mandaean diaspora. According to recent statistics, there are approximately seventy Mandaean families in the New York City area, including New Jersey, and others in Florida, Michigan, and California. There is also a large community of Mandaeans in Australia, while smaller groups and individuals may be found in Glasgow, Scotland; Odessa, Ukraine; and other cities. Increasingly, Mandaeans encounter the challenges of assimilation, modern technology, and a radically different physical environment.

Mandaeans around the world maintain contact with one another and with their home communities in the Middle East. They are led by a priesthood still recovering from a devastating cholera epidemic in 1831, which killed all of the adult priests but spared a handful of their sons. In recent years, priests from Iran have traveled to Australia and the United States to perform baptisms, weddings, and other rituals. As the Mandaeans enter the twenty-first century, they face the future strengthened by a long history of tenacious survival and cultural creativity.

35

The Ginza

The most significant holy book of the Mandaeans is the Ginza. The Ginza, whose title means "treasure," is also known as the "great book." It is divided into two parts, the right Ginza and the left Ginza, the former containing mythological and theological materials, the latter songs for the rituals for the dead.

In the selections from the Ginza presented here, the Mandaean vision of the world of light and the world of darkness is portrayed with beautiful and powerful images. In the beginning was "a sole enormous fruit" (the pleroma), and from the fruit came the world of light and life. Also in the beginning were the black waters, and from the waters came the world of darkness, with Ruha, "false wisdom," and her entire entourage. Ptahil the demiurge and the planets create Adam: "They made Adam and laid him on the ground, but he had no soul." With the intervention of Mana, the exalted heavenly spirit, Adam is given a soul, "is clothed in the radiance of life and stands firm on his feet." The savior Manda dHayye, the knowledge of life, declares his role as messenger of light, that Adam—and people of knowledge—may be saved. In contrast to a Christian gospel like the Gospel of John, here it is John the baptizer who assists the light, not the sorcerer Jesus. In the end the souls that strive for the light come to the light.

THE GINZA[1]

THE WORLD BEYOND

Before all the worlds came into being
there was a sole enormous fruit,
and when the enormous fruit entered a fruit,
the great and glistening king of light began.
An ether of radiance existed.
From the ether of radiance came the living fire.
From the living fire
there was a light.
By the power of the king of light

came the great fruit and life.
The great fruit came alive
and in it rolled the Jordan, which is also a garden.
The great Jordan came alive,
and the living water was in it.
Luminous water came alive from the living water.
I, life, came alive
and all the uthras—the light beings—found space.

ORIGIN OF THE WORLDS OF LIGHT

When the fruit was in the fruit, when the ether was in the ether,
when the great and glorious Mana[2]
was there[3] from whom powerful *manas*[4] came,
whose radiance is enormous and light is great,
no one was before them in the fruit abundant and without end,
whose radiance is too abundant for the words of the mouth,

---

1. The Ginza: translated by J. F. Hendry, in Robert Haardt, *Gnosis: Character and Testimony*
(Leiden: E. J. Brill, 1971), pp. 360–371, 379, 388–390; revised in verse by Willis Barnstone.
Reprinted by permission of Brill Academic Publishers.
2. Heavenly spirit.
3. In the pleroma.
4. Spirits.

and whose light, which was in that fruit, too great for telling
with the lips.

From the fruit came a thousand thousand fruits without end
and a myriad myriad of beings of light, the shkinas,[5] beyond count.
In each fruit were a thousand thousand beings of light.
They stand and praise the great and glorious Mana,
who lives in the great ether,
within the Jordans[6] of white water made by the Mana,
whose aroma is fragrant
and inhaled on all the roots of light
and on the great first radiance.

The long Jordan was made to go on uncounted and endlessly.
Plants grow next to it. They are happy.
They praise and stand in perfection,
and from the great Jordan came uncounted Jordans endlessly.[7]

THE WORLD OF DARKNESS

I saw the rebels and Hewath the serpent woman.[8]
When I was standing in the house of life, I saw the rebels.
I saw their gates of darkness.
I saw their destruction and the lords of the gloomy house.
I saw their fighters buried in darkness.
I saw the gates of fire and their burning glow,
    how the wicked burn and glow,
deliberately imperfect and in error.
I saw Hewath the woman,
    how she speaks in darkness and malice.
She speaks in malice and is expert in witchcraft and sorcery.
She talks with illusory wisdom on her throne of lies.[9]
I saw the gate of darkness

---

5. Heavenly realms, aeons; similar to the Hebrew shekhinah.
6. Baptismal water.
7. The earthly baptismal water comes from the heavenly baptismal water.
8. Nickname for Ruha.
9. Ruha is, after all, false wisdom.

and the arteries[10] of the earth, Siniawis the underworld,
    just as it is.
I saw the black water that rose up, boiled, and bubbled.
Whoever enters dies, and whoever sees it is scorched.
I saw the dragons
who were hurled there and writhe on the ground.
I saw the wicked rebels sitting in their chariots.
I saw the wicked of every type and species.
I saw a chaos of chariots of darkness.
I saw the wicked rebels arrayed in weapons of evil.
With weapons of evil they conspire against the place of light.

WHERE IS THE DARKNESS FROM?

Who are these hideous creatures?
Where is the darkness from?
Who are the inhabitants sitting there?
How were their actions born,
which are hideous and fearful?
And their enormous flaws?
Their frightening ugliness?
They are disfigured and deformed.

WHERE ARE THE MONSTERS FROM?

Where are the mighty and evil monsters from
who live in fire?
And the black waters seething and boiling?
Enter and you die, see it and you burn.
Where are the dragons from,
cast and contorted on the ground?
And their chariots, and the wicked sitting there,
and Hewath the serpent woman?

---

10. Rivers.

LIFE QUESTIONED

Life, since you went there, how did darkness get there?
How did darkness get there?
How were imperfection and flaws born?

ORIGINS OF LIGHT AND DARKNESS

There is no boundary for light.
It was unknown when it began.
Nothing was when light was not.
Nothing was when radiance was not.
Nothing was when life was not.
There was never a boundary for light.
Nothing was when water was not.

WATER IS PRIOR TO DARKNESS

Water is prior to darkness.
Prior to darkness is water.
Nothing is without an end.[11]
No number is before the uthras were.
Light beings are prior to darkness.
Prior to darkness are uthras
and older than their inhabitants.
Goodness is prior to the malice
of the place of darkness.
Gentleness is prior to the bitterness
of the place of darkness.
Living fire is prior to the consuming fires
of the place of darkness.
Praise is prior to the practice
of sorcery and witchcraft.
Hymns and books are prior to the sorcery
of Hewath, the terrible woman.

---

11. According to Kurt Rudolph, this is a Mandaean proverb (Foerster, *Gnosis*, vol. 2, p. 165).

DARKNESS

Water doesn't mix with tar,
and darkness can't be measured by light.

Darkness can't be measured by light.
The house of gloom isn't lighted.
The house of gloom isn't lighted, and turbid waters
    have no sparkle.
Darkness grew and creatures formed.
Darkness formed, and when it formed it tested its force.
It harbored malice in its mind.
It imprisoned its own *kanna*, the place of the soul.
It imprisoned its own *kanna*,
and everything it did was nothing.
The children of darkness are nothing,
but the children of life stay.
The house of evil is nothing,
and its consuming fires die.
Its sorcery dies and ends, since it has no place
    in eternity.
It comes to nothing.
The generations of life stay forever.
The living instruction rises and illuminates
    a perishable living place.

THE ARCHDEMON RUHA

The mind of Ruha dQudsha[12] is evil. She lies.
She is a sorcerer.
The mind of Ruha, the liar, is sorcery.
She is all sorcery, witchcraft, and fake wisdom.
Hewath the woman, who is Ruha, sits with her stone amulets
and tears clumps of hair from her head.
She is sitting, engaged in false magic,

---

12. Spirit of false wisdom, here the "holy" spirit, who is quite unholy.

along with her women spirits. They all practice false magic,
    possessed, evil, and ensnared.
She concocts a commotion of false magic.
Her mind is confused.
Who were her imperfect and disfigured instructors
who taught her lies?
Who is this woman, mother of the base monster?[13]

PTAHIL, ANGEL OF LIGHT

When I, Ptahil,[14] was shaped and came to be, I issued
    from a source of huge radiance.
When my father[15] decided to call me out, he called me
    out of the huge radiance.
He dressed me in a radiant robe and wrapped me
    in a covering of light.
He gave me a major crown in his whose luminosity
    the worlds glisten,
and he said to me, "Son, go to the Tibil earth[16]
    and make the black waters solid.
Solidify the Tibil earth and inscribe Jordan rivers
    and canals upon its face."

PTAHIL MAKES EARTH AND ITS INHABITANTS

With my first cry I solidified the earth from the waters
and stretched the firmament into perfection.
With my second cry I inscribed Jordan rivers and canals
    all over its face.
With my third cry I called into being fishes in the sea
and feathered birds of every shape and species.

---

13. She is mother of the monstrous lord of darkness, as Sophia is the mother of Yaldabaoth in
gnostic sources.
14. The demiurge.
15. Abathur, the divine judge.
16. Tibil is the physical world.

With my fourth cry I made every plant and its seeds,
and each one was distinct from another.
With my fifth cry sinister reptiles came into being.
With my sixth cry there came a full structure of darkness.
With my seventh cry I made Ruha
    and her seven sons, who are the planets.[17]
Ruha the mother of evil and her seven sons came into being
    and appeared before me.
When I saw them, my heart fell out of my body.

CREATING ADAM

After the angel Ptahil came he said to the planets, "Let us create Adam and make him king of the world." The planets conferred. They agreed to tell him that they wanted to create Adam and Eve. After all, he belongs to them.

"Yes," the planets said, "we will make Adam and Eve the head of the human family."

After they said what they were planning to do, Ptahil was profoundly shaken. He thought, "If I myself create Adam and Eve the head of the whole family, what will Adam's role be in the world?"

Then Ptahil Uthra[18] spoke to the planets, asking them. "Whom can we trust? What is our authority in the world?" And he said to them, "Planets, you will be his guardians and serve him in all ways."

They made Adam and laid him on the ground,
    but he had no soul.
When they made Adam they couldn't cast a soul into him.
They called on the wind of the ether to hollow out his bones.
To hollow out his bones and let marrow form in them,
    to let marrow form,
to make him strong and stand firm on his feet.

They called on the splendor of the living fire
    to make his robe luminous.

---

17. On false wisdom and the planets see the cosmogony presented in the Secret Book of John and other gnostic texts.
18. Ptahil, the demiurge, is also a light being (*uthra*).

To make his robe luminous,
to make him strong and stand firm on his feet.
They called on the mists over the brook
and smoke of the ravenous fire
to flow into his torso so he could clench his fist
    and spread his arms
and yell and shake himself awake,
to make him strong and stand firm on his feet.

Then the planets spoke, turning to Ptahil,
"Allow us to cast spirit into him,
which you took with you from your father's house."
All the planets urged him,
and the lords[19] of the world urged him,
and though they tried,
they couldn't stand him upright on his feet.[20]

BRINGING SOUL TO ADAM

In his illuminated state Ptahil rose to the place of light.
He came before the father of light beings, who are
    the uthras,
and his father asked him, "What have you done?"
He answered, "Once I worked well, but your image
    and mine have failed."
Then the father of light beings got up and hurried
    to a secret place.
He found the great Mana, the hidden Adam,[21] and urged him to
    light the corruptible, to light every varying coat of the body.[22]

Then the father wrapped him in his clean turban
and evoked the name that life gave him.
He seized him at the ends of his turban
    and carried him here.

---

19. Lord or lords.
20. As in other gnostic texts, at first Adam cannot stand up.
21. Adakas.
22. "Coat" probably refers to the flesh of people.

He gave him to his son, Ptahil. When he gave him
   to the light being Ptahil,
life summoned his helpers.
He summoned the light beings Hibil, Sitil, and Anosh,[23]
who are astonishing and immaculate.
He called them, ordered them, and warned them
   about their souls.
He told them, "Guard them and let no one know."
Don't let evil Ptahil learn how soul falls into body,
   how soul falls into body
and the blood speaks in it as the radiance fills him.[24]
How the blood speaks in it and how the vein channels
   permeate it.
Let the carrier of Adakas Mana, the hidden Adam,[25]
   be his soul's[26] protector.
When Adam is clothed in the radiance of life
   and stands firm on his feet,
when he speaks with a clean mouth,
you, Adakas, restore him to his place and protect him
   against enemies.

PTAHIL AND MANDA DHAYYE WORK ON ADAM

Ptahil wrapped Adam in his clean turban.
He wrapped him in his robe.
The light being quickly descended, and his helpers
   all went down with him.
His helpers who went down are men in charge of souls.
When they reached the Tibil,[27] which is the world
   and where his bodily torso is,
when Ptahil wanted to cast soul into his body,
I, Manda dHayye, removed the soul from his pocket.

---

23. Heavenly Abel, Seth, Enosh.
24. Conjectural reading.
25. Adakas is Adam Kasya, hidden Adam.
26. "Soul" is uncertain here. "His" may refer back to Adakas Mana.
27. Physical world.

When Ptahil lifted Adam up, I raised his bones.
When he laid his hands on him, I made him breathe
    the fragrance of life.
His body filled with marrow,
and the radiance of life spoke in him.
When the radiance of life spoke in him,
he opened the eyes of his bodily torso.
When the radiance of life spoke in him,
Adakas Ziwa, the radiant Adam, rose to his place.[28]

MANDA DHAYYE, MESSENGER OF LIGHT

I led Adam up to his place.
I led Adam up to his place, the house of powerful life,
the house where the great life is on his throne.
I handed him over to the guardians of the treasure,
the light beings who take care of the Jordans.[29]
Life thanked the light beings who brought the soul.
The great summoned me and commanded me, saying,
"Go down and shout a sublime call!
Shout sublimely so the wicked learn nothing of the soul!"

I came and found the wicked, all of them sitting there,
and while they were sitting there
I spread witchcraft and magic around the soul,
and the wicked wanted to chop the soul into tiny parts.
I saw them and I shone in my pure garments.
Before the world I glowed in a huge radiance
    given me by my father.
I appeared to Ptahil Uthra, who howled and wept.
He howled and wept over what he had done.
I appeared to Ruha, the seductive mother of planets
    and evil creatures,
who seduces the worlds.

---

28. Adakas is hidden Adam and Ziwa is radiance, hence "radiant Adam."
29. Heavenly baptismal water.

I showed her the great mystery that subdues rebels.
I showed her the great mystery, but she was blind
    and didn't see it.
I showed her a second mystery.
Then I threw a camel bridle on her and showed her
    a third mystery
and with a blow I split her head open.

WHEN THEY SAW ME THEY TREMBLED

When they saw me they trembled and called out,
saying they were guilty.
The seven called out, saying they were guilty.
They called out, saying they were guilty,
and fell headlong and landed on their faces.
They fell headlong and landed on their faces,
putting their hands before their faces,
and they cried, "Master. We were in error and sin.
    Forgive our sins."
But when the wicked spoke I cut through their phalanx.
I made them swear by the great mystery
    not to wrong the soul.
I hid before their seven souls.
I stopped and took on a body. I took on a body
and thought I would not terrorize the soul,
and in her garment she would not know terror.
I took on a body for her
and sat near her in splendor.
I spread radiance of the great Mana over her.
From that light, Adam was planted.
I sat by him and taught him what life had stored in me.
I sang to him sublimely,
more sublimely and luminous than the worlds.
I sang to him in a soft voice
and raised his heart from sleep.
I spoke to him in the speech of the light beings
and taught him out of my wisdom.
I taught him out of my wisdom. I told him to rise

and pray on his knees and praise the mighty.
He should praise the high place where the good sit.
He should praise Adakas Ziwa, the radiant Adam,
      the father from whom he came.

ADAM SAVED

As I sat and instructed him, he bowed down and praised
      the mighty. He praised his father, Adakas Ziwa,
the Mana by whom he was planted.
When he bowed down and praised his father the light being,
the father came to him from his secret place.
When he saw his father he overflowed with holy songs.
He sang in a loud voice and overturned the planets.
He overturned the planets
and overturned the lord of the world.
He disowned the sons of this world's house,
and everything
they had done.
He witnessed the name of life
and the light being who let him hear his voice.
He disowned the works of the Tibil
and raised his eyes to the place of light.

THE LIGHT BEING OF LIFE REWARDS ADAM

For what he had done the light being of life was kind,
the father of light was full of kindness to him
and commanded a building be erected for him.
He commanded a building be erected for him
and commanded a planting be planted for him.
He commanded a Jordan river be prepared for him
so at the ripe instant when his measure was full,
he would ascend and inhabit his building and inhabit
      the place of light
with Adakas Ziwa his father,
      and become a light being in the place of light.

JOHN THE BAPTIZER AND JESUS THE SORCERER

For nine months Nbu Christ[30] is in the womb of his mother,[31] the virgin, and he is hidden there. Then he came out of her body, along with blood and menstrual discharge, and grew up at her breasts and sucked her milk. When he was grown, he entered the temple of the Jews and became perfect in all wisdom. He perverts the Torah and alters its doctrine and all its work. He leads some of the descendants of the Jews into error and turns them into god fearers and shows them magical forms, which they believe in. He clothes them in colored tunic, tonsures their heads, and veils them like darkness.[32] And on Sunday[33] they keep their hands from work. He tells them,

> I am the true god. I have been sent here from my father.
> I am the first messenger and I am the last.
> I am the father, I am the son, I am the holy spirit.
> I came out of the city of Nazareth.

He demeans himself humbly, goes to Jerusalem, and there captivates some Jews through sorcery and deceit, showing them great deeds and magical forms. Some devils who are with him he inserts in a dead body, and they speak in the dead body. He cries to the Jews and tells them,

> Come and see, I am he who wakes the dead,
> performs resurrections and deliverances.
> I am Anosh[34] the Nazorean.

Then Ruha[35] screams in Jerusalem and testifies against him. He snares people by sorcery and befouls them with blood and menstrual discharge. He baptizes them in blocked waters[36] and perverts the living baptism and baptizes them in the name of the father and the son and the holy spirit. He alienates

---

30. Nbu is the planet Mercury (Roman counterpart of the Greek Hermes).
31. This is actually Ruha, the spirit of false wisdom.
32. That is, the followers of Jesus become monks and priests.
33. *Habshaba,* the Mandaean holy day, Sunday.
34. Heavenly Enosh.
35. The spirit of false wisdom.
36. That is, not living or flowing waters, as in Mandaean baptism.

them from the living baptism in the Jordan of living waters, with which you, Adam, were baptized.

Also in that generation a child was born, who was called by the name of John,[37] the son of the venerable Zachariah, who was born to him in his old age at the end of one hundred years. His mother, the woman Elizabeth, became pregnant with him. She gave birth to him in her old age. When John grows up in that generation of Jerusalem, faith will find a place in his heart and he will receive the Jordan and carry out baptisms for forty-two years, before Nbu, who is Hermes Christ, dresses in a body and enters the world. When John is in Jerusalem, Jesus Christ arrives, moves about in humility, is baptized with the baptism of John, and becomes wise through John's wisdom. Then Jesus proceeds to pervert the word of John and change the Jordan baptism, altering the words of truth,[38] and summoning wickedness and lies into the world.

MANDA DHAYYE BRINGS TRIUMPH TO JOHN

On the day that John's measure is full, Hibil Manda dHayye[39] comes to him. But I appear to John as a small boy, three years and a day old, and I converse with him about baptism and I instruct his friends. Then I take him out of his body and cause him to rise up in triumph to the world that is filled with radiance, and I baptize him in the white Jordan of living and brilliant waters,[40] clothe him in garments of radiance, and cover him in turbans of light and place praise in his pure heart from the praise of the angels of light.

THE LIGHT BEING ANOSH UNMASKS JESUS

After John, the world will go on in lies and Christ the Roman[41] will split the peoples; the twelve seducers[42] wander the world. For thirty years the Roman appears in the world. . . . And when the great one chooses, the light being Anosh comes. He will expose the lies of Jesus the liar, who makes himself equal to the angels of light. He will accuse Christ the Roman, the liar, the son of a

---

37. John the baptizer.
38. Truth is *kushta*, which is ritualized through a handshake.
39. Hibil is heavenly Abel; Manda dHayye is knowledge of life as heavenly messenger.
40. Heavenly baptism.
41. A reference to the Roman or Byzantine context of the Christian church.
42. The twelve messengers or apostles, linked to the twelve signs of the zodiac.

woman, who did not come from the light, that he is one of the seven seducing planets who roam the world,[43] and that he is wandering among the celestial spheres. He will unmask Christ the Roman as a liar, he will be bound by the hands of the Jews, his devotees will bind him, he will be fastened to a cross, and his body will be slain. His devotees will divide him up into many pieces.[44] He will be bound on the hill of Mara.[45] When the sun rises, it unleashes its heat against him, because he cast error and persecution into the world.

Soul Songs

THE SOUL'S QUESTIONS

The soul, the soul has words:
Who cast me into the Tibil?
Who cast me into the Tibil?
Who chained me to the wall?
Who roped me in the stocks
equal to the fullness of world?
Who threw a chain around me
that is unmeasured on earth?
Who clothed my soul in a coat
of every fabric and color?

ADAM ENVELOPED IN SLEEP

I am enveloped in sleep
in a robe without error.
In a robe without error
in which nothing lacks.
Life knew about me:
Adam asleep. I woke.
The soul took my hand.
Light hurled me into darkness,

---

43. Mercury.
44. This may refer to relics of Christ or the elements of the eucharist.
45. Mount Moriah? "Lord" (from Syriac)?

darkness filled with light.
On the day the light rises
darkness will go to its cave.
She came to clouds of light,
going to the place of light.

MY SOUL YEARNED FOR LIFE

The soul in me yearned for life.
Knowledge blossomed in my eyes.
The soul in me yearned for life.
I floated and wandered up
till I reached the first planet.
Her slaves came to meet me.
"Seize him, seize that man.
He will keep us company.
Seize him, seize that man,
and ask where he is from."
"Friend, where are you from
and where are you going?"
"I come from earth, the Tibil,
the house the planets built.
The soul in me yearned for life
and aimed for the place of life."
"This is the house of life.
This is the way!
Where are you going?"

When you go among enemies
they will perform anything
imaginable against you.
"That is not what I desire
and not what my soul wants."

The soul in me yearned for life.
Knowledge blossomed in my eyes.
The soul in me yearned for life.
I floated and wandered up
till I reached the second planet,

and the third and the fourth.
When you go among them,
they will shout the name of death,
and chain and torment you.
I floated and wandered up
the fifth, sixth, and seventh planets
till I reach the house of life.
When I reach the house of life,
life came out to meet me.
Life came out to meet me
and dressed me in radiance
and covered me with light.
He counted me, gave me
his number. The good
came out of his midst.

Among the lamps of light
your lamps will float and shine.

THE SAVIOR TALKS TO THE SOUL

Soul, if you hear what I say
and do not oppose my word,
for you I will throw a bridge
over the great sea.
For you I will lay a dam
and guide you to the watchtower
where the rebels hold out.
I will guide you past the fire
and smoke touching the sky.
I will take you past the double pits
where Ruha has dug her way.
And over that high mountain
I will smooth the path for you.
In this wall, this wall of iron,
I will hack a breach for you,
hug you with all my strength,
and take you to the place of light.

LOVING LIFE, PERFORMING GOOD DEEDS

Loving life, I let Manda dHayye,
the messenger of light,
calm my innermost thought.
Late Saturday evening
and before the good Sunday,
I stuffed alms in my pocket
and went to the temple gate.
I piled alms and bread
on the common plate.
I found an orphan. I fed him.
I found a widow. I filled her pocket.
I found a naked man
and gave him a garment
for his nakedness.
I found a prisoner and found a way
to free him to his village.

36

Hibil's Lament from the Book of John

The gnostic text called Hibil's Lament is from the Mandaean Book of John. The Book of John, also referred to as the "book of the kings" (meaning the angels), contains discourses of John the baptizer, who occupies a significant place within Mandaean thought.

In Hibil's Lament the main character is Hibil Ziwa, a heavenly figure who has come down to earth to instruct, punish, and save. His initial failures and dejection dominate the book as he reports to the major Mandaean savior figure, Manda dHayye ("knowledge of life"). The scene is established in the opening words, "I am happy, very happy, though I am hurt in the house of the wicked." In his plaintive discourse, Hibil emphasizes the gnostic struggle of light over darkness and asks how many adulterers and thieves—as well as those poor beings who live in darkness and temptation and fail to find the way to knowledge and light—he will have to send into darkness. He tells us that he made darkness and light, and that he chose Abathur as the high judge to stand at the dread toll stations where he determines what souls are worthy to enter the house of light. By those stations—and there are a stream of them, we learn in other texts—are pots bubbling with liquids to cook the souls of the wicked.

Hibil's Lament describes a Job-like litany of suffering that affects both the punisher and the punished. As Job questions the afflictions cast on him by god, so does Hibil question Manda dHayye's stern mandates. Hibil both condemns and feels compassion for those whom he must send on to the toll keepers to weigh and destroy: of the frightened and eager souls who reach the toll stations, only one or two among ten thousand will rise to the house of light. Hibil is weary of his duty to punish multitudes of unredeemables. Rather than harm, he would save. "When will they give up killing?" he asks. "When will combat fade, and my heart heal?"

By the tract's end, Hibil is pleased with his report to Manda dHayye, and his speech rises in poetic transport before those virtuous humans to whom he offers ascension to and communion with the father of light. As for the rest, he states, "There is no rising for those who fall, and the mountain of darkness swallows them."

HIBIL'S LAMENT FROM THE BOOK OF JOHN[1]

How long must I sink between worlds?
In the name of a better life, may light be everywhere.
I am happy, very happy, though I am hurt in the house
　　of the wicked.
In my heart I will be pleased by the works
I have created in this world.
How much longer must I sink between worlds?
How long should I pour light into the world?
How long shall I raise treasure to the house of the leaders?
I will be happy! My soul looks to the father.
I will be pleased by working with the poor and the young.
I will quiet my heart and be calm.

How long must I nourish powerful light world messengers
　　and the leaders' rhetoric?
How long should I combat demons and murder rebels?

---

1. Hibil's Lament from the Book of John: translated by Jorunn Jacobsen Buckley ("Professional Fatigue: 'Hibil's Lament' in the Mandaean Book of John," *Le Muséon* 110, nos. 3–4 [1997], pp. 367–81); revised in verse by Willis Barnstone.

Will one of you release me from Abathur the high judge?
How long must I walk with weights on my neck?
How long will I tramp on Sunday, our holy day,
and expel it from existence?
When will I bring authority to the tollhouses?[2]
How long must I tame stallions and harness them?
How long must I plow and disperse seed around the world?
How long sow, reap, and give away the perishable?
How long must I counter wicked fools, hurl them into pots
     and cook them?
How long must the scale weigh and Abathur judge us?
How long must I batter Shamish the sun and condemn
     his earthly appearance
and berate him in favor of the select good ones in this world?
How long must I attack tollhouse guards and suffocate them
     with Sin the moon?
Must I keep hurling him each month into pots of boiling liquids?

How long will the earth accept seed and fruit dropped across
     horizons?
When will ships no longer sink and rise to the realm of light?
How long must I restrain the living water
and throw it into still water?
How long must the messengers of light claw through pollution
     and wrongdoing?
How long can they stand it?
When will darkness end and light come?
When will I not waste pearls on transitory life?
How many will hang in my fishing nets,
and when can I cease dragging up the poor and the hurt?
How long will I punch mountains?
How long will I dress the perishable in darkness?
When will I stop hanging chains on earthly adulterers
     and thieves?

---

2. Hibil sends people to the high judge at the toll houses or guard posts, where their souls will
be weighed and their fate determined.

When will I stop waving my fists,
killing, stomping on the bad and the liars?
How soon will I give up disorienting them?
When will they give up killing?
When will combat fade, my heart heal?
When will Tibil's earthly world end, so I can conceal
    my nets?

MANDA DHAYYE'S RESPONSE

After Hibil Ziwa spoke these words,
Manda dHayye responded, saying to him,
"When will you no longer stumble, Hibil Ziwa?
When will your pain in this world end?
And the works of the sick, when will you no longer
    bear them on your neck?"

HIBIL ANSWERS

After Hibil Ziwa heard this, he sprang from his carpet,
stood, and opened his mouth to candor, uttering to Manda dHayye,
"I created Tibil, the earthly world. On whose neck is it now?
Those I created, what light carriers will have them?
After I made Adam and his wife, Eve, I formed
and condemned them and sent them into exile.
To them I was persecution.
I made the toll stations and chains for the Jews
and inside them placed everyday officials.

"I have smoothed a road from darkness to the dwelling place
    of permanence.
I have appointed witnesses in the tollhouse of Abathur.
I made Abathur the judge of the world.
I placed him among scales
and gave him power over events on earth.
I made the river Ksas flowing between earth and the light world,
and by it I placed Abathur.

I created white fruit into which souls are placed.
From it they shoot out to sit on the scales.
I created brooks of brisk water, like Jordan waters,
in which souls are baptized.
I made a way so that all souls float on the streams and rise.
I made a ship for the good,
a ferry for souls crossing to the house of Abathur.
Therein strength and permanence will enter them everlasting.

"I brought the holy day, Sunday, and placed it above the customs men,
and I said to them, 'Whoever brings this letter of passage
    will reach you,
but who ventures without it you will hide.
All wrongdoers and liars will be interrogated in your tollhouse
until a letter of passage with all its contents
rises from Tibil, the earth, to life in its being.
When the letter and its contents ascend to life,
a letter from life will come.
When it reaches Abathur they will ascend.'

"I made works and death and life in the world.
Those with avid souls rise to light,
but the adulterers and thieves collapse in the dark.
Erotic Ruha[3] is here to seduce the entire earth.
When I heard the blatant alarm, I warned against her.

"I made a rope of cable and planted a pole.
I told the Mandaean scholars to shimmy up the rope,
to hang from the rope;
to rise and see the precinct of light.
Whoever ignores the rope must climb the pole.
Whoever ignores both rope and pole falls
and will find no ascension.
There is no rising for those who fall,
and the mountain of darkness swallows them.

---

3. As the spirit of false wisdom, Ruha is both fallen and erotically compelling, like Sophia in
some gnostic texts.

Whoever wishes a second death,
but who is dead to light,
his eye will see no light and his foot feel no firm earth.

"You have prevailed, Manda dHayye, as those who love your name.
Life wins."

37

Songs from the Mandaean Liturgy

From Mandaean liturgical texts, collected together under the rubric Mandaean Liturgies, come the lovely songs for the poor, the persecuted, and the soul given here. Particularly poignant is the song of the poor man from the fruit (the pleroma), who is dragged from the dwelling of the good to the world of the wicked, "where all is malice and fire." He suffers, a stranger in this strange and terrible world, "like a fatherless child," until a messenger from the realm of life and light arrives to deliver the poor man. The messenger promises splendid clothing, an exalted seat, and freedom. Thus, "Welcome to anyone life knows, and sorrow to whomever life ignores." All of this is reminiscent of the Song of the Pearl, in Part Two of this volume.

SONGS FROM THE MANDAEAN LITURGY[1]

Song of the Poor Man

A POOR MAN TAKEN FAR

I am a poor man from the fruit.
They took me from far away. I am far.
I am a poor man whom life spoke to.
I am far. The light beings took me away.
They carried me here from the good
to where the wicked live.
They installed me in the world of the wicked
where all is malice and fire.

I didn't ask for it. I didn't want to come
to this awful place.
By my strength and light I suffer through
this misery. By illumination and praise.
I remain a stranger in their world.
I stand among the wicked like a child without a father.
Like a fatherless child, an untended fruit.
I hear the voice of the seven planets.
They whisper. They say among themselves,
"Where does this alien come from?
He doesn't speak like us."
I didn't listen to their speech raging against me.

THE KINDLY LIGHT BEING

Life heard my cry and sent an angel,
a kindly light being who was prepared for me.

---

1. Songs from the Mandaean Liturgy; translated by Kurt Rudolph, ("Mandaean Sources" in Foerster, ed., *Gnosis: A Selection of Gnostic Texts*, vol. 2, pp. 121–319); revised in verse by Willis Barnstone.

He told me in a pure voice
as light beings speak in the house of perfection.
He said, "Poor man, don't be alarmed or fearful.
Don't say, 'I am utterly alone.'
For you we spread the firmament above.
For you we spread the firmament above and made dry land.
We made dry land,
and solid land came and stood in the water.
For you the sun came,
for you the moon came into the firmament,
for you, poor one, the seven planets
and twelve creatures of the zodiac were set in orbit.
Radiance sits at your right hand
and glittering light on your left.
Be strong in your seed until you are fulfilled.
When you are fulfilled
I will come again.
I will bring you splendid clothing,
the envy of the world.
I will bring you a lovely shawl of light,
abundant and boundless.
I will deliver you from the wicked,
free you from the sinners.
You will sit in your own heavenly place.
I will free you in that pure place."

THE POOR MAN DELIVERED

I hear the voice of the seven planets,
who whisper to one another,
"Blessings on the father of the poor one:
he is the one who tends the fruit tree.
We have no father and no one to tend our tree."
Welcome to anyone life knows,
and sorrow to whomever life ignores.
Welcome to anyone life knows,
and who stays on earth free
from the world of imperfection

where the planets live.
They sit on rebel thrones and work with a whip.
Gold and silver excite them,
and they cast war into the world.
They cast war into the world, and they will roast in fire.
The evil will roast in fire, their glory gone.
But my family and I will ascend and see
the place of light where the sun does not go down,
where lamps of light never dim,
the place, the house to which your souls
are called and invited in,
souls of our kin, of the good,
and of our believing brothers and sisters.
There life is extolled.

Advice for the Persecuted

You came from the house of life.
You came from the house of life,
you came. What did you bring us?
I came with you so you won't die,
so your souls won't be erased.
I brought life on the day of death,
happiness on the day of gloom.
I brought you rest. There disquiet
of the nations is not raging.
Good one, you came to the true
man carrying this? And only this?
I made him my treasurer.

I made him my treasurer and
the master over all I possess.
I gave him the keys of truth
to enter the world and leave it
as a man with longing filled.
My chosen ones,
my chosen ones, you looked

and found, again and again.
My chosen ones, you looked
and found as our ancestors
looked. Life is victory.

A Letter Looped around One's Neck

Here is a sealed letter
leaving the world,
a letter written with truth
and marked with the seal
of mighty life.
Perfect ones wrote it,
and believers insured it.
They looped it around
the soul's neck
and sent it to the gate
of life. The soul wisely
used her finger
to mark the open letter.

Be Like Wine Jars

You of my blood, speak the truth.
Close your lying lips.
Don't be a pomegranate whose outer face is fresh.
Its outer face is fresh, but inside it is full
of rotting corn seed.
Be like wine jars filled with redolent wine.
Their outer shells are clay and pitch,
but inside is redolent wine.
The message of life shouts. Ears of my chosen,
come and hear me.

PART FIVE

Manichaean Literature

INTRODUCTION

PAUL MIRECKI

Manichaeism was one of the major world religions and the only such religion to align itself closely with late antiquity's Near Eastern gnostic tradition. Previously considered by Western scholars to be a Christian heresy, Manichaeism is now properly understood in the context of third-century Mesopotamian religions. The religion was founded by the Iranian prophet Mani (216–77 CE), who deliberately created a universal and propagandistic religion that incorporated Christian, Zoroastrian, and Buddhist concepts. Whether Manichaeism is properly designated as gnostic, as Hans Jonas and others have suggested, is being debated by scholars. The religion moved east toward India and west into the Roman Empire already in Mani's lifetime, reaching as far west as Algiers and southern Europe and as far east as Central Asia and southeast coastal China, where traces of the religion datable to the early seventeenth century can be identified. The focus of this introduction is on western Manichaeism.

LIFE OF MANI

Mani was born on April 14, 216, near the Mesopotamian city of Ctesiphon, Parthia. His parents were of Iranian descent. His mother, Maryam, was related to the ruling Arsacid dynasty, and his father, Patik, was a devotee in an Elkesaite Mughtasilist community, a Jewish-Christian baptismal sect with gnostic and ascetic features that derived from the popular religious movement founded by the obscure figure Elkesai. Mani entered the baptismal group at the age of four, but the most striking incident of his early life was a revelation he received at the age of twelve, when an angel he called "the twin" appeared and ordered him to leave the baptismal group at an unspecified later date. The crucial second revelation came at the age of twenty-four, when the angel ordered him to begin his public ministry by openly preaching the newly revealed doctrine. This novel public teaching put Mani at odds with the traditional community, and he was forced to leave with only the support of his father and two faithful followers. Although Mani's new doctrine contained many elements that were rejected by the baptismal community, the primary point of contention was probably his argument that ritual purity through baptism was of no avail and that true redemptive purity comes only from the physical and moral separation of light from darkness, spirit from matter, and good from evil.

Mani proclaimed himself the messenger (or apostle) of light, the comforter (or paraclete) incarnate (see John 14:16, 26), and the seal of the prophets who would bring the final revelation to the world. Mani viewed all previous religious traditions as contaminated versions of the originally true though incomplete teachings of the prophets Buddha, Jesus, and Zoroaster. Mani, as the seal of the prophets, proclaimed the final revelation, the true universal religion that would unite all people through his teaching. This grand plan required propagandistic methods designed to overcome the cultural and linguistic barriers that prevented the revelations of the earlier prophets from reaching a universal audience. Mani emphasized the need for the translation of Manichaean texts into all languages in order to propagate his teaching as effectively and quickly as possible. In contrast to the earlier prophets, whose teachings were put into written form by their followers, who contaminated those teachings with their own interpretations, Mani himself produced a corpus of seven canonical works. Perhaps Mani's most effective propaganda tool was his ability to instill in his followers a sense of the absolute necessity to devote their lives to propagating the religion. Mani himself traveled extensively during his own lifetime and was influenced by the popular image of the Christian messenger Thomas, who, tradition holds, traveled as far as India to spread the Christian faith.

Mani's canon of seven works, written in the eastern Aramaic language, consists of the Living Gospel, the Treasure of Life, the Pragmateia, the Book of Mysteries, the Book of the Giants, the Letters, and the Psalms and Prayers. Mani also wrote the Shaburagan, which replaces the Psalms and Prayers in some canonical lists. None of these texts is known to survive today in a complete form. Much previous research in Manichaeism has depended on a considerable number of quotes and descriptions in the writings of heresiologists and historians. The most important works were the *Acta archelai*, the writings of the former Manichaean Augustine of Hippo, and the works of the Arab authors al-Biruni and Ibn al-Nadim.

Mani's first mission was eastward, like that of Thomas before him, and he met an early success in what is now southeast Iran with the conversion of Turan-shah, the Buddhist king of Turan, and his entourage. He continued to meet success during his return journey through Persia, Susiana, and Mesene. Mani returned to the Persian Sassanid empire when the emperor Ardashir I died and his son Shapur I assumed the throne. He met with Shapur and was granted the freedom and protection to propagate the religion throughout the empire. Manichaeism was adopted by the emperor's family and influential political figures. During this period of imperial favor, Mani wrote the Shaburagan, a summary of his teachings in the Middle Persian language, and dedicated it to Shapur. Manichaeism then spread throughout Persia, beyond its borders, and even westward into the Roman Empire. Mani accompanied Shapur in the victorious Persian campaign against the Roman forces in which the Roman emperor Valerian was captured at Edessa in 260.

Although Mani enjoyed imperial favor under Shapur, the Magian clergy of the official state religion, Zoroastrianism, grew intent on persecuting the prophet. When Shapur I died, his successors Hormizd and Bahram I both favored the traditional state religion. The Zoroastrian high priest Kerder (or Karder), now strengthened by widespread nationalistic aspirations, was successful in convincing Bahram to begin official persecution of the minority movement. By order of the emperor, Mani was arrested, brought to Gundeshahbur (Susiana), interrogated for one month under Kerder, and died in prison.

MANICHAEAN SACRED TEXTS

The success of the intense heresiological polemic against Manichaeism resulted in the effective censorship and eventual elimination of Manichaean texts from the western and eastern manuscript traditions. Heretics of all types throughout the medieval period were uncritically slandered as Manichaeans. Even Luther's Catholic detractors spoke of a revived Manichaeism. The Protestant response demanded a more objective understanding of Manichaeism, investigated known Manichaean evidences, and so initiated the modern study of the religion.

From the sixteenth through the eighteenth centuries, the works of Christian and pagan heresiologists were studied in depth, resulting in the interpretation of Manichaeism as primarily a Christian heresy, rather than as an independent religion in its own right. This interpretation was proposed in the eighteenth century by the Calvinist theologian Isaac de Beausobre, who argued that Mani was a brilliant precursor of Luther and thus part of the history of reformed Christianity. Although this position was ultimately rejected, the great contribution of Beausobre's study was that it drew attention to the previously ignored eastern sources. About a hundred years later, Ferdinand Christian Baur emphasized the significance of the Buddhist, Indo-Iranian, and Zoroastrian elements in Manichaeism, thus bringing the study of Manichaeism into its natural interpretive context: that of the history of Eastern religions. Thereafter scholars began to recognize the significance of the newly discovered and less biased Arab authors, such as the historian Ibn al-Nadim, for a more objective understanding of Manichaeism. It was argued that Mani's eclectic Eastern religion was primarily based on Zoroastrianism and Mughtasilism, which Mani then creatively reinterpreted, using biblical models. Another study pushed Manichaean origins even further back in time to the pre-Zoroastrian beliefs of Babylonian religion. This study argued that Mani was concerned with recovering the original sources of Zoroaster's beliefs in an attempt to undercut his Magian opponents in the Sassanid court. To these ancient Babylonian beliefs it was suggested that Mani added elements from Buddhism, Christianity, and Mithraism.

During the twentieth century several great discoveries of Manichaean sacred texts have revolutionized our knowledge of Manichaeism. Those texts form three groups: Central Asian and Chinese sources, writings in Greek and Latin, and Coptic scriptures.

Central Asian and Chinese Texts

Between 1904 and 1914, German archeological teams were engaged in four expeditions of ruined Manichaean monasteries at Turfan and Qoco in Sinkiang, China, north of Tibet. The teams recovered thousands of fragments from heavily damaged Manichaean manuscripts. These Turfan fragments (many of which could not be conserved) are the disintegrated remains of what were once high-quality illuminated manuscripts that had suffered mutilation under Muslim conquerors. The texts are written in several Central Asian languages, and they are now conserved in the collection of the German Academy of Sciences in Berlin. Sir Aurel Stein discovered the remains of a large hoard of Buddhist and Manichaean manuscripts in the Temple of the

Thousand Buddhas at Tun-huang (east-southeast of Turfan). Stein recovered a long Manichaean confessional text entitled Confessional for the Hearers. Also discovered were three Manichaean texts translated into Chinese from Iranian-language originals, including the Treatise on Cosmogony and Its Implications for the Everyday Life of Manichaeans (now conserved in Beijing), the Hymn Scroll (now in London), and the Compendium of the Teaching of Mani, the Buddha of Light (now in London and Paris).

Western scholars are now informed of the numerous recent discoveries of Manichaean archaeological sites, artifacts, and texts in Central Asia and China through the works of S. N. C. Lieu and Geng Shimin. As an example of a most recent discovery of a Manichaean text in Chinese, Lin Wu-shu of Sun Yat Sen University (Guangzhou, China) published a fragmentary Manichaean inscription that was found in Fukien Province. The inscription on the large stele dates from 1315 to 1369, originally consisted of sixteen calligraphic Chinese characters, and is similar to another Manichaean inscription in Chinese in the famous Manichaean temple in Ch'üan-chou, also in Fukien Province. That temple, discovered in the 1950s, is today the only known intact Manichaean temple site and contains an intact low-relief statue of "Mani the Buddha of Light." Near the temple were found inscribed (ritual?) bowls and three Manichaean tombstones.

Greek and Latin Texts

Sensational discoveries of Manichaean manuscripts have also been made in the West. Albert Henrichs and Ludwig Koenen announced in 1970 the successful decipherment of a small parchment codex acquired by the University of Cologne. The Cologne Mani Codex dates from the end of the fourth or the beginning of the fifth century, or possibly later, and contains a Greek translation of a previously unknown Manichaean text originally written in Syriac, with the title On the Origin of His Body. The text seems to be an anthology containing quotations from the works of several of Mani's early disciples edited by a final redactor around a core of Mani's own autobiographical statements. The traditions contained in the Cologne Mani Codex concern Mani's latter days with the baptismal sect and his early missionary journeys after the age of twenty-four, and thus they constitute some of the most important sources of information on Mani's early life.

A fragmentary Manichaean parchment codex, the Tebessa Codex, was discovered in a cave near Theveste, Algeria, in 1918 and placed in the National

Library of Paris. Only twenty-five damaged leaves and the slight remains of four others are preserved from this codex, with each page originally carrying two columns of Latin text. The extant text contains two sections: an apologetic discussion on the relationship between the two major groups in the Manichaean church, the elect and the auditors, with allusions to and quotations of relevant canonical gospel texts; and a discussion in which the unknown Manichaean author defends the "nonwork ethic" of the Manichaean elect (who had their practical needs met by the auditors), apparently as an apologetic response to Christian charges that the messenger Paul had clearly condemned such dependent lifestyles in 2 Thessalonians 3:10b ("If anyone will not work, let that person not eat"). The Manichaean apologist begins with the Pauline text and then continues to defend the dependent lifestyles of the Manichaean elect, quoting or alluding to nearly every letter in the Pauline (and deutero-Pauline) canonical corpus.

Coptic Texts

Seven papyrus codices with Manichaean texts in the Coptic language were discovered by local workers digging through the ruins of an ancient house in the Fayyum town of Medinet Madi probably sometime in 1929. These books were all purchased in the next three years through a series of acquisitions by Sir Chester Beatty, an American businessman and art collector residing in England (two codices and parts of two others are now the property of the Chester Beatty Library, Dublin), and by the noted German papyrologist Carl Schmidt of Berlin (three codices and parts of two others are now the property of the State Museums of Berlin). A few leaves are in the national collections of Vienna and Warsaw. The seven books include a book of Psalms; a heavily damaged book of homiletical material (Greek, *synaxeis*), which may reflect or even be identified as the lost Living Gospel of Mani; two books of central principles (Greek, *kephalaia*); a book of Homilies; a book of Acts; and a book of Letters. Some of these Manichaean texts have been published, some still await publication, and some have been lost, owing to the confusion in Europe after World War II.

Manichaean literary and documentary texts dating to the fourth century have recently been discovered in the ancient town of Kellis in the Dakhleh Oasis of Egypt's western desert. Texts include Manichaean liturgies, doctrinal works, psalms, biblical texts, Syriac-Greek glossaries, and numerous private letters providing rare insights into Manichaean personal lifestyles. The texts may indicate that the earliest form of Christianity to enter the Oasis was in fact Manichaeism portraying itself as a type of Christianity.

MANICHAEAN TEACHINGS

Mani's teaching embraced a highly complex historical drama of supracosmic proportions in which humanity's past origin, present predicament, and future possibilities are described. The drama centers its theological concern on the existential question of the origin of evil in human experience. Mani employed a typical apocalyptic scheme in which cosmic history was divided into three time periods: past, present, and future.

In the past time there existed two eternal principles, one all good and the other all evil. The good principle exists exclusively within the kingdom of light and finds its focus in the father of greatness, whose fourfold majesty embraces divinity, light, power, and goodness. His throne is surrounded by at least 156 peace-loving entities: twelve aeons (or eternal realms, in three groups of four each) and 144 aeons of aeons. The kingdom of light is constructed of five elements or *stoicheia* (air, wind, light, water, and fire) and contains five peaceful "dwellings" (intelligence, knowledge, reason, thought, and deliberation). (In Manichaeism many things are given in five, even the five trees of paradise reminiscent of Gospel of Thomas 19.) The evil principle and the kingdom of darkness are the complete antitheses of the good principle and the kingdom of light. The many monstrous and agitated inhabitants of the kingdom of darkness are ruled by five evil archons (demon, lion, eagle, fish, and dragon), who are in constant opposition to each other and who, collectively, make up the hellish prince of darkness. They are sexually preoccupied and controlled by their passions, and they dwell in an ominous netherworld of smoke, fire, wind, water, and darkness. The two kingdoms are completely distinct yet eternally coexistent.

The "present time" begins when the evil inhabitants of the kingdom of darkness drive a wedge into the kingdom of light in a lustful desire to mingle with the light. The kingdom of darkness is thoroughly aroused, and its terrifyingly vicious inhabitants enter the light in a full-scale invasion. The father of greatness responds by evoking a series of entities who may need to be sacrificed to the invaders so as to satisfy them and stop the assault. The first evocation is the mother of life, who then evokes the primal man, who fights the incoming forces of darkness but loses his battle. The five evil archons (who constitute the prince of darkness) then consume some of the light elements of the primal man's armor. Having unwittingly fallen into the trap of the father of greatness, they are now dependent on the light for their continued existence. The primal man awakens from his sleep of forgetfulness, remembers his divine origins, and prays for his rescue. The father of greatness responds by evoking a series of beings who initiate the rescue of the primal man: the friend of lights evokes the great architect, who then evokes the living spirit, who evokes his five sons (the custodian of splendor, the great king of honor, Adamas of light, the king of glory, and Atlas). The living spirit cries out from the kingdom of light into the darkness to the primal man, who answers. The cry and answer (representing the divine word of salvation and the positive human response) are hypostasized, that is, they become divine beings who ascend to the kingdom of light. The living spirit then grasps the primal man by the hand and rescues him from the kingdom of darkness.

The rest of the drama in the "present time" focuses on the work of the father of greatness to regain all of the light particles swallowed by the five evil archons. The living spirit first creates ten heavens and eight earths out of the material corpses of the slain demons. He separates the swallowed light particles into three types: the first is undefiled, and from these he creates the sun and the moon; the second is only partly defiled, and from these he creates the stars; the third is completely defiled, and so he creates an elaborate cosmic mechanism to distill the light from the matter. The living spirit then evokes the third messenger, who evokes the zodiacal twelve maidens, collectively the maiden of light, who operate the cosmic three wheels created to distill the light particles out of the material universe. Another evocation is the column of glory (the Milky Way), which transports the recovered light particles from the distilling three wheels to the moon and then the sun, which function as ships transporting the light particles to their temporary haven (the new earth created by the great architect). The third messenger and the maiden of light then excite the sexual nature of the male archons, causing them to ejaculate the light particles from within them. The sin that excites the archons falls to the earth, becoming the source of all plant life. The female archons miscarry their light-bearing fetuses, which fall to the earth and copulate among themselves, becoming the source of all animal life. The sum total of all of these precious light particles trapped in deadly matter, including plants and animals, is called the suffering Jesus (Jesus *patibilis*), who is on the light cross (*crux luminus*).

The prince of darkness, in an attempt to frustrate the cosmic distillation of light particles, gives birth to the two evil demons, Sakla (Ashqulan) and Nebroel (Namrael), who eat the monstrous offspring of the miscarried fetuses in order to ingest their light particles. The two demons then copulate, and Nebroel gives birth to exact miniature replicas (the "image of God" of Genesis 1:26–27) of the confused light-matter macrocosm: Adam and Eve. In a typically gnostic "inverted exegesis" of Genesis 1–5 (a hermeneutical feature shared with some forms of gnosticism), the sexually oriented evil creator can create only by copulation and birth, and so can create only matter (which is inherently evil). He is unable to create in the manner of the father of greatness, by asexually evoking pure spiritual entities. Consequently, Adam (representing humanity) is specifically designed by the evil creator in his own image (Genesis 1:26) to procreate sexually (Genesis 1:27–28). Thus, Adam can only continue the evil cycle of birth, copulation, and rebirth, and in so doing he fulfills his natural evil inclination to "be fruitful and multiply" (Genesis 1:28; 5:4b). Adam's evil material nature (representing human sexuality) thus entangles the precious light particles, transmitted through male seed, in potentially endless generations of material bodies (representing human history; see Genesis 5:1–32).

But Adam is ignorant of the light within him and his true origin in the kingdom of light and so is unable to recognize and redeem the light particles. The evocations of the father of greatness then send Jesus of light to awaken Adam (Genesis 3:1) to inform him of his true nature (Genesis 3:4–5) and to lead him to self-recognition (Genesis 3:7, 11a, 22a). Jesus of light helps Adam eat of the salvific tree of life (Genesis 3:22), warns him of the dangers of sexual procreation with Eve, and so encourages a sexually abstinent lifestyle (the ideal model of behavior in Manichaean ethics). Then Eve and a male archon copulate, and Eve gives birth to Cain (Genesis 4:1), who then copulates with his mother Eve, who gives birth to Abel (Genesis 4:2), and so begins the incestuous interaction of Cain (Genesis 4:2a) and Abel with Eve and with each other's daughters borne by Eve (Genesis 4:17). Eve then receives magical knowledge from an evil archon, which enables her to copulate with the ascetic Adam. She succeeds in her desire and bears Seth (Genesis 4:25a), who, as the first true son of Adam (Genesis 5:3, 4b), contains a significantly larger amount of light particles than the other offspring of Eve. The ascetic Adam and Seth, self-conscious particles of light entrapped in innately evil material bodies, become the exemplary human figures for Manichaean ethics (Genesis 4:26b; 5:1–32).

The "future time" is the third and final act of the historical cosmic drama, and it provides for Manichaean ethics a preview into the system of reward and punishment. The final and great war will break out among the unenlightened powers of darkness when the distillation of light particles from the material cosmos has neared its completion. Jesus will return at a decisive eschatological moment as the great king and will judge humanity and the infernal powers. The elect will become angels, the auditors will be judged righteous, and the sinners will be cast into hell with the sexually promiscuous woman Eve and her hellish offspring. The cosmos will disintegrate and burn in a conflagration for 1,468 years. The remaining light particles will be gathered and finally return by ascent to the kingdom of light, while the prince of darkness and his diabolical minions will be cast into a bottomless pit permanently sealed with a huge stone for all eternity. The two principles of light and darkness will again be two separate and distinct entities, never again to commingle.

THE MANICHAEAN CHURCH

Just as Jesus of light was the prime evocation of liberation for Adam, so the great mind (*nous*) is the prime evocation of Jesus of light for the liberation of Adam's descendants throughout human history, thus providing the unique Manichaean solution to the human predicament. The primary redemptive function of the great mind is to reveal the true knowledge of the origin and destination of the human soul (self-recognition), and the two central precepts of Manichaean belief: the three periods of cosmic history, and the existence of two eternally antithetic and supracosmic principles.

Individual human beings are replicant microcosms of the confused "light-matter" macrocosm. As such they endure an eternal struggle within their own souls for release from matter and return to their true home in the immaterial kingdom of light. After the individual human soul has been awakened by the great mind (a typical experience of regeneration), that individual is conscious of the eternal dualistic realities that control its fate, and it then can hope to succeed against influences from the lower nature. This internal struggle was described by Mani in Pauline terms concerning the "new person" (1 Corinthians 3:9–10) and the "old person" (Ephesians 4:22–24), who are locked in mortal combat. The individual can succeed in this struggle through the continued protection of the great mind, which is accessible only in the teaching of Mani and the guidance of the Manichaean church. Strict adherence to the extreme ascetic requirements (sexual abstinence, poverty, vegetarianism) is impossible to enforce on the popular level and, were such strict adherence to succeed, would result in the eventual extinction of the human race. Knowing that such commitment could only be expected from himself and a few choice believers, Mani divided his church into two basic classes, the elect and the auditors.

The elect are required to keep the "five commandments" (to be pure and poor and not to lie, kill, or eat flesh) and to adhere to the "three seals." First, the seal of the mouth (*signacula oris*) includes the avoidance of evil speech, the drinking of alcohol, and the eating of meat. The vegetarian requirement was imperative for the elect because plants contain more light particles than flesh. The light particles are digested through the bodies of the vegetarian elect, released through their belches into the atmosphere, distilled by the cosmic machine of the three wheels, and finally sent on their homeward journey along the column of glory (Milky Way) to the kingdom of light. For this belief heresiologists ridiculed the Manichaean elect as "saviors of god" (*salvatores dei*). Second, the seal of the hands (*signacula manuum*) forbids the elect from any activity that might injure material objects containing light particles. Thus killing animals, planting, harvesting, or even walking over the smallest plants could prevent the liberation of the light particles (the divine suffering Jesus). Because the procuring and preparation of vegetable foodstuffs often required the damaging or partial destruction of light-bearing plants, the elect were not permitted to prepare their own meals, and instead were served by the auditors, who were pardoned for the unavoidable destruction of plants. Even bathing with water was not allowed for the elect, since water could be defiled by contact with material bodily substances. Third, the seal of the breast (*signacula sinus*) focused especially on the avoidance of sexual intercourse, since the process of birth, copulation, and rebirth was directly related to Adam's lower material nature and was meant by the evil creator to enslave light particles in material bodies. The "three seals" were required for all Manichaean elect, while the auditors were given lesser requirements, allowing them to acquire wealth and to marry and maintain mistresses, but were urged to avoid sexual relations. Only the elect would return to the kingdom of light directly after death, while the auditors could only hope to enter into the bodies of vegetables after death and finally be freed through the digestive systems of later elect. All humans who are not awakened by the great mind will be forever damned into an inescapable cycle of reincarnation in the bodies of animals, culminating in their permanent entrapment in the kingdom of darkness.

The leadership of the Manichaean church comprised the elect. Extant Manichaean texts in Latin, Greek, Middle Persian, and Chinese are unanimous in documenting the four classes within the church hierarchy: the central figurehead or pope (Greek, *archegos*; Latin, *princeps*), who is Mani's successor;

the twelve messengers; the seventy-two bishops; and the 360 elders. Only males could be enrolled in these four classes. Apart from this governmental hierarchy is the larger body of the elect and the even larger group of auditors. Modern research on the place and function of women in Manichaeism has only recently begun.

The complex mythological structures inherent in Manichaean theology are the result of Mani's own creative genius and his diverse theological sources. This complexity first begs the question as to why Mani, wishing to communicate to the masses, would create such a difficult system reminiscent of the "fables and endless genealogies" previously decried by the author of the First Letter to Timothy in the New Testament (1:4). One suggestion concerns point of view. Today we see Mani as a creative theologian, but he saw himself as a receptive vehicle of divine revelation, so that the complexity was not his invention but was given to him by the spirit of revelation, as he was merely the prophet of god.

Mani's theological complexity also begs the question as to who could understand the fantastic mythological structures. Did the complexity inadvertently function to limit the number of converts to Mani's religion? No doubt it did, since the heresiological responses indicate that educated theologians, such as Alexander of Lycopolis, struggled to understand Mani's system. That Mani should summarize his own teachings in the Shaburagan indicates that the complexity of the system was already a problem Mani himself tried to overcome. The problem is further indicated within Manichaean social structure itself and the existence of two classes of Manichaean devotees, the elect and the auditors. This bifurcated structure demonstrates that the ability to live the more difficult life of the elect was coupled with their ability to search the Manichaean scriptures and arrive at a full knowledge of the truth, while the auditors understood less and thus less was required of them. Those who ultimately rejected the teaching were considered to be blind, not simply confused by the complexity.

The Manichaean texts that follow present these sorts of issues in the life of Mani, Manichaean teachings, and Manichaean mythology and theology. As with many religious texts, these Manichaean texts may outlast the traditional keepers of the word. The glory is that the word may remain for readers to discover.

38

On the Origin of His Body

O n the Origin of His Body is the title of the text in the Cologne Mani Codex, a miniature parchment manuscript written in Greek and dated to the late fourth or early fifth century. The text's chief significance is what it says about the life of Mani, including his time, early in his life, among the Jewish-Christian Elkesaites. The Elkesaites, named after their legendary prophet and founder Elkesai (or Elchasai; his name is said to designate the "hidden power of god"), constituted a baptizing religion with Jewish and Christian affinities. Like Jews for Jesus or Messianic Jews of the present day, the Elkesaites and other Jewish Christians tried to practice both Jewish and Christian piety, thereby seeking to avoid having to choose one and reject the other. Christian Jewish observance was—and is to the present day—a creative piety, but one that is hard to maintain in the face of religious, social, and political pressures. Mani's father belonged to an Elkesaite community, and Mani himself was initiated into this baptizing group when he was four years old. The Mandaeans are also a part of this Middle Eastern world of baptizing religions.

On the Origin of His Body may be so named because of its concern for the life and body of Mani, or it may be given its title in reference to the Manichaean church (according to the apostle Paul the church is the body of Christ). According to the portion of this text translated here, Mani declares in his own writings that he came to a knowledge of secrets and the truth, and his twin was sent to him. Various of his students, it is suggested in the headings of the text, also document features of Mani's career: his life among the baptizers, the coming of his twin, his teachings and debates with the Elkesaites. Mani appealed to the words and deeds of Jesus and to the baptists themselves to formulate his arguments against Elkesaite teachings and observance of the law, particularly the food laws and laws of cleanliness. Mani was judged by his followers to be an innovative teacher with an innovative message, and eventually he went out to found a new Manichaean church.

ON THE ORIGIN
OF HIS BODY[1]

SECRETS WERE REVEALED TO MANI

Also in this way, it is fitting for the all-praiseworthy messenger[2] Mani, through whom and from whom has come to us the hope and inheritance of life, to write to us and to provide interpretation for all posterity, the householders of faith, and those who are spiritual offspring, increasing through his most limpid waters, so that his rapture and revelation may be known to them. For we know, brothers, with this arrival of the comforter[3] of truth, how great the magnitude of his wisdom is in relationship to us. We acknowledge that he has received it neither from people, nor from the reading of books, just as our father Mani himself says in the letter that he sent to Edessa. For he says thus:

"The truth and the secrets that I speak about—and the laying on of hands that is mine—not from people have I received it nor from fleshly creatures, not even from studies in the scriptures. But when my most blessed father, who called me into his grace, saw me, since he did not wish me and the rest who are in the world to perish, he felt compassion, so that he might extend his well-

---

1. On the Origin of His Body: revised by Willis Barnstone mainly from the translation by Ron Cameron and Arthur J. Dewey, *The Cologne Mani Codex* (*P. Colon. inv. nr. 4780*): *Concerning the Origin of His Body*. Texts and Translations Early Christian Literature Series 15.3 (Missoula, MT: Scholars Press, 1979), pp. 49–79. Reprinted by permission of Society of Biblical Literature. Also revised from Ellen Bradshaw Aitken, "The Cologne Mani Codex," in Richard Valantasis, ed., *Religions of Late Antiquity in Practice*, Princeton Readings in Religions (Princeton and Oxford: Princeton University Press, 2000), pp. 169–70. Reprinted by permission of Princeton University Press.
2. Or "apostle," here and throughout the text.
3. Or "paraclete," also referred to in the Gospel of John.

being to those prepared to be chosen by him from the sects. Then, by his grace, he pulled me from the council of the many who do not recognize the truth and revealed to me his secrets and those of his undefiled father and of all the cosmos.[4] He disclosed to me how I was before the foundation of the world, and how the groundwork of all the works, both good and evil, was laid, and how everything of this aggregation was engendered according to its present boundaries and times."

I, MANI, HAVE SEEN THE TRUTH

He wrote thus again and said in the gospel of his most holy hope,[5]

"I, Mani, a messenger of Jesus Christ through the will of god, the father of truth, from whom I also was born, who lives and abides forever, existing before all and also abiding after all. All things that are and will be subsist through his power. For from this very one I was conceived, and I am from his will. From him all that is true was revealed to me, and I am from his truth. The truth of ages that he revealed I have seen, and that truth I have disclosed to my fellow travelers; peace I have announced to the children of peace, hope I have proclaimed to the immortal race. The elect[6] I have chosen, and a path to the height I have shown to those who ascend according to this truth. Hope I have proclaimed, and this revelation I have revealed. This immortal gospel I have written, including in it these eminent mysteries, and disclosing in it the greatest works, the greatest and most august forms of the most eminently powerful works. These things that he revealed I have shown to those who live from the truest vision, which I have seen, and from the most glorious revelation revealed to me."

Again he said,

"All the secrets that my father has given to me, while I have hidden and covered them from the sects and the pagans, and still more from the world, to you I have revealed according to the pleasure of my most blessed father. And if again he would be pleased, once more I shall reveal them to you. For indeed, the gift that was given to me from the father is very great and rich. For if the whole world and all people obey it, I would be able from this very possession and advantage, which my father has given to me, to enrich them and establish wisdom as sufficient for the entire world."[7]

---

4. This claim to revelation recalls Paul's claim in Galatians 1:11–17.
5. This most likely refers to Mani's Living Gospel.
6. The elect, or the perfect, are the leaders in the Manichaean church.
7 Manichaeism is intended to be a universal religion.

MANI'S TWIN

Again he said,

"When my father was pleased and had shown compassion and care for me, he sent out from there my most unfailing twin,[8] the entire fruit of immortality, that he might redeem and ransom me from the error of those followers of that law.[9] In coming to me, he has provided me with the best hope, redemption, which is based on immortality, true instructions, and the laying on of hands from my father. Now, when that one came, he preferred and chose me, severed and pulled me out of the midst of those followers of that law in which I was reared."

Now, very many other extraordinary things like these are in the books of our father, which demonstrate both his revelation and the rapture of his position as messenger.[10] For very great is the abundance of this coming that, through the comforter, the spirit of truth, is coming to us.

Now, concerning these things, why are they sifted thoroughly by us, who are once and for all convinced that this position as messenger excels in its revelations? For this reason we have repeated from our forefathers their rapture and the revelation of each one, namely, for the sake of the considerations of those who have put on unbelief and who think they know something about this revelation and vision of our father Mani, that they might acknowledge that such was also the commission given to the earlier messengers. For when each of them was snatched up, all these things that he saw and heard he wrote down and set forth, and he himself became a witness of his own revelation. But his students became seals of his position as messenger.[11]

BARAIES THE TEACHER: MANI IS CHOSEN FROM AMONG THE ELKESAITES

We, then, brothers, being children of the spirit of our father Mani, who also have heard and listened to these things,[12] thus let us rejoice in them and

---

8. Mani's twin is his heavenly double or alter ego. The twin also figures prominently in the Gospel of Thomas and other Syrian literature.
9. The followers of the law (or Torah) are the Jewish-Christian Elkesaites.
10. Or "apostleship."
11. This paragraph establishes Mani's students as authorities on his teaching—hence the headings that follow.
12. In this and succeeding sections, teachings about Mani are presented in the name of his students, as the headings indicate.

recognize his coming spiritually, how he was sent by a command of his father and in what way he was conceived in the body, and how his most august twin came to him and set him apart from the law in which his body was reared. For in his twenty-fifth year the twin was revealed magnificently to him.[13] For while he was still in that sect of the baptists, he was like a lamb dwelling in a strange flock, or like a bird living with other birds of a different song. For always with wisdom and skill he dwelt in their midst during all that time: none of them recognized him as to who he was, or what he had received, or what had been revealed to him. Rather, they regarded him among themselves in this manner, according to the standards of the body.

ABIESOUS THE TEACHER AND INNAIOS BROTHER OF ZABED: MANI REJECTS EARTHLY TREASURES FOR DIVINE ONES

The lord Mani said,

"When I was dwelling in their midst, one day Sitaios, the elder of their council, the son of Gara, took me by the hand, because he greatly loved me and regarded me as a beloved son. He took me, then, by the hand—no one else was with us—and went, dug up and showed me very great treasures, which he kept secretly buried. He said to me, 'These treasures are mine and I have control of them. From now on they will be yours. For I love no one else like you, and to you I shall give these treasures.' When he had thus spoken to me I said in my heart, 'My most blessed father preferred me and has given to me an immortal treasure that does not pass away. Whoever inherits it will receive immortal life from it.'[14]

"Then I spoke to Sitaios the elder: 'Where are the forefathers, who acquired these earthly treasures before us, they who inherited them? For, consider, they are dead and gone and they did not keep them as their own, neither did they carry them off with themselves.'"

He, Mani, spoke to him:

"'What good, then, are these treasures to me, which introduce sins and offenses to everyone who acquires them? For the treasure of god is very great and exceedingly rich and will bring everyone who inherits it to life.'[15] When

---

13. When Mani was twenty-four, his twin appeared and told him to begin preaching the new thought.

14. Or "from him" (the father).

15. Earthly treasures and the treasure of god are also discussed in the teaching of Jesus in Matthew 6:19–21; Luke 12:33–34; Gospel of Thomas 76; Gospel of Mary.

Sitaios saw that my mind was not persuaded to the acquisition of the treasures that he showed me, he was altogether astonished at me."

TIMOTHY: THE DROWNING OF SITA

"Then after a little while I, Mani, determined thus to declare to Sita and those of his council what my most blessed father had revealed to me, and to show them the path of holiness.[16] But while I was considering these things, there appeared to me the entire world, which had become like a sea full of very dark waters; and I saw thousands and tens of thousands brought down into it, plunged down, bobbing up, and spinning about the four corners of the sea. I saw in the midst of it a foundation laid and of very great height, and over it alone a light rising, and a road laid upon it, and myself walking on this. When I turned round I beheld Sita, holding on to some person who was held by someone else, and perishing in the midst of the sea and the darkness, after he had fallen and gone under the surface. I could see only a little bit of his hair, so that I was distressed greatly on account of Sita. But that one who cast him out said to me, 'Why are you distressed about Sita? For he is not of your elect, nor will he walk on your way.' Then, when I saw these things, I revealed nothing to him, Sita. But later, when I was preaching the word of truth, I saw him opposing my teaching."

BARAIES THE TEACHER: MANI DEBATES THE ELKESAITES ABOUT OBSERVANCE

My lord Mani said,

"I have had enough debating with each one in that law, rising up and questioning them concerning the way of god, the commandments of the savior, the washing, the vegetables they wash, and their every ordinance and order according to which they walk.[17]

"Now, when I destroyed and put aside their words and their mysteries, demonstrating to them that they had not received these things that they pursue from the commandments of the savior, some of them were amazed at me, but others got cross and angrily said, 'Does he not want to go to the Greeks?'[18] When I saw their intent, I responded, gently, 'This washing by which you wash

---

16. Sita as an opponent of Mani is discussed below.
17. These matters of law and observance are key concerns in the life and thought of the Elkesaites.
18. That is, to nonobservant gentiles.

your food is of no avail. For this body is defiled and molded from a mold of defilement. You can see how, whenever someone cleanses his food and partakes of that food that has just been washed, it seems to us that from it still come blood and bile and flatulence and excrements of shame and the defilement of the body. But if someone were to keep his mouth away from this washed food for a few days, immediately all these offals of shame and loathsomeness will be recognized as lacking and wanting in the body. But if that one were to eat of food again, in the same way the offals would again abound in the body, so that it is clear that they swell from the food itself. But if someone else were first to partake of food that is washed and cleansed, and then partake of food that is unwashed, it is clear that the beauty and the power of the body is recognized as the same in either case. Likewise, the loathsomeness and dregs of both types of food are seen as not differing from each other, so that what has been washed, which the body rejected and sloughed off, is not at all distinguishable from that other, which is unwashed."[19]

WHAT PURITY REALLY IS

"'Now the fact that you wash in water each day is of no avail. For having been washed and purified once and for all, why do you wash again each day? So that also by this it is manifest that you are disgusted with yourselves each day and that you must wash yourselves on account of loathsomeness before you can become purified. And by this too it is clear most evidently that all the foulness is from the body. And indeed, you also have put the body on.[20]

"Therefore, make an inspection of yourselves as to what your purity really is.[21] For it is impossible to purify your bodies completely, since each day the body is disturbed and comes to rest through the excretions of feces from it, so that the action comes about without a commandment from the savior. The purity, then, which was spoken about, is that which comes through knowledge, a separation of light from darkness, of death from life, of living waters from turbid, so that you may know that each is different from the other and you may keep the commandments of the savior, so that he might redeem the soul from annihilation and destruction. This is in truth the genuine purity, which you were commanded to do; but you departed from it and began to bathe, and have held on to the purification of the body, a thing most defiled

---

19. Washing food does not remove defilement. See Gospel of Thomas 14 and parallels.
20. Washing or baptizing the body does not make it pure. See Gospel of Thomas 29, 56, 80, 87, 112.
21. Part of this paragraph is restored; see Cameron and Dewey, *The Cologne Mani Codex*, 67.

and fashioned through foulness; through foulness the body was coagulated and, having been built up, came into existence."

THE ELKESAITES DEBATE ABOUT MANI

"When I said these things to them, and destroyed and demolished that very thing they were zealous for, some of them, marveling at me, praised me and regarded me as a leader and teacher; but there arose much slander in that sect on account of me. Some of them regarded me as a prophet and teacher. Some of them were saying, 'A living word is uttered by him; let us make him a teacher of our doctrine.' Others were saying, 'Has a voice really spoken to him in secret, and does he say those things that it revealed to him?' Some were saying, 'Did something appear to him in a dream, and does he tell of what he saw?' Others were saying, 'Is this really the one about whom our teachers prophesied, saying, "A certain young man will rise up from our midst and a new teacher will come forth to overturn all our teaching in the way our forefathers spoke concerning the rest[22] of the garment"?' Others were saying, 'Surely, then, is it not error that speaks through him, and does he not wish to lead our people astray and divide our teaching?' Others of them were filled with jealousy and rage, some of whom were voting for my death.

"Others were saying, 'He is the enemy of our law.' Some were saying, 'He wishes to go to the gentiles and eat Greek bread, for we have heard him saying, "It is necessary to partake of Greek bread." Likewise, he says it follows to partake of drink, bread, vegetables, and fruit, which our fathers and teachers enjoined us not to eat. Further, the washing by which we wash ourselves he destroys and does not wash himself like us, nor does he wash his food as we do.'

"So, then, when Sita and his companions saw that I would not give in to their testing, but that little by little I was destroying and rejecting their own law and the food that they rejected, and that I was not practicing the washing as they were; when they saw me opposing them in all these things, then Sita and the group of his fellow presbyters set up a synod on my account. They also summoned the master of the house, Pattikios, and said to him, 'Your son has turned aside from our law and wishes to go into the world. Wheat bread and fruit and vegetables, which we exclude and do not eat, all these things he does not follow and says it is necessary to overturn these things. He makes of no

---

22. Greek *anapausis,* divine rest or repose.

avail the washing in the way it is practiced by us.[23] And he wishes to eat Greek bread.' Now, Pattikios, because he had seen their very great uproar, said to them, 'Summon him yourselves and persuade him.'"

WHAT HAPPENED TO YOU, MANI?

"Then, when they summoned me to them, they gathered around and said to me, 'From youth you have been with us, doing well in the ordinances and customs of our law. You have been like a demure young girl in our midst. Now what has happened to you, what has appeared to you? For you oppose our law and destroy and reject our teaching. You have adopted a different way of life from ours. We hold your father in greatest esteem. Why, then, do you now destroy the washing of our law and that of the fathers, in which we have walked from of old? You even destroy the commandments of the savior; you even wish to eat wheat bread and vegetables, which we do not eat. Why do you live so, not submitting to till the earth like us?'"

MANI APPEALS TO THE EXAMPLE OF
JESUS AND HIS STUDENTS

"Then I said to them, 'In no way would I destroy the commandments of the savior. But if you reproach me on account of wheat bread, because I have said, "It is necessary to eat of it," this the savior has done; as it is written, that when he had blessed it and shared it with his students, "over bread he said a blessing and gave it to them."[24] Was not that bread from wheat? The scripture points out that he reclined to eat with tax collectors and idolaters.[25] Likewise, he also reclined to eat in the house of Martha and Mary on the occasion when Martha said to him, "Lord, do you not care enough for me so as to tell my sister to help me?" and the savior said to her, "Mary has chosen the good portion, and it will not be taken away from her."[26] Consider, moreover, how even the students of the savior ate bread from women and idolaters and did not separate bread from bread, nor vegetable from vegetable; nor did they eat, while laboring in

---

23. Or "But he does not wash himself in the way we do" (reconstruction by Walter Burkert in Cameron and Dewey, *Cologne Mani Codex,* 73).
24. See Matthew 26:26; Mark 14:22; Luke 22:19; 1 Corinthians 11:23–24.
25. Matthew 11:19; Luke 7:34.
26. Luke 10:38–42.

the toil and tilling of the land, as you do today. Likewise, when the savior sent his students out to preach in each place, neither mill nor oven did they carry with them, but made haste, taking one garment. . . .'"[27]

ZACHIAS: MANI APPEALS TO THE TEACHINGS OF ELKESAI

"If, then, you accuse me, Mani, about the washing, look, again I prove to you from your law and from those things revealed to your leaders that it is not necessary to wash. For Elkesai, the founder of your law, points this out. When he was going to bathe in the waters, an image of a man appeared to him from the source of the waters, saying to him, 'Is it not enough that your animals injure me, but do you yourself also mistreat me without reason and profane my waters?'[28] So Elkesai marveled and said to it, 'Fornication, defilement, and impurity of the world are thrown into you and you do not refuse them, but are you grieved with me?' The water said to him, 'Granting that all these have not recognized me as to who I am, you, who say that you are a servant and righteous, why have you not guarded my honor?'

"And then Elkesai was upset and did not bathe in the waters.

"Again, a long time after, he wished to bathe in the waters. He commanded his students to look out for a place not having much water, so that he might bathe. His students found such a place for him. As he was about to bathe, the image of a man appeared to him again, a second time, from that source, saying to him, "We and those waters in the lake are one. You have come, therefore, even here to wrong and injure us."[29] Trembling greatly and upset, Elkesai allowed the mud upon his head to dry, and thus he pointed it out."[30]

Again he, Mani, demonstrates that Elkesai had plows in storage and went to them. The earth spoke to him, saying, "Why do you make your living from me?" Elkesai, having taken soil from the earth that spoke to him, wept, kissed it, and placed it upon his breast and began to say, "This is the flesh and blood of my lord."[31]

---

27. Matthew 10:5–15; Mark 6:8–11; Luke 9:2–5; 10:3–12.
28. The water complains about being polluted.
29. The water complains again.
30. Or "he wiped it off" (reconstruction by Walter Burkert in Cameron and Dewey, *Cologne Mani Codex*, 77).
31. The soil complains about being used by people, and Elkesai confesses that the soil is of the lord.

Mani said again that Elkesai found his students baking bread. The bread spoke with Elkesai, and he commanded them to bake no longer.[32]

MANI APPEALS TO THE EXAMPLES OF THE VEGETABLES AND DATE PALM TREE

Again Mani points out that Sabbaios, the baptist, was carrying vegetables to the elder of the city. And immediately that produce said to him, "Are you not righteous? Are you not pure? Why do you carry us away to the fornicators?" Thus Sabbaios was upset on account of what he heard and returned the vegetables.

Again Mani points out that a date palm tree spoke with Aianos, the baptist from Koche, and commanded him to say to the date palm's owner, "Don't cut me down because my fruit is stolen, but grant me this year. And in the course of this year I shall give you fruit proportionate to what has been stolen, and in all the other years hereafter." But it also commanded him to say to that man who was stealing its fruit, "Do not come at this season to steal my fruit away. If you come, I shall hurl you down from my height and you will die."[33]

TIMOTHY: MANI IS CONFRONTED AND BEATEN BY THE BAPTISTS

Then Mani said to them, "Consider these famous men of your law, those who saw these visions, who were moved by them and proclaimed them as good news[34] to others. Likewise, I too practice everything I was taught by them."

"While I was speaking to them, reducing their words to nothing, suddenly they became angry and violent, and one of them even got up and hit me. They huddled around me and beat me. They grabbed my hair as though I were an enemy. They shouted at me in a loud voice that grew bitter and angry as at someone who was superstitious. Out of malice, they wanted to strangle me. Because Pattikios, the master of the house, begged them not to be impious toward people among them, they were ashamed and released me. After I went through this trial, I withdrew to one side and stood praying. I prayed for our lord to come to my aid."

---

32. The bread complains about being baked.
33. The vegetables and the palm tree complain about being treated badly, and the palm tree threatens to throw down the person stealing its dates.
34. Or "gospel."

THE TWIN APPEARS AND COMMISSIONS MANI

"When I finished praying and was filled with grief, my most blessed twin,[35] who is my master and supporter, appeared before me. He said to me, 'Don't be upset and don't cry.'

"I told him, 'Why shouldn't I be upset? The people of this sect, with whom I lived since my youth, have changed and become enemies to me because I stood apart from their law. Where shall I go? All the sects and parties are hostile to the good, and I myself am a stranger and solitary in the world. When I was in the sect of those who study chastity, flagellation of the flesh, and self-control, and who all still know me by name, I also had a certain connection with its leaders and elders during the training of my body.[36] If these men have not given room to receive the truth, how will the world, its leaders, or its teachings receive me and hear these ineffable matters and accept these weighty commandments? And how shall I act before the rulers of the world and the leaders of the sects? Look, they are high and mighty in wealth, confidence, and possessions, and I am alone and poor.'

"The most honored one[37] said to me, 'You have not been sent to this sect alone, but to every nation and teaching and city and place. Through you will hope be clear and preached in all regions of the world. Many will accept your word. So travel about, for I myself am with you as an ally and protector wherever you speak what I have revealed. And do not be distressed or grieved.'"[38]

---

35. On Mani's twin, see above.
36. This fragmentary sentence is paraphrased here.
37. Again, Mani's twin.
38. This commission by the twin resembles the commission of the students of Jesus in Matthew 28:16–20 and at the conclusion of the Letter of Peter to Philip. With this commission and promise Mani goes forth to preach.

39

The Story of the Death of Mani

T he various descriptions of Mani's last days and death range from the one here, which says nothing of Mani's suffering and emphasizes his disciplined calm and salvation, to others that speak of his torture and martyrdom. While Mani had enjoyed support from the Persian king Shapur I, with the advent of Bahram I his fate changed. The Zoroastrian magi were eager to consolidate their national religion and to halt the spread of Manichaeism and Christianity. The high priest Karder, who appears in the text, may have engineered Mani's imprisonment and death. After the unfortunate audience with the king, Mani was fettered and taken away in chains. While in his cell, he was apparently able to speak to his close followers, and during these days he designated his twelve messengers and seventy-two bishops, who would form the clerical structure of his church. The story of his execution parallels the story of the death of Jesus in the New Testament gospels, including the Gospel of John. In John 17, the so-called high priestly prayer, Jesus discusses with god his accomplishments on earth, even as Mani does in his prayer to Ohrmizd, below.

By some accounts Mani died by fasting and mortification and "at eleven o'clock ascended out of his body to the great sanctuary on high." Other documents say the messenger of light was flayed alive or was crucified. A song from the Coptic Manichaean Songbook has the king ordering a burning torch thrust through Mani's body to insure that he is dead; he then orders the body cut up and the head set on a pike high over the city gate. This burning torch may be compared to the spear jabbed into Jesus' side to guarantee his expiration according to the Gospel of John.

THE STORY OF THE DEATH OF MANI[1]

BAHRAM I AND MANI

Mani came to the audience of Bahram I, after the king had summoned me—Nuhzadag the interpreter—and Kushtai the scribe, and Abzakhya the Persian. The king was at the dinner table and had not yet washed his hands nor finished his meal.

The courtiers entered and said, "Mani has come and is standing at the door."

The king sent the lord the message, "Wait awhile until I can come to you myself."

Then the lord again sat down to one side of the guard and waited there until the king had finished his meal, when he was to have gone hunting.

The king stood up after his meal. After putting one arm around the queen of the Sakas and the other around Karder,[2] son of Ardavan, he came to the lord. His first words to the lord were, "You are not welcome here."

"Why? What wrong have I done?" replied the lord.

"I have sworn an oath not to let you come to this land!" And then he angrily told the lord, "What good are you? You don't fight or go hunting. Perhaps you are needed for doctoring and healing, but you don't even do that!"

Then the lord told him, "I have done you no evil. I have always done good in tending you and your family. And I have freed a multitude of your servants from demons and witches. And I caused many to rise from their sicknesses. I have held down the fever of many. And many who died I brought back to life."

---

1. The Story of the Death of Mani: translated by Jes P. Asmussen, *Manichaean Literature: Representative Texts Chiefly from Middle Persian and Parthian Writings*, UNESCO Collection of Representative Works: Persian Heritage Series 22 (Delmar, N.Y.: Scholars' Facsimiles & Reprints, 1975), pp. 54–58, from M 3 verso, M 5569 recto, and M 5569 verso; revised in verse by Willis Barnstone. Reprinted by permission of Bibliotecha Persica.
2. The high priest.

MANI'S SPIRITUAL VOYAGE TO THE FATHER IN THE SKY

Like a sovereign who removes and lays his weapons aside
and also his clothes and puts on another royal garment,
so the messenger of light laid aside the warlike dress of the body
and took his seat in a ship of light,[3]
where he received the divine garment, the diadem of light,
and the beautiful garland.
Then in great joy he flew with the light gods
who were on his right and on his left,
with the music of the harp and songs of happiness.
He flew because of holy miraculous power
like swift lightning and a star darting to the column of glory,[4]
the path of the light, and the moon chariot[5]
where the gods meet.
And there he remained with god, Ohrmizd the father.[6]
Yet below him, Mani had left the whole flock
of the just-orphaned and sad.

PRAYER TO OHRMIZD

The ever powerful one stood in prayer, imploring the father with praise:[7]
I have cleaned the earth and spread the seed
and the fruit full of life I have brought you.
I have built a palace and a quiet monastery
for your spirit.
And the holy spirit I sowed in a green flower garden
and brought you a delightful garland.
Brilliant trees I made fruitful
and showed the road leading to the sons high in the air.
I entirely fulfilled your holy commands

---

3. The moon and sun are ships of light to transport the light to the realm above; on riding the moon, see below.
4. The Milky Way.
5. The moon as a ship of light.
6. Ohrmazd, or Ahura Mazda, the good god in Zoroastrianism.
7. Note also the prayer of Jesus in John 17.

and for them I was sent into the world.
Take me now into the peace of salvation
where I will no longer glance at the figures of enemies,
nor hear the voice of tyrants.
For the time of this birth,
unlike my earlier ones,
affords me the garland of victory.

THE EARTH TREMBLES AS HE ENTERS NIRVANA

On the fourth of the month of Shahrevar, on Monday at the eleventh hour, when he had prayed, Mani shed the wonted garment of the body.

Like the swift lightning he gleamed
brighter than the light of the sun, the chariot glittered,
and the messengers spoke and greeted the just god.
The sides of the house of the sky broke.
The earth trembled. A mighty voice was heard,
and people who saw this sign were confused
and fell on their faces.[8]
It was a day of pain and a time of sorrow
when the messenger of light entered death,
when he entered the complete *nirvana*.[9]

COMMANDS FROM THE CHARIOT OF WATER

He left behind the leaders guarding the church. Mani the noble prince has fulfilled his promise, telling us,

For you I shall wait above in the chariot of water,
on the moon, my resting place until the world is saved,
and always send down help to you.

---

8. This description finds parallels in the apocalyptic signs accompanying the death of Jesus in the New Testament gospels, especially Matthew, and in accounts of transfigurations and heavenly ascents in 1 Enoch and other Jewish and Christian literature.
9. This is *parinirvana*, the Buddhist realm of death and liberation. Here is one of many authenticating references proving the centrality of Buddhism in Mani's formulation of gnosticism.

Whoever strikes you, do not strike back.
Whoever hates you, do not hate back.
Whoever envies you, do not envy again.
Whoever strikes you with anger, always return him kindness,
and what you deplore in others do not yourself do.[10]
No, you must endure insults and abuses
from those of higher station, from equals and those below,
because you who are devout and endure will not waver.
If someone throws flowers against an elephant,
these flowers cannot smash an elephant.
If raindrops fall on a stone,
these raindrops cannot melt the stone.
So insults and abuses can in no way make the devout
and of good endurance waver.

---

10. The golden rule (here in a negative formulation), found also for example in Gospel of
Thomas 6.

40

The Kephalaia

The Kephalaia (sing., Kephalaion), meaning the headings or central principles, is a series of chapters of varying length that present Mani discussing basic Manichaean doctrine with his students. Iain Gardner provides a good, succinct description of the style of the chapters:

> In general they follow a standard pattern wherein a disciple (occasionally an opponent) asks a question of the apostle, the "enlightener" (various epithets are used). Usually contextual or historical detail is missing. The body of the chapter is then taken up with a summary of doctrine on that particular question which convinces all listeners; and may then end with a prayer of praise for Mani and thanks for his revelation.[1]

Here two Kephalaia are given, 26 and 38. In Kephalaion 26 Mani tells five stories or parables about the primal man, the third messenger, and the role of the living spirit in bringing redemption. In Kephalaion 38 Mani offers a Manichaean cosmogony. He describes the universe in human form, and he relates the cosmic human to the individual human. Thus the cosmogonic account, for all its complexity, becomes the story of the individual person living out his or her life. The gods in the outer zone are remote, transcendent, but the actions of the light mind are intimate and accessible.

---

1. Gardner, *The Kephalaia of the Teacher*, xx–xxi.

THE KEPHALAIA

Kephalaion 26 [2]

Mani speaks:

The primal man is a great distinguished figure
whose treasure has been stolen
and who tries to recover it.
So he descends from the skies to find his sons,[3]
to liberate them and regain his treasure
which is scattered among his enemies.[4]
Again he is someone whose two sons are kidnapped.[5]
He comes to liberate them.
So the primal man glows in the skies
for his sons who are lost to him.

They are his soul of life, each one in two powers, making four of them.

Again the ship of the day[6] is a powerful spear.
Inside the ship the great spirit is a wise artisan
who adorns and lines up all the weapons for combat.[7]

Again the living spirit is a warrior
who comes to a prince made prisoner of war
and liberates him from the hands of his enemies.[8]

The messenger[9] too is someone rare
because of the treasure . . . hand
of his prisoners . . . these light powers,

---

2. Kephalaia 26 and 38: translated by Iain Gardner, *The Kephalaia of the Teacher: The Edited Coptic Manichaean Texts in Translation with Commentary* (Leiden & New York: E. J. Brill, 1995), pp. 77–78, 93–105; revised in verse by Willis Barnstone. Reprinted by permission of Brill Academic Publishers.
3. The sons are light trapped in darkness.
4. The forces of darkness.
5. Light trapped in darkness, again.
6. The sun.
7. Arrangements are made for the cosmic struggle between light and darkness.
8. The living spirit liberates the primal man.
9. The third messenger.

the sons and their soul,
and the soul may be shown
in the land where it is imprisoned.

Again Mani turns and speaks to his students:
You must become purifiers and liberators
of your soul that lives everywhere
so you may be courted in the company
of the fathers of light,
of the kingdom in the new eternity
and in the place of joy.[10]

Kephalaion 38

THE LIGHT MIND AND THE SOLITARY MAN

A student asks the messenger[11] Mani about the light mind:

You said the light mind will come and be a saint
and he too is a god and many gods
are with him, and when he enters the body of the flesh
he binds the old man with his five counsels
(the five sleepless guardian sons of living spirit
in whose human form the cosmos is made)
and he inserts those five intellectual qualities
into the five limbs of his body.
Where is he now?
The old man stands chained in the body!
And though he is in bondage,
I see how demonic rebellions surge in him.[12]

---

10. The students, too, are to be liberators of souls.
11. Or "apostle," here and throughout.
12. The light mind is the divine that enters a person, but the struggle with the old man continues. On the struggle between the new man and the old man, see Paul's discussion in 1 Corinthians and Romans, as well as the (deutero-Pauline?) letter to the Ephesians.

Second, I ask, if he is a great god,
unchanging and immeasurable,
how could he come and be found in the pettiness
of the body?

Third, tell me, how is a holy one the mind,
and how is he pure despite the defilement of the body?

Fourth, if the light mind exists in saints,
why can't we see his likeness as he is?
I beg you, can you be persuasive and tell me
what I ask you?

Fifth, tell me about your mission.
Look, it isn't clear to me.
In this world they oppress and persecute you.

Mani offers his student a vision:

The whole revelation I have unveiled
and declared to the church. In your presence
I declare this revelation alone.

The student asks:

Everything you unveiled, you did so in our presence
yet I want to know about the light mind.
What is the light mind?

ABOUT THE LIGHT MIND

The messenger responds:

If I tell you these things you care about
and they become true after your concern,
will you understand what you must do?
I will give vision to those who see!
I will make the living fountain overflow
so the thirsty may drink and live.

BODY OF THE LIGHT MIND IN HUMANS

The messenger speaks to the student:

All that error comes from the enemy of the lights,
who construed it and made it[13] look like a man.[14]
The head of the cosmos has the first garments.
His neck is the nape of the garments.
His stomach is the five unfolded ones,
which are of the same garments.
His ribs are the firmaments.
His navel is the sphere of the stars
and the signs of the zodiac.
And also the parts coming from the navel to his hips
are the same that come
from the sphere to the corners of the four worlds.
His loins are the three earths on Atlas's head.
His . . . to the earth on which Atlas stood firm.
His shins and his feet are . . . and the whole zone
belongs to. . . .
His heart is human.
His liver is quadruped animals.
His lungs are the race of birds floating in the air.
His kidneys are the world of reptiles creeping
on the earth. His outer skin is the wall
surrounding the piercing and great fire.
His . . . are the vessels of the great fire.
His . . . darkness. His gall is . . . great intestine
and the breath of the great . . . of the worlds.
His veins . . . all the springs and wells.
His eyes. . . . His feet are his. . . .

This is how each of the worlds stands in harmony.
Five gods[15] are fastened in him: they are his soul

---

13. That is, error.
14. The universe is said to resemble a human.
15. These are the five sons of the living spirit.

and his life. The living spirit and
the envoy and the five sleepless guardians.

CUSTODIAN OF SPLENDOR

The custodian of splendor[16] knows the mind in
the world of the mind that is above.
He has the whole of the powers of heaven
that are in the great king of honor,[17]
who is the thought that is in the seventh firmament.
He has also humbled . . . Adamas of light[18]
who is the insight . . . because of lust.
The king of glory,[19] who is the counsel,
has patience over the three images
of wind, of fire, and of water.
He has him . . . and over those who do evil.
Atlas,[20] who is the consideration
of wisdom in the world below.
He made him and the foundation below.

And the envoy refined from the five intellectuals of life.
The summons and the obedience were there.
Now they made six sons of the living spirit
who were together with six sons of the first man.
And the envoy placed in them the great mind
who is the column of glory, the perfect man.[21]

THE YOUNG JESUS IS SENT DOWN

And the young Jesus was set there. He is the image
of the living word, of the utterance and obedience.

---

16. Or "keeper of splendor," one of the sons of the living spirit.
17. Another son of the living spirit.
18. The third son.
19. The fourth son.
20. The fifth son. Together the five sons of the living spirit are the intellectual qualities of the universe.
21. This is the mind of the universe. In Manichaean thought the column of glory is the Milky Way.

He has made these camps strong, those above
and below. Each of them will be safe in the circle
of his vigil, and there will be no uprising or betrayal.

And look, look! The custodian of splendor is firmly
set in the great mind, in the camp above the prison
of the bound ones.[22] He turns the gloom of death
into nothing! Yet there was a betrayal and an uprising![23]
Sin aborted, it tangled in the soul. It mixed
with light that it expelled toward the image of the envoy.
It entered the third firmament above the watchtower
of the custodian of splendor. From there
it tangled with the light. It came loose and fell down
to what is dry and moist. It fashioned trees on dry land,
but in the sea it gathered form
and caused a great uprising in the sea.

THOUGHT, THE GREAT KING OF HONOR

Look, look, again. The great king of honor, who is thought,
is in the third firmament.[24] He is made . . . with anger.
And there was an uprising![25] A betrayal and anger
happened in his camp. The watchers of heaven,
who descended to earth in his circle of vigil,
performed all the acts of treachery.
To the people they revealed in the world crafts
and heavenly mysteries. An uprising happened,
and on the earth came destruction.

THE ABORTIONS PLUNGE DOWN TO EARTH

Adamas of light, the fulfillment.
He is set firmly on the earth,

---

22. The custodian of splendor and the other sons of the living spirit are set over realms of the universe.
23. The story of the history of the universe is a story of invasions and uprisings on the part of darkness. Here a demonic uprising occurs, in the realm of the custodian of splendor.
24. Probably read "seventh firmament."
25. Another demonic uprising occurs, in the realm of the great king of honor.

and a betrayal came about in his camp.[26]
It happened when the abortions plunged down to earth.
They formed Adam and Eve. They conceived them
to rule through them in the world.
They fashioned every object of lust on the earth.
The entire world was filled with their lust.
They persecute churches. They kill the messengers
and just Adamas of light's circle of vigil,
again and again, and from generation to generation.

IN THE VIGIL OF THE KING OF GLORY

Again, in the vigil of the great king of glory,
who is the grand counsel reigning over the three wheels,
a disturbance occurred, and an affliction.[27]
They were oppressed and pained in the three earths.
After the envoy displaced his image,
the paths were closed and their ascent was blocked by them.
The wind, water, and fire ascend to them.

Again, in the vigil of Atlas, who humiliates
the uprising of the abysses down below.
He bent low and the fastenings underneath
were loosened in the foundation below.[28]
Because of the earthquake that happened during the vigil
of the custodian of splendor, the column of glory
came out as the helper of the custodian of splendor.
And he survived under all burdens.

BETRAYAL AND UPRISING ON THE KING'S WATCH

Conversely, since the betrayal and the uprising
that occurred in the watch of the great king of honor,
these watchers came down to earth from the skies.
Four angels were called to contend with them.

---

26. Another demonic uprising occurs, in the realm of Adamas of light.
27. Yet another uprising, in the realm of the king of glory.
28. A fifth and final uprising, in the realm of the carrier Atlas.

They bound the watchers with an eternal chain
and thrust them in a prison of the darkened ones,
and they obliterated their children from the earth.

Again the abortions descended in the watch
of Adamas, and they conceived Adam and Eve.
Because of that great betrayal and the mystery
of evil, Jesus was sent the prayer of the five sons.[29]

He seized them, those abortions,
and he fastened them under the mind of Adam.
Because of the earthquake in the three earths,
and because the paths were blocked, and springs
of wind and water and fire were stopped,
Jesus came down to the world. He seized Eve,
and he straightened the tracks of the wind,
the water, and the fire. He opened the springs
for them and established the way of their ascent.

Again, since the earth below Atlas was loosened
from the fastenings, because of this too,
Jesus went down, seizing Eve until he reached that place.
Then he came to his rest.

THE LIGHT MIND HUMBLES THE BODY

Look at all these vigils of the zones
where great gods are masters watching over them.
Uprisings have happened and treachery.
From time to time there is a great humiliation
until they humble the powers of enmity.

So also is this body.[30] Though small, here a great power lives.
The old man also inhabits it.
He is cruel and moves with great cunning
until the light mind finds how to humble
and control this body as it sees proper.

---

29. See the discussion of the place of Jesus within Manichaean thought in the introduction to
Part Five. Also note the role of young Jesus, just above.
30. Mani now compares the cosmic struggle between light and darkness to the struggle between the light mind and the old man in human life.

So they are the masters in the watched districts
of his outer brothers. There, in the great body,
the earthquakes and betrayal happened again and again.
There is the mind's watched district,
which is the body of the flesh.
But sin looms incessantly, agitating in the body.

POWERS OF LIGHT ARE GOOD

Now you understand that the powers of light are good
and the beginning and the end are unveiled to them.
Whatever they do is with good judgment.
For this reason they allow the enmity
of initial error and follow its pleasure for a moment.
Then they seize. They have acted first
with a well-tempered judgment.[31]

HOW MAY THE LIGHT MIND COME?

As for the other question you ask me,
how may the light mind come, this great and honored
holy one, and assume this little body of flesh?[32]
Again, look, look. These gods are great and mighty.
Each is enclosed and hard pressed in the place
where he is set like trees holding to their taproot.
So this is also how each one holds his taproot.
So this is how each one has held on
to his taproot in the world and where he is set.

Now, as you already know, the world is set firm,
ordered by the five sons of the living spirit
in all its members.
Sin took this body from the land,
constructed it in its members.
It took its body from the five bodies of darkness.
Sin constructed the body. Yet its soul it took
from the five shining gods. Sin bound the soul

---

31. The triumph of the light in human life is assured.
32. See Gospel of Thomas 29 and John 1.

in the five members of the body.
It bound mind in bone, thought in sinew, insight in vein,
the counsel in flesh, and consideration in skin.[33]

SIN FINDS THE SOUL

Sin set its five powers, its mind on the mind of the soul,
its insight on insight of the soul,
its counsel on counsel of the soul,
its consideration on consideration of the soul.
It placed its five angels and authorities
on the five members of the soul,
which it brought in and bound in flesh.
Others spoke to the soul and led it on
to all that is evil, to all the sins of lust,
to the worship of idols, to wrong opinions,
to humiliation in the humiliation of slavery!
As it is set fast, worshiping things impermanent,
bowing before idols of wood and gold and silver,
worshiping beasts unclean and polluted!
Think of them. How ugly in form and appearance!

The soul assumed error and forgetting.[34]
It forgot its essence and its race and its kin.
It didn't know the door of the place to pray to him.
It grew hostile to the father.
It was wicked in its own light.

THE LIGHT MIND FINDS THE SOUL AND RELEASES THE NEW MAN

The light mind comes and finds the soul
and assumes it into wisdom. He will become
for it . . . the bonds and members of the body.
He will loosen the mind of the soul

---

33. The body is made by sin from evil matter. The soul comes from the divine but is trapped in the body.
34. The soul becomes forgetful of its nature and origin—the fundamental problem of life in the world, according to gnostic and mystical texts.

and release it from the bone.
He will release the thought of the soul from sinew
and bind the thought of sinew in sinew.
He will release insight of the soul from the vein
and bind insight of sin in the vein.
He will loosen the counsel of the soul
and release it from the flesh
and so bind the counsel of sin in the flesh.
He will release consideration in the soul from skin
and bind consideration of sin in the skin.[35]

HOW HE WILL RELEASE THE MEMBERS OF THE SOUL

This is how he will release the members of the soul
and free them from the five members of sin.
Conversely, these five members of sin
that were loose he will bind.
He will make right the members of the soul,
and form and purify them,
and construct a new man from them, a child of justice.
And when he fashions and constructs
and purifies the new man,
he will bring forth five great living members
from the five great members and place them
in the members of the new man.
He will place his mind, which is in love,
in the mind of the new man.
And thought, which is faith, he will place
in the thought of the new man, whom he will purify.
His insight, which is perfection, he will place
in the insight of the new man.
His counsel, which is patience, he will place in his counsel,
and wisdom, which is his consideration,
he will place in the new man.
He will make an image of the pure word

---

35. The light mind comes and liberates, enlightens, and saves the soul.

from the word of sin, and add it to his word
so he becomes the nourisher and strengthener.[36]

WHEN HE IS PERFECT

When he is perfect. The twelve members
and his wisdom. He becomes just
as he perfects. Formerly he was running aimlessly,
but now he runs up his road and his path
and mount to the heights, to the great aeons.
So the old man is bound in lust,
foolishness in these five members of the body; the dark
spirit is imprisoned with them in a bond
and in severe misery.

THE NEW MAN REIGNS BY LOVE

And the new man reigns by love, by faith, by perfection,
by patience, and by wisdom.
Yet his king is the light mind, who is king of all.
He reigns over it as he wishes. The members' sin
is imprisoned, yet the light mind is king,
and an affection often rises in the body.

FOOLISH SIN CLIMBS UP

There are instances when sin will climb up
and show off its foolishness.[37]
It disturbs consideration and clouds wisdom
and understanding. It splits truth
and puts doubt in him, uttering foolish words.
When this kind of foolishness enters the church,
the teachers and elders gather.

---

36. All of this describes the process whereby a person becomes renewed, sanctified by the light.
37. A person may still backslide into sin, in spite of the best efforts and intentions of teachers
and friends.

They inform wisdom and consideration.
Wisdom is set in place and well.

SIN WILL RISE AND LIGHT MIND WILL CONTEND

If the new man will not accept blame
and edification from his brothers and helpers,
then sin will rise again, moving
from consideration to the counsel.
Sin will take patience from him and feed him
cowardice and pain. And sin shows off
among the brothers. It does what it wants,
ignoring advice, and becomes its foolishness.
But a battle and a war materialize between light mind
and sin in the counsel. They assemble and
silence him and take him away to another time.
These are his companions in his struggle.[38]

NOW A SOLITARY MAN

If in that place, then sin will rise again
and clothe him with lust and vanity and pride.
He breaks off from his teacher and the brothers.
He always wants to go in and come out alone,
a solitary man. He will always walk alone.
It is a sign that the closeness of his brothers
does not persuade him.

If he again does not keep his heart from lust,
again sin will rise in him,
the thought of death will enter his thought.
He will yield to vanity,
causing his faith and truth to leave him.
When the sign of his foolishness is displayed,

---

38. These last lines are garbled as to person, and there are lacunae, but the sense is detectable.

and his reputation spreads in the church,
the wise in the church will come to him
to straighten out his heart,
encourage it with god's edification.
If he took his brothers' advice and listened,
and freed himself from anger,
he might live and conquer sin and all its wars.

AN EARTHLY MAN

But if he fails to make this watch secure,
sin will rise and assume his mind
and disturb his mind, which earlier was calm.
It will disrupt his love and take it away
from his teacher and instructor.
It will take love from his heart and his church
and fill it with hatred.
Then all his brothers become hateful before him.
His brothers and loved ones and friends
who love him will be like enemies before him.
He is disturbed and lets his love and his will turn from him.
He will be a vessel of loss; he will leave the church
and drop down to the world. Mind who was in him
will scatter away and go to the envoy who sent him.
He will be filled with evil spirits,
and they will drag him about.
He will be like worldly men.
He will change and become like a bird
with its feathers plucked out.
He becomes an earthly man.

INSTRUCTION ON THE WAYS OF
THE LIGHT MIND

I, Mani, have taught you and opened your eyes
about confusion in the zone.
How can it rise in the camps of the mighty gods?
Such disturbances happen in the light mind
and in the keepers of the watch,

for they are set firmly in the zone, though not visible.
This too is the way of the light mind,
for he is not visible in the body.

And these keepers of the watch are great,
yet they are twisted. They have become small
with their appropriate tasks. The process is like mind
who was great and exalted, and now he is bent over
and become small in this small worthless body.
While the gods in the outer zone are transcendent and pure,
they are involved in the mingling into the entirety
but are not defiled. This too is like the light mind.

Consider the might and actions of the light mind.
How vast he is over the keepers of the watch of the body!
He stays in his camp. He closes down the body's
deliberations from the temptations of sin.
He limits them and scatters them.
He puts them down at his will.

He does another work surpassing the others.
He bestows a great spirit over the elect.
Now you may find him standing on the earth,
rising up in his heart and ascending to the father,
the god of truth, he who exists and is established
above all things without loss.
And again he may push down in his insight and consideration
and descend to the land where darkness poured out.
His heart will run and touch everything.[39]

Then Mani says to the student:
I have taught you the deeds of the light mind.
Whoever has an open and perceptive eye,
the light mind can appear to him.
Whoever lacks that eye,
the light mind cannot appear to him.
As for my work not manifest or revealed to you,

---

39. The cosmic struggle is like the struggle of the individual, and in the cosmos and in the individual the light ultimately wins.

I will teach you and open your eyes to this wonder
and my leadership.

MANI RECORDS HIS TRIUMPHS

Observe. I, a single Manichaean, have come alone
to the world. And the races and kin of the body,
and the gold, silver, copper, and breastplates,
the multitude's armor and a mass of people
submit to me, including many kinds of gods and idols
from the smelting furnaces!
You have seen the kingdom of the world.
Yet with all their advantages and gifts,
with breastplates and a violent war,
they have subdued no city or conquered no country.
But without breastplate or armor
I have conquered remote cities by the word of god,
and remote countries. And they bless my name,
which is glorified in all countries.

And there is another thing I shall teach you.
Kings have worked with me, and the nobles
and their officials and their powers,
so they might bring their truth to nothing.
They lacked the strength to work against me.
Since I am now alone, why were they impotent
before me, all those who opposed me?

And I have a third message. No one in this world
has freed his children and brothers and kin
from the circumstance of all things as I have.
I have freed all my children from labor.

And I have a fourth thing. I have covered them
with the breastplate of wisdom,
and so among humans you will not find one
who has been victorious. No one is victorious
over me in the whole world. Nor upon
my children. No one can conquer them.

And as a fifth feat, with my power I've chosen
the entire election. I have given my children
my emblems of authority and great springs of wisdom,
so that as the messenger of the church I have
made it mine. I have strengthened the church
and embellished it with all beneficial qualities.
I have planted the good and sown truth
in every far and near land. Messengers and envoys
I have sent to all countries. So messengers before me
have not done what I have in this harsh generation,
except for only Jesus, the son of greatness,
who is the father of all messengers. No envoy
has been like me! Look and see me now.
How great is my power and my actions?
No earlier envoy in the flesh has reached my likeness.
The great doors have been opened by me
to the gods and angels and people,
and all spirits and living souls who are prepared
for life and for eternal rest.

After his students heard what Mani proclaimed, they answered him, saying:

All you have uttered to us is great and mighty,
which you accomplished with your powers,
and the power of the one who sent you.
Who could fully thank you for the grace
you have given us, except the one who sent you?
We have but one gift for repaying you.
We will become strong in your faith,
persevere in your commandments, and,
of the word you proclaimed to us, be persuaded.

41

The Coptic Manichaean Songbook

S ome of the most strikingly beautiful Manichaean literature is poetry, presented in songs and hymns. A substantial number of songs
are to be found in the Coptic Manichaean Songbook, or Psalmbook,
which is preserved in Coptic but has only partially been translated and edited.
Here several songs from the Coptic Manichaean Songbook are offered. The
Songs of Thomas may refer to Mani's student of that name and seem to be
based on Mandaean poetry, as Nathaniel Deutsch also mentions above in his
introduction to the Mandaean literature in Part Four. The Song of Herakleides
may recall one of Mani's twelve messengers. The names cited at the conclusion
of some of the songs may be names of saints or martyrs.

THE COPTIC MANICHAEAN SONGBOOK[1]

Songs of Thomas

Song 1   My Father Evoked Holy Fire

MY FATHER THE PLEASURED LIGHT

My father the pleasured light,
the pleasured light, the glory,

my father the pleasured light,
the pleasure, the holy light,

my father the pleasured light,
the pleasure, the esteemed light.

He summoned the aeons of light,
he chose them to enjoy his greatness.

He summoned the aeons of peace
in whom no flaw or loss lives.

He summoned the aeons of light
and his sons in whom he put the aeons.

He summoned the aeons of peace.
He called his wealth, set it in them.

He summoned the aeons to repose.
He called his angels, set it in them.

He founded places for life.
He set living icons in them.

---

1. Songs from the Coptic Manichaean Songbook: translated by C. R. C. Allberry (Allberry, ed., *A Manichaean Psalm-Book*); revised in verse by Willis Barnstone.

He set living icons in them,
which never disappear.

He summoned clouds of brightness,
dripping with dew and light.

He evoked holy fire
that burned sweet.

He evoked wind and air
that breathed a living breath.

He evoked holy mountains
pouring out fragrant roots.

They are all concord and melody.
In them no flaw or loss lives.

They were ecstatic in brightness[2]
filled and inhabiting eternity.

I SAW THE EVIL ONE

I couldn't see where the son of evil saw them.
I stood up, saying, I want to be like them.

Where did the son of evil see them?
Did the poor one own nothing?

No diamonds are in his possession,
no eternity in his estate.

He took the hand of his seven companions
and his twelve helpers.

He took the hand of seven companions
and went and looked at still aeons

so if any fell and came down
he would go and be like them.

---

2. Or "glory."

The father took the first step.
He empowered his angels and said,

Come together, all of you. Beware
of the evil one's eye. It glanced up.

A SON OF LIGHT LOOKED DOWN

A son of light looked down from high
and saw him. He said to rich brethren,

O my brethren, sons of light
in whom no flaw or loss lives,

I looked down into the abyss.
I saw the evil one, the son of evil.

I saw the evil one, the son of evil,
who wanted to get into war.

I saw his seven companions too
and his twelve helpers.

I saw their tent pitched
and a roaring fire in it.

I saw miserable myrmidons[3] living there,
plotting war.

I saw their hanging armor
ready for the campaign.

I saw the traps all put in place
and the nets cast and spread

to catch a bird if it comes
and fish not escape them.

They lay around drinking stolen wine
and devouring plundered meat.

---

3. This may refer to the "ant people" of Aegina, created by Zeus when the island inhabitants were killed in a plague, who later fought under Achilles in the Trojan War.

THE CHILD ARMED AND THE SON OF EVIL

The child got through his months
until he could walk.

The little one among the tall stepped in.
He took up arms. He armed his waist.

He leapt and raced into the abyss.
He leapt and got to their center to battle them.

He humiliated the son of evil
and his seven companions and twelve slaves.

He wrecked their camp and cast it down.
He put out their roaring fire.

He bound the miserable myrmidons there,
who plotted to make war.

He grabbed their armor hanging there, readied
for war, destroyed their readied traps.

He ripped up their outspread nets.
He released the fish to go out to sea.

He let the birds fly up into space.
He let the sheep into their folds.

He seized the evil one's wealth. He went off
with it and took it up to the land of rest.

So he saved what the living took.
They will come back to what is theirs.

Song 9   The Lion and the Beautiful Daughter[4]

The lion took my beautiful daughter. He seized her,
dragged her into his lair with his great dragon.

When she was in the pit, the lion screamed.
His companions gathered. The dragon whistled

and hissed. All the beasts gathered near him
and roared. They hid from my daughter,

roaring elsewhere, lest their powers diminish.
So my cry calls up to the mighty one,

who excels among the powers. I the son ask
my father. My garment hangs

on the universe, saying, If I have wronged
the great lion, let him eat me now in his lair.

If I've wronged the great dragon, let him swallow
me here. But if I haven't wronged the lion

here in his midst, let me escape his lair and take
my daughter from him. Father of us all . . .

place the garment over us all. I pounded. Ranks
even their nets I cracked open their lair.

I cast stones on it. I seized the great dragon and his
consort I enmeshed in a trap. I took my daughter

---

4. This song is very fragmentary.

from them and placed her high above them all.
I hurled stones at their wheel till it collapsed

under them, and my daughter and I destroyed
all their nets. We drove the great lion

and the dragon out of the cosmos, and we came
to the village land of the just. They know

it too. From the heart of a second lair I
took my daughter into the land. They now

are also happy. And it will happen soon
just as the bride enters the bridal chamber.

Song 12   Jesus Dug a River

Jesus dug a river in the cosmos. He dug a river,
even he of the sweet name. He dug it with a spade

of truth. He dredged it with a basket of wisdom.
The stones he dredged from it are drops

of incense from Lebanon. All the waters in it
are roots of light. Three ships sail.

They voyage in the river, testing. One is full,
one half freighted. The third is empty.

The full ship sails fearlessly. One half full.
The empty one comes empty

and leaves nothing behind. It will suffer
at the customs. It has nothing to give,

nothing on board. They will tear it apart
wickedly and send it back to the port.

The ship will suffer what corpses suffer. Empty.
They called it and it heard nothing.

Song 20   Cry of Pamoun the Ox[5]

Hear an ox. The cry of Pamoun, an ox. Mercy.
I make the worlds weep.

What have the children of the earth given me?
They grabbed two-edged axes

and stuck me in marshes. They felled fat trees
and even thin ones.

They didn't leave alone. With the fat tree
they cut out a plow.

From the thin one they made a sharp goad.
Then took it to an artist

who in his own hand fashioned a yoke,
stuck it on my neck,

and hooked the plow hanging behind me.
They used the goad

to pierce my ribs. Then they carried me
to the butcher's son,

the fattener of oxen; it was the butcher's
son who chopped me up,

scattered me to foreign tents, hung me
in far markets, and

before anybody tossed my bones to stray
beasts.[6] Release me

from the owners. They don't buy me. They burn
what is inside me,

---

5. This song has many lacunae.
6. Stray beasts or dogs, a conjecture.

even that. Don't beat Pamoun, the ox.
Shake the spirit vessels

in you. I will make you sit in a place
where generations

will pass through you, planting, repaying,
making you the living.

Freedom. Even they who are my kin. On
a day of the great.[7]

Song of Herakleides

COME TOGETHER

Come together, O sons of the earth, and hear
the angel who was sent out

with the message[8] of the skies.
You came and were a gathering, you came

and they gathered in you.
Tell us the message of the skies.

You came and the aeons were in rank,
you came and they gathered in you.

Tell us
the message of the skies.

Wake, you who sleep.
Wake, you who sleep. Sleep in the cavern[9]

that you can receive the sky's message.
The carrier of the message is on his way

---

7. The song's last words are missing. The last word is "amen."
8. The "message" may be thought of as good news, but the word is neutral and permits the long song to develop theme and suspense. Here and throughout the song there are clear parallels to the Song of the Pearl.
9. The symbolic meaning of the cavern or pit is uncertain, but it is clearly a place to receive a heavenly message.

with the message from the land of light
to speak out the message of the skies.

He was sent out. He raced laughing
to the first man to tell him the message.

He came and knocked on the gates
and shouted, Open up at once.

I have the message of the skies!

FIRST HUMAN ON EARTH

Stand up, O first human on earth,
open your gates that are shut

so I can tell you the message! Stand up,
O first human on earth,

let the trumpet of peace resound
so I can tell you the message!

Stand up, O first human on earth, spread
the logos of the good news

so I can tell you the message! Stand up,
O first human on earth,

build up the bricks of the tower
so I can tell you the message!

Stand up, O first human on earth, and go
with the troops to your city

so I can tell you the message!
Stand up, O good shepherd,

grab the lamb from the vengeful wolf
that I can tell you the message!

WHO ARE YOU? MY DOORS ARE LOCKED

Who are you? My doors are locked,
give me a sign so I'll open to you

and you can tell me the message.
Who are you for me to open

so you can tell me the message?
I am the son of the son

of the father. The son of the father has sent me
to you about the message.

Open, open up at once! Open the closed gates
so you can be given the message!

As the gates were about to open he was
already inside the gates

to tell him the message of the skies.
The first man found him at his side.

He was happy and said to him,
Tell me the message!

What is my father doing now?
Father of the lights beyond him?

Tell me my father's message.
What are the twelve aeons doing now

who were round the father when I left?
Tell me the message!

How are things with the living air, the breath
of life around the father?

Tell me the message! The great spirit
of the land of light, the cupbearer

of all the aeons? Tell me the message!
The land of light, the house of the father,

bridal chamber of all the aeons?
Tell me the message!

The walls that were dug in the earth
when I went away,

the sentinels on the towers who guard them,
tell me the message!

How is the mother of the living,[10]
whom I left behind? How are her kin?

Tell me the message!
The first man on earth is happy

but is asking, and tells the envoy:
Tell me the message!

THE CALL IS HEARD

The call, the call, is once again heard.
I came and they were gathered.

I came and the gods were happy.
I came and they were gathered round me.

Look, this is the message!
I came and the father was gathered.

The aeons were gathered round the father.
Look, this is the message!

I came and the aeons were gathered.
They were a garland around the father.

Look, this is the message!
The harpists were gathered and the pipes were sonorous.

I was sent out, and the father was happy.
He lived in the bridal chamber

of the land of light so I might tell the message!
I was sent out, and the aeons of the aeons were gathered.

They played music for the father
of the lights so I might tell the message!

---

10. Or "mother of life." This epithet is also used to describe Eve in Genesis and gnostic texts.

I was sent out, and harpists were gathered and sang
of the father so I might tell the message!

I was sent out, and the air was ecstatic
to be all gathered and round the father

so I might tell the message! I was sent out,
and the bridal chamber was happy,

the land with light, the house of the father.
Look, this is the message of the skies!

I was sent out, and the walls were dug in the earth,
and the sentinels of the towers

were guarding them.
Look, this is the message!

I was sent out, and the mother watched,
and her kin were assembled round her.

Look, this is the message!
I was sent out, and the feast was prepared,

the lavish feast around the father.
Look, this is the message! I was sent out,

and the father was happy,
and pleasure was round him.

Look, this is the message!
I was sent out, and the father was gathered.

He was sleeping in his quarters in the land of light.
Look, this is the message! I was sent out, and the father

was happy and the virgins encircled him.
Look, this is the message! I was sent out,

and the harps were in their hands,
and they played for the father of the lights.

Look, this is the message!
I was sent out, and the pipes were sonorous

on the mooring places.
Look, this is the message! I was sent out,

and the sea was placid,
and the raft of heaven was towed out.

Look, this is the message!
I was sent out, and ships touched land,

and the seaports were secured.
Look, this is the message! I came, and the walls

were set in foundations,
and the sentinels on the tower guarded them.

Look, this is the message!

FORSAKING THE FIVE LIMBS OF THE FATHER OF TRUTH

I abandoned reason, since it guarded the father,
pleasure of the land of light.

Look, this is the message! I abandoned thought,
since it guarded faith

and the aeons who are round the father.
Look, this is the message!

I abandoned insight, since it guarded the father.
Look, this is the message!

I abandoned desire, since it guarded resolution
and gave life to the aeons.

Look, this is the message!
I abandoned reflection

at the floor and foundation of the land of light.
Look, this is the message!

I CAME FROM THE HOUSE OF HAPPINESS

I came from the house of happiness. I brought you
joy by my coming.

Look, this is the message! I came from the house
of abundance. I brought you abundance

by coming to you. Look, this is the message!
I came, since the mother

looked for you and her kin were with her.
Look, this is the message!

I came, since the mother was looking for you
and her kin were with her.

Look, this is the message! They are at the frontier,
waiting for you. Look, this is the message!

GOD HAS COME WHOLLY

Look, god has come wholly. Call and he will answer.
Look, this is the message!

They are weighed down with garlands and palms,
a gift for you, the leader.

Look, this is the message! Tell me the message,
arm your loved ones,

your garlanded troops. I will carry the message
from all the aeons.

and with those words and your son, go out
and carry the message!

COSMIC BATTLE

His troops are firmly entrenched. He seizes the ruler
of the land of darkness.

Look, this is the message!
The air is fixed over the smoke. His troops are in chains,

they are fettered.
Look, this is the message!

The wind guards the king of storms.
His troops lie in chains, fettered.

Look, this is the message!
Look, the waters have surrounded the king

of the flood of death.
Carry the message!

The virgin, the living fire has become master
of the land of darkness.

Carry the message!
Look, the land of darkness we have wasted.

We wait for you with a garland.
Carry the message!

We bought dens of the hungry. We got their land
for five loaves of bread.

Carry the message!
We gave water. They drank. They were drunk

and frittered away their wages.
Carry the message!

The robe of light was set on them. For them
it was a bond, a shackle.

Carry the message!
They lusted over the breath of the wind.

It was a fetter on their neck.
Carry the message!

They smelt the breath of the air.
It was death for all of them.

Carry the message!

LIGHT HAS SURROUNDED DARKNESS

Let's go. They are expecting you. The light
has surrounded darkness.

Let's go. They are expecting you. They live
on the border. They are waiting.

Look, god has wholly come. Call him.
He will answer you.

Carry the message!
They come heavy with garlands and palms for you,

victorious captain.
Carry the message!

The envoy heard the good news. He took it
to him who sent him.

Carry the message!
The fathers of light have come to help

their loved one.
Carry the message!

They helped the first human,
and he shouted happily,

"Look at me! Look at my merchandise!"
There was enormous joy, the first man among them,

covered with garlands and palms.
This is the message!

May it happen to us together, be counted in his merchandise
and pleasure with the aeons.

This is the message!
May we be counted with those on his right hand

and inherit our kingdom.
This is the message!

May we live with our families forever.
This is the message!

Glory to the first man, honor to the living spirit
and their unceasing work. Victory

to the soul of blessed Mary, Theona![11]

Song of the Bema, 223
Let Us Worship the Spirit[12]

Let us worship the spirit of the comforter,
bless lord Jesus who sent us the spirit of truth.

He came and split us from the world's error.
He came with a mirror, we looked.

In it was the cosmos. When the holy spirit came
she disclosed the way of truth.

It taught us two natures, light and darkness,
distinct from the beginning.

The kingdom of light has five greatnesses:
father and his twelve aeons,

and the aeons of aeons, the living air, the land of light,
and the enormous spirit through whom

they breath and which nourishes them with light.
But the kingdom of darkness has five storehouses:

smoke and fire and wind and water and darkness.
Their advocate creeps in them, inciting them

to make war on each other. When making war
they dared attack the land of light. They supposed

---

11. The Coptic uses the Greek word *theona*. Theona is identified by Allberry as one, along with Mary, of a pair of martyrs. The name also suggests Mary as a female god.
12. The Bema was a rostrum on which Mani's picture was displayed during the Bema feast. The Bema celebration commemorated the death of Mani in the early spring of the year (just as the death and resurrection of Jesus were commemorated during the Christian holidays of Good Friday and Easter, also in the spring of the year). At the Bema celebration, songs like this song of the Bema were sung. In the song the comforter (or paraclete) is Mani.

they could vanquish it and didn't know that their plans
would crash down on their own heads.

There was a horde of angels in the land of light,
ready to pour out and break the father's enemy.

They were pleased to have the father's word
to rout those rebels who saw themselves exalted.

The angels were like a shepherd who sees
a lion padding near to destroy the fold,

who cunningly takes a lamb and sets it as a snare
to catch the lion. With a single lamb he saves

his fold, heals the lamb, and wounds the lion.
Such is the way of the father who sent forth his strong son

and made from himself his virgin armed
with five powers to fight the five abysses of the darkness.

When the watcher stood at the borders of light, he showed
them to the virgin who is his soul. In their abysses

they stirred, desiring her. They opened their mouth to swallow her.
He held her power fast. He spread her over them

like nets over fish. He had her rain down on them
like purified clouds of water. She stabbed inside them

like piercing lightning. She crept into
their inner parts. She bound them. They knew nothing.

When the first man finished his war, the father sent
his second son. He came, lifted his brother

out of the abyss. He made the whole world out of
that mixture of the light and darkness.

He spread all his powers of the abyss to ten heavens
and eight earths. He shut them up

into this cosmos and made it a prison for all
powers of darkness. It was also a place

of purification for the soul swallowed in them.
He established the sun and moon and set them high

to purify the soul. Daily they took in refined parts
up to their height, yet however they mixed the dregs

they couldn't move them up or down.
The whole world halts for a season. A great building

is being built outside the world.
As soon as the workers finish, the cosmos will dissolve,

catch fire, and flame will melt it away.
All life, the relic of light wherever it is, he will take

to himself and then project an image.
The counsel of death—it is all darkness—will meet

and create a likeness of itself and the ruler,
but in a flash the living spirit comes, succors the light,

and will lock up the counsel of death
and darkness in a house made to hold them there forever.

There is no other way to freeze the enemy. He won't be
received to the light, for he is a stranger,

yet he can't be left in his land of darkness. He must not
engage in a war greater than the first one.

A new aeon will be built in the place of the cosmos
that will dissolve. In the aeon the powers

of light may reign, since they have performed and fulfilled
the will of the whole father, subdued the hated

over him forever.
This is Mani's knowledge. Let us worship and bless him.

Whoever trusts him will be blessed and live
with justice. Glory and victory to our lord Mani. Spirit

of truth from the father. He reveals to us
the beginning, the middle, and the end. Victory to the soul

of the blessed Mary, Theona, Pshaijmnoute.[13]

---

13. Another Manichaean name or epithet. In Coptic *noute* means "god."

Song to Jesus, 254
Ferry Me to the Sun

Take me, firstborn. The path of light
spreads before me from my own first city.

I look for someone. The dissolving image
of the savior comes to me. O first one, the light

of the virgin touches me, the brightest
picture of truth with her three angels

who give grace. Firstborn, the portals of
the sky fly open before me in the rays

of my savior and his portrait of light.
I left my garment on the earth.

Senile diseases were mine. I dress in the deathless
robe. Ferry me to the sun and the moon.

Ferry of light at peace over three earths.
Firstborn, I am a holy bride in her chamber

of light, resting. I keep my victory gift. I have worked;
it is good. My end is happy eternal possession.

O firstborn, glory and conquest for lord Mani,
his holy elect, and for blessed Mary's soul.

Wanderer Song
You Are a Spring[14]

You are a spring, Jesus. You come from the aeons, king.
You are a spring of living water.

The mysteries of the father you know.
You are the clothing of the aeons, which is the church's robe.

---

14. The meaning of the word translated "wanderer" is uncertain.

You are the cane of the kingdom. It leans on you.
You are the gate of the land of light

The father's name is your glory.
You are the blossoming fruit of the imperishable tree.

You are the holy dove floating over clouds,
with the three-branched anesh[15] in her mouth.

Jesus, the virgin, the mind become the perfect church.
The tree, the fruit are good and sweet.

Love wears the garments of the fair commandment and knowledge.
Grace circles around the name of Jesus.

Whoever finds you is blessed and lucky.
One who knows does not taste death

but reposes in life forever.
Glory and honor Jesus, the king and the holy.

Victory to the soul of the blessed Mary, Theona.

Wanderer Song
O Soul, Sleeping[16]

O soul, sleeping. You who sleep, you who
doze, wake. Sun rises on you.

Morning is the truth of the commandments
the dead, the corpses have risen.

Here is the habitat of robbers,
the house of cares and sadnesses.

They are merciless scavengers,
hearing no call. They have no heart

---

15. Meaning uncertain.
16. This poem is fragmentary. As before, the meaning of the word translated "wanderer" is
uncertain.

for the condemned. They flatter you
the tree. The good man has come

Jewel garland, you. Wandering sheep,
your shepherd seeks you. Noble and despised,

your king wants you. Where are
your angelic cloths, robes that don't age?

Where are your cheerful wreathes
and crowns that don't fall? The clay mold

of your kin, your father's seal? When you
were saved, your first jewel, your mind

was collected, familiar, unfailing to you.
How many of your blood has the world . . .

for you? The humble you have loved
and the great you have humbled.

You were not yet ashamed. Forever
and ever the blessed soul of Mary.

42

Parthian Songs

Here we encounter two more collections of Manichaean songs, or hymn cycles, in this case songs from Parthia, an ancient empire, originally corresponding to the northeastern Iranian province of Khorasan. During the first centuries BCE Parthia was a vast empire extending from the Indian Ocean through Afghanistan, Persia, and east to Syria, but it declined when it was finally conquered by the Persians in 226 CE. The first song, entitled *Huyadagman* (after the opening line, "How good for us," or "How fortunate we were"), is a long poetic composition originally of four hundred verses, which are divided into cantos. It is preserved in a Parthian version, a Sogdian version (from Sogdiana, a province of Persia that included Bukhara and extended through Samarkand), a Chinese version (with a good deal of Buddhist language), and Turkish fragments. Sections from the Parthian version are translated here. The second collection of songs, entitled *Angad Rosnan* (after the opening line, "Deep companion of the beings of light," or "Bountiful friend of the beings of light"), is also a long composition, and some of its apocalyptic themes are paralleled in the Apocalypse of Thomas. Both hymn cycles are said to have been composed by Mani's student Mar Ammo in the mid-third century. These songs (all fragments from larger lost compositions) contain the essential range of themes in the life of a practicing gnostic. They speak of a soul in distress that is threatened by personal weaknesses and surrounded by dangers from all sides, the soul's fervent longing for salvation, the coming of the savior, and hence the promise to begin a journey to the new paradise. Its verse, like that of the New Testament Apocalypse, is a major extended poetic achievement.

PARTHIAN SONGS[1]

Huyadagman

PARADISE OF MONASTERIES

How good for us to have known your teaching!
Please have mercy on us, generous ruler.
The messenger of the father heals souls,
draws joy in all of us, and carries away sorrow.
Lofty and limitless, where darkness never comes,
all the monasteries and the dwelling places are great
in beauty, for they are happy in the light
and know no pain. Those who enter remain
forever. No blow or torture ever reaches them.
The clothing they wear no one made by hand.
They shine with light, and no ants crawl in them.
The green wreathes on their heads never lose color.
Their bodies are unfamiliar with dead weight
and don't droop. Their limbs are not paralyzed.
Heavy sleep never overtakes their souls,
and deceptive dreams and delusions are unknown
among them. In that land hunger and anguish
are not known. There is no thirst. The waters
of all its lakes give out a wondrous fragrance
everywhere. No one knows floods and drowning.
Their walk is quicker by far than lightning.

In their bodies there is no sickness. The actions
of all the dark powers leave them completely alone.
Fear and horror do not live in those lands,
nor does destruction. The trees don't shake down
their fruit. Decay is foreign to their fruit.

---

1. Parthian Songs: translated by Jes P. Asmussen, *Manichaean Literature: Representative Texts Chiefly from Middle Persian and Parthian Writings*, UNESCO Collection of Representative Works: Persian Heritage Series 22 (Delmar, N.Y.: Scholars' Facsimiles & Reprints, 1975), pp. 81–86; 88–97; revised in verse by Willis Barnstone. Reprinted by permission of Bibliotecha Persica.

Within and outdoors it is replete with brilliance,
the gardens aromatic and no stray bricks
or thorns. Those who ascend to those precincts
and have knowledge will extol his manifestation.
No one suffers a dark shadow. Its earth and face
are radiant. Precious forms are free from hurt.
Their limbs don't become feeble with age.
They are happy. They speak well. They revere
the high generous one. There is glad sweet song
in splendid monasteries. No fear, no dogs howling,
no bird squawking, no confusing evil
and dreadful screeching. Nothing coarse in that land.
Darkness and fog have not marked pure paradise.
The self lives in light. The virtues of joy, love,
and beauty are shared. No living being dies.[2]

PITS AND PRISONS

Who will release me from the pits and prisons
of assembled lusts that I loathe? Who will take me
over the flooding sea, the mouths of conflict
that give no rest? Who will save me from the jaws
of pitiless beasts who destroy and terrify?
Who will lead me beyond the walls and over
the moats that boil with fear and trembling
from ravaging demons? Who will take me
beyond rebirths, and free me from the waves
which give no peace? I weep for my soul,
saying, May I be saved from this, from grotesque
beasts who eat each other! The human body,
birds of the air, fish of the ocean, quadrupeds
and insects, who will take me beyond them?
Who will save me so I won't turn and plunge
into those hells, so I won't live in their muck
or suffer rebirth devoid of living plants?

---

2. Asmussen, *Manichaean Literature*, Canto 1.

Who will save me from the swallowing height
and the devouring deeps of hell and distress?[3]

THE CALL

And while I wept on the ground,
I heard the voice of the beneficent king.[4]

DELIVERANCE

I shall save you from the powers of revolution
who terrify. I will release you from deception,
a field of turbulence, and the torment of death.
I will end the forces that destroy. I will ban
sickness, which has dismayed you, and death.

FROM THE HANDS OF HELL'S GUARDIANS

I will take you from the hands of hell's guardians,
who treat the spirit and soul without mercy.

PRIMEVAL CALM OF NEW LAND

I will take you eagerly, and we'll soar on wings
high over dark powers and recalcitrant princes.
I will take you into the primeval calm of new land,
the new paradise, and will show you
the design of the father's being.
You will know joy and praise, go beyond pain,
and in luminous dress you will gird on light.
On your head is your diadem of authority.

Spirit spoke and built on that structure the vast
fortress of the noble emperor. The primeval
firstborn merits a palace as his dominion.

---

3. Asmussen, *Manichaean Literature*, Canto 4a.
4. This and the next two sections are from Asmussen, *Manichaean Literature*, Canto 6.

The first human clothes himself in gladness
and binds on the diadem of sovereignty.
On his friends he binds
the diadem and clothes their bodies in the garment
of gladness. And those faithful elect he clothes
in praise, binds the diadem on them. They reign
happily as once they were in shackles just for
their name and were horribly punished by enemies.
Their victory was their return from hell.
Their enemies are subdued, and before them cliffs!
On that day when the father reveals his form,
the caring father, lord of the aeons of light,
he will show his illuminated shape. It's a glorious
bright form to all the gods who will live there.

Angad Rosnan

THE SHIP OF GOD

Deep companion of the beings of light!
In your mercy, give me your strength and help me
with your own hand. Dress my soul, O lord,
and speak to me. Help me when enemies
close in. Their deceitful body would ravage
and torture me. Beneficent friend, free me.
My soul is crying in my body at every blow
and dagger stab. My hour of life and this form
in flesh is over, and all its days of turbulence.
My hour tumbled about as on troubled water,
pain after pain ravaging my inner place.
I walked in anguish, fire at my ankles, fog
a smoke in my face. Springs of darkness opened,
and the giant fishes transfixed me with fear.
My soul fainted before those dreadful forms,
hideous to look at. Their bodies lack a human
shape. These are the demons, the banished princes,
transfixing me with terror. Their fury assembled

like sea bodies of fire. They rose to drown me.
In every neighborhood there were storm winds.
Rain, the mist of all fogs, lightning and drums
of thunder, shores of clouds, hail, crashing sea.
The skiff rose over the crest of a wave and glided
into a hidden trough. All the clamps got loose,
iron rivets fell out. With the drownings the sails
swallowed water, and the masts shook together
in the turmoil. The rudders dropped into the sea.
Those left on board turned to stone. The helmsmen
and his pilots wailed bitterly at the top of their lungs.

THE COMETS QUIVERED

Redemption became a habit. From every source
the wind blew the prison locks loose.
Stars whirled wildly about, planets fell out of orbit.
The earth shuddered, as did my foundation.
Lofty heavens sank. My veins were all the rivers
that dried in my body. My limbs no longer
were connected and broke, wondering if
they existed. I could no longer count
my days and months. The wheel of the zodiac
lost its course. The seal of my feet and joints
of my toes, every link of my soul's life
was loosened. Each joint of my hands and fingers
was loosened and its seal taken off.
Their meaty life grew feeble. My limbs fell cold.
My knees froze together in fear. In my legs
the strength was struck and drained away.

MY LIMBS COLLAPSED, MY SOUL MOANED

When I saw the dark, the strength in my limbs collapsed,
and my soul moaned at all its opposing forms.

Who will save me?
Who will save me; make a new way?
Who will set me straight on that way?

Who will rip off this body?
Who will rip off this body
and dress me in a new one?

After I spoke with trembling soul I saw the savior.
After I spoke with trembling soul I saw the savior
and saw his helmsmen, who came down to dress my soul.
I raised my eyes that way and saw deaths hidden by the envoy.
Hurt was remote. So too sickness and distress.
Their vision left, their darkness fled.
Everything was holy and unsurpassed.
Light shone elating and lovely,
swelling my mind with gladness.

HE SPOKE TO ME THROUGH JOY

He spoke to me through joy,
lifting my soul from hell. He said, Come, spirit,
and don't fear. I am your mind,
your hope. You are the garment of my body,
which dismayed the powers of darkness.
I am your primeval light, your great mind
and total hope. You are my word,
my panoply of war, saving me from struggle
with sinners. I will release you from dungeons,
carry you far from your wounds. I will lead you
from physical torment.
You will not fear encounter.

First human, you will have the portals of heaven.
Beloved! beauty of my bright nature!
From filth and corrosion I will cleanse you
through perfect light.

You are my beloved, the love in my limbs,
and I am the light of your whole structure,
your soul and base of being.

From the holiness of my limbs you descended in the beginning
into dark places and became their light.

For your sake the gods went down and became apparent
and slaughtered death and darkness.
First human, I shall open before you the portals of heaven.
Fear and death will not trail you.

They will not ravage you with pain and wretchedness.
No, you will rest in the lofty precincts of salvation,
here with the gods and those who live in placid quiet.

LET THERE BE NO DESIRE

Come, spirit. Death has fallen, and sickness fled away.
Let there be no desire for the house of affliction,
which is wholly destruction and anguishing death.
You were cast out from your native abode. You suffered in hell.
Come nearer in gladness. Don't turn back
to regard the shapes of the bodies. See, they return
through every rebirth, and through every agony
and every choking prison where they burn and sigh.
Come nearer. Don't be fond of perishing beauty
in any of its forms. It falls and melts like snow in sunshine.
The beautiful doesn't abide. It withers
and fades like a broken rose that dries in the sun,
its grace destroyed.
Princes and dead souls lie shackled in the tomb
where all is blackness.

MY SOUL IS SAVED

My soul is saved.
I am dressed in light.[5]

---

5. The last five brief parts of this hymn cycle (not included here) largely repeat previous passages.

43

The Great Song
to Mani

The Great Song to Mani is a late piece of Manichaean poetry, probably composed in the thirteenth or fourteenth century. It was written in Turkish and is included in the same manuscript as another song to Mani, this one copied in two different languages (Tocharian B and Turkish). This second song, not given here, is much shorter. It rehearses much of the same material about Mani, but adds references to the god Ohrmazd and the god Zurvan, figures equated with aspects of the divine in Persian Manichaeism (for example, the first man) and derived from the Zoroastrian good god Ohrmazd (Ahura Mazda) and the divine principle of infinite time Zurvan. Both songs praise Mani in terms that are distinctly Buddhist, reflecting the years of exile that Mani was said to have spent in India, where he was exposed to the word and worship of the Buddha.

In the Great Song, Mani is described as teacher of what Jesus taught and author of a gospel book (probably the Living Gospel), but he is also addressed as Buddha Mani. The song alludes to aspects of the three jewels of Buddhism, the Buddha (who is Mani), the *dharma* (or law), and the *sangha* (or religious community). The four Buddhas of the song are most likely four prophets or messengers, Seth, Zoroaster, Buddha, and Jesus. After the four comes Mani, who attains his own incomparable buddhahood. He (and others) will escape the cycle of suffering (*samsara*) and attain *nirvana*.

THE GREAT SONG TO MANI[1]

MY BUDDHA MANI

O teacher of the original doctrine of the noble Jesus!
We are here to worship and revere you.
O my respected and famous father, my Buddha Mani!
We are here alone
to worship you from our heart of humility.
Be our hope and refuge
and receive the worship of each one of us.
Before you we bow with internal faith.
May each of our prayers be pure.[2]

You told us the consequences of evil
. . . you blocked the road to hell
. . . preaching good laws.
. . . You rescued eight kinds of suffering beings
in poisonous savage animals. . . .

Unendingly submerged in the dust
of forgetting rebirths
and in a state of poisonous savage animals,
they were always mad.
When the passion of greed[3] poisoned them
and they were dying,
you prepared a medicine for them
from the herb of meditation.

YOU FREED FROM IGNORANCE
AND GAVE WISDOM

They raved in the passion of anger;
they lacked sense or coherent thought

---

1. The Great Song to Mani: translated by Hans-Joachim Klimkeit (*Gnosis on the Silk Road: Gnostic Texts from Central Asia*, 280–84); revised in verse by Willis Barnstone.
2. Of the next eleven lines, which are badly preserved, five line fragments are here given.
3. The Pali Buddhist term for greed is *lobha* (a vice also in Manichaeism), for anger *dvesa,* for ignorance *moha.*

and you assembled their thoughts,
and so they understood their origin
in the realm of light.
Those living beings in the five states of existence[4]
you freed from ignorance
and gave them wisdom,
leading them to *parinirvana*.[5]

Many differing passions—hatred and bitterness—
troubled these thinking beings
and scattered their thought,
but holy father, when you descended from the sky,
the families of all thinking beings
reached the peace of *nirvana*.[6]

YOU RESCUED FROM SAMSARA[7]

We who are miserable and with no hope
would have stayed in the torture of *samsara*,
not finding the end of your path.[8]
You set up the ladder of wisdom,
you let us supersede the five forms of being,
and you delivered us.

We who were fettered in suffering
were rescued from rebirth
to see the Buddha-like sun god
who is like you.
For those tied to transitory pleasure,
you preached the true law.

---

4. In Buddhism these are the states of gods, humans, hungry spirits (*pretas*), animals, and beings of hell.
5. This Buddhist *nirvana* is the Manichaean realm of light.
6. The next six verses are badly preserved and are reconstructed.
7. The cyclical process of metempsychosis, that is, the transmigration of the soul by way of rebirths and deaths, is called *samsara*. This transmigration extends from the lowest insect to the
Brahma, the highest of the gods. The rank of one's new birth, after passing through a hell or a
heaven, depends on one's karma in the previous life. In Sanskrit *samsara* means "the running
around."
8. The realm of light.

You carried them across the sea of suffering
to the good *nirvana.*
For those tied to the root of attachment to the world,
you revealed the road to the realm of the Buddhas,[9]
you raised a Sumeru mountain[10] of virtue,
you let them find endless happiness.
For those plunged in the water of pride,
you showed the bridge of the true law.
You took understanding of the good law into their hearts.
You entrusted them to the holy assembly.
For those confused by the six organs of perception[11]
you showed the rising and falling states of being.
You revealed what is the suffering of those in the Avici,
the deepest Buddhist hell.
You let them be reborn in the blessed fivefold heaven[12] of light.
Look for the ways of salvation,
you crossed lands going to every side.
When you found humans needing salvation,
you rescued all.

YOU PREACHED THE JEWEL OF THE GOSPEL

To those like us who were lazy,
you preached details of the jewel of the gospel book.[13]
We come on the ways of freedom and salvation
when we know them in the book.
If you hadn't preached the pure law so fully,
wouldn't the world and its thinking beings
have come to an end by now?
After the four Buddhas[14] you went down

---

9. Again, the realm of light of the previous prophets.
10. The Sumeru mountain is the central mountain of the universe in the Buddhist and Hindu cosmology.
11. The six organs of perception (*sadayatana*) in Buddhism are the five sense organs and *manas,* the mind.
12. The realm of light.
13. Probably Mani's Living Gospel.
14. The four Buddhas are probably Seth, Zoroaster, Buddha, and Jesus. "Four" is not in the original text.

and attained truly incomparable buddhahood.[15]
You saved thousands
and saved them from dark hell.
You purged them of masterly cunning and deception
and caused them to help others.
You were a guide leading those in error.
You saved them from the claws of evil Mara.[16]
You rescued the malevolent,
you healed the blind,
you caused them to do works of honor,
you showed them the right path to the land of the gods,
You were born the hope and refuge of the world.
You taught the seven precious books[17]
and held back those about to join evil.[18]

YOU DO GOOD TO ALL

Walking on foot and calling your name,
praising you with their tongues,
they would all love the same as children
who love their mothers and fathers.
Hugging them with your compassionate heart,
you brought them great help and prosperity.
Not distinguishing between relative and stranger,
you made them yours.
You counseled numberless people.
With your heart you do good to all,
and through your good
the afflicted overcome their sorrow.
You brought them great help and prosperity
in this way always.
Because of your virtue
you come into full buddhahood.

---

15. Buddhist technical term for highest stage of enlightenment (*anuttara-samyakasambodhi*).
16. The Buddhist Satan.
17. Mani's seven canonical books.
18. The next twenty-one verses are badly preserved and have been reconstructed.

Through your insuperable tongue and generosity
you gave the jewel of the good law to us the miserable.

The families of the living lost their minds
through their dark passions,
yet they were reborn.

YOU EMBRACE EVERYONE

Through your great and compassionate heart
you put your arms around everyone
and rescued them from the cycle of rebirth,
saving them from *samsara*.

The blessed of pure heart
slowly came upon insight,
overcame malevolence,
and came to the statue of the *arhats*.[19]
But pleasure, tying them to the world,
gave them mastery of cunning and trickery.
You brought them help and prosperity.

For those who forgot their origin,
you revealed who you are,
changing your form.
When all living beings saw your revelation,
they were inspired and desired only
to escape from the suffering of cyclical *samsara*.
To children you came in a benevolent form
and turned them from evil
and love of the world, to which they had succumbed.
Before the blue sky of the whole kingdom
you were born as the Buddha god of teachers.

KNOWLEDGE SHINES, COMPASSION GROWS

On seeing you, the living were happy
and with firm minds no longer doubted.

---

19. Ideal figures or saints of Theravada Buddhism.

They obeyed your commandments.
Their good thoughts increased every day
and shone like the sun god.[20]
The knowledge of light shone.
In their hearts compassion grew.
They obeyed the commandment to be sinless
and escaped the unending burning fires of hell.

They tried to keep the true law,
observe the true commandment,
and not fall into impure sin.

After knowing the transience of the body,
they left their houses and homes.
Following the good law, they were pure in body.
They made every effort to follow pure laws
and avoid the dangerous places.
To be reborn in the palace of immortality,
they observed the commandment to be pure in mouth.[21]
They prayed for blessing
and to walk along the road of blessing
and escape terrible *samsara*.
They followed the commandment of blessed poverty.[22]
In fear of the perceived transitory doctrines
and of the three evil ways,[23]
they followed the three seals[24]
to be reborn in the highest place.[25]

GATHER, MEDITATE, SING

You agreed to command them,
to praise and sing songs,
to repeal their evil,

---

20. Probably Jesus.
21. Purity of mouth is one of the three seals in Manichaeism.
22. Blessed poverty is a Manichaean commandment of the elect.
23. The three evil ways or forms of existence in the Buddhist sense are existence as animals, hungry spirits, and beings in hell.
24. Commandments of the heart, mouth, and hands.
25. The realm of light. The next twenty verses are badly preserved and are reconstructed.

to gather and meditate.
The living had been confused,
but when they heard your command,
their virtue was a teeming stream and river,[26]
and they were reborn in the land of the Buddhas.[27]
Other unworldly people
walked in pure paths
and meditated
and were reborn in the palace of immortality.[28]

We bow our heads
and we worship before you, our highest god.
May the living on earth
be forever reborn in *nirvana!*
We worship. Our heart is steady.
May all the living on earth
escape dangers.
May they find the peace of *nirvana.*

So through the virtue of our praise and worship
may all holy forces
of the gods above and below
and of the diverse spirits
be magnified.[29]

---

26. A Buddhist image.
27. The realm of light.
28. Again, the realm of light.
29. A colophon typical of Turkish Buddhist texts from the silk road.

PART SIX

Islamic Mystical Literature

INTRODUCTION

MARVIN MEYER

In the final two parts of this volume we present literary texts of two traditions that are somewhat later in origin than the traditions of gnosis we have encountered thus far. These texts of Islamic mysticism and Cathar dualism are powerful examples of later gnostic or neomanichaean literature. In this part we consider Islamic mystical literature in general, and the Mother of Books in particular, as an example of the rich and diverse mystical heritage of Islam.

MUHAMMAD THE SEAL OF THE PROPHETS

In the cultural and religious mix of late sixth-century Arabia, Muhammad was born into the Hashimite clan of the Quraysh tribe in Mecca. The religious climate of Arabia during his day was substantially Semitic, with a variety of expressions. The faiths of Arabia were faiths of the desert, faiths that developed from Babylonian and Zoroastrian roots and from Jewish and Christian faiths of one sort or another. Caravans had traversed the trade routes of Arabia for a very long time, and with the caravans came cultural traditions and connections. Hence, some of the deities of Arabia had even been accorded Greco-Roman names and identities.

In Mecca three such goddesses were called daughters of the god Allah. These goddesses are al-Lat, a mother goddess who may be linked to the sun; al-Manat, the goddess of fate; and al-Uzza, the goddess of the morning star. Al-Uzza—sometimes connected to Venus (Aphrodite), Fortuna, and Isis—ruled the stone city of Petra, with Dushara, and the three daughters of Allah still assert themselves in Salman Rushdie's book *The Satanic Verses*. Allah, in turn, was the creator god. His name means "god" or "the god," and he was worshiped in Mecca by Muhammad and the members of the Quraysh tribe.

Muhammad was a reflective, brooding person of around forty, it is said, when he wandered off to a cave near Mt. Hira, just north of Mecca, fell into meditation, and received a revelation from Allah. The vision is described in sura 96 of the Qur'an: "In the name of god, the merciful, the compassionate. Recite: in the name of your lord who created, created man of a blood clot. Recite: and your lord is the most generous, who taught by the pen, taught man what he knew not."[1] Later Muhammad reflected upon the circumstances of his vision at Mount Hira: "One night," the prophet says, "Gabriel came to me with a cloth as I slept and said, Recite! I answered, I cannot recite. So he choked me with the cloth until I believed that I should die. . . . I awoke from my sleep, and it was as if they had written a message in my heart."[2] Muhammad went out of the cave and saw a vision of Gabriel, who appeared everywhere on the horizon.

Such visions, which recurred over a period of time, could take different forms. Once, thinking about his visions, Muhammad observed, "I hear loud noises, and then it seems as if I am struck by a blow. I never receive a revelation without the consciousness that my soul is being taken away from me." Again, "The revelation comes to me in two ways. Sometimes Gabriel visits me and tells it to me as though one man were speaking to another, but then what he speaks is lost to me. But sometimes it comes to me as with the noise of a bell, so that my heart is confused. But what is revealed to me in this way never leaves me."[3]

Gradually Muhammad came to the realization that he was a prophet (*nabi*) and messenger (*rasul*, apostle) of Allah, and his visions became the basis for the Qur'an. So Muhammad proclaimed Islam, submission to Allah, who is acclaimed the one and only god, the god of Jews, Christians, and Muslims.

According to Islam, Muhammad is a prophet and the seal of the prophets, the prophet whose distinction is that the Qur'an was revealed through him. Yet the Qur'an insists that Muhammad is the last in a long series of prophets. The prophetic line is said to include such venerable people of god as Adam, Noah, Abraham, Moses, John the baptizer, Jesus—and, of course, Muhammad. This concept of the prophetic line recalls similar emphases on a series of prophets in other traditions, particularly in Manichaeism. Manichaeism professed that a series of people in the past functioned as messengers (apostles)

---

1. Adapted from Arberry, ed., *The Koran Interpreted.*
2. Adapted from Andrae, *Muhammad: The Man and His Faith,* 43–44.
3. From ibid., 49–50.

of light, including Seth (Sethel), Noah, Enosh, Enoch, Shem, Abraham, Buddha, Aurentes, Zoroaster, Jesus, Paul—and Mani, the consummate messenger of light.

This observation leads Kurt Rudolph, the prominent scholar of gnosticism, to draw a provocative conclusion:

> Manichaeism, which flourished longer in the Orient, found its reflection in early Islamic theological trends, apparently most effectively in the book of the Arab prophet himself. Mohammed, according to the Qur'an, advocates the same cyclic theology of revelation as the gnostic prophet Mani from Mesopotamia, and stands similarly at the end of a series of forerunners who proclaimed the same as he did, but with less success, and whose teaching was falsified by their followers. Mohammed has the same predilection for the Old Testament figures from the Pentateuch as has Mani. But their view of the world and their doctrine of salvation are almost in opposition and separate them; they are united in their claim to be the last prophet of a very ancient history of salvation. Mani's work has vanished in history, while Mohammed's foundation, thanks to a different point of departure that had a more positive attitude to the world, developed into the greatest post-Christian world religion, a fame which Mani was also able to claim for a time.[4]

JESUS THE SAGE IN ISLAM

The role of prophet Jesus (in Arabic, 'Isa) in Islam may be secondary to that of prophet Muhammad, but Jesus remains a glorious prophet and sage. Within Islam Jesus is confessed to be not only a prophet of god but also the messiah, servant, spirit, and word of god, the son of Mary, who spoke words of wisdom and performed mighty deeds as he taught submission to Allah. At the end of a remarkable life he died—or perhaps he only to seemed to die, says the Qur'an, in terms that bring to mind the unreal death of Jesus in the Second Treatise of the Great Seth and the Revelation of Peter in the Nag Hammadi library, as well as other gnostic sources. Features of prophet Jesus in Islam recall aspects of

---

4. Rudolph, *Gnosis*, 376.

Jesus in Christian traditions, particularly in the wisdom traditions and wisdom gospels discussed above, and so bear brief examination here.

Of particular interest are the sayings of Jesus found in Islamic literature. The sayings of Jesus in the Qur'an, through relatively few in number, are readily available in editions and translations of the Qur'an. Many more sayings of Jesus are collected in other Islamic sources, and they merit close examination.[5] Many are wisdom sayings. Taken together, these Islamic sayings of Jesus present a picture of Jesus that may be compared to that of Q and the Gospel of Thomas, discussed at the beginning of this volume.

The Muslim who collected and edited many of these sayings of Jesus is Abu Hamid Muhammad al-Ghazali. Al-Ghazali was an eleventh- to twelfth-century Muslim scholar, theologian, and mystic who wrote numerous books, the greatest of which is *Ihya' 'ulum al-din* (The revival of the religious sciences).[6] He composed this book following a period of turbulence in his life, when he had retired from his professorial position in Baghdad and had begun a life of meditation as a Sufi. This magnificent work, four volumes in length, is divided into four major "quarters," which deal with issues of religious practice, social customs, vices, and virtues, and contain ten books each, for a total of forty books. In this massive work al-Ghazali discusses the provisions of the Shari'a (Islamic law), and he addresses the reader on the devout life of a Muslim, including the mystical life. Within the work al-Ghazali cites sayings of Jesus.

The following are a few of the sayings of Jesus quoted in al-Ghazali's *Revival of the Religious Sciences:*

> Jesus said, "Whoever knows and does and teaches will be called great in the kingdom of heaven." (1.8)

> Jesus said, "Do not offer wisdom to those who are not worthy of it, or you might harm it, and do not withhold it from those who are worthy of it, or you might harm them. Be like a gentle doctor who puts the medicine in the diseased spot. Whoever offers wisdom to those who are not worthy of it is a fool, and whoever withholds it from those who are worthy of it is an evildoer. Wisdom

---

5. Collections of these sayings of Jesus have been published by Asin y Palacios, *Logia et Agrapha Domini Jesu;* Dunkerley, *Beyond the Gospels;* Jeremias, *Unknown Sayings of Jesus;* Margoliouth, "Christ in Islam"; Khalidi, *The Muslim Jesus;* Meyer, *The Unknown Sayings of Jesus;* Morrice, *Hidden Sayings of Jesus;* Robson, *Christ in Islam;* and Ropes, "Agrapha."
6. On al-Ghazali see Meyer, "Did Jesus Drink from a Cup?" in Asgeirsson, De Troyer, and Meyer, ed., *From Quest to Q.*

has rights and rightful owners, so give each what is appropriate." (1.30; compare Matthew 9:12; Mark 2:17; Luke 5:31)

Jesus said, "Evil scholars are like a rock that has fallen at the mouth of a brook: it does not drink the water, nor does it let the water flow to the plants. And evil scholars are like the drainpipe of a latrine that is plastered outside but filthy inside; or like graves that are decorated outside but contain dead people's bones inside." (1.49; similar sayings are found in Matthew 23:27–28 [Q]; Luke 11:44 [Q]; Gospel of Thomas 39, 102; and in Aesop's fable of the dog in the manger)

Jesus was asked, "Who taught you?"
He answered, " No one taught me. I saw that the ignorance of the fool was shameful, so I avoided it." (3.52)

Jesus was asked by some people, "Show us the way by which we may enter paradise."
He said, "Do not speak at all."
They said, "We cannot do that."
He said, "Then say only what is good." (3.87)

Jesus passed by a pig and said to it, "Go in peace."
They said, "O spirit of god, why do you speak like this to a pig?"
He answered, "I do not want my tongue to grow accustomed to evil." (3.64)

One day Jesus was walking with his students, and they passed by the carcass of a dog.
The students said, "How this dog stinks!"
But Jesus said, "How white are its teeth!" (3.108)

One day Jesus was greatly troubled by the rain and thunder and lightning, and he began to seek shelter. His eye fell on a tent some distance away, but when he came to it, he found a woman inside, so he turned away from it. Then he noticed a cave in a mountain, but when he came to it, there was a lion in it. Laying his hand on the lion, he said, "My god, you have given everything a resting place, but to me have you given none."

Then god revealed to him, "Your resting place is the house of my mercy." (3.153; see also Matthew 8:20 [Q]; Luke 9:58 [Q]; Gospel of Thomas 86)

Jesus said, "Whoever seeks the world is like one who drinks sea-water. The more he drinks, the more his thirst increases, until it kills him." (3.161)

The students said to Jesus, "How is it that you can walk on water and we cannot?"

He said to them, "What do you think of the dinar and the dirham?"[7]

They answered, "They are precious."

He said, "But to me they are the same as mud." (3.175; see also John 6:16–21 and other gospel texts regarding Jesus' walking on water)

Jesus the messiah used to take nothing with him except for a comb and a jug. Then he saw a person combing his beard with his fingers, so he threw away the comb, and he saw another person drinking from a river with his hands, so he threw away the jug. (4.182; a similar story is told about Diogenes the Cynic philosopher)

Additionally, in an inscription from a mosque at Fatehpur Sikri, India (also known from the Clerical Instruction of Petrus Alphonsi), Jesus says, "This world is a bridge. Pass over it, but do not build your dwelling there." This resembles, as much as any other saying, Gospel of Thomas 42: "Be passersby."

ISLAMIC GNOSIS AND THE MOTHER OF BOOKS

The Muslim devotees of the party (Shi'a) of Ali, now commonly called Shi'ites, emerged from the bleak and bloody times that saw the assassination of Ali, cousin and son-in-law of Muhammad, and Ali's sons Hasan and Husayn. The commitments of these partisans of Ali included an insistence that the leaders of the Muslim community—the caliphs—be direct descendants of Muhammad, and that these leaders were legitimated by Allah and given knowledge by Allah. Among the early adherents of Shi'a were certain thinkers, called *ghulat*, "exaggerators" or "extremists," who were referred to in this way because of their extreme devotion to the figure of Ali and whose perspective could be messianic, mystical, even gnostic. Advocates of such *ghuluw*,

---

7. Pieces of money.

"exaggeration," included Abdallah ibn Saba, described by Ioan Culianu as "the archheretic of Islamic ghuluw"—a figure comparable to Simon Magus in the history of Christian gnosticism— who was devoted to Ali in Kufa, Iraq, and continued to be a proponent of Ali even after Ali's assassination. Eventually forms of Islamic exaggeration led to the development of several thinkers, activists, and schools of thought, some of them quite radical: Isma'ilites, Assassins, 'Alawites, Nusayris, Druzes, Sufis.

Ioan Culianu speculates on the roots of these *ghulat* in Islam:

> How might gnostic myths have reached the Ghulat and the Isma'iliyah? They were probably transmitted by the so-called *mawali*, or "clients," from Kufa. The *mawali* were foreigners converted to Islam after the conquest of Persia's capital, Seleucia-Ctesiphon . . . and its transfer to Kufa under the Umayyads (637–638 C.E.). Among the *mawali*, Jewish, Christian, Zoroastrian, gnostic, and Manichaean ideas were represented.[8]

Some of the *ghulat* put their speculative thought into literature. Two revelatory texts that stem from these traditions are the Mother of Books (*Umm al-kitab*)[9] and the Book of Shadows (*Kitab al-azillah*). A portion of the former work, the Mother of Books, is presented here. The Mother of Books comes from the late eighth century, from the town of Kufa, famous for its *ghulat*. It is a text that deals, like so much of the literature of gnosis in this volume, with creation and the proper interpretation of creation. The strongest case for a gnostic understanding of the Mother of Books has been made by Heinz Halm.[10] Halm understands the Mother of Books to present a gnostic mythological account in Shi'ite form. The divine manifests itself in a fivefold fashion, reminiscent, suggests Halm, of the divine father's realm of five (pentad) in the Secret Book of John, but in the Mother of Books the five are identified with prophet Muhammad; his son-in-law, Ali; his daughter, Fatima; and his grandsons, Hasan and Husayn. In Manichaean literature one of the ways the five is expressed is in five trees of paradise, a motif that also occurs in the Gospel of Thomas (saying 19). Five trees of paradise are also discussed in the Mother of Books. The arrogance of the gnostic world ruler, so central to gnostic cosmogonies, finds its corollary in the Mother of Books in the arrogant Azazi'il.

---

8. Culianu, "Gnosticism," in *The Encyclopedia of Religion* 5:575.
9. The epithet "Mother of Books" is also commonly applied to the Qur'an itself.
10. Halm, *Die islamische Gnosis*.

Azazi'il seems to have developed from a figure of Jewish lore, Azazel, the chief of the fallen angels (see 1 Enoch and the Apocalypse of Abraham), who also makes an appearance among the Mandaeans and who is somewhat reminiscent of the gnostic demiurge Yaldabaoth.

The selection from the Mother of Books presented here includes the major, revelatory section of the text, in which a revelation (in dialogue form) about the origin and meaning of the world is given (from Baqir, as revealer, to Jabir, as the recipient of the revelation and the dialogue partner who raises questions). The names of many of the figures in the revelation are derived from famous characters in Islamic and Shi'ite history. The revelation is a brilliant text of epic poetry, with mythic color, apocalyptic fire, and mystical power. This revelation describes the glories, angels, and colors of the cosmic realm, along with the god who remains exalted above it all. Beginning with a long mystical exegesis of the *Bismillah*, the opening phrase of every sura in the Qur'an ("In the name of Allah, the compassionate, the merciful"), the text proceeds to demonstrate its points with reference to proof texts in the Qur'an and figures in Islamic lore. Throughout the revelation there are sections that relate the cosmogonic descriptions to the individual and to the inner mystical quest for the divine. The revelation uses imagery that sometimes brings to mind the opening chapters of Genesis and gnostic interpretations of Genesis as it maintains that the world below comes from the arrogant, rebellious Azazi'il.

Eventually the world below literally becomes colorless. The benevolent will of god for the cosmos and the people in the cosmos is realized, however, through the actions of Salman, god's regent, who recalls the first human or Sophia (wisdom) in gnostic texts and who is described, as is the first human in many gnostic texts and Sophia in some gnostic texts (for example, Valentinian texts), as a higher figure and a lower figure. At last, the text proclaims, people may come to knowledge and be liberated. The Mother of Books provides four conditions for such salvation; a postscript to the revelation, part of which is presented here, adds an account of how the individual person may embrace mystical knowledge. In the postscript it is said that the one who seeks perfect knowledge will find it:

The one who knows arises
and testifies to spirit as to himself.
The student will be perfect, and ten spirits
are spoken for. God says, "These are the perfect ten."

44

The Mother of Books[1]

THE ESSENTIAL MYSTERY

Jabir rose to his feet, saying, "My lord,
tell me the meaning of the holy phrase,
Bismillah al-rahman al-rahim.
These words meaning 'In the name of Allah,
the compassionate, the merciful' begin
each chapter of the Qur'an. And many
recite them before doing anything.
All know them as the essential mystery."

Baqir said, "They are from the high king, who is god.[2]
He wrote them as the loftiest line on earth:
seven and twelve parts the king made for himself.[3]
Overhead he made a sea of a thousand colors
and below another sea named godliness.[4]
Between the seas the king placed seven and twelve deathless

---

1. The Mother of Books: translated into German by Heinz Halm, *Die islamische Gnosis,* 113–98; translated from the German by Heather TerJung; retranslated as blank verse by Willis Barnstone.
2. High or exalted king, throughout the text, is god. On Jabir, the student, compare Jabir ibn Yazid al-Ju'fi. On Baqir (or al-Baqir), compare Muhammad al-Baqir, the fifth imam, as revealer of knowledge. Al-Baqir means "the one who opens," for example, the one who opens knowledge. See below.
3. The numbers seven and twelve also occur in the Secret Book of John and other gnostic texts.
4. Another heavenly body of water, a luminous spring of living water, is described near the opening of the Secret Book of John.

uncreated lights, his ears and eyes. As written in the Qur'an,
'He let two great bodies of water flow. They meet
with a barrier to halt their commingling.'[5]

"Jabir, the large bodies of water are two seas,
the barrier is the king, their pearls and coral
are the Naqib and Najib angels.[6] They are dazzling
lights and lamps joining realms to believers' hearts.
By the highest god, here is knowledge[7] flowing
from paradise to paradise and hell to hell,
and nothing has been written of these events.

THE SEVEN AND TWELVE LIGHT OUR FORM AND BODY

"Jabir, the seven and twelve also light our form
and body.[8] So the brain is the white sea,
and the spirit of speech is the high king
found in the medulla. Two eyes, two ears,
two nostrils, and the mouth are seven parts
of the high king. Two hands with ten fingers
are the twelve parts dividing the white sea
and remote eternal sphere. And in that sphere
is the high king's canopy over our heads.

"The sphere is the great spirit of a thousand colors.
The brain is the white earth over seven skies
as the white sea lies over seven realms
of a heavenly palace. As it is written, 'A revelation
from him who created the earth and heaven.
The merciful one sat on the throne possessing
all in the skies, on earth, and in between
and underground.'[9] God is on the white sea
as the high king's throne—he is all powerful!

---

5. Qur'an sura 55.
6. Two classes of angels. The term Naqib means "leader"; the term Najib means "noble one."
7. Elsewhere, gnosis.
8. This and other sections that focus on the body as the locale of divine mystical activity may be later additions to the text, applying this story of the godhead and its evolution to the individual's inner mystical experience.
9. Qur'an sura 20.

"He made the houris,[10] castles, torches, lights,
and young men of eternal youth, his pearls
scattered on the earth.[11] Jabir, *Bismillah al-rahman
al-rahim* at the beginning of the Qur'an
is the holy palace. *Ba* and *sin* and *mim* and the dot
under the *ba*[12] are four angels. In our tongue
they are Salman, Miqdad, Abu Zarr, and Ammar.
Two *lams* and *ha* describe three other angels:
Komayl, Abu Horayra, and Jondob,
and *alif* in the middle of seven letters
is the high king. He is all powerful![13]

OUR FEATURES ALSO REFLECT BISMILLAH'S LETTERS

"Our human features were created to prove
this mystery. The right ear, eye, nostril,
and language reflect *ba* and *sin* and *mim*,
and language is the dot under the *ba*.
The left ear, eye, and nostril become *lams*
and *mim* and *ha*. The holy spirit of life
on the forehead is the sign and proof
of *alif* in the middle, and these parts
figured on our head are the spirit's tools.[14]
The ears are set at both sides for eternity.
Quicker than a wink they inform life spirit.
The eyes, nose, and mouth are set so Salman,
Miqdad, Ammar, Abu Zarr, Jondob,
Abu Horayra, and Komayl obey
the high king. They remain his subjects, girded
before him. They are carrying his throne.[15]

---

10. Young women of legendary beauty who live in paradise.
11. Qur'an sura 76.
12. *Ba, sin,* and *mim,* with *lam* and *ha* (below), are the Arabic letters of *Bismillah.*
13. The Arabic letters of the *Bismillah* indicate angelic powers, with god (the letter *alif*) in the middle. Here the names of the angels derive from names of followers of Ali: Salman, Miqdad, Abu Dharr, Ammar, Kumayl, Abu Hurayra, and Jundub.
14. The Arabic letters of the *Bismillah* also reveal the head's powers.
15. Qur'an sura 40.

BISMILLAH ALSO MEANS GOD'S THRONE AND GREATNESS

"Jabir,[16] *Bismillah al-rahman al-rahim*
is greater than people say. A mere heart
cannot imagine god's name and his throne
and the godhead. Here we have the high king's
complete magnificence. And so his seven
and twelve attributes appear in the letters
and they are also concealed inside them.

"The twenty-eight lights of the Najib angels
and light of four angels give life to heaven
and earth, and also slip it away from them.
They hide in the clothing of the twelve letters
that make up *al-rahman al-rahim*,
and *Bismillah* is the throne of god."[17]
The revealer of knowledge[18] said, "This word
and image is written on a silver tablet:
Bismillah al-rahman al-rahim."

BISMILLAH'S NINETEEN LETTERS

Jabir said, "Be visible to your weak servant, lord.
Let thousands of lives and their possessions
be sacrificed, all for the life of the lord."
The revealer of knowledge answered him,
"I must save your life. Be careful, Jabir.[19]
Bismillah stands for the most remote realm,
and *al-rahman al-rahim* is the white sphere.
Bismillah has nineteen letters: *ba* two,

---

16 . Or "Jafar," another student.

17. This description is reminiscent of the pleroma or fullness of holy glory in gnostic texts. On god's throne, compare the merkavah (god's chariot) in Jewish mystical literature. The use of letters to signify virtues is characteristic of Kabbalah.

18. The gnostic revealer plays a prominent role in numerous texts.

19. The dangers of mystical inquiry are fully documented.

sin three, *mim* three, *alif* three, and *lam* three,
second *lam* three, *ha* two. Nineteen letters.[20]

THE SEVEN AND THE TWELVE AS MUHAMMAD AND HIS FAMILY

"The seven are parts of the high king: Muhammad,
Ali, Fatima, Hasan, Husayn, Abdallah,
and Abu Talib.[21] There is nothing above
or beside the seven. With a hundred thousand lights
and sparks and the glow of every color
and type, the seven appear in the white sea.
The other twelve are twelve lights of the people
of the house, lined in a row as incomparable
members of this realm. 'God commands the hosts
of heaven and earth. He is almighty and wise.'[22]

THE SEVEN AND THE TWELVE AS HEAVENLY FEATURES

"The seven and the twelve lie hidden in the raiment
of the seven angels, signifying the seven letters
of the *Bismillah*, namely, Salman, Miqdad,
Abu Zarr, Ammar, Abu Horayra, Jondob,
and Komayl. The seven mantles and curtains
come from the seven and twelve in the same way
that *Bismillah* is the seven and the twelve.
Seven and twelve secret letters lie hidden
deep in the seven, and from east to west
in the world, no one is reliable but the reader

---

20. The sum of nineteen is found by counting the numbers of letters in the *names* of the letters in *Bismillah*.
21. Muhammad is the prophet, Ali his cousin and son-in-law, Fatima the daughter of Muhammad, Hasan and Husayn the sons of Ali, Abdallah the father of Muhammad, and Abu Talib the father of Ali and uncle of Muhammad. The first five represent the five powers or lights or angels, the last two seem to be later additions. See below.
22. Qur'an sura 48.

of this book or someone who has learned
by hearing words spoken by the believers.

"*Al-rahman al-rahim* is the twelve Naqib
of the white sea, and their raiment conceals
twenty-eight Najib and four familiar angels.
They are hidden, but if you add the letters
of *al-rahman al-rahim* you come up with
the thirty-four letters: twenty-eight Najib,
the two Yatim, and four familiar angels.[23]

"The twelve hidden letters are *Bismillah*
as *Bismillah* is *al-rahman al-rahim*.
The most remote realm is the high king's canopy
over the white sea, and the twelve Naqib,
special beings before the high king, carry
the white sea. The high one says, 'Each day
the eight in the sky carry the lord's throne.'[24]
The twenty-four posts of god's throne are the twelve
Naqib, the seven angels of the throne,
and five special beings from Muhammad
to Abu Talib are two groups of seven.

THE BODY AS A MICROCOSM OF THE UNIVERSE

"'And we told seven stories and cited from
the powerful Qur'an.'[25] 'We' are the twelve,
the people of the house after the seven angels
of the throne. Seven and twelve. It is written,
'God created heaven and earth in six days
sitting on his throne.'[26] Jabir, see the microcosm."[27]

Jabir said, "My lord, I ask you to inform me."
The revealer of knowledge answered,

---

23. More ranks of angels. The two Yatim (orphans or single ones) may be Miqdad and Abu
Zarr. See below.
24. Qur'an sura 69.
25. Qur'an sura 15.
26. Qur'an sura 7.
27. The following lines may be an addition to the text.

"These seven lights made a circle around
the faces of the believers and imams.[28]
The seven and twelve virtues hide in them.
If one is missing, then the body's clothing
and form are incomplete. The right ear hears
three words of knowledge. The right eye sees
three tools, white, black, and yellow. The right nostril
smells three aromas, good, bad, and mixed.
The left ear and nostril are similarly set,
and the tongue speaks the three words of knowledge.
They are nineteen. As it is written, 'It burns the skin.
Nineteen over them.'[29] The twenty-eight Najib angels
are ten fingers and two hands confirming
the twelve and twenty-eight of the white sea.

"Here you have the meaning of *Bismillah
al-rahman al-rahim*. Jabir, here is
the knowledge that heaven and earth cannot know
and in the book there is no explanation."

WHAT IS THE CREATOR OF THIS WORLD LIKE?

Jabir rose to his feet, wiped his face with his hand,
and asked, "My lord, is the creator in heaven
or on earth? What is he and where is he from?
What does he look like? What virtues has he?
Where is he from and what has he created?"[30]

The revealer of knowledge—may our salvation
come from him—said, "Jabir, these are hard questions.
Forget them. It's wrong to open the curtain
before the high king. It is a grave sin.
No prophet or spirit has ever drawn open
the curtain, even a slit, to reveal the king.
No book has ever recorded his face.
Keep this book for yourself and the believers."

---

28. Leaders of the Islamic community.
29. Qur'an sura 74.
30. Such a list of questions to be answered by the revealer is attested in other gnostic texts.

Jabir was still awhile. He paused, stood up,
murmured a prayer, praised god, and then he said,
"My lord, lord of all lords, speak to your weak,
helpless servant. Answer my question." And all
close to him arose and pleaded with him.

The revealer of knowledge said, "Jabir,
could we move the curtain and the veil
the slightest bit and make the high king visible?
If someone did this, their spirit would leave their body
and enter that of the listener. Jabir, these words
must not be overheard. It is dangerous.
Jabir, be careful! I will write them on a paper.
May god guard you and guard the messenger,
and Muhammad and Ali, and Salman, Miqdad,
and Abu Zarr, and the Naqib and Najib angels.
I leave it to you to read and to be silent.
Then believers who own this book will read
and learn and not spread the word disastrously."[31]

The revealer of knowledge—may we be blessed—
wrote it on paper and placed it in Jabir's hands.
He wrote, "Our lord and creator is in heaven
and on earth, in heaven's highest spheres
and in the microcosm of the curtain
of believers and imams who live in time."

THE FIVE PREEXISTENT LIGHTS

"Before the sky or earth or any creature,
there were five preexistent lights in five colors
like the rainbow.[32] Sublime air issued like sun
from sparks of light and spread over the sky
and earth. The five lights stood in this air,
and a glow came out of the belly of light
continuously and in five colors: hearing,
sight, smell, taste, and speech. The five lights

---

31. For a similar statement, see the Secret Book of John.
32. The father's realm of five is presented in the Secret Book of John.

are Muhammad, Ali, Fatima, Hasan,
and Husayn. They came from nothing. As it is written,
'Speak out that he is god, one sovereign god.
He did not father children, nor was he fathered;
there's none like him.'[33] Around believers' heads
these five lights swim around the throne of god.

THE SPIRIT OF SPEECH SITS IN THE SEA ON THE BRAIN

"The spirit of speech sits among them.[34] He is the god
of truth. He creates and appears in each name
and body, from the loftiest of summits
down to the profoundest depths. Jabir,
I said, the lord is spirit through his godliness
and sun through light. Through spirituality
he has been called the spirit of speech. He sits
in the white sea on the brain of the believers.
His is color of lightning, clouds, and moon.

GOD'S FORM AND ATTRIBUTES

"Here is god's form. His right hand is retention
that comprehends and is the color of sun.
His left hand is the spirit of thought. From it
comes the full propagation of all light.
'No. Spreading his hands, he gives as he wishes,'[35]
and this spirit is the color violet.
God's head is the grandest spirit composed
of all kinds of colors, a thousand of them.
There is nothing higher than he, neither
in heaven nor on earth. 'There is nothing
that might be his equal. He hears and sees.'[36]

"His right eye is a huge spirit, the color
of white crystal. His left eye is the spirit

---

33. Qur'an sura 112.
34. The following lines may be an addition to the text.
35. Qur'an sura 5.
36. Qur'an sura 42.

of the intellect, color of red yellow fire.
The two spirits see all heaven and earth,
both this world and the next. He says, 'God sees
through what they do.'[37] Elsewhere he says, 'Their vision
does not comprehend him, but he their vision.'[38]

"His two ears are an intense mixing of
the rays of color from the holy veil.
They hear the voices of all living creatures
and bring them from all spheres and palaces
into this spirit in the form of god.
As it is written, 'We gave them hearing and sight
and understanding. Yet their ears and sight
and even understanding couldn't help them,
for they rejected the emblems of god
and they were seized by him whom they had mocked.'[39]

"The lord's nostrils are the spirit of knowledge,
one the color of red carnelian, exuding everywhere
a floating holy perfume. The other nostril
is the spirit of the almighty, green
from god's breath and radiance. His tongue
is the voice of holy spirit, the color of red rubies,
and by whom all creation was affected.
As it is written, 'Praise him who holds dominion
and to whom all of you will be returned.'[40]

"The heart of the lord is the spirit of faith,
whose name is the confessor of one true faith
and who is the color of the sphere of the moon.
The faith of all believers shines through him,
and guidance and trust in our god of spirits
comes from him. It is written, 'Whoever trusts
in god will find fulfillment. God brings his own
desires to completion. He has set the measure

---

37. Qur'an sura 2.
38. Qur'an sura 6.
39. Qur'an sura 46.
40. Qur'an sura 36.

and goal for all things.'⁴¹ And the lord's two feet
reveal the holy and the believer's view
in this house of speech where he is connected
to the heart and spirit of the body's life.

"On the day of resurrection the lord
will place his foot across hell and freeze it.
The heart is not based on any perception
and bears no witness till the holy is revealed
and a believer's vision appears in him,
and that vision will testify to the true
and present and existing lord, and wake
at night and fast by day. 'Our god affirms
there is no other god. A truth for angels
and the wise. He provides us with justice.'⁴²

"The lord's throne is this godly seat, the brain.
The right half of the brain is the spirit
of wisdom, and the left is the spirit of abundance.
The lord sits in his majesty. As it is written,
'The merciful set himself on the throne.'⁴³
These five lights, visible from eight angles,
are reflected on the believers' faces
and compose the lord's throne: of two eyes, ears,
nostrils, speech, and spirit perceiving taste.

BE CAREFUL, JABIR

"By god, the highest and most powerful god!
We wrote these words in no other book.
Careful, Jabir! The spirit of anyone openly
speaking these words will quit its bodily form."

Then Jabir read the tablet and he fell
to the ground, bowed, and said, "I testify.

---

41. Qur'an sura 65.
42. Qur'an sura 3.
43. Qur'an sura 20.

Praise and honor Muhammad and Ali,
the lord of angels and spirit, the glorified
and chosen one, and his governor as-Salsal[44]
and Abu al-Hattab."[45] Baqir said, "Jabir,
all the believers who receive this book,
let them take care! They must read it silently
and only at night. By day they should seek
each single believer who knows the lord
and witnesses him. He'll find deliverance
from the imprisonment of heart. Jabir,
I mean every believer who knows the lord
and his majesty, who witnesses him
and gives up life, money, and his possessions."

WHAT OF THOSE WHO DENY GOD'S ATTRIBUTES?

Jabir asked, "My lord, what does it mean
when fallen creatures say that god cannot
be described and he is without attributes?"
Baqir answered, "Jabir, these are god's words
of wrath. The high king is near and is called near
and rejects the worship of cursed Iblis: [46]
'They see him distantly; we see him close.' [47]
Watch out, Jabir. I tell you, when the Qur'an
states, 'Say, he is one god,'[48] this is the speech
of unbelievers. What do you say to that?"

Jabir said, "Lord of all lords, you know best."

Baqir said, "God is as we have described him,
as he appeared to Iblis. The cursed Iblis said,
and full of loathing, 'You are not our lord.

---

44. Salman.
45. A Muslim mystic from among the *ghulat*. Perhaps a later addition to the text.
46. The devil.
47. Qur'an sura 70.
48. Qur'an sura 112.

There is only one god and a godhead, but he
is in heaven. There is no likeness or image
of him.' Yet this is a shallow explanation
of the verse, 'Say, he is one god.' The words
also signify enormous anger.
May Iblis be far from you, from all Muslims
and believers. Jabir, for all the faithless
he is far and difficult, but for believers
he is near and plain. Believers know he is,
but the unbelievers see nothing there.

"When you worship what is not, it rejects
your worship. When something is not, the worship
is refused. As it is written, 'He rejects repentance
of the unbelievers.'[49] Jabir, for us
there is no room for what is not. Apart
from god as he's described, we see no other.
The high king is the spirit in the godhead.
In light he is the sun coming from god.
From realm to realm that light kisses light
all the way down into the holy seat
of the believers' brain, like rope or path.
When light and spirit fade, believers wed
the truth, and through the light return to body."

THE ORDER OF THE HEAVENLY REALMS

Jabir[50] said, "My lord, if you will, enlighten me.
Tell your servant the face, sense, and majesty
of holy realms, of light joining realm to realm."

Baqir said, "First comes the curtain of eternity
on the white sea and the form of the high king.
Muhammad, Ali, Fatima, Hasan, and Husayn
are of this realm, finished by Abu Talib

---

49. Qur'an sura 9.
50. Or "Jafar."

and Abdallah. These five angels' five lights
join the white sea like trees of paradise.[51]

"Five creatures sit in five trees in the first, white sphere:
The lion, Boraq, the white falcon, the royal phoenix,
and Duldul, who is the sign of godliness,
sit on the top of five trees,[52] singing praise,
happiness, honor, and glory from the leaves:
'All on heaven and earth glorify god,
most holy king, the powerful and wise."[53]
Boraq comes from the light of Muhammad,
Duldul from the light of Ali, the lion
from the light of Fatima, the white falcon
from the light of Hasan, the royal phoenix
comes from the glittering light of Husayn.

"The white sea is decorated with them.
In all this vastness in the white sphere,
a thousand times greater than other realms,
lies 'a garden as great as sky and earth.'[54]
The high Duldul is proof for the believers,
and Naqib and Najib for the high king.

"Boraq beams light across this holy sea
for seven angels. The lion and falcon
spread a hundred thousand feathers of light,
and holy radiance brightens the white dome.
The royal phoenix spreads his shadow over
the heads of Naqib and Najib angels,
the stream of living water flows majestic,
'and shadows scatter and the waters gush.'[55]

---

51. On the five trees of paradise see Gospel of Thomas 19, and Manichaean literature. Here in this text the legendary trees of paradise are called tuba trees (*tuba* means "happiness").
52. An eagle is perched on the tree of knowledge in paradise according to the Secret Book of John. In Islamic tradition Boraq is the winged horse on which prophet Muhammad rode on his night journey, and Duldul is Muhammad's white mule.
53. Qur'an sura 62. The revealer proceeds to describe the seven heavenly spheres, from the first, white sphere to the seventh, lapis lazuli sphere.
54. Qur'an sura 57.
55. Qur'an sura 56.

THE RUBY RED CURTAIN

"Below this white dome is a curtain red
like a ruby. In this curtain five creatures
appear in five Tuba trees. The ruby curtain
is believable down to the last sphere.
In rainbow colors 124,000 lights
on the white sea glitter to the last sphere
where 124,000 white lights
came to the ruby curtain. As it is written,
'Have you not seen that god created seven layers
of skies and how he placed the moon as light
and sun as lamp? God made you grow in earth
like plants.'[56] The high one fastened many lights
and spirits to these spheres, and then he placed
the sun and moon and glowing trees as beauty.

THE FIERY CURTAIN

"Below this curtain is a curtain the color
of fire. Five figures from the ruby curtain
show on this cloth. Their names are Gabriel,
Michael, Israfil, Azra'il, and Sura'il.
One hundred twenty-four thousand lights from the ruby curtain
shine in the sphere. As written, 'Light on light.
God chooses whom he leads into the light,
with allegories to describe his people.'[57]
Light has been described as the color fire.
The fire-colored sea is like an ocean,
and firelight glows in a white crystal of
an indescribable beauty and brilliance,
a sphere showing unnumbered lights and spirits.

---

56. Qur'an sura 71.
57. Qur'an sura 24.

THE CARNELIAN SPHERE

"Below this sphere is a curtain the color
of carnelian, and five lights of five angels
from the fire-colored sphere appear in this sphere
of carnelian color, five splendid figures
inhabiting the sphere. Their names are mind,
soul, victory, happiness, and imagination.
'A row and row of angels.'[58] In this sphere
the aura from 124,000 lights dazzles
like 100,000 suns and moons
mixed with red. Holiness shines in good food.
As it is written, 'A spring where the lord's
servants drink and let water gush endlessly.'[59]

THE EMERALD SPHERE

"Below this curtain is a sphere the color
of emeralds. One hundred twenty-four thousand lamps
and glimmering green torches. Five great lights
from the carnelian line up in a row.
A hundred thousand birds of color float,
and the bright peacocks stand majestically
in rows and rows of feathers. In their sphere
they are on fire. They sing and echo praise
to the high king and chant endlessly
to affirm the word of god: 'Have you not seen
how birds spread their wings and pull them back in?
Only the merciful one keeps them aloft.'[60]

THE VIOLET DOME

"Below is a violet dome called the gardens
of paradise. A hundred thousand luminous

---

58. Qur'an sura 89.
59. Qur'an sura 76.
60. Qur'an sura 67.

rivers and fragrant herbs and babbling brooks
mark this violet sphere, as well as castles
of paradise below where the four rivers
of wine, milk, honey, and pure water flow.
They are called the water of life. Five great
lights of this sphere, who are known as the houris,
float over these castles. As it is written, 'Houris
locked up in tents.'[61] Their words are the water
of life when praising the exalted king.

"The river of wine is practical knowledge,
the river of milk their esoteric knowledge,
the river of honey their inspired knowledge
of the eternal and ultimate sphere.
As it is written, 'The paradise promised to those
in awe of god is in this way created.
In it are rivers with unpolluted water,
another river with milk of constant taste,
another with wine a delight to drink,
another fashioned of transparent honey.'[62]
In this curtain 124,000 lamps dazzle.

THE SUN-COLORED SPHERE

"Below this sphere is a curtain of the color
of sun, and from the violet curtain come
124,000 bright candles and lamps
glowing in this curtain colored by sun.
Five other lights are masters in this sphere,
commanders of these lights, 'holding a lamp
surrounded by a glass as if it were
a glittering star.'[63] This sphere is a great sea
intrinsic with holy light. One hundred twenty-four thousand suns
flow into this sea, and the earthly world
cannot suffer its heat. As it is written,

---

61. Qur'an sura 55.
62. Qur'an sura 47.
63. Qur'an sura 24.

'We've made the sun the pilot, drawing him
gently to us. God made the night your mantle.'[64]

THE MOON-COLORED CURTAIN

"Five colors have dropped down from this curtain
to the next one, the color of the moon,
and 124,000 rainbow lights
hang in garlands with an aura of sunlight
over this curtain colored like the moon.
In this curtain are 100,000 moons,
with 24,000 full moons in rows
marking the fourteenth night. All praise five lights,
confirming the words of god: 'To catch the moon,
the night must still enter before day.
All hover in the firmament.'[65] Rezwan,
angel of paradise, has the five lights,
and the five colors of the angel soar,
fulfilling words of god: 'The good dwellings in
gardens of Eden. But the peace of god
conjures up more: supreme felicity.'[66]

THE SEVENTH SPHERE

"The fire lights from the veil colored by moon
appeared in the next sphere, which is the color
of lapis lazuli. Praise and adoration
reverberate from 100,000 lights
and spirits that are constellations shining
with stars orbiting around the five lights.
From the blue curtain 124,000
luminaries appeared across the earth
and joined the hearts of prophets and the saints
and magistrates, and in their hearts the lights
ignite so brilliantly the veil is raised,
giving them strength for anything they wish.

---

64. Qur'an sura 25.
65. Qur'an sura 36.
66. Qur'an sura 9.

GOD'S LIGHT EXTENDS TO US

"Jabir,[67] god is light joined to imams' hearts,
extending to the far end of the spheres,
from the brain of the blue dome to the spirit
of speech.[68] From the brain it has sent a shadow
over the dark heart. Though the arrogant say
god's shadow does not fall over the earth,
the earth is the heart, and god is light
joined with the heart.[69] The spirit of speech,
a symbol of the king, comes from this light.

"When light cares to, it travels to the heart,
the canopy of the king's farthest dome,
and the five lights of the blue dome are joined
to the spirit of speech and final mixture
of holy breath, sun rays, a holy union,
believing glance, and each group of five in the world
springs from this light: Muhammad, Ali, Fatima,
Hasan, and Husayn, and their shadows fall
over the earth. These five lights join the spirit
of speech, of god who has radiated shadow
over the earth that is called heart. The spirit
of senses in the chamber of the water
and vacillating spirit in the chamber
of limpid wind are beautified with light.
Then all the seven palaces and heavenly
far spheres are joined—clear down to the heart—
by chains of light as by a rope or cable.

"The spirit of speech now commands the human spirits,
'Grasp this holy cord, and by this heavenly
journey rise higher.' So god's word is fulfilled:
'He holds on to the firm handhold.'[70] The heart
is earth where all the waverers live.

---

67. Or "Jafar."
68. The following lines may be an addition to the text.
69. Here god's shadow is not meant negatively but is like a reflection of the divine.
70. Qur'an sura 2.

Half is the dark and disbelief, half light
and mercy. The spirit of the senses means
disbelief. Dark is the rebuked Adam.
The vacillating spirit lies in the chamber
of wind and sun, and the spirit of senses in
the chamber of the water and the moon.
As it is written, 'the sun rises, the moon soars.'[71]

"The journey from below and up to heaven
is tied to spirit in the way Muhammad
was joined to Ali. There is a blue curtain
comprising the believers' spirit of speech,
so all these parts join right up to god.
This is the meaning of the sovereign as
shadow of god. This sign of life comes from
the brain casting a shadow on the heart.
God on the throne, his shadow fell to earth,
and the five special beings cast their shade,
spanning from realm to realm on tested spirit.

"These five are never absent from the world.
Everywhere their names are Muhammad, Ali,
Fatima, Hasan, and Husayn. From the high throne
of god and down below to earth, nothing
and no one's ever free of them. Each group of five
in the world springs from these five glowing lights.
Five lights, originating in the faces
of humans, prove the hand contains five fingers,
the eye five layers. Orders of Muhammad
are five. As it is written, 'Prophet, we have sent you
to testify as a messenger of good news,
to warn; with his permission you call out
to god and are a bright light. Tell the believers.'[72]
Such is the meaning of heavenly spheres."

---

71. Qur'an sura 6.
72. Qur'an sura 33.

THE BEGINNING OF CREATION
SPRINGS FROM AZAZI'IL

Then Jabir[73] stood, prayed, and said, "My Lord,
how did the high king create all these spheres
and palaces? From where did he make the spirits?
What was the origin of his creation?"[74]

The revealer of knowledge—may we be blessed—
said, "The creation of these realms is hard
to fathom. Not everyone knows the way
to knowledge, and its secret's well concealed.
Jabir, in the beginning there was god,
only eternal god and nothing else,
but in the middle of five special lights
the high king shone, as told in the beginning
of this book. All the heavens and the earth
were nothing but pure clear fine spiritual air.
From five specific elements came five
lights of the farthest realms, and they contained
some 124,000 hues,
and every moment was another color.

"Those special elements were members of
the farthest dome. A hundred thousand shining
lights, candles, and lamps emerged from the depths
of the high king in that dome, moving from
nonbeing to being. As it is written, 'Questions of
the hour are but a second.'[75] No one knows
the majesty of angels, of angelic beings
and creatures. If the seas turned into ink
and trees were writing instruments, the seven
heavens were paper, and the spirits and beings

---

73. This reference to Jabir, like some later references, may indicate the name of another student
(Jabir ibn Abdallah al-Ansari).
74. Another typical list of questions.
75. Qur'an sura 16.

of lights, jinns, and humans began to write
and wrote about the appearance and majesty
of the eternal farthest dome, all would be used,
less than a thousandth of it written down,
fulfilling words of god, 'Look, if the sea
were ink for words of my lord, it would
dry up before seizing words of my lord.'[76]

"Then the high king's cries echoed left and right.
The two cries then converted into beams,
and these two beams were pure uncounted spirits.
Each spirit was made of seven colors, each
color a million colors like the rubies
from Badahshan, carnelian, coral,
turquoise, emerald, and pearls. And each joint beamed
its light like a clear star, and as our fingers
and toes have nails, so every moon or sun
shone from each nail. They were in six circles,
and each group had a leader and an elder.
The master was Azazi'il, and his
six ranks of elders went from one to six.

IN HIS IMAGE AND ARROGANCE AZAZI'IL CREATES FROM LIGHT

"The high king lent Azazi'il light, and using
this light he shaped his creations.
In his image he made spirits. The king
shouted about what he had done. Azazi'il shouted
his creation of place, aeon, and spirit into being,
and no one but the high king knows how many.[77]

"The high king said to Azazi'il, 'Old man,
tell me who you are and what I am
and what all these creatures are.' Azazi'il

---

76. Qur'an sura 18.
77. The gnostic demiurge (for example, Yaldabaoth in the Secret Book of John) creates in a similar fashion in other texts.

answered, 'You are a god and I'm a god,
and all these spirits both of us have made.'[78]

"The high king said, 'There cannot be two gods.
You're my creation. I'm the one who's made
these spirits,' in fulfillment of god's word;
'I will create a person out of clay.'[79]

"Azazi'il said, 'What I've made is more
than yours; yes, I've made ten times more than you.
How can you dare claim your divinity?'

THE HIGH KING TAKES BACK THE LIGHT FROM AZAZI'IL

"The high king captured Azazi'il's light,
saying, 'These creatures you have made I made
also. If I withdraw the gift I loaned you,
how will you create?' He took from Azazi'il
the light he'd loaned him and the creatures
that had been made with it, and from it
he made a dome of a white sea a thousand times
larger than the blue dome of earthly sky.
He made 124,000 lamps,
flickering candles, and brightly burning lights
appear, and painted palaces and castles
out of white crystal in 100,000 colors,
and he adorned them with the flowing rivers
of the water of life and on the riverbanks
the Tuba tree. In branches of the trees
the royal phoenix sat, and in its shade
were young men and boys. The white falcon, Duldul,
Boraq, and the lion adorned this white sphere.
On branches he created the wood pigeon,
turtledove and nightingale, beautiful

---

78. Azazi'il's boastful statement recalls the arrogant claim of the demiurge in gnostic texts.
79. Qur'an sura 38.

beyond description. 'Nothing had been made
like him. He is the one who hears and sees.'[80]

"After the high king fashioned the white dome
in all its beauty, he told Azazi'il,
'Make another sea equal to the one
that I have made.' After the king said this,
Azazi'il was shocked. He could not make
such a creation. And as it is written, 'Those
who won't believe are doomed to nothingness.'[81]
'God doesn't lead those lacking faith in him.'[82]

THE HIGH KING CREATES MORE GLORIOUS BEINGS

"The high king wanted to create more beings
and showed this, shouting out his echo ahead
and behind, and when it reached the horizons
of the holy realm, everything rebounded
the echo of the two shouts, and from them
arose six tiers of spirits a thousand times
more delicate and pure. They were embellished
with pearls, corals, and rubies. A light shone
from every joint, a sun from every sinew.
A clear moon sparkled out of its navel.

"The high king glorified himself and from him
all learned to glorify and became glorifiers.
The senior in these six ranks was his Salman.[83]
The others said, 'This place is beautiful,
and the form god has given us is beautiful.
If the godhead who created us appeared,

---

80. Qur'an sura 42.
81. Qur'an sura 18?
82. Qur'an sura 16.
83. As the manifestation of the divine Salman resembles Sophia, wisdom, or even the first human, in gnostic texts.

we'd testify he gave us paradise
and beauty's forms would be with us forever.'

"Then the high king turned to them, saying, "I am
Allahu akbar, I am *Allahu akbar.*"
The spirits were amazed, not knowing whether
the high king spoke for himself or someone else.
When some time passed, the high king said again,
"I am *Allahu akbar,* I am *Allahu akbar,*"
which means, 'I am your great god and creator.' [84]

THE RANKS AFFIRM GOD AND HIS MESSENGER AND REGENTS

"Soon Salman understood. Turning to the king,
he said, 'I testify that there's no god but god,
you are our god, and none but you exists.'
No other spirit understood when he said,
'I testify there is no god but god.' [85]

"Miqdad caught on and said, 'I testify
Muhammad is the messenger of god,
and you are god. The one who glorifies,
preparing us and singing praise, is Salman.
He is your prophet and has gone ahead
and is the one who's made us know your name.'

"No other spirit testified but Salman:
'Muhammad is the messenger of god.' [86]

"Abu Zarr got it, and standing up, he turned
to his right and left, saying, 'Let us pray.
Come quickly, you spiritual beings and brothers,
and witness your creator and his regent.

---

84. As the text indicates, *Allahu akbar* is Arabic for "great god" or "god is great."
85. The profession of monotheism is the first part of the *shahada,* or Islamic creed.
86. The second part of the *shahada.*

I testify. He is our god, and Salman
his regent, and Miqdad is Salman's regent."
And once again he uttered, 'Let us pray.'

"Twelve spirits who are called our leaders[87]
said in a single voice, 'Grace be with you. Come
and quickly hear and testify to obtain redemption,
and testify to the witnessing of Salman,
Miqdad, and Abu Zarr.' They listened awhile.
No one answered, and they repeated, 'Grace
be with you.'
Then came twenty-eight pure spirits,[88]
flawless, and turning to the king, they said,
'God is most great, god is most great, you are
the great god. There is no other god but you.'
These five ranks reaffirmed it absolutely.
As it is written, 'Those who go ahead are first,
and they have proved themselves closest to god.'[89]
Those nearest the high king were these five ranks.

"But then the 124,000
vacillating spirits, who had turned
away and were suspect, spoke in one voice,
'Maybe we learned the joy of chanting praise
from him, maybe from his manner of speech.'
Yet then they said, 'It's wrong that one of us be god.'
As it is written, 'They had lapsed between two parties
and never could decide.'[90] Yet in the end
they bore certain witness and spoke these words,
'There is no god but god,' and rose up shouting
as the prayer caller in the muezzin's voice.

"These words are why they too stood up. Their ranks
were six. The first Salman, second Miqdad,

---

87. Naqib.
88. Najib.
89. Qur'an sura 56.
90. Qur'an sura 4.

third Abu Zarr, fourth Naqib,[91] and fifth Najib.
These first five special ranks are the foremost,
and the sixth rank belongs to waverers.
The elected recognized the high creator.

AZAZI'IL REBELS AND FALLS FROM GLORY

"The king said to Azazi'il, 'Azazi'il,
lie on the ground before Salman. All followers
lie on the ground before the foremost who
confirm Salman or I will cast you down
below.' As it is written, 'When we said to the angels,
lie down before Adam, they all lay down
except for Iblis, who arrogantly refused.
He was faithless.'[92]

"Then Azazi'il
turned to the king. He was a fool and claimed
divinity.[93] A second and a third
arose and came to aid Azazi'il.
They claimed divinity, calling the king
a common liar and a thief, a trickster,
and then they said that 'god is one of three.'[94]

"The six denying ranks turned on Salman
and battled him at length with arrogance.
The high king said, 'You, unbelieving demons,
corruption, rebels! You attempt to rule
this realm and the eternal far white sea,
but you cannot rule unless you will affirm
me and my regent.' This fulfills god's word,
'Jinns and humans! You try to penetrate

---

91. Halm, *Die islamische Gnosis*, 160, reads Najib, probably in error.
92. Qur'an sura 2.
93. As noted before, he acted like the gnostic demiurge.
94. Qur'an sura 5. This claim may recall the Christian trinitarian confession.

the precincts of the sky and of the earth,
but without my permission you will fail!'⁹⁵

THE DENYING RANKS ARE CONFINED

"Then the high king gave orders to Salman,
'We cannot leave these beings in this state.
From seven lights I made to cloak the faithless,
turn ruby light into a ruby curtain.
Transform the fire light, and make a curtain
from it, and keep them muffled in the cloth
and cover the white eternal farthest sea
with this curtain, color of ruby.' As it is written,
'We told you all to fall from paradise.'⁹⁶

"Right then Salman began to terrorize,
seizing the ruby light, and cloaking them
as by a ruby dome, cloaked the white sea
and farthest dome. He stripped them of their fire,
spreading it out below them. They lived
between these curtains for a thousand years.

THE HIGH KING APPEARS

"After a thousand years the high king shone
in Salman's curtain, with his special beings,
the pure-hearted Naqib, Najib, and waverers,
and he shouted, 'These are my creatures. Bow
before them. As lord over them and you,
I command all who sprang out of the loins
of Adam's children, I command you now
to testify, for am I not your lord?'⁹⁷

"Then select beings and all the pure of heart
recognized the high king: 'Yes, we declare.'⁹⁸

95. Qur'an sura 55.
96. Qur'an sura 2.
97. Qur'an sura 7.
98. Qur'an sura 7.

And 124,000 vacillators
also affirmed, declaring he was god,
but others froze. Six ranks of unbelievers
rebelled against the powerful Salman
and the high king. They started a new war,
fulfilling words of god: 'We made and formed
you and we told the angels, "Bow to Adam."
All bowed but Iblis. Iblis wouldn't bow.'[99]

THE FAITHLESS FALL FURTHER

"Then the high king commanded Salman, 'Hurl
these beings out of the fire-colored sea,
and take the carnelian light away from them,
and spread it below them.' Salman struck terror
into them, hurled them below the curtain,
color of fire. He took carnelian light
from them. They howled. He spread it under them
like earth. He made a dome of colored fire
their heaven, hiding the ruby dome from them.
And for another thousand years they lived
between these curtains.
But in the same month
and year in this new realm, they forgot all
they did under the fire-colored realm,
and then the war and battle disappeared
from monastery and from sanctuary
and from their memory. Every thousand years
they fell from realm to realm until they landed
in this despicable world, unknowing where
suddenly they were. As it is written, 'So it is.
Our signs came to you and you forgot them
and hence you too will be today forgotten.'[100]

"Then the high king appeared with all who had
affirmed him, and at Salman's carnelian cloth

---

99. Qur'an sura 7.
100. Qur'an sura 20.

and realm, he ordered them to testify,
'Bow down before my regent, my right hand.'

"Some waverers chose Salman. They were saved.
But the faithless Iblis rebelled. His second,
third, and all the followers of Iblis showed
their stupid disbelief a thousand times.
This denial of the realm reads in the Qur'an,
'We have created people of damp clay.' [101]

"Then the high king said to Salman, 'Remove
the covering of emerald green from the faithless
and unjust, make it earth, and then transform
the carnelian realm, now earth, into their sky,
and keep these wretched beings prisoners there.' [102]

"Salman struck them with terror, removed them
from clarion green light. He made a green curtain
and held them prisoners, blind to the fire realm.

"After a thousand years the high king shone
again, and as confronting them before,
he asked them to affirm divinity.
But Azazi'il said, 'I will never do it,
for you are as I am and cannot be our god.
There's only one god in the highest realm.'

THE TRANSCENDENCE OF THE DIVINE

"God stands beyond all 'when' and 'how,' beyond
description, and beyond known qualities.
He was not made by anyone. No one made him. [103]
The words, 'Say, he is god,' [104] are words
of Azazi'il in that emerald realm,
but only superficially. The prayer
of all confessors of the one who is not

---

101. Qur'an sura 15.
102. Human beings are imprisoned in this world, according to gnostic texts.
103. The Secret Book of John opens with such a statement of divine transcendence.
104. Qur'an sura 112.

is founded on the words, 'Say, he is god,'
and true for all those nonexistent ones.
But the prayer of unity of the confessor
and of those confessing the existing one
is also founded on 'Say, he is god.'
'Say, he is god' is true for all that is."

Then Jabir said, "My lord, reveal and tell me
what it means that we servants escape
from every doubt and from uncertainty."

The revealer of wisdom answered, "Jabir,
the meaning of 'Say, he is god' concerns
five angels about whom we've often spoken:
Muhammad, Ali, Fatima, Hasan,
and Husayn, who lead the believers' prayers
and who appear before believers' eyes.
These five lights with the spirit of speech join
the pious. But for nonbeings, 'Say, he is god
and the sole god' displays the cunning of
those who avow extremes of seeing nothing,
nothing in heaven or on earth apart
from the always existent god
who stands before us in this book. Even
the unbelievers see that seven heavens
and earth came out of him. God says, 'He made
no child, nor was he made.'[105] He did not come
from anyone, and he never gave birth
to anyone. They should not be so stupid
as to suppose that he's derived from lust
or luscious food, that he had made himself
from some vile drop of what exists in heaven
and on the earth. The drop, however, is
the noxious water that he took from beings
and transformed into water, clay, and dust.
From it he made seven heavens and earth.
Jabir, does all this go against the truth?"

---

105. Qur'an sura 112.

Jabir said, "Lord, let your servant hear how
the Iblis tale unfolds and how it ends."

Baqir said, "Jabir, the elder of the beings
told the godhead, 'There's only one true god,
and he stands in the highest realm.' The others
gathered in groupings of six ranks. They called
the king a liar, and every rank took up
a diverse blasphemy against the king.

THE FAITHLESS FALL TO THE EARTH

"Then the high king was furious and ordered
Salman to hurl the beings out of the green sea.
He removed their violet mantle and spread
it out below them, making it the earth
under their feet. He made the violet sea
from it, decking it with a million lights
and spirits and mountains made of crystal
with running waters, and called it paradise.
This is the fourth paradise. Three realms above
is the sea colored ruby, a paradise
named palace of glory; the sea color
of fire that is the paradise named 'the palace
of dominion'; and the emerald-green sea,
that is the paradise named 'the palace
of eternity.' But the three realms
below them are named the gardens of Eden
and gardens of refuge. Sun-colored sea
is palace of dominion. Moon-colored sea
is paradise of gardens of refuge;
and the blue sea is the garden of Eden,
and every realm was one time called the heaven
of beings, and then they turned into the earth.
The paradise of the high king has no
borders or end, fulfilling words of god:
'a garden huge as heaven and the earth.'[106]

---

106. Qur'an sura 57.

AZAZI'IL CONTINUES HIS REBELLION

"Azazi'il stayed with six groups of beings
locked in this paradise a thousand years.
After the thousand years the high creator
appeared behind the curtain of Salman
and said clearly, 'I am god.' Azazi'il
denied him and again he was the fool.
This denial is mentioned in the Qur'an,
where it says, 'When we said to the angels,
"Lie down before Adam," they all lay down
except for Iblis. He said, "Should I bow
before one whom you fashioned out of clay?"
He asked, "What kind of king is this? You showered
more honor on him than me. If you'll grant me
a chance to wait until the resurrection,
I'll murder his descendants, save a few."
God said, "Go away. Whoever follows you,
hell will be his reward. Wake whom you can,
use your armies to incite them, take up
their fortune and their children, promise them
all kinds of things. Satan makes lying vows.
But you have no command over my servants."'[107]

"They fought a horrid and horrific battle
against the high king. Then the high creator
ordered Salman, 'We have no use for them
in paradise. Take the sun-colored light
from them and spread it out below them all.'
Salman struck terror in their ranks. He cut
them off from sun-colored light and turned
it into sun water, spread it below,
adorned it with great tons of light and color,
the sun and moon. Azazi'il was imprisoned
with all his beings. He cloaked his violet realm
with realms of sun. His beings stayed behind
the curtain of the sun a thousand years.

---

107. Qur'an sura 17.

"Then the high king appeared among them, saying,
'I am your god, and Salman is my regent
and curtain.' Azazi'il and his beings
of course denied him and began to fight,
saying, 'Salman is not the high king's regent
and he's not god. Our creator is elsewhere
in the highest realm.' As it is written, 'They see him
far off, but we perceive him close.'[108] They stayed
denying in disbelief. The struggle filling
this realm appears in the Qur'an where
it says, 'When we said to the angels, "Lie down
before Adam," they all lay down except for Iblis.
He was a jinn sinning against himself.
He did not follow the one lord's command.
Do you choose him and demons of his seed
as friends instead of me? They're enemies
who are an awful trade for the offenders!'[109]

"At the command of the supreme creator,
Salman screamed and terrorized the enemy,
and threw them down. He cut them from the light,
color of moon, and spread a curtain made
from it and pulled them down below. They spent
a thousand years imprisoned in this realm.

MORE DIVINE APPEARANCES, MORE ARROGANCE

"Then the high king appeared again, demanding
a confirmation of divinity.
He said, 'I am your god. Now witness it.'
Humbly some of them bore witness and became
the undefiled. And some vacillators
relinquished doubt, and yet denial of

---

108. Qur'an sura 70.
109. Qur'an sura 18.

the unbelievers just increased. The story
of denial in the realm colored with moon
is in the Qur'an, meeting god's word,
'We earlier heard Adam. He forgot;
we found him undecided and we said,
concerning angels, "Lie down before Adam."
Then they lay down except for Iblis. Then
Satan whispered to him sinister thoughts.
He said, "Adam, shall I show you
the tree of life? Shall I reveal to you
the one dominion that will never end?"'[110]

"Then the high king commanded Salman, 'Take
the turquoise-colored cloak away from them
and let it be their place of habitation.'
Salman regarded them with awful anger;
he took away their turquoise-colored mantle
and sent them back to live in ghastly realms
below, all in fulfillment of god's word,
'So it is. Our revelations came to you
and you forgot them. So you'll be forgotten
today,"[111] until the thousand-year cycle
of this realm elapses. Then the high king
appeared out of the curtain of Salman
with all the special beings and faithful ones
in this realm, and among them and clearly visible,
he said, 'I am your god, I who in each place
and palace have demanded truth from you,
I am your god and lord of ancestors.[112]
Witness my divinity so you won't fall
lower than this realm. I've taken six colors
away from you and only the color blue
is left. If I take blue from you, you'll fall
from highest peaks into the deepest pits.'

---

110. Qur'an sura 20.
111. Qur'an sura 20.
112. Qur'an sura 37.

A LESSER SALMAN IS DISTINGUISHED FROM THE GREAT SALMAN

"The prince of the believers spoke. A spirit
left Salman, him they called lesser Salman.[113]
At once he answered the high king, saying,
'We are believers, and I bear witness
that you are god and that no other god
but you is here or anywhere exists.
I say it for Muhammad, high Ali
the chosen one, for his regent Salsal,
those gifts of god, our light. I testify
there is no other god but he, holy
and powerful.' When the lesser Salman
testified with Miqdad, Abu Zarr, Naqib,
and Najib of the faithful, some wavering
spirits also swore faith, and humbly they,
a mob of waverers, were so redeemed.

AZAZI'IL AND HIS RANKS CALL GOD A LIAR

"Then Azazi'il and all he had produced
grew skeptical, as were the second, third,
fourth, fifth, and sixth ranks. And so the six ranks
of unbelievers proved their doubts, their errors,
and called the king a liar and a fool.
This denial and rejection is that mentioned
in the Qur'an. It's there and it confirms
the word of god, 'When the lord said to angels,
I'll make a man from clay, but when I've made him,
and breathed my spirit into him, lie down
before him. Then the angels all lay down
before him—except Iblis. He was proud,
belonging to the mob of unbelievers.'[114]

---

113. The distinction between a greater and a lesser Salman recalls two wisdoms, Sophia and Achamoth, in Valentinian literature, or two primordial humans, one heavenly and one earthly, throughout gnostic texts.
114. Qur'an sura 38.

"The oldest of the faithless denied
seven times more than he had done before
in every other realm. And seven sparkling
colors made of millions of colors were seized
from him by Salman in the seven realms:
one from the realm of divinity, one
from the curtain manifesting the kingdom,
one in the curtain of glory, one in the sea
of the high lord, one in the sea of divinity,
one on the carpet of light, and one more sea,
which is the sanctuary of the spirit.

So the cursed Azazi'il, and those
who proceeded from his cry fell down
from the high king, down into the curtain,
and fell for seven thousand years because
of seven harsh denials and rejection.
These are noted in the Qur'an: denial
of the divinity, denial of
the kingdom, denial of the glory,
denial of the highest god, denial
of his godliness, denial of light,
and denial of the spirit's mind.

"The high king had bestowed each particle
of his inherent light to the rash fool,
who used it to create his filthy creatures.
From bellowing screams they made spirits,
filling them with disbelief, denial, lies, error,
rebellion, and corrupting avarice.

AZAZI'IL GOES BY MANY NAMES

"The name of this curse changes in each realm.
In god's realm he was called Azazi'il,
and in the time of humans was called
Harith,[115] at the time of Adam, Ahriman,[116]

---

115. A name for the devil in Druze sources.
116. The name of the evil god in Zoroastrian sources.

at the time of Noah and David, Suwa,[117]
at the time of Abraham, Nimrod,[118]
at the time of Moses, it was the pharaoh,
at the time of Jesus, it was the tempter,
and at the time of Muhammad, Abu Jahl.[119]
In our time he is called Satan. All names
are sounds invented by the cursed one,
who with the others in the turquoise dome
refused to witness, while the ones who came
before, whose leader is Salman, accepted
manifestation of the highest king."

THE EARTH IS CREATED

Then Jabir said, "My lord, what do you say
to commentary on the following verse
from the Qur'an? 'Once we offered treasure
that was to be entrusted to the world,
to heaven first, then to the earth, and then
to mountains. Yet none of them make it his,
since they were petrified. Some humans did,
although it was the sacrilege of fools.'"[120]

Baqir spoke, "Jabir, the high king states in verse,
We stored our treasure in heaven and they took it.
We put it on earth and they took it.
We put it on the mountains and they took it.
Everyone between the skies and earth took it,
but nervously, cautiously, and after
the high creator's warning. Only a group of humans
took it with hardship. As for all the rest,
the unbelievers, hypocrites, and heathen,
they snubbed the warning of the lofty king,

---

117. One of the idol gods in Qur'an sura 71.
118. Genesis 10:8–12.
119. In Arabic, "father of folly," nickname of an opponent of prophet Muhammad.
120. Qur'an sura 33.

who castigated them four thousand years.
If the humans speak again, they will return
to the high king, who in mercy
will pardon them. This is the warning for
the treasure that had once been in our charge.

"Jabir, the demonstration of the princes
among believers happened in the place
of god, thereby increasing his divinity.
The heavens are Salman, Miqdad, Abu Zarr,
Ammar, Jondob, Horayra, and Komayl,
who undertook the tasks. The earth is angels
of Naqib, one step below the seven angels.
The mountains are the Najib and a few
waverers whose example was held up
before the people, and they all accepted.

MOUNTAINS, ROCKS, ANIMALS APPEAR

"The other six ranks of the faithless with
their leaders—curse and punish them—refused
the holy gift. So he made them appear
shaped as mountains and rocks, and he transformed
them into animals not to be saved.
But if the faithful and the lingering waverers
in this world keep the pact with the high king,
receiving the holy manifestation,
they will be free from every punishment.
This is the commentary on that verse.

"When these poor faithless, fastened to denial,
quarreled and went to war with the high king,
he terrified them, 'You the unbelievers,
the impure and ungrateful, you seek victory,
rule and control in precincts of the sky.
But you can do nothing without full faith,
without witnessing me. I am the lord.'
As it is written, 'You jinns and humans! If you
have power to penetrate the skies and earth,

do so. But you will fail unless I give you
powers.'[121] This is my proof and testimony.

"Then the high king—whose majesty is great—
said to Salman, 'You are my gate, my book,
the Qur'an is the word of god, and you
are my right hand in all my palaces,
realms, and curtains. You are my ambassador
and throne of which I'm god. You are the treasure
and faithful keeper of treasure; my spirit
shows on your curtain, through you; I am lord,
and you the lord of believers. I've placed
the guidance of the earth and heaven in
your hand; I am the lord and you the lord
of all heavens and earth. These unbelievers
who won't revere or think of me in awe,
who quarreled and who warred against me,
I'll turn to mountains, rocks, deserts, rivers,
I'll make them into animals and birds.
You, Salman—with Miqdad, Abu Zarr, Ammar,
Jondob, Horayra, and Komayl—turn them
into the seven parts of earth.' Then he
commanded the Naqib, 'Make of them twelve
countries of the dark earth.' He ordered the Najib,
'Make twenty-eight islands out of your body.'

THE SEAS AND LANDS APPEAR

"Suddenly the huge Salman terrified them,
howled at them. And they screamed back like
a hundred thousand basins and gold bowls
clashing together. All light and spirit fled,
and from it he spread out the blue curtain.
At once the waverers asked miracles
from the high king, and unbelievers went
into the dark, and he curtained this horde

121. Qur'an sura 55.

of faithless, and these happenings fulfilled
the word of god, 'the day on which the smoke
of heaven could be clearly seen.'[122] The terror
of Salman turned each being into water,
and water into sea. Small particles
were clay, and seven angels made the seven
parts of the earth from their own matter.

First, Salman made the east coast of Africa
with all mountains and rivers made of those
who had denied. Miqdad made Hindustan
from the second rank, Abu Zarr made Turkestan
from the third rank, Ammar made Horasan
out of the fourth, and Jondob made Iraq
out of the fifth, Abu Horayra made Egypt
from the sixth, and Komayl made Byzantium
from the seventh rank. Komayl completed
creation of the earth, and it was finished.
The twelve Naqib created the twelve countries:
Sind, Hind, Tibet, Berber, Russia,
Abyssinia, Hazar, Turkestan, Bahrain,
Kuhestan, Armenia, Persia, Maghreb, and Slavia.

ALL THE ELEMENTS OF THE WORLD ARE MADE FROM THE UNBELIEVERS

"The twenty-eight Najib angels created
the twenty-eight islands of Hind and Sind,
the island of Ceylon, Alexandria, Constantinople,
Barqius, Ferghana, Arrajan, Sawad, Macin,
the Ionian islands, Gilan, Ifriqia, Askalon,
Nisibin, Malatia, Samarkand, Antiochia,
Tartus, Kis, Oman, the island of Karak,
and Masqat. From them and around the mountains
he also made seven great seas. From matter
he made oil, sulfur, tar, pitch, zak, salt,

---

122. Qur'an sura 44.

and limestone. He made every mountain, rock,
piece of gravel, and mineral in the world
out of those unpeaceful with the high king
and those who fought his regents. May his blessing
be on us. As it is written, 'So we reward those
who are not sober or who do not believe
signs of the lord. Their punishment will be
a hereafter of extreme enduring pain.
Did you not understand when you look at
the homes of generations we destroyed?'[123]

"All waters of the world were made from them.
Followers of those beings, outsiders,
consider those waters not as waters that the
regents of the high lord made from them but as
rains from the firmament, yet if such rain
came down it would have rained a thousand years
and all the world would long have turned to water.
These waters were made by Salman out of
the faithless, which he poured into the world
and put into the seaways of the earth. They flow
through the earth's arteries, and four elements
of nature rise into the air and fall as rain
to keep the earth damp and fresh.

"All this Salman created, every mountain,
rock, and beast. All vegetation and plants.

SALMAN TURNS THE FAITHLESS INTO ELEMENTS AND CREATURES

"All those who fought against the high creator
he degraded. All those who reproached the high king
he made into fine clay. All those who turned
against the lofty king he turned into bronze.
All those who'd practiced soothsaying he made
into iron. All those who called the king
traitor he turned into mountains and rocks.

---

123. Qur'an sura 20.

All those who said the king was a magician
he turned into the deserts of the world.
All those who called the high king ignorant
he made as fire. All those who hurled insults
at the high king he turned into gold
so in this world they could be minted coins.
All those who turned against him in six realms
he made into a dinar and six dangs.[124]
All those who saw the high king as sorcerer
he made into silver. All those who questioned
the high king he made into copper. And those
who wondered who the high king was he turned
to lead. All who contested him were trees
and tree trunks. All who treated the high king
with violence he turned into minerals
of varying colors. All who mocked him became
cattle, beasts, and wild animals, and all
who called the king a trickster became birds.
All who were boorish to the lord were echoes.
All who did not hold the word of our high king
in awe he made as snakes. And all who called
the high king arrogant he made as fish.
And all who uttered hateful things became
small creatures. All who used stinging sarcasm
he made into wolves and hyenas. All who
were cruel to him he made as pigs and bears.
All who turned the evil done to the high king
into sweet presents for themselves were lions,
and all who uttered shabby slurs were treated
shabbily. If we keep telling all this,
this book will be absurdly long.

THIS WORLD IS MADE COLORLESS

"God made the world framed with appalling mountains,
expansive deserts, profound seas, and beasts

---

124. Monetary amounts.

and birds from substances of the six ranks
of faithless. Then he took away the color
of the world. Prolonged time passed without day
or darkness, when there was no time or name
or any soul across the dry cracked earth.

THE WORLD COMES TO LIFE

"Then the high king flung out denying spirits,
the faithless minds, flung them out of the kingdom
down onto earth, and then he gave the world
a breath, a spirit, and it came to life.
Vegetation and plants sprang from the earth,
and through his force vegetation and plants
were fashioned from the substance of the cursed,
proceeding from the shout of Azazi'il.

"This vegetative spirit spread everywhere
across the earth. And then the high king chose
to regenerate the seven colors taken
from Azazi'il: red, black, blue, violet,
indigo blue, yellow, and white. He called
them clouds and returned water to the streams
and rivers, scattering them over the earth,
keeping the earth moistened and fresh. And steam
in the spirit's world became the angel whom
the high king consigned to the clouds. He fulfilled
his words, 'The thunders praise him, as do angels.'[125]

"But the beasts, the mountains and the rocks,
the vegetation and the plants and bodies
all issue from the pot of Ahriman,
and even now Ahriman comes with clouds
and thunder. And obeying the high king
he brings his creatures their daily bread."

---

125. Qur'an sura 13.

THIS DESCRIBES THE BODY AS MICROCOSM

Jabir said, "My lord, what can be the proof
that the highest command descends from clouds?"[126]

Baqir answered, "Here is truth. Each particle
of holy light sent through this cloud down to
the path of breathing earth is consonant
with the highest command. The cloud itself
consists of substance of Azazi'il.
Jabir, if clouds were not from Azazi'il,
the sun and moon sloping along their spheres
would not be hidden to the waverers.
Azazi'il shows in the microcosm
with seven faces: evil thoughts and greed,
jealousy, doubt, uncertainty. The glow
of faith's spirit and the intelligible sun
are also hidden from the spirit of lust.

"Clouds of the macrocosm are combined
with light of the high king as a nude body
combines with spirit. And the other cloud,
highest in the command, is spirit's speech,
color of cloud, the thunder and lightning
and the moon's rain are knowledge of the light.
The earth on which it tumbles is the heart,
the sky from which it comes is spirit's faith,
its sphere is language: 'All float in a sky.'"[127]

SOULS ARE CREATED

Jabir said, "My lord, please tell us the rest
about the meaning of the macrocosm."

Baqir said, "Jabir, when this cloud kept the world
moistened and fresh, yellow and green, and it issued

---

126. The following lines may be an addition to the text.
127. Qur'an sura 36.

vegetation and green plants, no one ate
the plants combined with vegetative power.
The being that rebelled again against
the high king seized the vegetative power,
implanted it in hearts of animals
and everything this earth produced. It was
eaten by the spirit of the senses, and both
rose with the lusting mind of the deniers.

"The waverers were in the blue curtain
and praised the high king. The high king's justice
did not permit doubters and waverers
to be in the same place, on the same carpet
of the almighty, as the pure and honest.
Then the high creator said to waverers,
'I want to create people in this world
and grant them dominion of the world.'
This happened, meeting his words, 'When your lord
said to the angels, "I will place a successor
on earth," they said, "Do you want someone who
will harm and spill blood, while we sing out
our hearts of praise to you and glorify?"'[128]

"Then Salman, Abu Zarr, Miqdad, Ammar, Jondob,
Abu Horayra, Komayl, and the Naqib
and Najib said, 'God will do what he wants,'[129]
and 'He decides as he wishes.'[130] The waverers
in the seven curtains and some who testified
in each curtain were still, since they were saved.
The prophet says, 'Who knows silence escapes.'

"But other vacillators said, 'Our lord,
should you who make the vices in this world
instill decay and bloodshed? When we must,
we'll praise, sanctify, glorify all you want.'

---

128. Qur'an sura 2.
129. Qur'an sura 3.
130. Qur'an sura 5.

"Then the high king said, 'Your sins went too far.
You must be dismissed from the blue curtain.
I know how far it goes with you, though you
don't know. I know all things you do not know.'[131]

"The waverers shouted and wept, 'We gave
advice that was a sin. Why was it so?'
A mob below them festered with remorse
and penitence. They begged for intercession
and complained to the king, 'You mustn't grieve
one time but often.'[132] But the king forgave,
freed them of doubt, created spirits of them,
and spread them over all the earth: 'He made
their spirits by mixing fire.'[133] The waverers
received the name confessors of the one
and only. Degradation was made from them.
There were four thousand of them, and in rank
they made their home below the Najib angels.

"The other waverers who remained did not
complain or demand intercession. No,
they praised the king, and turning to him
said, 'Lord, what can you do for us who were
transgressors?[134] Lord, we know that we have sinned
against ourselves. If you will not forgive us,
we'll stay among the lost. If we repent,
pardon us, lord, or else we are the lost.'

THE WAVERERS LEARN PRAISE

"The high king said to Salman forgivingly,
'Cast these waverers out from the blue dome
down to a heavenly airy covering.' Salman
transformed them into air and held them firmly
up in the air. They formed pairs, two and two,

---

131. Qur'an sura 2.
132. Qur'an sura 25.
133. Qur'an sura 55.
134. Qur'an sura 7.

and reproduced amazingly, beyond
moderation and limit. The high king
in self-praise shone among them to confirm
what he had told them in his highest realm
so they would learn to praise. They said to him,
'You are our elder and speak for us. Show us
the god you praise.' The high king said to them,
'I will show you your lord, provided you
enter a covenant with me. When you see him—
his power is great—you'll testify and he
will move you to the place of the undefiled.
However, one who doubts or disclaims him
will be sent down to earth.' So vacillators
entered into a covenant with him—
his power is great—and they agreed with it.

"Then the high king said, 'I am *Allahu akbar*,[135]
the great god that you seek. And I am he.'
Nine hundred ninety-nine spirits stepped forward
and testified to the high god and said,
'We do believe, affirm, and witness you
as god of grace and mercy and that you
showed in the seven realms and palaces.
We do believe, affirm, and witness you.'
Through this confession they again were saved.
The one who declares clearly and sincerely,
'There is no other god but he,' will rise
to paradise. He took the dregs in them
and made of it a horde of ghosts and demons.
God made the unbelievers from the dregs
of the believers. The spirits, sons of spirits,
he created from the lowness of believers,
the demons from the lowness of the tested.
'A multitude belonged to earlier time,
and a multitude belonged to later time.
What is the fate of those fixed on the left?
A searing heat and boiling water, shade

---

131. On *Allahu akbar*, see above.

of the black smoke.'[136] And they received the name
'the tested,' and he kept them there below
the confessors of the one and only.

THE SEVEN RANKS OF SPIRITUAL BEINGS

"In this way the former were seven ranks.
The first is Salman's level, second Miqdad,
third Abu Zarr, fourth the Naqib, fifth the Najib,
sixth the confessors of the one and only,
and seventh the tested, fulfilling his word,
'The patient and truthful and humble who
give alms and pray for pardon in the dawn.'[137]

"For other vacillators the high king
commanded Salman, 'Send them out of here,
keep them on earth.' 'We told you to get out,
all of you, go. True guidance comes from me.'[138]
Immediately 313 of them screamed
as someone screams when thrown into a prison.
That's how they howled, and loud as they could.
The high god pardoned them again, cut them
from doubt and wonder. He made seventy thousand
angels from them, and now these waverers,
as pure, received the name of messengers,
and they were worthy of his grace and pardon
through the mercy of the exalted king.
'After I was afraid I fled from you.
My lord endowed me with the power of judgment
and I became one of the messengers.'[139]

IBLIS APPEARS

"Among the low ones who were called angel
the cursed Iblis appeared. He belonged to the low ones,

---

136. Qur'an sura 56.
137. Qur'an sura 3.
138. Qur'an sura 2.
139. Qur'an sura 26.

but it was the high one's will that spirits
and sons of spirits would fall into his hands.
Then the high king commanded that the low
go down to the earth. And after many years
he commanded the destruction of Iblis,
his spirits, and the sons of spirits. Iblis
and all the angels and the low ones warred
on other spirits and the sons of spirits.
They all plunged into seas, and some of them
became sea creatures. They were whales, snakes, fish,
some wild animals and birds, some Gog
and Magog,[140] some turned into shells, pigs, limestone,
everything in the seas is of their substance.
Iblis emerged among the angels and painted
their coverings and shapes in all the colors
of the seven heavens and earth. He made them.

"The covering and form of these angels
was like fire. They were haughty in their form
and arrogant, but Azazi'il became
a thousand times prouder even than they.

THE HIGH KING WANTS TO CREATE PEOPLE ON EARTH

"Then the high king told them, 'I want to make
people on earth, endowing them dominion
over the world.' 'When the lord told his angels,
I will send a successor to the earth,'[141]
they became three nations. One nation said,
'God does what he wants to.'[142] 'And he decides
his ways. You want it solely at god's desire.'[143]

---

140. On Gog and Magog as powers on the earth, see Ezekiel 38–39; Revelation 20:8; Qur'an sura 18. Magog is also mentioned in Genesis 10:2 and 1 Chronicles 1:5.
141. Qur'an sura 2.
142. Qur'an sura 3, 5.
143. Qur'an sura 76.

"Others said, 'Why place someone on this earth
who unjustly sheds blood, who commits acts
of shame?' 'Azazi'il rebelled and others rose
in the madness of his misery, and said,
"If you create someone else in this world,
we will not prostrate ourselves before him."' [144]
"The high king said, 'Come before waverers
and bow down before everything above you,
and before those who know the earth and heavens
and those who know the plants and growing things.'
The angels could not comprehend, but waverers
explained the knowledge of the earth and heavens,
the names of plants and growing things, mountains
and all on earth. 'He taught Adam the names
and then he showed them to the angels.' [145]

IBLIS REBELS; SHADOWS AND PHANTOMS APPEAR

"Iblis and his people who had the form of fire
rebelled and showed their disbelief. 'We won't
bow down before them, we're better than they.'
'You fashioned me of fire but him of clay.' [146]
The high king grew furious. He said to them,
'The covering will fall off all of you—
and this is hell—and you will wander proud
no longer, but you'll linger in those tight
and black and body-hugging darkest forms.'

"Iblis and his people said, 'We have praised you.
How can you let our efforts go in vain?'
The high king answered, 'I am not reducing
your wages. I have turned you into women,
beauties among the skeptics and the dregs.
Amuse them and keep them from staying on

---

144. The madness of Yaldabaoth is described in the Secret Book of John.
145. Qur'an sura 2.
146. Qur'an sura 7.

the right path. You appear to right and left
of them. Then I will send you down to hell
for this sin. Seven thousand years you'll keep
the shape of flesh and blood of animals.'
As it is written, 'We created you and gave
you form. Then we said to the angels, "Bow
before Adam." All bowed except for Iblis.
He wouldn't bow. God said, "What stops you from
bowing as I have ordered?" Iblis said,
"I am better than he. From fire you made me,
but he is only clay." God said, "Go
down from him to the earth. Pride and arrogance
are not permitted here. Leave! You belong
in the future to those who are disdained."
Iblis said, "Grant me a reprieve until
the day they are awakened." God said,
"You will linger among those whose fate
will be made apparent later." Iblis said,
"Since you let me go wrong, I'll wait for them
on the straight path. I'll conquer them from front
and from behind, from right and left. You'll see
that most of them are ungrateful to you."' [147]

"Then the high king transformed Iblis's people
into a form of shades, a hell of shadows
where they were fixed. But waverers he turned
into phantoms. As it is written, 'Some will be
in paradise and some will burn in hell.' [148]

THIS DESCRIPTION RECALLS THE HEART IN THE BODY

"Now, paradise is in the form of phantoms,
but hell takes on the form of those in shadow. [149]

---

147. Qur'an sura 7.
148. Qur'an sura 42.
149. The following lines may be an addition to the text.

And hell consists of lowness of believers,
which is their punishment. If form were not
of shadows, they would have no place to be.
Without the earth, there'd be no place for phantoms
here in the world. So if the body had
no heart, the wavering spirit couldn't find
existence in this form; if in the heart
there were no chambers for his blood, there would
be no place for rebuked Adam to exist.

DO NOT EAT OF THIS TREE

"Then the high king said to the vacillators,
'Live in this paradise of phantoms, and eat
only from what you have been commanded
to eat from. From this one tree do not eat.'
That means, do not fall into any act
of lechery. He made a covenant
with them: 'I will send Gabriel to you.
He is my holy guidance. And you who follow
my guidance need not live in fear. You won't
be sad.'[150] You'll stay in paradise as phantoms,
but if those formed of shadow become women,
beautiful women, do not touch their bodies.
As it is written, 'Do not come close to this tree,[151]
or you will be a party to transgressors.'[152]

FATIMA

"Then Gabriel led the inspired spirit to
a place in paradise and saw a figure,
painted in millions of colors, sitting on
a throne, a crown on its head, and two rings
in its ears, girded with a shoulder sword,

---

150. Qur'an sura 2.
151. Or "structure"?
152. Qur'an sura 2.

and paradise glowed with light from this being.
The waverers were eager to discover
what kind of being it was. The inspired spirit
appeared to them. 'This being is from the first
and farthest realm. The figurehead of Fatima
is of the highest majesty that lives
in paradise. Her crown is Muhammad,
her earrings are Hasan and Husayn,
and the girded sword is the prince who is
faithful Ali. Her throne is the lord's seat
on which the high king—great is his power—sits
in splendor.' All praised and glorified this being.

MEN ARE TEMPTED BY WOMEN

"After some time, Iblis became a woman,
a beauty. And everyone with him became
beautiful women before the waverers.
They all were tempted; for a man there is
nothing more tempting than a woman he
might have. Sensual lust caused them to touch
and lay their hands on them and grope around
their bodies. After nine months, out of them
emerged another being.
                    The snake and peacock
lived in the second and third paradise
of those who followed Iblis's insanity.

HUMANS ARE EVICTED FROM PARADISE

"When the high king came in, he howled against
the lingerers, 'Get out of here, all of you.[153]
Get out of paradise. Assume the form
of thin dark shadows.' He hurled them away

---

153. Qur'an sura 2.

into their shadowy shape, and had women
appear with deep vaginas and with breasts.

"The vacillators fell under the cover
of shadows, and they hollered day and night.
The prince of unbelievers shone among
them as a stunning woman and seduced them,
and they attained destruction. The high king fumed
against them, 'Curse you. My curse is on you
until the day of judgment,[154] till you leave
the form of shadows and are flesh and blood,
and skin and hair.'

HUMANS NEED TO BE FREE FROM BODY

"Then the vacillators grieved
and said, 'Our lord, if only you command us,
we will be washed and clean of sin, even
in this, our present form.' The high lord said,
'Atonement for such sin I won't accept
as you are in your bodily form. Doubt hangs
on you.' They answered him, 'What can we do
to become pure again while in our bodies?'

HUMANS MUST FULFILL GOD'S FOUR CONDITIONS

"The high king said, 'You must fulfill my four
conditions to exist closer to me.
The first is that in every each shape and form
you see me, testify in all the tongues:
Arabic, Farsi, Greek, Hindi, Sindi,
Georgian, Slavic, Syrian. And with decision,
prove that you are upright.

---

154. Qur'an sura 38.

The second is
you recognize the proper imams and holy
and enlightened ones who know,[155] and learn
from them about my knowledge and my nature;
witness the deity with their words and spirit.

"Third is that all of you must become brothers
and sisters to each other, and not withhold
your life or limb; give up possessions, wealth,
and blood for our religion and believers.
Hold to religion and your worldly life
in proper order, and never choose the ways
of evil and of violence—neither in public
nor in your heart share food and sustenance
or time with them. Witness the deity
and spirit and be as friendly as you can,
so fellowship is real because you testify.
'Believers are brothers.'[156] These three conditions
are triple witness to the exalted king:
one to the prophets, one to right imams,
and one to brothers and sisters who keep faith.

"The fourth is that you must not live by profit
and worldly fancy. Do not indulge desires.
When you've fulfilled these three conditions I
assign you, I will grant you one last pleasure:
I'll pardon you and give you back eternal
paradise. As it is written, 'But the believers
who do what's right will go into gardens
whose hollows are filled with flowing streams, and stay
forever.'[157] And elsewhere it says, 'He must
behave with honor,'[158] and elsewhere it reads,
'those of good works.'[159] If you keep my covenant,

---

155. Gnostics?
156. Qur'an sura 49.
157. Qur'an sura 4.
158. Qur'an sura 18.
159. Qur'an sura 18.

I also will. Be dutiful to me
and I will do my duty toward you.'"[160]

HOW THE INDIVIDUAL COMES
TO KNOWLEDGE AND IS SAVED[161]

Then Jabir said, "My lord, when will the spirit
and heart be saved?"

    Baqir answered, "A spirit
of conviction living in the heart is witness
to divinity and leaves the heart and goes
into the brain, if it has witnessed clearly.
And even after worship from the highest
heaven and from the earth, it won't accept
anything but witnessing described as just
in Muhammad's Qur'an,[162] a testimony
for current imams, whose appearance is
the paradise of the exalted king.

"Their speech provides the gate to paradise,
the place of Salman, and the site where orphans
bow and where seven angels say their prayers,
the realm of the Naqib, the palace of the Najib,
the dome of Adam and the ark of Noah,
the priestly robes of Abraham, the tablets
of Moses, the summit of Jesus, and the throne
where Muhammad the chosen lives, along
with the thirty-legged footstool of Ali,
the prince of the believers, and the garden
of Fatima, and paradise of Hasan and Husayn,
the bridge of the believers. They make up
the refuge of the cherubim, the spheres
of beings of light, direction of the prayer
of spiritual beings. The high king said,

---

160. Qur'an sura 2.
161. These final passages, perhaps an addition to the Mother of Books, describe how a person is liberated from the body and comes to wisdom, knowledge, and perfection.
162. Qur'an sura 18.

I do not wish you to turn east and west
to say your prayer. The eternal god prefers
you turn to the good imams and believe
in their prophetic light, in every show
of light, and every palace, realm, aeon,
and cycle, each location of the deity,
the kingdom, the great lord, the glory and
eternity of godliness, the light,
spirit, humanity, the flesh, and imam.

"Everywhere you must testify to him
and sacrifice possessions, blood, and power
to build a dam to hold back death and need,
hunger and poverty, grave sicknesses
and all the world's catastrophes. What happens
to you in any form, be patient; suffer it.
In all things fear judgment, try to grow nearer to god,
and be on guard against this awful world.
Have faith. And thus you fulfill god's word,
'Goodness does not require you to turn
your face to east or west. It asks you to believe
in god and the last day, the angels, scripture,
and prophets.'[163] The last day is a great day.
Believe in these words and believe in light
of the high king's regent, Salman, who is
the word of god. For everything in heaven
and on the earth is also in the word of god,
and nothing on dry land or in the sea
is not part of his word, 'and there is nothing,
wet or dry, not recorded in his word.'"[164]

WHERE DOES THIS SECRET KNOWLEDGE COME FROM?

Then Jabir said, "My lord, is the final testimony
from us or from the will and glory

---

163. Qur'an sura 2.
164. Qur'an sura 6.

of the high king? When the inspired who know
sit on the carpet of the great lord, the curtain
of light is raised and your students testify.
Where does this secret knowledge[165] come from?"

Baqir answered, "Get away from bad students[166]
as from the avarice of those who know."[167]

Jabir said, "My lord, explain to your low servant."

Baqir said, "Be careful. These words are difficult.
By Muhammad and the glorified, by Ali
the highest, these are words not written in
a book. One keeps them secret. Jabir, if
the right imam and the inspired who knows
reveals the truth to students, the pupil
would not accept it and the heart's spirit
could not absorb it. The speaking spirit
of life is all alone. Then at the bidding
of the high king, with the purpose and will
of the imam, a spirit of lightning color
will come down from the blue dome and enter
the student's brain and spirit of the heart.
The spirit of the heart believes in glory
and words of one who knows and testifies
in truth of the convinced. At the will of the
high king, the shining spirit descends from
the moon-colored curtain and searches out
the tested spirit, speaker for the teacher.
The spirit of the heart of students hears
this word and testifies to godliness
of one who knows, but his rank is incapable
of holding the word in his memory.[168]

"Then by the will of one who knows, the spirit
of retention descends from the sun-colored

---

165. Gnosis?
166. Or "disciples."
167. Gnostics?
168. Literally, "monastery and sanctuary."

curtain, and it enters faith's spirit.
The word remains in memory, but he
has not the strength to think of it. But sent
by the high king, thought's spirit comes down from
the violet-colored curtain and resides
in his retention. The spirit of the heart
thinks of this thought and understands the words
of one who knows but who lacks strength to speak
before the one who truly knows the word.

"Then the almighty's spirit descends from
the emerald green curtain and enters thought.
The student's heart floats overhead and in
his limbs he clearly sees the holy realm.
These words are clear but are not from the curtain
until the will of one who knows the light
of spirit and of wisdom descends from
the agate-colored realm and joins the spirit
of the high lord. This spirit is gifted with language,
and light of knowledge speaks before the one
who knows. It is not perfect yet, and one
who knows has not approved it. Then intellect
comes down from the realm, the color of fire,
and enters knowledge. Finally the student
understands clearly and hears the words
of one who knows. He cannot yet transcend
his sensual soul, the spirit of desire, and the rebuked Adam,
until the holy spirit appears from the dome
of red ruby and enters his spirit.

"The spirit of the student's heart crushes
the three souls tempting sin in him, kills them,
and as the seven components, heart, head, lungs, liver,
spleen, bladder . . . he destroys the seven
unbelievers who have lived in his soul,
and Iblis's cycle is over now.
The lusting in his penis and testicles
is dead, the spirit of the heart awakes
at night and fasts by day. A human still is
not about to rise to heaven. He'll get there

if by the will of the high king and through
the light of one who knows and the resolution
of the disciple a great universal spirit
descends from the white dome and enters in
the student's holy spirit. Then spirit of
the student's heart will climb a few steps higher
from the house of wind and hover in
the commanding arteries of his chest.

"Body and matter will be bright and light
because of light of godliness and holy
revelation. God says, 'Is there anyone
whose chest god has expanded for Islam
so he's enlightened by the lord?'[169] But spirit
of the heart still can't reach the brain. Great spirit
descends from under the high king's canopy,
in the remotest realm, at the command
and by the will of the high king and with
the purpose of good imams, landing perfectly
on the great universal spirit. Then
the spirit of the heart can move from chest
to lips, tongue, and mouth, and end up on
the holy throne. The one who knows arises
and testifies to spirit as to himself.

"The student will be perfect, and ten spirits
are spoken for. God says, 'These are the perfect ten.'[170]
The ten stanzas of the Qur'an also
convey the ten Islamic[171] ranks, ten days
of feast,[172] the counting going up to ten
and when it gets to ten begins again,
and every number ten around the world
stands for it too. That's why we call this book
the ten speeches, and this description resides
uniquely in this book and in no other."

---

169. Qur'an sura 39.
170. Qur'an sura 2.
171. Or "Salmanic" (the text is unclear).
172. Ten feast days to celebrate the martyrdom of Husayn.

PART SEVEN

Cathar Literature

INTRODUCTION

WILLIS BARNSTONE

The Cathars represent the last major flourishing of gnosis in western Europe in the early eleventh, twelfth, and thirteenth centuries. They are also called Albigensians, a geographical reference, because among their main converts were the people in the Languedoc city of Albi. When the pope declared the crusade against the Cathars in 1209, he called it the Albigensian Crusade. The epithet Cathar was probably derived from the Greek *katharoi* (clean, pure) and designated the class of the perfect or elect. The name was already applied to the dualist community at Monteforte in Italy as early as 1030.

The Cathars first appeared in northern Italy, and then in western Germany, England, and Flanders, but soon their major concentration was in Provençal-speaking southwestern France. By the end of the tenth century we hear of Gerbert of Aurillac, archbishop elect of Reims, who issued a declaration of faith that included Manichaean dualistic doctrines and a rejection of the Old Testament.[1] There is evidence of a continuity of Manichaean groups in France from the time (c. 370s CE) when Augustine, in his earlier Manichaean period, was exiled in Champagne and was actively proselytizing. Whatever the size and significance of these interesting relics of classical Manichaeism, however, the reappearance of a radical dualism in the region can be attributed to the Bogomils, a neomanichaean group from Macedonia and Bulgaria who, like the original adherents of Mani, quickly spread the fire of their doctrine from Europe and North Africa to China. This time the Bogomils carried their message through the Balkans and western Europe. Such was their impact that by the twelfth century the Cathars had their own network of bishoprics reaching

---

1. The declaration was made in 991. Gerbert of Aurillac, *Epistolae*, no. 180, ed. Havet, 161–62.

from southern to northern France, Catalonia, and the whole of northern Italy, with scattered communities from Lombardy down to Rome.

The spread of gnosticism in this area of western Europe also coincided in twelfth-century Languedoc with the emergence of Kabbalism. The *Sefer ha-Bahir* (Book of Bright Light) is, as Gershom Sholem demonstrates, an example of gnostic Kabbalism as well as the most significant extant document of medieval Jewish mysticism and symbolism. The many dissenting religious movements in this area of southern France made it a new Alexandria, where, as in the ancient hellenistic capital, diverse religions and philosophical movements flourished, including neoplatonism, hermeticism, Judaism, Christianity, and, a child of this diversity, gnosticism.

BOGOMIL ROOTS OF THE CATHARS

The legendary founder of Bogomil neomanichaeism was the tenth-century Slavic priest Bogomil, also called Theophilos. The Bogomils, who owed many ideas to the earlier Paulicians[2] in Armenia and the Near East, were the most powerful sectarian movement in the history of the Balkans. Predominantly Slavs with some Greek followers, they were a powerful force in Constantinople, Macedonia, and Bulgaria, and especially in Serbia and Bosnia, where they persisted for five centuries and for a period vied for dominance with orthodoxy. In the capital city of Constantinople the Bogomils were a powerful populist movement that vigorously opposed Byzantine culture and theocracy. They fell into obscurity in the fifteenth century with the Ottoman conquest of Byzantium, but in their active years the Bogomils in the east, together with the Cathars in the west, formed a network of dualist communities from the Black Sea to the Atlantic.

---

2. A Christian sect that appears in Armenia in the sixth century and was associated with Nestorianism. This "heretical" sect favored Luke and the letters of Paul, hence the epithet Paulicians. By the seventh century it had spread through the Byzantine Empire. After being persecuted by the Byzantines, the Paulicians sided with the Muslims in their struggle against the Eastern Roman Empire. In the mid-ninth century they had their own state at Tephike (in present-day Turkey). In 871 the Byzantine emperor Basil I attacked them and they fled to Syria, and a century later they were expelled from Syria and combined with the Bogomils, largely Slavs, who were considered a barbaric menace to the Orthodox of Constantinople. After the eleventh century the Paulicians disappeared as a separate identity, but as a sect, now merged with the Bogomils, their missionaries emigrated to southwestern Europe, where they brought the essential neomanichaean texts, in Latin translation, that became the basic scriptures of Catharism.

BOGOMIL DUALISM, DOCETISM, AND POPULARISM

Bogomillian and later Catharist ideas go back to the grand confusion of many earlier heretical sects, including the Marcionites, Borborites, Bardaisans, Messalians, Montanists, Adoptionists, and Monarchians, and the later sect in Dioclea and Bosnia called the Patarenes (who after a migration to the west were eventually the Cathars of northern Italy). Many of these sects shared with the monophysites, and the Nestorians,[3] who still survive in large numbers in Mesopotamia and India, the essential docetic notion of Christ and Jesus as two figures, one divine and one human, and Christ as a phantom on the cross who only seemed to be human.

Like earlier gnostics, the Bogomils held a dualistic view of soul and body, and of good and evil deities as evinced in the struggle between the good god of light and the demonic biblical god of darkness and error who created and trapped our souls in material, perishable bodies. Christ was an angel messenger of god. On earth, following the docetic interpretation of Jesus Christ, the Christ was not real flesh but a phantasm, his sufferings an illusion. The man Jesus was a prophet, the earthly counterpart of Christ the angel spirit. The Bogomils replaced biblical myth, as did the earlier gnostics, with an elaborate cosmogony and theogony of their own, and rejected much of the Old Testament, whose deity they considered to be Satan. They utterly opposed most of the church structure, symbology, and doctrine—hierarchy, saints, sacraments, relics, the cross, the trinity, and the divinity of Mary. They detested the cross as the instrument of Christ's murder. They aimed early Christian iconoclasm at Orthodox icons, which they called idols. As for their comportment, they drank no wine, ate no meat, and were essentially pacifists practicing passive resistance. And they took a politically populist view, denouncing

---

3. The Nestorians, who believed that the human and divine natures remained distinct in Jesus, hold a position that may be contrasted with the Catholic view pronounced by Saint Cyril of Alexandria that Jesus was two natures inseparably joined in one person, and the monophysite belief that Jesus Christ was composed of a single nature, a belief that, in certain expressions, could tend toward docetism. Monophysite christologies are to be found in eastern churches of the Levant to the present day. Docetic interpretations, such as those represented among some of the gnostics discussed in this volume, suggest that the real Christ only seemed to be human. At times docetists maintain that Jesus was human and represented a human being, while Christ was a phantom, appearance, or illusion of Jesus, whom people mistook for Jesus, and whose appearance represented god.

the wealth and opulence of the Byzantine Church and seeking to liberate the Slavic serfs from serfdom.

THE BOGOMILS SPREAD TO THE WEST

In the eleventh century the Bogomils sent missionaries to spread their reform—or heresy, in the eyes of the established church—into northern Italy and France, where the new orders retained the essential Bogomil theology and personal practice. The Cathars, however, extended the more restrictive reading of the Bogomils to include Paul, the gospels, and the Hebrew Bible, to which, in the manner of the earlier Alexandrian exegetes, they gave their own distinctive interpretation. In 1167 the Bogomils sent to Toulouse a major bishop, Nicetas, who instructed and gave prestige to the developing Cathar movement. And Bogomil scriptures appeared in Latin, one of which survives today: the Gospel of the Secret Supper, or John's Interrogation. This key and influential book came into hands of the French and Italian Cathars in Latin translation, probably from Byzantine Greek (the original was lost). It exists in two slightly different versions, one preserved in the archives of the Office of the Inquisition at Carcassonne and the second in the National Library of Vienna.

CATHAR BRANDS OF DUALISM

The Cathars of France and Italy are normally divided into two sects: absolute dualism and mitigated dualism.[4] Absolute dualism is more purely Manichaean, varying less from its Bogomil roots and using the traditional terms of Manichaean cosmogony. Mitigated dualism was dominant among the Cathars, however. Even the present form of the Gospel of the Secret Supper, or John's Interrogation, the major Bogomil text imported into France and used by the Cathars, the dualism is decisively mitigated, and the usual terms and personages of Manichaean dualism—aeons, archons, Sophia—are not used. Not even the name of Mani appears in it. Instead, the text is based on the gospels and a gnostic interpretation of them, and especially of the Gospel of

---

4. Normally the term Albigensians, the geographical epithet of the Cathars, is used interchangeably with Cathars. René Nelli, however, distinguishes philosophically between the Albigensians, who had a more absolutist form of dualism that was closer to Manichaean roots, and the Cathars, whose dualism evolved toward their own interpretation and tends to be mitigated.

John, which throughout has been favored among the canonical gospels by gnostics as one of their own. As a rule the gnostics have vigorously interpreted the Gospel of John, through elaborate exegesis, as gnostic scripture. The Cathars saw the Gospel of the Secret Supper, or John's Interrogation, as a purely Johannine gnostic text. It is a conversation between the evangelist John and god (*le Seigneur*) in which John interrogates *le Seigneur* about Satan before the fall, the creation, Adam and Eve, the descent of Jesus Christ, baptism by water and by spirit, and Satan's lake of fire and the invisible god's heaven. It is a Cathar variation of Christian myth.

In contrast, the major extant Cathar text, known as the Book of the Two Principles, is a perfect example of absolute dualism, showing the relentless struggle between the god of goodness and the god of evil for dominion and belief among the unknowing. The god of goodness will be conquered in time but will be victorious in eternity when captive souls escape evil and return to light. Only then will evil be annihilated. As in classical Manichaean texts, a Cathar primordial human will also fight against evil and fail, as will the good angels. But their victory is not in defeating and punishing evil now—which they say is the way of the *romains* (the Catholics)—but in waiting until matter annihilates itself, when nonbeing is truly nonexistent and light lives in eternity.

In the absolute dualism of the Albanenses (an epithet for the absolute dualists), the principle of good is entirely opposite to the principle of evil, as being is to nonbeing. The absolutists' god is limited ontologically to the good, without free will, because his power (*la puissance*) and his will (*la voluntée*) are one and the same. He cannot and does not want to do evil. Nor can the good god create anyone with free will, such as a human who might do evil or a favored angel Lucifer, who has the free will to become the evil devil. That task of creating evil, free will, and the demon god is left to the entirely separate entity of the principle of evil. It must be remembered that the principle of evil is the eternal principle, preceding the demon god of evil.

The absolute and mitigated dualists also differed in their myths, though these differences are less significant than the conceptual differences of absolute versus relative separation of the good and evil principles. As an example of the mythic differences, the absolutist Albanenses believed that the demon of evil never managed to invade any of the seven levels of heaven and their corresponding angels. The mitigated dualists believed that only the higher levels of heaven resisted the temptations of the fallen angel Lucifer, but that Lucifer could ever have been at any level of god's heaven was an idea abhorrent to the absolute dualists. The good god could never have been the creator of a Lucifer who has the free will to become wicked.

More prominent in mitigated dualism than in absolute dualism is the essential theory of emanation. For the mitigated dualists, there is only one original principle: the good god, from whom both Christ and Lucifer emanate. Lucifer, carrier of light, was originally good and sat next to god, but he became corrupted and corrupted his angels and they all became demons. For the absolute dualists, there are two principles: the principle of good and the principle of evil, which is nothingness. Lucifer is Satan, the creature of nonbeing, of earth, which is the inferno where souls must wait for the possibility of redemption and return to the light. Satan has always been evil, and of his own free will has imprisoned the good spirits (who lack free will) into earthly matter. The good spirits on earth have not willingly sinned but have been forced into human bodies.

Some modern scholars attempt to reconcile the two systems, saying that these two theses do not reflect fundamentally different worldviews but are simply different ways of explaining how Satan was tempted and absorbed by matter, how evil entered heaven, and how being was contaminated by nonbeing, all of which was inevitable when god chose to create. Such an argument is wrong, however, and reflects only the mitigated branch of Catharism. It must be remembered that the good god of absolute dualism is absolutely separate from any creation that could have led to evil. This separation from evil, however, has interesting consequences in limiting the true god's power. God cannot create evil, and to that extent is not omnipotent like the good god of mitigated dualism. The absolute god seems to be "all powerful" yet remains limited because of his inability to concoct an evil universe. His purity and goodness limit him. Yet he still has contact with evil: the good god will spend eternity struggling with evil, and ultimately, as Jean de Lugio, the probable author of the Book of the Two Principles, assures us, this good principle will overcome the wicked principle, being will vanquish nonbeing, and every soul infected with evil, except the principle of evil itself, will be redeemable, including Satan.

Among the firm dualists, the devil's domain was this world of evil matter. This is why the good spirit will ascend to the spiritual domain while the material body must remain in this world. The Old Testament was the domain of the creator god and his patriarchs Abraham and Moses, who were villainous, although the other Old Testament prophets as well as the Songs (the Psalms) and the Song of Songs were accepted. Other gnostic sects (such as the Mandaeans) made John the baptizer a true rival of Jesus, but while some Cathars saw John as a false prophet because he baptized with water rather than spirit, others held him to be an angel, as we note in the Book of the Two Principles. As for creating more evil bodies, the perfect (or elect) chose abstinence. Some of the perfect even chose *endura*, meaning they committed suicide through starvation. The believers, however, were freer than their Catholic counterparts. They could have sex outside of marriage, particularly if it did not lead to the conception of children and more trapped sparks of light. So marriage contained a dubious expression of sexuality, where conception was accepted as inevitable but regrettable. These reversals of Catholic principles were deeply repugnant to the established church.

THE ROLE OF CHRIST

In general the Cathar mythology of god and creation is, as in diverse gnostic texts, poetic, fantastic, and contradictory. With so much of our knowledge still dependent on summaries in archival documents of the Inquisition in France and Italy, the nature of Cathar thought is difficult to classify neatly. Christ, for example, is seen in sundry ways. All Cathar texts agree that he is not the son of god, nor is he god by another name. He is god's first angel. Some declare that because he fought the demon and was not contaminated, he earned the title—but just the title, not the fact—of son of god. Others among the mitigated dualists claim that Christ's soul is god. All agree that to save souls he had to come to earth and suffer—either by giving the appearance of suffering and sacrificing himself in the phantasm of a Christ figure, or, as some believed, by becoming a man and truly suffering the passion. Another reason Christ was sent below by the father was to instruct people that the god they worshiped in the churches, the god of the Bible, was none other than the devil.

LES BONNES-HOMMES AND POPULARISM

The Cathars also adopted from the Bogomils a populist mode that esteemed beggars, itinerant monks, and the common good people, which is to say, the peasants. Indeed, while the Cathar theologians and ascetics also had their inevitable hierarchy, they held on to modest titles, even for the perfects, as in *la bona gen* (Provençal) and *le bon homme* (French), both meaning "a good person." The notion of the good everywhere in the celestial realm was at the core of Catharism and has led scholars to speak of a pantheistic good. In the words of Steven Runciman, "The Cathars were essentially believers in pantheism throughout the celestial realm. That is to say, good to them was God."[5] And on earth that good should be fairly shared, including a knowledge by the people of the scriptures, which speak the good, meaning that holy text is not the sole province of clergy. Hence the abundant translation of texts into the vernacular tongue (Provençal). It is fair to say that this anticlerical, populist strain in the middle ages was not restricted to the Cathars.

The Lollards in England and the Carmelite *descalzos* (the unshod) in Spain were other attempts to return to the truth or legend of the early Jewish-Christian peasant movement, derived from the communal poor, for whom spirit was stronger than gold or power. All were swiftly denounced and persecuted as heresy.[6]

THE PERFECT AND THE BELIEVERS

Among the ordinary people of Toulouse and other cities in Languedoc, there were two groups of the faithful Cathars: the perfect (also known as the *parfait, bon-homme*, elect, or purists) and the much larger ranks of believers (also known as the *credentes* or hearers). The perfect were ascetic clergy, devoting themselves to contemplation and following strict moral rules, who forswore meat, cheese, sex, and other worldly pleasures. To pass into the ranks of the perfect, one received the sacrament of *consolamentum*, a laying on of hands. The believers were the lay people, who were peasants, a mobile merchant class, and even a majority of the southern lower nobility as well as greater nobles such as Count Raymond VI of Toulouse, Count Raymond-Roger of Foix, and Roger II, Viscount of Béziers and Carcassonne. The movement also included an unusually large number of very active women, both at the perfect and believer levels. There was a clear division of acceptable behavior for the two divisions of Catharists, and the believer caste was exceptionally free from ascetic restraints.

The devotion by Cathar *credentes* to diverse regional arts was not only tolerated but encouraged. Consequently, the arts flourished in Toulouse and other Cathar cities when northern France lived under a darker light. Southern France had the song of the aristocratic troubadour composer and the *joglar*

---

5. Runciman, *The Medieval Manichee*, 149.
6. There were even French crusade leaders from the poor, leading armies of the poor, Peter the Hermit (c. 1050–95) and his disciple Walter the Penniless (Gautier Sans-Avoir, d. 1096). But like the titled leaders, they brought hell and havoc wherever they could plunder, from Belgrade to Jerusalem.

(jongleur) performer and singer—*albas, cansos, sirventes, plancs, pastorals* (morning songs, songs, political lyrics, dirges, pastorals); the north had grave epic and the trouvères, who imitated the troubadours. Out of this mélange of Cathar and Catholic and poetry, the troubadours gave us an age of cosmopolitan, witty, and wildly satiric song. In short lyric or ballad, they recounted adventures and misadventures of carnal and spiritual love. Their cult of courtly love commingled with a fully secular expression in an accessible vernacular tongue, and they opened worlds of courtly love from which we have, fortunately perhaps, never recovered. Indeed, it is a commonplace to say that the first lights of the renaissance, even before the radiant sonneteers of the royal courts of Sicily, shone in the free-spirited Midi of southern France.

CATHAR AS HERESY AND PAPAL RESPONSE

From the point of view of church orthodoxy in France and Italy, however, this popular religion was increasing at an alarming rate. Its dualistic, anticlerical, and worldly stance was a diabolic heresy and its suppression inevitable. When it came, the punishment was catastrophic. The fall of the Cathars had levels of political complexity, with diverse Spanish, northern French, Italian, and even English interests vying for a piece of the destruction. Pope Innocent III made the first decisive move, proclaiming the Albigensian Crusade in 1209 against the gnostic heresy, calling in secular forces against the dualists, whom he offered the same indulgences as given to crusaders: spiritual salvation and material riches. The papal troops ravaged Toulouse, and in southern France thousands were slaughtered or burned at the stake. Churches and monasteries were razed, and scriptures burned. Many of the nobility lost their lands and were also burned. Later the northern barons, under the French king Saint Louis IX, invaded, and in 1244 they captured the last Cathar fortress, the famous mountaintop Montségur in the Pyrenees, bringing the independent region of the south into a larger France. For the French king his invasion was not a crusade against Cathar heresy but a war of annexation.

With the fall of the citadel at Montségur and the capitulation of the nobility, the Catharist communities went underground. There was a large immigration to Catalonia and Lombardy, and also to Bosnia, where the Bogomils offered them sanctuary. As for the Cathar church in France, it was not yet completely crushed, but the great cities of the south—Toulouse, Béziers, Carcassone, and Narbonne—lay in ruins. After a hundred years of war and executions, there was almost everywhere in southern France a drop in population of more than half.

As a legal instrument to complete the job of rooting out Catharism in Albigensian centers, Pope Gregory IX in 1233 established the Inquisition. He gave the task to the Dominicans friars. So was born the medieval Inquisition, which later spread to northern Italy and Germany. (The Spanish Inquisition established by Ferdinand and Isabella in Spain in 1478, with its notorious autos-da-fé, was independent of the medieval Inquisition elsewhere in western Europe and was finally abolished in 1834.) The Dominican inquisitors labored through southern France in the thirteenth and fourteenth centuries to extinguish virtually all discoverable remnants of the heretical religion. The Inquisition kept records of their activities and preserved the documents of heresy in their archives. We owe our detailed historical knowledge of these events and of Cathar scripture to these documents.

The Inquisition and the Vatican found not only Catharism subversive, but also the troubadours, the great symbol of Occitanian and general Provençal culture. Many of the troubadours were Cathars, and of these, some of the best known, such as Peire Cardenal, were strongly anticlerical, that is, *anti-romains* (anti-Catholic). The troubadour composers—and the jongleurs who performed the troubadour songs—vanished as their noble patrons had vanished in the massacres of the great families. With the destruction of the two dissenting movements, the Cathars of inner light and the troubadours of outer light, along with the supporting peasants, nobility, and their political protectors, power and culture in France moved from the prevailing *langue d'oc* (in Provençal, *lenga d'oc*) in the south to the bleak *langue d'oïl* north, and the brilliant Provençal civilization faded forever.[7]

SURVIVAL OF SCRIPTURES

The literature of the Cathars awaits the discovery of its own Nag Hammadi library of original gnostic scripture. We rely principally on five treatises, including the Gospel of the Secret Supper (*La Cène secrète*), the Anonymous

---

7. While Provençal was destroyed, its legacy was unstoppable. Meg Bogin summarizes: "The troubadour's use of *lenga d'oc* spurred the development of poetry in all the other nascent languages of Europe. By the beginning of the thirteenth century, imitations of the Provençal *chanson*, or love song, were being written in Italian, German, Spanish, *langue d'oïl* [French] and even English. This medieval poetry produced a double legacy, which continues to determine a good portion of the western world of feeling. Through Dante's Beatrice, love was proclaimed the supreme experience of life, and the quest for love, with the lady as its guiding spirit, became the major theme of western literature" (Bogin, *Women Troubadours*, 10).

Cathar Treatise (*Le Traité cathare anonyme*), the Cathar Ritual (*Le Rituel cathare*), the Ritual of Dublin (*Le Rituel de Dublin*), and the extensive Book of the Two Principles (*Le Livre des deux principes*), as well as writings of the heresiologists deposited in the offices of the Inquisition, which were written to record the central doctrines, practices, and heresies of the Cathars. The Anonymous Cathar Treatise, for example, is a scholastic interpretation of absolute dualism, probably the work of Barthélemy of Carcassone, an antipapist Cathar who employed reason to prove his heretical faith. The treatise is included in the Book against the Manichaeans (*Liber contra Manicheos*), written in 1222 or 1224 and attributed to Durand de Huesca, in which the author cites Cathar texts and then point by point refutes them, converting the book into a Catholic essay in itself. The most important heresiological work by far is the work of a former Cathar priest, Raynier Sacconi, who became a *romain*, a church Catholic, and an articulate inquisitor, whose seminal work against the Cathars is the *Summa de Cataris*. We also possess twelfth- and thirteenth-century works with Catharist influence.

From the rituals of the Cathars, the pivotal work is the *Consolamentum* in the Book of Ritual, which contains the sacramental words an initiate must recite in order to become a perfect. The core of the ritual is a reading from parts of the canonical Gospel of John. As we have seen throughout this volume, John was the favorite gospel among the gnostics: from the Alexandrian gnostics, who explained and allegorized John as a gnostic gospel, to the Cathars, for whom John was at the heart of their ceremony and scriptures. The book of John persisted as a key source in the last centuries for all those major groups who speculated on the alien god, and who looked for the light of knowledge in its verse:

> The light was the true light
> which illuminates every person
> who comes into the world. (John 1:9)

45

The Gospel of the Secret Supper

The Gospel of the Secret Supper, or John's Interrogation, is not an original Cathar text. It exists as a gift from the Bogomils, in Latin translation from a text in old Bulgarian from the twelfth century or earlier, that in the thirteenth century was obtained and taken to Italy by the Patarene emissaries of Bosnia to the bishop of Concorezzo and thereafter dispersed through Italy and Provence. There may have been a Paulician scripture behind it, in Greek rather than Armenian, some centuries before, now lost, on which the Secret Supper was based and shaped to accommodate Bogomil doctrine. It exists in two slightly different versions, one preserved in the archives of the Office of the Inquisition at Carcassonne and the second in the National Library of Vienna. Both come from one source, but the Vienna version appears to be altered to make it clearer in sense and interpretation. It is not complete, breaking off forty-three lines from the end (in René Nelli's French translation). The Vienna has definite virtues. It clarifies passages and adds colorful language. However, it reads almost as a gloss of the Carcassone and lacks its majesty. Where the Vienna version seems to solve a problem of meaning, this is recorded in the notes.

The Secret Supper is a gospel of the invisible father, his son the angel Christ, and John of the canonical gospels, who questions the lord (Jesus Christ) and the invisible father at a Last Supper (Passover meal). Structurally, it is dialectic, at times like a platonic dialogue, but without debate; at other moments it is a genesis narration. It begins with a creation of the world. The imagery is as striking as that of Genesis or Revelation. The main character is Satan, shining white before his fall and burning red thereafter. Then Adam and Eve are created. After Satan and his reptile provoke the first couple's sin, the world, which is a mistake, is reigned over by Satan and his own angels. Jesus Christ descends. There is baptism by water and spirit, the eucharist, last judgment, and punishment of Satan. In the last part the invisible father speaks and controls the scene.

The work begins as a strongly dualist text, immediately introducing two conflicting deities. The invisible father is not to be confused with the demiurge creator in Genesis. There is the creator of good, who is the true lord, and the creator of evil, who is Satan and his contaminated creations. Humans have a spirit or soul, however, which permits them to return from the evil of the prison of earthly matter. This gospel or treatise is thus a mitigated dualist document, in that god is not entirely separated from the possibility of creating figures who might do evil. There is an element of free will, which permits Adam and Eve to make their fatal choice. In a text like the Book of the Two Principles, which is considered an absolute dualist document, however, free will does not exist. Otherwise god would have been guilty of creating angels and ultimately humans capable of choosing evil, which he cannot do or even wish to do. God is limited to doing good, and therefore there is a second presence who can and desires to do evil—the second absolute deity, the principle of evil. In absolute dualism there is an absolute distinction between good and evil and their mutual divine authors.

After earlier gnostic conversation and narration, the scripture continues, moving toward a more conventionally Christian gospel, albeit with a reference to the crucifixion in which Christ is an angel, an illusion, a phantasm rather than the suffering Jesus. The last judgment, while it is linguistically fresh and the details of Satan's punishment are rich in apocalyptic images from late apocrypha, varies little, or not at all, from what it means and how it sounds in the New Testament. The way there is different, the deity above is other, but the conclusion is recognizably alike, with the invisible father substituting for the Christian god. In the early part the references are to Genesis and Isaiah, in the later part to the gospel of John, the preferred gospel in gnostic treatises. The Secret Supper and the Book of the Two Principles, which escaped the fire of wars and Inquisition, constitute the two main extant Cathar scriptures.

THE GOSPEL OF THE
SECRET SUPPER[1]

WHO BROUGHT YOU HERE?

I, John, who am your brother and share with you the tribulation of having shared the kingdom of the skies, since I was lying on the chest of our lord Jesus Christ, asked him, "Lord, who brought you here?"

And he answered me, "He who put his hand in the plate with me.[2] So Satan entered in him, and he, Judas, had already betrayed me."

BEFORE SATAN FELL

And I said, "Lord, before Satan fell, what was his glory beside your father's?"

And he told me, "Such was his glory that he governed the virtues of heaven. As for me, I sat next to my father. Satan was the master of all those who imitated the father, and his power descended from the sky to the inferno and rose again from the inferno to the throne of the invisible father. And he observed the glory of him who transformed the skies. And he dreamed of placing his seat on the clouds of heaven, because he wanted to be like the very high.[3]

Then, having descended into the air, he said to the angel of the air, "Open the gates of the air for me."

And the angel opened the gates of the air.

And he went on his way to the bottom. There he found the angel who guarded the waters, and he said to him, "Open the gates of the waters for me."

And the angel opened the gates of the waters.[4]

Going ahead, he found the whole face of the earth and saw two fish who were stretched over the waters.[5] They were like two oxen joined together for plowing and, at the invisible father's order, they held up the earth, from sunset to sunrise.

---

1. The Gospel of the Secret Supper: translated by Willis Barnstone, from the French translation by René Nelli, *Écritures cathares,* 146.
2. Mark 14:20. The reference is to Judas Iscariot.
3. Isaiah 14:13–14.
4. The angels who guard the gate of the sky are found in Revelation 16:5. The angels of the waters are in 1 Enoch 66:1–2.
5. These fish appear in Job 15:10, 40:15, and 41:1.

When he descended farther down, he found himself in the presence of clouds weighing on the tidal waves of the sea. He went on until he got to his *ossop*, which is the principle of fire.[6] After that he could not descend farther because of the intense flame of the fire. Then Satan came in from behind and filled his own heart with malice, and reaching the angel of the air and the one who was above the waters, he said to them, "Everything belongs to me. If you listen to me, I will place my seat on the clouds and I shall be similar to the very high. I will withdraw the waters of the upper firmament and assemble all the areas occupied by the sea into one entity of vast seas. That done, there will be no water on the face of the entire earth, and I shall reign with you through the centuries of the centuries."

After he said this, the angel Satan rose toward the other angels to the fifth heaven, and to each of them he said, "How much do you owe your masters?"

"One hundred measures of wheat," one of them answered.

"Take pen and ink," he said to him, "and write forty."

He told the others, "And you, how much do you owe the lord?"

"One hundred jars of oil," he answered him.

"Sit down," Satan said to him, "and write fifty."[7]

He climbed into the skies, and with such words seduced the angels of the invisible father up to the fifth heaven.

THE FATHER PITIES SATAN

But a voice came out of the throne of the father, saying, "What are you doing, denier of the father, you who are seducing the angels? Creator of sin, hurry with what you hope to do!"[8]

Then the father ordered his angels, "Rip off their robes!"

The angels stripped all those angels who had listened to Satan of their robes, their thrones, and their crowns. And I questioned the lord further.

"When Satan plummeted, where did he make his living place?"

And he responded to me, "My father transformed him because of his pride, and he withdrew the light from him.[9] His face became like red fire and

---

6. In the Vienna version a marginal notes says that *ossop* is the same as the Valley of Josaphat, although the text reads "principle of fire."

7. Luke 16:5–7.

8. John 13:27.

9. Satan was also the angel Lucifer, carrier of the light.

was fully like that of a man. He dragged with his tail the third part of the angels of god, and he was hurled from his seat and from his domain in the skies. Descending to the firmament of the fallen angels, he found no place to rest for himself or for those who were with him.

And he begged the father, saying, "Be patient with me and I will return everything to you!"[10]

The father pitied him and gave him and those with him rest and permission to do what he wished to do on the seventh day.

SATAN REVEALS DRY LAND AND CREATES MAN AND WOMAN

So he installed himself in his heaven and commanded his angels who were above the air and above the waters. He lifted two parts of the water, from bottom to top, into the air, and from the third part he made the sea, which became the mistress of the waters, but, according to the father's commandment, he also prescribed that the angel who was above the waters hold up the two fish. And he lifted the earth from bottom to top and dry land appeared. He took the crown of the angel who commanded the waters and from one half made the light of the moon, from the other the light of the stars. With precious stones he made the army of stars. Then he chose the angels for his ministers according to the celestial hierarchies established by the very high. And by command of the invisible father, he made thunder, the rains, the frosts, and the snows. He placed his angels as ministers over them to govern them. And he commanded the earth to produce every kind of great beast, all reptiles, and trees and grasses. And he commanded the sea to produce fish and the sky birds.

After that he reflected, and he made a man so that he might have a slave. He ordered the angel of the third sky to enter this body of mud, from which he then took out a part for making another body in the form of a woman. And he commanded the angel of the second sky to enter the body of the woman. But these angels wept when they saw that they had there an external mortal form and that they were dissimilar[11] in that external form. Satan joined them in this act of turning their bodies of mud into flesh. The angels did not perceive that in this way he also committed a sin.

The announcer of coming evils meditated in his spirit on a way he would

---

10. Matthew 18:26–27.
11. I.e., were man and woman.

fashion paradise. Then he ordered the people to enter it and his angels to lead them to it. The devil planted a reed in the middle of paradise. And in one spit he made the serpent, whom he commanded to live in the reed. In such way the devil concealed his evil design so they might not know his trickery.

And he entered paradise and spoke with them.

He said to them, "Eat from all the fruit that is found in paradise, but beware of eating the fruit of the knowledge of good and evil."

However, the devil slipped into the body of the evil serpent and seduced the angel who was in the form of woman and he spread over her head the powerful desire of sin, and he satiated Eve with his bodily desire while he attended to the serpent's tail.[12] That is why humans are called the children of the devil and children of the serpent, because they serve the desire of the devil, who is their father, and will serve it until the consummation of this century.

ADAM AND EVE CHOOSE SIN AND BECOME MORTAL

Then, I, John, questioned the lord, "How can one say that Adam and Eve were created by god and placed in paradise to obey the father's orders, but they were then delivered to death?"

The lord answered me, "Listen, John, beloved of my father, it is the ignorant who say, in their error, that my father made these bodies of mud. In reality he created all the virtues of heaven through the holy spirit. But it is through their sin that they found themselves with mortal bodies of mud and were consequently turned over to death."

And again I, John, questioned the lord, "How can a man become born in spirit in a body of flesh?"

And the lord answered, "Descended from angels fallen from the sky, men enter the body of a woman and receive the desire of the flesh. Spirit is born then from the spirit and flesh from the flesh.[13] So Satan accomplishes his reign in this world and in all nations."

He told me further, "My father permitted him to rule seven days, which are seven centuries."

---

12. The serpent's tail here suggests the penis.
13. Nelli comments on this passage that the spirit that man receives from on high is sperm (seed) of an angelic nature. The mitigated dualists teach that a person's soul derives from a fallen angel, the body from bodies created by Satan that serve as a prison to house the spirit (*Écritures cathares*, 52).

SATAN'S ANGEL CHOOSES THREE TREES FOR THE CRUCIFIXION

And again I asked the lord. I said to him, "What did he do during all that time?"

And he told me, "From the instant the devil was expelled from the glory of the father and was forbidden to take part in affairs of heaven, he sat on the clouds and sent his ministers, angels burning with fire, down below to the people. He did so from the time of Adam to Enoch. And he raised his minister Enoch above the firmament and revealed his divinity to him.[14] He had pen and ink brought to him. And once seated, Enoch wrote sixty-seven books under the devil's dictation, and the devil ordered him to carry them back to earth.

Enoch kept them safely on the earth and then transmitted them to his children, and he began to teach them the way to celebrate sacrifices and iniquitous mysteries. So he concealed from people the kingdom of the skies.

And Satan said to them, "See that I am your god and that there is no other god but me."[15] That is why my father sent me into the world, that I make known and teach people to perceive the wicked spirit of the devil. But then Satan, having learned that I had descended from the sky to this world, sent his angel, and he took the wood of three trees and gave it to Moses so that I might be crucified on a cross made from the wood, which is at this time waiting for me. And he made his divinity known to his people, and ordered the law to be given to the children of Israel, and that he cross dry through the middle of the Red Sea.

THE LORD INSEMINATES THE ANGEL MARY

When my father thought of sending me to the earth, he sent before me his angel named Mary to receive me. Then I came down,[16] entered her by the ear, and came out of her ear.[17]

---

14. In the Vienna version, the devil ravishes Enoch with ecstasy as he sends him on high.
15. Isaiah 45:5–6, 21; 46:9. This arrogant claim is commonly made by the creator of the world (for example, Yaldabaoth) in gnostic texts.
16. The Vienna version adds, "she became my mother."
17. The notion that Mary was inseminated through the ear is based on noncanonical apocrypha and is found in medieval painting. Here Jesus as an angel inseminates his mother the angel Mary with his sperm through her ear. This notion of purity is doubly reinforced, since Mary will not have been inseminated normally, and the child will issue from her pure ear rather than from her loins.

And Satan, prince of this world, knew that I had come down to seek and save the beings who had perished, and he sent his angel the prophet Elijah down to earth to baptize in water. He is called John the baptizer. Then Elijah asked the prince of this world, "How can I recognize the Christ?"

And the lord himself answered, saying, "He on whom you will see the holy spirit descend like a dove and remain there, he is immersed in the holy spirit for the remission of his sins. He alone has the power to lead astray and to save."

IS IT A SIN TO MARRY?

Again I, John, ask the lord, "Can one be saved by John's immersion without your immersion?"

And the lord answered me, "If I have not immersed one through the spirit for the remission of sins, no one by only immersion in water can see the kingdom in the skies, because I am the bread of life descendant from the seventh heaven.[18] Only those who eat my flesh and drink my blood are called the children of god."

And I asked the lord, "What must one understand by your words, eating my flesh and drinking my blood?"[19]

The lord told me,[20] "Before the devil was driven out with all his troops from the glory of the father, his angels prayed and glorified the father, saying in their prayers, 'Our father who is in the skies,' and so all their canticles rose before the throne of god. But since their fall, they cannot glorify god, at least not in their prayer."

And I asked the lord, "How is it that all receive John's immersion and not yours?"

The lord made this response to me: "Because their works are bad and they do not reach the light. John's students[21] take husbands and wives, but my students do not marry and are like god's angels in the sky."

I said then, "If it is a sin to know a woman, is it wrong to marry?"

The lord replied to me, "Not everyone understands the sense of this word unless he has been given grace to understand. There are eunuchs who have come out of their mother's stomach, there are men who have become eunuchs,

---

18. John 6:33–35.
19. This question is not answered in either version. It is answered in the New Testament passages on the eucharist.
20. From the Vienna version.
21. Disciples.

and there are those men who have become eunuchs by renouncing marriage in exchange for the kingdom in the skies. Whoever can understand this should understand."

HEAVEN OR THE LAKE OF FIRE

And then I asked the lord about the day of judgment, "What will be the sign of your coming?"

He answered me, "It will be when the name of the just will be consummated[22] according to the name of the just ones who have been crowned and fallen from the sky. Then Satan will be freed and will leave his prison,[23] a prey to great anger, and he will make war on the just and they will cry to the lord god in a great voice. And the lord will immediately command his angel to sound the trumpet. The voice of the archangel, in the trumpet, will be heard from heaven to the inferno. And then the sun will darken and the moon give no more light. The stars will fall and the four winds will be torn from the foundations, and they will make the earth tremble, and also the mountains and hills. Immediately the sky will tremble and the sun darken until the fourth hour.[24] Then will appear the earthly son,[25] and with him all the saintly angels. And then the son rises, and he will place his seat on the clouds and will sit on the throne of his majesty,[26] with twelve messengers[27] seated on twelve chairs of glory.

The books will be opened and he will judge the universe according to the faith they revealed. And then the earthly son will send his angels to gather the elect—from the four winds and the summits of the skies and to the corners of the world—and bring them before him. The earthly son will send for the bad demons to bring all the bad nations with him, and he will say to them, "Come here, you who say, 'We have eaten well and drunk and enjoyed the goods of this world.'"

Then he will direct them all before the tribunal, and they will be shaking with terror. And the books of life will be opened, and there will be known the thoughts of all the nations and of their impieties. And the lord will glorify the just in their patience and good deeds. Those who have followed the angelic

---

22. The Vienna version reads "accomplished."
23. Revelation 20:7.
24. See Luke 23:44–45.
25. Matthew 24:30.
26. Matthew 25:31.
27. Apostles.

prescriptions will gain glory, honor, and imperishability. Those who have obeyed the iniquity of the devil will share in anger, indignation, and the torments of anguish. The earthly son will take the elect from the midst of the sinners and say to them, "Come, you who are blessed by my father. Receive the kingdom that has been prepared for you since the organization of the world."[28]

He will say to the sinners, "Go far from me, cursed ones, into the eternal fire that has been prepared for the devil and for his angels."[29]

Then all the others, seeing that the time has come for the ultimate separation, will pity the sinners in their inferno, who will be there by order of the invisible father.

The souls will leave the prison of the unbelievers and also my voice will be heard, and there will be no more than one sheepfold and one pastor. And there will issue from the depths of the earth a dark gloom, which is the dark gloom of the Gehenna of fire, and fire will consume the universe from the abysses of the earth to the air of the firmament.[30] And the lord will reign from the firmament to the infernos of the earth. The lake of fire where the sinners will live is so deep that a stone that a thirty-year-old man lifts and drops to the bottom will barely reach the floor of the lake after three years.[31]

SATAN IN FIRE AND THE ELECT IN HEAVEN

Then Satan will be bound with all his troops and placed in the lake of fire. But the son of god and his elect will stroll on the firmament, and he will lock the devil, lying there, in strong, indestructible chains. The sinners weeping and lamenting will say, "Earth, take us back and hide us in you."[32]

The just will glow like a sun in the kingdom of the invisible father. And the son of god will take them before the throne of the invisible father and say to them, "Here I am with my children whom you have given me. Just father, the world has not known you, but I have truly known you, because it is you who sent me on my mission."[33]

---

28. Matthew 25:34.
29. Matthew 25:41.
30. At this point the Vienna version breaks off. The conclusion is lost.
31. This passage has been identified in a Bogomil Bulgarian version and also in an early apocryphal apocalypse. The man of thirty years may be Jesus.
32. The suggestion is that they wish to return to their painless death in the annihilating earth.
33. John 17:25.

Then the father will answer his son with these words, "My beloved son, sit down to my right until I place at your legs, as a stool,[34] your enemies who have denied me and have said, 'We are gods and besides us there are no other gods.' They have killed the prophets and persecuted the just. It is you now who will pursue them into the remote gloom, where there will be tears and the grinding of teeth."[35]

Then the son of god will sit at the right of the father, and the father will govern his angels and govern the elect. He will place them in choirs of angels, dress them in imperishable garments, and give them unfading crowns and immutable seats. And god will be seated in the middle of them. They will not know hunger or thirst. The sun will not strike them, nor any burning heat. And god will banish all tears from their eyes. The son will reign with his saintly father, and his reign will have no end from centuries to centuries.[36]

---

34. Matthew 22:44; Mark 12:36; Luke 20:43; Psalm 110:1–2.
35. Matthew 13:42; 22:13.
36. Since this manuscript was found in the Office of the Inquisition in Carcassone, two concluding lines, rejecting the truthfulness of the treatise, were added by the Carcassone inquisitors concerning the Gospel of the Secret Supper. They are omitted here.

46

The Book of the Two Principles

The Book of the Two Principles is the centerpiece of Cathar scripture. The single incomplete manuscript in Latin is preserved in the National Library of Florence. This book, in all about the length of a canonical gospel, is perfectly unified and consistent in its doctrine. It is an argumentum, always precise, sometimes colorful, but without prayers or rituals or songs, in favor of absolute dualism. The seven sections are "Treatise on Free Will," "On Creation," "On Universal Signs," "A Shorter Version for the Instruction of the Unknowing" (part of which is translated here), "Against the Garatenses" (an argument about the superiority of absolute dualism over mitigated dualism),[1] "On Free Will," and "On Persecutions."

The two treatises on free will (the first and sixth sections) detail a theme constantly alluded to in "Instruction of the Unknowing": the god of goodness cannot commit evil. This obviously limits the god's freedom of will and power. But, the treatise explains, since the god of goodness wants only to do good, he has no conflict within him: he and his will are one. The syllogistic reasoning is relentlessly consistent through the book.

---

1. The Book of the Two Principles represents the Albanenses' view in favor of "absolute dualism," which the probable author, Jean de Lugio, proposed, as opposed to "mitigated dualism," which the Garatenses held to be true. In other ways the Albanenses and Garatenses were in agreement. The Albanenses, here represented in the Book of the Two Principles, were the only main Cathar sect to accept the authority of the entire Bible.

The good god's sole wish to do good—the principle of good—and the evil god's desire to inflict wickedness—the principle of evil—are elaborated throughout "Instruction of the Unknowing." We have chosen this seminal and longest treatise in the Book of the Two Principles, with its focus on the two principles of the title, to represent the Cathar branch of absolute dualism.

The author of these seven treatises, composed around 1250, is likely to have been Jean de Lugio (Giovanni de Lugio) of Bergamo, an absolute dualist, who was a *vicaire* of the Cathar church and major assistant to the bishop of Desenzano in Italy. Our scant information about the author and even the attribution to Jean de Lugio comes from Rainier Sacconi, an Inquisitor and former Cathar priest, whose denunciations of the Cathars are contained in his *Summa de Catharis*. Sacconi discusses the rigorously philosophical basis of the writings. His summary and response actually refers to a larger, more inclusive volume. Preserved, however, is only this highly systematized metaphysical and polemical part—the rest is lost.

Unlike the Gospel of the Secret Supper, which contains some pages of a cosmology and myth, the Book of the Two Principles is a scholastic argument, repeatedly documenting its message in biblical evidence. Proven by biblical example, Lugio's elaborate and logical argument will, he believes, inexorably lead all adversaries to reject the ways of the unknowing and to accept the Cathar truth. The reader is so instructed at the end of each segment. The treatise's gods mirror the deities of gnostic scriptures in which the invisible father is good and nameless while the biblical creator god, who takes on many notoriously evil-sounding names, is evil. In brief, since god wants to do good and cannot do evil, he is not omnipotent but all powerful with regard to the good. Since there exists evil in the world, in the temporal and material world if not in his own eternal world, and since he the god of goodness cannot do evil or even create a being with free will to do evil, it follows that the evil, as well as the temporal world itself, has been created by a principle of evil. This principle precedes the god of evil, Satan, and is unredeemable. But in the day of reckoning, even Satan the god of evil has a soul, and when free of the body, it may be elevated to spirit and find redemption.

To prove that the biblical god is not the god of goodness, Lugio cites holy scriptures, seeking to demonstrate that the creator of the temporal universe is actually the demon, the principle of evil and creator of the infernal earth and its bodily inhabitants, in which our souls are imprisoned. The biblical god, he claims, is all iniquity: a fornicator, a destroyer and plunderer of village and city, a murderer of adults and little children, a liar who breaks oath promises. Once having understood these proved assertions, "our adversaries" should abandon the god of darkness, "who is the cause and the principle of all iniquity and malice, of all bitterness and injustice," and turn to the true lord and god, "who is the light, who is good and saintly, who is the living fountain and the origin of sweetness, of all tenderness and justice."

In a typical passage of "Instruction of the Unknowing" Lugio takes a passage from Deuteronomy (3:3–7) to show how the biblical god, principle of evil, urged his people to murder and plunder. "So when king Sihon came out against us, he and all his people for battle at Jahaz, the lord our god gave him over to us; and we struck him down, along with his offspring and all his people. At that time we captured all his towns, and in each town we utterly destroyed men, women, and children. We left not a single survivor."

The late scholar René Nelli, who wrote about Cathars and troubadours, comments astutely on this passage, finding parallels between biblical slaughter and the fate of the Cathars before the Catholics:

> During the Crusade against the Albigensians, the Roman Catholics might have been able to authorize on the basis of these passages in the Bible the right to sack cities and castles and to exterminate the inhabitants, as they did many times. The Cathar morality, by contrast, formally condemned wars and massacres wherever they took place. Whatever one may say about it, Catharism represented then an indisputable moral progress. And even their refusal to attribute to a good god the horrors reported in the Bible is a measure of the change that they infused at that time in the conscience of the best of them.[2]

The Cathars stood, then, in utter contrast to the crusading power-and-pillage portraits of soldiers of Christendom who dominated society during centuries of failed but devastating rampages to Jerusalem. Their inner light and obsession with goodness, peace, and justice are witnessed in the tragic history of their massacre and disappearance and in the luminous remnants of their song and scripture.

---

2. Nelli, *Écritures cathares*, 159.

THE BOOK OF THE TWO PRINCIPLES[3]

GOD HAS NOT MADE THE WORLD[4]

My proposal is to give here a résumé of what has been said previously on the creation of the sky, the earth, and the sea for the instruction of the unknowing.[5] I think that skies[6] and earth in the holy scriptures sometimes designate real creatures of the true god, who are endowed with mind and capable of comprehending and perceiving, and not only the elements, which always change and are deprived of reason. As David said in the Psalms, "The skies recount the glory of god, and the firmament proclaims the works of his hands."[7] We read in Deuteronomy, "Skies, listen to what I am going to say: that the earth understands the words of my mouth."[8] And in Isaiah, "Skies, listen, and you earth, lend me your ear, because the lord has spoken."[9] Again in Jeremiah, "Earth, earth, hear the word of the lord,"[10] and in the Psalms, "You have made yourself a road in the sea. You have walked amid the waters."[11] David refers to these ways when he says in the Psalms, "All the ways of the lord are but mercy and truth."[12]

Then by sky, earth, and sea we understand celestial beings. Saint John says in Revelation:

> And every creature which is in the sky,
> on the earth and under the earth and on the sea,
> and everything in these, I heard them saying:

---

3. A portion of the section "A Shorter Version for the Instruction of the Unknowing" from the Book of the Two Principles; translated by Willis Barnstone from the French translation by René Nelli, *Écritures cathares*, 143–48.

4. Except in this first section, where the two subtitles are provided, the subtitles are found and translated from the original text.

5. Conveying knowledge to those who do not know was a central gnostic concern.

6. Or "heavens."

7. Psalms 19:1. The French text numbers the Psalms one less than the English Psalms. The English numbering is followed in the notes.

8. Deuteronomy 32:1.

9. Isaiah 1:2.

10. Jeremiah 22:29.

11. A free version of Psalm 77:19, also containing elements from Isaiah 43:16.

12. Psalm 25:10.

"To the one seated on the throne and to the lamb,
blessings and honor and glory and dominion forevermore."[13]

And David in the Psalms, "I believe I see the goodness of the lord in the land of the living."[14] He also says, "Let your good spirit lead me on a level path."[15] Solomon declares, "But the just will inherit the earth and live on it forever."[16] Christ has ordered "not to swear by any part of the sky because it is the throne of god."[17] When he says "throne" he is surely thinking of David in Psalms when he says, "O god, your throne exists eternally,"[18] and again Matthew, "not on earth, for earth is god's footstool."[19] It is our lord himself who adds, in Hebrews, "because it is his footstool."[20] David continues the footstool allusion in Psalms:

Fear the lord, our god, and worship
the footstool at his feet, for he is holy.[21]

About creation, I wish to confess that our lord god is the creator and author, but not of the elements of the world, which are impotent and empty, and as Paul said in Galatians, "How can you now turn back to the impotent and empty elements under which you suffer a new slavery?"[22] The messenger[23] also says in Colossians, "If with Christ you died to the elemental spirits of the universe, why do you live as if you still belonged to the world? Why do you submit to regulations: 'Do not handle, Do not taste, Do not touch'? All these regulations refer to things that perish with use."[24]

GOD HAS NOT MADE DEATH

Even less can we admit that our lord is the creator and author of death, and of the things that are, by their essence, in death, because, as it is written in the

---

13. Revelation 5:13.
14. Psalm 27:13.
15. Psalm 143:10.
16. Psalm 37:29.
17. Matthew 5:34.
18. Psalm 45:6.
19. Matthew 5:35.
20. Hebrews 1:13, from Psalm 110:1.
21. Psalm 99:5.
22. Galatians 4:9.
23. Apostle.
24. Colossians 2:20–22.

book of Wisdom, "God has not made death, and he does not rejoice at the loss of the living." [25] There exists, then, with no doubt whatsoever, another creature or factor, who is the principle and cause of death, of perdition, and of all evil, as we have explained above with sufficient clarity.

ON THE OMNIPOTENCE OF THE TRUE LORD GOD

I wish to speak now of the omnipotence of the true lord god, which so often permits our adversaries[26] to play the glorious one when they claim against us that there is no other force or power than theirs.

Although in the testimony of the holy scriptures, the true lord god may be called all powerful, one must not believe that he is called that because he can do and does all evils, because there exist many evils that the lord cannot and will never do. As the Letter to the Hebrews says, "It is impossible for god to lie." [27] And the same messenger declares in the Second Letter to Timothy, "If we are unfaithful to him, he will not cease being faithful, since he cannot deny himself." [28] Nor must one believe that this good god has the power to destroy himself, and to commit all kinds of wickedness against wisdom and justice. That is even more impossible for him, since he is not the absolute cause of evil. And if one objects to us, saying, "We have the right to say that the true lord god is all powerful, and not only because he can do and does all the good things, but also because he could do all the wicked things, if he wanted to, even to lie and destroy himself, if he cared to. But he does not want to," the answer to them is easy.

THAT GOD CANNOT DO EVIL

If god does not want to do all the wicked things, if he does not want to lie or destroy himself, surely he cannot. Because what god in his unity does not want to do, he cannot do. And what he cannot do, he does not want to do. And in this sense, one must say that the power of sinning and of doing evil does not belong to the true lord god. All that is thought to be god's attributes and conduct is not accidental, as the learned know. It necessarily follows,

---

25. Wisdom of Solomon 1:13.
26. Roman Catholic clergy, usually referred to as *les romains.*
27. Hebrews 6:18.
28. 2 Timothy 2:13.

then, that god himself and his will are one and the same. The good god cannot lie or commit every kind of evil, if he wants to, because this true god cannot do what he does not want to, we repeat, since he himself and his will are one and the same.

THAT GOD CANNOT CREATE ANOTHER GOD

I can say again, very reasonably and without fear of deceiving myself, that the true god, with all his power, cannot, nor ever could, nor ever will, neither willfully or involuntarily, nor by any other means, create another god, lord, and creator resembling and equal to himself in any way. I prove that it is impossible for the good god to be able to make another god like himself with regard to every quality: the eternal and sempiternal, the creator and author of all his goodness, without beginning or end, the one who was never made or created or engendered. But in the holy scriptures it does not say that the true god is a weak god. One must believe with assurance that the good god is not endowed with omnipotence because he would then be able to or might commit all the evils that have been, that are, and that will be, but because he is truly all powerful concerning the good that has been, that is, and that will be. Moreover, he is the absolute and principle cause of all the good, and he is never, in any way, by himself and essentially, the cause of evil. It follows that the true god is called all powerful by the sages, in everything he does, has done, or will do in the future, but that those who think accurately cannot call him all powerful with regard to his supposed power that he might have to exert and that he has never exerted, that he never will exert, with regard to creating a god of evil. As for the argument that says that if he does not do it, it is because he does not want to, we have already shown that such a track is meaningless, since he, himself, and his will are only one.

THAT GOD DOES NOT HAVE THE POWER TO BE EVIL AND THAT THERE EXISTS A FORCE THAT IS EVIL

Since god is not powerful in evil, nor has the power to appear to be evil, we must believe firmly that there is another principle, which is he who is powerful in evil. From him come all evils that have been, that are, and that will be. About him David surely wanted to speak when he said, "Why do you glorify yourself in your malice, you who are powerful only for committing an iniquity? Your language has contemplated injustice. You have sharpened your razor to let trickery sneak in. You have more evil than good, and you have preferred a language of iniquity to that of justice."[29] And Saint John says in Revelation:

> The great dragon, the ancient snake, who is called
> devil and Satan, the deceiver of the whole,
> lived in the world and was flung down to earth.[30]

And Christ in the Gospel of Luke has said:

> The seed is the word of god.
> The ones on the side of the road are those who heard.
> Then comes the devil, who takes away the word from their heart
> so they will not believe and be saved.[31]

The prophet Daniel says, "As I looked, this horn from the fourth beast made war with the holy ones and was prevailing over them, until the ancient one came; then judgment was given for the holy ones of the most high."[32] And he says further, "As for the ten horns, out of this kingdom ten kings will arise, and another will arise after them."[33] And then, "But from one of those four horns a small one emerged, which began to grow toward the south and then toward the east, and then toward the glorious land. He raised his great horn toward the armies of the sky, and it cast down some of the armies and some of the stars to the ground and trampled them down."[34]

> We read in the Apocalypse of Saint John:
> And another portent was seen in the sky,
> look, a great fire-red dragon with seven heads
> and ten horns, and on his heads seven diadems.
> His tail dragged a third of the stars of heaven
> and hurled them to the earth.[35]

---

29. Based on Psalm 52:1–3.
30. Revelation 12:9.
31. Luke 8:11–12.
32. Daniel 7:21–22.
33. Daniel 7:24.
34. Daniel 8:9–11.
35. Revelation 12:3–4.

And again in John:

> And he was given dominion
> to act for forty-two months. Then he opened
> his mouth to utter blasphemies against god,
> blaspheming his name and his tenting place,
> and those who have set their tent in the sky.
> He was given powers to battle the saints
> and to overcome them.[36]

Leaning on such testimonies, the sages decided it impossible that this powerful god, and his might and force, had been created, essentially and directly, by the true lord god, since our god works feverishly every day against that force and vigorously combats him. And the true god would not respond in this fashion if evil had derived from him, in any way, as almost all our adversaries claim.

ON THE DESTRUCTION OF THE POWER IN EVIL

In the holy scriptures it is clearly expressed that the true lord god will destroy the powerful[37] and all his forces who work feverishly every day against him and against his creation. David has indeed said of the one who is a powerful malignancy, "That is why god will destroy you forever. He will tear you out of your place, drag you out of your tent, and strip your roots from the land of the living."[38] And for asking help from his god against the powerful, David again says, "Break the arm of the impious and the wicked. You will punish him for his lies and he will be no more. The lord will reign forever and into eternity."[39] David also sings out, "In a moment the wicked will be no more. You will look at the place where he was and you will no longer see him there."[40]

---

36. Revelation 13:5–7.
37. Nelli observes that Jean de Lugio calls the principle of evil the powerful but never the all powerful. So the principle of good and the principle of evil are never equal (*Écritures cathares*, 46–59).
38. Psalm 52:5.
39. Psalm 10:15–16.
40. Psalm 37:10.

In Solomon's Proverbs it is written, "The wicked are overthrown by their evildoing."[41] The messenger Paul alludes to the destruction of the powerful through the coming of our lord Jesus Christ when he says to the Hebrews, "in order to destroy him through his death, he who has the empire of death and who is the devil."[42] Likewise, our lord is forced to destroy not only the powerful but also all forces or dominations who through the powerful have appeared at times to dominate the creatures of the good god who has been exposed to the empire of evil. That is what the holy virgin says in the Gospel of Luke:

> He has toppled monarchs from their thrones
> and raised the poor to their feet.[43]

And the messenger in the First Letter to the Corinthians tells us, "Then comes the end when he hands over the kingdom to god the father, after he has destroyed every rule and every authority and power. For he must reign until he has put all his enemies under his feet. The last enemy to be destroyed is death."[44] The same messenger says to the Colossians, "Give thanks to the father, who has enabled you to share in the inheritance of the saints in the light. He has rescued us from the power of darkness and transferred us into the kingdom of his beloved son."[45] And Paul also says, "And when you were dead in sins and the uncircumcision of your flesh, god made you alive together with him, when he forgave us all our sins, erasing the record that stood against us with its legal demands. He set this aside, nailing it to the cross. He disarmed the rulers and the powers, and he made a public example of them, triumphing over them."[46] And likewise Paul was sent by the lord Jesus Christ to strip this power, as it is written about him in Acts: "For I have appeared to you for this purpose, to appoint you to serve and testify to the things in which you have seen me and to those in which I will appear to you. I will rescue you from your people and from the gentiles, to whom I am sending you to open their eyes so that they may turn from darkness to light and from the power of Satan to god,

---

41. Proverbs 14:32.
42. Hebrews 2:14.
43. Luke 1:52.
44. 1 Corinthians 15:24–26.
45. Colossians 1:12–13.
46. Colossians 2:13–15.

so that they may receive forgiveness of sins and a place among those who are sanctified by faith in me."[47] And Christ says in the Gospel of Matthew:

> Have you come to arrest me with swords and clubs
> as if I were a robber?
> Day after day I sat in the temple, teaching,
> and you did not take hold of me.[48]

And in Luke, "But this is your hour, and the power of darkness."[49] From all this one must believe that the power of Satan and of darkness cannot proceed directly and immediately from the true god. Since if the power of Satan and of darkness proceeds directly and immediately from the true god, with all the other powers, virtues, and dominations of evil—which is what the unknowing say—then one would not understand how Paul and all others faithful to Jesus Christ could have "removed power from darkness," nor how they could have transferred this power of Satan to the true lord god. Above all, if one considers that in removing power from darkness, they become in reality, properly and essentially, attached to our lord god, since all powers and virtues, according to the belief of our adversaries, emanate properly and essentially from the good god. How then would the good god be able to strip and eliminate another power than its own, if it is true that there can exist no other before him, as all our enemies say of these true Christians whom one calls, by their right title, Albanenses?[50]

---

47. Acts 26:16–18.
48. Matthew 26:55.
49. Luke 22:53.
50. The name for the absolute dualists.

47

A Nun's Sermon

The anonymous poem "A Nun's Sermon to Ladies Carenza, Iselda, and Alais on Priority of Knowledge and Light over Earthly Body" is an example of a commingling of sacred and secular poetry among the troubadours. The poem in Provençal (*langue d'oc*) is anonymous, in a woman's voice, purportedly by a nun, who with humor, satire, and delicious skill advises the ladies of her concern of the perils of family, of the physical degradation of the temporal body, and of the greater satisfaction and thrill to be gained from marrying god, who is the crown of knowledge and light.

A NUN'S SERMON[1]

My lady Carenza of the lovely body,
please offer sisters your profound advice,
and since you know what's best, tell us precisely what to do. You know. Your ways embody
all ways of woman. Please say: shall I wed
someone we know? Or stay a virgin? I've said

---

1. A Nun's Sermon: translated from the Provençal by Willis Barnstone. Originally published as "My Lady Carenza of the lovely body" in *Voices of Light*, edited by Aliki Barnstone. ©1999 Aliki Barnstone. Reprinted by arrangement with Shambhala Publications, Inc., Boston, www.shambhala.com.

that would be good. But having kids—what for?
To me a marriage seems a painful bore.

Lady Carenza, I'd like to have a man,
but what a penance when you have a clan
of brats. Your tits hang halfway to the ground;
your belly is discomfited and round.

My lady Iselda and my lady Alais,
you have youth, beauty; your skin a fresh color
and you know courtly manners; you have valor
beyond all other women in your place.

Hear me. And for the best seed from a cod,
marry the crown of knowledge, who is GOD.
And you will bear the fruit in glorious sons,
saving your chastity like married nuns.

My lady Iselda and my lady Alais,
remember me and may my light transcend
all fears. Please ask the king of glory,
when you enter heaven, to join us once again.

THE INNER LIGHT OF GNOSIS: A HISTORICAL MEDITATION

WILLIS BARNSTONE

The specific origin of gnosticism is unknown—and may be unknowable. It is unknown not because gnosticism sprang from nowhere and nothing. Indeed, we know approximately when and where this dualistic movement of a god of light spirit and a god of dark matter began in antiquity, and also the names of the possible sources. But there are deeply conflicting theses, ancient and modern, about the relevance of these sources to the origin of the widespread and enduring global sect. The story of the origin of most of the world's spiritual movements—Daoism, Hinduism, Buddhism, Zoroastrianism, and Judaism—is blurred in possibility, and reaches us more as legend than history. Even highly documented early Christianity, born of two essential Jewish scriptures, the Old and New Testaments, is steeped in the legends of the New Testament gospels, its core source, that disguise rather than reveal historical probability. So the word is still out on gnosticism. It has backers who speak of elements of Jewish, Christian, Zoroastrian, Buddhist, platonic, Alexandrian neoplatonic, and Egyptian hermetic ancestry.

Is there one or are there multiple progenitors of gnosticism? While many favor a multiple-source thesis, the diverse appearances of gnostic thought in the Near East and Alexandria have enough commonality to suggest a unifying spirit in the air, transcending sect, language, and geography. Two singular ideas separate the dualistic gnostics from the old Greco-Roman theologies, Judaism, and emerging Christianity: (1) an assumption of two divinities finding their way into us—one of spirit and eternal light, the other of darkness and temporal body; and (2) a transcendent principle of light that may be found during one's lifetime, in a flash of gnosis, bringing divinity into one's solitude.

In gnosticism, salvation, as the flash of gnosis, may be achieved *now* and not only as a reward after death, as in Christianity. Christian salvation—unseeable, untestifiable, unexperienced by humans—is uniquely associated with an afterlife. Its elusive nature gave rise to those great organized clergies who claimed possession of a knowledge of salvation through their interpretation of scripture that usually they alone could read. The gnostic can go it alone, without clergy, and arrive now. In this sense the pervasive ideas of Plato and the neoplatonists, who offer us metaphors and allegories of immediate mystical salvation, seems to be the common stuff that links all the diverse eruptions of gnosticism.

Gnosis, meaning "knowledge," becomes the quest of those competing sects, deriving from diverse sources, who have been called the gnostics. When, through Plato, Socrates declares, "Know yourself,"[1] one tenet of gnosticism was born. But much earlier, in the Hebrew Bible, Eve chose the fruit of gnosis from the tree and is treated thereafter—as is woman—as the flawed, outsider heretic in the Judeo-Christian-Islamic family of religions. Conversely, among the gnostics she is praised for her courage to choose knowledge rather than innocence (ignorance) and to defy the authority of the creator god of earth and people, who guards knowledge as his own. Eve is the hero of the light and the Promethean liberator from god's tyrannical authority. In Genesis and in later gnostic myth (such as the Origin of the World and the Reality of the Rulers), Eve is the mythical mother of gnosticism.

In Mesopotamia and along the Mediterranean, all the way from Alexandria to Rome, from about 200 BCE to 200 CE, we witness a rich ferment of spiritual movements, all seeking answers to the enigmas of existence. This is the intertestamental period, in which appear most of the noncanonical apocrypha and pseudepigrapha, the Dead Sea Scrolls of the Essenes and the Corpus Hermeticum of Egypt. In this period of the mystery religion, messianic charismatic, philosopher, theologian, and mystic also fashioned those systems of wisdom sayings, doctrines, and myth, often recorded on scrolls, that have been classified as gnostic scripture. But until the twentieth century this gnostic scripture survived only as disparate fragments in Greek, Latin, Syriac,

---

1. This is also the admonition inscribed on the temple of the Delphic Oracle, according to Plutarch.

Coptic, old Persian, and even Chinese, along with a few major works in Greek and Syriac, notably the pagan Corpus Hermeticum, dating from the second and third centuries, which includes Poimandres, attributed to Hermes Trismegistos, and the Songs of Solomon, a book of gnostic psalms. For many generations of scholars and seekers, knowledge of gnosticism came primarily from the works of early church fathers, whose writings, even when fairly reliable in terms of stating gnostic tenets, were composed as fiercely unsympathetic refutations of gnosticism. Then in 1945 in the sands of Egypt was found the Nag Hammadi library, consisting of the great treasure of fourth-century translations into Coptic of earlier Greek texts. These fifty-plus documents constitute a bible of classical gnosticism.

Among modern scholars who have had their say about gnostic parentage, Bentley Layton, in *The Gnostic Scriptures*, sensibly sees gnosticism rooted primarily in classical Sethian philosophers, but he also speaks of the gnostic presence in the Greek-speaking synagogues and in early Christianity (notably in Simon Magus, Acts 8:9–12). The leading scholar of Jewish mysticism and Kabbalah, Gershom Sholem, looks to a Jewish origin of gnostic notions in his *Jewish Gnosticism, Merkabah Mysticism, and Talmudic Tradition*, and his near contemporary, Hans Jonas (gnosticism's first major interpreter), asserts that gnosticism began in radical circles in Samaria. The Italian historian Giovanni Filoramo notes that "many scholars propose a Jewish origin for Gnosticism," and that the Nag Hammadi gnostic texts confirm a Jewish influence, yet he finds the whole Jewish thesis shaky, for lack of corroborating scripture.[2] Yet some major corroborating scriptures strengthen a Jewish thesis of origin: the Book of Baruch of Justin, the Secret Book of John, and parts of the Gospel of John. The Book of Baruch is primarily a Jewish-gnostic text (Baruch is an angel of Elohim), with Christian and pagan main characters, including Moses, Jesus, and Hercules. It may be that Baruch in its earliest form was a purely Jewish scripture, and the extraordinary work we have now is a somewhat Christianized version redacted during the Christian-Jewish period. Even the Christianizing effort is tentative, since its ecumenical editors have generously acknowledged the pagan origins of gnosticism by bringing the god Hercules into the cast.

As for the views of early church fathers on the source of gnosticism, Irenaeus of Lyon, in his *Adversus haereses* (Against Heresies), excoriated both the

2. Filoramo, *History of Gnosticism*, 145.

followers of Alexandrian Valentinos as well as the heresiarch and magician Simon Magus, among many others. The church fathers "simply traced back the rise of Gnosis to the devil."[3] The gnostics returned the favor by making the god of the Old and New Testaments the demiurge—or more bluntly, the devil.

Not all the church fathers' polemics against the gnostics were uninformed, however. The Alexandrian fathers Clement (d. 215?) and Origen (185?–254?) were well informed and, to counter the readings of the Valentinian school of biblical scripture, developed their own hermeneutics, which were based on an allegorical reading of scripture. Tertullian was called "the Christian gnostic," since he was said to have found the true gnosis while the gnostics propounded false gnosis. Clement's student Origen, the most prolific theologian before Augustine, edited the *Hexapla Bible* and developed a threefold reading of scripture: literally, ethically, and allegorically. Imitating the gnostics in looking for esoteric meanings in scripture, he developed an exegesis of the Bible that would find approval in the church. Origen was also linked to gnosticism by his elevation of knowledge over mere faith.

But what most enraged early Christians about the gnostics was not only their unsympathetic portrait of the traditional creator god and the rivalry for dominion in this emerging religion—there were many serious heretical rival sects posing threats to primitive Christianity—but their rejection of the essential creed that in Jesus there existed two natures: the human and the divine. For the orthodox, Christ was at once man and god, and after suffering on the cross he was resurrected and ascended as the son of god to heaven.

The gnostics denied Christ's two natures of human and divine, and labeled his human semblance merely that—a semblance, not a reality. For them Jesus was a celestial body incapable of human misery. They shared the second-century docetic belief that during his life on earth, Christ was a divine phantom, who only seemed to inhabit a human body and to die on the cross.[4] Since Jesus Christ did not die a human death or a divine death, his resurrection and ascension to heaven never took place. Likewise, his lifetime ministries, miracles, and suffering were mere appearances. In the Nag Hammadi library's First Apocalypse of James, the exalted Christ straightens out a commiserating James after his crucifixion: "I am the one who was in me. Never have I experienced any kind of suffering."[5] As for those who thought

3. Rudolph, *Gnosis*, 275.
4. Second-century docetism (from Greek *dokein*, "to seem") affirmed Christ's divinity and scoffed at the idea that made Jesus both man and god.
5. The First Apocalypse of James, Codex V, 3, 15–20 (*Nag Hammadi Library*, 3d ed., p. 268).

they could cause him pain, we see Jesus laughing at his would-be tormentors: "I laughed at their ignorance."[6] In sum, most of the gnostic sects rejected the usual symbolic interpretation of "the word became flesh" (John 1:14) in which the word of god resided in Jesus, who was at once the holy word and a human being. These rejectionist ideas were an anathema to the church, and the gnostics and docetists were examined at length and denounced for their terrible heresies by Irenaeus of Lyon, the bishop Ignatius of Antioch, and Hippolytus and Clement of Alexandria.[7] Later the gnostics were condemned by Augustine, who knew gnosticism from the inside, since he had been a fervent Manichaean in his youth.

The church fathers were concerned. Here we have the earthly Jewish messiah of Isaiah, who in the gospels becomes salvific Jesus, turned by the gnostics into a divinity who resembles an angel but is neither man nor god. And above Jesus is the gnostic god of light at odds with his rival, the ignorant god of the Bible. The creator god of the Bible has earned his title of darkness by creating man and woman as a prison containing the divine particles of light that fell from the pleroma, the fullness (the highest principle in the gnostic theogony). While the biblical god made light, that external light is a temporal illusion. True light is in the human spirit. The gnostic earned the title of illumination by seeking the inner light. And to know and become these particles of light though gnosis is to disappear into eternity. Clearly, the gnostics were heretics. They could become light or god—or whatever one calls the divine principle— in their own person, and without need of the angry church that saw them as evil and would eventually annihilate them.

THE JEWISH MOMENT AT THE BEGINNING OF GNOSTICISM

One of the intriguing hypotheses about why and how gnosticism developed remains the earlier-noted Jewish one as described by Scholem and Grant. Grant suggests that the earliest gnostics operated in the first century before

---

6. The Second Treatise of the Great Seth, Codex VII, 2, 56 (*Nag Hammadi Library*, 3d ed., p. 365).
7. The question of whether Jesus had two natures (human and divine) or one (divine) divided orthodox Christians and divergent sects for more than a thousand years. For example, in the sixth century the Byzantine emperor Justinian wavered, giving some leeway to the Monophysites, who taught that Jesus Christ was only divine. There were many sects who insisted on the docetic or monophysistic creed that Christ had only a divine nature, from the early Montanists, gnostics, and docetists to the tenth- and eleventh-century Bogomils in Constantinople and Bosnia, and their later Cathar adherents in northern Italy and southwestern France.

the common era as a turn elsewhere or inward by Jews disappointed that their foretold messiah had not come. But there were messianic figures who did come to parts of Israel, were not as radical as Jesus, or at least as Jesus' interpreters created and made him, and whose lives were recorded in historical detail, which Jesus, outside the gospels, was not. In the Mishnah and the Talmud we find numerous examples of religious figures operating beyond the fold of the main Jewish sects. Rebellious Galilee had produced not only Jesus but Hasidic messianic figures contemporary with Jesus, of whom the two outstanding healers and miracle makers were Honi and Hanina. Probably Jesus himself was a Hasidic messianic, as Geza Vermes suggests in *The Changing Faces of Jesus*, but these charismatics were extrinsic, as apparently was Jesus, to the traditional religious parties.[8] In this period of change and anxious searching for messianic figures of spiritual enlightenment, the gnostics added their message of personal salvation.

Incidentally, it must be remembered that the faces of Judaism, like that of the rabbi Jesus, were also changing and multiple. They changed again with each new interpreter, and their scriptures changed according to the eyes of each interpreter. Among those changing faces, whom Scholem, Grant, and others describe, were the Jewish gnostics who, as noted, were to give us the earliest extant gnostic scripture, the Book of Baruch.

THE JEWISH BOOK OF BARUCH

Gnosticism's main Christian speculations were preceded by heterodox Judaism and early Jewish-Christian gnostic systems. Of the latter, Irenaeus declares the oldest to be the three doctrines of Simon Magus, Menander, and Saturninus. They reject the god of the Bible as the creator of the world, which they say was the work of angels. The Book of Baruch attributed to Justin, preserved only as a paraphrase in Hippolytus's *Refutation of All Heresies*, represents one of the earliest stages of gnostic evolution. Grant calls it "an example of a gnosis almost purely Jewish . . . which owes its origin to three principles, two male and one female."[9] It contains a fascinating mixture of traditions, in which the first male is hellenic Priapos, father of the cosmos, while Jewish Elohim is father of this world and a lover of Edem (Eden), the female principle. Elohim breaths spirit into Adam, while Edem breathes soul into the first

---

8. Vermes, *The Changing Faces of Jesus*. When gnosticism embraced Jesus in various guises—messiah, angel, and god—their docetic Jesus was interpreted as a gnostic figure just as the Gospels of John and of Thomas became central to the gnostic canon.
9. Grant, *Gnosticism and Early Christianity*, 19.

man. Baruch ("blessed" in Hebrew) is the tree of life and the chief angel. Naas, the serpent, is the tree of the knowledge of good and evil and the chief maternal angel. Eden is many: garden, earth, Israel, a symbol of Eve, and the earth mother. In later speculations the unknown god in his various guises has a male and female element and is called the mother-father of us all, or god with a female principle or emanation. The female emanation is usually Sophia, who is wisdom. Because of a disturbance and inadequacy in god, she is separated from him, falls from the pleroma, and creates the world. In referring back to Christian gnosticism's Jewish origin and early ties between gnosticism and early and late Kabbalah, Grant observes that Justin's variation of Judaism "is like the mystical Judaism we find in the [medieval Spanish] Zohar, where Yahweh is called the father and Elohim the mother."[10]

DESPAIR AND TURN TO LIGHT

The calamitous Roman occupation of Israel surely influenced the Jewish turn to gnosticism. After the failure of the Jewish rebellion in Jerusalem (66–70 CE), the misery of the Jews increased with the destruction of the Second Temple (70 CE). The utter failure of god to intervene on their behalf dashed their apocalyptic hopes for external help and opened a way to gnosticism. Grant describes the mess of destruction and despair: "For all practical purposes, the Gnostics must have been ex-Jews, renegades from their religion, for they had abandoned the deity of the Creator."[11] While the destruction of the Temple and the city of Jerusalem devastated and exiled the Jews, the later Christian Jews who composed the gospels turned that historic horror into a punishment for those Jews who failed to recognize their messiah and a reward and hope for those who did. In reality both Jews and Christian Jews were slaughtered and driven out of the razed city. This diaspora led to the spread of both gnosticism and Christianity. With Christian Judaism now in the gentile world, the new sect's laws of the Sabbath, circumcision, and diet were quickly altered, making large-scale conversion to Christianity a popular possibility. At the same time the original persecution and calamity, having been experienced equally by Jew and Christian Jew, led many to a gnostic solution, which is seen in the sudden eruption of gnosticism in all the new Christian terrains.

Rather then pinning hope on clergy and traditional places of worship, these heterodox Jews as well as Christian Jews chose to look for a light inside.

---

10. Ibid., 23.
11. Ibid., 26.

For the gnostic that light is spirit, and its contemplation can lead to a knowledge of god, or even for one to adhere to or be god within oneself.[12] Then the body is left behind, and escape is possible from earthly time through the inner light. To know that light of being signifies escape from temporal and bodily captivity on the material earth and a return to origin, to the precinct of eternal light from which the spark of the spirit came.

In the religions of the world the escape from ordinary time and matter, through the mind, into an extraordinary dimension of spirit and revelation has come under the label of mysticism.

NATURE OF THE MYSTICAL LEAP

Mysticism is a phenomenon appearing in many forms, in East and West and in all continents, and each religious sect carries its own terminology to describe it. Sometimes it is regulated by shamans or carried out as a personal heterodoxy at the fringes of an established religion (Paracelsus, Teresa of Avila, Boehme). Sometimes it is at the heart of the creed itself, which may be said of Buddhism, gnosticism, or ancient Hasidism and later Kabbalah. The mystical instant may be called illumination or extinction through *nirvana*, or the light following the annihilation of annihilation. The Persian Sufis call it a conference of birds and the Japanese Zen Buddhists *satori*. The process itself takes on many descriptive metaphors, such as "the four levels of cognition" in Plato, "the negative way" in Pseudo-Dionysios and John of the Cross, and "the steps of the ladder" in Philo and again John of the Cross. Each rung of the ladder may signify darkness, illumination, and union that is an ineffable ecstasy of oblivion. These various steps usually suggest a cosmic ascent from sensations of the body through the soul to the light and loss of earthly consciousness. The ascender dies from ordinary time on the way to the source of spirit. Then the major question is with what or with whom is the union. With god? A pantheistic all? A Buddhist void? A Plotinian One? A gnostic particle of light? But perhaps the most obscure question in mysticism is the nature of that union. The two essential but discrete types of union are the monistic and the theistic.

If god is postulated as the universal principle to be reached at the end of ascent, then the monistic mystic seeks identity with god and total immersion in god, while the theistic mystic seeks a communion with or adhesion to god, but no loss of personal identity. In monism subject and object become one; the mystic is absorbed into the deity—Saint Teresa speaks of a drop falling into a

---

12. See Scholem for more on gnosticism as a self-centered religion in *Jewish Gnosticism,* 21ff.

river—and thereby achieves union (*enosis*) and divinization (*theosis*). Monism is typically neoplatonic and Christian. John of the Cross (Juan de la Cruz) seeks self-abolition, being lost in god, one with god, and with one identity, god. The most common Christian gnostic articulation of mystical experience is the monistic model, where one moves from initial unknowing (the *agnosia* of darkness and error, as opposed to *gnosis*) to full illumination and total union. The notion of being deified, of passing into and becoming the light, is found in Plotinos, whose "one becomes the One," and similarly in the writings attributed to the pagan gnostic Hermes Trismegistos. In Hermes the soul rises on an ascending scale of mental states though the spheres. Hans Jonas describes the journey of the self, while still in the body, which "attains the Absolute as an immanent, if temporary condition." In that instant there is a translation "of objective stages into subjective phrases whose culmination has the form of ecstasis, gnostic myth has passed into mysticism (neoplatonic and monastic), and in this new medium it [the attainment of the Absolute] lives on long after the disappearance of the original mythological beliefs."[13]

By contrast with platonist mystical fusion and oneness, Martin Buber in *I and Thou* rejects the monistic notion of "I am god." For the theist the notion of becoming the godhead is shameful and deprives the creator of independent existence. Theistic mysticism—characteristic of the Bible, Jewish gnosticism, the Kabbalist Zohar, and a majority of postmedieval seekers—holds to an ultimate separation of the human and the divine. As Scholem states, the Jewish mystic "retains a sense of distance between the Creator and His creature."[14] This dualism of person and god is frequently symbolized in the merkabah, the divine throne-chariot that carries the soul skyward to god, which is illuminated by god's presence but does not disappear into and become god. There is the ascent, adhesion but not the fusion.

The divine chariot draws its inspiration from Ezekiel 1:10 and provides the metaphor at the origins of Jewish mysticism. In the Dead Sea Scrolls is a striking picture of cherubim blessing the chariot as it ascends, with its cargo of spirit, near god in his precincts. In reading this description of the cherubim and the merkavah, note that a cherub (a little angel) in the Jewish tradition would not resemble the sentimentalized plump children in Raphael's Sistine Madonna but perhaps a multi-faced Picasso grotesque, since the model in Ezekiel for cherubim and seraphim flitting about in god's court has four faces and four wings:

---

13. Jonas, *Gnostic Religion*, 165–66.
14. Scholem, *Major Trends in Jewish Mysticism*, 14.

The cherubim bless the image of the Throne-Chariot above the firmament, and they praise the majesty of the fiery firmament beneath the seat of his glory. And between the turning wheels, angels of holiness come and go, as it were a fiery vision of most holy spirits; and about them flow seeming rivulets of fire, like gleaming bronze, a radiance of many gorgeous colors, of marvelous pigments magnificently mingled.[15]

The theistic tradition of Jewish ascension goes from its biblical sources, through the Jewish gnostics and the ancient and medieval Kabbalists, to modern interpreters who visit god but do so, as once the biblical Enoch made that ascent, without losing his person and spirit. In the sixteenth century this way continues in the work of the Spanish mystical poet Luis de León (1527/8–91). An Augustinian monk of New Christian (*converso*) origin, whose great-grandmother Leonor de Villanueva was burned to death in an auto-da-fé in 1512, León chose musical and celestial metaphors to reveal the soul's adhesion to god. But there is no immersion in the deity's blinding light. As the chariot pierces the highest sphere, the soul still hears and feels as it passes into oblivion and peace. It retains its human qualities as it comes into the presence of its divine maker:

> Here the soul sails around
> inside a sea of sweetness, and finally wheels
>   about and then is drowned
>   so that it hears or feels
> nothing that foreign accident reveals.
>   O happy deep collapse!
> O death conferring life! O sweet oblivion!

ASCENSION DURING ONE'S LIFE TO THE ETERNAL

The gnostics developed their own lexicon to map the experience of self-knowledge, which drew on the philosophical speech of Alexandrian platonism as well as the mythologies of the Bible and of classical Greek and

---

15. Vermes, *Dead Sea Scrolls*, 212–13.

Egyptian antiquity. From these sources they formed their own cosmogony (creation of the world) and theogony (creation of the gods) and their fantastic symbolic legends.

While confined to the earth, the gnostics believed, each human being consists of a vital trinity of material body, temporal soul, and eternal spirit. Within that physical and mental trinity, one is free to ascend from body and soul to eternal spirit, even before death, from darkness to the freedom of full illumination. These powerful, radical ideas opened interior ways of endless possibility. Nothing is all new, yet the specific articulation of gnosticism was a new, alluring alternative to the normative religion that locked ideas into dogma, bureaucracy, and worldly power to defeat infidels and banish creative solitude. The attractive equation of knowledge, light, spirit, and god was at the heart of gnosticism as it developed in differing modes all over the ancient world.

Around the time of the crucifixion, gnosticism rose in the Near East, Egypt, and the European Roman Empire. In this turbulent period of diaspora, dispirit, intense speculation, and self-proclaimed prophets and messiahs, the gnostics chose the meditative gaze. Their dualism was not only of two conflicting gods but of external flesh and internal spirit, and these two human attributes lived in absolute separation. There is nothing new about the Cartesian split of mind and matter, but in the instance of the gnostics mind is all and the rest an encumbrance. The body is matter. Their turn from the body is not Asian asceticism or flesh-loathing puritanism. It is simply that mind is the only reality that can turn into light. In this sense we see how close the gnostics are to Plotinian immersion in the all, the sun, the good, where all the rest is illusion. In gnosticism (which Plotinos derided) the ascent is inward to the fullness, to a glimpse of and participation in the light of the pleroma. Other than the jargon and metaphor, there is little difference in the mystical leap to immediate salvation in gnosticism and the Plotinian way. Both offer salvation now in one's life, in contrast to the three orthodox Abrahamic religions, which hold out some form of salvation as a reward after death. The Kabbalist and Christian mystics, who have operated on the borders of heresy, also report ascension and adhesion to or immersion in god, and their voyage is immediate and presumably outside time. The meaning of their experience differs specifically from that of the gnostic, however, in that their communion or union with god is not consummated as a confirmation of eternal salvation—all that must occur as a reward in the afterlife—while the gnostic does find eternal salvation in the now, which even later death will not erase.[16] While this is not usually recognized, gnostic salvation now makes mortality not only secondary but also, as in the Judaism of the Torah, final, with no probability of afterlife or heaven. For the Torah-based Jews, however, reward is closeness to god and a good, virtuous, long life on earth; for the gnostics it is a flash of disappearance of the spirit from body and earth to return to the original light source, to become that light source or god or whatever name one attaches to the most significant creative principle, and then to return to earth, body and soul, consoled by the knowledge of that glimpse and participation.

JEWISH, CHRISTIAN, AND GNOSTIC GODS

In Judaism god is the principle force, and Satan (meaning "adversary") is a scarcely mentioned member of god's court (Job 1–2 and Zechariah 3:1–2). He is god's enforcer among humans, and only in 1 Chronicles 21:1 is there ambiguity as to whether he is an adversary of god or of humans. In this one instance of possible evil and opposition, he is at worst a minor digression. Judaism is not dualistic with regard to divine powers, and apart from the early rival Canaanite gods of the Torah, god has no rival within the ranks of Jewish divinities. Probably through the influence of Persian (Zoroastrian) dualism, Christianity drove Satan out of heaven into the underworld but gave him only limited powers. Satan and his demons caused physical and mental sicknesses and were a pervasive temptation, but wicked Satan never tasted the omnipotence of god. His inferno was not another great firmament, a site not of cosmic creation but of punishment. In fact Satan himself was usually a prisoner in his own realm, in Apocalypse fire or Dante's ice, and no match for the magnificent Almighty of Jews and Christians, whose Hebrew Bible name, *El Shaddai*, "god of the mountains" or "god the bountiful," resounds his grandeur.[17]

In contrast to the feeble Satan of Judaism and the fearful devil of the later Christians comes the gnostic demiurge, who is no other than the great and

---

16. After distinguishing between spiritual leaps of the gnostic and others, we may note that these are descriptive, not evaluative, distinctions. The lives and poems of the sixteenth-century Spanish mystics Fray Luis de León and San Juan de la Cruz (Saint John of the Cross) have been and remain a lifelong summit.

17. The "Almighty" of the English Bible (the term appears thirty-one times in Job alone) is an unfortunate mistranslation of the Hebrew *El Shaddai* in which a strong metaphor of diverse human qualities is replaced by a pious, conceptual adjective of disquieting omnipotent power.

good creator god of the Bible,[18] now operating demonically down in the realm of sinister evil. While the creator god loses virtue, he remains almighty, for it is he who created the world. With his command "Let there be light" (the light of illusion), Eve and Adam were trapped on earth, and god becomes the warden of their human spirit.

By these shifts of power and province, the attributes of the Judeo-Christian god are divided between the two polar gods. There is the god of spirit, whose attributes are light and knowledge, and the god of matter, whose attributes are darkness and error. In varying texts, from China to western Europe, Yahweh takes on nasty and fearful-sounding names, such as Yaldabaoth, Sakla, and Samael. Like fallen Lucifer, he is the boss and patron of evil, whose main business occurs on his creations, the earth under its revolving sun star.

Replacing the creator god of illusion at the top is the interior god of light whose domain is everywhere there is mind. The earth-bound are not pure matter and darkness, which should be seen as impediments to transcendence, but also particles of light, which are reached not through the church or the outer firmament but through meditation. The inner god of light represents the hope of return.

Clearly, the gnostics turned Judeo-Christian theology upside down. They had the audacity to make Yahweh into a vain creator of the earth and its imprisoned inhabitants and, in many scriptures, simply into the devil. This extreme turnaround must be understood in the historic complexity of gnostic rivalry with Christian orthodoxy and the need of each sect to hide its ancestry. The earliest Christians were Jews. Yet in slipping away from Judaism, Christianity demonized the Jews. So in John 8:44 we have Jesus, a rabbi, addressing the Jews, saying, "You are from your father the devil." Developing Christianity essentially deconstructs Judaism, diminishing all, from its Torah to its "temporal" god. And though it debases the Jews, speaking of their prophets "whom they murdered" and their god of wrath and revenge as opposed to the New Testament god of love and mercy, it must denounce the Jewish god in a confused fashion, since without a scripture of their own, the early Christian Jews and Christian gentiles of the first and second centuries depended on the Jewish Bible as their own book, as a book that foretells the coming of the Christian messiah. Ultimately, that Jewish earthly messiah will be in the name of Jesus Christ (Yeshua Mashiah), the foremost god, the immediate

---

18. In some main gnostic treatises Sophia, rather than the biblical god, creates the world and humans.

god, clearly replacing the Hebrew Bible deity and, in practice and in popular understanding, god himself. While in the gospels Jesus will sit to the right of god's throne, in popular thought and iconography god and salvation are more understood through Jesus. The tripartite nature of god explains away this popular misunderstanding, but the perception persists that Jesus is not only god but also, for all practical purposes, the immediate god to address in prayer.

If the Christian god must share his realm of significance with Jesus and to a much lesser extent with the holy spirit, then the gnostics carry sectarian rivalry with an ancestral father religion in the Hebrew Bible radically further. The gnostics deconstruct both Judaism and Christianity and reconstitute them both to conform to their own creation myths. In both Christian and gnostic reconstruction of precursors, however, these ritual killings of the founding father contain astonishing inconsistencies. The Christians demonize the Jews but exempt all the early Christians, who were also Jews, by ignoring or dissembling their religious identity as Jews. While the gnostics demonize the original god of the Jews, they pay less attention to the Jews themselves, who are seldom mentioned—though they are not well treated when they *are* mentioned. Classical gnosticism sees the creator god of the Bible not only as the god of the Jews but principally as the demiurgical tyrant of misguided Christians, who have appropriated and interpreted the Hebrew Bible as their own Christian Bible. And insofar as Christians worship that biblical god, they also obey the demon of darkness. But the misguided Christians have a way out. They can become true Christians if, as Christian gnostics, they renounce the god of the Bible and turn to the invisible father of all.

JESUS AMONG THE GNOSTICS

How does Jesus fit into this revisionism? Among the Christian gnostics, Jesus is the mediating figure. He is often the envoy (or angel) of the invisible true father. This position makes him higher than a human, less than the godhead. He is normally monophysitic, which is to say that he is only spirit and his body on earth is illusion. He has no human body but only *appears* to have died on the cross. In his highest position as envoy, he appears as an eternal being (an aeon) sent to earth to instruct humans in the ways of light and redemption.

While the Christian gnostics, including the later Cathars, claim that their Jesus is the true Jesus, he is so different from the Jesus of orthodox Rome and Byzantium as to make his gnostic articulation impossible for Christians to accept. On at least two major issues there could be no compromise. Christianity had already thrashed out the docetist notion of the phantom Christ with more than a dozen other early sects. The docetist heresy would take the humanity, the generous suffering, and the miracle from the gospel Jesus. Jesus has to be both man and god, and not an apparent man-god. Secondly, and equally important, in gnosticism Jesus does not hold that strange relation of being both son of god and, surely in popular perception, god himself. For the gnostics Jesus is only one of the divine emanations of the invisible father of all, and not near the top of the hierarchy in the pleroma. The Greek word for angel is *angelos*, a translation of the Hebrew *mal'ach*, meaning "messenger" or "envoy" and originally applied to Hermes, the messenger of the gods. In gnosticism Jesus is frequently referred to as a mere angel (messenger) of god, and this low station is counter to basic Christian doctrine. In Christianity, as said, the Jewish messiah has become the divine Christ, and Christ or Jesus often replaces god in icon and prayer. So the gnostic Jesus who mocks the clergy for supposing him human, vulnerable to pain, and mortal definitely has no place in the church.

PAGAN GNOSTICS

There were also classical gnostics who did not derive from Judaism or Christianity. These were the pagan gnostics. Largely in Alexandria, they adapted neoplatonism and local hermetic mystery religion into a new mythical dualism in which flesh is dark temporal matter while mind (*nous*) is knowledge and sunlike. Knowledge will make us better than the gods, for once we have acquired it we are both mortal and immortal. The pagans believed that the great hermetic philosopher is Hermes Trismegistos (the thrice greatest), who sprang from the Egyptian god Thoth and Greek Hermes. In Poimandres (Shepherd), a superb literary tractate attributed to this Hermes, he gives his severely dualistic view of the cosmos, expressed as visionary experience. The demiurge is the maker who originally emanates from the androgynous father of all. The maker makes humans, whom he sets in the prison of the material earth. But an androgynous primal person (*anthropos*) descends to earth and mingles with the cosmos, offering spiritual promise. He carries in him a spark of holy light. The human creature, by the act of gnosis in his or her life, can rise from the body through interior light to join the light-body of god.

Long after the myth of cosmic return to the light principle has disappeared, the technique of spiritual ascent, while alive and in the body, lives on as a later development of neoplatonic and Christian mysticism. In addition to the ascension to the interior sun in Plotinos (205–70), there is an outstanding example of early Christian ascension in the super-luminous gloom and ray of blackness of the Syrian Pseudo-Dionysios (6th c.?). The first a philosopher, the second a church theologian, each used a different lexicon to translate the phenomenon, but the experience of the ecstatic and of mystical ascension, whether among gnostics, Jews, Christians, or Muslims (and most of the rest of the world, including the shamans of most continents) is a universal commonplace.

ZOROASTRIANISM, A PRECURSOR OF GNOSTICISM

Among these diverse sources of gnosticism, Iranian Zoroastrianism (Mazdaism) had a paramount influence in eastern gnosticism. While it did not directly reach the earlier Syrian-Egyptian gnostics, Zoroastrian structure and notions of salvation profoundly affected third-century Mani and Manichaeism. Led by Ahura Mazda, the Zoroastrian good spirits (*ahuras*) contend against dark evil spirits (*daevas* or *divs*), led by Ahriman, for the fate of the human soul. The people of light are pitted against the people of darkness. When Mazda (meaning "wise") wins, the soul ascends to the realm of light. Particularly during the sixth-century BCE Babylonian captivity, when Jews were in a region where Zoroastrianism was practiced, this dualistic religion also affected Judaism. There is obviously a coincidence of idea and word in the Essenes of *The Manual of Discipline*, with their sons of light warring against the sons of darkness. The Iranian dualism coincides with the essential character of the gnostic speculation, which emerges as a system of antinomies.

GNOSTICS AS DANGEROUS HERETICS

The majority of gnostics saw themselves as the enlightened Christians, at least in the first periods of their growth. By the end of the second century of the common era, while traditional Christianity was becoming a powerful independent religion, the gnostics were converting and spreading in great numbers and across many borders of Asia, Africa, and Europe. To convert traditional Christians to their intelligence, the gnostic philosophers developed an allegorical exegesis of the gospels to prove that Christian gospel revealed gnostic truths. They produced the first theological Christian literature, and in the second century their writings were apparently significantly more extensive than those of the Catholic and Orthodox churches.[19] Their favored text to comment on was the Gospel of John (see Herakleon), which they treated as their gospel. In the first lines of the Gospel, John establishes the notion of the essential interior light and tells the role of John the baptizer:

> He was not the light.
> but came to testify about the light.
> The light was the true light
> which illuminates every person
> who comes into the world. (John 1:8–9)

John the baptizer was not the light, meaning that Jesus was the light and John merely the lamp carrying the light. So John's role is defined as prophetic but secondary to that of Jesus, who is the divine. All this suggests intense rivalry between early followers of a messiah, some favoring John, who electrified Judaism with his arrival as a human messiah in ways seemingly foretold in Isaiah (Isaiah 7:14, 9:2–7, 42:1–4), others, the majority, favoring Jesus as a divine messiah. There is considerable evidence that by the second century the number of those favoring John—apart from the gnostics who favored him—was increasing alarmingly. The Mandaean gnostics aggressively chose John the baptizer over Jesus and made Jesus into the so-called Nbu Christ, who is a sorcerer, who fouls baptism and people with menstrual discharge but claims to be the true god.

The high clergy in Rome, Antioch, and Constantinople was alarmed. Not only were the gnostics converting newcomers by appropriating the gospels as their own, but they were also converting Christians to their heresy and spreading from land to land as an unquenchable fire. These gnostics seemed to turn every sacred notion on its head, from Eve, who could be seen as virtuous for choosing knowledge, to the creator god, who was denigrated as proud, legalistic, and ignorant and assigned the lowest demonic place in the cosmic hierarchy. In those ostensibly Christian schools of the gnostics, especially pernicious were the intellectual and mystical notions of Alexandrian Valentinos (Valentinus), Basilides, and the Sethians, which, from at least 135 to 450, were prominent. To the initially decentralized networks of the early Christians, these were formidable heretics. These Alexandrians, along with Mani and his followers,

---

19. See Rudolph, *Gnosticism*, 25.

were reviled and furiously opposed as usurpers of their salvific terrain. By the end of the fifth century, the heterodox sects were in large part muted. However, as late as Saint Augustine (354–430), the battle of numbers for possession of the Christian heart lingered. An emblem of those times is Augustine's protean persuasions, the gnostic who saw the light of Christianity. Though later he wrote abundantly against the gnostics, early in his career the theologian was a fervently active and roaming gnostic in Italy and North Africa, one who proselytized and preached the message of Manichaeism. His *Against Faustus*, in which he denounces his former Manichaean master Faustus, is one of many important works, along with those by Irenaeus, Hippolytus, Origen, Epiphanius, and Tertullian, that summarize and refute the gnostic heresy.

For the witnessing Christians, for whom Jesus Christ and God were father and son, and Christ both human and divine, these people of light were dangerous hypocrites insofar as they called themselves Christians. The gnostics did not accept the humanity of Jesus (Jesus was a phantom), nor the trinity of father, son, and holy spirit, nor god himself as their god. To the Christians, gnosticism was not only a threat to their dominion but also a negation of the conceptual frame of Christianity. The traditional Christians were also in a period of anxiety, instability, and danger. Christianity was still at odds with Judaism and with imperial Rome, which persecuted it. From Rome to Cappadocia in Anatolia (present-day Turkey), the Christians were living in caves and underground to escape the Roman sword. They lacked a mainstream church (from the start there were internal feuds, as their own beginning had been a feud with fellow Jews), and they were struggling to confirm their own doctrine and domain. Above all, the lack of a defined Bible created a scriptural vacuum. There would not be an official selection of books to be included in the New Testament until the Nicaean Council in 325.[20] The Hebrew Bible history of the Jews, which they either denied or interpreted as their history, was a scriptural dilemma and a plague to them even till this day.

So while the gnostics were creating abundant scripture with extravagant myths that made god the counterfeit creator of the world, the Christians wandered in a maze of overlapping apocrypha, epistles, and apocalypses, all competing for inclusion in a yet to be determined canon. The Jews were less of a

---

20. In *The First Edition of the New Testament*, David Trobisch states that by the middle of the second century the essential New Testament was defined and being copied. Nevertheless, while the core texts of the Gospels, Acts, and some of the letters may have been set in their final form, the question of which other texts would be included remained a matter of dispute until well into the fourth century.

threat, except for the unchangeable fact that their Hebrew Bible, though interpreted throughout as a prophecy of Christianity, had been appropriated to
stand alone as the Christian Bible. It was odd and surely discomforting that
the one established book of the Christians was still the Book of the Jews,
whether read in Hebrew, in Septuagint Greek, or in the Old Latin translation.
While the Jewish Bible had long been set, New Testament scriptures (written
by Christian Jews, about and for Jews) remained in flux, and a Christian Bible,
containing Old and New Testaments, was still nearly four centuries away.

In response to these many challenges to the church, Christian apologists
forcefully rejected "the abominable writings of the demonic heretics." Ironi-
cally, in the course of angry refutation, the heresiologists imitated the gnostic
philosophers and developed their own Christian exegesis. For its part, gnosticism with immense vitality challenged and widely subverted Christian theology—which had its own divisions—and remained Christianity's most serious
rival, even when muted, until the birth of Islam.

THE DESTRUCTION OF RIVAL GNOSTICS
AND CLASSICAL CIVILIZATION

Christianity responded to rivals of their dominion by silencing the gnostics
along with the religious and philosophical remnants of the Greco-Roman
world. As early as the second century, Christian clerics destroyed gnostic texts,
burned meeting places, and went after the pagan arts and philosophers with a
fury. But how did the syncretistic hellenistic ethos disappear in the West? The
classical Greek civilization of Alexandria had given us Euclid and his principles of geometry, Longinos describing Sappho's religious ecstasy in "On the
Sublime," the philosophers Philo and Plotinos keeping platonism alive, and
the main schools of classical gnosticism. But after this great flowering, the
city's culture was violently shut down. Christians under the command of the
Alexandrian patriarch Theophilos of Alexandria (later saint), with approval
by the Byzantine emperor Theodosios I, leveled the major temple complex of
the Sarapeum in 391. In the Sarapeum was lodged the Mouseion (museum) library, the greatest library of antiquity, holding about 700,000 rolls. After raz-
ing the buildings, Theophilos used the temple stone to construct Christian
churches. His nephew Bishop Cyril (later saint), attacked Egyptian Christian
and hermetic gnostics as heretics, burned synagogues, and drove the Jews out
of Alexandria. In 415 Cyril ordered a mob of Nitrian monks to stone to death
the woman philosopher, astronomer, and mathematician Hypatia, the last

major platonist in Alexandria.[21] In Constantinople the bishop went after the Nestorians and Arianists orders. All perceived rivals of the church were slaughtered—classical neoplatonists, Christian and pagan gnostics, and Jews, as well as the "heretical" orders within the Christian compass.

After Constantine, a votary to the pagan sun god, converted to Christianity in 306, the Roman Empire possessed its first Christian monarch. As Emperor Constantine I he continued fighting brutal wars among other self-acclaimed emperors in order to consolidate a greater Rome, whose new center would be Byzantium (later Constantinople). But before Constantine could establish the Eastern Roman Empire in Byzantium he had many civil wars to attend to, the last of which resulted in his victory in 324 over Licinius, a competing claimant to the title of emperor. General Licinius was Constantine's sister's husband and his ally in wars against the other western pretenders to the throne. When there were only two claimants left, Constantine and Licinius, Constantine defeated Licinius in decisive battles at Adrianople and Anatolia, and executed him and his son. When Christianity became the state religion, replacing the Roman gods whose highest deity had been humanly embodied in the emperor, the churches and monasteries ceased being persecuted and thereafter received favors. In 330 Constantine officially moved the center of the empire to the city of Byzantium, which he rebuilt as Constantinople.

Despite the triumph of Constantine over the Roman gods, the internal doctrinal disputes in Christianity that had preceded its political triumph never ceased. Apart from the outsider gnostics, whom the Church saw not as Christians but as Satanists, there were the Roman bishops (a disagreement that was to culminate in the great schism of Orthodox Constantinople and Catholic Rome), the Nestorians, the Donatists, and the Arians, among others, who also demonized each other. The Arians under Bishop Arios of Alexandria claimed that Christ was not divine but a created being. To quell dispute, Constantine optimistically convened the first ecumenical Council of Nicaea (now Iznik, Turkey) in 325. Despite such accomplishments as the Nicaean Creed, which condemned Arianism and affirmed the equality of the trinitarian son and father, the doctrinal struggles only intensified. The wavering neophyte Constantine was finally baptized on his deathbed by an Arian bishop.

During his life in Rome of the East, the emperor took the role of Christianizing his adopted city of Constantinople seriously. Though unbaptized, he

---

21. For a discussion of Hypatia see Mary R. Lefkowitz and Maureen Fant, *Women's Life in Greece and Rome*, 107–12.

put on the robes of a Christian prelate and preached to the high clergy. Ignorant of Greek, he wrote his sermons in Latin and had them translated into Greek words written in the Latin alphabet, so he could preach his sermons in Greek to his audiences. Nevertheless, Constantine held together Rome and Constantinople as the twin pillars of the empire. With a Latin-speaking emperor in Byzantium, the West and East, Rome and Greece, were at last one, politically and religiously—at least for a while.

With Christianity now the state religion of the Roman Empire, there seemed a chance for religious and political stability in Christendom. The Christians were no longer persecuted by Rome. Rather, a new theocracy set out to combat heretics within the empire, and the war against the gnostics was waged from the top. The long campaign was only partially successful. Hellenism was in tatters, the marble Roman gods of the pantheons crushed, and the parent religion Judaism disenfranchised and insignificant, but the faith was still caught up in doctrinal struggles. The foremost enemy remained the great gnostic heresy. The gnostics in Alexandria were early on fiercely persecuted by a church tolerated by Rome. When the Roman Empire under Constantine became both the political as well as the religious master of the ancient world, the destruction of the "acosmic heresy" seemed to be nearly total. Christian clerics burned the writings of the heretics. The light people buried many scrolls of their scripture, which in at least one Egyptian site, at Nag Hammadi, was to be discovered sixteen hundred years later. The gnostics themselves were killed or hounded out of one place but would appear elsewhere, even in Constantinople nearly a thousand years later as the Slav Bogomils, and gnostic speculation would outlast the Roman Empire, the Eastern Roman Empire, and the Byzantine Empire.

A few gnostic texts survived, quoted at length in the diatribes of their accusers. But though Alexandria, North Africa, and Syria ceased being gnostic centers, the religion of light persisted in other areas, mainly remote ones: in western China, in pockets of Mesopotamia, and in the Balkans and southwestern Europe until well into the fifteenth century. But after repression by early Catholic heresy hunters and a Persian king, by later crusaders and inquisitors in France and Italy, and finally by conquering Mongol and Turkish armies, their light was put out and their dominion of influence a memory.[22]

---

22. In about 276 the Persian king Shapur I, at the behest of Zoroastrian clerics who felt threatened by the rise of Mani and the Manichaean gnostics, had Mani tried and executed. Yet some villages of Mandaeans survive even today in remote areas of Iran and Iraq.

HAD ALEXANDRIA TRIUMPHED

There followed centuries of silence. Gnostic texts were found beginning in the Italian renaissance, but only in the twentieth century did we come upon the equivalent of a Dead Sea Scrolls resurrection with the great find near the town of Nag Hammadi in Egypt, which afforded us texts to comprehend, for the first time, the literatures and thought of the gnostics. Jorge Luis Borges points out that it might not have been this way had history been different, favoring a gnostic majority. In an early essay, Borges spoke about the Alexandrian gnostic Basilides, whose work we still have only in fragmentary and corrupt form as bequeathed to us by his condemners. In "A Defense of Basilides the False" Borges writes, "Had Alexandria triumphed and not Rome, the extravagant and muddled stories that I have summarized here would be coherent, majestic, and perfectly ordinary." But Alexandria did not triumph. A philosopher of the knowledge of nonbeing and the abyss, Basilides was one of the most fascinating of the gnostic thinkers, but he is preserved only in the writings of his opponents, and their summaries contradict each other on significant points. That his works were not included in the Nag Hammadi library or in other finds is lamentable. Were we to uncover a major original text, on the basis of existing evidence, we would have the writings of an essential ancient philosopher. There is a strange fact of survival. We have abundant texts by two neoplatonist philosophers from Alexandria—Philo, a Jew, and Plotinos, a pagan—yet no original text of their fellow Alexandrian philosopher Basilides. This strongly implies that to Christian apologists, the gnostics were held to be more dangerous than the Jews or the classical philosophers. So the gnostic writings of their greatest rival had to be destroyed. It is some comfort that at least their refutations in the works of Christians fathers, such as Irenaeus and Augustine, do exist and inform, if not satisfy, us.

A RESURFACING OF GNOSTIC COMMUNITIES

With the iconoclastic rage unleashed by Christian orthodoxy in Alexandria, Athens, Rome, and the Eastern Roman Empire against classical antiquity and the gnostic heresy, by the middle of the fifth century even the widespread gnostics began to fade. Western culture moved into its darkest centuries. Yet much light still shone at the eastern and western edges of Europe, in Byzantium on the east and Muslim Spain on the west, and especially among the more structured Manichaean gnostics, whose message of light survived with vigor. Within a century after Mani's death, in about 276, the founder's religion spread throughout the Roman Empire and Asia and was the sturdiest of the gnostic sects. Even after the earlier dismal suppression of other gnostic schools in North Africa and most of Europe, areas of ascetic neomanichaeans survived largely beyond the grasp of pope and emperor or at the outer reaches of their dominion, from Turkestan to Carthage—in Persia, in the Arabic Near East, in western China, and in southern France, where persecution was initially less extreme. These were also the Islamic gnostics in central Asia. And there was the amazing trail of the neomanichaean Paulicians, who from the sixth to the tenth centuries were in Armenia and the eastern provinces of the Byzantine Empire and who later merged with the neomanichaean Bogomils, who were driven out of Constantinople and persisted in Syria and Armenia; it was Bogomil missionaries who in the eleventh century brought their form of Manichaeism to the Cathars in France. The Manichaeans in Chinese Turfan became the leaders of the state religion of the important Uigur empire in Turkestan, western China (762–840). In its territorial range, in its cultural multiplicity, no religion has been so internationally receptive as has gnosticism. Into its diversity of sects and scriptures it incorporated essential figures from the world's major philosophies and religions: Buddha, Plato, Ahura Mazda, Apollo, Moses, Jesus, and Muhammad.

The thirteenth century was tragic for the gnostic speculation, both in the Far and Middle East and in the European West. In Asia it was Genghis Khan's horsemen who from 1218 to 1224 stormed over the gnostics in Chinese Turkestan; in Provence it was Pope Innocent III's Albigensian crusade (1209) into southern France that cleansed the "Manichaean scourge of god" from the earth. The crusade was followed by a century of the newly formed Inquisition (1231). After another century of murder, torture, seizure of properties, and forced conversion, by the end of the fourteenth century the Cathars (or Albigensians), who flourished in the Occitan region in southwest France, were wiped out, their meditation extinct. Only small numbers of Cathar gnostics survive today, making up the Cathar church in parts of France and Canada. They have their own website. There are more Mandaeans (also known as Nasoreans and Christians of Saint John), a largely non-Christian sect that looks back to Babylonia for its astrology and to John the baptizer for his cleanliness rite of immersion. The holy book of the Mandaeans, which means "knowers" or gnostics, is the *Ginza*. This fertile, nonascetic religion of the living water is practiced by groups in villages and cities of Iraq and Iran, and some, far from their roots, have migrated to cities in America.[23]

RECOVERY OF GNOSTIC SCRIPTURES

Gnosticism lives beyond the existence of a contemporary school in a chance Mesopotamian village or city or in assimilated Catharist communities in Montreal or Detroit. Principally, it has survived as sacred texts. A gnostic bible has emerged, gradually assembled out of the church fathers' imperfect Greek and Latin refutations, from tombs in Persia and China, from a pot under the sands near the ancient hamlet of Chenoboskion in which was discovered the great Coptic Nag Hammadi library, and also from documents held in the Coptic Museum at Cairo and in the British Museum and Berlin Museum. These are some of the sites where words of gnosticism have been located and stored.

Some heresiological literature had survived, but altogether not more than fifty printed pages. But by the end of the Middle Ages the long reconstruction of that gnostic memory was in full swing. A large collection of writings known as the Corpus Hermeticum (or the Hermetica), attributed to Hermes Trismegistos, was repeatedly copied. The central work of the Hermetica is the Poimandres, a Socratic dialogue between the dark body and the enlightened mind, or *nous,* whose purpose is the soul's escape and ascent. Cosimo de Medici ordered the Poimandres to be translated into Latin; this appeared in 1471, translated by Marsilio Ficino. In the late eighteenth century the Coptic text Pistis Sophia (Faith Wisdom), going back to the third century, found its way into English libraries. This collection contains interminable gnostic conversations by the risen Jesus with his companions about the fall and redemption of a heavenly aeon Pistis Sophia. In the next hundred years Pistis Sophia was translated into Latin and European languages. In 1896 more came out of Egypt: a Coptic papyrus volume containing the Gospel of Mary, the Secret Book of John, and the Sophia of Jesus Christ. Five songs of a major collection, the Songs of Solomon (or Odes of Solomon), were in the Pistis Sophia.

---

23. In modern times Mandaeans have moved from villages to medium-sized towns and cities between Baghdad and Basra and in Iran to cities like Ahvaz and Shustar, where ceremonies are attended but knowledge of the old languages and scripts is diminishing.

Then in 1909 J. Rendel Harris discovered an old Syriac (Aramaic) manuscript of the Songs of Solomon comprising forty songs (originally forty-two; the first two are missing). These songs, carrying the false attribution to Solomon, are among the most beautiful and profound songs of world religious literature. Another long poem is the Song of the Pearl, contained in the apocryphal Acts of Thomas, a Syriac text that also exists in Greek. It is an extraordinary narrative of a prince who seeks a pearl in Egypt, which he finds, thereby bringing the soul from darkness into the kingdom of light. To these we must add, again from Egypt, the Coptic Songbook of Manichaean poems, as well as collections of Mandaean poems, songs, prayers, and narrative cosmologies that first came into Europe through Portuguese monks returning from Asia.

Despite these accumulating discoveries, the quilt of gnostic scriptures was thin. Because the destruction of the great ancient libraries and specifically of gnostic sacred texts was so complete, our knowledge of essential ideas of gnosticism still had to be detected from Christian writings against them. Then in 1945 in Egypt a farmer discovered near Nag Hammadi a buried cache of thirteen codices containing some fifty texts, in fourth-century Coptic translation from Greek second- and third-century compositions. After a few decades of hijinks, high adventure, and even the intervention of Carl Jung, these splendid texts were finally translated into French, German, Italian, and English under the title of the Nag Hammadi library.[24] Gnosticism had found a new voice. When the Dead Sea Scrolls were found on the west bank of the Dead Sea in 1947 near Wadi Qumran, suddenly a fringe sect of Essenes, opposed to Jerusalem, had abundant scripture from out of a vase. Similarly the gnostics, a religion on the fringe, but one that had extended from the east coast of China to the west coast of Portugal, came, after being concealed because of critical danger, into light. These two instants of discovery were supreme in the resurrection of an apparently extinguished body of thought.

GNOSTIC STORIES AND TERMINOLOGY

Most of the gnostic texts have an engaging literary clarity. In these, abstraction yields to striking metaphor. One example is the unsurpassed allegorical adventure in the Song of the Pearl, or the divine orgy in the Origin of the World.

---

24. Robinson, ed., *Nag Hammadi Library in English*.

In the latter, the romping creator god holds dominion over Eden as he chases and rapes the virgin Eve, who represents courage, defiance, and knowledge; as a result of an abominable gang rape by the creator god and his angelic aids, Eve begets generations of trapped demigod souls, who are our ancestors. But after the fiercely discrediting deeds by the demiurge, the mountains of the first father will blaze and fire will turn on its maker, who will burn inside the forests. Then "light will cover darkness." There are constants to these wild tales that slip in allegorically or emerge in plain description: a radical and alien stance to traditional creed; a mystical encounter with invisible spirit; and a flight from initial ignorance and darkness to silent freedom and light.

Other tales fare less well in transcription. Confusion is inevitable with so many schools, conflicting symbolism, and variation of a mythic story. Consider the common theme of the fall and enslavement of the soul in the body's prison and its longing for return to its source. What is that holy source? It has a babel of names: the androgynous god of light, god the father/god the mother, the Sethian unknowable god, the Valentinian father of truth, the Manichaean original light, the abyss of nonbeing that in Basilides means the demiurge. Often there is a mishmash of hierarchical names, titles, and abstractions, where the author appears seduced by the glory of language to the detriment of meaning (and delight of scholars) as in a fascinating scripture called the Foreigner (Allogenes in Greek and Coptic).

In this adventure the foreigner goes off on a platonic journey and ascent to salvation. He is aided by divine figures who generate other crucial helpers: the aeon of Barbelo and her triadic emanation of Kalyptos, Protophanes, and Autogenes. They prepare him with wings of internal ascent for the coming visions when his liberated soul will merge joyfully with the unknowable god of light. The Foreigner is a complex tale of metaphysical acrobatics and meta-realities, a far cry from the apocalyptic journey in Revelation with its beasts from the sea, splashes of angels, and jeweled decorations of heaven. Deprived of the high rhetoric of Revelation or Daniel, this flight to joyful extinction falters in turgid overload of abstract exclamations. The worthy thought is not always matched by dramatic means.

Here it is appropriate to acknowledge the terminological problems in reading gnostic texts, complicated not only by the diversity of sects but the multiple ways these terms are translated into English and other languages. Mandaean texts demand a glossary of terms just to decipher the main figures and concepts, beginning with Anosh or Enosh for "man" and Kushta for "truth." Perhaps this diversity is inevitable and right for a religion that fed on freedom from conventional stricture and had a flair for inventing myth to verbalize withdrawal and meditative flight. Even the current term *gnosticism* (a fine umbrella term, today under fire) is largely, but not entirely, an eighteenth-century invention for the ancient dualistic critique of the world. For the polemical church fathers, the label "heretics," as in Irenaeus's *Adversus haereses*, was commonly sufficient. Yet even Irenaeus was acutely aware that gnosis was intrinsic to this group that dared to tamper with Christian monotheism. The bishop's longer title for his attack reads *On the Exposure and Refutation of their Falsely Called Gnosis.*

GNOSTIC DESPAIR AND INNER LIGHT, AND THE EMERGENCE OF A SELF-CENTERED RELIGION

From the gnostics' very inception, their inner light came as a response to oppression and dismay. The circumstance of despair with the material world that impelled their original alienated vision as well as their turn inward to dissident knowledge and meditation probably had its beginnings with first-century Jews who were shaken by the destruction of their temple in Jerusalem and the forced diaspora into neighboring lands. With their apocalyptic vision and hope arrested by exile and the failure of god to halt Roman armies and their endless crucifixions, some Jews from Palestine and Alexandria turned from faith in the outside creator god to a revelatory knowledge attained in solitude. A similar dashing of apocalyptic hope also stirred early Christians who were finding their way and from whose ranks was to come the main body of converts to gnosticism.

From these multiple strands of Jewish and Christian hopelessness and from hermeticism in Egypt, mythical theologies in Babylonia, and Zoroastrian dualisms in Persia came a new self-centered religion, based no longer on the creator god of the Jewish Bible but on imaginative forces of mind seeking a personal awakening of the spirit to light. It is imperative to remember that gnostics distinguish between soul and spirit. Spirit is higher, also associated with breath (*pneuma*), while soul is still hylic, that is, connected to body and the earth, dependent on their form but capable, through gnosis, of rising to the salvific level of spirit.

In the notion of a self-centered religion we have the essence of gnosticism's most radical contribution to the history of ideas. There is no longer only a social contract between god and humans in which obedience to the master god is virtue. Now the *self* is valuable. The self may become divine. The self may become god. Such flouting of authority is of course suppressed as heresy. To understand this universal push by the gnostics toward self-realization, we may remember the sixth-century BCE pre-Socratic philosopher Herakleitos, exiled for his radical disagreements with his native Ephesos, one of whose surviving sayings centers the search for mind in "I looked for me."

Consider the rationalist lens grinder from the Amsterdam ghetto Baruch Spinoza (1623–77), whose central ideas pronounce the words of discordant gnosis. In his day he could not say that the creator god did not exist. He said something equally radical, which he conveyed by correspondence to Leibnitz and other philosopher friends, which is that the universe is a single substance capable of an infinity of attributes, including physical extension and thought. God is not the creator of nature beyond himself. God is nature in its fullness, its *plenum* (Latin for the Greek *pleroma* of the gnostics). In Spinoza's ethical system the intellect is active and escapes earthly desires through knowledge, *scientia* (Latin for *gnosis*). A human is equal to god because all is god, which is understood in solitude by the active intellect. For his ideas, and for his higher criticism of the Jewish Bible, which he was translating, he was early excommunicated (1656), and his blasphemous pantheism could not be published during his lifetime.

Elaine Pagels speaks of the gnostics' independence from the authority of orthodox religion and of god, and of god's divinity, which can be, through knowledge, found within us. She writes, "Orthodox Jews and Christians insist that a chasm separates humanity from its creator: God is wholly other. But some of the gnostics who wrote these gospels contradict this: self-knowledge is knowledge of God; the self and the divine are identical."[25]

In the Gospel of Thomas, a gnostic Jesus (in parabolic words resembling a Daoist saying or a Zen koan) states that while the orthodox leaders separate humans from god's heaven by placing it outside and up in the sky, god and his realm are actually inside us and everywhere outside. In the pantheism of the living Jesus, god's realm and self are identical and everywhere:

> If your leaders tell you, "Look, the kingdom is in heaven,"
> then the birds of heaven will precede you.
> If they say to you, "It's in the sea,"
> then the fish will precede you.
> But the kingdom is inside you and it is outside you.

---

25. Pagels, *Gnostic Gospels*, xx.

While early Christianity was replete with conflicting creeds and many gospels circulating and competing for authority and a place in the canon, including the Gospel of Thomas, the Gospel of Mary, the Gospel of Philip, the Gospel of Truth, and the Book of Thomas, the church fathers were seeking to squelch secret teachings and dissent from an emerging canon. And despite a later sentimental view that early Christians had a unanimity of belief and charitable tolerance of outsiders, the times were intensely dangerous for dissenting Christians and especially for gnostic Christians. In comparing the dissidence of John the baptizer with that of gnostic revolutionaries in those divisive times, James M. Robinson, the editor of *The Nag Hammadi Library in English*, observes that as the ingredients of Christianity coalesced and became a set doctrine, the followers of the radical Christian Jews soon became powerful, comfortable, and conventional and took on the "basic stance ... of the myopic heresy-hunters."[26] As for the gnostics, they in turn appeared to abandon traditional god and church for a personal mythopoeia to accompany, in image and word, their turn inward. Robinson writes,

> [Their] outlook on life increasingly darkened; the very origin of the world was attributed to a terrible fault, and evil was given status as the ultimate ruler of the world, not just a usurpation of authority. Hence the only hope seemed to reside in escape. Because humans, or at least some humans, are at heart not the product of such an absurd system, but by their very nature belong to the ultimate. Their plight is that they have been duped and lured into the trap of trying to be content in the impossible world, alienated from their true home. And for some, concentrated inwardness undistracted by external factors came to be the only way to attain repose, the overview, the merger into the all which is the destiny of one's spark of the divine.[27]

These rebels, trying to make sense of the trap of an impossible world and move from alienation to a divine spark, were, as were so many, influenced by platonic thought. They were affected by both Plato and platonism, in the writings of Philo, and Greek revelation-wisdom texts from Egypt, in the Corpus Hermeticum. Other sources were Jewish mysticism as elaborated by Scholem

---

26. Robinson, ed., *Nag Hammadi Library in English*, 3.
27. Ibid., 4.

in *Jewish Merkabah Mysticism and Talmudic Tradition* and the mysterious "Fourth Gospel" of John. The prologue of the book of John, "In the beginning was the word," gave gnostics a concordance with Genesis, the philosopher's logos, and platonic light. The Sethian texts carried on the Essene "antithesis of light and darkness, truth and lie, a dualism that ultimately went back to Persian dualism."[28] Of this turbulent and creative moment, where heterodoxy and disappointment seemed everywhere, Robert M. Grant wrote about a self-centered religion: "In the period when gnosticism arose, apocalyptic-minded Jews might have sought signs of the creator's power and his intervention on their behalf; philosophically minded Greeks might have looked for speculative wisdom, more or less rational in nature; but the gnostic preached himself and his true spiritual origin, both of which he had come to know by revelation."[29]

So after the late first century through at least the fourteenth and fifteenth centuries, in Northern Africa and virtually all of Europe, and from Asian Syria to Chinese Turkestan, gnostics were writing books of spiritual search and illumination that made self-knowledge a virtue rather than a sin. In the Origin of the World, Eve herself is not the servant of a devil snake who leads her to original sin. Rather, she is the primal heroine of self-knowledge. She also ceases to be a mere rib taken from Adam but his creator. By breathing spirit into the mouth of an inert clay figure of Adam on the ground, she gives life to the first man. As for the conniving snake, he is no longer a disguised devil but a luminous god who helps Eve snatch gnosis from the demiurge. In freeing Eve from shame and abuse, the gnostics—alone among major faiths—made woman an equal.

REVIVAL IN THE WORKS OF DISSIDENT PHILOSOPHERS AND POETS

After its centuries of flourishing growth and then its virtual obliteration, gnosticism in the West found its true revival in the works of dissident poets, playwrights, philosophers, alchemists, and scientists. Traces of gnostic knowledge was basic to intellectual history. The Swiss physician and alchemist Paracelsus (1493?–1541) was the first modern doctor of chemical medicines and was also a student of gnostic thought. As an alchemist he sought to purify and transform nature's elements, freeing them of their low level of matter, so that nature in its purest forms could be used for curing the body and mind. In

---

28. Ibid., 7.
29. Grant, *Gnosticism and Early Christianity,* 38.

the Italian renaissance the Poimandres was popularly published by Lorenzo de Medici and later absorbed into the writings of the philosopher Giordano Bruno (1548–1600), who for his opposition to traditional Catholicism and his "cosmic theory of deity" was accused of gnostic perversions, among other heresies, and burned at the stake in the Piazza dei Fiori. The German mystic Jakob Boehme (1575–1624) was imbued with gnosticism. In his work he spoke of the blemished but ever creating Sophia who fell from the pleroma (Valentinos), the seven divine source spirits (Basilides' seven cosmic spheres), god as nothingness (Basilides' nonexistent god), and god as abyss (Valentinos).

William Blake (1758–1827) is the only writer in English letters to create his own complex gnostic system. His cranky and enlightened anger against clerical orthodoxy runs throughout the early *Songs of Innocence and Experience*. It is in his long prophetic poems, however, that Blake ventures fully into gnostic cosmogonies and theogonies. The god of Reason in *The Book of Urizen* recounts how in the prison of earth the mind is captive and has been deprived of eternity and light:

Forgetfulness, dumbness, necessity!
In chains of the mind locked up,
Like fetters of ice shrinking together
Disorganized, rent from eternity.

In Goethe we find this mocker of convention and religion choosing Faust as his wayward hero (Saint Augustine's Manichaean teacher was Faustus) and retelling the Manichaean myth of the messenger and his distracting but redemptive angels. In a fantastic cosmos, Faust's soul is, at the end, appropriately rescued from error and flown off to the realm of light.

The writer of gnostic themes, seeking inner knowledge in a condemned world, persists widely into more recent times. Herman Melville's "Fragments of a Lost Gnostic Poem" uses the words *fragment* and *lost* in the title to bespeak the sad paucity in his day of original gnostic texts. Melville's allegorical white whale may be seen as the monster of evil out of a gnostic dualistic bestiary, while his alien figure Ishmael, an orphan tossed on a hostile ocean, seeks knowledge of redemption as he clings to the wreckage of survival. The gnostic revival in literature and philosophy is found in Nietzsche's nihilism and the alienated hero of his *Thus Spake Zarathustra*, in Carl Jung's *Seven Sermons to the Dead*, and in the existentialist philosophers to whom Hans Jonas dedicates his chapter "Gnosticism, Nihilism, and Existentialism" in *The Gnostic Religion*.

To this list of modern gnostics who, having rejected orthodoxy and its creator god, chose acosmic solutions and transcendence, we can add many major figures, as Richard Smith does in his afterword to *The Nag Hammadi Library in English*, including "the good alien Superman battling forces of evil," whom Umberto Eco sees as clearly reflecting "Manichaean incontrovertibility"; Hermann Hesse's novels embodying the allegory of Jungian archetypes; and the alienated Beat Generation of Kerouac on the road and Ginsberg's outsider attack on convention as in his "Plutonian Ode," where he chants a fitful gnostic dirge, using Valentinian and Sethian epithets: "I salute you . . . Ialdabaoth, Aeon from Aeon born ignorant in an Abyss of Light." The leading contemporary critic Harold Bloom tells us in *The Anxiety of Influence* (1973) that authors must extinguish their literary fathers in order to find voyage. For Bloom the Kabbalah is his spiritual home, and Kabbalah's ally gnosticism is his "religion of belatedness."

The figure who everywhere shares qualities of gnosticism—probably by coincidence or knowledge of the unorthodox—is Franz Kafka. His castle is the domain of the unknowable god, and his climber antihero is, as in all of Kafka's novels, a humorous, depressed, skeptical orphan, without hope of fulfillment on earth, who must climb forever seeking, but not finding, an interior light that lies still concealed in dark error.

THE CHANGING FACE OF GNOSTICISM

For many centuries "Manichaean" was an abusive term applied indiscriminately to all gnostic sects, and often to any dualistic heresy. But the Enlightenment—its very epithet means "entering light"—changed all that. It welcomed gnosticism as a powerful weapon against orthodoxy. It had its secular Voltaires and Humes who used a gnostic lexicon to trash conventional religion. For the irascible skeptic Hume, whose *An Enquiry into Human Understanding* (1748) by its name commends knowledge, religious convention was erroneous, dark, and ignorant. He summed up religion as "Stupidity, Christianity, and Ignorance." In that century, which had science and reason as well as Blake's "Self-annihilation & the grandeur of Inspiration" (*Milton*), Hume was simply drawing from an arsenal of gnostic charges to battle received tradition and its prevailing theologies.

For most of the last century, however, gnosticism may be seen not merely as a secret doctrine discovered by writers to bring the esoteric into their work or as an instrument to counter convention, but as a developing field with its own scriptures, increasing dramatically through archeology and scholarship. Whatever its appellation, gnosticism is for real. It represents a world religion with fundamental notions and an extraordinary history. Today, gnosticism is surprisingly alive. Since the uncovering of the Nag Hammadi library in Egypt and the possession of a treasure of original gnostic scripture, gnosticism as an alternative intellectual and spiritual body of knowledge finds itself at a summit. This is evidenced in the quality of the historical and religious studies that gnosticism has generated, the many new translations of core scripture, and the general esteem and curiosity that gnosticism elicits, though in-depth knowledge of the history and nature of gnostic speculation is still rare. Apart from genuine coincidences in thought, gnosticism and Kabbalah find themselves in a similar period of revival and respect.

Contemporary interest in gnosticism is especially awake in France, where the Cathar past has become a pleasant obsession. The joy of free-spirited gnostic troubadours who sang of imperfect love as well as the massacres of a gnostic region capture the French and world imagination. The fortresses, castles, texts, and the Inquisition's city archives remain. The latter document some horrendous events in the years of the Cathar extermination, during which it is estimated that half the population of this dense region in southwestern France may have been killed. Historians, anthropologists, and novelists have turned their attention to the papal crusade in 1209, in which a northern French army of twenty thousand came down under the crusade commander Simon de Montfort and sacked the city of Béziers, slaughtering twenty thousand men, women, and children, including Cathar perfects and Catholics priests, indiscriminately, all for the possession of the rich lands of the south and a secure place in heaven. On one violent afternoon in 1308 in the mountain village of Montaillou, all the inhabitants who were not slaughtered were arrested. A bishop named Jacques Fournier was the inquisitor in the city of Pamiers who interrogated the surviving heretics. Some of those who confessed under torture were given penances, others went to the stake. (In 1320 in this same area, a center of Kabbalism, more than a hundred Jews—both forced converts wearing the yellow cross and professing Jews— were burned in mass.)[30] The Cathar incident took on greater meaning when

---

30. "Confession of Baruch, once a Jew, then baptized and now returned to Judaism," translated by Nancy P. Stork of the English department at San Jose State University, found in the Jacques Fournier Register on the Jacques Fournier Home Page, <http://www.sjsu,edu/depts/english/Fournier/Baruch.htm>, pp. 1.10.

in 1334 the inquisitor became Pope Benedict XII. Every word of his interrogations was stored in the Vatican. In the last years, after modern historians pressed the Vatican successfully for the publication of the Fournier Register, a slew of remarkable historical studies on the politics and religion of the Cathars have appeared. They include the classic *Montaillous: The Promised Land of Error* by Le Roy Ladurie, *The Perfect Heresy: Revolutionary Life and Death of the Medieval Cathars* (2000) by Stephen O'Shea, *The Cathars and the Albigensian Crusade* (2001) by Michael Costen, and a retelling of events revealed in the Fournier's interrogations, *The Good Men: A Novel of Heresy* (2002) by Charmaigne Craig, who traces three generations of a Montaillou family in her novel of misery, love, and trial within doomed walls.

The pained but extraordinary history of the gnostic speculation, with its external misadventures with church and civil powers that it rejected and its spirit-filled solitude of shining darkness, is every year a more articulate memory in books and images. The energy of discovery, as vital as that generated by archaeological and old temple finds, is apparent, from the *Pays cathare* (Cathar Land) signs that have popped up all over southern France to the growing band of serious thinkers and creative writers who have assumed the gnostic experience as their intellectual heritage.

DISCOVERING THE BOOK OF THE MIND

The gnostics endured. The many schools of gnosticism are of supreme interest. Now the loot at Nag Hammadi has given us works of Sethians as well as Valentinians, the latter including the Gospel of Truth, possibly by Valentinos himself. Other major finds from the Egyptian earth are the Gospel of Thomas, those wisdom sayings of Jesus that are now increasingly printed as and called the Fifth Gospel, and the non-Christian Sethian works the Three Steles of Seth, the Paraphrase of Shem, and the Foreigner/Allogenes. The Sethians, like the Essenes before the discovery of the Dead Sea Scrolls, were largely unknown except through commentators and opponents.

Whatever the school, there are general principles that go through all the gnostic teachings. We are confined to the earthly cycles of birth and death in a materialist universe, captive in the innermost dungeon that is the earth. We are remnants of spirit fallen into bodies, but bodies that retain a tiny element of salvation in them. That salvific hope is precisely the spark, the light of the spirit in the darkness of the flesh, but it remains unconscious and unknown until gnosis, a secret, revelatory knowledge, can extricate its light from cosmic involvement. Then, free of matter, the liberated spirit can rise and be reintegrated into the unknowable god.

Man and woman of the earth were originally eternal spirits, aeons, who fell tragically from the acosmic pleroma, the spiritual realm of light, into a cosmos of sensation where they are completely alien to their real being. Each spirit is invested in a decaying body. To escape from that declining flesh, the gnostic's gaze is directed inward to the spark, to the intuited mystery of the unconscious self that was once consubstantial with the unknown god. In this split of mind and body lies the conflictive dualism between spiritual good and material evil, and ultimately between the self and the planetary world, whose discord yields the human condition of alienation. Only knowledge (gnosis) of spiritual light—not faith prescribed by clergy—offers escape from the earthly dominion and return to the realm from which we have fallen.

Gnosis is a personal activity, and through reading, meditation, and search, its instant of appearance is probably as wordless as it is revelatory. Such is the nature of mystical experience, of ecstatic information, of epiphany wherever it is found—whatever previous information has been fed into the instant and however the ineffable is then translated back into speech, reason, or myth. In gnostic and other mystical meditations, there is a distinctive and different preparatory word, a darkness, illumination, and union, and after the oblivion of absence a new translation of the mystical experience for the world.

The gnostics were, like the Kabbalists, irredeemably bookish, and both engaged in elaborate mythology to map their transcendental journey. The Kabbalists even had god create the alphabet before creating the world so he would have speech to call the world into being. The gnostics were obsessed with recording the experience of gnosis and were prolific in creating, copying, and preserving libraries of scripture. Unfortunately, rival sects erased their books, just as they burned or obscured the heretical nine books of Sappho's poems to her ally, the god Aphrodite, or time and neglect effaced the music and number theory of the pre-Socratic philosopher Pythagoras. But now, with the existence and wide translation of the Nag Hammadi library of gnostic scriptures and other seminal texts from China to Mesopotamia, from Alexandria to Languedoc, we have at last an intimate garden with its tree of gnosis and a pleroma of scripture detailing the gnostic word of return. We have the writings of a gnostic bible. Perhaps these books may generate another, preferable bible, without sect or text, without cipher or sound, which is the light in the book of the mind.

GLOSSARY

MARVIN MEYER

Abathur Fallen light being, judge, and father of Ptahil, in Mandaean thought.

Abdallah Father of Muhammad the prophet, figure of the divine realm in the Mother of Books (perhaps a later addition).

Abel Son of Adam and Eve in Genesis, sometimes thought to be the son of Eve and the demiurge in gnostic thought. *See also* HIBIL.

Abrasax Name of a power in a variety of traditions, including gnostic traditions. The numerical value of the name Abrasax in Greek totals 365, the number of days in the solar year. The name may be derived from the Hebrew *Arba* ("four," for the tetragrammaton, the ineffable four-letter name of god, YHWH, Yahweh) *Sabaoth* ("hosts" or "armies," shortened), hence "lord of hosts."

Abu Jahl Arabic, "father of folly," a nickname for an opponent of prophet Muhammad and a name for Azazi'il in the Mother of Books.

Abu Talib Father of Ali and uncle of Muhammad the prophet, figure of the divine realm in the Mother of Books, perhaps a later addition.

Achamoth Lower wisdom in Valentinian texts. *See* ECHAMOTH and SOPHIA.

Adakas Contraction of Adam Kasya, "hidden Adam." Adakas is heavenly Adam, whose soul animates earthly Adam in Mandaean thought. Also called Adakas-Mana. *See* ADAMAS, GERADAMAS.

Adam Legendary first father of human beings in Genesis and many gnostic texts. The name means "human being" in Hebrew, and in Genesis it is connected to *'adamah*, "earth." *See also* ADAMAS, GERADAMAS.

Adamantine Steel-like, diamond-like. Sometimes connected to the name Adamas.

Adamas Heavenly Adam, father of heavenly Seth in the divine pleroma. *See also* GER-ADAMAS.

Adamas of light One of the five sons of the living spirit, sent out to help the primal man, in Manichaean thought. Referred to in the Kephalaia. *See* ADAMAS, GERADAMAS.

Adon, Adonai Hebrew for "lord," "my lord." The root is used to form names of powers of this world in gnostic texts, for example, Adonaios. The Jewish god is known as Adonai in Mandaean sources.

Adonaios One of the powers of this world, linked to Sabaoth and Yaldabaoth. The name Adonaios derives from Adonai, Hebrew for "my lord."

Adonis Lover of Aphrodite and a young man who dies and rises. Adonis means "lord" in Semitic languages; *see* ADON. Referred to in the Naassene Sermon.

Aeon Eternal realm. As an eternal realm, an aeon is an emanation of the divine in gnostic texts, and a ruling entity in the pleroma. Sometimes the realms of the demiurge below are also called aeons, but they are poor imitations of the eternal realms above.

Afterthought Greek *epinoia*, which can be translated "thought, intelligence, creativity." Emanation of the divine and a heavenly aeon closely connected to Sophia in Sethian texts. Afterthought is called life (Zoe) and is sent as a revealer to enlighten Adam in the Secret Book of John.

Ahriman Evil god in Zoroastrianism, a name for Azazi'il in the Mother of Books. *See also* ARIMANIOS.

Albanenses Name for absolute dualists in Cathar religion. Referred to in the Gospel of the Great Supper.

Albi City and Cathar center in Languedoc, southwestern France. The Albigensian Crusade, declared by Pope Innocent III in 1201 to exterminate the Cathars, takes its name from Albi, which became synonymous with the Cathars.

Ali Cousin and son-in-law of Muhammad the prophet, martyr of Shi'ite Islam, figure of the divine realm of five in the Mother of Books.

All Or the all, the entirety, the universe. "All" may refer to the totality of the divine realm, the pleroma.

Allahu akbar Arabic, "god is great," an acclamation of the greatness of Allah. Referred to in the Mother of Books.

Anasses Duses Name addressed to the revealer Derdekeas in the Paraphrase of Shem. It probably derives from the Greek words for "rising" (or "east") and "setting" (or "west"), to indicate the rising and setting of the light.

Androgyny State of being male-female, with complete sexual identity. According to early traditions Adam was created as an androgynous human, and gnostic traditions describe numerous powers as androgynous. Gospel of Thomas 22 proclaims androgyny as salvific union. *See* HERMAPHRODITE.

Anointed one Messiah, Christ (Greek *christos*). One who has been anointed with oil, literally or metaphorically, and thus has been given a special place of prominence. Some early followers of Jesus saw him as the messiah, the anointed one of god, hence the phrase Jesus (the) Christ or Jesus the messiah. In the Gospel of Philip chrism, or anointing with oil, is considered one of five sacraments. Anointing with oil is still practiced in some Christian churches, often as a sacrament, to the present day.

Anosh Heavenly Enosh, a messenger of light, in Mandaean thought. Enosh means "person" or "humankind." In Genesis Enosh is described as the son of Seth, and it is said that at this time people began to call on god's name.

Aphrodite Goddess of love in Greek mythology. Referred to in the Book of Baruch, the Exegesis on the Soul, and the Naassene Sermon.

Archigenitor Chief creator of this world as in the Three Forms of First Thought.

Archon Ruler, especially an angelic ruler of this world, in the entourage of the chief archon, the demiurge.

Arhat Ideal figure, saint, in Theravada Buddhism, referred to in the Great Song to Mani.

Ariael Name of the demiurge or creator of the world in On the Origin of the World. The name closely resembles Ariel, which in Hebrew means "lion of god." See Gospel of Thomas 8.

Arimanios Name of a Pharisee in the Secret Book of John. Ahriman is the name of the evil god in Zoroastrianism.

Arrogant one Greek *authades*. Epithet of the demiurge in the Letter of Peter to Philip and elsewhere.

Asklepios Greek hero and god of medicine and healing, identified with the deified Egyptian architect Imhotep. Aklepios is described as a hermetic initiate and student, and a hermetic text called the Revelation of Asklepios survives in Greek and Latin, along with Coptic selections from the Nag Hammadi library.

Astaphaios Son of Yaldabaoth in On the Origin of the World.

Atlas Greek god who carries the world on his shoulders. Atlas is one of the five sons of the living spirit, sent out to help the primal man, in Manichaean thought. Referred to in the Kephalaia.

Attis Phrygian eunuch and lover of Cybele in the mysteries of the Great Mother and Attis. Attis reflects the interests of dying and rising deities throughout the mystery religions and early Christianity. Referred to in the Naassene Sermon.

Autogenes Greek for "self-conceived," "self-created," "self-begotten." Epithet of the divine in many gnostic texts.

Avici Deepest Buddhist hell, referred to in the Great Song to Mani.

Azazi'il Arrogant angel who resembles the gnostic demiurge, in the Mother of Books. Azazi'il seems to have developed from Azazel, the chief of the fallen angels in later Jewish sources (1 Enoch, Apocalypse [Revelation] of Abraham). This angel is also referred to in the Mandaean tradition.

Babel Angel of Edem in the Book of Baruch. In Genesis the Tower of Babel is a site of legendary human pride (from the ziggurat of Babylon?).

Bacchos Dionysos, Greek god of fertility, ecstasy, and wine. Referred to by Hippolytus of Rome in connection with the Naassene Sermon.

Baqir Or al-Baqir. The revealer in the Mother of Books, whose name means "the one who opens." The name derives from Muhammad al-Baqir, the fifth imam in Shi'ite Islam.

Barbelo The divine mother and the first emanation of the father of all in Sethian texts. She is also described as the forethought (Greek, *pronoia*) of the invisible spirit, and she is given the nickname "human." The name Barbelo may well derive from Hebrew. A possible translation is "god (compare *el*) in (*b-*) four (*arb(a)*)," with reference to the tetragrammaton, the ineffable four-letter name of god.

Baruch Paternal angel of Elohim, identified with the good tree of life, in the Book of Baruch. In Hebrew the name means "blessed."

Bema Rostrum on which Mani's picture was displayed during the Manichaean Bema celebration, which commemorated the death of Mani, in the spring. At the Bema celebration, songs of the Bema from the Coptic Manichaean Songbook were sung.

Bismillah Arabic for "in the name of Allah." This expression, and what follows, is written at the opening of suras in the Qur'an: *Bismillah al-rahman al-rahim*, "In the name of Allah, the compassionate, the merciful." Discussed in the Mother of Books, where *Bismillah* may also be connected to the throne of god. *See* MERKAVAH.

Bloodless food Vegetarian food, referred to in the Hermetic Prayer of Thanksgiving. The elect within Manichaeism were also vegetarians.

Bogomils A neomanichaean gnostic group in Bulgaria, the Balkans, and especially Constantinople, who flourished between the tenth and fifteenth centuries. *See* CATHARS.

Boraq Or Buraq, "lightning." The winged horse on which Muhammad rode on his night journey to Jerusalem and up to heaven, and a heavenly creature in the Mother of Books.

Boundary *See* LIMIT.

Bridal chamber Referred to as one of five sacraments in the Gospel of Philip and mentioned elsewhere in gnostic texts. The ceremony of the bridal chamber typically emphasizes the spiritual meaning of heavenly union.

Brimo In the Naassene Sermon there is a saying from the Eleusinian mysteries: "Brimo has borne a holy child, Brimos." Lady Brimo ("strong one," "terrible one") probably is to be understood as Kore, or Persephone, who had intercourse with Zeus and gave birth to Dionysos, "Brimos."

Buddha Indian sage and founder of Buddhism, designated as a prophet within Manichaeism. Mani is addressed as Buddha Mani in the Great Song to Mani.

Bulls Two famous bulls, Apis and Mnevis, were revered in ancient Egypt. Referred to in On the Origin of the World.

Cain Son of Adam and Eve in Genesis, sometimes thought to be the son of Eve and the demiurge in gnostic texts.

Cathars Cathari, from Greek, *katharoi*, "pure ones." The Cathars were a gnostic group, largely in southwestern Europe and especially in southwestern France, who flourished between the eleventh and fourteenth centuries.

Cave The allegory of the cave in Plato's *Republic* and its teaching about human knowledge may be referred to in the Secret Book of John. According to the allegory of the cave, people may be described as being bound in a cave and seeing only shadows of realities, until they break free and see the true, unseeable sun, the source of light.

Cerinthos Christian teacher who taught in the early second century and who may be referred to as the recipient of the Secret Book of James (the name needs to be restored in the text).

Cherubim Angels around the throne or merkavah of god in Ezekiel 1 and elsewhere, including gnostic texts. *See* MERKAVAH.

Colors In gnostic texts, descriptive language is used to depict light and darkness in graphic terms and accentuate the contrast between them. In the Mother of Books, the glory of the divine fullness is portrayed with brilliant colors, and the heavenly spheres are characterized by these colors. On the other hand, it is said that this world is drab and colorless until god the high king empowers it spiritually and makes it come alive with color.

Column of glory Milky Way, a cosmic vehicle to help transport the light on its way back to the kingdom of light, in Manichaean thought.

Corybant Korybant, ecstatic celebrant sometimes linked to the mysteries of the Great Mother and Attis. Referred to in the Naassene Sermon.

Cosmogony Account of the creation of the cosmos or universe.

Credentes Cathar hearers or believers, general members of the Cathar religion, who were not obliged to hold to the strict ascetic rules of the perfect, the leaders. Both *credentes* and the perfect (*les parfaits*, or *perfecti*) came under the populist title of "the good men," *la bona gen* (Provençal), *les bonhommes* (French), but originally "the good men" referred solely to the "perfect."

Custodian of splendor One of the five sons of the living spirit, sent out to help the primal man, in Manichaean thought. Referred to in the Kephalaia.

Danae Young woman raped by Zeus, who took the form of a shower of golden rain, in Greek mythology. Referred to in the Book of Baruch.

Daphne Young huntress pursued by Apollo and changed into a laurel tree in Greek mythology. The theme is applied to gnostic mythology and referred to in the Secret Book of John, the Reality of the Rulers, and On the Origin of the World.

Darkness Gloomy expression of the loss of divine light, in general, in gnostic texts. In the Paraphrase of Shem, darkness is the primal power or root below.

Daveithai One of the luminaries in gnostic thought.

Deficiency The lack of divine fullness that results from the fall from divine glory. Deficiency stands in direct contrast to the pleroma as the main problem in the cosmos.

Demeter "Grain mother," or, less plausibly, "earth mother," from the Greek mysteries, especially the Eleusinian mysteries. Her daughter is Kore, or Persephone. Referred to in the Naassene Sermon.

Demiurge Greek, *demiourgos*, "artisan." In Plato's *Timaeus*, the demiurge orders or fashions the material world out of chaos. In the creation stories in Genesis and other sources, the creator god or gods also fashion the world, and often from chaos. In Genesis 1 and the Mesopotamian story called the Enuma Elish ("When on high"), the divine creates out of watery chaos, the primal ooze. In gnostic texts the demiurge creates people and the material world and is often viewed as the originator of evil, as the biblical creator who traps particles of light in material flesh. *See* AZAZI'IL, NEBROEL, PRINCE OF DARKNESS, PTAHIL, SAKLA, SAMAEL, SATANAS, YALDABAOTH.

Depth Greek *bythos, bathos*. Infinite divine manifestation, from which the pleroma of divinity emanates, in Valentinian texts. With thought, depth constitutes the first Valentinian pair of beings. For Sethian texts, *see* INVISIBLE SPIRIT.

Derdekeas Gnostic revealer in the Paraphrase of Shem. The name Derdekeas may derive from the Aramaic for "male child."

Deucalion Hero of the great flood who survives the deluge brought by Zeus in Greek mythology. Referred to in the Revelation of Adam.

Dharma Buddhist law, referred to in the Great Song to Mani.

Diospolis One of two cities in Upper Egypt. Diospolis Magna is Thebes (modern Luxor), Diospolis Parva is Heou (near Nag Hammadi). In the Discourse on the Eighth and the Ninth there is a reference to a temple at Diospolis.

Docetists From Greek *dokeo*, "appear, seem to be." Early Christians who claimed that Christ only appeared or seemed to live in the flesh and suffer and die on the cross were dubbed docetists. Many gnostics shared this view. See, for instance, the Second Treatise of the Great Seth.

Dositheos First-century Samaritan religious leader and the teacher of Simon Magus. Referred to in the Three Steles of Seth, which is said to be the revelation of Dositheos.

Duldul The white mule of Muhammad, and a heavenly creature in the Mother of Books.

Ear In Gospel of Thomas 33, Jesus refers to one ear and the other ear. In the Gospel of the Great Supper, Jesus, as an angel, inseminates Mary through her ear. He enters by her ear and he leaves by her ear.

Earthly son *See* HUMAN CHILD.

Echamoth A form of wisdom in the Gospel of Philip, from Hebrew *hokhmah*. Achamoth is lower wisdom in Valentinian texts. *See* SOPHIA.

Echmoth "Little wisdom" in the Gospel of Philip, from the Hebrew and Aramaic for "like death." *See* SOPHIA.

Edem Or Eden, name of the divine mother in the Book of Baruch. The name derives from the Hebrew for "earth" (*edem*) or the place of paradise (garden of "Eden," perhaps garden of "delight"); in the Septuagint the garden of Eden is referred to as *edem* in Greek.

Eight Ogdoad, the realm of eight aeons. The eighth can also refer to the realm of the fixed stars, beyond the seven planetary spheres, hence the realm of the demiurge or of wisdom, as in the Discourse on the Eighth and Ninth and elsewhere. Sometimes the eighth sphere is thought to be the abode of the ruler of the cosmos; sometimes it is considered a higher level for spiritual advancement and perfection.

El Eloah, Elohim (plural ending), etc., Hebrew for "god." The root is used to form names of powers of this world in gnostic texts, for example Eloaios or Poimael.

Elect Common epithet of those chosen by god, including gnostics. In Manichaeism the elect are the strict adherents to Manichaean regulations and the leaders of the Manichaean church. They may be compared to the perfect in Cathar thought (*see* PERFECT).

Eleleth One of the luminaries in gnostic thought. Eleleth is called a great angel in the Reality of the Rulers and plays a revelatory role in that text.

Elements The four traditional elements in Greco-Roman thought are earth, water, air, and fire. Spirit replaces fire in the Book of Thomas, probably because of the association of fire with ignorance and passion. According to Manichaean thought there are five elements in the kingdom of light (air, wind, light, water, and fire—no earth, of course).

Eleusis Sacred site near Athens, at which the Eleusinian mysteries were celebrated. The mysteries featured the grain mother Demeter and her daughter Kore, or Persephone. Referred to in the Naassene Sermon.

Elkesai Elchasai, "hidden power," designating the hidden power of god. Elkesai is described as the prophet and founder of the Elkesaites, a Jewish-Christian baptizing group to which Mani's father belonged and in which Mani was baptized. Referred to in On the Origin of His Body.

Eloai Son of Yaldabaoth in On the Origin of the World. *See* EL.

Elohim Hebrew word for "god." Elohim is the divine father in the Book of Baruch; Elohim is the child of Eve and the demiurge in some Sethian texts.

Emmacha Seth Name of heavenly Seth in Sethian texts.

Enoch Character in Genesis who is said to have walked with god and to have been taken away, mysteriously, by god. Several revelatory books are attributed to Enoch on the basis of his remarkable experience with god. Referred to in the Gospel of the Great Supper and elsewhere.

Eros God of love and lover of Psyche in Greek mythology. Referred to in On the Origin of the World.

Error In the Valentinian Gospel of Truth, error (female in gender) is personified and plays roles usually assigned to wisdom and the demiurge in gnostic texts.

Esthesis-Ouch-Epi-Ptoe Mother of the demons in the Secret Book of John. The name is a philosophical saying from Greek and seems to mean "sense perception is not in an excited state." See Bentley Layton, *Gnostic Scriptures*, 43. Another version is also given: Esthesis-Z-Ouch-Epi-Ptoe, which may mean "the seven senses (?) are not in an excited state."

Eve Legendary first mother of human beings in Genesis and many gnostic texts. The name is sometimes said to be related to the Hebrew word for "life." In the Septuagint Eve is called Zoe, Greek for "life."

Fate Greek *heimarmene*. In the Greco-Roman world fate was considered to be the overwhelming force that determines the destiny of all that is earthly and heavenly. Coming to expression in the inexorable movements of the heavenly bodies, fate was commonly understood astrologically, and the power of fate was often thought to exceed that of the gods and goddesses. Fate, then, may be the ultimate bondage. Referred to in the Secret Book of John, On the Origin of the World, and elsewhere.

Father of greatness Eternal divine manifestation of good in Manichaean thought.

Fatima Daughter of Muhammad the prophet, figure of the divine realm of five in the Mother of Books.

Female Gender category used symbolically to designate what is physical and earthly (for example, the divine described as mother earth).

First thought *See* PROTENNOIA.

Five Pentad, quintet; realm of the divine father, consisting of Barbelo and four personified attributes (foreknowledge, incorruptibility, life eternal, and truth) in Sethian texts. Since the five is androgynous, it is also called the ten, and it constitutes the divine father in emanation. In the Mother of Books the divine realm of five includes Muhammad, Ali, Fatima, Hasan, and Husayn, and ten is a perfect number. In the Valentinian Gospel of Philip there are five sacraments. Five trees of paradise are referred to in Gospel of Thomas 19, Manichaean sources, and the Mother of Books. In Manichaean and neo-manichaean texts many things are presented in groups of five. *See also* FIVE SEALS.

Five seals Part of the Sethian ritual of baptism. In Three Forms of First Thought the five seals may be linked to gnostic ecstatic ascent to the divine.

Forethought Greek *pronoia*. *See* BARBELO.

Fullness Pleroma, or state of being filled with the divine.

Gabriel Angel and archangel in Jewish, Christian, and Islamic tradition. Gabriel is an angelic minister to the luminary Oroiael in the Gospel of the Egyptians and elsewhere. Gabriel plays a prominent role within Islam and is referred to, along with other angels, in the Mother of Books.

Gamaliel Angelic minister to the luminary Harmozel in the Gospel of the Egyptians and a prominent angelic figure in Sethian texts.

Ganymede Youth of great beauty kidnapped to become the cupbearer for Zeus in Greek mythology. Referred to in the Book of Baruch.

Garment Symbol of the body that is put on at birth and taken off at death.

Gehenna Valley of Hinnom, an unholy ravine near Jerusalem, often identified with hell. Referred to in the Gospel of the Great Supper and elsewhere.

Geradamas Geradama, heavenly Adam in Sethian texts. The name Geradamas probably derives from Hebrew, and it may mean "Adam the stranger" (Hebrew, *ger adam*). See Howard M. Jackson, "Geradamas, the Celestial Stranger"; Goehring and Robinson, "The Three Steles of Seth," in Pearson, ed., *Nag Hammadi Codex VII*, 388. Another suggestion:

"holy Adam" (Greek *hier-adamas*). Others have related Geradamas to the name Adam and the Greek word for "old" (*geron*), thus indicating "old Adam."

Ghuluw "Exaggeration," radical thinking within Islam, including mystical and gnostic reflection. One of the leading *ghulat*, or "exaggerators," was Abdallah ibn Saba, who lived in Kufa, Iraq, where the Mother of Books came from.

Ginza Treasure, also called the Great Book. Sacred text of the Mandaeans, with two main sections, the Right Ginza and the Left Ginza.

Glossolalia Ecstatic speech, understood to be the language of the heavenly realms, as in the Baptismal Ceremony of the Gospel of the Egyptians, the Paraphrase of Shem, and the Discourse on the Eighth and the Ninth.

Gnosis Knowledge, especially mystical knowledge and insight. Knowledge of god and self offers the way of salvation in gnostic texts.

Gog and Magog Powers on the earth, referred to in the Bible (Genesis 10:2; 1 Chronicles 1:5; Ezekiel 38–39; Revelation 20:8), the Qur'an (sura 18), and the Mother of Books.

Good Name of the transcendent deity in the Book of Baruch, also in the Book of Thomas. The Good is an ethical and metaphysical principle in Greco-Roman philosophy, especially platonism, and an attribute of the divine in Judaism and other religions.

Great king of honor One of the five sons of the living spirit, sent out to help the primal man, in Manichaean thought. Referred to in the Kephalaia.

Habshaba Sunday, observed as a holy day in Mandaean religion.

Hades God and realm of the dead in Greek thought. *See also* TARTAROS.

Harith Druze name for the devil, a name for Azazi'il in the Mother of Books.

Harmozel One of the luminaries in gnostic thought.

Hasan Son of Ali, grandson of Muhammad the prophet, martyr of Shi'ite Islam, figure of the divine realm of five in the Mother of Books.

Hebdomad *See* SEVEN.

Helen Helen of Troy, for whose sake the Trojan War was fought, in Homer. Sometimes connected to Helena, companion of Simon Magus and expression of the first thought of the divine. Referred to in the Exegesis on the Soul.

Herakles Hercules, hero of Greek mythology, who accomplished twelve mighty labors. Referred to in the Book of Baruch.

Hermaphrodite Character in Greek mythology who is androgynous, that is, male-female. Referred to in On the Origin of the World. *See* ANDROGYNY.

Hermes Messenger god in Greek mythology. Hermes Trismegistos is the divine father of hermetic religion. Hermes is identified with the Egyptian god Thoth, god of wisdom and divine scribe, and with the planet Mercury in the Discourse on the Eighth and Ninth. *See also* NBU.

Herodotos Greek historian of the Persian Wars. Referred to in the Book of Baruch.

Hewath Possibly "serpent," nickname of Ruha in Mandaean sources. *See* SERPENT.

Hibil Heavenly Abel, a messenger of light, in Mandaean thought.

High king Transcendent deity, in the Mother of Books.

Himeros God of desire who was linked to Eros in Greek mythology. Referred to in On the Origin of the World.

Homer Greek poet, author to whom the *Iliad* and the *Odyssey* are attributed. Referred to as "the poet" and cited in the Exegesis on the Soul and the Naassene Sermon.

Houris Young women of legendary beauty who live in paradise. Referred to in the Mother of Books.

Human child Son of man, earthly son, Semitic idiom (Hebrew, *ben adam* or *ben enosh*, "son of man") used to designate a human, an offspring of the group of humankind. The phrase can designate any human being, or it can be used to refer to oneself (Gospel of Thomas 86), or it can be employed apocalyptically to refer to the human one coming with god at the end of time. In Sethian texts "human" is an epithet of Barbelo and may also refer to Geradamas, and the human child may be the divine child of the invisible spirit and Barbelo, or heavenly Seth.

Husayn Son of Ali, grandson of Muhammad the prophet, martyr of Shi'ite Islam, figure of the divine realm of five in the Mother of Books.

Hylic Material person, person of earthly matter (Greek, *hyle*). Lowest of three divisions of humanity, especially in Valentinian texts. Also sometimes called fleshly person (sarkic, Greek *sarkikos*) or earthly person (choic, Greek *choikos*). *See also* PNEUMATIC, PSYCHIC.

I am god Monotheistic revelation of god in Isaiah and ignorant boast of the demiurge in gnostic texts: "I am god, and there is no other god but me." Note also the monotheistic confession in the *shahada*, or Islamic creed, referred to in the Mother of Books: "There is no god but god (Allah)."

"I am" statements Aretalogical self-predications, statements in which gods or goddesses reveal their divine features. Used in the Gospel of John, Thunder, and many other gnostic texts.

Iblis "Devil" in Arabic. Referred to in the Mother of Books.

Imam Religious leader in Islam, especially Shi'ite Islam. Referred to in the Mother of Books.

Inquisition Established by Pope Gregory IX in 1233, during the Albigensian Crusade to annihilate the remaining Cathar heretics in Languedoc. Not to be confused with the Inquisition established in Spain by Ferdinand and Isabella in 1478. *See* ALBI.

Invisible spirit Infinite divine manifestation, from which the pleroma of divinity emanates, in Sethian texts. Also referred to as the invisible virgin spirit. *See* ONE. For Valentinian texts, *see* DEPTH.

Isis Egyptian goddess of fertility, royal continuity, and magical power, and the wife of Osiris. Referred to in the Naassene Sermon.

Jabir The student in the Mother of Books. The name derives from Jabir ibn Yazid al-Ju'fi; but compare also Jafar al-Ju'fi and Jabir ibn Abdallah al-Ansari.

James the just James (Yaakov) the righteous, brother of Jesus and the leader of the early church in Jerusalem, acclaimed for his piety and observance. Apparently thought to be the author of the Secret Book of James, referred to in the Gospel of Thomas and elsewhere.

Jesus Yeshua, Jewish teacher and exorcist from Nazareth, commonly considered a revealer and savior in Christian gnostic texts. In the Gospel of Thomas and the Gospel of John, Jesus is a teacher of wisdom who speaks in brief sayings (in Thomas) or mystical discourses (in John). In the Book of Baruch, Jesus cooperates with the angel Baruch and proclaims the Good, until an angry Naas has him crucified. In Manichaean texts Jesus is said to be a Manichaean prophet, and Jesus is described variously, as young Jesus

(Jesus as a boy anticipating the salvation of the light), suffering Jesus (Jesus as light suffering in matter), and Jesus of light (or Jesus of splendor, Jesus as heavenly revealer of light), who in turn evokes the great mind (*nous*) for the revelation of knowledge and the final liberation of the light. Jesus is often called messiah or Christ, "the anointed," or is linked to Christ. In the Secret Book of John the anointed child of god dwells in the heavenly fullness, along with heavenly Seth. In Three Forms of First Thought heavenly Seth puts on Jesus as a garment. In Valentinian texts Christ is an aeon in the divine pleroma, and a distinction is made between the heavenly Christ and the earthly Jesus. In Mandaean sources, conversely, Christ (Nbu-Christ) is described as a liar and false messiah who distorts the gnosis of John the baptizer.

Jinn Arabic for "spirit," especially a spirit of this world, referred to in the Mother of Books.

John the baptizer Yohanan the baptizer, the Jewish teacher who initiated Jesus by baptizing him in the Jordan River. He is assigned a secondary place to Jesus in the New Testament gospels, including the Gospel of John, but it is clear from the Acts of the Apostles and the Pseudo-Clementine Recognitions that he was acclaimed as a great teacher and even a messianic figure by some. In Gospel of Thomas 46 he is given high praise. In Mandaean texts it is said that John's wisdom is true wisdom, and Jesus perverts the true ways of John the baptizer and brings falsehood and wickedness into the world.

Jordan River (in Hebrew, Yarden) in Palestine, flowing from the Sea of Galilee to the Dead Sea, near which such Jewish baptizing movements as those of John the baptizer and the covenanters or Essenes of Qumran were located. In Mandaean religion a Jordan (*yardna*) is baptismal water, consisting of living or flowing water, and there are heavenly and earthly Jordans. The use of the word Jordan may indicate that the Mandaeans derive from Jewish baptizers of the Jordan valley.

Kabbalah Jewish mystical tradition that developed from earlier mystical conceptions and has flourished since medieval times.

Kanna Place, home, often of the soul, in Mandaean sources.

Kaulakau, Saulasau, Zeesar Three words derived from the Hebrew of Isaiah 28:10, 13: *sav la-sav, sav la-sav, kav la-kav, kav la-kav, ze'ir sham*, meaning uncertain, translated in the revised Standard Version as follows: "it is precept upon precept, precept upon precept, line upon line, line upon line, here a little, there a little." Referred to as words of power in the Naassene Sermon. Sometimes these words are linked to the three words or sayings of Gospel of Thomas 13.

Kephalaia Greek for "headings, central principles." Sacred Manichaean text in which Mani discusses the basic tenets of the religion with his students.

King of glory One of the five sons of the living spirit, sent out to help the primal man, in Manichaean thought. Referred to in the Kephalaia.

Know yourself Greek *gnothi sauton*. Maxim from the oracular shrine of Apollo at Delphi. Gnostic texts reflect extensively upon the meaning of knowing oneself.

Kore "Maiden" in Greek, identified with the cycle of life of grain and people, from the Greek mysteries, especially the Eleusinian mysteries. Her mother is Demeter, and she herself is often identified with Persephone. Referred to as Persephone in the Naassene Sermon.

Kouretes Ecstatic celebrants of the mysteries, originally linked with Zeus and Crete. Referred to by Hippolytus of Rome in connection with the Naassene Sermon.

Kronos Divine ruler of the Titans in Greek mythology. Referred to in the Naassene Sermon.

Kushta Truth, ritualized by means of a handshake, in Mandaean religion.

Laughing Jesus Jesus is described laughing at the world in the Gospel of Philip, the Round Dance of the Cross, the Second Treatise of the Great Seth, and elsewhere, because, though the world thinks him a vulnerable human being, he is divine and cannot suffer and die.

Leda Woman ravished by Zeus, who took the form of a swan, in Greek mythology. Referred to in the Book of Baruch.

Letter Symbol of divine call to revelation and knowledge in the Song of the Pearl. As a winged divine messenger the letter functions as a form of the gnostic revealer.

Light Glorious expression of the divine, in general, in gnostic texts. In the Paraphrase of Shem, light is the primal power or root above, perhaps like the sun. This concept is paralleled in platonic and neoplatonic thought.

Limit Greek *horos*, "limit, boundary." In Valentinian thought, a limit or boundary separates the world inside the pleroma from the world outside and thus protects the integrity of the divine fullness.

Living Gospel Sacred book written by Mani, now lost. Referred to in On the Origin of His Body and the Great Song to Mani.

Living spirit Light being sent to rescue the primal man in Manichaean thought, who had fallen into the kingdom of darkness. Father of five sons: the custodian of splendor, the great king of honor, Adamas of light, the king of glory, and Atlas. Referred to in the Kephalaia.

Living water Flowing water, water connected to life and to baptism.

Logos Word; the word of god, commonly personified, is comparable to the wisdom of god in gnostic and other texts. In Judaism the divine logos is the creative word of Genesis, and in Greco-Roman philosophy, including stoicism and forms of platonism, the divine logos is the reason and rationality that permeate the cosmos. In the Johannine tradition the logos is particularly prominent, and Jesus is said to be the manifestation or incarnation of the divine word. In the Mother of Books Salman is called the word of god. In the Second Treatise of the Great Seth the word translated as "treatise" is *logos*.

Lucifer "Lightbearer," an angel identified with the morning star (Venus) and later with Satan, as in the Gospel of the Great Supper.

Luminaries Four lights in gnostic thought, especially in Sethian texts, which shine in the pleroma. They are named Harmozel, Oroiael, Daveithai, and Eleleth.

Male Gender category used symbolically to designate what is spiritual and heavenly (for example, the divine described as the heavenly father). The epithet "triple male" as a superlative can be used of either male or female powers.

Mana Spirit of the divine and spirit in people, in Mandaean thought. The great Mana is the heavenly spirit, the highest divine manifestation.

Manda "Knowledge," gnosis, in Mandaean thought.

Manda dHayye "Knowledge of life," gnostic revealer and important messenger of light, sometimes linked to Hibil, in Mandaean thought.

Mani Founder of Manichaeism and messenger of the light. Mani proclaimed a universal religion, based on the teachings of the prophets Buddha, Jesus, and Zoroaster, which he was convinced would unite the people of the world.

Mara Buddhist demonic tempter, referred to in the Great Song to Mani.

Mary of Magdala Galilean woman, a student of Jesus, one of his closest followers according to the Gospel of Philip and the Gospel of Mary. Later discredited by being called a prostitute. One of several Marys mentioned in early Christian gospels.

Masbuta Mandaean baptism by immersion.

Mathaias Person claimed to be the compiler of the Book of Thomas. Mathaias may be considered the apostolic replacement for Judas Iscariot according to Acts 1:26, or the apostolic author of the Gospel of Matthew, or some other person.

Mercury *See* HERMES.

Merkavah Divine throne-chariot, depicted in Ezekiel 1, which functions as a goal of contemplation in Jewish mysticism.

Messenger Apostle.

Micheus, Michar, Mnesinous Heavenly powers connected to Sethian baptism in the Gospel of the Egyptians and elsewhere.

Middle Realm of Achamoth, lower wisdom and mother of the demiurge, between the spiritual realm of the divine above and the realm of creation below, according to Valentinian texts. The middle thus is the region between the pleroma and this world, and as such it is termed a place of death in the Gospel of Philip.

Mirothea Sethian name or epithet for the divine in Three Forms of First Thought, the Three Steles of Seth, and elsewhere. The meaning is uncertain; perhaps "divine anointed one" (from Greek *myro-theos*) or "divine destiny" (from Greek *moiro-theos*—compare Moira, destiny in Greek mythology). Mirothea is a feminine form, Mirotheos a masculine form. Mirothea can be used to denote Barbelo and the mother of Geradamas. See Turner, *Sethian Gnosticism and the Platonic Tradition*, 211.

Mirotheos Masculine form of Mirothea. Mirotheos can be used to denote Geradamas.

Monad *See* ONE.

Moon Ship of the night, a cosmic vehicle to help transport the light on its way back to the kingdom of light, in Manichaean thought.

Moses Hebrew lawgiver, said to be the author of Genesis (which is particularly important to gnostics) as well as the other books of the Pentateuch.

Muhammad Prophet of Islam, figure of the divine realm of five in the Mother of Books.

Naas Maternal angel of Edem, identified with the evil tree of the knowledge of good and evil, in the Book of Baruch. The term derives from *nahash*, Hebrew for "serpent" (as with Naassenes). *See* SERPENT.

Naassenes Serpentine gnostics, whose name derives from *nahash*, Hebrew for "serpent." The Ophites are gnostics given a similar name, from *ophis*, Greek for "serpent." *See* NAAS, SERPENT.

Nag Hammadi City in Upper Egypt near which the Nag Hammadi library was discovered by Muhammad Ali of the al-Samman clan, reportedly in 1945. The Nag Hammadi library contains gnostic texts representing Sethian, Valentinian, Thomasite, hermetic, and other traditions.

Najib Class of angels in the Mother of Books. The name means "noble one."

Naqib Class of angels in the Mother of Books. The name means "leader."

Nbu The planet Mercury, one of the planetary powers of this world, in Mandaean thought. The power Nbu may be linked to Christ, considered a liar and false messiah, as Nbu-Christ. *See* HERMES.

Nebroel Namrael, demonic creator of the material world in Manichaean thought. *See* PRINCE OF DARKNESS.

Nimrod Mighty warrior referred to in Genesis, a name for Azazi'il in the Mother of Books.

Nine The ninth refers to the realm beyond the seven planetary spheres and the eighth realm of the fixed stars, hence the realm of the divine, as in the Discourse on the Eighth and Ninth and elsewhere.

Nirvana State of final liberation and bliss in Buddhism. Complete nirvana is termed *parinirvana*. Referred to in the Story of the Death of Mani and the Great Song to Mani.

Noraia The First Book of Noraia, the First Account of Noraia, referred to in On the Origin of the World. Perhaps related to the Nag Hammadi text entitled the Thought of Norea. *See* NOREA.

Norea Virgin daughter of Eve in Jewish lore and gnostic texts, especially Sethian texts. Perhaps compare Naarah, "girl" in Hebrew. Sometimes Norea is linked to Naamah in Genesis 4:22 (and Genesis 6:2), and in gnostic traditions she resembles Sophia in some respects. Referred to in the Reality of the Rulers and elsewhere. *See also* OREA.

Nous Mind, the primary manifestation of the divine. This Greek word also can be used to form names of aeons in gnostic texts, for example, Nousanios in Three Forms of First Thought. *See also* JESUS.

Oannes Mesopotamian god of wisdom, part man and part fish. Referred to in the Naassene Sermon.

Ogdoad *See* EIGHT.

Ohrmazd Ahura Mazda, the good god in Zoroastrianism, sometimes identified with the primal man in Manichaean sources.

Omphale Queen of Lydia to whom Herakles was enslaved, in Greek mythology. Referred to in the Book of Baruch.

One Monad. In Greco-Roman texts, for example, platonic texts, the divine is frequently characterized as embracing oneness, and within Judaism the divine is confessed as being preeminently one. The divine is often addressed as the One in gnostic texts.

Orea Variant spelling of Norea in the Reality of the Rulers and possibly On the Origin of the World. Orea resembles the word "beautiful" in Greek. Possibly a misspelling of Norea?

Oroiael One of the luminaries in gnostic thought.

Osiris Egyptian god of moisture, kingship, and underworld, and the husband of Isis. Osiris dies and yet lives as the king of underworld in Egyptian mythology. Referred to in the Naassene Sermon.

Pan Greek god of the wild, half man and half goat. Referred to by Hippolytus of Rome in connection with the Naassene Sermon.

Papas Name connected to Attis and the mysteries of the Great Mother and Attis. The name resembles "papa." Referred to in the Naassene Sermon.

Paraclete From Greek *parakletos*, "comforter, helper, counselor." In the Gospel of John, Jesus promises that god will send another comforter, the spirit of truth. Mani is acclaimed as being the comforter of truth in On the Origin of His Body.

Pearl Symbol of the soul in the Song of the Pearl and elsewhere.

Perfect Cathar leaders, who must adhere to strict ascetic rules. *See also* CREDENTES.

Persephone Greek goddess and queen of the underworld, often identified with Kore in the Eleusinian mysteries. Referred to in the Naassene Sermon.

Peter Petros (Greek), Kefa (Aramaic), "rock"; student of Jesus traditionally connected to the founding of the church in Rome and the establishment of the papacy. Depicted as a misogynist in the Gospel of Mary and Gospel of Thomas 114.

Phoebos "Bright one" in Greek; epithet of Apollo, Greek god of wisdom and beauty. Referred to by Hippolytus of Rome in connection with the Naassene Sermon.

Phoenix Legendary bird that lives for centuries, dies by fire, and rises, renewed, from its own ashes, according to Egyptian tradition. Referred to in On the Origin of the World and the Mother of Books.

Pistis Faith; in On the Origin of the World, Sophia Zoe is the daughter of Pistis, or Pistis Sophia. *See* PISTIS SOPHIA.

Pistis Sophia Faith wisdom, in the Reality of the Rulers and other gnostic texts. *See* SOPHIA.

Place Place of god, a circumlocution for god.

Pleroma Fullness, the sum total of the aeons and emanations of the divine in gnostic texts. The divine pleroma is thus the full manifestation of the glory of the transcendent god.

Pneuma Greek for "spirit," the immortal divine presence within the world and within people. In the Paraphrase of Shem, spirit is the primal power or root between light and darkness.

Pneumatic Spiritual person, person of divine spirit (Greek, *pneuma*), gnostic. Highest of three divisions of humanity, especially in Valentinian texts. *See also* HYLIC, PSYCHIC.

Poimael Heavenly power connected to Sethian baptism in the Gospel of the Egyptians. The name Poimael resembles Poimandres and includes the common suffix -*el* ("god").

Poimandres Divine mind that reveals itself in the hermetic text Poimandres. The name Poimandres probably derives from the Greek for "shepherd (*poimen*) of men (*aner*, nominative plural *andres*, genitive plural *andron*)." Another suggested derivation: from Coptic for "the knowledge of the sun-god Ra" (*p-eime nte Re*). See Layton, *Gnostic Scriptures*, 450.

Priapos Greco-Roman fertility god, famous for his prodigious phallus. Identified with the Good in the Book of Baruch.

Primal man Heavenly first human in the kingdom of light in Manichaean thought. The primal man becomes entrapped in the kingdom of darkness, loses some of his light, and needs to be rescued. *See* ADAMAS, BARBELO, GERADAMAS, LIVING SPIRIT.

Prince of darkness Transcendent divine manifestation of evil in Manichaean thought. The prince of darkness produces two demons, Sakla and Nebroel, who create the creatures of the material world through sexuality.

Prison The body is the prison or tomb of the soul according to a platonic and Orphic teaching reflected in gnostic texts.

Pronoia Forethought. *See* BARBELO.

Protennoia First thought; first female manifestation of the divine in Sethian tradition, specifically in Three Forms of First Thought. Protennoia closely resembles forethought, *pronoia*. *See* BARBELO.

Proteos Greek god, connected to Poseidon and the sea, who could foretell the future and change his shape. He spent much of his time around the island of Pharos near Alexandria, Egypt. Referred to in the Naassene Sermon.

Psyche Greek for "soul," sometimes the animate soul that brings breath and physical life, sometimes the immortal soul within people (*see* PNEUMA). Personified as a young woman loved by Eros in Greek mythology and the Exegesis on the Soul.

Psychic Psychical person, person of animating soul (Greek *psyche*). Middle of three divisions of humanity, especially in Valentinian texts. In Christian gnostic traditions these are ordinary Christians. *See also* HYLIC, PNEUMATIC.

Ptahil Demiurge in Mandaean thought. The name Ptahil may derive from the name of Ptah, the Egyptian patron of artisans and creator god of Memphis, and the Semitic suffix *-il* (in Hebrew, *-el*). Jonas, *Gnostic Religion*, 98, connects this Egyptian basis for the name of the Mandaean demiurge with the broader Mandaean interest in Egypt as symbolic of the material world (as also in the Song of the Pearl). The name Ptahil may also mean "El who creates"; see Kurt Rudolph, "Mandean Sources," in Foerster, ed., *Gnosis*, 2.146. Sometimes called Ptahil-Uthra.

Q From *Quelle*, German for "source." Collection of sayings of Jesus used in the composition of the Gospels of Matthew and Luke.

Qur'an Al-Qur'an, "the recitation," the sacred book of Islam. Muslims believe that the Qur'an was revealed to prophet Muhammad in Arabic by Allah through the angel Gabriel. It consists of 114 suras and is cited extensively in the Mother of Books.

Rebouel Woman who is beheaded, in the Paraphrase of Shem. Perhaps to be interpreted allegorically as separation from the emerging orthodox church and its baptismal practices. See Roberge, *La Paraphrase de Sem*, 90.

Redemption Or ransom; referred to as one of five sacraments in the Gospel of Philip and mentioned elsewhere. According to heresiologists, the ceremony of redemption involves the use of oil and water in a ritual for the dead to aid them in their transition to the realm of the divine. Such ceremonies are also known from the Mandaeans.

Rest Greek *anapausis*. Divine rest or repose, the blessed state of those who are at peace. In gnostic thought rest is reserved for people who attain gnosis. In the Secret Book of John it is said that the transcendent One is in silence and at rest.

Rhea Divine wife of Kronos in Greek mythology. Referred to in the Naassene Sermon.

Right In Valentinian thought, those of the right are psychical people, as opposed to those of the left, who are material people. In the Gospel of Truth, reference is made to the Roman system of counting on the fingers of the left hand for numbers 1–99 and switching to the right hand at 100. Right and left are also referred to in the Gospel of Philip. In general right was considered fortunate and left unfortunate in ancient thought. In Matthew 25:31–46, Jesus is said to separate the sheep from the goats (that is, the righteous from the unrighteous) by putting the sheep on the right and the goats on the left.

Rubbing Image used to refer to sexual intercourse in the Paraphrase of Shem.

Ruha Spirit of wisdom who falls and gives birth to her son, the lord of darkness. Together they create the powers of this world. Also known as Ruha dQudsha, "holy spirit," as in Christian thought, though she is anything but holy. *See* SOPHIA.

Sabaoth Son of Yaldabaoth and a prominent power of this world in gnostic texts. The name is from the Hebrew for "hosts" or "armies," as in "lord of hosts."

Sabbath Shabbat, the seventh day of the week and a day of rest in the Jewish calendar. Referred to as such in a variety of texts. The root is also used to form names of powers of this world in gnostic texts, for example, Sabbataios and Sambathas.

Sakla Or Saklas, demiurge or creator of this world, especially in Sethian texts. In Manichaean texts Sakla is a demonic creator of the material world, along with Nebroel, on behalf of the prince of darkness. The name Sakla means "fool" in Aramaic. Also called Samael, Yaldabaoth.

Salman A follower of Ali, and the spiritual regent of god the high king in the Mother of Books. Salman shows similarities to wisdom and the heavenly human in gnostic texts. As in Valentinian texts, where there is a distinction between higher wisdom (Sophia) and lower wisdom (Achamoth), and as in many gnostic texts, where there is a distinction between the heavenly human and the earthly human, the Mother of Books distinguishes between great Salman and lesser Salman. Salman is described as a being of light and the word of god.

Samael Demiurge or creator of this world, especially in Sethian texts. The name means "blind god" in Aramaic. Also called Sakla, Yaldabaoth.

Samsara Cycle of incarnation and reincarnation in Buddhism and other religions, referred to in the Great Song to Mani.

Sangha Buddhist religious community, referred to in the Great Song to Mani.

Saphaia Power invoked in the Paraphrase of Shem. Perhaps *see* SOPHIA.

Saphaina Power invoked in the Paraphrase of Shem. Perhaps *see* SOPHIA.

Satanas Satan, in Cathar thought. In Cathar texts Satanas is also the demiurge and creator god.

Serpent Mythical deceiver in paradise according to the story of the fall in Genesis, derived from earlier serpent stories (for example, the story of Utnapishtim, the Babylonian hero of the great flood, in the epic of Gilgamesh). In gnostic texts the place of the serpent in the story may be reinterpreted and the serpent itself rehabilitated, when the serpent, as dispenser of gnosis, is considered an instructor in knowledge. The names Ophites and Naassenes, both derived from words for serpent or snake, are used to refer to gnostic groups.

Sesengenbarpharanges Word or name of power known from magical texts. Referred to in the Baptismal Ceremony of the Gospel of the Egyptians, where Sesengenbarpharanges is described as a purifier. The word or name probably derives from Aramaic (Sesengen, son of [*bar*-] Pharanges); John G. Gager, *Curse Tablets and Binding Spells*, 269, suggests a connection with a drug from a fig tree in "the Baaras ravine" (Greek *pharangos* [genitive]).

Seth Son of Adam and Eve after the death of Abel and the banishment of Cain. In Genesis, in the Septuagint, Seth is called "another seed." The Sethian gnostics describe themselves as the seed or offspring of Seth. As a heavenly being, Seth is also described as the son of Geradamas in the divine pleroma. *See also* SITIL.

Seven Hebdomad. Seven is the ancient number of completeness, commonly used to indicate what is full and complete. Seven indicates the number of days in a week, the number of planetary spheres (sun, moon, Mercury, Venus, Mars, Jupiter, Saturn) in ancient astronomy, and so the number of kings stationed over the spheres of heaven in the

Secret Book of John. The seventh or hebdomad refers to the realm of the planetary spheres, over which the demiurge is stationed.

Seventy-two Or seventy, the traditional number of nations and languages in the whole world. The title of the Septuagint, the Greek translation of the Hebrew Bible, means "seventy," for the number of translators. Since seventy is seven times ten, *see* SEVEN for the symbolism of seventy. Since seventy-two is six times twelve, *see* SIX and TWELVE.

Sexual organs In the Exegesis on the Soul, the soul is described as a female who has an external womb and is seduced and defiled by wanton males. In the Paraphrase of Shem the cosmogonic drama is depicted in graphically sexual terms as an orgy of cosmic sexuality. Nature is described as womb, hymen, vagina, and afterbirth, the demons are described with penises, and the sexual activities include rubbing, masturbation, intercourse, and the production of bestial offspring. Sexuality also plays a significant role in Mandaean, Manichaean, and neomanichaean texts.

Shamish Sun, an evil power identified with Adonai the Jewish god, in Mandaean thought.

Shem Son of Noah and legendary father of Semites. Referred to in the Revelation of Adam (as Sem) and the Paraphrase of Shem (as Seem).

Shi'a "Party" of Ali, Shi'ites, within Islam. Shi'ites look for leadership in the Islamic community to come from the descendants of prophet Muhammad, who are legitimated by Allah.

Shkina Heavenly home, eternal realm, aeon of uthras and light beings, in Mandaean thought. Shkina derives from *shekhinah*, Hebrew for "dwelling, presence, glory."

Silence Expression of the transcendence of the divine in mystical traditions. In the Secret Book of John, for instance, the divine invisible spirit is said to be ineffable, "dwelling in silence, at rest, before everything." Silence is an aeon in the Valentinian pleroma.

Simon Magus First-century Samaritan religious teacher claimed by heresiologists to be the founder of gnosticism. Simon Magus seems to have designated himself the great power of god, and he associated with a woman named Helena, whom he called first thought. He is portrayed as a mere magician in the Acts of the Apostles and the Acts of Peter.

Simon of Cyrene In the New Testament gospels, Simon of Cyrene carried the cross of Jesus to the place of crucifixion. In the Second Treatise of the Great Seth, Simon is also said to have carried the cross, and "another" (either Simon or the body that Jesus adopted) was crucified instead of Jesus. According to Irenaeus of Lyon, Basilides taught that Simon of Cyrene was mistakenly crucified in place of Jesus. According to the Qur'an, sura 4, Jesus only appeared to be crucified, and another may have been crucified instead.

Sin Moon, an evil power, in Mandaean thought.

Siniawis Underworld, in Mandaean thought. *See* HADES.

Sitil Heavenly Seth, a messenger of light, in Mandaean thought.

Six Number of incompleteness, used as a numerical symbol for matter in Herakleon's Commentary on John.

Sodom City near the Dead Sea. In Genesis Sodom is punished for wickedness with destruction by fire and brimstone. In the Paraphrase of Shem Sodom is praised for its gnostic inhabitants.

Soldas Demon in the Paraphrase of Shem, referred to along with another demon. May be identified with Jesus, otherwise with John the baptizer. In the text Soldas may be crucified by the power of nature. See Roberge, *La Paraphrase de Sem*, 87–89, and Wisse, "Paraphrase of Shem," 88.

Solomon Son of David and king of Israel, of legendary wisdom. A text titled the Book of Solomon is referred to in On the Origin of the World. While the identity of this text remains unknown, several known texts are attributed to Solomon, including (in addition to the biblical texts Ecclesiastes and Song of Songs) the Testament of Solomon, which discusses how Solomon built the temple with the help of demons.

Son of man *See* HUMAN CHILD.

Sophaia Power invoked in the Paraphrase of Shem. Perhaps *see* SOPHIA.

Sophia Divine wisdom, personified, who falls from glory and is restored in gnostic myths. In Valentinian texts she is said to be manifested in higher wisdom (Sophia) and lower wisdom (Achamoth; *see also* ECHAMOTH and ECHMOTH).

Spirit *See* INVISIBLE SPIRIT, PNEUMA.

Stele Ancient monument in the form of a tablet, often with an inscription, well known in the world of the Middle East. In gnostic texts steles are sometimes thought to be sources of revelation preserved from antiquity. Referred to in Three Steles of Seth, the Discourse on the Eighth and the Ninth, and possibly the Revelation of Adam.

Sumeru mountain Central mountain of the universe in Buddhist cosmology, referred to in the Great Song to Mani.

Sun Ship of the day, a cosmic vehicle to help transport the light on its way back to the kingdom of light, in Manichaean thought. *See also* SHAMISH.

Suwa One of the idol gods in the Qur'an, a name for Azazi'il in the Mother of Books.

Syzygos Partner or companion, especially in a heavenly syzygy or union of a pair of aeons in the pleroma.

Tartaros Hades, the underworld, the realm of the dead. Often Tartaros is the lower realm of Hades, hence hell, the place of punishment.

Tartarouchos "Controller of Hades," ruler of Tartaros. Referred to in the Book of Thomas.

Tat From Thoth, Egyptian god of wisdom and divine scribe. Tat is described as an initiate and student in Hermetic texts.

Telmachael Telmachael Eli Eli Machar Machar Seth Name or epithet of heavenly Seth in the Gospel of the Egyptians.

Theogony Account of the creation of the gods and goddesses.

Theona Female martyr referred to, along with Mary and others, in the Coptic Manichaean Songbook. The name Theona may derive from a form of the Greek word *theos*, "god," or a related word.

Thomas Aramaic or Syriac for "twin"; compare Didymos, Greek for "twin." Nickname for Judas, brother of Jesus, thought by Syrians to be the twin brother of Jesus, the compiler of Gospel of Thomas, and a collaborator in the Book of Thomas.

Those people Phrase apparently designating gnostics, the seed of Seth, in the Revelation of Adam.

Three hundred sixty-five Number of days in the solar year, and the numerical value of the name Abrasax. In the Secret Book of John three hundred sixty-five angels assemble the body of Adam.

Tibil Earth, physical world, in Mandaean thought.

Tomb The body is the prison or tomb of the soul according to a platonic and Orphic teaching reflected in gnostic texts.

Torah Hebrew for "instruction," the Jewish law.

Triple male *See* MALE.

Trismegistos Greek for "thrice greatest." Superlative epithet of Hermes in hermetic texts.

Twelve Number of signs of the zodiac, and so the number of cosmic authorities produced by the demiurge in the Secret Book of John. Also the number of tribes of Israel, and the number of students (disciples) and messengers (apostles) of Jesus in the early church.

Twin Gnostic texts include various references to a twin. Judas Thomas is the twin brother of Jesus in the Gospel of Thomas and the Book of Thomas. The angel who appears to Mani and gives revelation as his heavenly double is called the twin. Behind such references may be the conviction that one's divine counterpart is the twin, alter ego, or true self that one knows when one knows oneself in gnostic thought.

Umm al-kitab Arabic for "Mother of Books," a text of mystical, gnosticizing ghuluw.

Uthra Any of the light beings who are forces for good and inhabitants of the realm of light or the pleroma in Mandaean thought.

Veil A veil separates the world within the pleroma from the world outside, in the Gospel of Philip and On the Origin of the World. *See* LIMIT. The veil also refers to the curtain that separates the holy of holies from the holy place in the Jewish temple.

Vine Grapevine, the plant of Dionysos, the Greek god of fertility, ecstasy, and wine, linked to Eros in On the Origin of the World.

Virgo "Virgin," constellation referred to in the Discourse on the Eighth and the Ninth.

Wisdom *See* SOPHIA.

Word *See* LOGOS.

Yahweh YHWH, the ineffable name of god in Hebrew. Yahweh is the child of Eve and the demiurge in the Secret Book of John.

Yaldabaoth Demiurge or creator of this world, especially in Sethian texts. The name probably means "child of chaos" or "child of (S)abaoth" in Aramaic. See Layton, *Gnostic Scriptures*, 74–75; Scholem, *Jewish Gnosticism, Merkabah Mysticism, and Talmudic Tradition*, 71–72. Also called Sakla, Samael.

Yao A form of Yahweh, especially in Greek. Yao is a power of this world in some gnostic texts and a son of Yaldabaoth in On the Origin of the World.

Yatim Class of angels in the Mother of Books. The two Yatim ("orphans" or "single ones") mentioned there may be Miqdad and Abu Zarr/Abu Dharr.

Yeshua Aramaic for Jesus.

Yoel Heavenly dignitary and luminary connected to Sethian baptism in the Gospel of the Egyptians.

Zeus Father god and the ruler of Olympian deities in Greek mythology. Referred to in the Book of Baruch and the Naassene Sermon.

Ziwa "Radiant," a common epithet of beings of light, for example, Adakas-Ziwa, in Mandaean sources.

Zoe Greek for "life," the name of Eve in some traditions. Zoe is the enlightened afterthought hidden within Adam in the Secret Book of John, the daughter of Pistis Sophia in the Reality of the Rulers, and one of the aeons in the Valentinian pleroma. *See* AFTERTHOUGHT.

Zohar Sefer ha-Zohar, "Book of Splendor," Jewish mystical text of Kabbalah.

Zoroaster Prophet of Zoroastrianism, referred to in the Secret Book of John and other gnostic texts. In Manichaean texts Zoroaster is said to be a Manichaean prophet.

Zostrianos Traditional grandfather or uncle of Zoroaster. Referred to in the text titled Zostrianos.

Zurvan God of infinite time in Zoroastrianism, sometimes identified with the father of greatness in Manichaean sources. *See* AEON.

BIBLIOGRAPHY

FURTHER READING

Please see "Sources Cited" for full facts of publication regarding the works in this section.

Gnosticism, Gnostics, and *The Gnostic Bible*

Ugo Bianchi, ed., *Le origini dello gnosticismo*; Ioan Culianu, "The Gnostic Revenge"; Ioan Culianu, *The Tree of Gnosis*; Werner Foerster, ed., *Gnosis*; Harry Y. Gamble, *The New Testament Canon*; Robert M. Grant, *Gnosticism*; Robert Haardt, ed., *Gnosis*; Adolph von Harnack, *Marcion*; Hans Jonas, *The Gnostic Religion*; Hans Jonas, *Gnosis und spätantiker Geist*; Karen L. King, *What Is Gnosticism?*; Bentley Layton, *The Gnostic Scriptures*; Gerd Lüdemann and Martina Janssen, *Bibel der Häretiker*; Bruce M. Metzger, *The Canon of the New Testament*; Elaine H. Pagels, *Beyond Belief*; Elaine H. Pagels, *The Gnostic Gospels*; Birger A. Pearson, *Gnosticism, Judaism, and Egyptian Christianity*; Pheme Perkins, *Gnosticism and the New Testament*; James M. Robinson, "Nag Hammadi: The First Fifty Years"; James M. Robinson, ed., *The Nag Hammadi Library in English*; Kurt Rudolph, *Gnosis*; Hans-Martin Schenke, Hans-Gebhard Bethge, and Ursula Ulrike Kaiser, eds., *Nag Hammadi Deutsch*; Wilhelm Schneemelcher, ed., *New Testament Apocrypha*; Walter Schmithals, *Gnosticism in Corinth*; David M. Scholer, comp., *Nag Hammadi Bibliography, 1948–1969*; David M. Scholer, comp., *Nag Hammadi Bibliography, 1970–1994*; Alan F. Segal, *Two Powers in Heaven*; Jonathan Z. Smith, *Drudgery Divine*; Michael A. Williams, *Rethinking "Gnosticism."* For a very helpful and accessible collection of texts written by gnostics, mystics, apocalypicists, Kabbalists, and other creative religious people, see Willis Barnstone, ed., *The Other Bible*.

The Gnostic Bible and Literary Translation

Willis Barnstone, ed., *The Other Bible*; Willis Barnstone, *Poetics of Translation*; Geddes MacGregor, *Literary History of the Bible from the Middle Ages to the Present Day*; J. F. Mozley, *William Tyndale*; George Steiner, *After Babel*.

Part One: Early Wisdom Gospels

Jon Ma. Asgeirsson, Kristin DeTroyer, and Marvin W. Meyer, eds., *From Quest to Q*; John Dominic Crossan, *The Historical Jesus*; Stevan Davies, *The Gospel of Thomas and Christian Wisdom*; Robert W. Funk, *Honest to Jesus*; Ronald F. Hock and Edward N. O'Neil, *The Chreia in Ancient Rhetoric*; John S. Kloppenborg, *The Formation of Q*; John S. Kloppenborg, *Q Parallels*; John S. Kloppenborg, Marvin W. Meyer, Stephen J. Patterson, and Michael G. Steinhauser, *Q—Thomas Reader*; John S. Kloppenborg-Verbin, *Excavating Q*; Burton L. Mack, *Logos und Sophia*; Burton L. Mack, *The Lost Gospel*; Marvin Meyer, *The Unknown Sayings of Jesus*; Stephen J. Patterson, James M. Robinson, and Hans-Gebhard Bethge, *The Fifth Gospel*; James R. Pritchard, ed., *Ancient Near Eastern Texts*; James M. Robinson, Paul Hoffman, and John S. Kloppenborg, eds., *The Critical Edition of Q*; James M. Robinson and Helmut Koester, *Trajectories through Early Christianity*; Albert Schweitzer, *The Quest of the Historical Jesus*.

1. The Gospel of Thomas

Critical editions of the Gospel of Thomas, with introduction, Coptic text, English translation, and notes: Marvin Meyer, *The Gospel of Thomas*; Helmut Koester, Bentley Layton, Thomas O. Lambdin, and Harold W. Attridge, "The Gospel According to Thomas," in Bentley Layton, ed., *Nag Hammadi Codex II, 2–7*, 1.37–128. The latter volume also includes the Greek fragments of the Gospel of Thomas, Papyrus Oxyrhynchus 1, 654, and 655, along with testimonies in the church fathers. English translation: Helmut Koester and Thomas O. Lambdin, "The Gospel of Thomas," in James M. Robinson, ed., *The Nag Hammadi Library In English*. Scholarly studies: Stevan Davies, *The Gospel of Thomas and Christian Wisdom*; Marvin Meyer, *Secret Gospels*; Stephen J. Patterson, *The Gospel of Thomas and Jesus*; Richard Valantasis, *The Gospel of Thomas*. The Gospel of Thomas has also attracted a great deal of popular interest, and it was portrayed as a significant and suppressed collection of sayings of Jesus in the film *Stigmata*.

2. The Gospel of John

The books and articles published on the Gospel of John are legion. Representative scholarly studies: Raymond E. Brown, *The Gospel According to John*; Rudolf Bultmann, *The Gospel of John*; Ernst Käsemann, *The Testament of Jesus*. Each of these important books includes significant reflections on the question of the Gospel of John and gnosticism. Raymond Brown's commentary is a comprehensive, two-volume work with excellent, balanced surveys of the literature and discussions of the issues.

Part Two: Literature of Gnostic Wisdom

Willis Barnstone, ed., *The Other Bible*; Walter Bauer, *Orthodoxy and Heresy in Earliest Christianity*; Robert M. Grant, *Gnosticism and Early Christianity*; Charles W. Hedrick and Robert Hodgson, Jr., eds., *Nag Hammadi, Gnosticism, and Early Christianity*; Hans Jonas, *The Gnostic Religion*; A. F. J. Klijn, *Seth in Jewish, Christian, and Gnostic Literature*; Bentley Layton, *The Gnostic Scriptures*; Bentley Layton, *The Rediscovery of Gnosticism*; Elaine H. Pagels, *The Gnostic Paul*; Elaine H. Pagels, *The Johannine Gospel in Gnostic Exegesis*; James M. Robinson, ed., *The Nag Hammadi Library in English*; James M. Robinson and Helmut Koester, *Trajectories through Early Christianity*; Kurt Rudolph, *Gnosis*; Francois Sagnard, *La Gnose valentinienne et le témoignage de Saint Irénée*; Hans-Martin Schenke, "Das sethianische System nach Nag-Hammadi-Handschriften"; Hans-Martin Schenke, "The Problem of Gnosis"; Hans-Martin Schenke, Hans-Gebhard Bethge, and Ursula Ulrike Kaiser, eds., *Nag Hammadi Deutsch*; Jonathan Z. Smith, *Drudgery Divine*; G. C. Stead, "The Valentinian Myth of Sophia"; Gedaliahu A. G. Stroumsa, *Another Seed*; John D. Turner, "Sethian Gnosticism: A Literary History"; John D. Turner, *Sethian Gnosticism and the Platonic Tradition*; Michael A. Williams, *The Immovable Race*; Michael A. Williams, *Rethinking "Gnosticism."*

3. The Book of Baruch

Critical editions of the Book of Baruch, in Hippolytus of Rome, *Refutation of All Heresies*: Miroslav Marcovich, ed., *Hippolyti refutationis omnium haeresium librorum decem quae supersunt*; Paul Wendland, ed., *Refutatio omnium haeresium*. English translations: Robert M. Grant, *Gnosticism*, 94–100; Robert M. Grant, "Baruch by Justin," in Willis Barnstone, ed., *The Other Bible*, 637–47; Robert Haardt, ed., *Gnosis*, 108–16. Scholarly studies: Robert M. Grant, *Gnosticism and Early Christianity*; Ernst Haenchen, "The Book Baruch," in Werner Foerster, ed., *Gnosis*, 1.48–58, as well as his article under the same title; Michael A. Williams, *Rethinking "Gnosticism,"* 18–23.

4. The Secret Book of John

Critical edition of the Secret Book of John, with introduction, Coptic text, English translation, and notes: Michael Waldstein and Frederik Wisse, eds., *The Apocryphon of John*. English translation: Frederik Wisse, "The Apocryphon of John," in James M. Robinson, ed., *The Nag Hammadi Library in English*. Scholarly studies: Karen L. King, "The Apocryphon of John: Part II of the Gospel of John?"; Karen L. King, "Sophia and Christ in the Apocryphon of John"; Bentley Layton, *The Gnostic Scriptures*, 23–51; Michel Tardieu, *Écrits gnostiques: Codex de Berlin*. The volume by Michael Waldstein and Frederik Wisse contains a lengthy bibliography.

5. The Reality of the Rulers

Critical edition of the Reality of the Rulers, with introduction, Coptic text, English translation, and notes: Roger A. Bullard and Bentley Layton, "The Hypostasis of the Archons," in Bentley Layton, ed., *Nag Hammadi Codices II, 2–7*, 1.219–59. English translation: Bentley Layton, "The Hypostasis of the Archons," in James M. Robinson, ed., *The Nag Hammadi Library in English*. Scholarly studies: Bernard Barc and Michel Roberge, eds., *L'Hypostase des archontes*; Roger A. Bullard, *The Hypostasis of the Archons*; Francis T. Fallon, *The Enthronement of Sabaoth*; Bentley Layton, "*The Hypostasis of the Archons*; or, *The Reality of the Rulers*"; Bentley Layton, *The Gnostic Scriptures*, 68–76.

6. The Revelation of Adam

Critical edition of the Revelation of Adam, with introduction, Coptic text, English translation, and notes: George W. MacRae, "The Apocalypse of Adam," in Douglas M. Parrott, ed., *Nag Hammadi Codices V, 2–5 and VI*, 151–95. English translation: George W. MacRae, "The Apocalypse of Adam," in James M. Robinson, ed., *The Nag Hammadi Library in English*. Scholarly studies: Charles W. Hedrick, "The Apocalypse of Adam"; Bentley Layton, *The Gnostic Scriptures*, 52–64; Françoise Morard, *L'Apocalypse d'Adam*.

7. Three Forms of First Thought

Critical edition of Three Forms of First Thought, with introduction, Coptic text, English translation, and notes: John D. Turner, "Trimorphic Protennoia," in Charles W. Hedrick, ed., *Nag Hammadi Codices XI, XII, and XIII*, 371–454. English translation: John D. Turner, "Trimorphic Protennoia," in James M. Robinson, ed., *The Nag Hammadi Library in English*. Scholarly studies: Yvonne Janssens, *La Prôtennoia trimorphe*; Bentley Layton, *The Gnostic Scriptures*, 86–100; James M. Robinson, "Sethians and Johannine Thought: The Trimorphic Protennoia and the Prologue of the Gospel of John."

8. The Three Steles of Seth

Critical edition of the Three Steles of Seth, with introduction, Coptic text, English translation, and notes: James E. Goehring and James M. Robinson, "The Three Steles of Seth," in Birger A. Pearson, ed., *Nag Hammadi Codex VII*, 371–421. English translation: Goehring and Robinson, "The Three Steles of Seth," in Robinson, ed., *The Nag Hammadi Library in English*. Scholarly studies: Paul Claude, *Les trois stèles de Seth*; Bentley Layton, *The Gnostic Scriptures*, 149–58; Konrad Wekel, "Die drei Stelen des Seth."

9. The Vision of the Foreigner

Critical edition of the Foreigner, with introduction, Coptic text, English translation, and notes: Antoinette Clark Wire, John D. Turner, and Orval S. Wintermute, "Allogenes," in Charles W. Hedrick, ed., *Nag Hammadi Codices XI, XII, and XIII*, 173–267. English translation: Antoinette Clark Wire, John D. Turner, and Orval S. Wintermute, "Allogenes," in James M. Robinson, ed., *The Nag Hammadi Library in English*. Scholarly studies: Karen L. King, *Revelation of the Unknowable God*; Bentley Layton, *The Gnostic Scriptures*, 141–48.

10. The Sermon of Zostrianos

Critical edition of Zostrianos, with introduction, Coptic text, English translation, and notes: Bentley Layton and John H. Sieber, "Zostrianos," in Sieber, ed., *Nag Hammadi Codex VIII*, 7–232. English translation: John H. Sieber, "Zostrianos," in James M. Robinson, ed., *The Nag Hammadi Library in English*. Scholarly studies: Catherine Barry, Wolf-Peter Funk, Paul-Hubert Poirier, and John D. Turner, eds., *Zostrien*; Bentley Layton, *The Gnostic Scriptures*, 121–40; John H. Sieber, "The Barbelo Aeon as Sophia in Zostrianos and Related Tractates."

11. The Baptismal Ceremony of the Gospel of the Egyptians

Critical edition of the Gospel of the Egyptians, with introduction, Coptic text, English translation, and notes: Alexander Böhlig and Frederik Wisse, eds., *Nag Hammadi Codices III,2 and IV,2*. English translation: Böhlig and Wisse, "The Gospel of the Egyptians," in James M. Robinson, ed., *The Nag Hammadi Library in English*. Scholarly study: Bentley Layton, *The Gnostic Scriptures*, 101–20.

12. Thunder

Critical edition of Thunder, with introduction, Coptic text, English translation, and notes: George W. MacRae, "The Thunder: Perfect Mind," in Douglas M. Parrott, ed., *Nag Hammadi Codices V,2–5 and VI*, 231–55. English translation: George W. MacRae, "The Thunder, Perfect Mind," in Willis Barnstone, ed., *The Other Bible*, 595–609; George W. MacRae, "The Thunder: Perfect Mind," in James M. Robinson, ed., *The Nag Hammadi Library in English*. Scholarly studies: Hans-Gebhard Bethge, "'Nebront'"; Bentley Layton, *The Gnostic Scriptures*, 77–85.

13. The Letter of Peter to Philip

Critical editions of the Letter of Peter to Philip, with introduction, Coptic text, English translation, and notes: Marvin Meyer, *The Letter of Peter to Philip*; Marvin Meyer and Frederik Wisse, "Letter of Peter to Philip," in John H. Sieber, ed., *Nag Hammadi Codex VIII*, 227–51. English translation: Meyer and Wisse, "The Letter of Peter to Philip," in James M. Robinson, ed., *The Nag Hammadi Library in English.* Scholarly studies: Hans-Gebhard Bethge, *Der Brief des Petrus an Philippus*; Hans-Gebhard Bethge, "The Letter of Peter to Philip," in Wilhelm Schneemelcher, ed., *New Testament Apocrypha*, 1.342–53; and Jacques-É. Ménard, *La Lettre de Pierre à Philippe.*

14. The Gospel of Truth

Critical edition of the Gospel of Truth, with introduction, Coptic text, English translation, and notes: Harold W. Attridge and George W. MacRae, "The Gospel of Truth," in Harold W. Attridge, ed., *Nag Hammadi Codex I*, 1.55–122, 2.39–135. English translation: Harold W. Attridge and George W. MacRae, "The Gospel of Truth," in James M. Robinson, ed., *The Nag Hammadi Library in English*; Robert M. Grant, "The Gospels of Truth," in Willis Barnstone, ed., *The Other Bible*, 286–96; Scholarly studies: Kendrick Grobel, "The Gospel of Truth"; Bentley Layton, *The Gnostic Scriptures*, 250–64; Jacques-É. Ménard, "L'Évangile de vérité"; Hans-Martin Schenke, "Die Herkunft des sogennanten Evangelium Veritatis."

15. The Gospel of Philip

Critical edition of the Gospel of Philip, with introduction, Coptic text, English translation, and notes: Wesley W. Isenberg and Bentley Layton, "The Gospel According to Philip," in Bentley Layton, ed., *Nag Hammadi Codex II,2–7*, 1.129–217. English translation: Wesley W. Isenberg, "The Gospel of Philip," in Willis Barnstone, ed., *The Other Bible*, 87–100; Wesley W. Isenberg, "The Gospel According to Philip," in James M. Robinson, ed., *The Nag Hammadi Library in English*. Scholarly studies: Bentley Layton, *The Gnostic Scriptures*, 325–53; Jacques-É. Ménard, *L'Évangile selon Philippe*; Hans-Martin Schenke, "The Gospel of Philip," in Wilhelm Schneemelcher, ed., *New Testament Apocrypha*, 1.179–208; Walter C. Till, *Das Evangelium nach Philippos*; R. McL. Wilson, *The Gospel of Philip*. The study by Hans-Martin Schenke includes good bibliographical entries.

16. The Letter to Flora

Critical edition of Ptolemy's Letter to Flora: Gilles Quispel, ed., *Ptolémée, Lettre à Flora*. English translation: Robert M. Grant, *Gnosticism*, 184–90. Scholarly study, with English translation: Bentley Layton, *The Gnostic Scriptures*, 306–15.

17. Commentary on the Gospel of John

Critical editions of the fragmentary sections from Herakleon, preserved in Origen's Commentary on the Gospel of John and Clement of Alexandria's Miscellanies: A. E. Brooke, ed., *The Fragments of Heracleon*; W. Völker, ed., *Quellen zur Geschichte der christlichen Gnosis*. English translation: Robert M. Grant, *Gnosticism*, 195–208. Scholarly studies: Werner Foerster, ed., *Gnosis*, 1.162–83; Elaine H. Pagels, *The Johannine Gospel in Gnostic Exegesis*. Related to Herakleon's

Commentary on John is the work of the Valentinian Theodotos, whose writings survive in fragments: critical edition, R. P. Casey, ed., *The Excerpta ex Theodoto of Clement of Alexandria.*

18. The Treatise on Resurrection

Critical edition of the Treatise on Resurrection, with introduction, Coptic text, English translation, and notes: Malcolm L. Peel, "The Treatise on the Resurrection," in Harold W. Attridge, ed., *Nag Hammadi Codex I,* 1.123–57, 2.137–215. English translation: Malcolm L. Peel, "The Treatise on the Resurrection," in James M. Robinson, ed., *The Nag Hammadi Library in English.* Scholarly studies: Bentley Layton, *The Gnostic Scriptures,* 316–19; Bentley Layton, *The Gnostic Treatise on Resurrection;* Jacques-É. Ménard, *Le Traité sur la résurrection.*

19. The Prayer of the Messenger Paul

Critical edition of the Prayer of the Messenger Paul, with introduction, Coptic text, English translation, and notes: Dieter Mueller, "The Prayer of the Apostle Paul," in Harold W. Attridge, ed., *Nag Hammadi Codex I,* 1.5–11, 2.1–5. English translation: Mueller, "The Prayer of the Apostle Paul," in James M. Robinson, ed., *The Nag Hammadi Library in English.* Scholarly study: Bentley Layton, *The Gnostic Scriptures,* 303–5.

20. Valentinian Liturgical Readings

Critical edition of the Valentinian Liturgical Readings, with introduction, Coptic text, English translation, and notes: John D. Turner, "On the Anointing," "On Baptism A," "On Baptism B," "On the Eucharist A," "On the Eucharist B," in Charles W. Hedrick, ed., *Nag Hammadi Codices XI, XII, and XIII,* 94–95, 142–51, 170–72. English translation: John D. Turner, "On the Anointing," "On Baptism A," "On Baptism B," "On the Eucharist A," "On the Eucharist B," in James M. Robinson, ed., *The Nag Hammadi Library in English.*

21. The Secret Book of James

Critical edition of the Secret Book of James, with introduction, Coptic text, English translation, and notes: Francis E. Williams, "The Apocryphon of James," in Harold W. Attridge, ed., *Nag Hammadi Codex I,* 1.13–53, 2.7–37. English translation: Ron Cameron, "The Apocryphon of James," in Ron Cameron, *The Other Gospels,* 55–64; Ron Cameron, "The Apocryphon of James," in Willis Barnstone, ed., *The Other Bible,* 543–49; Francis E. Williams, "The Apocryphon of James," in James M. Robinson, ed., *The Nag Hammadi Library in English.* Scholarly studies: Ron Cameron, *Sayings Traditions in the Apocryphon of James;* Dankwart Kirchner, "The Apocryphon of James," in Wilhelm Schneemelcher, ed., *New Testament Apocrypha,* 1.285–99; Donald Rouleau, *L'Épître apocryphe de Jacques.*

22. The Round Dance of the Cross

Critical edition of the Round Dance of the Cross, in the Acts of John: Eric Junod and Jean-Daniel Kaestli, *Acta Johannis*. Scholarly studies: Arthur J. Dewey, "The Hymn in the Acts of John"; Knut Schäferdiek, "The Acts of John," in Wilhelm Schneemelcher, ed., *New Testament Apocrypha*, 2.152–212.

23. The Songs of Solomon

Editions of the Songs of Solomon: Rendel Harris and Alphonse Mingana, *The Odes and Psalms of Solomon*; English translation: Willis Barnstone, ed., *The Other Bible*, 275–85; James H. Charlesworth, *The Odes of Solomon*. Scholarly studies: James H. Charlesworth, *Critical Reflections on the Odes of Solomon*; Gerald R. Blaszcak, *A Formcritical Study of Selected Odes of Solomon*.

24. The Song of the Pearl

Translations and scholarly studies of the Song of the Pearl: Günther Bornkamm, "The Acts of Thomas," in Edgar Hennecke and Wilhelm Schneemelcher, eds., *New Testament Apocrypha*, 2.498–504; English translation: Willis Barnstone, "The Hymn of the Pearl," in Willis Barnstone, ed., *The Other Bible*, 299–307; Han J. W. Drijvers, "The Acts of Thomas," in Wilhelm Schneemelcher, ed., *New Testament Apocrypha*, 2.380–85; Robert M. Grant, *Gnosticism*, 116–22; Bentley Layton, *The Gnostic Scriptures*, 371–75. Layton's book includes additional bibliography.

25. The Book of Thomas

Critical edition of the Book of Thomas, with introduction, Coptic text, English translation, and notes: John D. Turner and Bentley Layton, "The Book of Thomas the Contender Writing to the Perfect," in Bentley Layton, ed., *Nag Hammadi Codex II,2–7*, 2.171–205. English translation: John D. Turner, "The Book of Thomas the Contender," in James M. Robinson, ed., *The Nag Hammadi Library in English*. Scholarly studies: Raymond Kuntzmann, *Le Livre de Thomas*; Hans-Martin Schenke, "The Book of Thomas," in Wilhelm Schneemelcher, ed., *New Testament Apocrypha*, 1.232–40; John D. Turner, *The Book of Thomas the Contender*.

26. The Exegesis on the Soul

Critical edition of the Exegesis on the Soul, with introduction, Coptic text, English translation, and notes: William C. Robinson, Jr., and Bentley Layton, "The Expository Treatise on the Soul," in Bentley Layton, ed., *Nag Hammadi Codex II,2–7*, 2.135–69. English translation: William C. Robinson, Jr., and Maddalena Scopello, "The Exegesis on the Soul," in James M. Robinson, ed., *The Nag Hammadi Library in English*. Scholarly studies: Hedda Bethge, ed., "Die Exegese über die Seele";

Frederik Wisse, "On Exegeting the Exegesis on the Soul"; Scopello, *L'Exégèse de l'âme*, with introduction, French translation, and commentary.

27. On the Origin of the World

Critical edition of the text On the Origin of the World, with introduction, Coptic text, English translation, notes, and presentation of the British Library and Nag Hammadi library fragments: Hans-Gebhard Bethge, Bentley Layton, and Societas Coptica Hierosolymitana, "On the Origin of the World," in Layton, ed., *Nag Hammadi Codex II,2–7*, 2.11–134. English translation: Bethge, Layton, and Societas Coptica Hierosolymitana, "On the Origin of the World," in James M. Robinson, ed., *The Nag Hammadi Library in English*. Scholarly studies: Hans-Martin Schenke, "Vom Ursprung der Welt"; Michel Tardieu, *Trois mythes gnostiques*; Michael A. Williams, *Rethinking "Gnosticism."* Hans-Gebhard Bethge, who has collaborated on the English scholarly edition and whose comments are quoted, has done his doctoral dissertation on this text ("Vom Ursprung der Welt").

28. The Paraphrase of Shem

Critical edition of the Paraphrase of Shem, with introduction, Coptic text, English translation, and notes: Frederik Wisse, "The Paraphrase of Shem," in Birger A. Pearson, ed., *Nag Hammadi Codex VII*, 15–127. English translation: Michel Roberge and Frederik Wisse, "The Paraphrase of Shem," in James M. Robinson, ed., *The Nag Hammadi Library in English*. Scholarly studies: Michel Roberge, "Anthrogonie et anthropologie dans le Paraphrase de Sem"; Michel Roberge, *Le Paraphrase de Sem*.

29. The Second Treatise of the Great Seth

Critical edition of the Second Treatise of the Great Seth, with introduction, Coptic text, English translation, and notes: Gregory Riley, "The Second Treatise of the Great Seth," in Birger A. Pearson, ed., *Nag Hammadi Codex VII*, 129–99. English translation: Roger A. Bullard and Joseph A. Gibbons, "The Second Treatise of the Great Seth," in James M. Robinson, ed., *The Nag Hammadi Library in English*. Scholarly studies: Hans-Gebhard Bethge, "Zweite Logos des grossen Seth"; Louis Painchaud, *Le Deuxième Traité du Grand Seth*.

30. The Gospel of Mary

Critical edition of the Gospel of Mary, with introduction, Coptic text, English translation, and notes: George W. MacRae and R. McL. Wilson, "The Gospel of Mary," in Douglas M. Parrott, ed., *Nag Hammadi Codices V, 2–5 and VI*, 453–71. English translation: Karen L. King, MacRae, and Wilson, "The Gospel of Mary," in

James M. Robinson, ed., *The Nag Hammadi Library in English*. Another English translation, with introduction and notes: King, "The Gospel of Mary," in Robert J. Miller, ed., *The Complete Gospels*, 351–60.

31. The Naassene Sermon

Critical editions of the Naassene Sermon, in Hippolytus of Rome, *Refutation of All Heresies*: Miroslav Marcovich, ed., *Hippolyti refutationis omnium haeresium librorum decem quae supersunt*; Paul Wendland, ed., *Refutatio omnium haeresium*. Translations: Robert M. Grant, *Gnosticism*, 105–15; Robert Haardt, ed., *Gnosis*, 99–100; Revision: Willis Barnstone, "Naassene Psalm," in Willis Barnstone, ed., *The Other Bible*, 635–36. Scholarly studies: Werner Foerster, ed., *Gnosis*, vol. 1; Josef Frickel, *Hellenistische Erlösung in christlicher Deutung: Die Naassenerschrift*; Marvin Meyer, *The Ancient Mysteries*.

Part Three: Hermetic Literature

A. J. Festugière, *La Révélation d'Hermès Trismégiste*; Hans Jonas, *The Gnostic Religion*; H.D., *Trilogy*; Bentley Layton, *The Gnostic Scriptures*; Jean-Pierre Mahé, *Hermès en Haute-Égypte*; Arthur Darby Nock and A. J. Festugière, eds., *Corpus Hermeticum*; Birger Pearson, "Jewish Elements in *Corpus Hermeticum I (Poimandres)*."

32. Poimandres

Translations and scholarly studies of Poimandres: A. J. Festugière, *La Révélation d'Hermès Trismégiste*; Bentley Layton, *The Gnostic Scriptures*; Arthur Darby Nock and A. J. Festugière, eds., *Corpus Hermeticum*. English translation: Willis Barnstone, "Poimandres," in Willis Barnstone, ed., *The Other Bible*, 567–74.

33. The Discourse on the Eighth and Ninth

Critical edition of the Discourse on the Eighth and Ninth, with introduction, Coptic text, English translation, and notes: Peter A. Dirkse, James Brashler, and Douglas M. Parrott, "The Discourse on the Eighth and Ninth," in Douglas M. Parrott, ed., *Nag Hammadi Codices V, 2–5 and VI*, 341–73. English translation: Brashler, Dirkse, and Parrott, "The Discourse on the Eighth and Ninth," in James M. Robinson, ed., *The Nag Hammadi Library in English*. Scholarly studies: Jean-Pierre Mahé, *Hermès en Haute-Égypte*, vol. 1; Karl-Wolfgang Tröger, "Die sechste und siebte Schrift aus Nag-Hammadi-Codex VI."

34. The Prayer of Thanksgiving

Critical edition of the Prayer of Thanksgiving, with introduction, Coptic text, English translation, and notes: Peter A. Dirkse and James Brashler, "The Prayer of

Thanksgiving," in Douglas M. Parrott, ed., *Nag Hammadi Codex V, 2–5 and VI*, 375–87. English translation: Brashler, Dirkse, and Parrott, "The Prayer of Thanksgiving," in James M. Robinson, ed., *The Nag Hammadi Library in English*. Scholarly studies: Jean-Pierre Mahé, *Hermès en Haute-Égypte*, vol. 1; Jean-Pierre Mahé, "La Prière d'actions de grâces du Codex VI de Nag-Hammadi et le discours parfait"; Karl Wolfgang Tröger, "Die sechste und siebte Schrift aus Nag-Hammadi-Codex VI."

Part Four: Mandaean Literature

Jorunn Jacobsen Buckley, *The Scroll of Exalted Kingship (Diwan Malkuta 'Laita)*; Nathaniel Deutsch, *Guardians of the Gate: Angelic Vice Regency in Late Antiquity*; E. S. Drower, *The Canonical Prayerbook of the Mandaeans*; E. S. Drower, *The Haran Gawaita and the Baptism of Hibil-Ziwa*; E. S. Drower, *The Mandaeans of Iraq and Iran*; Werner Foerster, ed., *Gnosis*; E. S. Drower, *The Secret Adam: A Study of Nasoraean Gnosis*; S. Gündüz, *The Knowledge of Life: The Origins and Early History of the Mandaeans and Their Relation to the Sabians of the Qur'an and to the Harranians*; Mark Lidzbarski, *Ginza: Der Schatz oder das grosse Buch der Mandäer übersetzt und erklärt*; Mark Lidzbarski, *Das Johannesbuch der Mandäer*; Kurt Rudolph, *Die Mandäer I. Prolegomena: Das Mandäerproblem; II. Der Kult*; Kurt Rudolph, *Theogonie, Kosmogonie und Anthropogonie in den mandäischen Schriften*; Georg Widengren, ed., *Der Mandäismus*; Edwin Yamauchi, *Pre-Christian Gnosticism*.

35. The Ginza

English translations of portions of the Ginza: Kurt Rudolph, in Werner Foerster, ed., *Gnosis*, vol. 2; Robert Haardt, ed., *Gnosis*; Werner Foerster, "A Selection of Gnostic Texts," in Willis Barnstone, ed., *The Other Bible*, 692–702. Scholarly study: Mark Lidzbarski, *Ginza*.

36. Hibil's Lament from the Book of John

English translation of Hibil's Lament: Jorunn Jacobsen Buckley, "Professional Fatigue: 'Hibil's Lament' in The Mandaean *Book of John*." Scholarly study: Mark Lidzbarski, *Das Johannesbuch der Mandäer*.

37. Songs from the Mandaean Liturgy

English translations of Songs from the Mandaean Liturgy: Kurt Rudolph, in Werner Foerster, ed., *Gnosis*, vol. 2. Scholarly study: Mark Lidzbarski, *Mandäische Liturgien*.

Part Five: Manichaean Literature

C. R. C. Allberry, ed., *Manichaean Manuscripts in the Chester Beatty Collection*, vol. 2, *A Manichaean Psalm-Book*, Part II; Willis Barnstone, "Mani and Manichaeism," in Willis Barnstone, ed., *The Other Bible*, 669–74; Ferdinand Christian Baur, *Das manichäische Religionssystem*; Isaac de Beausobre, *Histoire critique de Manichée et du manichéisme*; Jason BeDuhn, *The Manichaean Body*; Geng Shimin, "Recent Studies on Manichaeism in China"; Hans-Joachim Klimkeit, *Gnosis on the Silk Road*; Ludwig Koenen and Cornelia Römer, eds., *Der Kölner Mani-Kodex*; S. N. C. Lieu, *Manichaeism in the Later Roman Empire and Medieval China: A Historical Survey*; Lin Wu-shu , *Manichaeism and Its Spread to the East* (in Chinese; English review by P. Bryder in *Manichaean Studies Newsletter* 1 [1989]: 15–19); Lin Wu-shu, "A New Find of [a] Manichaean Stone Carving in Fujian, China"; Lin Wu-shu, "On the Joining between the Two Fragments of 'The Compendium of the Teachings of Mani, the Buddha of Light'"; Reinhold Merkelbach, *Mani und sein Religionssystem*; Reinhold Merkelbach, "Der manichäische Codex von Tebessa"; Paul A. Mirecki, "The Coptic Manichaean Synaxeis Codex: Descriptive Catalogue of Synaxis Chapter Titles"; H. J. Polotsky, *Manichäische Handschriften der Sammlung A. Chester Beatty*. Band 1. *Manichäische Homilien*; H. J. Polotsky and Alexander Böhlig, *Manichäische Handschriften der staatliche Museen Berlins. Kephalaia*; J. Ries, *Les Études manichéenes: Des Controverses de la Réforme aux découvertes du XXe siècle*; James M. Robinson, "The Fate of the Manichaean Codices of Medinet Madi, 1929–1989"; Carl Schmidt and H. J. Polotsky, "Ein Mani-Fund in Ägypten: Originalschriften des Mani und seiner Schüler."

38. On the Origin of His Body

Critical editions of the text On the Origin of His Body: Albert Henrichs and Ludwig Koenen, eds., "Ein griechischer Mani-Codex"; Ludwig Koenen and Cornelia Römer, eds., *Der Kölner Mani-Kodex*. English translations: Ron Cameron and Arthur J. Dewey, *The Cologne Mani Codex*; Ellen Bradshaw Aitken, "The Cologne Mani Codex." On the Elkesaites: Hans-Joachim Schoeps, *Jewish Christianity*; Hans-Joachim Schoeps, *Theologie und Geschichte des Judenchristentums*.

39. The Story of the Death of Mani

English translations of the Story of the Death of Mani: Jes P. Asmussen, *Manichaean Literature*, 54–58; Jes P. Asmussen, "Mani's Death," in Willis Barnstone, ed., *The Other Bible*, 690–91; W. B. Henning, "Mani's Last Journey," 948–53.

40. The Kephalaia

English translation of the Kephalaia: Iain Gardner, *The Kephalaia of the Teacher*, 77–78, 93–105; Robert Haardt, "The Kephalaia of the Teacher," in Willis Barnstone, ed., *The Other Bible*, 668–69. Scholarly study: H. J. Polotsky and Alexander Böh-lig, *Kephalaia*.

41. The Coptic Manichaean Songbook

English translation of the Coptic Manichaean Songbook: C. R. C. Allberry, *A Manichaean Psalm-Book*. Scholarly study: Torgny Säve-Söderbergh, *Studies in the Coptic Manichaean Psalm-Book*.

42. Parthian Songs

English translation of the Parthian Songs: Jes P. Asmussen, *Manichaean Literature*. Scholarly study: Hans-Joachim Klimkeit, *Gnosis on the Silk Road*, 99–122.

43. The Great Song to Mani

English translation of the Great Song to Mani: Hans-Joachim Klimkeit, *Gnosis on the Silk Road*, 280–84.

Part Six: Islamic Mystical Literature

A. J. Arberry, ed., *The Koran Interpreted*; Michael Asin y Palacios, *Logia et Agrapha Domini Jesu*; Ioan Culianu, "Gnosticisim"; Roderic Dunkerley, *Beyond the Gospels*; Heinz Halm, *Die islamische Gnosis*; Heinz Halm, *Kosmologie and Heilslehre der frühen Isma'iliya*; Joachim Jeremias, *Unknown Sayings of Jesus*; Tarif Khalidi, *The Muslim Jesus*; D. S. Margoliouth, "Christ in Islam"; Marvin Meyer, "Did Jesus Drink from a Cup?"; Marvin Meyer, *The Unknown Sayings of Jesus*; William G. Morrice, *Hidden Sayings of Jesus*; Geoffrey Parrinder, *Jesus in the Qur'an*; James Robson, *Christ in Islam*; James Hardy Ropes, "Agrapha"; Kurt Rudolph, *Gnosis*; Salman Rushdie, *The Satanic Verses*. The passages quoted from al-Ghazali are from Marvin Meyer, *The Unknown Sayings of Jesus*.

44. The Mother of Books

German translation of the Mother of Books: Heinz Halm, *Die islamische Gnosis*.

Part Seven: Cathar Literature

Aliki Barnstone and Willis Barnstone, *A Book of Women Poets from Antiquity to Now*; Aliki Barnstone, *The Shambhala Anthology of Women's Spiritual Poetry*; Meg Bogin, *The Women Troubadours*; René Nelli, *Écritures cathares*; Rayenius Sacconi, *Summa de catharis*; Christine Thouzellier, ed., *Le Livre des deux principes*; Christine Thouzellier, ed., *Rituel cathare latin*.

45. The Gospel of the Secret Supper

French translation of the Gospel of the Great Supper: René Nelli, *Écritures cathares*.

46. The Book of the Two Principles

French translation of the Book of the Two Principles: René Nelli, *Écritures cathares*.

47. A Nun's Sermon

English translation: Willis Barnstone, in Aliki Barnstone, ed., *The Shambhala Book of Women's Spiritual Poetry*, 66.

The Inner Light of Gnosis: A Historical Meditation

Willis Barnstone, *The Other Bible*; Willis Barnstone, *The Poetics of Ecstasy: Studies in Ekstasis from Sappho to Borges*; Willis Barnstone, *The Poems of Saint John of the Cross*; Jean Doresse, *The Secret Books of the Egyptian Gnostics*; Giovanni Filoramo, *A History of Gnosticism*; Robert M. Grant, *Gnosticism and Early Christianity*; Hans Jonas, *The Gnostic Religion*; Karen L. King, *Revelation of the Unknowable God*; Bentley Layton, *The Gnostic Scriptures*; Marvin Meyer, *The Unknown Sayings of Jesus*; Marvin Meyer, *The Gospel of Thomas*; Stuart Holroyd, *The Elements of Gnosticism*; James M. Robinson, ed., *The Nag Hammadi Library in English*; Kurt Rudolph, *Gnosis*; Gershom Scholem, *Jewish Gnosticism, Merkabah Mysticism, and Talmudic Tradition*.

SOURCES CITED

Aitken, Ellen Bradshaw. "The Cologne Mani Codex." In *Religions of Late Antiquity in Practice*, edited by Richard Valantasis, 161–76. Princeton Readings in Religions. Princeton, N.J.: Princeton University Press, 2000.

Allberry, C. R. C. *A Manichaean Psalm-Book*. Stuttgart: W. Kohlhammer, 1938.

———, ed. *Manichaean Manuscripts in the Chester Beatty Collection*. Vol. 2. *A Manichaean Psalm-Book, Part II*. Stuttgart: W. Kohlhammer, 1938.

Arberry, A. J., ed., *The Koran Interpreted*. 2 vol. Spalding Library of Religion. London: Allen & Unwin, 1963.

Asgeirsson, Jon Ma., Kristin De Troyer, and Marvin W. Meyer, eds. *From Quest to Q: Festschrift James M. Robinson*. Leuven, Belgium: Leuven University Press/Peeters, 2000.

Asin y Palacios, Michael. *Logia et agrapha Domini Jesu: Apud moslemicos scriptores, asceticos, praesertim, usitata, collegit, vertit, notis instruxit*. 2 vols. Turnhout, Belgium: Brepols, 1926–74.

Asmussen, Jes P. *Manichaean Literature: Representative Texts Chiefly from Middle Persian and Parthian Writings*. UNESCO Collection of Representative Works: Persian Heritage Series 22. Delmar, N.Y.: Scholars' Facsimiles & Reprints, 1975.

Attridge, Harold W. *Nag Hammadi Codex I*. 2 vols. Nag Hammadi and Manichaean Studies 22–23. Leiden: E. J. Brill, 1985.

Attridge, Harold W., and George W. MacRae. "The Gospel of Truth." In *Nag Hammadi Codex I*, edited by Harold W. Attridge, 1.55–122.

———. "The Gospel of Truth." In *The Nag Hammadi Library in English*, edited by James M. Robinson, 38–51.

Barc, Bernard L., and Michel Roberge, eds. *L'Hypostase des archontes: Traité gnostique sur l'origine de l'homme, du monde et des archontes (NH II,4); Norea (NH IX,2)*. Bibliothèque copte de Nag Hammadi, Section "Textes" 5. Québec: Presses de l'Université Laval; Louvain: Peeters, 1980.

Barnstone, Aliki, ed. *The Shambhala Anthology of Women's Spiritual Poetry*. Boston: Shambhala, 2000.

———, and Willis Barnstone, eds. *A Book of Women Poets from Antiquity to Now*. New York: Schucken Books, 1980; 1992.

Barnstone, Willis. *The New Covenant, Commonly Called the New Testament: The Four Gospels and Apocalypse*. New York: Riverhead/Penguin Putnam, 2002.

———. *The Other Bible*. San Francisco: Harper & Row, 1984.

———. *The Poems of Saint John of the Cross*. New York: New Directions, 1972.

———. *The Poetics of Ecstasy: Varieties of Ekstasis from Sappho to Borges*. New York: Holmes & Meir, 1983.

———. *The Poetics of Translation: History, Theory, Practice*. New Haven, Conn.: Yale University Press, 1993.

Barry, Catherine, Wolf-Peter Funk, Paul-Hubert Poirier, and John D. Turner, eds. *Zostrien (NH VIII,1)*. Bibliothèque copte de Nag Hammadi, Section "Textes" 24. Québec: Presses de l'Université Laval; Louvain: Peeters, 2000.

Bauer, Walter. *Orthodoxy and Heresy in Earliest Christianity*. 2d ed. Philadelphia: Fortress Press, 1971.

Baur, Ferdinand Christian. *Das Manichäische Religionssystem nach den Quellen neu unter-sucht und entwikelt.* Tübingen: Ostander, 1831.

Beausobre, Isaac de. *Histoire critique de Manichée et du manichéisme.* Amsterdam: J. F. Bernard, 1734–39.

BeDuhn, Jason. *The Manichaean Body: In Discipline and Ritual.* Baltimore: Johns Hopkins University Press, 2000.

Bethge, Hans-Gebhard. *Der Brief des Petrus an Philippus: Ein neutestamentliches Apokryphon aus dem Funde von Nag Hammadi (NHC VIII,2), herausgegeben, übersetzt und kommentiert.* TU 141. Berlin: Academie-Verlag, 1997.

————. "'Nebront': Die zweite Schrift aus Nag-Hammadi-Codex VI: Eingeleitet und über-setzt vom Berliner Arbeitskreis für koptisch-gnostische Schriften." *Theologische Liter-aturzeitung* 98 (1973): 97–104.

————. "The Letter of Peter to Philip." In *New Testament Apocrypha*, edited by Wilhelm Schneemelcher, 1.342–53.

————. "'Zweite Logos des grossen Seth': Die zweite Schrift aus Nag-Hammadi-Codex VII eingeleitet und übersetzt vom Berliner Arbeitskreis für koptisch-gnostische Schriften." *Theologische Literaturzeitung* 100 (1975): 97–110.

Bethge, Hans-Gebhard, Bentley Layton, and Societas Coptica Hierosolymitana. "On the Origin of the World." In *Nag Hammadi Codex II, 2–7*, edited by Bentley Layton, 2.11–134.

————. "On the Origin of the World." In *The Nag Hammadi Library in English*, edited by James M. Robinson, 170–89.

Bethge, Hedda. "'Die Exegese über die Seele': Die sechste Schrift aus Nag-Hammadi-Codex II: Eingeleitet und übersetzt vom Berliner Arbeitskreis für koptisch-gnostische Schriften." *Theologische Lituraturzeitung* 101 (1976): 93–104.

Bianchi, Ugo, ed. *Le origini dello gnosticismo: Colloquia di Messina, 13–18 Aprile 1966.* Stud-ies in the History of Religions (Supplements to Numen) 12. Leiden: E. J. Brill, 1970.

Blaszczak, Gerald. *A Formcritical Study of Selected Odes of Solomon.* Atlanta: Scholars Press, 1985.

Bogin, Meg. *The Women Troubadours.* New York: Paddington Press, 1976.

Böhlig Alexander, and Frederik Wisse. "The Gospel of the Egyptians." In *The Nag Ham-madi Library in English*, edited by James M. Robinson, 208–19.

————, eds. *Nag Hammadi Codices III,2 and IV,2: The Gospel of the Egyptians.* Nag Ham-madi Studies 4. Leiden: E. J. Brill; Grand Rapids, Mich.: Eerdmans, 1975.

Bornkamm, Günther. "The Acts of Thomas." In *New Testament Apocrypha*, edited by Edgar Hennecke and Wilhelm Schneemelcher, 2.498–504.

Brashler, James, Peter A. Dirkse, and Douglas M. Parrott. "The Discourse on the Eighth and Ninth." In *The Nag Hammadi Library in English*, edited by James M. Robinson, 321–27.

————. "The Prayer of Thanksgiving." In *The Nag Hammadi Library in English*, edited by James M. Robinson, 328–29.

Brooke, A. E., ed. *The Fragments of Heracleon.* Texts and Studies 14. Cambridge: Cambridge University Press, 1891.

Brown, Raymond E. *The Gospel According to John.* Anchor Bible 29–29A. Garden City, N.Y.: Doubleday, 1966, 1970.

Buckley, Jorunn Jacobsen. "Professional Fatigue: 'Hibil's Lament' in the Mandaean *Book of John*." *Le Muséon* 110 (1997): 367–81.

———. *The Scroll of Exalted Kingship (Diwan Malkuta 'Laita)*. New Haven, Conn.: American Oriental Society, 1993.

Bullard, Roger A. *The Hypostasis of the Archons: The Coptic Text with Translation and Commentary*. Patristische Texte und Studien 10. Berlin: De Guyter, 1970.

Bullard, Roger A., and Bentley Layton. "The Hypostasis of the Archons." In *Nag Hammadi Codices II, 2–7*, edited by Bentley Layton, 1.219–59.

Bullard, Roger A., and Joseph A. Gibbons. "The Second Treatise of the Great Seth." In *The Nag Hammadi Library in English*, edited by James M. Robinson, 362–71.

Bultmann, Rudolf. *The Gospel of John: A Commentary*. Translated by G. R. Beasley-Murray. Philadelphia: Westminster, 1971.

Cameron, Ron. *Sayings Traditions in the Apocryphon of James*. Harvard Theological Studies 34. Philadelphia: Fortress Press, 1984.

———. *The Other Gospels: Non-Canonical Gospel Texts*. Philadelphia: Westminster Press, 1982.

Cameron, Ron, and Arthur J. Dewey. *The Cologne Mani Codex (P. Colon. inv. nr. 4780): Concerning the Origin of His Body*. Texts and Translations, Early Christian Literature Series 15.3. Missoula, Mont.: Scholars Press, 1979.

Casey, R. P., ed. *The Excerpta ex Theodoto of Clement of Alexandria*. Studies and Documents 1. London: Christophers, 1934.

Charlesworth, James H. *Critical Reflections on the Odes of Solomon*. Vol. 1. *Literary Setting, Textual Studies, Gnosticism, the Dead Sea Scrolls and the Gospel of John*. Journal for the Study of the Pseudepigrapha Supplement Series 22. Sheffield: Academic Press, 1998.

———. *The Odes of Solomon*. Oxford: Oxford University Press, 1973.

Claude, Paul. *Les Trois stèles de Seth: Hymne gnostique à la triade (NH VII,5)*. Bibliothèque Copte de Nag Hammadi, Section "Textes" 8. Québec: Presses de l'Université Laval, 1983.

Crossan, John Dominic. *The Historical Jesus: The Life of a Mediterranean Jewish Peasant*. San Francisco: HarperSanFrancisco, 1991.

Culianu, Ioan Petru. "Gnosticism from the Middle Ages to the Present." In *The Encyclopedia of Religion*, edited by by Mircea Eliade, 5.574–78. New York: Macmillan; London: Collier Macmillan, 1987.

———. "The Gnostic Revenge: Gnosticism and Romantic Literature." In *Religionstheorie und Politische Theologie*, Band 2, *Gnosis und Politik*, edited by Jacob Taubes, 290–306. Munich: Wilhelm Fink/Ferdinand Schöningh, 1984.

———. *The Tree of Gnosis: Gnostic Mythology from Early Christianity to Modern Nihilism*. Translated by H. S. Wiesner. San Francisco: HarperCollins, 1992.

Davies, Stevan. *The Gospel of Thomas and Christian Wisdom*. New York: Seabury, 1983.

Deutsch, Nathaniel. *Guardians of the Gate: Angelic Vice Regency in Late Antiquity*. Brill's Series in Jewish Studies 22. Leiden: E. J. Brill, 1999.

Dewey, Arthur J. "The Hymn in the Acts of John." *Semeia* 38 (1986): 67–80.

Dirkse, Peter A., and James Brashler. "The Prayer of Thanksgiving." In *Nag Hammadi Codex V, 2–5 and VI*, edited by Douglas M. Parrott, 375–87.

Dirkse, Peter A., James Brashler, and Douglas M. Parrott. "The Discourse on the Eighth and Ninth." In *Nag Hammadi Codices V, 2–5 and VI*, edited by Douglas M. Parrott, 341–73.

Doresse, Jean. *The Secret Books of the Egyptian Gnostics: An Introduction to the Gnostic Coptic Manuscripts Discovered at Chenoboskion*. Translated by Philip Mairet. London: Hollis & Carter, 1960.

Drijvers, Han J. W. "The Acts of Thomas." In *New Testament Apocrypha*, edited by Wilhelm Schneemelcher, 2.380–85.

Drower, Ethel S. *The Canonical Prayerbook of the Mandaeans*. Leiden: E. J. Brill, 1959.

———. *The Haran Gawaita and the Baptism of Hibil-Ziwa*. Studi e Testi 176. Vatican City: Biblioteca Apostolica Vaticana, 1953.

———. *The Mandaeans of Iraq and Iran: Their Cults, Customs, Magic, Legends, and Folklore*. Oxford: Clarendon Press, 1937.

———. *The Secret Adam. A Study of Nasoraean Gnosis*. Oxford: Clarendon Press, 1960.

Dunkerley, Roderic. *Beyond the Gospels*. Middlesex: Penguin Books, 1957.

Fallon, Francis T. *The Enthronement of Sabaoth: Jewish Elements in Gnostic Creation Myths*. Nag Hammadi Studies 10. Leiden: E. J. Brill, 1978.

Festugière, A. J. *La Révélation d'Hermès Trismégiste*. 4 vols. Paris: Gabalda, 1949–54.

Filoramo, Giovanni. *A History of Gnosticism*. Oxford: Blackwell, 1990.

Foerster, Werner. *Gnosis: A Selection of Texts: Coptic and Mandaean Sources*. Translated by R. McL. Wilson. 2 vols. Oxford: Clarendon Press, 1974.

Frickel, Josef. *Hellenistische Erlösung in christlicher Deutung: Die gnostische Naassenerschrift*. Nag Hammadi Studies 19. Leiden: E. J. Brill, 1984.

Funk, Robert W. *Honest to Jesus: Jesus for a New Millennium*. San Francisco: HarperSanFrancisco, 1996.

Gager, John G., ed. *Curse Tablets and Binding Spells from the Ancient World*. New York and Oxford: Oxford University Press, 1992.

Gamble, Harry Y. *The New Testament Canon: Its Making and Meaning*. Guides to Biblical Scholarship. Philadelphia: Fortress Press, 1985.

Gardner, Iain. *The Kephalaia of the Teacher: The Edited Coptic Manichaean Texts in Translation with Commentary*. Leiden: E. J. Brill, 1995.

Goehring James E., and James M. Robinson. "The Three Steles of Seth." In *Nag Hammadi Codex VII*, edited by Birger A. Pearson, 371–421.

———. "The Three Steles of Seth." In *The Nag Hammadi Library in English*, edited by James M. Robinson, 396–401.

Grant, Robert M. *Gnosticism and Early Christianity*. 2d ed. New York: Columbia University Press, 1966.

———, ed. *Gnosticism: An Anthology*. New York: Harper, 1961.

Grobel, Kendrick. *The Gospel of Truth: A Valentinian Meditation on the Gospel, Translation from the Coptic and Commentary*. Nashville, Tenn.: Abingdon Press, 1960.

Gündüz, Sinasi. *The Knowledge of Life: The Origins and Early History of the Mandaeans and Their Relation to the Sabians of the Qur'an and to the Harranians*. Oxford: Oxford University Press, 1994.

H.D. *Trilogy*. Edited by Aliki Barnstone. New York: New Directions, 1998.

Haardt, Robert, ed. *Gnosis: Character and Testimony.* Leiden: E. J. Brill, 1971.

Haenchen, Ernst. "The Book Baruch." In *Gnosis: A Selection of Texts,* edited by Werner Foerster, 1.48–58.

———. "Das Buch Baruch: Ein Beitrag zum Problem der christlichen Gnosis." *Zeitschrift für Theologie und Kirche* 50 (1953): 123–58.

Halm, Heinz. *Die islamische Gnosis: die extreme Schia und die ʿAlawiten.* Die Bibliothek des Morgenlandes. Zürich: Artemis, 1982.

———. *Kosmologie und Heilslehre der frühen Ismaʿiliya: Ein Studie zur islamische Gnosis.* Abhandlung für Kundes des Morgenlandes 44.1. Mainz: Deutsche Morgenländische Ges.; Wiesbaden: Steiner in Komm, 1978.

Harnack, Adolf von. *Marcion: The Gospel of the Alien God.* Translated by John E. Steely and Lyle D. Bierma. Durham, N.C.: Labyrinth Press, 1990.

Harris, Rendel, and Alphonse Mingana. *The Odes and Psalms of Solomon.* 2 vols. Manchester: University Press; New York: Longmans, Green, 1916–20.

Hedrick, Charles W. *The Apocalypse of Adam: A Literary and Source Analysis.* SBLDS 46. Chico, Calif.: Scholars Press, 1980.

———, ed. *Nag Hammadi Codices XI, XII, and XIII.* Nag Hammadi and Manichaean Studies 28. Leiden: E. J. Brill, 1990.

Hedrick, Charles W., and Robert Hodgson, Jr., eds. *Nag Hammadi, Gnosticism, and Early Christianity.* Peabody, Mass.: Hendrickson, 1986.

Henning, W. B. "Mani's Last Journey." *Bulletin of the School of Oriental and African Studies* 10 (1942): 941–53. Reprinted in Henning, *Selected Papers.* Acta Iranica 14–15. Leiden: E. J. Brill; Teheran: Bibliothèque Pahlavi, 1977, 2.81–93.

Henrichs, Albert, and Ludwig Koenen, eds. "Ein griechischer Mani-Codex." *Zeitschrift für Papyrologie und Epigraphik* 4 (1970): 97–216.

Hock, Ronald F., and Edward N. O'Neil. *The Chreia in Ancient Rhetoric.* Vol. 1. Atlanta: Scholars Press, 1986.

Holroyd, Stuart. *The Elements of Gnosticism.* Shaftesbury, Dorset: Element, 1994.

Isenberg, Wesley W. "The Gospel According to Philip." In *The Nag Hammadi Library in English,* edited by James M. Robinson, 139–60.

Isenberg, Wesley W., and Bentley Layton. "The Gospel According to Philip." In *Nag Hammadi Codex II,2–7,* edited by Bentley Layton, 1.129–217.

Jackson, Howard M. "Geradamas, the Celestial Stranger." *New Testament Studies* 27 (1981): 385–94.

Janssens, Yvonne. *La Prôtennoia trimorphe (NH XIII 1): texte établi et présenté.* Bibliothèque Copte de Nag Hammadi, Section "Textes" 4. Québec: Presses de l'Université Laval, 1978.

Jeremias, Joachim. *Unknown Sayings of Jesus.* 2d ed. Translated by Reginald H. Fuller. London: S.P.C.K., 1964.

Jonas, Hans. *The Gnostic Religion: The Message of the Alien God and the Beginnings of Christianity.* 2d ed. Boston: Beacon Press, 1963.

———. *Gnosis und spätantiker Geist.* Part 1. 3d ed. FRLANT 51. Göttingen: Vandenhoeck & Ruprecht, 1964.

Junod, Eric, and Jean-Daniel Kaestli. *Acta Johannis.* Corpus Christianorum, series apocryphorum 1,2. Turnhout, Belgium: Brepols, 1983.

Käsemann, Ernst. *The Testament of Jesus: A Study of the Gospel of John in the Light of Chapter 17*. Translated by Gerhard Krodel. Philadelphia: Fortress Press, 1968.

Khalidi, Tarif. *The Muslim Jesus: Sayings and Stories in Islamic Literature*. Cambridge, Mass.: Harvard University Press, 2001.

King, Karen L. "The Apocryphon of John: Part II of the Gospel of John?" Paper presented at the annual meeting of the Society of Biblical Literature, Denver, Colo., November 2001.

———. "The Gospel of Mary." In *The Complete Gospels*, edited by Robert J. Miller, 351–60.

———. *Revelation of the Unknowable God: With Text, Translation, and Notes to NHC XI,3 Allogenes*. Santa Rosa,Calif.: Polebridge Press, 1995.

———. "Sophia and Christ in the Apocryphon of John." In *Images of the Feminine in Gnosticism*, edited by Karen L. King, 158–76.

———. *What Is Gnosticism?* Cambridge, Mass.: Belknap Press/Harvard University Press, 2003.

———, ed. *Images of the Feminine in Gnosticism*. Studies in Antiquity and Christianity. Philadelphia: Fortress Press, 1988.

King, Karen L., George W. MacRae, and R. McL. Wilson. "The Gospel of Mary." In *The Nag Hammadi Library in English*, edited by James M. Robinson, 523–27.

Kirchner, Dankwart. "The Apocryphon of James." In *New Testament Apocrypha*, edited by Wilhelm Schneemelcher, 1.285–99.

Klijn, A. F. J. *Seth in Jewish, Christian, and Gnostic Literature*. Leiden: E. J. Brill, 1977.

Klimkeit, Hans-Joachim. *Gnosis on the Silk Road: Gnostic Texts from Central Asia*. San Francisco: HarperSanFrancisco, 1993.

Kloppenborg, John S. *The Formation of Q: Trajectories in Ancient Wisdom Collections*. Philadelphia: Fortress Press, 1987.

———. *Q Parallels: Synopsis, Critical Notes, and Concordance*. Sonoma, Calif.: Polebridge Press, 1988.

Kloppenborg, John S., Marvin W. Meyer, Stephen J. Patterson, and Michael G. Steinhauser. *Q—Thomas Reader*. Sonoma, Calif.: Polebridge Press, 1990.

Kloppenborg-Verbin, John S. *Excavating Q: The History and Setting of the Sayings Gospel*. Minneapolis: Fortress Press, 2000.

Koenen, Ludwig, and Cornelia Römer, eds. *Der Kölner Mani-Kodex: Abbildungen und diplomatischer Text*. Papyrologische Texte und Abhandlungen 35. Bonn: R. Habelt, 1985.

Koester, Helmut, and Thomas O. Lambdin. "The Gospel of Thomas." In *The Nag Hammadi Library in English*, edited by James M. Robinson, 126–38.

Koester, Helmut, Bentley Layton, Thomas O. Lambdin, and Harold W. Attridge. "The Gospel According to Thomas." In *Nag Hammadi Codex II, 2–7*, edited by Bentley Layton, 1.37–128.

Kuntzmann, Raymond. *Le Livre de Thomas (NH II,7): Texte établi et présenté*. Bibliothèque copte de Nag Hammadi, Section "Textes" 16. Québec: Presses de l'Université Laval, 1986.

Layton, Bentley. *The Gnostic Scriptures: A New Translation with Annotations and Introductions*. Garden City, N.Y.: Doubleday, 1987.

————. *The Gnostic Treatise on Resurrection from Nag Hammadi: Edited with Translation and Commentary.* HDR 12. Missoula, Mont.: Scholars Press, 1979.

————. "*The Hypostasis of the Archons; or, The Reality of the Rulers:* A Gnostic Story of the Creation, Fall, and Ultimate Salvation of Man, and the Origin and Reality of His Enemies, Newly Edited from the Cairo Manuscript with a Preface, English Translation, Notes, and Indexes." *Harvard Theological Review* 67 (1974): 351–425.

————. "The Hypostasis of the Archons." In *The Nag Hammadi Library in English,* edited by James M. Robinson, 161–69.

————. ed. *Nag Hammadi Codex II, 2–7, Together with XIII, 2*, Brit. Lib. Or. 4926(1), and P. Oxy. 1, 654, 655.* 2 vols. Nag Hammadi Studies 20–21. Leiden: E. J. Brill, 1989.

————, ed. *The Rediscovery of Gnosticism: Proceedings of the International Conference on Gnosticism at Yale, New Haven, Connecticut, March 28–31, 1978.* Studies in the History of Religions (Supplements to Numen) 41. Leiden: E. J. Brill, 1980–81.

Layton, Bentley, and John H. Sieber. "Zostrianos." In *Nag Hammadi Codex VIII,* edited by John H. Sieber, 7–228.

Lefkowitz, Mary R., and Maureen B. Fant, eds. *Women's Life in Greece and Rome.* London : Duckworth, 1982.

Lidzbarski, Mark. *Ginza: Der Schatz oder das grosse Buch der Mandäer übersetzt und erklärt.* Göttingen: Vandenhoeck & Ruprecht, 1925.

————. *Das Johannesbuch der Mandäer.* Giessen: A. Töpelmann, 1905–15.

————. *Mandäische Liturgien: Mitgeteilt, übersetzt und erklärt.* Berlin: Weidmannsche Buchhandlung, 1920.

Lieu, S. N. C. *Manichaeism in the Later Roman Empire and Medieval China: A Historical Survey.* 2d ed. Tübingen: Mohr, 1992.

Lin Wu-shu. "A New Find of [a] Manichaean Stone Carving in Fujian, China." *Manichaean Studies Newsletter* 1 (1989) 22–27.

————. "On the Joining Between the Two Fragments of 'The Compendium of the Teachings of Mani, the Buddha of Light.'" In *Manichaean Studies: Proceedings of the First International Conference on Manichaeism,* edited by P. Bryder. *Lund Studies in African and Asian Religions* 1. Lund, Sweden: Plus Ultra, 1988, 89–93.

————. *Manichaeism and Its Spread to the East.* In Chinese; English review by P. Bryder in *Manichaean Studies Newsletter* 1 (1989): 15–19.

Lüdemann, Gerd, and Martina Janssen. *Bibel der Häretiker: Die gnostischen Schriften aus Nag Hammadi.* Stuttgart: Radius, 1997.

MacGregor, Geddes. *Literary History of the Bible from the Middle Ages to the Present Day.* Nashville, Tenn.: Abingdon Press, 1968.

Mack, Burton L. *Logos und Sophia: Untersuchungen zur Weisheitstheologie im hellenistischen Judentum.* Göttingen: Vandenhoeck & Ruprecht, 1973.

————. *The Lost Gospel: The Book of Q and Christian Origins.* San Francisco: HarperSanFrancisco, 1993.

MacRae, George W. "The Apocalypse of Adam." In *Nag Hammadi Codices V, 2–5 and VI,* edited by Douglas M. Parrott, 151–95.

————. "The Apocalypse of Adam." In *The Nag Hammadi Library in English,* edited by James M. Robinson, 277–86.

———. "The Thunder: Perfect Mind." In *Nag Hammadi Codices V,2–5 and VI*, edited by Douglas M. Parrott, 231–55.

———. "The Thunder: Perfect Mind." In *The Nag Hammadi Library in English*, edited by James M. Robinson, 295–303.

MacRae, George W., and R. McL. Wilson. "The Gospel of Mary." In *Nag Hammadi Codices V, 2–5 and VI*, edited by Douglas M. Parrott, 453–71.

Mahé, Jean-Pierre. *Hermès en Haute-Égypte*. Bibliothèque copte de Nag Hammadi, Section "Textes" 3. Québec: Presses de l'Université Laval, 1978

———. "La Prière d'actions de grâces du Codex VI de Nag-Hammadi et le Discours parfait." *Zeitschrift für Papyrologie und Epigraphik* 13 (1974): 40–60.

Marcovich, Miroslav, ed. *Hippolyti refutationis omnium haeresium librorum decem quae supersunt*. New York: Walter de Gruyter, 1986.

Margoliouth, D. S. "Christ in Islam: Sayings Attributed to Christ by Mohammedan Writers." *The Expository Times* 5 (1893–94): 59, 107, 177–78, 503–4, 561.

Ménard, Jacques-É. *L'Évangile de vérité: Rétroversion grecque et commentaire*. Paris: Letouzey & Ané, 1962.

———. *L'Évangile selon Philippe: Introduction, texte, traduction, commentaire*. Strasbourg: Letouzey & Ané, 1967.

———. *La Lettre de Pierre à Philippe: Texte établi et présenté*. Bibliothèque copte de Nag Hammadi, Section "Textes" 1. Québec: Presses de l'Université Laval, 1977.

———. *Le Traité sur la resurrection (NH I,4): Texte établi et présenté*. Bibliothèque copte de Nag Hammadi, Section "Textes" 12. Québec: Presses de l'Université Laval, 1983.

Merkelbach, Reinhold. "Der manichäische Codex von Tebessa." In *Manichaean Studies: Proceedings of the First International Conference on Manichaeism*, edited by P. Bryder, 229–64. *Lund Studies in African and Asian Religions* 1. Lund, Sweden: Plus Ultra, 1988.

———. *Mani und sein Religionssystem*. Opladen: Rheinisch-Westfälische Akademie der Wissenschaften, 1986.

Metzger, Bruce M. *The Canon of the New Testament: Its Origin, Development and Significance*. New York: Oxford University Press, 1987.

Meyer, Marvin. "Did Jesus Drink from a Cup? The Equipment of Jesus and His Followers in Q and al-Ghazzali." In *From Quest to Q: Festschrift James M. Robinson*, edited by Jon Ma. Asgeirsson, Kristin De Troyer, and Marvin W. Meyer, 143–56. Leuven, Belgium: Leuven University Press, 2000.

———. *The Gospel of Thomas: The Hidden Sayings of Jesus*. San Francisco: Harper Collins, 1992.

———. *The Letter of Peter to Philip: Text, Translation, and Commentary*. SBLDS 53. Chico, Calif.: Scholars Press, 1981.

———. *Secret Gospels: Essays on Thomas and the Secret Gospel of Mark*. Harrisburg, Pa.: Trinity Press International, 2003.

———. *The Unknown Sayings of Jesus*. San Francisco: HarperSanFrancisco, 1998.

———, ed. *The Ancient Mysteries: A Sourcebook of Sacred Texts*. Philadelphia: University of Pennsylvania Press, 1999.

Meyer, Marvin, and Frederik Wisse. "Letter of Peter to Philip." In *Nag Hammadi Codex VIII*, edited by John H. Sieber, 227–51.

————. "The Letter of Peter to Philip." In *The Nag Hammadi Library in English*, edited by James M. Robinson, 431–37.

Miller, Robert J., ed. *The Complete Gospels*. 2d ed. Sonoma,Calif.: Polebridge Press, 1992.

Mirecki, P. A. "The Coptic Manichaean Synaxeis Codex: Descriptive Catalogue of Synaxeis Chapter Titles." In *Manichaean Studies: Proceedings of the First International Conference on Manichaeism*, edited by P. Bryder, 135–45. *Lund Studies in African and Asian Religions* 1. Lund, Sweden: Plus Ultra, 1988.

Morard, Françoise. *L'Apocalypse d'Adam (NH V,5): Texte établi et présenté*. Bibliothèque copte de Nag Hammadi, Section "Textes" 15. Québec: Presses de l'Université Laval, 1985.

Morrice, William G. *Hidden Sayings of Jesus: Words Attributed to Jesus outside the Four Gospels*. Peabody, Mass.: Hendrickson, 1997.

Mozley, James Frederic. *William Tyndale*. New York: Macmillan, 1937.

Mueller, Dieter. "The Prayer of the Apostle Paul." In *The Nag Hammadi Library in English*, edited by James M. Robinson, 27–28.

————. "The Prayer of the Apostle Paul." In *Nag Hammadi Codex I*, edited by Harold W. Attridge, 1.5–11, 2.1–5.

Nelli, René. *Écritures cathares; La Cène secrète; Le Livre des deux principes; Traité cathare; Le Rituel occitan; Le Rituel latin: Textes précathares et cathares présentés, traduits et commentés avec une introduction sur les origines et l'esprit du catharism*. New ed. Paris: Planète, 1968.

Nock, Arthur Darby, and A. J. Festugière, eds. *Corpus Hermeticum*. Paris: Sociéte d'édition "Les Belles lettres," 1945–54.

Pagels, Elaine H. *Beyond Belief: The Secret Gospel of Thomas*. New York: Random House, 2003.

————. *The Gnostic Gospels*. New York: Random House, 1979.

————. *The Gnostic Paul: Gnostic Exegesis of the Pauline Letters*. Philadelphia: Fortress Press, 1975.

————. *The Johannine Gospel in Gnostic Exegesis: Heracleon's Commentary on John*. Society of Biblical Literature Monograph Series 17. Nashville, Tenn.: Abingdon Press, 1973.

Painchaud, Louis. *Le Deuxième Traité du Grand Seth (NH VII,2): Texte établi et présenté*. Bibliothèque copte de Nag Hammadi, Section "Textes" 6. Québec: Presses de l'Université Laval, 1982.

Parrinder, Geoffrey. *Jesus in the Qur'an*. New York: Oxford University Press, 1965.

Parrott, Douglas M. *Nag Hammadi Codices V,2–5 and VI with Papyrus Berolinensis 8502,1 and 4*. Nag Hammadi and Manichaean Studies 11. Leiden: E. J. Brill, 1979.

Patterson, Stephen J. *The Gospel of Thomas and Jesus*. Sonoma, Calif.: Polebridge Press, 1993.

Patterson, Stephen J., James M. Robinson, and Hans-Gebhard Bethge. *The Fifth Gospel: The Gospel of Thomas Comes of Age*. Harrisburg, Pa.: Trinity Press International, 1998.

Pearson, Birger A. *Gnosticism, Judaism, and Egyptian Christianity*. Studies in Antiquity and Christianity 5. Minneapolis: Fortress Press, 1990.

————. "Jewish Elements in *Corpus Hermeticum I (Poimandres)*." In *Studies in Gnosticism and Hellenistic Religions: Presented to Gilles Quispel on the Occasion of His 65th Birthday*, edited by R. van den Broek and M. J. Vermaseren, 336–48. Leiden: E. J. Brill, 1981.

———. ed. *Nag Hammadi Codex VII.* Nag Hammadi and Manichean Studies 30. Leiden: E. J. Brill, 1996.

Peel, Malcolm L. "The Treatise on the Resurrection." In *Nag Hammadi Codex I,* edited by Harold W. Attridge, 1.123–57, 2.137–215.

———. "The Treatise on the Resurrection." In *The Nag Hammadi Library in English,* edited by James M. Robinson, 52–57.

Perkins, Pheme. *Gnosticism and the New Testament.* Minneapolis: Fortress Press, 1993.

Polotsky, H. J. *Manichäische Handschriften der Sammlung A. Chester Beatty.* Band 1. Manichäische Homilien. Berlin: Kohlhammer, 1940.

Polotsky, H. J., and Alexander Böhlig. *Kephalaia.* Stuttgart: Kohlhammer, 1940.

———. *Manichäische Handschriften der staatliche Museen Berlins. Kephalaia.* Berlin: Kohlhammer, 1940.

Pritchard, James R., ed. *Ancient Near Eastern Texts Relating to the Old Testament.* 3d ed. Princeton, N.J.: Princeton University Press, 1969.

Quispel, Gilles, ed. *Ptolémée, Lettre à Flora: Texte, traduction, et introduction.* SC 24. Paris: Cerf, 1949.

Ries, J. *Les Études manichéenes: Des controverses de la Réforme aux découvertes du XXe siècle.* Louvain-La-Neuve, Belgium: Centre d'Histoire des Religions, 1988.

Riley, Gregory. "The Second Treatise of the Great Seth." In *Nag Hammadi Codex VII,* edited by Birger A. Pearson, 129–99.

Roberge, Michel. "Anthrogonie et anthropologie dans la *Paraphrase de Sem* (NH VII,1)." *Muséon* 99 (1986): 229–48.

———. *Le Paraphrase de Sem (NH VII,1): Texte établi et présenté.* Bibliothèque copte de Nag Hammadi, Section "Textes" 25. Québec: Presses de l'Université Laval, 2000.

Roberge, Michel, and Frederik Wisse. "The Paraphrase of Shem." In *The Nag Hammadi Library in English,* edited by James M. Robinson, 339–61.

Robinson, James M. "The Fate of the Manichaean Codices of Medinet Madi, 1929–1989." In *Studia Manichaeica: Proceedings of the Second International Conference on Manichaeism,* edited by G. Wießner and H.-J. Klimkeit, 19–61. Wiesbaden: Harrassowitz, 1992.

———. "Nag Hammadi: The First Fifty Years." In *The Nag Hammadi Library after Fifty Years: Proceedings of the 1995 Society of Biblical Literature Commemoration,* edited by John D. Turner and Anne McGuire, 3–33. Leiden: E. J. Brill, 1997.

———. "Sethians and Johannine Thought: The Trimorphic Protennoia and the Prologue of the Gospel of John." In *The Rediscovery of Gnosticism,* edited by Bentley Layton, 643–62.

———, ed. The *Nag Hammadi Library in English.* 3d ed. San Francisco: HarperSanFrancisco, 1988.

Robinson, James M., Paul Hoffman, and John S. Kloppenborg, eds. *The Critical Edition of Q : Synopsis Including the Gospels of Matthew and Luke, Mark, and Thomas with English, German, and French Translations of Q and Thomas.* Leuven, Belgium: Peeters, 2000.

Robinson, James M., and Helmut Koester. *Trajectories through Early Christianity.* Philadelphia: Fortress Press, 1971.

Robinson, William C., Jr., and Bentley Layton. "The Expository Treatise on the Soul." In *Nag Hammadi Codex I,2–7*, edited by Bentley Layton, 2.135–69.

Robinson, William C., Jr., and Maddalena Scopello. "The Exegesis on the Soul." In *The Nag Hammadi Library in English*, edited by James M. Robinson, 190–98.

Robson, James. *Christ in Islam*. The Wisdom of the East. London: Murray, 1929.

Ropes, James Hardy. "Agrapha." In *A Dictionary of the Bible*, edited by James Hastings, ex. vol. 343–52. New York: Scribner's; Edinburgh: T. & T. Clark, 1904.

Rouleau, Donald, and Louise Roy. *L'Épître apocryphe de Jacques (NH I,2); L'Acte de Pierre (BG 4)*. Bibliothèque copte de Nag Hammadi, Section "Textes" 18. Québec: Presses de l'Université Laval, 1987.

Rudolph, Kurt. *Gnosis: The Nature and History of Gnosticism*. Translated by R. McL. Wilson. San Francisco: Harper Collins, 1983.

———. *Die Mandäer. Vol. 1. Prolegomena: Das Mandäerproblem*. Vol. 2. *Der Kult*. Göttingen: Vandenhoeck & Ruprecht, 1960–1961.

———. *Theogonie, Kosmogonie und Anthropogonie in den mandäischen Schriften*. Göttingen: Vandenhoeck & Ruprecht, 1965.

Runciman, Steven. *The Medieval Manichee: A Study of the Christian Dualist Heresy*. Cambridge: Cambridge University Press, 1995.

Rushdie, Salman. *The Satanic Verses*. London: Viking, 1988.

Sacconi, Rayenius. *Summa de catharis*. Edited by Franjo Sanjek. *Archivum Fratrum Praedicatorum* 44 (1974): 31–60.

Sagnard, Francois. *La Gnose valentinienne et le témoignage de Saint Irénée*. Paris: Vrin, 1947.

Säve-Söderbergh, Torgny. *Studies in the Coptic Manichaean Psalm-Book: Prosody and Mandaean Parallels*. Uppsala: Almqvist & Wiksells, 1949.

Schäferdiek, Knut. "The Acts of John." In *New Testament Apocrypha*, edited by Wilhelm Schneemelcher, 2.152–212.

Schenke, Hans-Martin. "The Book of Thomas." In *New Testament Apocrypha*, edited by Wilhelm Schneemelcher, 1.232–40.

———. "The Gospel of Philip." In *New Testament Apocrypha*, edited by Wilhelm Schneemelcher, 1.179–208.

———. *Die Herkunft des sogennanten Evangelium Veritatis*. Berlin: Evangelischer Verlag, 1958.

———. "The Problem of Gnosis." *Second Century* 3 (1983): 78–87.

———. "Das sethianische System nach Nag-Hammadi-Handschriften." In *Studia Coptica*, edited by P. Nagel, 165–72. Berlin: Akademie-Verlag, 1974.

———. "Vom Ursprung der Welt: Eine Titellose gnostische Abhandlung aus dem Funde von Nag-Hamadi." *Theologische Literaturezeitung* 84 (1959): 243–56.

Schenke, Hans-Martin, Hans-Gebhard Bethge, and Ursula Ulrike Kaiser, eds. *Nag Hammadi Deutsch*. Vol. 1. Berlin: Walter de Gruyter, 2001.

Schmidt, Carl, and H. J. Polotsky. "Ein Mani-Fund in Ägypten: Originalschriften des Mani und seiner Schüler." In *Sitzungberichte der Preussischen Akademie der Wissenschaften zu Berlin, philosophisch-historische Klasse I*, 4–90. Berlin: Akademie, 1933.

Schmithals, Walter. *Gnosticism in Corinth: An Investigation of the Letters to the Corinthians*. Translated by John E. Steely. Nashville, Tenn.: Abingdon Press, 1971.

Schneemelcher, Wilhelm, ed. *New Testament Apocrypha*. English translation edited by R. McL. Wilson. 2 vols. Cambridge: James Clarke; Louisville, Ky.: Westminster/John Knox, 1991–92.

Schoeps, Hans-Joachim. *Jewish Christianity: Factional Disputes in the Early Church*. Translated by Douglas R. A. Hare. Philadelphia: Fortress Press, 1969.

———. *Theologie und Geschichte des Judenchristentums*. Tübingen: Mohr, 1949.

Scholem, Gershom. *Jewish Gnosticism, Merkabah Mysticism, and Talmudic Tradition*. New York: Jewish Theological Seminary of America, 1960.

———. *Major Trends in Jewish Mysticism*. New York: Schocken Books, 1954.

Scholer, David M. *Nag Hammadi Bibliography, 1948–1969*. Nag Hammadi Studies 1. Leiden: E. J. Brill, 1971.

———. *Nag Hammadi Bibliography, 1970–1994*. Nag Hammadi Studies 32. Leiden: E. J. Brill, 1997.

Schweitzer, Albert. *The Quest of the Historical Jesus: A Critical Study of Its Progress from Reimarus to Wrede*. Translated by W. Montgomery. New York: Macmillan, 1968.

Scopello, Maddalena. *L'Exégèse de l'âme, Nag Hammadi Codex II,6: Introduction, traduction et commentaire*. Nag Hammadi Studies 25. Leiden: E. J. Brill, 1985.

Segal, Alan F. *Two Powers in Heaven: Early Rabbinic Reports about Christianity and Gnosticism*. Studies in Judaism and Late Antiquity 25. Leiden: E. J. Brill, 1977.

Shimin, Geng. "Recent Studies on Manichaeism in China." In *Studia Manichaeica: Proceedings of the Second International Conference on Manichaeism*, edited by G. Wiessner and H.-J. Klimkeit, 98–104. Wiesbaden: Harrassowitz, 1992.

Sieber, John H. "The Barbelo Aeon as Sophia in Zostrianos and Related Tractates." In *The Rediscovery of Gnosticism*, edited by Bentley Layton, 788–95.

———. "Zostrianos." In *The Nag Hammadi Library in English*, edited by James M. Robinson, 402–30.

———, ed. *The Nag Hammadi Codex VIII*. Nag Hammadi and Manichean Studies 31. Leiden: E. J. Brill, 1991.

Smith, Jonathan Z. *Drudgery Divine: On the Comparison of Early Christianities and the Religions of Late Antiquity*. Chicago: University of Chicago Press, 1990.

Stead, G. C. "The Valentinian Myth of Sophia." *Journal of Theological Studies* 20 (1969): 75–104.

Steiner, George. *After Babel: Aspects of Language and Translation*. 3d ed. Oxford: Oxford University Press, 1998.

Stroumsa, Gedaliahu A. G. *Another Seed: Studies in Gnostic Mythology*. Leiden: E. J. Brill, 1984.

Tardieu, Michel. *Écrits gnostiques: Codex de Berlin*. Sources gnostiques et manichéennes 1. Paris: Cerf, 1984.

———. *Trois mythes gnostiques: Adam, Éros et les animaux d'Égypte dans un écrit de Nag Hammadi (II, 5)*. Paris: Études augustinennes, 1974.

Thouzellier, Christine, ed. *Livre des deux principes: Introduction, texte critique, traduction, notes et index*. Paris: Cerf, 1973.

———. *Rituel cathare: Introduction, texte critique, traduction et notes*. Paris: Cerf, 1977.

Till, Walter C. *Das Evangelium nach Philippos*. Patristische Texte und Studien 2. Berlin: Walter de Gruyter, 1963.

Trobisch, David. *The First Edition of the New Testament.* New York: Oxford University Press, 2000.

Tröger, Karl-Wolfgang. "Die sechste und siebte Schrift aus Nag-Hammadi-Codex VI: Eingeleitet und übersetzt vom Berliner Arbeitskreis für koptish-gnostische Schriften." *Theologische Literaturzeitung* 98 (1973): 495–503.

Turner, John D. *The Book of Thomas the Contender from Codex II of the Cairo Gnostic Library from Nag Hammadi (CG II,7): The Coptic Text with Translation, Introduction and Commentary.* SBLDS 23. Missoula, Mont.: Scholars Press, 1975.

———. "The Book of Thomas the Contender." In *The Nag Hammadi Library in English,* edited by James M. Robinson, 199–207.

———. "On the Anointing"; "On Baptism A"; "On Baptism B"; "On the Eucharist A"; "On the Eucharist B." In *The Nag Hammadi Library in English,* edited by James M. Robinson, 482–89.

———. "On the Anointing"; "On Baptism A"; "On Baptism B"; "On the Eucharist A"; "On the Eucharist B." In *Nag Hammadi Codices XI, XII, and XIII,* edited by Charles W. Hedrick, 94–95, 142–51, 170–72.

———. "Sethian Gnosticism: A Literary History." In *Nag Hammadi, Gnosticism and Early Christianity,* edited by C. W. Hedrick and R. Hodgson, 55–86.

———. *Sethian Gnosticism and the Platonic Tradition.* Bibliothèque de Nag Hammadi. Section "Études" 6. Sainte-Foy, Québec: Presses de l'Université Laval; Louvain, Belgium: Peeters, 2001.

———. "Trimorphic Protennoia." In *Nag Hammadi Codices XI, XII, and XIII,* edited by Charles W. Hedrick, 371–454.

———. "Trimorphic Protennoia." In *The Nag Hammadi Library in English,* edited by James M. Robinson, 511–22.

Turner, John D., and Bentley Layton. "The Book of Thomas the Contender Writing to the Perfect." In *Nag Hammadi Codex II,2–7,* edited by Bentley Layton, 2.171–205.

Valantasis, Richard. *The Gospel of Thomas.* New Testament Readings. London: Routledge, 1997.

Vermes, Geza. *The Changing Faces of Jesus.* New York: Compass Viking, 2000.

———. *The Dead Sea Scrolls.* 2d ed. Reprint. New York: Penguin Books, 1962.

Völker, W., ed. *Quellen zur Geschichte der christlichen Gnosis.* Tübingen: Mohr, 1932.

Waldstein, Michael, and Frederik Wisse, eds. *The Apocryphon of John: Synopsis of Nag Hammadi Codices II,1; III,1; and IV,1 with BG 8502,2.* Nag Hammadi and Manichaean Studies 33. Leiden: E. J. Brill, 1985.

Wekel, Konrad. "'Die drei Stelen des Seth'; Die fünfte Schrift aus Nag-Hammadi-Codex VII: Eingeleitet und übersetzt vom Berliner Arbeitskreis für koptisch-gnostische Scriften." *Theologische Literaturzeitung* 100 (1975): 571–80.

Wendland, Paul, ed. *Refutatio omnium haeresium.* Die Griechischen christlichen Schriftsteller der ersten Jahrhunderte 26. Hildesheim: Olms, 1977.

Widengren, Georg, ed. *Der Mandäismus.* Darmstadt: Wissenschaftliche Buchgesellschaft, 1982.

Williams, Francis E. "The Apocryphon of James." In *Nag Hammadi Codex I,* edited by Harold W. Attridge, 1.13–53, 2.7–37.

————. "The Apocryphon of James." In The Nag Hammadi Library in English, edited by James M. Robinson, 29–37.

Williams, Michael. The Immovable Race: A Gnostic Designation and the Theme of Stability in Late Antiquity. Nag Hammadi Studies 29. Leiden: E. J. Brill, 1985.

————. Rethinking "Gnosticism": An Argument for Dismantling a Dubious Category. Princeton, N.J.: Princeton University, 1996.

Wilson, R. McL. The Gospel of Philip: Translated from the Coptic Text with an Introduction and Commentary. New York: Harper & Row, 1962.

Wire, Antoinette Clark, John D. Turner, and Orval S. Wintermute. "Allogenes." In Nag Hammadi Codices XI, XII, and XIII, edited by Charles W. Hedrick, 173–267.

————. "Allogenes." In The Nag Hammadi Library in English, edited by James M. Robinson, 490–500.

Wisse, Frederik. "The Apocryphon of John." In The Nag Hammadi Library in English, edited by James M. Robinson, 104–123.

————. "The Paraphrase of Shem." In Nag Hammadi Codex VII, edited by Birger A. Pearson, 15–127.

————. "On Exegeting 'The Exegesis on the Soul.'" In Les Textes de Nag Hammadi: Colloque du Centre d'Histoire des Religions (Strasbourg, 23–25 octobre 1974), edited by J.-É. Ménard, 68–81. Leiden: E. J. Brill, 1975.

Yamauchi, Edwin. Pre-Christian Gnosticism: A Survey of the Proposed Evidences. Grand Rapids, Mich.: Eerdmans, 1973.

INDEX OF PROPER NAMES

LINDEN YOUNGQUIST